BLACK HERITA

Beating Against the Barriers

Beating
Against the
Barriers

Biographical Essays in

Nineteenth-Century

Afro-American History

R. J. M. Blackett

LOUISIANA STATE UNIVERSITY PRESS   *Baton Rouge and London*

Copyright © 1986 by Louisiana State University Press
Manufactured in the United States of America
Designer: Patricia Douglas Crowder
Typeface: Linotron 202 Ehrhardt
Typesetter: G & S Typesetters, Inc.
Printer: Thomson-Shore, Inc.
Binder: John H. Dekker & Sons, Inc.

LIBRARY OF CONGRESS CATALOGING-IN-PUBLICATION DATA

Blackett, R. J. M., 1943–
  Beating against the barriers.

  Bibliography: p.
  Includes index.
    1. Afro-Americans—Biography—Addresses, essays,
lectures.   2. Abolitionists—United States—Biography—
Addresses, essays, lectures.   I. Title.
E185.96.B55   1986   973'.0496073022 [B]   85-23756
ISBN 0-8071-1281-X

The author is grateful to the following for permission to quote from materials in their possession:
American Philosophical Society Library, Philadelphia; Amistad Research Center, New Orleans;
The Beinecke Rare Book and Manuscript Library, Yale University, New Haven; Board of
Education, Harrisburg, Pa.; Chatham Public Library, Chatham, Ontario; Church Missionary
Society Archives, London; Cumbria Record Office, Kendal, England; Department of Rare
Books, Cornell University Library, Ithaca, N.Y.; Dr. Williams's Library, London; Friends
Historical Library, Swarthmore College, Swarthmore, Pa.; George Arents Research Library,
Syracuse University, Syracuse, N.Y.; The Historical Society of Pennsylvania, Philadelphia;
Hodgkin family, Warwickshire; The Huntington Library, San Marino, Calif.; The John Rylands
University Library of Manchester, Manchester; The Library, University College, London;
Massachusetts Historical Society, Boston; Massachusetts State Archives, Boston; The Methodist
Church Overseas Division (Methodist Missionary Society), London; The Mitchell Library,
Glasgow; Moorland-Spingarn Research Center, Howard University, Washington, D.C.; Oberlin
College, Oberlin, Ohio; Presbyterian Historical Society, Philadelphia; Rare Book and
Manuscript Library, Columbia University, New York; Rhodes House Library, Oxford University,
Oxford; Royal Geographical Society, London; Southern Historical Collection, Library of the
University of North Carolina at Chapel Hill; and Trustees of Boston Public Library.

Parts of Chapters II and III were published in *Journal of American Studies*, XII (April, 1978),
41–62, and in *Phylon*, XL (December, 1979), 375–86.

Publication of this book has been assisted by a grant from the Andrew W. Mellon Foundation.

To my parents

A small return for such huge sacrifices

Contents

Illustrations

Preface

In conversations with colleagues years ago, someone jokingly alluded to the fact that black Americans had finally achieved their due recognition with the appearance of Frederick Douglass on the cover of the telephone directory. The comment, though made in jest, raised some vital questions about the nature of contemporary American society and the road black Americans had traveled since 1776. More important, why was our knowledge of those who struggled against apparently insuperable odds limited to great leaders such as Douglass? The conversation took place when many were questioning the wisdom and utility of that concentration. Knowing what the inarticulate masses had done to improve their condition seemed much more significant than simply reciting the story of those whom pioneering black historians—like Carter G. Woodson, Charles Wesley, Benjamin Quarles, John Hope Franklin, and a handful of others—had already rescued from oblivion. Although the discussion generated considerable heat, a consensus emerged that both approaches had to be pursued if we were ever to understand the full range of black American history. We needed to know much more about the lives of other lesser-known black figures who labored for the elimination of inequality. That is the genesis of this study.

Such noble objectives seem to warrant carefully constructed criteria for selecting the individuals to be studied. Nothing of the kind occurred here: the cast of characters was determined simply by chance. I had only recently concluded my study of black Americans in the Anglo-American abolitionist movement and wanted to know what became of them after their return home. What ever happened to these men and women who had won acceptance in Britain? How were they received by America? And how did their time abroad affect their lives and actions? An in-depth analysis covering an extensive period seemed the best method of answering these and other questions. Their experiences were in many respects similar, since all lived through a period of American history that was both exciting and frightening. Such a study might help us understand how blacks responded to oppression in the antebellum period, to the euphoria of the late 1860s as slavery and legalized discrimination seemed to recede, and to the return of a more virulent oppression toward the end of the century. It appeared that white contemporaries in the abolitionist movement could claim that the job had been completed and the cause vindicated with the passage of the Thirteenth Amendment and so retire from the fray, but blacks could not afford to be that confident. Having borne the brunt of racial discrimination and oppression, they were understandably suspicious of America's intentions. There was work to be done: the cloud of ignorance created by more than a century of slavery and discrimination would take decades to dispel. The battle to secure passage of constitutional amendments, which was characterized by southern resistance and northern appeasement, spoke of American intransigence and demanded that blacks be vigilant.

The antebellum period witnessed the disproportionate growth of southern political power, the birth of independent black organizations, and the agitation against slavery and Jim Crow discrimination, all occurring at a time of American economic and geographical expansion. Those who came of age in that era of turmoil, though they were relatively optimistic that America would someday live up to its vaunted principles of equality, were never deluded into believing that hope was enough. Constant struggle was clearly necessary. Therefore even when victories were recorded during the first years of Reconstruction, one could discern a healthy cynicism about the country's true intentions. Blacks could not afford to lower their guard, nor would they entertain the idea of conceding rights so dearly won in blood. Such concessions would be made by a later generation, one largely ignorant of the battles already waged and of the distance the country had traveled since the 1820s, and by those who deliberately chose to disregard the lessons of history. There were many, however, like W. E. B. Du Bois, beneficiaries of earlier struggles, who continued the tradition. This book addresses itself to that tradition, and its title is derived in part from Du Bois.

It was also Du Bois who best captured the historical dilemma of being both black and American. Like him, most of the figures in these essays found it impossible to turn their backs on America. After all, this was their country, one they and their ancestors had fought for and cultivated; it was all they knew. Yet America, shackled by an unyielding racism, refused to allow them the full rights of citizenship. It therefore became the responsibility of blacks, in fighting for their own freedom, to save America from itself. They became the conscience of America, calling the nation back to first principles, badgering it to conform to the Founding Fathers' ideals of equality. Never content with just pleading, blacks actively sought to undermine the system by stirring up international public opinion; exploiting loopholes such as the absurd law in Ohio that gave the vote to blacks who could prove 51 percent white ancestry; protecting fugitive slaves; and developing black institutions. Ultimately, they hoped, America would either see the error of its ways and effect the desired reforms or be pressured by forces beyond its control to concede to blacks their constitutional rights. All of this presupposed that blacks would remain in America. Others contended, however, that America would not or was unwilling to recognize the rights of blacks. The chapter on Robert Campbell is a sort of counterpoint. A foreigner, he was not constrained by the same emotional attachment to America; when opportunity beckoned in Africa he moved, convinced that the "motherland" provided blacks freedom from racism.

I have tried to recount the lives of these figures in as unvarnished a manner as possible. This was not easy, for these exciting characters lived and worked during a time in American history that sorely tested their mettle. Yet they battled on against terrible odds at an unusually high personal cost. If there is a common feature to emerge from this study, it is that America has never taken kindly to those who challenged its racial hegemony. Refusing to bow to such oppression, many blacks were personally destroyed. James W. C. Pennington, John Sella Martin, and Ellen and William Craft went full circle, rising from slavery through their own efforts, only to die in relative obscurity and poverty; William Howard Day fared marginally better. And Campbell avoided a similar fate by moving to Lagos. As the record attests, however, they never flinched from what they considered their duty to uplift the race. This is what made them such interesting people and threatened to turn the study into hagiography. I hope I have avoided such pitfalls without losing totally the touch of filiopietism so essential to good biography.

Acknowledgments

I have incurred many debts in the preparation and completion of this study. Robert Penny, former Chairman of Black Studies, University of Pittsburgh, always managed to find unspent funds in the budget to help defray the cost of short research trips, and my friends Nancie and Anthony Dent gave me the run of their home whenever I visited Philadelphia. Sue Crosby of the Inter Library Loan department at Pittsburgh listened to my interminable complaints about the tardy arrival of requested material, ignored them, and did all she could to assist me. Equally helpful was Ms. Louise Rountree, librarian at Livingstone College, Salisbury, North Carolina, who employed the Victorian method of first frightening then enlightening the uninitiated. They and other librarians in both the United States and Britain contributed immeasurably to this study. So, too, did Dorothy Sterling, who kindly shared her materials on Ellen Craft, and David White of the Museum of Connecticut History, whose assistance helped to fill in some of the gaps in Pennington's biography. Finally, a special thanks to Dr. Clifton Johnson, who allowed me to work in the Amistad Research Center even while the packers were scurrying around, trying to get the center into its new quarters. This study owes a great deal to these and many others too numerous to mention.

The work also benefited from the criticism of Betty Fladeland, Robert Harris, and Larry Glasco, who read all or part of the manuscript. Barbara O'Neil Phillips, my editor at the Press, has my gratitude for her careful attention to my text. My thanks also to B. J. Grier and Brenda Smith-Vaughn, who typed many versions of the manuscript yet managed to remain calm. No sensible person would be brave enough to end an acknowledgment without recognizing the contributions of a spouse. My wife, Cheryl, was a tower of strength, and her support and sacrifices are greatly appreciated. Rather than stay at home, she accompanied me to New Orleans, and when the call of maternity beckoned, she gave up typing my manuscript to have two handsome sons. All historians should be so lucky.

Abbreviations

ACS	American Colonization Society Papers. Manuscript Division, Library of Congress.
AFASS	American and Foreign Anti Slavery Society Papers. Amistad Research Center, New Orleans.
AMA	American Missionary Association. Amistad Research Center, New Orleans.
ASP	American Anti Slavery Society Papers. Boston Public Library.
BAP	Black Abolitionist Papers. Microfilm Edition.
BFASS	British and Foreign Anti Slavery Society. Rhodes House Library, Oxford University, Oxford.
BRFAL	Bureau of Refugees, Freedmen, and Abandoned Lands. Record Group 105. National Archives.
CMC	Church Missionary Society Papers. Church Missionary Society Archives, London.
COD	British Colonial Office Documents. Public Record Office, London.
FDP	Frederick Douglass Papers. Microfilm. Library of Congress.
FOD	British Foreign Office Documents. Public Record Office, London.
GES	Glasgow Emancipation Society Papers. Smeal Collection, The Mitchell Library, Glasgow.
GSC	Gerrit Smith Collection. George Arents Research Library, Syracuse University, Syracuse, N.Y.
JNH	*Journal of Negro History.*

LGC   Leon Gardiner Collection. The Historical Society of
          Pennsylvania, Philadelphia.
MMS   Methodist Missionary Society Papers. The Methodist Church
          Overseas Division (Methodist Missionary Society), London.
OCA   Oberlin College Archives. Oberlin College, Oberlin, Ohio.
PHS   Presbyterian Historical Society. Philadelphia.
RED   Raymond English Deposit. The John Rylands University Library
          of Manchester, Manchester.
RGS   Royal Geographical Society Papers. Royal Geographical Society,
          London.
TCP   Thomas Clarkson Papers, Huntington Library, San Marino, Calif.
THP   Thomas Hodgkin Papers. In possession of Hodgkin family,
          Warwickshire.

Beating Against the Barriers

James W. C. Pennington
Reprinted from Wilson Armistead, *A Tribute to the Negro*

Chapter I

James W. C. Pennington

A Life of Christian Zeal

Nineteenth-century Afro-American history is strewn with veiled references to the many men and women who fought against slavery and discrimination. Because of this, our knowledge of their lives is usually found in obscure footnotes to larger events, and the implication is that in their time they influenced few developments. The life of the Reverend James William Charles Pennington is a prime example of this historical deficiency. This is even more alarming in view of the fact that Pennington, the fugitive slave who later received an honorary Doctor of Divinity degree from the University of Heidelberg and who was prominent in major black and abolitionist movements, was viewed by his contemporaries as an individual of considerable merit.

Born James Pembroke in January, 1807, on Upper Farm, one of four farms owned by James Tilghman of Queen Anne's County, Maryland, Pennington was the second child of Nelly, one of Tilghman's slaves, and Brazil, a slave from an adjoining plantation. James and his elder brother Robert spent their early years on Upper Farm in a small community of twelve slaves that was headed by Jack, who was quite likely James's grandfather and who Pennington later claimed was a Mandingo prince bought from slavers around 1746. James Tilghman was among the Eastern Shore's most prominent citizens. Like many young men of his class, Tilghman was sent to London to read law, and on his return, he set up practice in Annapolis. Within a few years he was elected chief justice of the Second Judicial District and appointed judge on the Court of Appeals.

Through inheritance and marriage to the daughter of an aristocratic Maryland family, Tilghman acquired 1,700 acres of land. By the time of his death in 1809, Tilghman owned sixty slaves who worked his four farms.[1]

James Tilghman's will was administered by his eldest surviving son, Frisby, who had emigrated to Washington County sometime before the turn of the century. Frisby was already well known in the area around Hagerstown, Maryland, where he had platted a number of new towns, one of which, Tilghmanton, was named after him, and where he successfully cultivated Rockland, a 189-acre farm. After settling his father's estate, Frisby returned to Washington County with Nelly and her two sons. The separation from his father was a devastating blow for young James. It began, he later wrote, "the first of our family troubles that I knew anything about, as it occasioned a separation between my mother and the only children she then had, and my father, to a distance of about two hundred miles." The family, however, was soon reunited when Frisby purchased Brazil and brought him to Rockland.[2] Like most other slave children, young James spent his time doing minor chores around the farm until 1816, when he was hired out to a Hagerstown stonemason. Robert was also sent to Hagerstown to work with a pump maker. After almost two years, James was returned to Rockland and soon became the assistant of Uncle Taff, the farm's skilled blacksmith. James was an attentive student and in a few years was considered a first-rate blacksmith.[3]

From what we can gather, Rockland was a rather prosperous farm and Tilghman was regarded as one of the more enterprising and innovative planters in the area. Neighboring planters generally followed a four-field system of crop rotation, but Tilghman employed an eight-field system, one each in wheat, corn, roots, hay, and oats and three in pasture, which he later claimed resulted in increased yields and profits. It is nevertheless impossible to determine exactly how profitable Tilghman's farm was during James's days in slavery. By 1830, however, there were few old slaves on the farm, which at least suggests the potential for future expansion. Of Tilghman's thirty-three slaves, eleven were under ten years, six under twenty; eight under thirty; seven under fifty-

1. Queen Anne's County, Maryland, Inventory, WHN, VII, 1810, in Maryland Hall of Records, Annapolis; New York *Evening Post*, quoted in *Frederick Douglass Paper*, June 9, 1854; *Pennsylvania Freeman*, June 1, 1854.

2. James W. C. Pennington, *The Fugitive Blacksmith; or Events in the History of J. W. C. Pennington Pastor of a Presbyterian Church, New York, Formerly a Slave in the State of Maryland, United States*, in Arna Bontemps (ed.), *Great Slave Narratives* (Boston, 1969), 207; J. Thomas Scharf, *History of Western Maryland* (2 vols.; Baltimore, 1968), II, 1287.

3. Pennington, *Fugitive Blacksmith*, 209.

five, and only one over fifty-five. Interestingly, the Pembroke family accounted for thirteen of the farm's thirty-three slaves.[4]

Sometime before his twentieth birthday, James started making plans for his escape from Rockland. The relative ease of the blacksmith's forge could not obscure the general cruelty of the slave system. Like William and Ellen Craft, Frederick Douglass, and so many other fugitives from slavery, James decided to escape because of the kind of treatment he received while in Hagerstown. During his two years there, James later wrote, he "enjoyed some relief from the peculiar evils of slavery."[5] Such kindness bred frustration with continued oppression; more important, it created hope, which could inspire resolute individuals like James. His return to Rockland and his separation from his older brother, to whom he was very attached, were ample confirmation of the system's scant regard for the people it enslaved. But James's distress was partially allayed by the joy of returning to his mother.

Cruelty, punishment, and oppression were never far removed from the Pembrokes' daily lives. When, for example, James's uncle and another slave were late returning from the customary weekend visit to their families on neighboring plantations, Tilghman, frustrated by his inability to control totally the activities of his slaves, threatened to sell Brazil, claiming there were too many slaves on the plantation. When Brazil requested an opportunity to find his own buyer, Tilghman replied with the whip. James witnessed this unwarranted punishment but did not run away immediately, "yet in my mind and spirit," he later wrote, "I never was a *Slave* after it." Relations between the Pembrokes and their master deteriorated rapidly after Brazil's flogging. Tilghman, fearing that the family was planning an escape, sent a "confidential slave," a "wretched fellow," Pennington called him, "who was nearly white, and of Irish descent," to inform on the family. Tilghman's vigilance soon led to an open break with James, who was also flogged for no apparent reason. Rather than making him more submissive, the unjustified beating only fired James's determination to flee.[6]

A few days after this incident in October, 1827, James decided that the time had come to escape from Rockland. Following a plan commonly employed by other fugitive slaves, he would start his journey on Sunday. His movements would raise no suspicions among whites, as that was the day slaves were allowed

4. *American Farmer*, June 3, 1840; Census of 1830, Maryland.
5. Pennington, *Fugitive Blacksmith*, 209.
6. *Ibid.*, 211–14.

to go visit their families and friends. On Sunday night, October 28, James went to Hagerstown, intending to see his brother Robert, but he quickly abandoned the idea because he feared he might be discovered. It was a wise decision, for Hagerstown was a favorite haunt of slave catchers, who usually laid traps there in hopes of intercepting fugitives just short of the Pennsylvania border and freedom. For two nights James traveled without the aid of the North Star, which was hidden by thick clouds. Early Wednesday morning he arrived at a toll gate on the National Road only to discover, to his utter dismay, that he was but eighteen miles from Baltimore. With better luck he would have been in Pennsylvania. Disoriented and convinced that slave catchers were on his heels, James immediately turned north, ignoring the friendly advice of a passerby not to travel the road during the day. James would have done well to heed the warning. He was captured hours later in a village four miles from Reisterstown.

His first attempt to escape was easily foiled, but he had not gotten that far only to be quietly returned to slavery. Later that day, when his captors were busy working their farms, James made another and this time successful bid for freedom. He traveled at night and hid during the day. By now Tilghman's advertisements offering a $200 reward for James's recapture had reached Reisterstown. In an attempt to cover all possible routes of escape, Tilghman even placed advertisements in the Lancaster and Philadelphia papers. All Tilghman's efforts were unavailing, however, for James eluded his pursuers, who dogged him for forty-eight hours, and finally crossed into Pennsylvania at Adams County.[7]

Exhausted and cold, the fugitive was directed to the home of William and Phoebe Wright in Petersburg. A Quaker family, the Wrights were for many years the leaders of the Underground Railroad in Adams County. They welcomed James and agreed to employ him on their farm. For the next four to five months, Pembroke split logs and did odd jobs. In his spare time William Wright, a retired schoolteacher, taught James to read, write, and cipher. By the time he left the Wrights in March or April, James had shown considerable improvement in reading and writing and could even do simple mathematical equations.[8]

But hanging like a pall over his freedom was the fear of possible recapture. It was obvious to James that Tilghman would never accept the loss of such valuable property. Advertisements announcing the escape offered $200 for the fugitive who, Tilghman said, "can read and I believe write, is an excellent

7. *Ibid.*, 215–34; *Torch Light and Public Advertiser*, November 8, 22, 1827.
8. William Still, *The Underground Rail Road* (Philadelphia, 1872), 692; Pennington, *Fugitive Blacksmith*, 235–38.

blacksmith, and a pretty good carpenter."[9] That was an asset Tilghman could hardly afford to lose. He also had to be concerned that James's family, who were almost half the slaves at Rockland, might follow his example. The frequency of advertisements for fugitive slaves which appeared in the local newspaper suggests that slaveholders had to be especially vigilant if they hoped to keep their slaves on the plantations. There were more than a dozen advertisements in the first few months after James's escape. Tilghman's alternatives were limited: he could either sell off some of the Pembrokes as a means of frightening others into acquiescence, or he could attempt to recapture James. He chose the latter, hoping both to recover his property and to set an example to those in the slave quarters who were dreaming of freedom.

Despite the complex system that warned the Underground Railroad of imminent danger, James was constantly afraid that he would be recaptured. The Wrights moved James to safer surroundings, where Pembroke adopted the name Pennington; later he would add two additional middle names, William for William Wright, and Charles possibly for another supporter during this time. From Petersburg, James traveled northeast across the Susquehanna River to the farm of Daniel Gibbons in Lancaster County. Both Daniel and his wife Hannah were active members of the Railroad, helping an estimated nine hundred slaves to freedom. The Gibbonses sent James farther east to the village of East Nautmeal in Chester County. There Pennington spent the next seven months, working on the farm of another Quaker agent of the Underground Railroad, furthering his education and reading the Bible in his spare time.[10] Toward the end of 1828, James undertook the last part of his escape from slavery, leaving East Nautmeal and settling finally in Brooklyn, New York.

James Pembroke was no ordinary slave—Frisby Tilghman's advertisement and his later claim that the former slave was worth at least $1,000 attest to that fact. He was a skilled artisan, a first-rate blacksmith, and a competent stonemason and carpenter who, stretching the boundaries of his enslavement, taught himself to "cipher" and write. He spent many Sundays trying to understand words in the overseer's daybook of work done at the forge. Using feathers he found in the yard as pens and making ink from berries, James spent hours transcribing letters and figures from the daybook. James became so involved in his writing that he made a steel pen at his forge. He was a proud young man who took his work seriously. During this period, he later remembered, "I frequently

9. *Torch Light and Public Advertiser*, November 8, 1827.
10. Still, *Underground Rail Road*, 647; Pennington, *Fugitive Blacksmith*, 241–42.

tried my hand at making guns and pistols, putting blades in penknives, making fancy hammers, hatchets, swordcanes, etc. etc." One suspects that this kind of determination, ambition, and pride could not long be stifled by Tilghman—or by antebellum America, which consistently denied blacks full equality. Pennington would devote the rest of his life to self-improvement and to the elevation of his people. By his death in 1870, this "5'5" high very black, square and clumsily made" slave who had "a down look, prominent reddish eyes, and mumbles or talks with his teeth closed," as Tilghman's advertisement so derogatorily described James Pembroke, was regarded as a black intellectual of some stature.[11]

Pennington settled in Brooklyn possibly because he thought it safer than New York City, where there were many more fugitives and, consequently, slave catchers. He apparently made no effort to find work as a blacksmith, taking instead a job as a coachman at the home of Adrian Van Sinderen.[12] Brooklyn's black community, though small (870 out of a total population of 8,800 in 1825), was nevertheless active. Like their contemporaries in other northern cities, Brooklyn blacks formed their first political organization to protest the plans of the American Colonization Society (ACS). Founded in 1816, the ACS promoted the expatriation of blacks to Liberia, its colony in Africa. In the summer of 1831, six months after a similar meeting in New York City, blacks in Brooklyn met to condemn the formation of a Brooklyn chapter of the ACS. Pennington took an active part in the proceedings, giving a speech and helping to write the session's address to the public. Colonization, the address warned, was "wholly gratuitous." How could colonizationists, it asked, be interested in charities thousands of miles away while refusing to grant blacks "christian instruction" at home? "How many of us," it continued, "have been educated in colleges, and advance into different branches of business; or taken into mercantile houses, manufacturing establishments, etc.? Are we not even prohibited from some of the common labor and drudgery on the streets, such as cartmen, porters, etc.? It is a strange theory to us, how these gentlemen can promise to honor and respect us in Africa, when they are using every effort to exclude us from all rights and privileges at home." Africa could not benefit if a "parcel of uninstructed, uncivilized and unchristianized people" with Bibles went to teach "the natives the truths of the gospel, social happiness, and moral virtue." Christianity could only succeed in Africa if the missionaries were first edu-

11. *Torch Light and Public Advertiser*, November 8, 1827; Pennington, *Fugitive Blacksmith*, 212, 236–37.
12. *Frederick Douglass Paper*, April 6, 1855.

cated in America. Among other things, the meeting called on those who wanted to emigrate to settle in Upper Canada rather than Africa, for Canada was a place "far better adapted to our constitutions, our habits, and our morals; where prejudice has not such an unlimited sway; where you will be surrounded by christians, and have an opportunity to become civilized and christianized."[13]

Pennington's speech, his first in public, shows clearly the distance he had traveled in four years. He condemned the ACS for pandering to prejudice and influencing a number of legislatures to enact laws for the expulsion of free blacks. Blacks, he argued, were not aliens, subject to laws restricting their activities, nor did the Constitution demand they become naturalized. In fact, he told the meeting, "our fathers were among the first that peopled this country. Their sweat and their tears have been the means in a measure of raising our country to its present standing. Many of them fought and bled and died for the gaining of her liberties." Blacks could neither forsake the graves of these brave ancestors nor ignore the dictates of history to stay and purge the American Constitution of the foul stain of slavery. Never throughout his long and active life would Pennington waver in his opposition to colonization, which he later wrote was "much like feeding a hungry man with a long spoon."[14] The speech also gives us a glimpse of Pennington's oratorical style, which he later perfected, but which already displays his penchant for historical references, and the logical sequence of argument.

Those assembled elected Pennington their delegate to the first annual meeting of the Negro Convention movement to be held a week later in Philadelphia. The convention, founded in 1830 under the leadership of the Reverend Richard Allen, bishop of the AME church, was organized ostensibly to marshal support for blacks forced to leave their homes in Cincinnati because of enforcement of Ohio's black code, which demanded bonds of $500 to ensure good behavior. The majority of those who left Cincinnati established the colony of Wilberforce in Upper Canada. The convention, however, quickly expanded its interests to include issues of broader concern to blacks. Education, temperance, and economy, the meeting declared, were "best calculated to promote the elevation of mankind to a proper rank and standing among men, as they enable him to discharge all those duties enjoined on him by his creator." This was Pennington's first major exposure to these crucial issues, all of which he avidly supported in subsequent years. It was an exciting time for Pennington:

13. William Lloyd Garrison, *Thoughts on African Colonization* (1832; rpr. New York, 1969), Pt. II, pp. 24–26.
14. *Frederick Douglass Paper*, April 6, 1855; Pennington, *Fugitive Blacksmith*, 245.

not only was he a participant in the first of these very important meetings, he also encountered for the first time whites like Arthur Tappan, William Lloyd Garrison, and Simeon S. Jocelyn, soon to be well known among abolitionists.[15]

Although his part in the convention brought obvious personal rewards, Pennington had to face the wrath of his employer, who was president of the Brooklyn Colonization Society. Much to Pennington's surprise, Van Sinderen wanted to explore black opposition to colonization plans, which he believed had been initiated out of a genuine desire to improve existing conditions. Pennington's arguments against colonization convinced Van Sinderen—at the society's next meeting, he influenced his friends to disband.[16] Buoyed by the decision, Pennington saw Van Sinderen's conversion as a first thin wedge against colonization. Unfortunately, victories would be harder to achieve in the future.

For the next three years, Pennington was an active and prominent participant at the annual convention meetings. The second meeting, held in 1832, also devoted considerable time to the issue of colonization and the advisability of blacks' emigrating to Canada. This time, however, there was no unanimity on the benefits of going to Canada. When the issue of buying land there came up for discussion, Pennington joined those who opposed the plan: "Any recommendation of the Convention to emigrate from the United States, was calculated to impress the public mind, that we relinquished our claim to this being the land of our nativity." Rather than cause an open rift, the meeting sent to committee a resolution to purchase land in Canada as "an Asylum" for blacks fleeing American persecution. In an obvious attempt at compromise, the committee reported that although the proposal to buy land was premature, the existence of antiblack laws necessitated the formulation of plans to aid financially those forced to leave their homeland.[17] Subsequent meetings decided against any participation in emigration schemes, but continued to support the efforts of the Wilberforce Settlement.

Pennington took an active part in resolving almost all the important issues addressed by the convention. He moved a motion recommending that auxiliary societies compile statistics on the number and condition of schools in their area, what courses were taught and how many students attended. Such information was essential for the future development of schools in areas where

15. "Minutes and Proceedings of the First Annual Convention of the People of Colour, 1831," in Howard H. Bell (ed.), *Minutes of the Proceedings of the National Negro Conventions, 1830–1864* (New York, 1969), 5–7.

16. *Frederick Douglass Paper*, April 6, 1855.

17. "Minutes and Proceedings of the Second Annual Convention for the Improvement of the Free People of Colour in These United States, 1832," in Bell (ed.), *Minutes*, 10, 15–20.

blacks were not permitted to go to public schools. This attempt to gather information on black communities throughout the North (the number of churches, schools, benevolent societies, etc.) would become a major objective of later conventions. The meeting also named Pennington to a committee of three to prepare its annual address, which, among other things, lauded education's positive effects on prejudice. Eliminating prejudice and building self-respect, the address concluded, could be achieved through the acquisition of "that classical knowledge which promotes genius, and causes man to soar up to those high intellectual enjoyments and acquirements, which places him in a situation, to shed upon a country and a people, that scientific grandeur which is imperishable by time."[18] This view informed all of Pennington's later activities as a schoolteacher and as a scholar; he firmly believed that without a classical education, blacks were incapable of fulfilling their potential.

While working for Van Sinderen, Pennington used every opportunity to acquire an education. There were, however, few schools for blacks in Brooklyn in the early 1830s. The city's only school for blacks, opened in 1817, was forced out of its segregated rooms in the public school building in 1827. So the African Woolman Benevolent Society, a black mutual aid society, built a new school for the displaced students. Although the school later received support from public school officials, money was always in short supply. As a result, the school had but one teacher at a time. It is not known if Pennington attended this school, but he likely got part of his formal education at Sunday schools, which traditionally provided many blacks with their first exposure to education. These schools, one authority has written, aimed to educate students of all ages in "reading and manners, to teach morality and acceptance of the status quo . . . and cultivate the intellect." From their inception, Sunday schools were intended to serve those who went neither to church on Sunday nor to school during the week. They were also inexpensive to run, as most teachers were volunteers. By 1820, Sunday schools had attracted a significant number of blacks. In New York City, for example, blacks were 9 percent of the population in 1821, but were 26 percent of the pupils in Sunday schools.[19]

To supplement his Sunday school instruction, Pennington paid private tutors and attended evening classes. An acquaintance later remembered seeing "the

---

18. *Ibid.*, 27, 34.
19. Pennington, *Fugitive Blacksmith*, 242; Carlton Mabee, *Black Education in New York State from Colonial to Modern Times* (Syracuse, 1979), 35–46, 51–52; Robert J. Swan, "Did Brooklyn (N.Y.) Blacks Have Unusual Control Over Their Schools? Period I: 1815–1845," *Afro-Americans in New York Life and History*, VII (1983), 26–29; Edwin Wilbur Rice, *The Sunday-School Movement and the American Sunday-School Union* (Philadelphia, 1971), 58–59.

quiet, meek looking boy" walking three miles on Sundays to attend the Reverend Samuel Cox's church and Sunday school across the river in New York City. It is not known who his tutors were, but by sheer application, Pennington managed in four years to become fairly proficient in Latin and Greek. In early 1833 a friend suggested that he apply for the teaching position at a recently founded school for blacks in Newtown, Long Island. Pennington, now twenty-six years old, applied, was examined, and was later offered the job at a salary of $200 per year. The school had been established with a bequest of $2,500 from Peter Remsen, a successful New York merchant, whose father had been one of the largest slaveholders on Long Island. Remsen's school was the first for the town's small black population of 375, whose children were refused admittance to the public schools.[20]

Pennington approached his first teaching job with the same dedication that characterized his escape and his early education. On the first day of school, he trudged seven miles through the snow from his home in Brooklyn and found that the school had not been cleaned since the builders left. Pennington purchased a broom and did the work himself. As he quickly found out, a schoolroom did not guarantee students. Pennington had to visit the homes of blacks and encourage reluctant, skeptical parents to send their children to school. Even those who did agree to let their boys attend, Pennington later recalled, were "ignorant of the benefits" and had little "knowledge of the merits of education." More difficult to address, however, was the parents' assumption that only whites were competent to teach. Some of these parents were surprised when Pennington appeared, for they had taken it for granted that the new teacher would be white. As if these obstacles were not enough, Pennington started his job without books or slates, which he had to buy with his own money. But he would not be denied—he was determined that his school would succeed. By the time he left for New Haven a few years later, he could claim with some justification that his efforts had ensured primary education for the black children of Newtown. Pennington was succeeded by Samuel Ringgold Ward, who would rise to prominence as a minister and an editor.[21]

This commitment to education was responsible in part for Pennington's decision to go to New Haven to prepare for the ministry. The move came after much soul searching and a profound conversion experience, triggered by his

---

20. *Frederick Douglass Paper,* July 30, 1852; *Anti Slavery Standard,* January 16, 1851.
21. *Colored American,* July 25, August 22, October 24, November 7, 14, 28, 1840; *Emancipator,* August 12, 1836; Samuel Ringgold Ward, *Autobiography of a Fugitive Negro* (1855; rpr. Chicago, 1970), 22–23.

growing awareness of the extent of American slavery. That discovery, he wrote, "entered into the deep chambers of my soul, and stirred the most agitating emotions I had ever felt." Wrestling with the problem of how best to act, Pennington prayed and fasted, hoping to be guided. But his efforts only created greater difficulties. How could a "lost sinner, and a slave of Satan" undertake the task of eliminating the sin of slavery without first escaping the tyranny of personal sin? For two weeks he labored without success. "My heart, soul, and body," he wrote, "were in the greatest distress; I thought of neither food, drink nor rest, for days and nights together. Burning with a recollection of the wrongs man had done me—mourning for the injuries my brethren were still enduring and deeply convinced of the guilt of my own sins against God." One evening during the third week he held a long discussion with Dr. Cox, who invited Pennington to attend his church. Some time later, Pennington "was brought to a saving acquaintance with him of whom Moses in the Law and the Prophets did write." Soon after, he decided to prepare himself for the church. Man, he believed, had been placed on earth specifically to contribute to God's grand design, which included the elimination of all sin. Men, God's "moral agents," the instruments of his "providential administration," Pennington wrote some years later, had to labor to "subserve his purpose."[22]

But America seemed determined to subvert the will of God by impeding progress toward the final elimination of sin and inequality. The authorities at Yale's School of Divinity, for example, refused to allow Pennington to enroll as a student because he was black. He could attend lectures, but he was not permitted to participate in classes or borrow books from the library. In spite of these restrictions, Pennington managed to complete a course of study and qualify for the ministry. He also gained invaluable practical experience by periodically officiating at the Temple Street Congregational Church.[23] Pennington returned to Brooklyn in 1837 and was licensed to preach the following year. He first assisted at the small black Presbyterian church in Newtown, and later served as minister of the town's recently formed black Congregational church. By the time he left for Hartford, Connecticut, in 1840, the little church, which had been struggling, had a congregation of twenty-six and a Sabbath school of thirty.[24]

22. Pennington, *Fugitive Blacksmith*, 242–45; J. W. C. Pennington, *A Text Book of the Origin and History of the Colored People* (Hartford, 1841), 68.
23. Robert A. Warner, *New Haven Negroes: A Social History* (New Haven, 1940), 83; *Anti Slavery Standard*, August 9, 1843.
24. Congregational General Association of New York, *Minutes* (Whitesboro, N.Y., 1839); *Scot-*

The years from 1835 to 1840 were a particularly trying period for the nascent black leadership, which had known relative harmony in the early years of the decade. Divisions in the ranks led to the cessation of the convention's annual meetings in 1835 and the establishment of the American Moral Reform Society, which had less specific objectives. Pennington and many of the original advocates of the convention yearned for the days when blacks spoke with one voice. But the debates over the Moral Reform Society, which continued through the latter half of the decade, were more than just the railings of misguided men. The question of how to achieve the agreed objectives of an end to slavery and discrimination tried the abilities of the best black minds, without producing any clearly defined solutions.

Pennington was deeply troubled by the breakup of the convention, and on his return from New Haven, he joined forces with those who were calling for the reinstitution of national meetings. The emergence of the Moral Reform Society, he believed, signaled a fundamental change in philosophy and policy. Assemblies no longer addressed problems besetting black communities; instead, they aired abolitionists' generalized concerns. This shift, Pennington later wrote, "suddenly turned our people from their noble work of improvement, and set them in chase after shadows fleeting in the wind." It was not that blacks were opposed to wider abolitionist objectives, only that they insisted that equal suffrage, the removal of segregation, and other matters were more pressing and deserved urgent attention. Those who argued against a return to first principles were, in Pennington's view, ignoring what was important to the communities they claimed to represent.[25]

More important, however, was Pennington's insistence that blacks had to play the pivotal leadership role in any struggle against oppression. He did not dismiss or underestimate the invaluable contributions of white abolitionists, but he maintained that only blacks could bring to the movement the sense of urgency and commitment so necessary to eliminate existing inequalities. Moreover, black leadership of the movement was symbolically significant, a demonstration of ability to direct and sustain their own organizations. It was precisely this factor that did so much, in Pennington's view, to defeat American colonizationists' efforts in Britain in the early 1830s. The Reverend Nathaniel Paul, a black minister from Albany who represented the Wilberforce Settlement, had been largely responsible for the colonizationists' failure to win Brit-

tish Press, June 28, 1851; *Colored American,* October 28, 1837, February 13, 1841; Congregational General Association of New York, *Minutes* (Hamilton, N.Y., 1840).

25. *Colored American,* March 28, 1840.

ish backing for the settlement of black Americans in Liberia. Paul made it abundantly clear that blacks opposed the work of the American Colonization Society. Without Paul's active leadership, Pennington argued, the ACS would have succeeded in gaining British support for their plans. It was obvious, then, that blacks had to continue to give direction to the movement if they hoped to eliminate slavery and discrimination.[26]

A return to the convention meetings, Pennington wrote, would do more than anything else "to inspire our people with proper feelings of self-respect, independence, and moral courage. . . . We in a great measure," he continued, "fail to command respect, because we do not respect ourselves. We are sometimes trodden down because we are not independent enough to stand on our feet. And so too we are cheated out of some precious privileges, only because we have not courage to demand them."[27] But the meetings would have to be more carefully organized if they hoped to address the pressing needs of the communities they represented. In order to achieve these ends, Pennington proposed that delegates be elected by local "associations of oppressed people of color," affiliated with the national convention. This approach would ensure ample attention to local problems as well as establish a system of equitable representation at national meetings. Dealing with specific issues, like the inadequacy of educational opportunities, national meetings would nonetheless act as advisors to state meetings, the real loci of power and action. Pennington's proposals were far in advance of those submitted by his contemporaries, and so met with little support. When a national council was finally established in 1853, it quickly fell victim to regional differences and competition.[28]

Frustrated at making little headway, Pennington called a meeting of Long Island blacks in April, 1840. Stressing the existence of discrimination in schools, segregation in transportation, and restrictions on their right to vote, those assembled wanted conventions held annually until "our objective is gained" and recommended Troy, New York, as the site for the first meeting. The call produced a flurry of opposition from those who disagreed with the timing and proposed location, as well as from those who disapproved of exclusively black meetings.[29] Although Pennington moved to Hartford soon afterward, he continued to promote the idea of a national meeting. In May he was named to a committee of three to correspond with blacks in other parts of the

26. *Ibid.*, June 30, July 21, 1838.
27. *Ibid.*, April 8, 1838.
28. *Ibid.*, April 19, May 3, 1838; *Frederick Douglass Paper*, July 22, 1853.
29. *Colored American*, May 9, July 25, April 4, 1840.

country on the best means of organizing such a conference. In reply to critics, they insisted that there was no other measure "better adapted to meet the necessities of our critical case than the concentration of our *energies, intelligence and sympathies*" in a national convention. It was proposed that the convention meet in New Haven in August.[30]

The Hartford proposals fell prey to differences among blacks. James McCune Smith, a consistent opponent of reconvening the national meetings, argued that the time was not propitious, and that the objectives could be attained by other means. Others, like C. B. Ray, editor of the *Colored American*, though not opposed to the call, recommended postponement. To complicate matters further, the National Reform Convention of the Colored Inhabitants of the United States of America, an ephemeral organization headed by David Ruggles, also called for a national meeting in New Haven in September. Surprisingly, Pennington endorsed Ruggles' plan, then unexpectedly withdrew his support, claiming that the call had been "issued before the correspondence in which we were engaged was matured." There were those, like Ray, who lightheartedly questioned Pennington's motives. But if Ray was skeptical, Ruggles was certain that opponents, who, he warned, were in the pay of West Indian colonizationists, had persuaded Pennington and others to change their minds. The cause of Pennington's reversal is unclear. His friend Amos G. Beman, who opposed Ruggles' plan, may have influenced his decision. It is also possible that Pennington was piqued that Ruggles had stolen a march on him, having won initial support for the New Haven meeting. Whatever Pennington's motives, the withdrawal did not signify a change of heart. In fact, he stepped up his attacks. Opponents of the meeting, he charged, harbored less than honorable intentions in their incessant calls for delay. "Some of these manifestoes," he wrote, "have reminded me of the heavy-handed Dutchman, who seeing a fly biting his neighbor's horse on the neck, smote it with the eye of a broad-axe; thus in killing the fly, levelled the horse to the ground to rise no more."[31]

Opposition from men like Pennington, Beman, William Whipper, and Robert Purvis totally undermined Ruggles' plan. Beman refused to allow the National Reform Convention to meet in his church, and Ruggles had no alternative but to use a private home. It was a convention in name only—there were five delegates and twenty onlookers. The first national meeting since 1835 foundered

---

30. *Emancipator*, June 12, 1840; *Colored American*, June 13, 1840; *Anti Slavery Standard*, June 25, 1840.
31. *Colored American*, August 8, July 25, 1840; *Anti Slavery Standard*, July 9, 1840.

because a disorganized and disunited leadership could not devise an acceptable plan of action. But what Pennington lost on the swings he gained on the roundabouts. Five days before the National Reform Convention met, he was elected president of the Connecticut State Temperance and Moral Reform Society. Although the society praised the work of British and American abolitionists, and stated its intention to cooperate with all those promoting human rights, there was no doubt that it was firmly committed to holding "conventions whenever circumstances require."[32]

Throughout the 1840s, Pennington continued to promote the Convention movement from Hartford, where he had moved to become pastor of the Talcott Street Colored Congregational Church, which was founded in 1826. It was his first important settled ministry. Like many other black churches associated with white denominations, Talcott Street was established in response to continued discrimination in white churches. For the first few years, church members met in the First Congregational Church and depended on support from the Sunday School Union. In May, 1826, the congregants formed the African Religious Society of Hartford to promote the interests of blacks in the city. Years later, when faced with possible eviction from the room in which they worshiped, the society decided to purchase a plot of land on which to build a church. With money raised through subscriptions from church members and donations from white supporters, the church on Talcott Street was built. Pennington was examined and installed as minister in July, 1840, and remained there until 1848, when he resigned to take up a pastorate in New York City.[33]

The new appointment also provided Pennington an opportunity to continue his work as a teacher. His arrival in Hartford coincided with a reorganization of the city's two black schools, the North African School, which met in the basement of the Talcott Street Church, and the South African School, whose classes were held in the Elm Street Methodist Church. Prior to 1830, black pupils were educated in the poorly equipped public schools. In spite of growing demands that one or two schools be opened, nothing was done until 1833, when Amos Beman, then of Middletown, became the teacher at the Talcott Street School. The following year, blacks formed the Hartford Literary and Religious Institution in an effort to raise funds for the establishment of a high

32. Jane H. Pease and William H. Pease, *They Who Would Be Free: Blacks' Search for Freedom, 1830–1861* (New York, 1974), 181; *Colored American*, September 19, August 15, 1840; *Anti Slavery Standard*, August 13, September 10, 24, 1840.

33. Faith Congregational Church, *Our 150th Anniversary 1826–1976* (Hartford, n.d.); *Colored American*, August 8, 1840.

school. The organization apparently accomplished little, however, and soon disappeared.[34]

There had been almost no improvement in the city's black schools since the early 1830s. For four years, Pennington and his wife Harriet struggled to keep the North African School afloat. When they resigned in 1844, they were replaced by Augustus Washington, a former student at Dartmouth and recently a teacher at Pennington's old school in Newtown. Washington did only marginally better. Although his teaching was praised by a visiting School Society inspector, attendance at the school fluctuated significantly from session to session. Fearing that the school promised them since 1830 would never be established, Pennington wrote the School Society on behalf of Hartford's blacks. He complained that appropriations for building the school and teachers' salaries had not even been passed. He also condemned the society for making no effort to improve conditions in existing schools. Because of this indifference, and the poverty of the community, blacks found it impossible to procure adequate rooms and competent teachers. In response, the School Society agreed to provide better supplies and equipment, but that was all. A few years later, blacks petitioned for a new schoolhouse, and when in 1852 they were given the choice of either attending the white public schools or having their own schools, they opted for the latter. This arrangement continued until 1868, when Connecticut education was finally desegregated.[35]

Education was, in Pennington's view, the cornerstone of the future of blacks: it would not only free them from the web of ignorance, it would also provide them the means to use fully the benefits of citizenship in a society unfettered by slavery and discrimination. The greater the opportunities for acquiring an education, the easier it would be to refute allegations that blacks were incapable of self-improvement. It was for these reasons that Pennington suggested in 1838 the formation of a black American educational society to aid in the establishment of schools and to promote classical education among black youth. The society would also send four or five of the brightest students to college in either America or Britain. In the interim, there would be a series of study groups, each led by an educated black man who would gather around him a dozen students. While working, the students could spend eight to twelve weeks a year for three years under their tutor. "This system," Pennington insisted, "would initi-

34. *Emancipator*, April 1, 1834.
35. David O. White, "Hartford's African Schools, 1830–1868," *Connecticut Historical Society Bulletin*, XXXIX (1974), 48; Warner, *New Haven Negroes*, 71–72; Javis Means Morse, *A Neglected Period of Connecticut History, 1818–1850* (New Haven, 1933), 146–47.

ate them into the art of systematic reading and study in the higher branches of education." Educated blacks had to leave "intellectual monuments," inspirations for future generations. Throughout his life Pennington struggled to build these monuments. He was, for example, an active member of the New York "Society for the Promotion of Education among Colored Children," which opened a number of elementary schools in the 1850s, but failed in its efforts to establish a secondary school.[36]

Wherever he lived, Pennington continued to promote similar efforts, insisting that blacks open their own seminaries and manual-labor and normal schools until such time as white America decided to provide its black citizens with equal educational opportunities. Black Americans had to see to their children's education until the struggle against segregation and lack of schools was successful. His suggestions were not always well received, especially by those blacks who maintained that their energies should be aimed at attaining integration. Although he supported the advocates of this position, Pennington nonetheless emphasized the necessity for black schools. "It has always seemed to me," he wrote in reply to his critics, "that the time wasted in waiting for admission to the existing institutions, and encountering the embarrassments of cruel caste, is worth more than the principle involved." He obviously surprised his colleagues when he said that black children learned more in segregated schools. "It was known that the blacks had black churches and black schools," he told an audience in Worcester, England, "not because they wished to be exclusive but for conscience' sake, for it was found that while black children did not learn so fast as white ones in mixed schools, they learned equally well with white children in schools where the pupils were all of their own colour, thus proving that the degradation to which they were subjected in mixed schools broke their spirits and rendered them unwilling to learn, which unwillingness in some instances had been distorted into incapacity." What mattered was "sound scholarship," not where one was educated.[37]

It was in order to promote these objectives that Pennington wrote *A Text Book of the Origin and History of the Colored People* in 1841. There is little of the textbook in this work, and it was too advanced for students in the elementary and secondary schools of the period. The book is, first and foremost, an attempt to refute the theories about the origin of blacks and the proslavery views of their inferiority. Following in the wake of Hosea Easton's *Treatise* (1837), Pennington's

36. *Colored American*, June 2, 1838; *North Star*, May 12, 1848; Mabee, *Black Education in New York State*, 63–67.
37. *Christian Freeman*, November 6, 1845; Worcester *Herald*, July 29, 1843.

Text Book continued the attack on such views and the arguments advanced by Dr. Josiah Nott, a Mobile physician, and others that Egyptians were not Africans. But the work also goes beyond Easton's limited aims, for Pennington was clearly attempting to establish an intellectual monument.

Employing a combination of biblical exegesis and "sacred" and "profane" history, Pennington leveled a broadside against those who argue that the Bible justifies slavery. Although Noah did curse Canaan, the curse was, Pennington maintained, explicit—Canaan alone, not his descendants, was to be a "servant of servants." Moreover, the words *servant* and *slave* are not interchangeable. To have made Canaan's posterity inherit the curse would have been to violate the sacred principle that "the son shall not bear the iniquity of the father, neither shall the father bear the iniquity of the son." Further, Pennington questioned whether blacks were direct descendants of Canaan, the youngest son of Ham. They were, he argued, descended from Cush, Ham's eldest son, whose children were the progenitors of the "Asiatic Cushites or Ethiopians." More specifically, blacks were "properly the sons of Cush and Misraim amalgamated," who settled Ethiopia and Egypt, respectively, at about the same time. The two nations subsequently joined in a confederation, so that they "became the same people in politics, literature and peculiarities" and together contributed to Egypt's fame as the originator of the arts and sciences. The notions that the Bible endorsed slavery, through the curse on Canaan, and that blacks were Canaan's descendants were dismissed by Pennington as totally without foundation.[38]

What, then, caused the ancestors of black Americans to fall from prominence? How did the source of the arts and sciences become victims of the slave trade? The answer, Pennington believed, was to be found in their adoption of polytheism and the consequent and predictable slide into heathenism, which, irrespective of its sophistication, blinds the mind, loosens the morals, and creates divisions and animosities. Reversing that trend and returning to the Kingdom of God necessitated accepting the God who led the Israelites out of bondage.[39]

Intellectual regression, another result of polytheist belief, was exacerbated by slavery. This did not in any way, Pennington argued, affect blacks' intellectual capabilities. Defining *intellect* as "those powers of the human soul, as distinct from mere instinct, which alone enable man to reason and reflect," he observed

38. Pennington, *A Text Book*, 5–17.
39. *Ibid.*, 32–38.

that it is in all cases "identical in human beings" and is what distinguished man from the animals. Further, because God created man "in his own likeness, and after his own image," and because there was no available evidence that God intended to "produce any change in the intellect," Pennington concluded that God created the intellect of black and white identically. Moreover, the "relation between himself and that intelligence" cannot be broken. Intellectual disparities therefore arise from the opportunities for development—namely, schools—and the extent to which individuals master different levels of education.[40] Blacks could not depend on the whims of a society that insisted on segregation; they had to open their own schools.

Expanding educational opportunities for black children was part of a broader movement for change and was symptomatic of a general improvement in the condition of blacks. In a speech to the second World Anti Slavery Convention in 1843, Pennington produced a mountain of statistics to show that blacks were demonstrating all the features of a civilized people, pursuing the "same conduct, and following the same avocations that white persons of European descent do." They were not simply aping the actions of whites, Pennington insisted, but had initiated a number of schemes and organized the necessary institutions to put them into effect. The Negro convention meetings, in which he had been an active participant, the establishment of independent denominations like the AME and AME Zion churches, the opening of schools for those denied admittance to public schools, and the founding of temperance, benevolent, and debating societies, all proved indisputably that blacks had taken the initiative and were not depending solely on the benevolence of white friends. These institutions, which responded to the needs of the black communities in which they were located, were also vehicles for attacking discrimination. Thus blacks, with invaluable support from whites, had managed to effect a measure of change in American society despite continued discrimination. As a consequence, a number of states had already removed certain legal restrictions. Although blacks were still not permitted to vote in Connecticut and Pennsylvania, they were allowed to do so in most of the New England states. Slowly but perceptibly, Pennington concluded, Jim Crow restrictions on streetcars and boats were being lifted.[41]

No one disputed Pennington's analysis of black initiative and industry, but

40. *Ibid.*, 54–63.
41. J. F. Johnson, *Proceedings of the General Anti Slavery Convention Called by the Committee of the British and Foreign Anti Slavery Society and Held in London from Tuesday, June 13th to Tuesday, June 20th, 1843* (London, 1844), 46–52.

some were startled by his optimistic view that discrimination was lessening. William Johnson of the New York Vigilance Committee felt compelled to dispute Pennington's interpretation. Blacks, he asserted, were still excluded from colleges, seminaries, trades, streetcars, hotels, churches, jury boxes, and even cemeteries where a "coloured man may not be buried by the side of a white." Johnson, at a loss to understand Pennington's conclusions, suggested that Pennington may have been unduly motivated by a desire not to "throw more odium on the country than was necessary." Nothing was farther from the truth; Pennington rarely missed an opportunity to heap scorn on America when he thought it necessary. What Johnson overlooked was Pennington's view of the nature of progress: "I am one of those . . . though a black man myself, who have long since adhered to the conclusion that he is capable of improvement equally with the white man."[42]

Although Pennington had few objections to Johnson's rebuttal, he was nonetheless groping for an analysis of black progress. The idea or law of progress, popularized by Auguste Comte, assumed that nature and man passed through stages of development from the past to the present and into the future, with the most recent (occasional regressions notwithstanding) superior to the most distant. The law posited, Robert Nisbet has written, that "mankind has advanced in the past—from some aboriginal condition of primitiveness, barbarism, or even nullity—is now advancing, and will continue to advance through the foreseeable future." For precisely this reason, Pennington devoted significant portions of his speeches and writings to discussions of the history of black Americans. During a lecture in Glasgow, for example, Pennington traced the history of free blacks since the War of Independence. It is the history of a people, he argued, "who have passed through scenes of untold cruelties and barbarism from the earliest moment of their existence in America; a people who have most skillfully practised the law of self-preservation until they are now numerically the dread of their oppressors; a people who at this moment stand largely connected with America's proud fame, *aiding largely to sustain her boasted school system, her agriculture, commerce, manufacture, mechanical arts, medical science, theology, popular literature, and taking the lead in all her great reforms.*"[43]

These attainments resulted from an expansion and an improvement of knowledge, prerequisites for progress. But this knowledge had to go beyond the mere acquisition of formal education; it also had to provide the tools for coping

42. *Ibid.*, 47, 55–57.
43. Robert Nisbet, *History of the Idea of Progress* (New York, 1980), 4–5; J. W. C. Pennington, *A Lecture Delivered Before the Glasgow Young Men's Christian Association; and Also Before the St. George's Biblical, Literary and Scientific Institute, London* (Edinburgh, n.d.), 20.

with the many problems presented by nature and by human groups. To reach this level, man had to be free from all unnecessary restrictions. One such restriction, which Pennington maintained had to be eliminated, was to be found in economic policies that impeded commerce. Borrowing from Adam Smith, he argued that economic growth was impossible if individuals were shackled by law or custom. There was no need for international laws "to compel men of different nations to come together for trade. The instincts of nature bring them—their natural love of gain." When it appeared in the mid-1850s that Fourierist socialism was attracting young blacks, Pennington lashed out. The "polluted elements of socialism," he warned, were only retarding "the progress of the cause of civilization."[44]

Blacks had not gotten this far in their fight against discrimination only to yield to socialist restrictions. Like all other oppressed people, blacks had to remain vigilant and be wary of all efforts to slow their progress. Back of Pennington's views was a strong conviction that, following Christ's example, blacks had to avoid a violent confrontation with their foes. In opposing inhuman restrictions, they had to practice "moral power," which he described as the "law of *forgiveness* and endurance of wrong," for, he argued, there was not a single case on record of a "minority, with justice on its side, being crushed, while adhering to the law of forgiveness and endurance." Moral power should not be confused with inactivity in the face of oppression, but should be seen as a form of passive resistance predicated on what Pennington called "Christian Zeal," or the Christian's commitment to work against all forms of evil and its hand-maiden, oppression. This is precisely why Pennington and so many of his contemporaries saw themselves as philanthropists opposed to all forms of social evil, including slavery and intemperance, and why he so avidly believed that blacks had to continue to lead the fight against American oppression. "The negro race," he told a Bristol audience in 1850, "had in the conflict proved to the world two things. It had proved that the race possessed vitality, and it proved, too, that the law of progress was incorporated in its constitution. The law of vitality had stood the test of two centuries of trial and endurance on the American soil; the law of progress was now beginning to be developed. Go where they would in America he would be able to show them pure negroes in the foremost ranks of the temperance platform, filling offices as commercial agents, and rendering service in all the departments of civil life."[45]

Progress imposed two related responsibilities on black Americans: one, they

44. *Anti Slavery Standard*, February 19, 1852; *Frederick Douglass Paper*, October 26, 1855.
45. Pennington, *A Lecture*, 20; Bristol *Mercury*, October 19, 1850.

must constantly rededicate themselves to the fight against oppression at home (this helps explain Pennington's opposition to colonization); and two, they, as the most advanced of the race, must promote the evangelization of Africa. The spread of Christianity would undo the harmful effects of polytheism and set Africa on a course by which it could rejoin the comity of civilized nations. Just before he left Newtown, an event occurred that, as it turned out, allowed Pennington to involve himself in the work of African redemption. In June, 1839, the fifty-one slaves of José Ruiz and Pedro Montez were transferred to the schooner *Amistad* for the trip from Havana to Guanaja in Cuba. Four days out to sea, the Africans, led by Cinque and Garbeau, mutinied, killed the captain and the cook, but spared the lives of Ruiz and Montez, who were to navigate the ship back to Africa. For the next few weeks the *Amistad* followed a zigzag course, sailing east during the day, then abruptly turning north at night, Ruiz and Montez hoping to reach the security of a port in the southern United States. Lost and short of provisions and water, the *Amistad* finally dropped anchor off Long Island. While Cinque and a small party were ashore searching for fresh supplies, the ship was captured by an American navy cutter commanded by Lieutenant J. R. Gedney. Cinque and the others were arrested when they returned and were taken to a prison in New Haven. As word of the mutiny and arrest spread, Lewis Tappan, Joshua Leavitt, and Simeon Jocelyn organized a committee to work for the Africans' release. The case wound its way through the courts, and the Supreme Court ruled in favor of the captives in March, 1841. The Mendians, as they were called, were settled on a farm in the town of Farmington, where they remained until their departure for Africa in November, 1841.[46]

Pennington had written the *Colored American* of his long interest in missionary work and the duty of black Americans to take an active part in the Mendians' return. The case of the *Amistad* captives and Sir Thomas Fowell Buxton's expedition to the Niger in 1841 rekindled an interest in Africa among black Americans. Buxton wanted to establish a string of settlements along the Niger, peopled mostly by skilled black agriculturalists from the New World; he hoped they would introduce farming practices, commerce, and Christianity to Africa. The editor of the *Colored American* praised this plan as a possible means of undermining the slave trade. Pennington's idea to use the Mendians as the nucleus of a missionary station on the west coast of Africa was influenced and

46. Bertram Wyatt-Brown, *Lewis Tappan and the Evangelical War Against Slavery* (Cleveland, 1969), 205–12; Clifton Johnson, "The American Missionary Association, 1846–1861: A Study of Christian Abolitionism" (Ph.D. dissertation, University of North Carolina, 1958), 52–55.

supported by A. W. Hanson, an African who had been studying and lecturing in America since 1838 and who was a member of Pennington's church in Hartford. Hanson subsequently returned to Africa, where he became a prominent figure, until his untimely death.[47] Pennington's letter to the *Colored American* and his suggestion that blacks form a missionary society to work with the returning Africans produced a flurry of letters in support of the idea.

Some of those interested in working with the Mendians met at Pennington's church on May 5 and decided to open correspondence with blacks in other parts of the country to determine the extent of support for establishing a missionary society. The response was overwhelmingly positive, and in July a committee consisting of Pennington, Hanson, and Samuel Serrington issued a call for a founding meeting in Hartford in August. Among other things, the call pointed out that blacks had no missionary societies through which they could put into effect Christ's command to "go into all the world and preach the Gospel to every creature." More important, they believed that it was time black Americans did something for the "land which our fathers loved as the land of their nativity."[48]

Forty-three delegates from six states, including five Mendians, attended the founding meeting of the Union Missionary Society (UMS) held at Pennington's church from the eighteenth to the twentieth of August, 1841. With Pennington as its president, the society aimed to enlist the support of blacks and whites in its work. Although its principal focus was Africa, which it believed offered blacks a "wider field of usefullness, and has greater claims upon our sympathy and benevolence than any other quarter of the globe," the UMS also spoke of carrying the gospel to all "benighted lands." Aware that American missionary societies had deliberately refused to exclude slaveholders, the society adopted a constitution that barred them from membership. In an obvious effort to be inclusive, the meeting created a board of managers consisting of forty-four members, larger than the total attendance at the sessions, and an executive committee of seventeen.[49]

Few blacks questioned the need to involve themselves in the work of taking the gospel to their ancestral home, where, in the words of the Reverend Daniel A. Payne, "charms and wizards fly." Such work was merely the fulfillment of God's design; blacks had been placed in America, many believed, as the

47. *Colored American*, August 24, 1839; Monroe Fordham, *Major Themes in Northern Black Religious Thought, 1800–1860* (Hicksville, N.Y., 1975), 91.
48. *Union Missionary Herald*, January, 1842.
49. *Ibid.*; *Anti Slavery Standard*, October 7, 1841.

means of accomplishing these ends: "[To] show to the unbelieving tribes of men, Gentile and Jew, civilized and barbarous," the UMS Executive Committee wrote, "that the gospel after the lapse of eighteen centuries, has lost nothing of its original power, to bless the injured, by enabling him to forgive the injurer; and to comfort the afflicted, by disposing him to become the instrument of good to still greater sufferers." But the God of the oppressed, who intervened to eliminate inequalities through his word, only came to the rescue of those who were determined to help themselves. It was therefore essential that blacks support the UMS. Demonstrating that they could originate and sustain an effort of this kind would both enhance their image throughout the world and redound to their benefit at home. Self-reliance, Pennington consistently reiterated, was indispensable to the progress of any people. Earlier that summer, in a preface to a book by Ann Plato, a young teacher and a member of his church, he wrote: "Our young authoress justly appeals to *us*, her own people, (though not exclusively) to give her success. I say the appeal is *just*. And it is just because her success will, relatively, be our own. A mutual effort is the legitimate way to secure mutual success."[50]

A black organization built by blacks had to rely almost totally, if not exclusively, on itself. From the beginning, the UMS insisted that it was primarily for blacks, though it did ask whites to join. Putting the principle into practice, however, proved much more difficult. Few black communities had the means to sustain the society's ambitious plans. The Executive Committee's suggestion that the one hundred black churches in the country each contribute $100 to the UMS met with little response. It was both exorbitant and impractical to request that kind of support from poor black communities. True to his word, Pennington sold a lot he owned in New Haven and gave the proceeds to the society's treasury.[51] Not many others could be that generous, and few whites contributed, preferring instead to send donations to the Mendian Committee, headed by Lewis Tappan.

In spite of efforts to present a public image of amiability and cooperation, relations between the two organizations were strained. Tappan saw the society, whose formation he considered exceedingly premature and rash, as a potential competitor. When offered the position of UMS auditor, he declined and, obviously attempting to steal a march on the society, suggested that Pennington

50. *Union Missionary Herald,* January, 1842; Ann Plato, *Essays; Including Biographies and Miscellaneous Pieces in Prose and Poetry* (Hartford, 1841), xix–xx.
51. *Union Missionary Herald,* February, 1842; *American and Foreign Anti Slavery Reporter,* May, 1843; J. W. C. Pennington to [?], January 12, 1842, in AMA.

accompany the Mendians as their missionary. Pennington in turn sidestepped the suggestion, insisting that he could best serve the cause and his people by remaining in America. "The Missionary Society which we have just formed," he reminded Tappan, "will need much labor to make it go. And I think I can do my duty by keeping this church up to the work and otherwise laboring here to train young men." The stalemate was not resolved. The committee still had to confront its organizational shortcomings, and the society made little headway in attracting greater financial support. With the Mendians pressing to return home, Tappan turned to the American Board of Commissioners for Foreign Missions for assistance. The board, however, refused because of the committee's insistence that it stop soliciting and accepting money from slaveholders. Yet Tappan continued to believe that the board could be influenced to adopt an antislavery position.[52]

An adamant board and the failure to compromise produced some rather bizarre situations in the following months. Pennington's attempts to elicit financial support for the society were continually frustrated, and he also had to face the fact that they had not attracted any qualified black missionaries to accompany the Mendians. Less than a month before the Mendians' proposed departure, Pennington wrote the committee and requested a delay of four to six weeks. That was totally impractical, however, given the Mendians' anxiety to leave America. The society had no alternative but to agree to send out two assistant missionaries under the supervision of the committee's missionaries. Yet the society and the committee met separately in New York to commission their respective missionaries, giving the false impression that they were acting independently. Finally, the groups boarded the ship *Gentleman*, which sailed for Africa on November 27.[53]

Jostling between the two organizations did not cease with the departure of the Mendians. The committee continued to attract the most contributions for the nascent missionary station, although it lacked the society's organizational structure. Unification obviously would improve efficiency and increase the African station's chances of success. Negotiations on the merger made little progress until the society agreed to an unstated constitutional change and to moving its headquarters to New York. Under the agreement the two executive committees were joined, the name of the society was adopted, Pennington re-

52. Pennington to Dear Sir, October 9, 1841, in AMA; C. Johnson, "The American Missionary Association," 27–28, 50, 56–57.
53. *Union Missionary Herald*, February, 1842; Pennington to A. F. Williams, November 1, 1841, in AMA.

mained president, and Tappan became treasurer and corresponding secretary. Tappan cheerfully reported to the September, 1842, meeting of the new society that it was in "delightful accordance with the spirit of the gospel that our colored fellow-christians should co-operate with their white brethren in extending the gospel to the unevangelized in heathen nations."[54] With Pennington in Hartford, and the UMS in New York under the daily supervision of the treasurer and corresponding secretary, it was obvious that Tappan had carried the day while conceding to Pennington the visible, but mainly honorific, position of president.

The UMS continued its efforts in Africa until it merged with the Committee for West Indian Missions and the Western Evangelical Missionary Society in 1846 to form the American Missionary Association (AMA). The West Indian Committee had been formed in 1844 to coordinate the efforts of American missionaries working in Jamaica, and the Western Society, formed the previous year, oversaw work among the Indians of the western United States. The plan of merger came only after repeated refusals by the American Board of Commissioners for Foreign Missions to accede to demands that it stop accepting money from slaveholders. Prior to the board's annual meeting in 1845, a group of twelve Presbyterians and Congregationalists, including Jocelyn, Beman, Henry Highland Garnet, Tappan, and Pennington, met to try to increase pressure on the board. The time had come, they asserted, for a new departure. Either the board must accept their demands, or they would establish a new organization that would have no connection with slaveholders. In February, while Pennington was on a visit to Jamaica, those in support of free missions gathered in Syracuse. In a letter to the meeting, Tappan, writing on behalf of the UMS, called for a complete break with the board and suggested that either the society be recognized as the free missions' agency or another society be formed. It was finally agreed to form the AMA as the new society of free missions.[55] Interestingly, the merger cost Pennington his office—Tappan assumed the presidency of the new organization.

In spite of these changes, Pennington maintained an active interest in missionary work, particularly in Africa. What that continent needed, he maintained, was not the founding of colonies under European or American auspices, but the spread of Christianity through missionary stations. That colonies in-

54. *American and Foreign Anti Slavery Reporter*, May, 1843.
55. *American Missionary*, October, 1864, May, 1868; Oberlin *Evangelist*, November 25, 1846, August 28, 1844; C. Johnson, "The American Missionary Association," 83–85, 60–61; *Emancipator and Weekly Chronicle*, May 21, 1845.

variably led to the destruction of aboriginal populations was exemplified, he argued, in the histories of American and British colonial experiments. Pennington perceived a clear relationship between the plans of British colonists and those of the American Colonization Society. Britain intended "to relieve herself from what she believed to be an over-grown population, America to relieve herself from what she calls an obnoxious population." Once settled, the colonists immediately turned against the natives, using superior military power to eliminate all opposition. These colonies of whites (and by the same token that of the Colonization Society), Pennington argued, paid no attention to the "African's love of home or veneration for his father's grave. The white in the land of Ham has been cruel and rapacious. He had outlawed the African in his own land, he has taken from him 30,000 square miles of maiden land, with the dash of a pen." Proud of African resistance to these incursions, and demonstrating real perspicacity, Pennington warned that if present colonial policies were not radically altered, Africa was "destined to be the theatre of bloody conflict, between her native sons, and intruding foreigners, black and white, for a century yet to come." What Africa needed, then, was a "pure system of Gospel Evangelization," the establishment of "Christian Theocracies," under which the native populations and their kings would receive the saving teaching of Christianity while being allowed to govern their countries as they deemed fit. Ultimately, Pennington concluded rather optimistically, this system would uplift those degraded by polytheist practices.[56]

Pennington's reputation grew dramatically after the formation of the Union Missionary Society (1841). At a period when the Negro Convention movement was relatively inactive, his presidency made him a national figure of some prominence. This may be one reason why the Connecticut State Anti Slavery Society named him a delegate to the second World Anti Slavery Convention in London in 1843. Accepting the appointment, Pennington was quick to recognize that he would be able to bring the problems of black Americans to the attention of a wider audience. He was aware that he had to uphold the tradition of black involvement in the transatlantic abolitionist movement, as established by his predecessors Nathaniel Paul and James McCune Smith in the 1830s and Charles Lenox Remond in 1840–1841.

Pennington left for New York in early May with endorsements from Hartford and Troy, New York, as the "accepted representative of the Colored People of

56. "Proceedings of the Colored National Convention Held in Rochester, 1853," in Bell (ed.), *Minutes*, 49–55.

the United States." In New York he attended the annual meeting of the UMS and was commissioned by the American Peace Society as one of its delegates to the first Peace Congress in London. Pennington set sail for England on May 10 on the packet *Montreal* in the company of William Johnson of the New York Vigilance Committee, the Reverend H. H. Kellogg of Illinois, and the Reverend Jonathan Blanchard of Ohio, all of whom were on their way to the convention.[57] In comparison to his return voyage, the trip was rather uneventful and Pennington thoroughly enjoyed the company and the fact that for the first time he had not been forced into segregated accommodations. On his arrival in London, Pennington wrote friends in Hartford almost ecstatic about the absence of racial discrimination in England. Throughout his stay, he never missed an opportunity to compare the friendly reception and his hosts' open hospitality with the discrimination he continually encountered in America. His treatment on the *Montreal*, he told a Leeds audience, was in stark contrast to what happened on his way from Hartford to New Haven, when he had to travel in a dingy carriage even though he had paid the full first-class fare. Pennington's criticism obviously annoyed many Americans, for on his return trip from Britain, he was refused a stateroom and had to take his meals by himself in the steward's pantry. His countrymen were determined to teach him a lesson. As he later reported, when he got on board he found "no berth, not even any tolerable protection from the weather provided for him—nothing but a sort of recess where merchandise had been tumbled in—affording not even a decent place for a beast."[58]

That kind of treatment only made Pennington more aware of the comparative hospitality of his English hosts and more sensitive to American discrimination. After a few days in London, Pennington was invited by the Reverend James Sherman to assist "at the table of the Lord" and to preach at Surrey Chapel, something none of Pennington's fellow ministers had dared to do in Hartford. No church in America, he told the congregation, would have issued such an invitation, nor could he attend without being reminded that he was black and, therefore, "not permitted to enjoy the privilege of worshiping God with them." The following Sunday he preached again, and in early July the church presented him with a gift and memorial.[59]

But most of Pennington's time was spent preparing for the convention. He had painstakingly collected a mass of data on black communities, in an effort to

57. Copy of the minutes of the Troy meeting, in BFASS; *Christian Freeman*, May 19, 1843.
58. *Christian Freeman*, June 22, 1843; Leeds *Mercury*, August 5, 1843; *Emancipator and Free American*, January 11, 1844, September 7, 1843.
59. London *Patriot*, August 3, 1843; *Emancipator and Free American*, September 14, 1843; *Anti Slavery Reporter*, June 1, 1851.

show that blacks had been largely instrumental in their own progress. But successfully removing impediments to advancement also depended, Pennington believed, on international moral pressure on America. More than any other country, Britain, having first introduced slavery in America and having now abolished it in the West Indian colonies, had a moral obligation to join Americans fighting for emancipation. The abolition of slavery in the West Indies had more than just symbolic value for the cause in America; victory over oppression in one place, he had argued years before, tended to weaken it elsewhere. Britain had benefited from slavery while it lasted and so owed the slaves' descendants a "debt of justice," which it could easily repay by taking a vigorous stand against American slavery. To achieve this, Pennington suggested that British philanthropists make every effort to educate potential emigrants on the nature of American slavery and discrimination and at the same time try to influence visiting American clergymen to join the ranks of the abolitionists on their return home. The convention voted to submit Pennington's recommendations to committee. Its report spoke of black progress in the face of continued oppression, and called for the removal of racial barriers, convinced that blacks would ultimately "rise to an equality with any other portion of the great human family, in arts, in science, in literature, and in everything which tends to elevate, ennoble, and render man happy and useful."[60] Pennington seemed to have carried the day.

Before leaving on a tour of the Midlands, Pennington attended the three-day conference of the Peace Congress. Years later he would look back with pride on having attended that first meeting. War, like slavery, he told the delegates, was both unchristian and impolitic; unchristian because it violated the teaching of the gospel, and impolitic because it failed to achieve its stated objectives. It was up to Christians, therefore, to work for the total elimination of the "repulsive, . . . unjust and pernicious" spirit that engendered wars.[61]

Pennington was due to lecture in Ipswich with William Johnson in mid-July, but for some reason he arrived a day late. He made a pilgrimage to Norwich to see Thomas Clarkson, the doyen of British abolitionism. The visit was the high point of his trip. Then he went to Worcester, where he was the guest of the Worcester Anti Slavery Society. In his speech he emphasized the theme of American prejudice and black attempts to undermine it. At the end of July he

60. J. W. C. Pennington, *An Address Delivered at Newark, New Jersey at the First Anniversary of West Indian Emancipation, August 1, 1839* (Newark, 1839), 7; *Anti Slavery Reporter*, June 21, 1843; J. F. Johnson, *Proceedings*, 54–55.
61. Peace Congress, *Report of the Proceedings of the First General Peace Convention Held in London, June 22nd, 1843, and the Two Following Days* (London, 1843), 39–40.

was guest of honor and delivered the main address to a large meeting of Leeds abolitionists. There he merely mentioned his view of black progress, choosing instead to attack slavery and those in the North who pandered to the spirit of discrimination. It was a patented Pennington speech, filled with historical information and accounts of recent developments, made all the more explicit and moving because of his controlled anger.[62]

On August 1, Pennington was the main attraction at the celebrations of the Birmingham Anti Slavery Society, and the next day he attended the first annual meeting of the Birmingham Peace Association, where he called on the members to work for the spread of the peace principle as the only guaranteed means of preventing future wars. Three days later he set sail for America, having completed a most successful trip. In its assessment of his visit, the *Anti Slavery Reporter* praised Pennington for his achievements and lamented that he could not remain longer "for the purpose of visiting the friends of the abolition cause generally, throughout the country."[63]

The visit increased Pennington's self-esteem. For the first time in his life he was cordially received by all, welcomed into their homes and churches, and he traveled freely, encountering no nagging racial restrictions. His abilities were never questioned, he told a Leeds audience, and in turn he derived "delight and instruction from his intercourse with Christian ministers, and Christian churches, and Christian circles in this country, whose conduct to him had exhibited such a strong contrast to the treatment he received in his own country, that he had been sometimes overwhelmed by it." That conduct verified the fact that "all the communities of the world were not afraid to act, and were not wedded to slavery" and fired his determination to continue the struggle against slavery and discrimination. After his return, Pennington spoke to a large and enthusiastic black audience at the Broadway Tabernacle in New York. They listened attentively and were obviously cheered by his report of English hospitality, the lack of prejudice, and the warm support for the cause of human rights in America. For the next few months, Pennington repeated these facts wherever he went, and this galled many Americans vulnerable to and angered by comparisons with Britain.[64]

62. Ipswich *Express*, July 25, 1843; *Nonconformist*, July 26, 1843; Samuel Drake to John Beaufort, July 20, 1843, in BFASS; *Anti Slavery Standard*, September 7, 1843; Worcester *Herald*, July 29, 1843; Leeds *Mercury*, August 5, 1843; Leeds *Times*, August 5, 1843.

63. *Nonconformist*, August 8, 1843; *Emancipator and Free American*, September 7, 1843; *Anti Slavery Reporter*, August 9, 1843.

64. Leeds *Times*, August 5, 1843; Leeds *Mercury*, August 5, 1843; *Anti Slavery Reporter*, September 20, 1843; *Christian Freeman*, October 26, 1843; *Anti Slavery Standard*, August 31, September 7, 1843.

Pennington's reception in England apparently affected some of Hartford's white ministers. Embarrassed, no doubt, by the ease with which he met leading English divines like James Sherman, John Angell James, and the bishop of Norwich, a few Hartford ministers invited Pennington to exchange pulpits. By mid-1844, Pennington reported to Clarkson that he had accepted a dozen such invitations since his return. That was a radical departure from the past. Some years earlier, his friend John Hooker, a Farmington lawyer, had asked him to attend service, and the result was a great many protests and dire warnings that such actions could destroy the church. In spite of this change in attitude, there were still those who thought it the better part of valor to keep their distance. One of the ministers who had given Pennington letters of introduction to friends in England declined to invite him to preach, fearful that "the whole white congregation would have walked out of the church." But there were irrefutable signs of progress. Four years later, Pennington was elected moderator of the Hartford Central Association of Congregational Ministers. In just seven years, he had moved from the relative obscurity of a small black church to the apparently exalted heights of moderator of the city's Congregational association.[65]

International and local recognition of his worth was a palpable sign, Pennington thought, of black progress. His optimism about the future of black Americans grew appreciably in the months after his return. Pennington decided to publish a newspaper catering primarily to blacks. Poorly conceived, the paper had little chance of succeeding. Hartford, with its small black population, was simply not the place to publish a newspaper intended to fill the void left by the demise of the *Colored American*. He named the paper the *Clarksonian*, in honor of his friend, but its name could not guarantee survival. Poor circulation and limited advertisements soon forced Pennington to merge his paper with the Albany *Northern Star*. That partnership, however, was dissolved after only a few issues because of differences between Pennington and Stephen Meyers, former editor of the *Northern Star*.[66]

But success in Britain also created problems for Pennington at home. With prominence came the increased risk of possible recapture as a fugitive. Haunted by the possibility, Pennington had kept his past a secret even from his

65. Pennington to Thomas Clarkson, September 25, 1844, CN 137–138, in TCP; *Union Missionary Herald*, May, 1844; John Hooker, *Some Reminiscences of a Long Life* (Hartford, 1899), 23; *Anti Slavery Bugle*, June 25, 1847; *Charter Oak*, June 10, 1847; *Anti Slavery Reporter*, June 1, 1851.

66. Pennington to Clarkson, September 25, 1844, CN 137–138, in TCP; *Christian Freeman*, May 2, 1844. There is only one extant copy of the *Clarksonian*, which is at the Yale University Library, but unfortunately has been misplaced.

wife. Now he was convinced that Tilghman would make every effort to return him to slavery if only to strike a blow at abolitionists. The evidence suggests that Pennington first disclosed his secret to English friends. While doing research on southern slave laws in the office of the Connecticut secretary of state, he wrote Joseph Sturge, the Birmingham abolitionist, he discovered a recent Maryland law in which his parents were actually mentioned. This was the first he had heard of them in fifteen years. His status was inadvertently betrayed when a portion of his letter to Sturge was published by the *Anti Slavery Reporter*. On his return to Hartford, Pennington disclosed his secret to John Hooker, who promised to open negotiations with Tilghman. Tilghman demanded $550 for his former slave but made no mention of either Brazil or Nelly, who, Pennington insisted, had to be included in the final sale. Pennington had already sold a considerable portion of his library—not a light decision for an avid book collector—in order to raise part of the money for the purchase.[67]

But no agreement materialized. Tilghman was stalling, hoping to force Pennington to increase his offer. He could have done with the money, for Rockland had fallen on hard times in the 1840s. By the time of his death in late 1846, there were fifteen slaves on the farm—more than a 50 percent drop since 1830—and they were worth only $1,433. Eleven were classified as old, crippled, lame, or invalid; and four had a total value of $3. None of the Pembroke family, with the possible exception of John, who was seventeen years old, was still at Rockland in 1847. Stephen, Brazil, Jr., and Daniel were sold locally; Emmeline and Nelly were sold to Missouri planters; Maria escaped to Canada with her husband; Robert fled to Pennsylvania, where he later died; Brazil went to Canada; and Margaret married a freeman who later bought her freedom.[68] Although it is impossible to determine the sequence of events with any precision, it is quite likely that neither Brazil nor Nelly was at Rockland, which may account for Tilghman's failure to mention them in his reply to Hooker's initial letter.

When Hooker and Tilghman could not come to terms, Pennington had to face the possibility of imminent recapture. This might have prompted him to request a two-year leave of absence from his church in August, 1845. The ostensible reason, however, was Pennington's desire to pursue a classical education. "I am still a young man," he told his congregation on the eve of his depar-

67. Hooker, *Some Reminiscences*, 39–40; *Anti Slavery Reporter*, November 27, 1844; Pennington, *Fugitive Blacksmith*, 250–51.

68. *Pennsylvania Freeman*, June 1, 1854; Washington County, Maryland, Inventory, Q, 1847, in Maryland Hall of Records.

ture. "Our part of this nation is yet in its elements, to be moulded. *And the last half of the present century will be our great moral battle day.* I GO TO PREPARE FOR THAT."[69] Yet three months later, Pennington was on his way to Jamaica for a short visit—and that, of course, kept him safely away from slave catchers.

Pennington was impressed with Jamaica. He divided his time among the American missionary stations, lecturing and promoting contacts between black Americans and Jamaicans. At the time of his visit, there were continuing efforts to employ black Jamaicans as missionaries in Africa, the first attempt having been made in 1844 by the Baptist Missionary Society at Fernando Po. Soon after, the Basel Missionary Society sent several Jamaicans to the Gold Coast. Just before Pennington returned to America in April, 1846, a group of Jamaican missionaries, sponsored by the Scottish Presbyterian church and supervised by the Reverend Hope Waddell, left for Old Calabar. Although none of the stations flourished, they continued to exist until the 1890s. During his stay in Jamaica, Pennington contacted local Scottish Presbyterian ministers and spoke about closer relations with the Union Missionary Society. Given the UMS's failure to attract black missionaries to accompany the Mendians, it is surprising that Pennington felt confident enough to suggest that black Americans were eager to join in the effort.[70]

The proposal was just one element in a more ambitious plan by which Pennington hoped to draw black Americans to Jamaica. This was indeed a curious turn for someone so strongly opposed to colonization, one who had voted against endorsing Canadian emigration because it tended to give the false impression that blacks were not citizens of the United States. Although America had not changed so dramatically in thirteen years that supporting emigration was warranted, Pennington had become an ardent proponent of black missionary endeavors. What was true for Africa was equally applicable to Jamaica— both needed to be exposed to Christianity. Pennington was also groping toward a free-produce position. Although the movement was still in its infancy in America, the notion that free-labor goods would displace slave-grown produce on world markets, and thus undermine slavery, had been a salient feature of abolitionist thinking for some time. In addition, Jamaican planters faced a critical shortage of manpower in the years after emancipation and had initiated a

69. J. W. C. Pennington, *A Two Years' Absence, or a Farewell Sermon, Preached in the First Congregational Church by J. W. C. Pennington, November 2nd, 1845* (Hartford, 1845), 6.
70. Bella Vassady, Jr., "The Role of the Black West Indian Missionary in West Africa, 1840–1890" (Ph.D. dissertation, Temple University, 1972), 57, 108, 128; *Union Missionary Herald*, July, 1846, September, 1846.

number of schemes to attract cheap labor from other parts of the world, including America. Pennington might have met W. W. Anderson, an English lawyer practicing in Kingston, who visited America in 1841 on a fact-finding tour for Lord Metcalfe, the governor of Jamaica. Although generally optimistic that blacks could be persuaded to settle in Jamaica, Anderson reported that existing opposition to colonization and emigration would severely curtail the number of emigrants. Anderson had little success in the 1840s, but efforts to attract black Americans to the island continued through the 1850s and were endorsed by Pennington.[71]

Not only were black Americans morally obliged to aid in the spread of Christianity, but their superiority in "point of education and civilization" forced on them the responsibility to work for the elevation of the race in other parts of the world. The fulfillment of this obligation would produce immediate and tangible rewards for those who emigrated: freedom from the racist impediments that stifled black American initiative. Although Pennington believed that the island's potential had been exaggerated by friend and foe alike, he was convinced that black Americans would seize the opportunity to distance themselves from American oppression. Pennington informed local editors that many of "his brethren of respectable talents and education" were "earnestly looking around them for a field to which they may flee." Impressed by what he saw, Pennington pledged to promote Jamaica as a place where the nature of black men and "their character and station among men" were recognized.[72]

On his return home, Pennington busied himself working for the new plan, which predictably won few supporters. He must have known that blacks were more interested in staying at home and battling discrimination. The following year, Pennington was named chairman of the Commerce Committee of the National Negro Convention held in Troy, New York, and he used the opportunity to promote the Jamaica Hamic Association, a society of black Jamaicans that was formed while he was in Kingston. Appealing to both racial pride and the commonly held view that commerce and profits were the indispensable prerequisites for development, the association called for closer ties with black

71. *Anti Slavery Standard*, March 29, 1849; *African Repository*, December, 1851; *Liberator*, July 16, 1852; *Frederick Douglass Paper*, December 25, 1851, June 10, 1853; Philip Curtin, *Two Jamaicas: The Role of Ideas in a Tropical Colony, 1830–1865* (Cambridge, Mass., 1955), 138; Joel Schor, *Henry Highland Garnet: A Voice of Black Radicalism in the Nineteenth Century* (Westport, Conn., 1977), 127–28.

72. *Jamaica Times*, n.d., quoted in Falmouth *Post*, January 27, 1846; *Union Missionary Herald*, June, 1846; *Anti Slavery Standard*, May 14, 1846; Pennington to Amos Phelps, February 26, 1846, in ASP.

Americans. These new commercial links would not only bring blacks together but would also attract white Americans, ultimately leading to a lessening of racial antipathies. Commercial intercourse, in the association's bold assertion, would substitute "civility and politeness" for antagonism and would provide the means through which "enlightenment can be carried forward, religious and philanthropic institutions sustained, and the natural resources which God has caused to be buried in the bosom of the soil . . . developed and made to contribute their quota to universal happiness, which is calculated to bind all mankind in one common brotherhood." The convention endorsed the idea that further contacts would be mutually beneficial, and established the Committee on West Indian Correspondence to report to the next meeting. There the matter died. In spite of this failure, the convention's endorsement did represent, as Howard H. Bell has argued, "the maturing of the concept that the free Negro should seek his fortune where opportunity beckoned."[73]

Although nothing came of these efforts, Pennington maintained a lively interest in missionary activity in and emigration to Jamaica. Three years later, during his second trip to Britain, he held a series of meetings with the Missionary Board of the United Presbyterian Church of Scotland, which was having considerable trouble attracting competent missionaries for its stations in Jamaica. His suggestion for cooperation with the American Missionary Association won the Scots' approval, but his letters home elicited no response from the association.[74] Pennington was not deterred. Soon afterward, he met privately in Berwick with the Reverend John Clarke, a former Baptist missionary in Jamaica. Clarke had already made arrangements with a local women's group that was planning several public meetings to promote cotton cultivation in Jamaica. In July, Pennington attended a gathering of Birmingham spinners and manufacturers who were debating the benefits of forming a joint-stock company for cultivating West Indian cotton. This would end their total dependence on supplies of American cotton, which they feared could be disrupted by wars or slave insurrections.[75]

The passage of the Fugitive Slave Law in September, 1850, gave new urgency to all these plans. At a meeting in Kelso, Scotland, in December, Pennington suggested that the estimated forty thousand fugitives in Canada

73. "Proceedings of the National Convention of the Colored People and Their Friends Held in Troy, New York, 1847," in Bell (ed.), *Minutes*, 23–25; Howard H. Bell, *A Survey of the Negro Convention Movement, 1830–1861* (New York, 1969), 132.

74. For example, see Pennington to George Whipple, March 20, 1850, in AMA.

75. *Anti Slavery Reporter*, August 1, 1850.

should be induced to go to Jamaica or some other West Indian island, where they could work cultivating cotton, rice, and other staples. Once again he asserted that black Americans could become the instruments of West Indian development. These "free laborers" who "had been well tried in many of the States of the union" would be better workers, he argued, than many others who went to the islands; they would prove that free labor was more profitable than slave labor. The benefits to the West Indies would be immediate, especially as these laborers "spoke better and purer English than the Creoles of Jamaica. Besides, they were men of strong muscle and sinews, and many of them had learned the first lessons of civilization; and, if placed on a soil suitable for the purpose, they might carry on production to a great extent." Soon afterward, the women's group in Berwick wrote Earl Grey, the colonial secretary, requesting the government's reactions to this proposal. They were informed that the American government would have to be canvassed before the plan could be entertained. Pennington endorsed the scheme in a letter to Grey, arguing that the South's interests and the government's partiality to African colonization guaranteed rejection of the proposal. Grey agreed, but suggested that the decision to emigrate to Jamaica rested ultimately with blacks themselves rather than with any specific policies of the British government.[76]

All Pennington's work on behalf of the Jamaica Hamic Association was overshadowed by the death of his thirty-six-year-old wife Harriet in June, 1846. We know absolutely nothing of Harriet Pennington's life, when they were married, or the cause of her death. For the next eighteen months, Pennington devoted his time to his studies and the attempts by Connecticut blacks to regain the vote. Between 1818, when blacks were denied the vote, and 1844, when Governor Roger S. Baldwin called for a reversal of that policy, Connecticut had systematically ignored all efforts by blacks and abolitionists to lift the ban. Baldwin's proposals were rejected by the legislature on the grounds that only Congress had the power to change the 1818 law. In 1846, however, a Democratic-controlled legislature passed a constitutional amendment removing the white-only clause. The following year, the Whigs, now a majority in the legislature, submitted the amendment to a popular referendum. Aware that a similar referendum had only recently been defeated in New York by more than 2 to 1, blacks marshaled all their energies toward winning a favorable vote.[77]

Pennington had been actively involved earlier in the enfranchisement struggle.

76. Kelso *Chronicle*, January 3, 1851; *Scottish Press*, March 1, 1851.
77. Hartford *Times*, June 6, 1846; *Anti Slavery Standard*, June 25, 1846; Warner, *New Haven Negroes*, 94–96.

When the Connecticut House of Representatives amended the tax-assessment laws in 1844, Pennington saw it as an attempt to remove blacks from the tax rolls completely. The object of this action, he warned, was to eliminate any arguments that blacks, as taxpayers, should have the right to vote. A meeting at the Talcott Street Church in June, 1846, praised the legislature for submitting the issue to the voters and expressed confidence that the people of Connecticut would "divest themselves of all prejudice, and give it that generous consideration which its merits demand." Knowing that the success of the proposition depended on significant white support, Pennington wrote a series of letters to the *Charter Oak*, the official organ of the state abolition society, arguing that the issue was much larger than the right of blacks to vote. The first tenet of political economy dictated that a well-governed state maximize all the resources of its people, and what better way, he asked, for Connecticut to achieve that goal "than that each man qualified by nature should bear his part in guarding, at the ballot box, the liberties of the State." Responding to white concerns, Pennington pointed out that a vote for the proposition would in no way threaten growing economic contacts with the South, nor would it justify the "scare-crow amalgamation" fears expressed by some local editors.[78]

Following a meeting in September, 1847, the Connecticut State Temperance and Moral Reform Society issued an address pleading for support of the proposition. Conceding that the initial exclusion may have been warranted because blacks were in a "comparatively degraded condition," the address argued that their progress had rendered the ban unjustifiable. Blacks also deserved the right to vote if only because of their historic contributions to the state. Finally, removing the restriction would bring Connecticut into conformity with the rest of New England, which permitted blacks to vote. All these efforts had little effect; Connecticut voted more than 3 to 1 in favor of keeping the white-only clause. Three districts—Farmington, Pomfret, and Harwinton—voted for removal; two—Meridian and Westbrook—voted against by narrow margins; and one—Chaplin—split evenly. The final vote of 5,323 for and 19,148 against was a massive defeat for blacks and abolitionists in the state.[79]

The defeat prompted Pennington to look for alternative fields in which to labor. There was almost a sense of despair about the future. Although "I have been a faithful and orderly citizen of Connecticut for eight years," he wrote an

78. *Northern Star and Clarksonian*, n.d., quoted in *Christian Freeman*, August 1, 15, 1844; *Charter Oak*, August 5, 12, 26, September 9, 16, 1847.
79. "To the Good People of the State of Connecticut" (Broadside, in Amos G. Beman Papers, Collection of American Literature, Beinecke Library, Yale University, New Haven); *Charter Oak*, November 4, 14, 1847.

English friend soon after the results of the referendum were announced, "the good people of this State are not willing to trust those of my brethren whom I have labored to elevate and myself to cast our votes." Connecticut, "the land of steady habits," had refused to waver in its determination to maintain the status quo in spite of all the pleadings and protests of blacks and their abolitionist supporters. When Pennington arrived at Talcott Street in 1840, churches and schools were segregated and blacks "lived apart from whites in poverty and squalor" and without guaranteed rights. By the time he left in 1848, there were few perceptible changes, a situation made even more onerous because Pennington had gained considerable personal recognition in the city.[80]

Harriet's death also contributed to his restlessness. But it seems that his decision to move resulted in large part from a desire to find a more lucrative pastorate. The year he took over at Talcott, the directors of the Missionary Society of Connecticut, an auxiliary of the American Home Missionary Society, described the church as "feeble" and appropriated $100 toward Pennington's salary. The church continued to rely on this support throughout his tenure; without it, Pennington would have had to beg to support his family. In his years at Talcott, he labored diligently to increase the number of communicants. Initially, there was optimism, as membership almost tripled in less than three years. But such growth could not be sustained, nor could Pennington predict with any certainty the rate of attrition. In 1843, for instance, there were 130 communicants, the number dropping to 118 the following year and rising again to 130 by the time of his departure in 1848.[81] Growth for a poor church like Talcott guaranteed solvency; otherwise, Pennington had to continue to depend on the charity of the American Home Missionary Society. And that was galling. When the pulpit at the First Colored Presbyterian Church (later known as Shiloh) in New York City became vacant following the death of the Reverend Theodore S. Wright, Pennington accepted the congregation's call to take his old friend's place.

But the move to Shiloh brought little financial security. The life of a black minister was precarious at best. Not only were there serious and sometimes heated debates over the merits of a learned ministry and its ability to fulfill blacks' spiritual needs, but most of the congregations were unable to provide

80. Pennington to Esteemed Friend, November 17, 1847, in BFASS; Lawrence Bruser, "Political Antislavery in Connecticut, 1844–1858" (Ph.D. dissertation, Columbia University, 1974), 11, 55.

81. Congregational General Association of Connecticut, *Minutes* (New Haven, 1844), *Minutes* (New Haven, 1845), *Minutes* (New Haven, 1848), *Minutes* (Hartford, 1841); *Christian Freeman*, April 21, 1843.

their ministers an adequate living. Small, poor, and often widely scattered, black congregations, Frederick Douglass argued, had to make unreasonable sacrifices first to build a church and then to meet the minister's paltry salary. "The minister and his family," Douglass wrote, "must be supported, though the members have scarcely the means of living, to say nothing of the means of educating and improving the minds of their children. We have known of churches composed of a dozen good colored women and as many men; the former gaining their living over the wash-tub, and the latter obtaining theirs by daily toil; at the same time supporting a minister and his family at an expense of from two to three hundred dollars a year." The solution, as far as Douglass was concerned, was a simple one: black churches ought to be disbanded and their congregations united with local white churches.[82] That, of course, was easier said than done, and it deliberately ignored both continuing white resistance to integrated churches and the question of what was to become of the black minister in a racist society.

For black ministers like Pennington, Douglass' recommendation was no help. Although relations with some white Hartford Congregationalist ministers had improved, Pennington was generally shunned by the larger community of ministers. Isolation was a spur to greater achievement, for he was determined to show that blacks could educate themselves despite discrimination. It was also a frustrating experience that dampened Pennington's enthusiasm, for he had only limited opportunities to grow intellectually through the mutual exchange of ideas. But in either case, Pennington and others had to depend on their small, poor congregations. Amos Beman continually lamented the fact that his congregation in New Haven found it difficult to pay his salary or to provide the necessary funds for church repairs. Alexander Crummell's experiences in Pennsylvania and Rhode Island captured the black minister's dilemma. In the wake of his decision to devote himself to missionary work in Liberia, Crummell wrote from England to his friend John Jay, bemoaning the poverty and racism under which he was forced to live in America. Not a year passed, he told Jay, "in which I had sufficient money to secure the clothes to cover me, and to keep me decent. Many a time my wife and myself have been so wretchedly poor that we have not known where to get a morsel of food." Although Pennington's experiences at Talcott Street were considerably better, it was a lament he would come to appreciate. For the moment, however, things looked hopeful. Soon after accepting the new position, Pennington married his second wife Elmira Way. The

---

82. *North Star*, March 10, 1848.

wedding took place on May 17, 1848, at the home of Edward Goodwin, former editor and publisher of the Hartford *Courant*, in whose home Elmira worked.[83]

Pennington's decision to go to Shiloh was only made after extensive discussions with his friends and his congregation in Hartford. Members of Shiloh had first approached him in April, 1847, but he had declined because of a commitment to return to Talcott Street at the end of his leave. There was additional pressure from friends who wanted him to remain in Hartford. One of them, Augustus Washington, the daguerreotypist and teacher, wrote of his regret that Pennington "should feel it his duty to leave this people whose pastor he has been for the last eight years. He has ever secured the confidence and respect of the whole community," Washington reported, and "has had one of the most orderly, respectable and intelligent audiences that I ever knew." But ambitious and eager for a larger and more lucrative pastorate, one that could possibly increase his influence on decisions affecting his people, Pennington finally accepted the call from New York and was installed in March, 1848.[84]

Within three weeks of his arrival, Pennington's new congregation voted to sell the church and move because William and Chatham streets were going to be widened. A new church costing $14,500 was purchased at Prince and Marion streets in the upper part of the city. One reporter praised the move, pointing out that the location was one of the best in the city, and that it brought the church closer to its congregation, making it possible to attract "a large portion of the destitute of the city." There was some merit to the claim, for the first three weeks at the new location the congregation increased and attendance at the Sunday school doubled.[85]

By the end of the year, it was rumored that Pennington was planning to visit Britain again. A perennial fear of possible recapture obviously influenced his plans. New York City seemed unusually crowded with slave catchers in 1848. There were reports that a cabal of Maryland slaveholders had decided to pool their resources so as to test the "strength of the Constitution and laws of Con-

83. Robert A. Warner, "Amos G. Beman, 1812–1874: A Memoir of a Forgotten Leader," *JNH*, XXII (1937), 204; Alexander Crummell to John Jay, September 21, 1851, in Jay Family Papers, etc., Rare Book and Manuscript Library, Columbia University, New York; Hartford Vital Records, I, 262, in State Archives, Hartford, Conn.; extract from the Hartford *Courant*, n.d., in Archives of the Connecticut Conference of the United Church of Christ, Hartford.

84. Records of the Third Presbytery of New York, March 7, 1848, April 19, 1847, in PHS; *North Star*, April 7, 1848; Edward H. Thomas, "An Analysis of the Life and Work of James W. C. Pennington, a Black Churchman and Abolitionist" (Ph.D. dissertation, Hartford Theological Seminary Foundation, 1978), 92–93.

85. *Charter Oak*, August 13, 1848; Records of the Third Presbytery of New York, April 5, 1848, in PHS.

gress on the recovery of fugitives." Although Pennington proposed the formation of a northern association to counter the slaveholders, these developments
caused him considerable alarm.[86] A tour of Britain would also give him an opportunity to raise money to pay off debts incurred by Shiloh after its recent
move. For some unknown reason, Pennington postponed his departure. But by
early spring he reactivated his plan, due mainly to the activities of the American Colonization Society and the determination of blacks to counter any new
moves by the society to win support in Britain.

Liberia's recent independence, the ACS argued, meant that the former
colony could now formulate and conduct its own policies and so deserved the
total backing of British and American philanthropists. Liberian president
Joseph J. Roberts had only recently completed a successful tour of Britain and
America, during which the British government recognized his country's independence. The society moved quickly to capitalize on Roberts' successes, using
the occasion of a private visit to Britain by the Reverend John Miller of Frederick, Maryland, to test British willingness to forget their earlier condemnation
of the ACS as a proslavery organization. This opposition had been led by Captain Charles Stuart, the Scots abolitionist, the Reverend Nathaniel Paul, and
William Lloyd Garrison in the early 1830s, and reconfirmed in 1840 through
the efforts of Charles Lenox Remond and James G. Birney. The society's
efforts in 1849, therefore, threatened to undermine almost two decades of successful opposition to its designs, a possibility blacks did not take lightly.

A large meeting was held at Pennington's church in April, 1849. Pennington
began with a stirring denunciation of recent colonization meetings in New
York City and the decision to grant Roberts the freedom of the city. Blacks,
who were still segregated on the streetcars and generally discriminated against,
could not fail to miss the irony of the black Liberian's status in a city that refused to grant its black inhabitants the full rights of citizenship. Pennington
concluded by calling for a renewed struggle against colonization. The ACS and
its schemes must be resisted, Charles Lenox Remond told the meeting, not because it could ever succeed in removing all blacks from the United States, but
because "so long as it shall exist, its tendency is to make more rabid the spirit of
caste and prejudice against the colored people in this country." The British, he
insisted, must be informed that blacks had not altered their views on colonization. The session ended with a resolution that friends in Britain not
"strengthen the hands of the slave holders, and aggravate the prejudice that

86. *North Star*, January 12, 19, 1849.

consumes" blacks by supporting the society, and commissioned Pennington as its emissary to Britain.[87]

Pennington sailed for England a few weeks later, anxious to renew the friendships he had made in 1843. His popularity in Britain, exemplified by the fact that his name headed the list of those to whom Wilson Armistead, the Leeds abolitionist, dedicated his book *A Tribute to the Negro* (1848), augured well for the success of Pennington's second visit. By the time he arrived in England, however, Miller was already considering returning to America, his efforts totally undermined by Crummell's opposition. With the colonizationists effectively out of the way, Pennington directed his efforts to lecturing against American slavery and discrimination, and raising money to pay off his church's debt.

Some weeks after his arrival, Pennington started preparing his narrative for publication. *The Fugitive Blacksmith* was an instant success, selling six thousand copies and going through three editions by July, 1850. It was also the first in a series of slave narratives, pamphlets, travelogues, and a novel published by visiting black Americans between 1849 and 1855. All these works were viewed as important instruments in the international movement against American slavery and racial discrimination. In an era that still paid homage to the ideal of self-improvement, these works argued convincingly that all men were capable of surmounting the most difficult of obstacles. Pennington was aware of his book's potential impact on a broad segment of British society. No American slave narrative had been published in Britain since Douglass' in 1846, and the public seemed ready for another account extolling the virtues of resistance to oppression. Pennington was not to be disappointed, for the book was widely read and circulated. Wherever he went on his lecture tours, he found a copy of his little book. In some cases, he reported, single copies were passed from one reader to another.

A captivating story, Pennington's narrative, like others of its genre, is in part an account of his life in slavery, his escape, his efforts to purchase his family, and a description of slave life on the plantation. It not only describes the events in the life of Pembroke the slave but presents them in such a way as to increase public aversion to slavery and, in so doing, win adherents to the abolitionist cause. In order to achieve this end, Pennington deliberately aimed his book at children "in point of matter" and at the masses "in point of price." It was an approach guaranteed to win instant success—as sales amply testified.[88]

Unlike his contemporaries, however, Pennington, always the educator, added

87. *Anti Slavery Standard*, May 3, 1849.
88. Pennington, *Fugitive Blacksmith*, 204.

to the second edition a lengthy preface in which he leveled a broadside against those who attempted to deflect criticism from slavery by arguing that not all forms of American slavery were as barbarous as abolitionists had argued. Such differentiations were false, he argued, for there was no such thing as a mild form of slavery. The system was governed by what he called the "chattel principle," which determined all relations between masters and slaves. It is this principle that produced the whips, the starvation, the nakedness, and the sexual exploitation of women so characteristic of all "forms" of slavery. Irrespective of the "ill or favored condition of the slave in the matter of mere personal treatment," the chattel principle robbed him of his manhood and transferred "the proprietorship of his wife and children to another. It is this that throws his family history into utter confusion and leaves him without a single record to which he may appeal in vindication of his character, or honor."[89]

The entire narrative is written explicitly with this point in mind. The history of Pennington's family, which was held together by a devoted father and a hardworking mother, epitomized the destructiveness of the chattel principle. In spite of Brazil's diligence, the master, an otherwise mild-mannered man, felt compelled to flog him in order to set an example to other slaves, who he feared were becoming unruly. The punishment was totally unwarranted, yet necessary if Frisby Tilghman was ever to maintain control of his slaves. When Tilghman failed to recapture James, he apparently had no choice but to sell members of the family. There was little doubt in Pennington's mind that Tilghman's decision was more than just the action of a vindictive man: it was, he firmly believed, dictated by the chattel principle, which compelled the master continually to demonstrate his absolute control over his slaves. For Tilghman to have acted otherwise would have been to confess openly that he was no longer master of the situation. *The Fugitive Blacksmith*, like the Crafts' *Running a Thousand Miles for Freedom* and other narratives of the period, is a rags-to-riches story set in the tradition of the odyssey, in which the protagonist achieves the ultimate goal of freedom despite the many obstacles thrown in his path. As I have argued elsewhere, this contributed considerably to their popularity. Young James's decision to escape was in part prompted by worsening relations between the master and his family after Brazil's flogging and in part by the flogging he received from Tilghman. In contemplating escape, James was torn between the hope of possible success and the fear of leaving the world he knew. Yet the possibility of betrayal forced him to act alone and to depend entirely on his own resolve, a

89. *Ibid.*, 201.

fact that only compounded his anxieties. "Hope, fear, dread, terror, love, sorrow, and deep melancholy" were intertwined in his sense of despair. Nevertheless, he had to "act and be free, or remain a slave forever." Having committed himself to an escape attempt, James was almost overcome by the serenity of the plantation, a mixture of a "strange and melancholy silence" and destitution, portents of imminent failure. Casually leaving the plantation on Sunday so as not to rouse any suspicions, James headed toward Hagerstown, the first obstacle behind him. The journey had now begun in earnest: "I felt like a mariner who has gotten his ship outside of the harbor and has spread his sails to the breeze. The cargo is on board—the ship is cleared—and the voyage I must make."[90] Pennington had to deal with many other difficulties before he reached free soil in Pennsylvania.

The Fugitive Blacksmith is also a poignant articulation of the Christian belief that the Lord helps those who help themselves. In other words, there could have been no Underground Railroad if there were no Pembrokes who braved the opposition to attain freedom. The narrative is punctuated by other, more direct moral apostrophes. When, for instance, James was captured by villagers, he lied, stating that he was free, and when it became apparent that his captors rejected his claims, he fabricated a fantastic story in which he was a member of a slave coffle heading south when it was discovered that many of the slaves had smallpox. Pennington entitled this section "Great Moral Dilemma" and felt it necessary to ask his readers' forgiveness for telling such lies. One assumes that Pennington was addressing his young readers, anxious to make a point against lying. This is Pennington the Christian minister talking, not Pembroke the slave, who we can safely assume had little compunction—if he thought of it at all—about lying his way out of a difficult situation.

The Fugitive Blacksmith's success was due in large part to Pennington's ability to tailor a captivating story to the tastes of an increasingly literate public eager for tales of success in the face of great adversity. The narrative, one rather besotted admirer boasted, wanting probably to reaffirm English superiority, "forms a splendid addition to proofs, already a thousand times more than enough, that difference of colour does not, necessarily, any more than difference of language or of stature, imply intellectual inferiority. No man, in the absence of information, could infer that the book before us was the production of a negro. The diction is so pure, the idiom so truly English, the observations generally so just and Christian, occasionally so penetrating and profound,

90. *Ibid.*, 216–17.

that they could do credit to an Englishman of superior ability and regular education."[91]

Soon after completing the narrative, Pennington left for Paris, where he joined his old friend William Wells Brown as a delegate to the second Peace Congress. Here and in subsequent meetings in England, Pennington returned to the views he had expressed six years earlier at the first Peace Congress. Although he agreed with Brown that slavery was a form of war, he nonetheless asserted that black Americans, as an oppressed group, had decided that their interests were best served if they kept the peace and chose "God as our arbiter," for physical force settled nothing. Pennington feared that the successes of the recent revolution in France would prompt oppressed people to advocate armed struggle—an approach he viewed as self-defeating—but he seemed genuinely more concerned to establish the principle of moral power, that is, the decision and the ability of the oppressed to suffer without reverting to arms. As I have shown, the principle did not advocate passivity; like the peace principle of which it was a part, it assumed that as man progressed toward perfection he would develop sophisticated systems of arbitration to which disputes could be referred. Pennington saw the development of this machinery as crucial to the survival of oppressed groups, like black Americans, who might be tempted to take up arms. The predictable defeat and decimation of such groups would reinforce the erroneous notion that might was right, and would also cloud the reasoning and circumstances that led the exploited to revert to armed struggle. As differences between nations should be submitted to impartial arbitration so as to avoid wars, so too, Pennington implied, should the issue of slavery, which as a system of war threatened the peace of the world. It was clearly an attempt to establish an international forum at which slavery could be discussed and pressure brought to bear on America to emancipate its slaves.[92]

Pennington quite thoroughly enjoyed himself in Paris, meeting prominent men like Victor Hugo and Abbé Deguerry and preaching one of the sermons at the congress. Speaking of Pennington and Brown, *La Presse*, a leading Paris newspaper, wondered whether "the revolution of February produced among the working classes of France, an orator of the power of either of these fugitive slaves."[93] Pennington's success in Paris and the rapid sale of his narrative in

91. *Christian Witness*, VI (n.d.).
92. Peace Congress, *Report of the Proceedings of the Second General Peace Congress Held in Paris on the 22nd, 23rd and 24th of August, 1849* (London, 1850), 84–85; Bristol *Mercury*, October 12, 1850; *Herald of Peace*, October, 1849.
93. London *Patriot*, August 27, 1849; William Wells Brown, *The Black Man: His Antecedents, His*

Britain brought increased invitations for lectures when he returned to England. Throughout his stay in Britain, he followed a hectic schedule, lecturing on slavery, peace, and temperance, preaching on Sundays, and speaking at Sunday schools. At Newark, for example, in just a few days he preached four times and gave one lecture each on slavery, temperance, and peace, and then he left for an adjacent town where he repeated the routine. His lectures were always well attended. Twelve hundred people attended his peace lecture in Newark; two thousand attended one of his lectures in Bristol; and "every available space" was occupied when he lectured to the Scottish Temperance League at the Reverend King's church in Glasgow. On several occasions he delivered a series of public lectures on slavery. His December, 1849, series in Edinburgh, for example, covered such topics as "Slavery as constituted by American laws," "Slavery as a system of Labour without wages," "The means by which Slavery is supported," and "Slavery considered as a war of minds." After one of his lectures at Stroud, Gloucestershire, on the Fugitive Slave Law, a local editor observed that Pennington's speech was "characterized by breadth of view, discrimination, carefully measured language, and Christian feeling." It is no surprise, then, that he was able to raise over one-half of his church's outstanding debt in less than four months.[94]

Pennington's lecture tours in 1849 and 1850 were in part undertaken at the invitation of Joseph Sturge and other supporters of the Free Produce Association (FPA). The free-produce principle had been an integral weapon of British abolitionism before West Indian emancipation and remained an important if peripheral one in subsequent years. With pledges of support from the American Free Produce Association, Joseph Sturge had attempted to reactivate the movement in 1843. The failure of British abolitionists to stop the rising importation of slave-grown sugar, following the reduction of import duties in 1845, prompted Sturge and others to issue a new appeal for the boycott of slave-grown products as a means of bringing about American emancipation. Led by Anna Richardson of Newcastle, the FPA invited Henry Bibb, the fugitive slave, to tour Britain as its agent in 1848, but the plans did not work out. Two years passed before Henry Highland Garnet agreed to fill Bibb's position. In the in-

---

Genius and His Achievements (1865; rpr. Miami, 1969), 277; *La Presse*, quoted in *Liberator*, September 28, 1849.

94. London *Patriot*, October 18, 1849; *Scottish Press*, February 13, 1850; Gloucester *Journal*, November 9, 1850; Pennington to Peter Bolton, November 13, 1849, in BFASS; Lincolnshire *Times*, November 6, 1849; Sunderland *Herald*, October 4, 1850; *Anti Slavery Reporter*, August 1, 1850; *Nonslaveholder*, December 9, 1850.

terim, Pennington acted as the association's informal agent. His free-produce credentials were well established. During a speech in 1839, Pennington confidently predicted that the day was "hastening when we shall see a combination of all the great and generous powers of the earth against the bloody slave system of this land, by the proscription of slave produce."[95]

Pennington took his duties seriously; during a five-week period in 1850 he lectured at Halefield, Newcastle upon Tyne, Alnwick, Berwick, Morpeth, Hull, Derby, Birmingham, Stourbridge, Manchester, Leicester, and Leeds. He adhered closely to the movement's economic argument that American slavery was sustained only by the continued patronage of countries like Britain, which bought cotton, and would end only when those countries decided that their interests were better served by procuring cotton from other sources. "Every farthing that is diverted from the pockets of slave holders," Pennington argued, "weakens the system; commercial patronage is the backbone, nay, the jugular vein, of the system." Cut off the flow of money, by boycotting slave-grown cotton, he insisted, and the system would be destroyed in twelve months.[96] This is why he supported schemes for settling black Americans in Jamaica. If one can judge solely from attendance at his lectures, then Pennington could claim some success for his efforts.

In late summer, 1850, Pennington broke off his busy schedule to join Garnet at the Frankfort meeting of the Peace Congress. Both addressed the congress on the need to form an organization that could cooperate with abolitionists in other parts of the world, promote the use of free-grown produce, and aid in the suppression of the slave trade. At the close of the congress, a public meeting was arranged so that they could speak specifically on American slavery. Soon afterward, a local free-produce society was organized. They also participated in the series of meetings that culminated in the formation of an antislavery society. At the conclusion of the congress, both accompanied the British delegation on the journey back to England.[97] These trips, free from the discom-

95. Joseph Sturge to John Scoble, July 20, 1849, in BFASS; *Anti Slavery Reporter*, January 1, 1846; Howard Temperley, *British Antislavery, 1833–1870* (Columbia, S.C., 1972), 165; Louis Billington, "British Humanitarians and American Cotton, 1840–1860," *Journal of American Studies*, XI (1977), 316–18; Pennington, *An Address*, 8.

96. Derby and Chesterfield *Reporter*, July 19, 1850; Pennington, *A Lecture*, 9; *Anti Slavery Reporter*, August 1, 1850; Birmingham *Mercury*, July 20, 1850; Henry Miles to Scoble, July 21, 1850, in BFASS; Leeds *Mercury*, August 3, 1850.

97. Peace Congress, *Report of the Proceedings of the Third Peace Congress, Held in Frankfort on the 22nd, 23rd and 24th August, 1850* (London, 1851), 63–69; *Anti Slavery Reporter*, December 1, 1850; *Nonconformist*, September 4, 11, 1850.

forts of segregated transportation to which they were accustomed in America, could not have failed to impress Pennington and Garnet. Such experiences further exposed the racist duplicity of American society and increased their determination to fight against slavery and discrimination.

Back in England, Pennington occasionally joined Garnet at free-produce lectures. At one meeting in Sunderland, the crowd was so large they were forced to use two adjacent churches, Pennington lecturing in one and Garnet in the other.[98] But thereafter Pennington turned his attention to wider abolitionist interests. The passage of the Fugitive Slave Law in September, 1850, gave visiting black Americans like Pennington, Brown, and Garnet ample means for winning over international public opinion. The law, which caused fugitives to pour into Canada in hopes of avoiding recapture, also created a new and pressing problem for British abolitionists. In the ensuing months the debate ranged over a whole series of proposals to deal with this new emergency, including suggestions for Jamaican emigration.

Pennington's active promotion of the Jamaican scheme was vigorously opposed by William Wells Brown, who was skeptical of all forms of emigration. It also brought to a head a dispute between Pennington and Scottish Garrisonians that had been simmering for some time. Earlier, Brown's friends had condemned him for participating in an Edinburgh meeting at which Pennington was present. As disputes between British Garrisonians and the British and Foreign Anti Slavery Society (BFASS) escalated in 1850, Pennington, the "special protege" of the BFASS, as John Estlin of Bristol called him, became the bête noire of Garrisonians on both sides of the Atlantic. They were convinced that Pennington was the main force behind the surge of anti-Garrisonianism in Scotland. As one opponent put it, the country was simply teeming with "Pennington adorers."[99]

Garrisonian suspicions of Pennington were in part due to the circumstances surrounding the honorary degree awarded him by the University of Heidelberg in December, 1849. The evidence suggests that the main movers behind the award were all members or supporters of the BFASS. Why Pennington was chosen above the host of other visiting black Americans is something of a mystery. The fact that he was a leading member of the American and Foreign Anti Slavery Society, an opponent of American Garrisonians, and had been working closely with the BFASS since his arrival might have influenced the choice. It

98. Sunderland *Herald*, October 4, 1850.
99. J. Estlin to Miss Wigham, May 3, 1851, M. Estlin to Ann Weston, May 12, 1851, both in ASP.

appears that British friends had attempted to arrange for a similar award from an English university during Pennington's visit in 1843. It was rumored that he had been awarded an honorary degree from the University of Surrey. As it turned out, no university by this name existed, and Pennington found it necessary to publish a disclaimer.[100]

Events leading up to the Heidelberg degree were equally mysterious. In supporting the award, the dean of the School of Divinity explained that Pennington had actually petitioned for it "not so much for himself, as for his color, which is represented by him, and which is so deeply disdained in America." In his request Pennington had written that he and others wished "to spread among our youth the higher branches of education. As a result of this I am in the process of founding a school as an adjunct of my parsonage. Would not Germany like to be the first one to give a strong push to our endeavors by recognizing the struggle of my people using all its power to educate my brothers and to evangelize them and to lift them up." The degree, usually given "in recognition of scientific achievements connected with personal worthiness"—criteria that Pennington could not possibly claim—was being awarded, the dean pointed out, in recognition of the "speedy and fortunate development of the intellectual abilities" of the recipient. Although Pennington publicly acknowledged that the degree was "in trust for my People, and as an encouragement to the Sons of Ham to rise with others in the acquisition of learning," suspicion that it was more the work of British friends than a recognition of his intellectual achievements was never allayed.[101]

Although the award gave Pennington's opponents, especially the leaders of the Glasgow Emancipation Society (GES), some convenient ammunition, they were really more concerned with the growing strength of Scottish "new" organizations and black support of them. Both Pennington and Garnet were agents of the Glasgow ladies' and men's "new" societies, and Pennington's active promotion of the New York Vigilance Committee was seen by Garrisonians as a major threat to their interests. These fears were not unfounded; throughout the 1850s, in fact, remittances to American Garrisonians from Britain dropped off sharply. Money and other gifts that previously went to Boston and Philadelphia, centers of Garrisonian abolitionism, were now being sent to Frederick Douglass in Rochester, the New York Vigilance Committee, and other organizations aiding fugitives.

100. *Christian Freeman*, August 10, 31, 1843.
101. Thomas, "An Analysis of the Life and Work of Pennington," 230–31, 337; *British Banner*, January 9, 1850; London *Patriot*, January 21, 1850.

The final split between Pennington and the GES did not occur, however, until late 1850. Initially the society welcomed him to its meetings where they discussed, among other topics, his position on "fellowshipping slaveholders and slaveholding Ministers." Evidently, Pennington's explanations were accepted, although there were some reservations concerning his fellowship with the General Assembly of the American Presbyterian Church. As a result, the GES Executive Committee declined to support Pennington publicly, in large measure because the society opposed the decision of the Free Church of Scotland to accept donations from slaveholding churches for its Sustentation Fund in 1843. The meeting instead agreed that it would be "most expedient" if during his lecture tours Pennington acted "independently of any Society," but with the clear understanding that individual members could cooperate with him. The decision was a veiled threat against Pennington's involvement in abolitionist squabbles; it also suggests that there were some on the committee who questioned the wisdom of such a policy.[102] There matters rested for the remainder of 1850, during which time Pennington continued to work with Scottish "new" organizationists and to promote the New York Vigilance Committe.

By the end of the year, William Smeal, secretary of the GES, was clearly worried that competitors, particularly the recently formed Glasgow New Association for the Abolition of Slavery, were making considerable inroads into traditional areas of GES support. Smeal wrote William Wells Brown in December of a plan to organize a "vigorous" antislavery meeting with Brown as the main speaker. His aim was to reactivate the GES (which had held only one public meeting since 1847) as a counter to the anti-Garrisonian new society. Smeal was concerned that "new" organizationists also intended to form another men's society and saw the Brown meeting as one means of taking the wind out of their sails. Prudence, a desire not to make abolitionist dissension a public spectacle, and the society's debts were largely responsible for Smeal's silence in the face of rising criticism from opponents. The meeting, he hoped, would rejuvenate the society. As far as Smeal was concerned, these divisions in the movement were "not a little aided . . . by Dr. Pennington."[103]

At the January, 1851, meeting organized by the GES for Brown and William and Ellen Craft, Smeal and other members of the society launched a blistering attack on their opponents. In response, R. Wright, a Glaswegian with no known abolitionist credentials, countered with a series of letters to the *Daily Mail*, accusing the GES of supporting radical abolitionists who advocated "un-

---

102. GES, Minute Book 4 (1845–1876), in Smeal Collection, The Mitchell Library, Glasgow.
103. William Smeal to William Wells Brown, December 12, 1850, in ASP.

Christian" views.[104] The dispute reopened old animosities between the competing organizations and achieved nothing of substance except to confirm the irreconcilability of the division. The GES leaders, however, were not to be denied; they were convinced that these problems were the work of Pennington, who had to be exposed if the society was ever to regain its influence. Rumors were floated that he had been collecting money under false pretenses, and American colleagues were urged to supply evidence to substantiate these claims.

Meanwhile, Pennington agreed to meet with the society to discuss their differences. But there was little chance of reconciliation, given some members' determination to expose Pennington. Why, they asked, was he collecting money to purchase his freedom if, as his narrative suggested, Jamaican friends had raised enough to meet Tilghman's demands? The trap was sprung. "The means I had acquired by the contributions of kind friends to redeem myself," Pennington had written, "I laid by, in case the worst should come; and that designed for the purchase of my parents, I used in another kind of operation, as a result of which, my father and two brothers are now in Canada." If this was the case, then Pennington was being duplicitous. There were other unexplainable points of contention concerning Pennington's "proceedings in different parts of the Country." But lacking hard evidence and unwilling to challenge Pennington publicly, the committee "resolved itself into a *confidential conversation* no vote being taken regarding the merits of the case each member of the Committee being left at full liberty in the meantime to form his own conclusion." Subsequent meetings failed to produce unanimity on the best way of dealing with Pennington.[105]

The committee's indecisiveness suggests that either Pennington had convinced some members that his actions were legitimate, or his opponents were unable to find sufficient evidence for their claims. Andrew Paton, a prominent member of the society, remained skeptical. But his suspicions that Pennington was hiding his true mercenary intentions behind a façade of abolitionist activities could not be substantiated. As he told his American friend Sydney Howard Gay, Pennington did "not exactly ask contributions directly, tho' there can be little doubt this is one object in view. I strongly suspect there is something decidedly wrong in this ransom business, could we only have it brought out, but unless clear evidence of wrong doing can be obtained, we can do nothing in it."

104. Later published as a pamphlet, *A Defence of the Glasgow Female Association for the Abolition of Slavery* (Glasgow, 1851).
105. GES, Minute Book 4 (1845–1876), in Smeal Collection; Pennington, *Fugitive Blacksmith*, 251–52; for Pennington's attempt to raise money in Jamaica, see Falmouth *Post*, March 17, 1846.

Paton prodded Gay to respond to an earlier letter requesting information on the religious affiliation of the dominant figures in the New York Vigilance Committee (NYVC) so as to determine their orthodoxy. Further, it was rumored that Pennington had already collected the £600 needed to meet his church's debts, and Paton wondered if any of this had been remitted to New York: "*If not* get some of them stirred up to insist on having what money he has collected remitted to them without delay. Ascertain what he writes them as to his money and generally inform me."[106]

This was clearly the action of a desperate man. Unable to find any chinks in Pennington's moral armor, and unwilling to challenge him publicly for fear of further alienating British support, Garrisonians retreated, biding their time, in the hope that his supporters, "the quakers and other," would soon realize that "Pennington has been taking them in." Nothing of the kind occurred, and Pennington continued to promote the NYVC, which throughout the 1850s received substantial support from British abolitionists.[107]

In the midst of the controversy, Pennington's friends in Dunse, Scotland, heightened tensions by starting a drive to raise money for his ransom. No new efforts had been made to purchase Pennington's freedom since the collapse of Hooker's initiative in 1844. Pennington's problems were increased substantially with the passage of the Fugitive Slave Law. Under the circumstances, he and the score of American fugitives who made their way to Britain after September, 1850, had few options. He could ignore the new law and return—one could imagine the elation that would greet the recapture of the fugitive doctor of divinity—or he could remain in Britain for a while until the excitement blew over. Pennington understandably chose the latter. But some members of his church were clamoring for his early return. Because of these difficulties, friends in Scotland decided to explore the possibility of opening a new round of negotiations with William Clarke, administrator of Tilghman's estate. Local committees were formed throughout Berwickshire to solicit contributions, every effort being made to keep the matter low-keyed so as not to jeopardize the negotiations. Hooker was contacted by the Dunse committee and asked to negotiate with Clarke on their behalf. Anxious to wind up the business of Tilghman's estate, Clarke agreed to accept the rather paltry sum of $150 for Pennington's freedom. Given that Maryland law forbade the direct manumis-

106. Andrew Paton to Sydney Howard Gay, January 30, March 21, 1851, both in Sydney Howard Gay Papers, Rare Book and Manuscript Library, Columbia University, New York.

107. M. Estlin to Anne Weston, May 8, 1851, in ASP; New York Vigilance Committee, *Report* (New York, 1853).

sion of slaves, it was agreed that Pennington would be purchased by Hooker. In May, Hooker sent one of his law partners, Joseph R. Hawley, later governor of Connecticut, to Maryland to finalize the transfer, which was completed on May 27.[108]

Word of Pennington's freedom reached Scotland in mid-June, and plans were made for a massive antislavery meeting in Dunse at which the former slave would be presented with his free papers. Berwickshire was understandably proud of its efforts. In less than three months it had raised almost £100 (£60 from Dunse, and almost £25 from other towns), £55 of which was sent to Hooker, the remainder going toward defraying expenses for Pennington's return to America. For the first time, Pennington told the meeting on the twenty-sixth, he was able to tell the full story of his life, without fear of recapture. Thanking the many friends in the audience, he observed, "A shackled man cannot think, feel, and act freely and fully as a man. This deliverance deepens my experience on the subject. I feel now that I can go and stand up among the men of my country. I shall ever esteem it to be one of the finest events in my whole life, that by your aid I have been delivered from this property principle of slavery." Soon after, Pennington and his family left Dunse for home, stopping first in Edinburgh, where temperance, peace, and abolitionist supporters gathered to bid them farewell.[109] Opposition from British Garrisonians did nothing to diminish Pennington's international stature. He left Britain a substantial figure in the Atlantic abolitionist, peace, and temperance movements, one whose achievements had been fittingly recognized by the University of Heidelberg.

It must have seemed to Pennington that during his two-year absence in Britain, little change had occurred in America; black New Yorkers were again in an uproar over a new colonization scheme. What made this proposal even more alarming was the fact that it originated among blacks (the vast majority of whom traditionally opposed colonization) and called for establishing settlements in Liberia, a country considered by many the embodiment of American racist schemes to expel blacks from their native land. The popularity of colonization appeared to be on the increase in 1851, due no doubt to the Fugitive Slave Law. Many now questioned the wisdom of staying in a country that so consistently reaffirmed its determination to continue the oppression of blacks.

---

108. John Dunlop to Scoble, January 29, 1851, in BFASS; Kelso *Chronicle*, January 24, 1851; Washington County, Maryland, Land Records, 1850–1851, in Maryland Hall of Records; Hartford Deeds, LXXVI, in State Archives, Hartford; New York *Independent*, quoted in *Liberator*, June 20, 1851; *North Star*, April 10, 1851; Hooker, *Some Reminiscences*, 40.
109. *Scottish Press*, June 28, July 2, 1851.

One of these was Augustus Washington, Pennington's old friend in Hartford, who sold his daguerreotypist shop and emigrated to Liberia, convinced that America held out few hopes for blacks. It was announced in the late fall that a group of New York City blacks had formed the "United African Republic Emigration Society" (subsequently known as the "Liberian Agricultural and Emigration Association") under the leadership of Lewis Putnam. Acting independently of the American Colonization Society, the association planned to send an agent, a "practical farmer," to negotiate with the government of Liberia for grants of land on which to establish a colony. The agent would then cultivate a portion of these lands, the proceeds from which would provide initial support for the first group of fifty emigrants, "who shall possess all the requisite stamina for the building up of our reputation as to agricultural ability." Their success, the association argued, would finally convince "by example" all of those who traditionally opposed colonization.[110]

The association's attempt to remain independent of the ACS was short-lived, however, for the black community failed to respond to its appeal. Were it not for the society's support the association's agent Abraham Cauldwell would not have left America in January, 1852. Unfortunately, Cauldwell's departure coincided with Governor Washington Hunt's proposal to the New York legislature to appropriate funds to aid the ACS. Slavery was so firmly entrenched, Hunt explained, that its abolition was unlikely "in a day or in a generation." Given this fact, the presence of free blacks only retarded progress toward ultimate emancipation. Furthermore, Hunt insisted, the inferiority of free blacks, which was a product of oppression, would lead to extinction of the race if they were not separated from whites. "The instinct of nature," Hunt baldly concluded, "too powerful to be countenanced by the refinements of abstract reasoning, proclaims that the two races must sooner or later be separated."[111]

If Putnam and his associates could be dismissed as deviants sailing too close to the wind, Hunt's call could not be so easily ignored. Shortly after Hunt's speech, blacks in the city organized the "Committee of Thirteen" to lead the resistance against this new wave of colonizationism. "There are traitors among us," they warned, "colored men allied with our oppressors—men who, to satisfy their selfish ends, to put money in their purses, are uniting their influence with those who would drive us from our country." It was an opportunity for these old anti-colonizationists to reaffirm their opposition to a movement they had always condemned. At a meeting called by the committee and held at the

110. *African Repository*, November, 1851, January, 1852, September, 1851.
111. *Anti Slavery Standard*, January 22, 1852.

Abyssinian Baptist Church, resolutions were adopted denouncing the new colonization schemes and calling on free blacks to remain in America and fight slavery and discrimination. The governor's plan was unchristian because it refused to call upon the oppressors to mend their ways, and unconstitutional "because there is no power given to the Legislature, by the constitution to make appropriations of public funds for the purpose of removing any portion of her law abiding and inoffensive citizens beyond the bounds of the State."

Whereas in the past Pennington had denounced unequivocally all forms of colonization, his association with W. W. Anderson and a number of Jamaican emigration schemes now forced him to question some of the meeting's resolutions. But of one thing he was convinced: the ACS was a society designed by oppressors for their selfish ends. The time had come for blacks to reaffirm their opposition to Liberian colonization. Africa, he argued, was well populated and needed no new emigrants. It did need "bibles, missionaries, well qualified teachers, and as many Christian families as can be spared to them, to go for the purpose of advancing the missionary enterprise. We must," he reiterated, "discriminate between colonization and christianization; they are two things, as distinct as the north and the south pole. Colonization has never done much for Christianity, in any part of the world; the history of colonization is a history of plunder and robbery." Samuel Cornish followed with a call for the organization of a lobby group to work in Albany. It was time, he asserted, that blacks form such a group to ensure the defeat of Hunt's proposal. The meeting agreed to establish the group, and called for a state convention meeting in Albany.[112]

The Committee of Thirteen then issued a rebuttal to Hunt's arguments and plan. Reminiscent of his speech at the World Anti Slavery Convention, the address was obviously prepared by Pennington. Based on refutation by historical facts, coupled with counterarguments, and reinforced by extensive use of statistics, it demonstrated that free blacks had progressed in spite of continuing discrimination. For example, there had been a gradual increase in the number of black ministers, who were slowly being accepted by their white counterparts, and in the number of black students who were now attending high schools and colleges. One result of this was that throughout New York, black men were "occupied, or employed, as farmers, blacksmiths, engineers, carpenters, shoemakers, merchant tailors, professors, clergymen, editors, teachers, physicians, lumber dealers, in short, in every calling, except the highly salaried offices of Government"; and all of this despite growing competition from European emi-

112. *Ibid.*

grants, who had on their side "the odds of complexional sympathy and political influence from the moment of their landing upon our shores." Given these facts, the address wondered whether Hunt had spent any time looking into black progress in the state, before condemning to expatriation the very people who in the previous election had overwhelmingly supported him.[113]

Pennington continued his onslaught on Hunt's plan in his presidential address to the Albany convention. He expanded on views expressed at the Abyssinian Church. These proposals, he warned, were analogous in intent to Governor George Clarke's orders to execute suspected participants, deport others, and ban meetings following rumors of a New York slave conspiracy in 1742. Both were the products of ignorance, founded upon a false philosophy. Contrary to Hunt's belief, the "instinct of nature" did not push men farther apart, but tended to bring them closer together through trade, travel, and the search for personal gain, education, and fulfillment. Furthermore, the Christian "instinct" of loving one's neighbor also dictated lessening the separation of men and nations. This "instinct," Pennington observed, had resulted in the perceptible narrowing of the gap between whites and blacks since 1742. If that fact of history was rejected, or attempts were made to thwart its progress, then liberty, religious and civil, "goes to the wall." For this reason, blacks had to be vigilant in their opposition to oppression. Some, he warned the meeting, would have blacks believe that the governor never meant to implement his suggestion. Such reasoning "is the old 'Lullaby, baby, daddy's gone a-hunting' story or song; and if we are soft and silly enough to be rocked to sleep while the artful song is being sung, we shall awake to find the Message DOES mean something." This organized resistance must have had some effect, for little more was heard of Hunt's proposal. Meanwhile, the association, in spite of Cauldwell's efforts, soon abandoned its plans—there had been opposition from the committee— for it could not raise sufficient support from the black community.[114]

Pennington was now at the zenith of his career, acknowledged as one of the leading black figures in America, a reputation undoubtedly enhanced by his honorary doctorate and his being pastor of the largest black Presbyterian church in the country. Early in 1853 his name headed the list of those who issued a call for a national convention meeting in Rochester. Pennington was elected president, in obvious recognition of his achievements. The election was even more significant given that the Rochester meeting represented a reunification, if only temporary, of the different factions that had separated in 1835. It

113. *Ibid.*, February 5, 1852.
114. *Ibid.*, February 19, 1852; New York *Tribune*, December 1, 1852.

also brought together many talented men, an array that no other national meeting could claim. It was, as Howard H. Bell has written, the "most outstanding assemblage of the entire era." Out of the meeting came four important committees set up under the general supervision of the National Council, a sort of "shadow cabinet." The Manual Labor School Committee was to carry on the search for the best means of establishing a national school for blacks; the Protective Unions Committee was to organize the cooperative purchase and distribution of consumer goods; the Business Committee, in addition to its obvious responsibilities, also had the duty of adjudicating disputes between blacks, a clear attempt to show that blacks did not have to rely totally on a biased judicial system; and the Press and Library Committee had tasks that were self-explanatory. Of these four only the School Committee got off the ground, and it continued to formulate plans for a school until 1855 when it disbanded. Even the National Council was short-lived, the victim of internal disputes as different factions jockeyed for control.[115]

Pennington also played an active role in the city's Underground Railroad. He became a member of the New York Vigilance Committee soon after he arrived in Brooklyn. In fact, one of his first duties as an ordained minister was to officiate at the wedding of Frederick Douglass, who had only recently escaped from slavery. His home in Hartford was one of the most active stations in Connecticut, receiving as many as twenty-five slaves in one day. Most of these were sent to him by the NYVC, and Pennington ensured their safe passage north. Through his efforts in Britain, thousands of dollars were raised for the NYVC. The committee raised $4,582.94 between January, 1851, and March, 1853, and $3,166.11 came from Great Britain, most of it from Scotland, where Pennington had his greatest success. Pennington continued his involvement with the movement after he returned to America. When James Snowden, a fugitive from Maryland, opted for imprisonment for theft, fearful that his master (who was also in court) would retake him, it was Pennington who journeyed to Albany two days before Snowden was due to be released, won an early pardon from the governor, and took the fugitive across the Canadian border.[116]

It therefore came as something of a surprise when Pennington and his colleagues in the Vigilance Committee allowed the recapture of three fugitives. What made it even more inexcusable was the fact that the fugitives were Pen-

115. Bell, *A Survey*, 166–67, 176; "Proceedings of the Colored National Convention Held in Rochester, 1853," in Bell (ed.), *Minutes*, 4–6.
116. Frederick Douglass, *Life and Times of Frederick Douglass* (1892; rpr. New York, 1962), 204–205; New York Vigilance Committee, *Report*, 5–6; Pennington to Esteemed Friend, November 17, 1847, in BFASS; *Frederick Douglass Paper*, August 5, 1853.

nington's brother Stephen and Stephen's sons Robert and Jacob. In his early for-
ties, Stephen was the slave of Jacob H. Grove, a Sharpsburg, Maryland, farmer,
and Robert, age seventeen, and Jacob, twenty, were slaves of David Smith,
a shoemaker in the same town, just a few miles from Rockland. Both Grove
and Smith were small slaveholders—Grove owned eight slaves; Smith, four.
Stephen, Grove's slave for almost twenty years, married his second wife Betsy, a
free woman, about the time he was bought from Tilghman. Sometime in early
1854, Stephen and his sons finalized their plans for an escape into Pennsylvania. When they left Sharpsburg on April 21, their aim was to reach Philadelphia as quickly as possible. Within twenty-four hours they and eight other
fugitives, seven from Maryland and one from Norfolk, Virginia, were being
hidden by William Still and the Vigilance Committee of Philadelphia. Concerned that so large a group would attract too much attention, Still and others
on the committee had them dispatched in different directions so as to minimize
possible recapture. Pennington was notified on the twenty-second to expect the
arrival of his family on the twenty-fifth and to be on the lookout for slave
catchers.[117]

Still's was no idle warning, for Grove and Smith, with the aid of Baltimore
slave catchers, were on the trail of the Pembrokes. In fact, unknown to either
group, the Pembrokes and their pursuers had traveled on the same train from
Philadelphia to New York. The Pembrokes were met by Pennington in New
York and hurried off to what was assumed to be a safe home on Thompson
Street. But the slave catchers soon discovered its location. Armed with a warrant for their arrest, the police broke into the home at 3:00 A.M. and removed
the Pembrokes to the Eighth Ward Station House. Five hours later and long
before the Vigilance Committee could arrange legal representation, the fugitives
were brought before a magistrate and summarily ordered returned to Maryland. Pennington had been initially informed that hearings would be held at
11:00 A.M., and subsequently that they had been postponed to 1:00 P.M. and
then to 4:00 P.M. The authorities were obviously stalling—they wanted the
Pembrokes taken from the city quietly. But word spread throughout the community that fugitives had been recaptured and were to be tried. A large crowd
of blacks gathered outside the courthouse, hoping to prevent their being returned to slavery. Aware of the threat, city officials ordered a large posse to

---

117. John Blassingame (ed.), *Slave Testimony: Two Centuries of Letters, Speeches, Interviews and
Autobiographies* (Baton Rouge, 1977), 167–69; Census of 1850, Maryland Slave Schedules; Still,
Underground Rail Road, 173–74.

escort the fugitives out of town. When the Pembrokes were removed in mid-afternoon, the crowd followed the posse all the way to the New Jersey state line, looking, unsuccessfully, for an opportunity to spirit them away. In New Jersey they were transferred to a local police force, which placed them on board a train for Baltimore. Seven days after their escape from Sharpsburg, the Pembrokes found themselves prisoners in a Baltimore slave pen.[118]

The recapture of the Pembrokes was a devastating blow to the Philadelphia and New York Vigilance committees, whose close partnership over the years had been very successful. The failure to keep the Pembrokes safe in New York marred the unblemished record of Still and his co-workers in Philadelphia. For some time after, the Philadelphia committee refused to send fugitives through New York City, preferring instead to use the line through Elmira, which they believed was more carefully monitored and protected. Still was particularly critical of the way the Pembrokes were guarded in New York. Warned that slave catchers were following, Pennington had ample time to move the fugitives out of the city. But the joy of seeing his brother caused Pennington to drop his guard, an error that proved to be costly.[119]

The day after the Pembrokes' recapture, a large group met at Pennington's church to discuss the next course of action. The meeting decided on raising a subscription to purchase Stephen and his sons. Four weeks later, Pennington received a reply from Grove, offering to sell Stephen if the price were right. Pennington responded by offering $600 for his brother. Recognizing a good thing when he saw it, Grove insisted that the price include expenses incurred in Stephen's recapture. When the transactions were finally completed toward the end of June, the price had climbed to $1,375—Pennington managed to raise $1,000 through public subscription. The elation surrounding Stephen's return was understandably subdued. Almost $1,400 had been wasted when a bit more care could have ensured the fugitives' successful escape. And Stephen's two sons had been sold to a North Carolina lumber merchant soon after their return to Baltimore. Smith obviously had no intention of risking another escape.[120]

In addition to his work with the Underground Railroad and his activities in the convention meetings, Pennington was one of the leading figures in the battle against segregated public transportation in New York City. With the

118. *Pennsylvania Freeman*, June 1, 1854; Still, *Underground Rail Road*, 175; Blassingame (ed.), *Slave Testimony*, 169; *Frederick Douglass Paper*, March 16, 1855; Baltimore *Sun*, May 29, 1854.
119. Still, *Underground Rail Road*, 176; *Provincial Freeman*, June 10, 1854.
120. *Pennsylvania Freeman*, June 22, 1854; Baltimore *Sun*, May 31, June 3, 1854; *Anti Slavery Reporter*, September, 1854; *Herald of Freedom and Torch*, July 4, 1854.

memory of his reception in Europe to fortify him, Pennington began his public attack on existing streetcar companies' policies soon after he came back from Britain. Why, he argued, should the pastor of one of the city's largest congregations be forced to travel on the outside of streetcars or, if he refused to accept such humiliating restrictions, be forced to walk in all kinds of weather, just because he was black? "It is not because I smoke cigars in the buses as I see some white men do," Pennington, always the gentleman, complained to the New York *Times*, "it is not because I chew and spit tobacco in the buses, as some white men do. . . . But it is simply and only because I am a black man, obediently carrying about my person the same skin with the same color, which the Almighty has seen fit to give me." The companies' arguments that public taste demanded such restrictions Pennington dismissed as archaic and unbecoming a society that prided itself on being civilized.[121]

Pennington's reasoning swayed few of the policy makers in the streetcar companies, for segregation was a well-established tradition in American public transportation. The efforts of blacks and abolitionists to reverse this policy were never well organized. Protests by men like David Ruggles in New Bedford, Massachusetts, and Henry Highland Garnet in New Hampshire and upstate New York were vigorous but sporadic, usually the spontaneous reactions of individuals angered by the refusal of train and streetcar companies to allow them the full privileges to which paying passengers were entitled. Abolitionist petitions and boycotts did lead to the end of segregation in Massachusetts in 1842, but this was a rare example of organized resistance. George T. Downing's decision to sue a railroad company for ejecting him from a car in December, 1840, was more characteristic of black and abolitionist protests against segregation.[122]

This form of protest met with only limited success; the plaintiffs won few of the suits brought against transportation companies. In early 1855, Pennington and other blacks in New York City decided that the time had come to create an organization to fight for the elimination of segregation on the city's cars. The Legal Rights Association was formed after Elizabeth Jennings, a young black schoolteacher, was expelled from a Third Avenue Railroad Company car in the summer of 1854. Jennings sued the company and was awarded $225 plus costs. The victory had little general application, however, as other companies, like the Eighth Avenue Railroad Company, continued to eject blacks from streetcars. Efforts by Pennington and his associates to pressure the mayor "to restrain said

121. New York *Times*, September 25, 1852.
122. *Anti Slavery Standard*, February 18, 1841.

Company and its conductors from such a course of conduct in the future, and require them to observe the law" were by and large fruitless.[123]

A few months later, when throngs of visitors came to the city to attend anniversary meetings, the Legal Rights Association decided to challenge those companies that continued to exclude blacks. In public statements and notices, Pennington announced that the Jennings ruling mandated equal access to all streetcars and ferries. It was a questionable interpretation of a narrow ruling that applied only to the Third Avenue Company. But the association seized the opportunity to press for a broader application of the decision. It was now up to blacks, Pennington told his congregation, to get other companies to adopt that ruling. Nothing "short of the utmost tameness and unjustifiable, indeed impious cowardice, would induce colored men and women, who valued their rights, to surrender the privilege of common transit along the regular thoroughfares of this busy City."[124]

Pennington then took up his own challenge. After his earlier speeches, a number of blacks had deliberately attempted to ride in the "white cars" of the Sixth Avenue Railroad Company and, when summarily ejected, had brought charges against the company. In defense of its policy the company argued that the majority of its white customers refused to ride in integrated cars and were opposed "to allowing the ladies of their families to mingle with blacks on public conveyances." Moreover, the company's secretary pointed out, "the more respectable portion of the colored people," which clearly did not include those of Pennington's ilk, had requested segregated cars, and in response the company had provided a car for blacks every half hour. Pennington rejected out of hand such spurious reasoning. On May 24 he took a seat in one of the company's cars and refused to leave when the conductor demanded that he move to the car for blacks. With the aid of the driver and the verbal encouragement of many passengers, the conductor forcibly removed Pennington from the car. But he did not go quietly—he held on to the railing and was dragged along beside the car. With the conductor stamping on his hands, Pennington was finally forced to give up his struggle.[125]

Backed by the Legal Rights Association, Pennington sued the company, claiming $1,000 in damages. On the day after the incident he called on blacks to suspend temporarily their protest against the company so the suit could be

123. *Ibid.*, March 3, 1855.
124. *Frederick Douglass Paper*, May 11, 18 (quoting New York *Tribune*), 1855.
125. *Ibid.*, June 8, 1855; New York *Times*, December 18, 1856, May 29, 1855.

heard. His strategy was based on the assumption that a favorable ruling by the courts would produce quicker results than sit-in protests would, because the latter depended on widespread public support and at that point the public seemed firmly committed to continued segregation. Facts, the law, and the people, Pennington announced (or possibly hoped), were on his side. The issues here were: "What is the law [and] Who has violated it in this case?" He insisted that the case "must be decided by a Judge of the Superior Court," for it was not a question "of prejudice, preference, or white or black, but it is a simple question of civil law."[126]

At an association meeting in September he reaffirmed his intention to take the case to the Supreme Court if necessary, and should that not work, he would "carry it to the ballot box." Either way of proceeding depended, however, on an expeditious decision from the courts. Unfortunately, the case was delayed until December, 1856, by which time the excitement caused by the initial protest had abated. At issue, Pennington's lawyer insisted, was not the conductor's violent action but a principle—whether blacks "can or cannot ride in these public conveyances." The company argued that the establishment of such a principle would not only allow "colored persons to ride in our cars, they must also be allowed to sit at the public tables in our hotels." Nature, the company's lawyer reminded the jury, "had made the race distinct, and they . . . must necessarily remain so." It was a shrewd move, for it shifted the case from the issue of the legality of segregated transportation, and challenged the jury to violate accepted social traditions and practices. When the jury retired, there seemed little hope for Pennington. To add insult to injury, the jury's decision in favor of the defendant skirted all legal niceties and simply observed that admitting blacks to the cars would severely diminish the company's profits. What that had to do with the suit, no one, not even Pennington, said. Although he considered appealing the decision to the Supreme Court, Pennington soon dropped the idea, probably because the costs were prohibitive. The fight to desegregate New York streetcars continued throughout the 1850s with only minor successes. Other companies were forced to desegregate their cars, but the Sixth Avenue Company continued to resist all efforts at integration. In April, 1858, the company won yet another case when a jury ruled that it had the right to eject blacks from its cars, so long as undue force was not used.[127]

The loss was symptomatic of the way things had gone for Pennington since

126. *Frederick Douglass Paper*, September 7, 1855; New York *Times*, May 26, 1855.
127. New York *Times*, December 18, 20, 1856, April 16, 1858; Pennington to Gerrit Smith, December 15, 1856, in GSC.

his return from Britain. By the time the case was heard in December, 1856, he was no longer pastor at Shiloh, and he had returned temporarily to Hartford to fill the vacant pulpit at Talcott Street. Pennington's problems had their origin in Britain precisely at the height of his popularity. His questionable use of funds collected for his ransom allowed opponents in the GES to launch an attack. But the time was not right; Pennington's reputation could not be undermined by suggestions of impropriety. Nor, one suspects, would public disclosures, supported even by concrete evidence, have had much effect either among those who viewed Garrisonians with considerable suspicion or those emotionally fettered to the sentimentalism created by *Uncle Tom's Cabin*. Unlike British Garrisonians, many of those who supported Pennington tended to be less critical of such foibles and more forgiving of weaknesses in character, all legacies, they insisted, of cruel, dehumanizing slavery.

It was not surprising, therefore, that Paton and others were reluctant to expose Pennington in Britain. But they nevertheless kept the issue of his misuse of funds alive, in the hope that developments would ultimately prove them right. Public questioning came mainly from America, where Pennington was less influential among abolitionists. Taking its cue from Scotland, the *Anti Slavery Standard* began asking about possible misappropriation of funds just as negotiations between Hooker and Clarke were being completed. Pennington's problems were compounded by "his manifest hostility to the American Anti Slavery Society," which had cost him "the confidence of many of the Anti-Slavery people in Britain and Ireland. Of course," the editor continued, "he has no one to blame but himself that the latter fact has been an obstacle in his path, as all those persons abroad who are not willing to sacrifice their Anti-Slavery to their Sectarianism naturally look to the American Society as the representative of the unadulterated Anti-Slavery of this country." Pennington's actions, the editor believed, had cast a deep shadow of doubt on his integrity.[128]

Initially his opponents were disheartened, for Pennington was warmly received on his return and appeared to be gaining in stature. But within two years he gave his patient detractors the opportunity they had been seeking. In January, 1853, the Third Presbytery of New York (of which he was a member) elected Pennington moderator, and surprisingly he accepted. He knew that his opponents would show little mercy. After all, the church had systematically refused to take an abolitionist stance and had openly endorsed slaveholding congregants' right to membership. Pennington tried to avoid the issues by pleading

---

128. *Anti Slavery Standard,* June 19, 1851.

with the church to institute new policies. He praised a resolution passed earlier that southern presbyteries provide statistics on the number of slaves in their churches as a "*manly vindication* of the principles of Christian discipline." "Some of us," he told his listeners, "who have travelled abroad have been made to smart under the odium of this commonfame report" of Presbyterians holding slaves. Regretting that some Presbyterian theologians had "undertaken to justify slavery from the Bible," he said the issue needed a "fair and open discussion." Pennington undeniably felt what he called "the uncomfortableness of his position," but he still trusted "in the workings of our system to bring us unanimously to the ground now occupied by our United Presbyterian brethren in Scotland, and other bodies of Christians in that country and this."[129] Pennington was whistling in the dark. Criticism could not be averted; American Garrisonians and some blacks gave him no quarter.

It was one thing to be a minister in a church that categorically refused to take an antislavery position, but quite another, Pennington's detractors argued, to accept office in it, for that was a clear acknowledgment of the legitimacy of its official stance. Pennington's accepting the position is even more inexplicable, given his past efforts to excommunicate slaveholders. It was this need, after all, that had prompted the formation of the Union Missionary Society. "I have serious scruples," he wrote in 1841 after attending a church in which there were "negro pews," "whether I do not sin in fellowshipping ministers and churches who tolerate these measures in the solemn season of a revival." What, then, would he say of those who refused to sever connections with churches that welcomed slaveholders? After he returned to Hartford from an 1843 meeting of the Christian Convention in Middletown, Connecticut, Pennington wrote an angry denunciation of the convention's acceptance of fellowship with slaveholders. There were, he argued, no "worthy exceptions among slave-holding Christians," for Christians were to be known only by their works. "Can we have any possible evidence," he asked, that the slaveholder is "saved by a living purifying faith until he does justly, loves mercy and walks humbly with God?"[130] No abolitionist, not even the most radical advocates of "come-outism," could fault such views.

Why had Pennington reneged on such principles? It is difficult to locate the genesis of this change in views. Late in 1848, Lewis Tappan submitted a motion

129. J. W. C. Pennington, *Christian Zeal. A Sermon Preached Before the Third Presbytery of New York, in Thirteenth Street Presbyterian Church, July 3, 1853* (New York 1854), 13–14.

130. *Clarksonian*, quoted in Thomas, "An Analysis of the Life and Work of Pennington," 137–38; Pennington, *A Text Book*, 84.

to the Executive Committee of the American and Foreign Anti Slavery Society, of which Pennington was a member, calling for the establishment of a special committee to investigate whether the society should communicate with or support churches and ministers who held fellowship with slaveholders, or ministers who maintained religious connections with slaveholding ministers, churches, or ecclesiastical bodies. It is impossible to ascertain the positions of individual members of the committee, many of whom, like Pennington, belonged to churches with southern members. But the motion did stir more than six hours of heated discussion at two later meetings, without producing any decision. The motion was finally tabled and never revived.[131] Pennington may have been influenced by, or he may even have influenced, the debate over Tappan's motion. Its intent was clear, and, more important, its sentiments were similar to those of Garrisonian abolitionists. Pennington's reiteration of his views against "Christian slave holders" in his narrative further suggests that his position remained fairly constant over the years.

If this is the case, then his acceptance of the position of moderator is difficult to fathom, and would become more so after the New School General Assembly meeting later in the year. Perhaps Pennington was flattered by the election, as he had been when elected moderator of Hartford's Congregational association, or maybe he saw it as further proof of black progress in America. The Third Presbytery might also have viewed his election as the best means of silencing opponents of its policies without endangering contacts with southern brethren. Whatever the reason behind the election, Garrisonians seized the opportunity to settle the score with Pennington. "That Dr. Pennington," one critic wrote, "who has felt in his own person the miseries and horrors of slavery, should be a member of that Presbytery, or any other forming a constituent part of the Presbyterian Church, is a fact which we cannot explain without supposing him to be either ignorant of the position of that Church in respect to slavery, or lacking in self-respect and sympathy for those in bond."[132] These were harsh words that demanded a response, yet Pennington chose to remain silent.

. Instead of abating as some might have hoped, the debate over the church's role in the fight against slavery quickened in 1853 and 1854. At the New School General Assembly in 1853, the Synod of Ohio moved that the church request statistics from southern presbyteries. In its report the committee on slavery also asked for information on the status of blacks in the South to determine the

---

131. AFASS, Minute Book, 1848–1859, in Amistad Research Center.
132. *Pennsylvania Freeman*, February 24, 1853.

degree to which slavery had proliferated in Presbyterian churches there. But the report was postponed under pressure from southern churches, and a modified version was accepted. Southern presbyteries were to so inform the next meeting and would thus answer and quiet "misapprehensions which may exist in many Northern minds." The Synod of New York and New Jersey, with which the Third Presbytery of New York was affiliated, condemned the assembly for overstepping its jurisdictional authority and demanded that the issue be left to the lower courts of the church. Continued agitation at this point, one resolution contended, was "undesirable and inexpedient."[133] Many clearly believed that it was to the church's advantage to maintain its traditional silence on this issue.

To compound Pennington's problems, the church's dispute with abolitionists was led by the Reverend Samuel Cox, an early friend, advisor, and mentor, or, as Pennington called him some years earlier, "my beloved old pastor." It was Cox who had led Pennington through those difficult days before his conversion, and who had welcomed the fugitive to his church and Sabbath school in New York. In the mid-1830s, Cox was considered one of the leading abolitionists in America and had gained some notoriety as an amalgamationist because of his condemnation of "negro pews" and his praise of black ministers like Theodore S. Wright. When in a series of sermons he argued that Christ was a dark-skinned Syrian, possibly blacker than most black Americans, and as such would have been relegated to segregated pews, one opponent, obviously beside himself, thundered, "He's against slavery, and the South, and the Union! And would you believe it? he called my *Saviour* a nigger! God damn him!" Although the causes are not clear, by 1846 Cox had openly broken with abolitionists. His attack on Frederick Douglass following the World Temperance Convention in London in the summer of 1846 only confirmed his apostasy for many. Cox subsequently became a leading proponent of the Fugitive Slave Law, denouncing as "wicked and unchristian men" those who advocated resistance to the law. When the Reverend I. S. Spencer, a fellow clergyman in the Old School Presbyterian Church of New York, preached a sermon in defense of the law, Cox wrote Spencer that the thanks of the "whole country are due to you for such a service." The law, he wrote the *Journal of Commerce*, was "properly inviolable and paramount or the shield of our safety is everywhere less than a sheaf of straw." It was Cox who led the move against the General Assembly's demand for information on blacks in southern churches, condemning the proposal for pan-

133. Victor Howard, "The Anti Slavery Movement in the Presbyterian Church, 1835–1861" (Ph.D. dissertation, Ohio State University, 1961), 185–86, 190.

dering to the "questionable and ambiguous principle which abolitionists are now labouring to force upon our acceptance."[134]

When Cox launched an attack on Presbyterian ministers who opposed the Kansas-Nebraska Act, many wondered how Pennington could allow himself to be associated with this "coxcomical, pedantic, windy weather-cocking" divine. To those who knew Pennington, his continued friendship with Cox was easily explicable. He was a man of fierce loyalty; a friendship once made was rarely broken, nor was he in the habit of publicly chastising friends. When, for instance, Dr. Hawes, a friend who had officiated at Pennington's installation at Talcott Street and at his second wedding, allowed his church to be used for a colonization meeting, Pennington, despite his strong anti-colonization views, remained silent.[135] Similarly, he could not just dismiss Cox's earlier aid and guidance.

This silence, however, could also have been the product of less noble motives. Pennington, like many other black ministers, became dependent on the few whites who were willing to ignore social traditions and openly support black ministers as Cox had done. Confined to small, poor churches, black Presbyterian ministers could not realistically expect their congregations to provide full financial support. Matters were made worse by church policy, which frowned on attempts by ministers to supplement their incomes by taking other jobs. Many, like Pennington, therefore, had to depend either on teaching and writing or on the private support of white friends to boost their meager incomes. "This pattern of dependence upon white support," one authority has observed, "was perhaps inevitable, given the economic disparity between white and Negro communities; but it could lead to an unwholesome paternalism on the part of whites and flattery and begging on the part of the Negro minister." Always struggling to make ends meet, Pennington might have chosen to remain silent on Cox's views and the policies of the Presbyterian church rather than alienate an old patron. Four years later, Cox, along with the committee of the Third Presbytery of New York, endorsed an application from the elders of the Colored Presbyterian Church of Newtown—at which Pennington then officiated—for $100 annually from the American Missionary Association for Pennington's salary.[136]

134. Pennington, *Two Years' Absence*, 8; Thomas, "An Analysis of the Life and Work of Pennington," 214; Leonard L. Richards, *"Gentlemen of Property and Standing": Anti-Abolition Mobs in Jacksonian America* (New York, 1970), 120–21; Howard, "The Anti Slavery Movement in the Presbyterian Church," 169–70.
135. *Frederick Douglass Paper*, April 8, 1852; *Anti Slavery Standard*, July 29, 1841.
136. Andrew E. Murray, *Presbyterians and the Negro: A History* (Philadelphia, 1966), 40–41; Elders of the Colored Presbyterian Church to the AMA, November, 1859, in AMA.

Pennington continued for some time to ignore the criticism from his Garrisonian opponents, hoping that the furor over the decisions of the Presbyterian church would soon dissipate. It not only persisted, but toward the end of 1854, Garrisonians began using these issues in an attempt to discredit Pennington and his supporters in Britain. During his tour of Britain, Parker Pillsbury, the Boston Garrisonian, in a letter to the Glasgow *Sentinel* commending Glasgow for its long commitment to abolition, argued that its efforts were "misdirected or . . . thrown away" on individuals and organizations such as vigilance committees that were not "in any way directly at war with slavery." Pennington, he claimed, had been principally responsible for this new shift; the same man accepted the arguments of the recent General Assembly of his church that there should be no discussion on slavery at a time when his family was being hunted by slave catchers. Hiding behind "his colour and his clerical connections," Pillsbury concluded, Pennington at once reviled Garrison as an infidel while saying nothing of his church's slaveholding connections. Pillsbury's letter was reprinted in most Garrisonian newspapers in Britain and America.[137]

This latest assault obviously stung Pennington sufficiently for him to break his silence. In late 1854, during a speech in Newport, Rhode Island, which one observer described as "calm but well placed," Pennington disowned all connection "with that class of Abolitionists, or reformers, called infidels." It was the kind of statement his opponents were waiting to hear:

That the Doctor should be anxious not to give offence to the church and clergy is quite natural, since, although a fugitive slave, he has so little moral principle and self-respect as to be willing to remain a member and a minister of the manstealing Presbyterian Church, half of whose clergy and membership would unhesitatingly consent to his re-enslavement, were it not for the fact that British gold had made him the owner of his own body. It is equally natural that a clerical associate and toady of the Rev. Dr. Cox should go about the country, uttering lying insinuations that real Abolitionists are "infidels". Is it our duty to spare such men on account of their complexion?

The patently gratuitous question aside, this was a most devastating indictment.[138]

Given the circumstances, it would have been in Pennington's interest to keep quiet; his comments at Newport only fueled the fire. He could not possibly hope to win such a debate, nor could he argue that his plans envisaged a day when the church would adopt an antislavery position, for it had resisted all abolitionist pressure. Some blacks also insisted that Pennington make his position

137. *Liberator*, September 29, 1854; *Anti Slavery Advocate*, October, 1854; *Anti Slavery Standard* October 28, 1854.
138. *Anti Slavery Standard*, January 13, March 24, 1855.

clear, and Douglass offered him space in his paper to respond to the charges. In a series of letters that appeared between February and May, 1855, Pennington attempted to defend his actions. The letters were surprisingly mild, although they were not infrequently spiced with ad hominem ripostes at his opponents. Pennington's initial thrust established the fact that he had always depended on his own resources in accomplishing his goals. Independence and self-reliance first drove him to seek his freedom and to work for an end to slavery and discrimination, long before most of his detractors were active in the movement. "Like a man," he wrote, "I have emancipated myself, I have educated myself, and have worked my way up to a standing among the *Men* of this land, and of the world; and I ask, why should these men pounce upon me as if I were an Alabama slave holder?" Pennington knew full well why he was under attack, but chose to ignore it, finding instead advantageous grounds on which to counter his opponents.[139]

It was a canny move, for success in this dispute would hinge on the issue of freedom of choice. The fugitive, who had freed himself, was self-educated, had struggled long and hard for emancipation and an end to discrimination, surely had some right to decide the best means of achieving his ends without being ridiculed by those who were ostensibly striving toward the same goals. Moreover, in what must have been merely a rhetorical aside, Pennington demanded of his adversaries that they state why he, of all other black Presbyterian ministers, was being singled out for attack. His opponents could not respond easily to that challenge, for they ran the risk of exposing themselves to the accusation that they were motivated by spite and a morbid desire for revenge for Pennington's successes in Britain. This right of choice, or "right of conscience," as Pennington called it, was a "sacred right" that no one could violate on the "pretence of fidelity to our cause." Anyone who usurped that right must be looked "upon as being as hostile to the interest of my race," he concluded, "as the man who binds chains upon our limbs, on pretence that he can take better care of us in the condition of slavery, than we can take of ourselves in a state of freedom."[140]

There the matter seemed to end, and it appeared Pennington had gotten the better of his opponents again. His letters, written more in pain than in anger, spoke of a proud man who cherished his struggles, attainments, and contributions to the advancement of his people, and who might therefore have defused

139. *Frederick Douglass Paper*, April 6, February 23, 1855.
140. *Ibid.*, May 4, 1855.

another potentially explosive dispute among abolitionists. But Pennington was careful also to attack his critics at their most vulnerable point, namely, their noted resistance to all attempts by others to assume governance over men, which, they argued, was solely within the province of God. "Each human being, man and *woman*," Henry C. Wright, a leading advocate of Garrisonian abolitionism and nonresistance, once argued, "is invested with sovereignty over himself—and no one over another. . . . Thus over our physical and spiritual natures God wields the sceptre of absolute dominion." Why, then, were his opponents, Pennington asked, insisting that he toe a line that he found unacceptable? From time to time, other blacks had found it necessary to chastise Garrisonians for their intransigence and their penchant for dictating the actions of others. Even some whites close to the Garrisonians, notably Sarah and Angelina Grimké, sometimes found them overweening: "They wanted us to live out William Lloyd Garrison," they complained, "not the convictions of our souls, entirely unaware that they were exhibiting . . . the genuine spirit of slave holding, by wishing to curtail the sacred privilege of conscience."[141]

Finally, Pennington could no more leave the church than his opponents could voluntarily submit to the authority of local synods. The church provided him the foundations on which he had built his entire life. As a pastor in Congregational and Presbyterian churches, Pennington was relatively free from the dictates of local synods. This freedom he exploited for the benefit of the black community, making his churches social agencies that promoted benevolence and education, gave aid to the poor, and assisted the fugitive. From his pulpits came sermons and lectures that dealt with topics ranging from temperance to the evils of socialism and free love. It is impossible to imagine Pennington relinquishing such a position for the unknown of life outside the church.

Although there were genuine differences of opinion over the church's role in abolitionism, the true reasons for these attacks on Pennington had their genesis in disputes between Scottish factions. The imputation that Pennington had been a little less than honest in handling the money raised in Jamaica was never far beneath the surface, however, and Pennington only encouraged further speculation by failing to give an adequate account of expenditures. Even if he had used these funds for some other purposes, it might have been well for him to admit his actions. As it stood, the suspicions of wrongdoing were never allayed. The pressures created by all these disputes soon took their toll. In early 1854 it was rumored that Pennington had become "a confirmed drunkard" and,

141. Wright and the Grimkés quoted in Lewis Perry, *Radical Abolitionism: Anarchy and the Government of God in Antislavery Thought* (Ithaca, 1973), 105, 53.

according to his colleague Lewis Tappan, had "used his friends wrongfully, is greatly in debt, is neglecting his parishioners, and contriving . . . to obtain money under false pretences." In April, Shiloh appointed a committee to confer with him "in relation to his personal affairs." Toward the end of the month, the committee reported that it had received from Pennington a "detailed statement of the transactions connected with the purchase of his freedom," which they found satisfactory. All of this sounded very much like the conclusions of the Glasgow Emancipation Society, and in both instances, the findings did nothing to remove suspicions against him.[142]

Confirmation of his alcoholism shattered Pennington's reputation. Temperance, after all, was an important feature of nineteenth-century philanthropy, a tool, many blacks believed, in the fight against oppression. Pennington had actively supported the cause. In 1833 he was a member of the committee that prepared the address on temperance for the third annual meeting of the Negro Convention movement. In calling for total abstinence, the address argued that there existed a proven association between disease and drink. Although it optimistically reported on the growth of temperance societies among blacks, it nonetheless warned that a great deal still had to be done to destroy the "rum system," which, like slavery, was "upheld by ignorance, avarice, and incorrect views of duty." Victory over intemperance was essential to black progress, for more than anything else, the address suggested, it "tends to perpetuate that *relentless prejudice*, which arrays itself against our dearest interests; frowns us away from the avenues of useful knowledge and wealth; and which with a cruel hand wrenches from us our political rights." By eliminating intemperance, blacks would provide America one less excuse for denying them their rights as citizens. Later, in New Haven, Pennington attended the organizational meeting of the Connecticut State Temperance and Moral Reform Society, which promoted total abstinence as the only "*safe* and *consistent* ground, which can be occupied by the friends of temperance." Not long after taking over at Talcott Street, he was elected president of the society's 1840 annual meeting, and throughout the years he continued to be a leading advocate of the cause.[143]

There was, therefore, a genuine sense of shock and loss among blacks and

142. Wyatt-Brown, *Lewis Tappan*, 307; Records of the Third Presbytery of New York, April 10, 24, 1854, in PHS.

143. Carol V. R. George, *Segregated Sabbaths: Richard Allen and the Emergence of Independent Black Churches 1760–1840* (New York, 1973), 127; "Minutes of the Proceedings of the Third Annual Convention for the Improvement of the Free People of Colour in These United States, 1833," in Bell (ed.), *Minutes*, 15–19; *Weekly Advocate*, January 28, 1837; *Colored American*, September 19, 1840; *Nonconformist*, October 3, 1849; *Teetotal Times and Essayist*, November, 1849.

abolitionists when it became known that Pennington had lapsed into alcoholism. But no one felt compelled to try to explain why this long-standing, devout believer in temperance had taken solace in the bottle; to many, such apostasy was a sure sign of a weak character unable to handle the normal pressures of life. It is obvious that his differences with British and American Garrisonians, his inability to account adequately for the money raised in Jamaica and elsewhere, and the reaction to his acceptance of the moderator's chair, all contributed to Pennington's problems. Proud of his accomplishments, and always anxious to show the world (especially America) that blacks were capable of attaining the highest ranks in society if only prejudice could be removed, Pennington found it impossible to understand his critics' stridency and vituperation. This explains the despair and disappointment so evident in his response to their criticism: disappointment that a man who had started with so little and achieved so much could become the victim of such bitter denunciation from those who should have been his supporters; and despair of ever gaining recognition in his own country. Foreigners lauded and lionized him, but his own countrymen castigated him on what he considered the flimsiest of pretexts.

His problems with alcoholism, which seem to have lasted until 1858, temporarily destroyed Pennington's self-esteem. Such wanderings from the path of righteousness were a clear indication of deep personal weaknesses. "Whatsoever teaches the believer to overcome the world, the flesh, and the Devil, tends to build him up," he once told his Hartford congregation. Failure to resist these weaknesses obviously tore him down. All of this damaged Pennington's relations with his congregation at Shiloh. Even though he was exonerated in April, 1854, Pennington's actions left a number of questions unanswered. Time, many in his congregation hoped, would absolve him from any blame. But for others, the sense of betrayal would never be eliminated. One suspects that some thought these problems were compounded by Pennington's "sit-in" on the Sixth Avenue car and the obvious ignominy of their pastor's being dragged through the streets. There were indeed many who viewed his protest as the action of a reckless man. Whatever the contending views within Shiloh, by December, 1855, the congregation was unanimous in their condemnation of his "conduct." Their request for "speedy relief" was referred to a committee by the Third Presbytery. The committee reported in early January, but a final decision was delayed to give Pennington an opportunity to defend himself. Afterward, the committee reported that the "confessions made by Dr. Pennington, his expression of penitence and his professed purpose carefully to guard against a repetition of the acknowledged offense, are satisfactory to the Presbytery and that, with their hearty forgiveness of the past, they commend him for the future to the grace of the Great Shepherd and Bishop of souls."[144]

Despite the conciliatory tone of the committee's report, it was obvious that Pennington could no longer continue to officiate at Shiloh. Less than one month later, he asked to be relieved of his duties in order to return to his old church in Hartford. Since his departure in 1848, Talcott Street had been without a settled pastor and the size of its congregation had fallen off considerably. Nothing is known of Pennington's activities during his two years at Talcott Street. It is possible that he viewed the return to Hartford as a form of retreat during which time he could overcome the personal ravages of alcoholism. In mid-1858 he returned as a stated supply minister to the small Presbyterian church in Newtown, where he had officiated briefly after his ordination twenty years before.

The return to Newtown also meant a return to the schoolroom after almost fourteen years. Rather than a vocation, teaching was now a necessity brought on by poverty. To make matters worse, Pennington's wife was ill and what little money he had went toward her medical bills. There was also the cost of tuition for his son at trade school in Albany. His paltry resources, Pennington wrote Gerrit Smith, came solely from selling his published speeches, and his salary of $200, which could not supply his family with its most basic needs. By the end of 1859, things had gotten so desperate that Pennington was reduced to begging from friends for assistance. To John Jay he sent a plaintive message: "I am much in want of a small amount of pecuniary aid. Can you give me $5."[145] It was the plea of a destitute man, too poor even to get to places where he had been invited to lecture; and it must have been a devastating blow to the proud spirit of one who just ten years before had been the toast of London, Paris, and Frankfort.

In spite of all these personal problems, Pennington never once reneged on his commitment to fight against American slavery and discrimination. Although he never regained prominence as a recognized national figure among black Americans, Pennington actively involved himself in the lives of the many communities in which he lived. Even while he was destitute he still found time to

144. Pennington, *Two Years' Absence*, 16; Records of the Third Presbytery of New York, December 10, 1855, January 28, 1856, in PHS.

145. Congregational General Association of Connecticut, *Minutes* (New Haven, 1856); Records of the Third Presbytery of New York, February 25, 1856, in PHS; Pennington to Gerrit Smith, March 1, 1858, in GSC; Pennington to John Jay, December 12, 1859, in Jay Family Papers.

work for the education of black youth, insisting, despite his own experiences, that "if the colored men in their several professions will prepare themselves to meet their white brethren as equals, they will find their level" in America. As late as 1868, he was trying to reactivate the defunct Presbyterian and Congregational Association, formed in 1843 as a means of promoting education for black youngsters. He also joined Martin R. Delany, James McCune Smith, Robert Campbell, and others in contributing articles to the *Weekly Anglo-African*, a literary journal that its editor Robert Hamilton hoped would provide blacks a medium through which they could hone their literary skills.[146]

The issue of emigrationism, which produced such bitterness in 1859, gave Pennington an opportunity to rejoin his old colleagues. Emerging earlier in the decade, it suggested an alternative to traditional policies that advocated staying in America. Emigration to Haiti, Jamaica, Central America, or Africa, its supporters contended, would remove blacks from the source of oppression, offer them ample space in which to develop their talents, and finally show the world that they were as capable as whites. Emigrationists, however, eschewed all affinity with colonizationists, arguing that they were opposed to the forced and total expatriation of blacks, preferring instead a partial, voluntary emigration of skilled black Americans to a country where their abilities could be fully expressed. By the end of the decade, there were three contending proposals, Delany's Niger Valley Exploring Party, Garnet's African Civilization Society, both promoting African emigration, and Haitian emigrationism led by a number of prominent figures.[147]

All of these schemes initially met with vigorous opposition from those blacks who saw them as devices to take away the best of the black leadership and thus rivet the chains of oppression more firmly on the black masses. The African Civilization Society (AFCS), however, generated the most bitter dispute. By the end of 1859 the battle lines were firmly drawn between pro- and anti-emigrationists. Given his known opposition to colonization, it is not surprising that Pennington would question the wisdom of establishing a colony in Africa. But his decision to join the anti-emigrationists occurred only after considerable debate. He found the strong missionary dimension of the AFCS very appealing and in many respects similar to those he had promoted earlier. Although he was

146. Pennington to Robert Hayden, December 14, 1869, in Omnium Gatherum Collection, Moorland-Spingarn Research Center, Howard University, Washington, D.C.; *Weekly Anglo-African*, October 15, 1859.
147. Floyd J. Miller, *The Search for a Black Nationality: Black Colonization and Emigration, 1787–1863* (Urbana, 1975), 186–87.

careful to disclaim all connections with the society, Pennington initially endorsed its objectives.[148]

His support was short-lived, however, and by early 1860, Pennington joined Downing, Douglass, and others in opposition to the society. He undoubtedly was influenced by his old friends Downing and Douglass, but it appears that other factors were more important in his final decision. The Reverend Theodore Bourne, the society's corresponding secretary, by the end of 1859 had managed to sway a number of British abolitionists to support African emigration under the auspices of the AFCS. That smacked too much of the earlier colonization activities of Elliot Cresson, R. R. Gurley, and the Reverend John Miller, representatives of the American Colonization Society, whose efforts in Britain to promote Liberian colonization Pennington and his contemporaries had done so much to undermine. Now Bourne was succeeding where others had failed, due largely to his convincing arguments that the AFCS, led by a black man, had the overwhelming support of black Americans, and the news that Delany and Robert Campbell had signed a "treaty" with the Alake of Abeokuta for the settlement of black Americans there. Bourne's claims were pure fabrication, but had the desired effect of winning the society considerable support in Britain.

Not only were a significant number of blacks opposed to the society, but the suspicion persisted that Garnet and other blacks in leadership positions were façades behind which colonizationists hid their true intentions. That impression became stronger when a society meeting in March, 1860, attracted many whites who supposedly held colonizationist sympathies. What, Pennington asked, was the purpose of such a meeting? "Is this great array of great names expected to silence all further questions in the minds of the colored people as to the desirableness of the African Civilization Society? This will fail. Is it expected that these names will be used as keys to the coffers of colonization monies? This too will fail." Two weeks after the March meeting, Pennington launched another attack, this time impugning the true motives of the society's supporters. Why, he asked, were the invitations extended to six speakers with known colonizationist sympathies? Such activities, he warned, were playing directly into the hands of those bent on the forced expatriation of black Americans. Pennington therefore called on Garnet to disband the society.[149]

148. *Frederick Douglass Paper*, July 8, 1859; *Douglass Monthly*, January, 1859; New York *Tribune*, December 10, 1858.
149. *Weekly Anglo-African*, March 3, 31, 1860.

As word of Delany's and Campbell's success in Abeokuta, and Bourne's in Britain, reached New York, Downing, Pennington, and others decided that more effective means had to be employed. In early April, Pennington added his name to the call for a public meeting to expose the society's operations, which its opponents believed were similar to the "old colonization scheme—a supporter of prejudice—and hence a co-worker in the ranks of our enemies." The April 12 meeting was a disaster for both sides in the dispute. A series of resolutions, which the gathering passed, concluded that the hope "for the emancipation of the slave in this country does not rest either on the cultivation of cotton in Africa, nor on the building up of a negro nationality there; but on the radical change of public opinion here, to be brought about by a continued anti-slavery agitation." What was actually said, however, seemed to matter little to the contending groups, who gave no quarter and who threatened on many occasions to come to blows. One observer sarcastically reported that "canes and fists became very unsteady . . . , in the possession of their owners, and everything betokened a representation of 'Donnybrook Fair.' Gentlemen might be seen everywhere jumping around in pantomime performances, which would have compelled the Ravel family to yield the hat." The meeting ended prematurely when the trustees of the church, hoping to avoid an open fight, turned off the lights. No attempt at reconciliation was made in the ensuing weeks, during which time the two groups continued to fire salvos at each other from the safety of their own retreats.[150]

Although never resolved, the issue of African emigration was finally settled by developments over which neither group had any control. Opposition from British missionaries in Abeokuta and British colonial interests finally forced the Alake to renege on the "treaty" arrangements. Many of those emigrationists who initially supported the proposed African settlement now turned their energies to the promotion of Haitian emigration led by James Redpath and the Reverend Theodore Holly. In negotiations with the Haitian government for the settlement of black Americans, Redpath had insisted that the emigrants be guaranteed freedom of worship, suitable land, free passage to the island, and freedom of political activity, demands which the Haitians accepted in the autumn of 1860.

Pennington's opposition to this scheme was unequivocal. The issue, he argued, was not the right of individual blacks to settle in any foreign country, or the right to trade with blacks in other parts of the world, or, for that matter,

150. *Ibid.*, April 28, 1860; *Liberator*, May 4, 1860.

black Americans committing themselves to missionary work in foreign fields, but rather the deliberate efforts of emigrationists "to dissolve the union of the race in this country." As he had done many times before, Pennington again employed his views on the ineluctable march of progress to show that in spite of continued discrimination, black Americans' achievements were significant— witness their many churches, schools, and societies. "In the great enterprise of agriculture, mechanic trades, and productive labor," he wrote, "our people have advanced, and are advancing, and yet you would have them leave this great progressive mark and go into the pell-mell game of chances for fortunes beyond the gulf." The natural increase in the numbers of black Americans was, for Pennington, irrefutable evidence that the "law of progress" was at work and that God had placed them here for a purpose. "Upon these," he concluded, "we sincerely predicate the belief, that this land is destined in the wisdom of God to continue one of the centers of the race."[151] Although seven different groups of emigrants went to Haiti by June, 1861, the movement soon petered out, due in part to the outbreak of the Civil War and in part to the difficulties many emigrants encountered in their new home.

Pennington's view that America was to "continue one of the centers of the race" was based on the conviction that the race's future was tied inextricably to that of the country. Years before, he had told a Glasgow audience that "our destiny is bound up with that of America, her ship is ours, her pilot is ours, her storms are ours, her calms are ours. If she breaks upon any rock, we break with her. We love America and hate slavery the more; and thus, loving the one and hating the other, we are resolved that they shall NOT LONG DWELL TO-GETHER."[152] The Civil War provided blacks with an opportunity to test this hypothesis. Black participation in the war, many argued, would force the North to recognize that slavery was the underlying cause of the dispute between the states, and would finally win them the rights of full citizenship. Pennington's decision to actively promote the Northern cause, and to call on blacks to join the armed forces, could only have been reached after much soul searching, for he took his peace principles seriously. As he had told so many meetings in Europe, wars singularly failed to resolve disputes between combatants. Civilized action dictated that the disputants submit their differences to international arbitration. In the case of the Civil War, however, these principles did not apply, for it was caused by the treacherous rebellion of a group bent on maintaining an

151. *Weekly Anglo-African*, January 19, February 2, 1861.
152. Pennington, *A Lecture*, 19.

oppressive racist system, one that also was responsible for the existence of discrimination in the North. Remove slavery, then, and America in all likelihood would also eliminate discrimination. It was, therefore, essential that blacks play an active role in the destruction of slavery if they ever hoped to prevent its reappearance in the future.

In order to ensure these results, Pennington joined other blacks in petitioning Congress to declare slavery illegal. "African slavery as it now exists at the South," the petition pointed out, "is the prime cause of the present Crisis," and a "permanent peace cannot be restored until said cause" is removed. But blacks also had to contribute actively to the defeat of the South to guarantee the race's future in America. "Let our able bodied men go to the United States service," he told an audience in Poughkeepsie two years later, for in the future the army would be the "great bulwark of our life, as a nation." Moreover, blacks should enlist in the "army in force for the sake of the strength it will give them, the education they will obtain, the pay they will get; and the good service they will do for God, the country and the race." Not to take part, he had written earlier, was "unpolitical, unphilosophical, unmanly," and even "traitorous to our own race," for the race was on the brink of a "grand heroic age" when "the last vestige of African Slavery shall be wiped out." Blacks, therefore, had to participate in its extirpation, if only because, unlike all other groups in the country, they had a vested interest in the final emancipation of their brothers in slavery. Twenty thousand black troops marching west "upon the rear of Jeff Davis, can recapture King cotton," he told a meeting in Yonkers, "or take that great gun which had been worth from $80,000,000 to $100,000,000 to the South per annum." Then, he believed, "the race will hold the position of the world. Because if cotton is King in the money market of the world, our race in America had by its blood, tears, and sweat crowned it king, and are therefore entitled to the benefit of his reign."[153]

The battle for the Union also had to be fought on the international front, especially in Britain, where the textile industry was almost totally dependent on southern cotton. Victory for the North, Pennington and others contended, was only possible if Britain could be persuaded to support openly the cause of the free states, or at least remain neutral in the dispute. Blacks who had done so much in the past to win British support for American abolition now had to harness their reputations to the interests of the North. Pennington obviously

153. James M. McPherson, *The Negro's Civil War: How American Negroes Felt and Acted During the War for the Union* (New York, 1965), 40–41; *National Principia*, January 7, 1864; *Weekly Anglo-African*, August 10, 1861; *Douglass Monthly*, June, 1863.

hoped to exploit his popularity to benefit the North when he left for Britain in October, 1861. But times had changed; no longer was he the popular figure who in 1849 had been awarded an honorary doctorate. His problems with alcoholism, and questions concerning misappropriation of money, tarnished his image. Pennington's difficulties were compounded by growing sympathy for the South among many who traditionally supported emancipation. By the time Pennington returned to America a year later, he had little to show for his efforts.

A few months after his arrival in Liverpool, where he seems to have spent most of his time, Pennington edited and published the narrative of J. H. Banks, a fugitive slave from Alabama, who was living in England. Pennington lectured only infrequently during this visit, and most of his speeches seemed totally out of place, given the changed circumstances in America. Of course, he might well have been simply acceding to British partiality for the sentimental account of slave life. It also appears that Pennington attempted to raise money "for carrying on the instruction of men of his own race for missionary purposes amongst the population." Such activity could only have raised suspicions about his motives, for no organization had commissioned him to raise money on its behalf. There were even rumors that he had gone to Britain "in behalf of some African emigration scheme."[154]

Whatever the reasons for his visit, the trip came to an abrupt and disastrous end in June, 1862, when Pennington was sentenced to one month's hard labor by a Liverpool court for the theft of a book. The events leading to his arrest are not clear, but from the testimony of the store clerk it appears that Pennington had attempted to leave a secondhand book store with a copy of Pope's translation of the *Odyssey* hidden in his coat pocket. In his defense Pennington claimed he had absentmindedly put the book in his pocket while reading others, that he had every intention of paying for it, and that he had offered to do so when accosted by the clerk. Pennington's account did little to sway the magistrate, who in sentencing him felt it necessary to express some discomfort at imprisoning someone who was so highly esteemed. When word reached America, few commentators questioned the outcome of the case; to them it was the logical consequence of Pennington's "intemperate habits."[155] It mattered little that he had overcome his problem with alcohol. It also seems particularly ironic that

154. J. W. C. Pennington (ed.), *A Narrative of Events in the Life of J. H. Banks, an Escaped Slave, From the Cotton State of Alabama, in America* (Liverpool, 1861); Manchester *Examiner and Times,* February 20, 1862; Manchester *Weekly Times,* February 22, 1862; *Weekly Anglo-African,* February 1, 1862; *Anti Slavery Standard,* July 26, 1862.

155. See, for example, Liverpool *Mercury,* June 26, 1862; Hartford *Courant,* July 2, 1862.

a man who was so enthralled by books should be imprisoned for taking a secondhand one that cost just three shillings.

Nothing is known of Pennington's activities in the months immediately after
his return to America in the summer of 1862. The records of the Presbyterian
church list him as "without charge" during 1863 and 1864, although he might
have assisted at his old church in Newtown. It is possible that he taught school
in Poughkeepsie in 1863, a year which saw some of the most vicious attacks on
northern blacks by white mobs. Just after Pennington came back from Britain,
a mob of Irish workers burst into a Brooklyn tobacco factory, which employed
twenty-five blacks, most of them women and children, and set it on fire, hoping
to burn the building and the workers with it. Although all escaped with their
lives, the mob's action set the tone for further attacks. The culmination was the
infamous Draft Riots of June, 1863, during which blacks were murdered in
their homes or lynched.

Although Pennington's family escaped the ravages of the mob, his wife was
consistently threatened by ruffians. This, and the death toll from the riots,
drove Pennington to abandon his cherished principle of "moral power," that
ability to suffer oppression peacefully while working diligently to ensure its cessation. Now, he told a Poughkeepsie audience, "we must study the use of arms,
for *self-defense*. There is no principle of civil, or religious obligation that requires us to live on, in hazard, and leave our persons, property, and our wives
and children at the mercy of barbarians. Self-defense is the first law of nature."
This was indeed a far cry from his earlier views. These riots, he warned, had to
be seen in their historical context as part of the society's traditional response to
the legitimate aspirations of blacks. These mobs, made up largely of Irish
Catholics, were bent on stemming the movement toward equality that would
result from a Union victory—they wanted to reap the benefits of continued
black oppression. In order to stymie the activities of future mobs and at the
same time secure equality for the race in America, blacks had to arm themselves for self-defense, and enlist in the army in increasing numbers.[156]

As history and self-interest dictated massive black involvement in the war so
the defeat of the South compelled all true Christians, especially free blacks, to
work for the elevation of the freedman. The task of improving the condition of
the former slaves, Pennington believed, would also close the circle of Christian
evangelization begun with the formation of the American Missionary Association in the 1840s, thus bringing to the South the work started in Africa and the

156. *National Principia*, January 7, 14, 1864; McPherson, *The Negro's Civil War*, 70.

Caribbean. Yet only the AME and AME Zion churches had moved expeditiously to supply the necessary ministers and teachers for the South in the months before the war ended. Impatient with Presbyterian indecisiveness, Pennington severed ties with the Third Presbytery of New York in November, 1864, and joined the Missouri Conference of the AME church.[157]

It was almost a year, however, before Pennington went south. In October, 1865, he attended the Missouri Conference meeting in New Orleans, where he was apparently ordained an itinerant minister and appointed station preacher in Natchez, Mississippi. Soon afterward, Pennington left for Natchez with the Reverend Javez Pitt Campbell, bishop of the Missouri Conference. Optimistic about the future, but fully aware of the many problems involved in reconstructing a battered society, Pennington devoted his energies to the education of the freedmen in the city. Lacking a schoolroom, he used his pulpit to deliver a series of lectures on the rights of the former slaves, firmly convinced that the aim of every "friend of human progress should be to educate and protect the colored race in the full employment of all their civil, religious and political rights." A full knowledge of these rights, he argued, was the only safeguard against the type of rebellion and bloodbath that had recently occurred at Morant Bay in Jamaica. Pennington was anxious to prevent any retaliation from Mississippi landholders for the zealous demands of former slaves that plantations be broken up and redistributed immediately. Arguing against wholesale land redistribution, which he saw as both impractical and dangerous, Pennington opted instead for purchasing and leasing of small tracts of land by the former slaves. Any other approach, he thought, would be only to the freedmen's detriment and would lead to further economic, social, and political turmoil.[158]

Pennington's stay in Mississippi could not have lasted more than a year. By the beginning of 1867 he was on the move again, this time to Portland, Maine, to fill the pulpit of the Newbury Congregational Church. Nothing is known of Pennington's activities in Portland except that he continued to promote education for black youth. In poor health and longing to return to the work of educating the freedman, Pennington left Portland after almost two years to accept an appointment from the Presbyterian Committee of Missions for Freedmen in Jacksonville, Florida. Soon after his arrival he founded a church and a Sabbath and day school. Attached to the East Florida Presbytery, the church grew

157. Records of the Third Presbytery of New York, November 7, 1864, in PHS.
158. Thomas, "An Analysis of the Life and Work of Pennington," 113–14; *Weekly Anglo-African*, December 23, 1865.

slowly and, at the time of his death, numbered fewer than thirty communicants. The school fared only marginally better.[159]

Pennington could do relatively little on his paltry salary of $200 and the small contribution his poor congregation raised. Yet he never once retreated in the face of mounting difficulties and personal hardship. Reconstruction in Florida would succeed only if planters and their "weak-kneed" political lackeys were frustrated in their efforts to return the state to the status quo ante. Careful attention also had to be paid to the freedmen who needed "a great deal of training to prevent them from being misled, on the one hand, by spurious Republicans, and on the other by their old enemies, who are growing bold, and do not hesitate to put in their claim for a share of whatever there is to be gained by the freedmen's vote." Pennington, however, died before he could begin the task he set himself. In "broken health, and bending under the infirmities of years," he died a lonely man, away from his family, in Jacksonville on October 22, 1870.[160]

All Pennington's activities through his long life were informed by a firm belief that God had placed him on this earth to work for the improvement of his fellow man. This duty, to do good by aiding others less favorably endowed or positioned, kept him working for so many causes, even after his reputation had suffered. This duty, he insisted, was predicated on Christian zeal, an "intense love for the objects of Christian labor with an impassioned and ever burning ardor to magnify, extend, and give prominence to these objects." The acquisition of all the necessary skills to aid in the improvement of mankind was the responsibility of strong-willed individuals who through self-reliance and drive achieved the stature of men of merit. He spared little time for those who resisted by inactivity this apparent law of nature. As a black minister, he was determined to disprove Frederick Douglass' statement that few black churchmen had the "mental qualification to instruct and improve their congregation; and instead of advancing, they retard the intellectual progress of the people."[161] Education was almost an obsession with Pennington, for without it, he argued, blacks would frustrate the "law of progress" and slow, if not subvert, the movement toward perfection. This is precisely why he was so involved in teaching

159. *Annual Report of the Presbyterian Committee of Missions for Freedmen of the Presbyterian Church of the USA* (Pittsburgh, 1871), 13; Pennington to Gerrit Smith, September 17, 1869, in GSC; *Palladium*, n.d., in Beman Papers.

160. Committee of Missions for the Freedmen, Presbyterian Church of the USA, Cash Book and Minutes, June 27, 1870, in PHS; *New National Era*, June 9, 1870; Census of 1870, Florida; *Palladium*, n.d., in Beman Papers.

161. Pennington, *Christian Zeal*, 5; *North Star*, March 10, 1848.

wherever he went. To Pennington, the consummate teacher, education was not simply formal learning, it was also the larger dissemination of information.

His efforts were facilitated by the fact that he was both a good teacher and an effective speaker. Always the educator, he usually directed his writings and speeches to correcting misperceptions even before he got to the core of the issue under discussion. Incisive, witty, and perspicacious, but ever under control, Pennington was capable of rising to anger when warranted. He was always immaculately dressed, and his appearance in the pulpit, in his long black gown and "snowy neck-band," was dignified and prepossessing. His sermons, an English newspaper reported, in no way resembled those caricatured by the popular minstrel shows. On the contrary "his manner and voice were rather subdued, and the genial warmth of heart-felt religion which seemed to pervade his discourses, never blazed out into extravagance or fanaticism. They were mild and chaste in language—earnest, but rational in sentiment—natural and unassuming in delivery, and altogether well calculated to touch the hearts of those who heard them."[162]

But all his work, commitment, and talents could not guarantee personal security in a country that simply relegated all its black citizens to the ranks of the inferior. Nor was his insistence on self-reliance and education always well received by his congregations, many of whom still questioned the efficacy of an educated ministry. Pennington, the Latin and Greek scholar, and the doctor of divinity, on many occasions found himself totally out of place among his congregations. Yet for the black minister, there was no other place to go; a fact that only bred increased frustration. Not only did he find himself intellectually isolated in his church, but the poverty of his congregation meant that Pennington had to struggle continuously to keep the wolves from the door. Economic insecurity was a reality for most ministers, black or white. Ann Douglas has shown that the more transient early-seventeenth-century white pastor tended to move only once; early-eighteenth-century pastors slightly more often. By the middle of the nineteenth century, however, the frequency rose to twice every decade. "Moreover," she writes, "the post-disestablishment minister tended not just to change place frequently, but increasingly to have no place, to be unattached to any particular pastorate."[163]

Pennington's experience clearly conformed to this pattern. In the years between his ordination and his death, he held eight positions, the longest being

162. Leeds *Times*, August 5, 1843.
163. Ann Douglas, *The Feminization of American Culture* (New York, 1977), 29–31.

Talcott Street, where he spent eight years. Between 1848 and 1870 he moved six times, in many cases acting only as stated supply for congregations left without a pastor. None of his pastorates paid adequate salaries, so that he was forced continually to supplement his income from lectures and the sale of his pamphlets. In fact the $200 he was paid in Jacksonville was no larger than his first teacher's salary in 1832. This struggle to make ends meet must have been responsible for his questionable use of funds collected in Jamaica and Britain, and for his trouble with alcoholism in the 1850s. By the time of his death in 1870, few of his contemporaries remembered the reverend doctor. Not one of the major black newspapers carried his obituary notice. Pennington's epitaph might have been written by a white small-town pastor who, in obvious desperation, wrote his own obituary: "At last he occupies an unminded grave in his own secluded churchyard, or he lives until another generation knows him not, knows nothing of the once glowing preacher in the old and jaded schoolmaster."[164]

164. *Ibid.*, 42.

William and Ellen Craft
Reprinted from William Still, *The Underground Rail Road*

Chapter II

The Odyssey of William
and Ellen Craft

Early on a December morning in 1848, long before any-
one stirred, two slaves, a man and woman, made their bid for freedom from a
plantation just outside Macon, Georgia. She, almost white, was dressed as a
slave master, he as her valet. In four days they were in Philadelphia; three weeks
later they moved to the safer city of Boston, where they remained until the passage of the infamous Fugitive Slave Law in September, 1850, forced them to
flee to England. They spent nineteen years under the "mane of the British
lion," where they were free from the "claws of the American eagle." Finally,
after the Civil War, they returned as farmers to their native Georgia. Their bold
odyssey in 1848 brought them fame and renown. It was a story of love, determination, and resilience, the virtues of frontier America, conquering all odds.
No other escape, with the possible exception of Frederick Douglass' and Josiah
Henson's, created such a stir in antebellum America as did the Crafts'. Their
journey was compared to Christian and Christiana's in Bunyan's *Pilgrim's Progress* and their love to Héloïse and Abélard's.

William and Ellen Craft, born in different parts of Georgia, were brought to
Macon when they were still young. William was apprenticed as a carpenter, and
Ellen was her mistress' servant. Although he did not experience the rigor of
plantation slavery, William soon witnessed the breaking up of his family. His
mother, father, a brother, and a sister were sold separately either to reduce expenses incurred in holding old, unproductive slaves or to pay off their master's
debts. At sixteen, William was mortgaged to the local bank to raise sufficient
capital to speculate in the cotton boom and, when the bottom fell out of the

market, was sold to the bank cashier to meet his master's mortgage payments. His new master, Ira H. Taylor, sent him back to the cabinet shop where he had been apprenticed.[1]

Ellen, born in Clinton in 1826, was the daughter of Major James Smith, a rich cotton planter and slaveholder, and Maria, one of his young house slaves. Mrs. Smith, angered by continuous references to Ellen's beauty and her resemblance to the major, made Ellen's life miserable. When one of her daughters, Eliza, married Robert Collins of Macon in 1837, Mrs. Smith took the opportunity to get rid of the constant reminder of her husband's infidelity. Ellen was given as a wedding present to Eliza and moved with her new owner to Macon.[2]

Macon was thriving by 1837—the town's economy was booming and the population was growing rapidly. Collins, who had moved there from North Carolina earlier in the decade, was a prominent member of the community. In December, 1840, he, Charles Collins, and Elam Alexander were awarded the contract for building the thirty-mile stretch of railroad from Macon to Oconee, which was completed in 1843 and linked Macon to Savannah. Eight years later he was responsible for bringing the telegraph system to Macon. At his death in 1861, Collins owned 102 slaves valued at $438,000; his landholdings included 1,120 acres in Macon, 5,390 acres "in joint account" in other parts of the state, and 23,343 acres in "Pine and Swamp land."[3]

The two slaves, who met in the early 1840s, soon fell in love and were eager to get married. Although Collins was considered a liberal master, advocating adequate rations and clothing, reasonable working conditions, and firm but fair discipline, he discouraged marriage between his slaves and those on adjoining plantations. "Taking wives and husbands among their fellow servants at home, should be as much encouraged as possible," he recommended, "and although inter-marrying with those belonging to other estates should not be prohibited, yet it is always likely to lead to difficulties and troubles, and should be avoided as much as possible. They cannot live together as they ought, and are constantly liable to separation, in the changing of property." It is no wonder that William and Ellen decided to postpone their marriage in the hope that conditions would

1. Samuel May, *The Fugitive Slave Law and its Victims* (1861; rpr. Freeport, N.Y., 1970), 12; *Anti Slavery Bugle*, December 7, 1850; William Craft, *Running a Thousand Miles for Freedom* (1860; rpr. New York, 1969), 13.

2. Craft, *Running*, 2; information on the Smith family kindly given by the Reverend Albert Foley, author of *Bishop Healy: Beloved Outcast* (New York, 1954).

3. J. C. Butler, *Historical Record of Macon and Central Georgia* (Macon, 1879), 115, 158, 161, 179; Census of 1860, Bibbs County, Georgia; Bibbs County, Record Book R, Georgia Department of Archives and History, Atlanta.

improve. But there were few signs of imminent change; rather than receding, slavery displayed vibrant health. Given these circumstances, the slaves had no alternative but to ask permission to marry. They were married sometime in 1846. Rather than calming their fears, marriage only heightened anxieties about possible separation. Accustomed to the relative ease and freedom they enjoyed in town and the "big house," both slaves were also haunted by the prospect of a loss of status. For the next two years, William later wrote, they "prayed and toiled on till December 1848" when they finally agreed on a plan of escape.[4]

The plan was ingenious, if not totally reckless: Ellen was to dress as a slave master traveling to Philadelphia for treatment for a rheumatic complaint and William was to accompany her as her valet. Working a second job as a waiter in a Macon hotel, William managed to save twenty dollars, which he used to purchase the necessary clothes for Ellen from different shops in town.[5] They would leave during the Christmas holidays, when they were more likely to be given passes to visit relatives and friends on neighboring plantations. When the day arrived, a nervous Ellen dressed in her planter's outfit. They took all possible precaution against exposure. Since Ellen could not write, her right arm was placed in a sling to dissuade officials from asking her to sign documents acknowledging ownership of her slave. William also put a poultice on his wife's face, hoping to limit conversation with strangers. Silence seemed the best guarantee of success. From Macon they caught a train to Savannah, then by a combination of boat, trains, and coaches, they traveled via Charleston, Wilmington, Richmond, Washington, and Baltimore to Philadelphia. Four days after escaping from Macon, they were being hidden by a Quaker family on a farm outside Philadelphia. Three weeks later they moved on to the safer environs of Boston.

Members of the Pennsylvania Anti Slavery Society and the local Underground Railroad came to their assistance immediately, well aware of the effect such a dramatic flight could have on antislavery sentiment. No other escape from slavery had been so well thought out and so precisely executed. The Boston *Chronotype* thought "the plan adopted displayed a degree of ingenuity which could not have been acquired under the ordinary circumstances of life." And the *Anti-Slavery Bugle* observed that the escape was "as difficult—and to them more glorious—than Bonaparte's journey from Egypt through a coast and sea studded with the British fleet."[6] The story of their escape was

4. Robert Collins, "Essay on the Management of Slaves," *Southern Cultivator*, XII (1854), 206; Craft, *Running*, 29.
5. Bristol *Mercury*, October 25, 1856; Boston *Journal*, June 7, 1878.
6. Boston *Chronotype*, quoted in *Anti Slavery Bugle*, July 14, 1849.

widely reprinted even by those newspapers opposed to the abolitionist cause.

Eager to capitalize on this notoriety, William Wells Brown invited the Crafts to join him on an abolitionist lecture tour. Brown would speak on the nature and effects of slavery and William would follow with the story of their escape. The alliance between Brown and the Crafts later became one of the most renowned and influential abolitionist combinations in both America and Britain. In early January, 1849, Brown wrote the *Liberator* from Pineville, Pennsylvania, of their plan to hold lectures in various New England cities—Norwich, Worcester, Pawtucket, New Bedford, Boston, Kingston, Abington, and Northborough. In late January, Brown introduced the Crafts and Henry "Box" Brown, another famous fugitive slave, to the annual meeting of the Massachusetts Anti Slavery Society, which unanimously pledged to protect them from possible recapture. An entire session was devoted to a discussion of the Crafts' escape and closed with a ringing statement from Wendell Phillips. "We would look in vain through the most trying times of our Revolutionary history," Phillips thundered, "for an incident of courage and noble daring to equal that of the escape of William and Ellen Craft; and future historians and poets would tell this story as one of the most thrilling in the nation's annals."[7] The Crafts' escape quickly became an abolitionist *cause célèbre.*

Although their popularity won plaudits and recruits for the movement, it also increased the probability that the South would attempt to retake the Crafts in an effort to silence critics. This may explain why the Crafts promptly disappeared from center stage at abolitionist meetings. Sufficient capital had been raised from publicly recounting the story of their escape; to continue would have been unnecessarily risky. For the next eighteen months the Crafts lived free, they thought, from possible recapture. William established himself as a cabinetmaker and Ellen worked as a seamstress. The black community of Boston, which numbered only two thousand in 1848, supported four churches and a host of benevolent associations and social clubs. Six years earlier, blacks, with the assistance of white abolitionists, had fought to prevent the extradition of George Latimer to the South, and when this failed, they raised sufficient money to redeem him. It was a community with a tradition of unified action against slave catchers and a commitment to protect the estimated four hundred fugitives who made the city their home.[8]

7. *Liberator*, January 12, February 2, 1849.
8. *Directory of the City of Boston, 1850–1851* (Boston, 1850); George A. Lavesque, "Inherent Reformers—Inherited Orthodoxy: Black Baptists in Boston, 1800–1873," *JNH*, LX (1975), 492, 510.

As in other black communities throughout the North, the Fugitive Slave Law threatened to dislocate the lives of blacks in Boston. Within three days of the bill's passage, forty fugitives left Boston for Canada. All of the city's black churches lost members in the wake of the new law. The construction of the small Fugitive Slave Church, begun in 1849, for example, had to be suspended by its pastor when a majority of members left for Canada. The African Methodist Church lost 85 communicants, the small Zion Methodist Church 10, and the Twelfth Baptist Church's congregation fell from 141 to 81. One contemporary observed that the result was a loss of property and jobs and "an uncertain and melancholy future" for many blacks in the community.[9]

But those who stayed rallied to defend their community and stem further erosion. On September 30, blacks organized the first in a series of protest meetings against the law. The recent capture of the fugitive James Hallet in New York lent a certain urgency to the meeting's deliberations and, as the *Liberator* observed, increased "the excitement already akin to that which characterized the Latimer case of 1843." Lewis Hayden, a fugitive and a leading figure in the black community, was elected chairman and in his address he emphasized the necessity of "united and persevering resistance to this ungodly antirepublican law." Resolutions were passed pledging mutual defense against the law, thanking concerned whites for continued support, and reminding the black community to be eternally vigilant, for "they who would be free, themselves must strike the blow." A committee, of which William was a member, was established to prepare the agenda for the next meeting, scheduled for October 4. This gathering discussed methods for defending the community, agreed to the formation of a "League of Freedom," and called on blacks to remain in Boston and resist any attempt to enforce the law. "The liability of ourselves and families becoming its victims, at the caprice of Southern mansteakers," they announced, "imperatively demands an expression whether we will tamely submit to chains and slavery, or whether we will, at all and every hazard, *live* and *die* freemen." The meeting also issued "The Fugitive Slaves' Appeal," which was circulated among the state's clergy and asked them to "exert a moral influence towards breaking the rod of the oppressor." Ten days later, 3,500 attended an abolitionist meeting held at Faneuil Hall, where it was decided to form a vigilance committee to coordinate opposition to the act. The subcommittee included some of the best legal minds in the state—Samuel Sewall, Charles

9. Benjamin Quarles, *Black Abolitionists* (New York, 1969), 199–200; Wilbur H. Siebert, *The Underground Railroad in Massachusetts* (Worcester, Mass., 1936), 40–41; John Weiss (ed.), *Life and Correspondence of Theodore Parker* (2 vols.; London, 1863), II, 92.

Sumner, R. H. Dana, Jr., and Charles C. Loring, among others.[10] Boston was
well prepared to combat any attempt by the South to retake its fugitives.

The city was thrown into a frenzy of activity a few days after the Faneuil Hall
meeting, when two slave-catchers arrived from Georgia, claiming the Crafts.
The black community and the vigilance committee promptly marshaled their
forces. Ellen was taken to the safety of Dr. Henry Bowditch's home in Brook-
line and a week later was transferred to the Reverend Theodore Parker's.
William, meanwhile, armed and barricaded himself in his shop while friends
stood watch. "No man could approach within 100 yards of Craft's shop," one
reporter observed, "without being seen by a hundred eyes, and a signal would
call a powerful body at a moment's warning." As tension mounted and it appeared the slave catchers were determined to test these defenses William was
taken to Lewis Hayden's, where kegs of gunpowder were placed in the basement in anticipation of an attack. According to an observer, black homes on
Belknap and Cambridge streets, the main thoroughfares, were fortified and the
occupants well armed with guns, swords, and knives: "The colored population
are really roused in this matter and are making their houses like barricades."[11]

Simultaneously, the vigilance subcommittee recommended exploring a series of legal approaches that would test both the constitutionality of the law and
its possible encroachment on state jurisdiction. These ranged from serving the
arresting marshal with a writ of *de homine repligeande* to arresting William on
criminal charges of violent assault. Either one, by establishing state jurisdiction
in criminal cases, would severely curtail the powers granted commissioners
under the Fugitive Slave Law. Should these moves fail to produce the desired
effect, the committee intended to have William arrested for violating the state's
anti-fornication law on the grounds that his slave marriage was not legal. It was
finally agreed to hold these plans in reserve and to employ instead other forms
of legal harassment. The vigilance committee also appealed directly to the public, posting handbills that described the slave catchers and warned Boston
against them. In many parts of the city they were met by hostile crowds shouting, "Slave-hunters, slave-hunters! There go the slave-hunters!" But not all of
Boston was opposed to the law, nor did everyone condone efforts to subvert its
enforcement. In promoting the Compromise of 1850, which included the law,

10. *Liberator*, October 4, 11, 1850; Siebert, *Underground Railroad*, 39–40; New York *Tribune*,
quoted in *Anti Slavery Bugle*, November 16, 1850; Harold Schwartz, "Fugitive Slave Days in
Boston," *New England Quarterly*, XXVII (1954), 192.

11. Nina Moore Tiffany, "Stories of the Fugitive Slaves, I: The Escape of William and Ellen
Craft," *New England Magazine*, I (1890), 528; *Anti Slavery Bugle*, November 16, 1850; *Pennsylvania
Freeman*, November 28, 1850.

Daniel Webster had won considerable support for this most recent attempt at northern appeasement. Nonetheless, there were significant pockets of resistance—not all of them dominated by abolitionists—to enforcing the law.[12]

The slave catchers Hughes and Knight adopted a number of strategies in their bid to recapture the Crafts. First, Knight, who had worked with William in the cabinetmaking shop in Macon, visited William and, feigning delight at renewing their acquaintance, suggested William take him on a tour of Boston. When William refused, Knight tried to lure the Crafts to his hotel, pretending to have news of Ellen's mother. These deceptions failed, and Hughes and Knight moved to obtain warrants for the Crafts' arrest under provisions of the law. But even with these warrants they were still faced with the problem of finding a marshal bold or reckless enough to venture into the black community in search of the Crafts. Hearing that warrants had been issued, blacks immediately called a meeting at Belknap Street Church. They repeated their pledge to protect the Crafts and appealed to the Massachusetts legislature to arrest the slave catchers on the grounds that their activities were creating a rebellious atmosphere in the state.[13]

Blacks and the vigilance committee promptly initiated a series of legal and physical harassments to force the slave catchers out of Boston. When Hughes and Knight accused the Crafts of being slaves, the committee had them arrested for slander. Bail was set at $10,000, and it was with considerable difficulty that they raised the bond. The following morning they were again arrested, this time for the attempted kidnapping of William; bail was set at $10,000. There was another arrest that same afternoon, this time for the attempted kidnapping of Ellen, with bail set at the same amount. Hughes later reported in utter disbelief that he was issued a total of five warrants in the space of a few days. But the slave catchers' troubles had only begun. After their third release on bond, a large and angry crowd of blacks charged the coach in which Hughes and Knight were traveling. The coachman, realizing the danger, whipped his horses into a gallop, but the crowd followed. He drove across the bridge to Cambridge, thinking that the toll would deter his pursuers, but someone paid the toll and still the crowd followed. Hundreds joined the chase, shouting abuse at the fleeing slave-catchers. Fearing for his life, the coachman

---

12. Weiss (ed.), *Theodore Parker*, II, 529, I, 91; Stanley J. Robboy and Anita W. Robboy, "Lewis Hayden: From Fugitive Slave to Statesman," *New England Quarterly*, XLVI (1973), 601; New York *Tribune*, quoted in *Anti Slavery Bugle*, November 16, 1850.

13. Weiss (ed.), *Theodore Parker*, I, 95–96; William Still, *The Underground Rail Road* (Philadelphia, 1872), 387.

decided to relinquish his passengers to the mob in West Cambridge. The hunters were now the hunted, and although they were not harmed, Hughes and Knight decided to abandon their mission. As if to confirm the wisdom of this decision, Theodore Parker visited the Georgians in their hotel and warned them of imminent danger from the angry crowd gathering outside. Hughes and Knight left on the next train.[14]

The black community and local abolitionists were understandably elated, and it appeared that Boston had struck the first major blow against the Fugitive Slave Law. "Not since the days of '76," wrote the *Liberator*, capturing the mood of the city's blacks, had there been "such a popular demonstration on the side of human freedom in this region. The humane and patriotic contagion has infected all classes. Scarcely any other subject has been talked about in the streets, or in the social circles." George Thompson, the British abolitionist, on an antislavery tour of America, told a packed audience at Faneuil Hall, "I see that the South demands of Massachusetts that the noble Craft and his equally noble companion should be given up, and I see that this demand is in derision of the established law of nations. Gentlemen, there is something on earth greater than arbitrary or despotic power. The lightning has its power, the whirlwind has its power; but there is something among men more capable of shaking despotic power than lightning, whirlwind and earthquake—that is the threatened indignation of the whole civilized world."[15]

Throughout the North, in Philadelphia, New York, Pittsburgh, Cincinnati, and Cleveland, black communities and their white supporters took heart from Boston's accomplishments; the South and its supporters looked on in dismay at these open violations of federal law. America followed developments in Boston with growing interest, for the Crafts' case was indeed a direct challenge to the government's authority to enforce a law many considered immoral. For others, the law had been duly enacted and was, therefore, inviolable. But southern concerns were even more immediate. Would the North, many wondered, use popular resistance to the law to abrogate the Compromise of 1850? For them, the significance of the compromise turned on the North's ability or willingness to enforce the law. Growing resistance to the law obviously irked some in Washington. President Fillmore, in reply to a letter from the Crafts' owners requesting federal assistance to recapture their "property," expressed his determination to fulfill both the letter and the spirit of the law by placing troops at the

14. *Anti Slavery Standard*, November 7, 1850; *Constitutionalist*, quoted in *Liberator*, December 6, 1850; Tiffany, "Stories," 529.
15. *Liberator*, November 1, 1851; *Anti Slavery Bugle*, December 7, 1850.

disposal of state and local authorities whenever necessary. Fillmore, however, saw little need for government intervention at this juncture. But his threat of federal intervention was an unmistakable signal to the Crafts and their supporters. Boston was alive with rumors that the president had already deployed roughly seven hundred troops to enforce the law. It was also becoming increasingly apparent that Collins would make another attempt to retake the Crafts, if only to save face following the ignominious retreat of Hughes and Knight. Boston was obviously no longer safe for the Crafts, and on the advice of friends they left for England in early November. For the next three weeks the Crafts followed a tortuous trail, in many ways reminiscent of their earlier escape, which took them to Portland, Maine; Saint John, New Brunswick; and Windsor and Halifax, Nova Scotia. After a delay of two weeks, they caught the steamer for Liverpool.[16]

This well-organized defense and escape created the tradition and machinery with which blacks and white abolitionists continued to oppose the execution of the law. The cases of Shadrach, Simms, and Burns soon followed, and although opponents of the law were not always successful, their activities helped to exacerbate sectional antagonisms between the North and the South. These actions also prompted Henry Clay to consider the formulation of a new bill to strengthen the Fugitive Slave Law, a bill that would determine "whether the government of white men was to be yielded to a government of blacks." The Augusta *Republic* captured the tenor of sectional antagonism over the law: "Massachusetts owes to the South the fugitive slaves within her limits; efforts have been made to get several of them back. We lost the two Crafts and Shadrach, and recovered Simms. A faithful execution of the law, indeed! When costs have been subtracted, we should like to know how much has been gained."[17]

In the months between their escape and the arrival of the slave catchers, the Crafts had established themselves as leading members of Boston's black community. William's cabinetmaking shop and Ellen's seamstress work had brought in sufficient money to give them a relatively comfortable if austere existence. They actively participated in the political and social life of the community, and it appears that William and Lewis Hayden acted as spokesmen for fugitives in Boston. William's lecture tour with William Wells Brown in January, 1849, and the Crafts' local political involvement meant that they were well grounded in

16. *Liberator,* November 29, 1850; Weiss (ed.), *Theodore Parker,* I, 99; Craft, *Running,* 100–107.
17. Thomas Wentworth Higginson, *Cheerful Yesterdays* (Boston, 1898), 136; Augusta *Republic,* quoted in Austin Bearse, *Reminiscences of Fugitive-Slave Days in Boston* (1880; rpr. New York, 1969),

the principles of Garrisonian abolitionism. This "delicate, almost white, quad-roon girl, with simple ladylike manners" and her husband, a strapping man, over six feet, "of marked natural abilities, of good manners, and full of pluck," were to have a dramatic and significant effect on British antislavery attitudes during nineteen years in exile.[18]

England was the safest, most logical asylum for the Crafts. It had harbored and welcomed fugitives from America for many years. Given the Crafts' noto-riety and the importance attached to their recapture by the government and by southern interests, exile in Canada was simply too dangerous. Treaties between the British and American governments had never clearly established the status of fugitives there. More important, both British and American abolitionists were well aware of the Crafts' potential impact on British antislavery senti-ment. Richard D. Webb, the Dublin abolitionist, hearing that the Crafts and Box Brown were to visit Britain, wrote to the editor of the *Anti Slavery Stan-dard*: "If they do come they will excite a hearty interest for American slaves and an increasing contempt and repugnance for their republican masters. There is no truer saying than 'by their fruits ye shall know them'—and a troupe of fugitive slaves—true heroes—lecturing through England must diffuse strange ideas of the peculiar institution."[19] This they were to do.

The passage of the Fugitive Slave Law provided British abolitionists with a new opportunity to condemn America's peculiar institution. Its enactment produced a dramatic increase in the number of American fugitives in England, and many of them attempted, as best they could, to whip up British public opinion against American slavery. Although not all found it easy to survive in England, some becoming beggars, the vast majority played a decidedly impor-tant role in rallying British support for the American slave. On August 1, 1851, one of their associations, the "American Fugitive Slaves in the British Metrop-olis," held a meeting in London to commemorate West Indian emancipation and to welcome George Thompson home from his tour of America. The gath-ering condemned the law and called upon British abolitionists to support the fight against American slavery. Simultaneously, four prominent black Ameri-cans, William Wells Brown, Henry Highland Garnet, J. W. C. Pennington, and Alexander Crummell, were on an antislavery tour of England, Scotland, and Ireland. Large audiences from every walk of life attended their lectures in

18. Still, *Underground Rail Road*, 354; Vincent Y. Bowditch, *Life and Correspondence of Henry In-gersoll Bowditch* (3 vols.; Boston, 1902), I, 203.
19. *Anti Slavery Standard*, December 26, 1850.

churches and town and village halls. In less than two years Brown delivered four hundred lectures to over 200,000 people; Garnet and Pennington followed as rigorous a schedule. By their extensive and successful lectures, these articulate products of American slavery and prejudice, like their predecessors Nathaniel Paul, Moses Roper, Charles Lenox Remond, and Frederick Douglass, profoundly influenced British attitudes against the peculiar institution.[20]

The Crafts' daring escape and Boston's successful resistance to the Fugitive Slave Law were widely reported in British newspapers. Soon after their arrival, William, reluctantly leaving Ellen in Liverpool, went to join William Wells Brown in Newcastle in an effort to exploit this popularity. The tensions and anxieties produced by developments in Boston, the escape, and the rigors of the transatlantic crossing had seriously undermined Ellen's frail health, so much so that William thought she would not survive. But the Liverpool abolitionist the Reverend Francis Bishop and his family had taken Ellen under their care and nursed her back to health. As soon as she recovered, Ellen left to join William and Brown in Scotland. For the next six months the Crafts and Brown toured the English and Scottish bastions of Garrisonianism, speaking against slavery and on temperance. From Newcastle, Brown and William went to the annual session of the Edinburgh Ladies Emancipation Society at the end of December. Their presentations were guaranteed to have the maximum impact on their audience. Brown spoke first, analyzing the development of American slavery in the South and prejudice in the North, which culminated in the Fugitive Slave Law. Everyone listening to him should, he said, sever all contacts with proslavery Americans, and American clergymen who did not openly condemn slavery should not be allowed to preach. And then William rose to speak about the escape from Georgia. Although William was not an experienced public speaker, his narrative was filled with suspense and wit.[21] British audiences knew about daring escapes from slavery—among them, Douglass, Roper, and Henson—but this tale involved unheard-of boldness and romance. And in a century still awed by the romance of the American frontier, this was strong stuff.

Brown and Craft gave three more lectures in Edinburgh before they went to

20. Henry Mayhew, *London Labour and the London Poor* (4 vols., 1851–64; rpr. London, 1967), II, 425–26; James Walvin (ed.), *Black and White: The Negro and English Society, 1555–1945* (London, 1973), 190; R. J. M. Blackett, *Building an Antislavery Wall: Black Americans in the Atlantic Abolitionist Movement, 1830–1860* (Baton Rouge, 1983), 13–25.
21. *Atheneum*, November 30, 1850; *National Instructor*, December 4, 1851; Liverpool *Mercury*, January 3, 1851; *Scottish Press*, January 1, 1851.

the annual meeting of the Glasgow Emancipation Society. The GES, relatively inactive since 1847, used the presence of Brown and the Crafts (Ellen had now joined them) to bolster its flagging fortunes and to counter the growing influence of local opponents. An audience of three thousand heard the fugitives' attack on American slavery. Then they held four days of lectures at the Glasgow Trades' Hall, where Brown's panorama on American slavery was displayed.[22]

From Glasgow they moved to Aberdeen, where large crowds flocked to their meetings and to Brown's panorama. Their schedule was full each day: in the morning, schoolchildren looked at the panorama and listened to speeches; in the afternoon and evening, sizable audiences heard them. Brown and the Crafts had by now refined their pattern. First, Brown spoke against American slavery, then William described their escape, and finally, in a tear-jerking scene, Ellen was invited onstage. This careful orchestration was guaranteed to provoke strong antislavery sentiments. What sort of country, newspaper reports asked, could enslave such articulate and obviously intelligent people? And, more important, if they were a sample of the sort of persons who were slaves, what a destruction of talent! Ellen's appearance on the stage increased the audience's dismay, for a black slave was one thing but a "white" woman enslaved was unconscionable.

Their initial tour in America had elicited similar responses. Observers wondered and abolitionists confirmed that blacks were the victims of slavery, but the nature of the peculiar institution did not preclude the exploitation of white labor if circumstances and the need to consolidate the system warranted it. Speaking of Ellen, one abolitionist lamented: "To think of such a woman being held as a piece of property, subject to be traded off to the highest bidder (while it is no worse or wickeder than when done to the blackest woman that ever was) does yet stir a community brought up in prejudice against color a thousand times more deeply than could be effected in different circumstances. She was a living proof," he concluded, "that Slavery has no prejudice about color, and is as ready to enslave the whitest and the fairest as any other, provided only the pretext be afforded." Ellen's enslavement became the symbol of slavery's barbarity (particularly its defilement of women) for British and American abolitionists. Sketches depicting her dressed as a man during her escape were widely circulated in the decade before the Civil War. After Brown and the Crafts left Aberdeen, a local newspaper commented, "Their visit to Aberdeen

22. *North British Mail*, January 7, 1851; GES, *Thirteenth Annual Report* (Glasgow, 1851); GES, Minute Book 4 (1845–1876), in Smeal Collection.

will be the means, we doubt not, of giving many a more vivid idea of the evils of slavery, and also, of leading them more forcibly to realize the enormous inconsistency and criminality of a professed land of liberty and Christianity holding 3 millions of intelligent and immortal beings in bondage."[23]

Brown and the Crafts campaigned successfully for three months in Scotland and the north of England, and then in April they went south to a meeting of the Bristol and Clifton Ladies Anti Slavery Society (BCLASS). Although their presentation followed the same pattern, William's lectures had become markedly sophisticated. The escape narrative was now part of an analysis of American slavery, in which he condemned the very notion of the happy slave. In a ringing voice he declared that no man was "so base, so low, so wretchedly degraded as to be content to drag out a miserable life in bondage for any tyrant on the face of the earth." Blacks in the South, whether free or slave, he said, had no legal rights against whites, and it was against the laws in the South to teach slaves. Using his own experiences, he told how easily families were broken up and sold separately. A local newspaper said that William's speech "with simplicity and feeling but without any attempt at display, produced quite a thrilling effect" on those present. Well into May, the Crafts and Brown toured the west of England, lecturing in such cities as Devonport, Exeter, Bridgewater, Gloucester, and Bath.[24]

As had happened with the GES, the Crafts and Brown helped to reanimate the BCLASS, which was founded in 1840 as an auxiliary of the British and Foreign Anti Slavery Society. Until William Lloyd Garrison and Frederick Douglass visited Bristol in 1846, the BCLASS existed largely on paper. But the society took on new life, establishing contacts with Garrisonian abolitionists, though it still held to neutrality between "old" and "new" organizations. After the visit, however, the BCLASS became increasingly distressed by what it saw as the inactivity of the BFASS. There were more and more contacts between Boston and Bristol between 1846 and 1850, and Brown's arrival in March, 1850, gave them significant reinforcement. Then the Crafts came to Bristol and, with the BCLASS, thoroughly explored American antislavery groups. It was after the Crafts visited that the society began to move perceptibly toward Garrisonianism. By September, 1851, with the arrival of the Boston aboli-

23. Samuel May, Jr., to J. B. Estlin, February 2, 1849, in ASP; Aberdeen *Journal*, February 12, 1851; for similar views, see *United Presbyterian Magazine*, February, 1851; Plymouth and Devonshire *Weekly Journal*, May 1, 1851; Kelso *Chronicle*, February 28, 1851.
24. Bristol *Mercury*, April 12, 1851; Plymouth and Devonshire *Weekly Journal*, May 1, 1851; Gloucester *Journal*, May 25, 1851.

tionists Maria Chapman and Anne Weston and George Thompson's lecture tour, Bristol was firmly established as a Garrisonian stronghold.[25]

In a special report published in 1852, the BCLASS attempted to explain its new stance by referring to the Crafts' emotional discussion of "the constant, self denying labours of the Boston abolitionists" and the kind treatment they had received when they had first come to Boston. But the Crafts were also being exploited in the "old" and "new" organizationists' disputes. The report, for instance, offered the improbable observation that the American and Foreign Anti Slavery Society was unknown to the Crafts until they came to Bristol. The reason was, the report claimed, that when the Crafts arrived in New York from Georgia, no one told them about the AFASS. In point of fact, however, the Crafts' escape route had not taken them through New York, and it seems highly unlikely that they would have made such a claim.[26]

Desperate to defend themselves against "new" organizationists, British Garrisonians were so concerned to keep Brown and the Crafts from being lured away by the opposition that they were not above bending the truth. The problem became even more pressing after a soirée in Edinburgh that Pennington also attended. In a letter to Eliza Wigham, secretary of the Edinburgh Ladies Emancipation Society, the Bristol abolitionist John Estlin warned that Pennington, the "special protege" of the BFASS, was untrustworthy. Wigham and others, however, did not agree. Estlin's daughter Mary felt that she had to defend Brown and the Crafts to friends in Boston. They thought their allegiances were clear to Wigham, she wrote, "but considered her judgment superior to their own from her intimate acquaintance with the parties with whom she had to deal." Wigham had evidently gotten wind of plans by Pennington's supporters to publicly protest his exclusion so as to embarrass Garrisonians.[27]

Although partial to the Garrisonian position, the Crafts were less concerned about ideological niceties and more interested in working with all sections of British abolitionism. They never allowed their support for Garrison to get in the way of that broader appeal. Not only did they work with the BFASS; in 1853, William publicly supported the purchase of a slave family, an action that violated Garrisonian principles. He argued that the Maryland slave family,

25. Bristol and Clifton Ladies Anti Slavery Society (BCLASS), Minute Book, February, March, June, September, November, 1851, in Estlin Papers, Dr. Williams's Library, London.
26. BCLASS, *Special Report of the Bristol and Clifton Ladies Anti Slavery Society; During Eighteen Months, from January 1851 to June 1852; With a Statement of the Reasons of its Separation from the British and Foreign Anti Slavery Society* (London, 1852), 14, 23, 61; Howard Temperley, *British Antislavery, 1833–1870* (Columbia, S.C., 1972), 239–42.
27. J. Estlin to Miss Wigham, May 3, 1851, M. Estlin to Miss Weston, May 12, 1851, both in ASP.

whom Garnet was trying to redeem, posed a unique set of problems. He was strongly "opposed to giving slaveholders money for refugees after they had fought their way through many perilous difficulties, and reached a land of liberty. However, the Weimms family does not come under this head, and therefore, I deeply sympathise with them: in fact were my dear wife and babe, or myself again in slavery, I should most heartily concur in any plan that might be devised for our restoration in liberty." Matters were made worse when William later ignored the advice of his friends in Bristol and decided to open a boardinghouse in London. He was determined to show that fugitives should not depend solely on the benevolence of British supporters—a position to which most British Garrisonians subscribed. Therefore, he was dismayed when Richard Webb attributed his decision to pride and secretiveness, and John Estlin wrote the Reverend Samuel May, Jr., rather condescendingly that William was "suspicious and self-willed, but is really a good fellow."[28]

These differences ultimately led to a cooling of relations between the Crafts and many British Garrisonians. But before this occurred they combined to launch another public attack on American slavery. The occasion was the opening of the Great Exhibition at London's Crystal Palace in the summer of 1851, which, along with the traditional influx of American clergymen attending religious conventions, was expected to attract a large number of American visitors. In February, 1851, Henry C. Wright, the American abolitionist, wrote James Haughton of Dublin, suggesting that British abolitionists use the exhibition as a forum to reveal the cruelty and inhumanity of American slavery, by displaying the whips, chains, and other tools of torture used by slaveholders. To further dramatize the issue, he recommended that the Crafts stand on an auction block, Henry "Box" Brown appear with the box in which he had actually escaped from slavery, and William Wells Brown show his panorama. On a visit to York in March, William Wells Brown and the Crafts announced that the Great Exhibition would be the scene for the public exposure of that American barbaric institution—they hoped to counter the façade of philanthropy and good will. "They [the Americans] would tell us," Brown told the meeting, "of their efforts to spread the gospel by sending missionaries and bibles to the heathen, whilst they forget the 3 or 4 million of slaves perishing for lack of knowledge at their own doors." Such duplicity had to be exposed. The Crafts and Brown were joined at the exhibition by some of the leading British abolitionists, among them, George and Jenny Thompson, Richard and Maria Webb, and

28. *Slave*, March, 1853; Richard Webb to Maria Chapman, May 29, 1953, J. Estlin to Samuel May, Jr., November 3, 1853, both in ASP.

William Farmer. They walked arm in arm through the grounds, openly discussing slavery, in the hope that some irate American visitor would take up the challenge; but none did. William Farmer reported that "the gauntlet, which was unmistakably thrown down by our party, the Americans were too wary to take up. We spoke among each other of the wrongs of slavery; it was in vain." William Craft and Brown kept up the effort for a few more days with little apparent effect.[29]

The Crafts and Brown separated soon after the demonstration at the World's Fair. Brown continued his exhausting lecture tour for the next three years yet still found time to write *Clotel*, the first novel ever written by a black American, which was well received by the literary public, and *Three Years in Europe*, a book about his travels. The Crafts, sponsored by John Estlin, Lady Byron, and Harriet Martineau, among others, spent the next three years at an agricultural school in Ockham, Surrey.[30]

The Ockham school was founded in 1835 by Lord Lovelace, a close relative of Lady Byron's, at a time when agricultural schools flowered throughout Britain in reaction to widespread unrest among farm workers. Established on the principles of Emanuel von Fellenberg's school at Hoffwyll, Switzerland, Ockham aimed to teach the youth of the rural districts "useful" ideas and skills. Both Lady Byron and Lord Lovelace believed that if young people were given the rudiments of an education, one that would fit them for an existence in agriculture, social stability would be enhanced. Lady Byron saw the extensive unrest of the 1830s as a direct consequence of the French Revolution, a symbol, in her view, of the moral decay of European societies. Education, as developed by Fellenberg, would counteract this dangerous Jacobin tendency: "There is a growing conviction that the great antidote to vice and crime, and therefore to political disturbances is to be found in an improved moral education in the mass of the people."[31]

The average school day at Ockham was tightly organized: the hours from 9:00 to 11:30 A.M. and from 2:00 to 4:00 P.M. were spent in school, and the rest of the day until 5:00 P.M., with the exception of one hour for lunch, was spent in the gardens and workshops. In the classrooms the students were given a basic

29. *Liberator*, February 28, 1851; Brown quoted in Yorkshire *Gazette*, March 29, 1851; Farmer quoted in Still, *Underground Rail Road*, 390.

30. Bristol *Examiner*, May 10, 1851; Craft, *Running*, 109; *Liberator*, January 2, 1852; Harriet Martineau to Dear Lucy [Aikin], April 5, 1851, WDX/482/4, in Harriet Martineau Papers, Cumbria Record Office, Kendal, England.

31. W. A. C. Stewart and W. P. McCann, *The Educational Innovators* (2 vols.; London, 1967), I, 156; Edward W. Brayley, *A Topographical History of Surrey* (5 vols.; Dorking, 1841–48), II, 120.

grounding in grammar, English, writing, and music, as well as a fair sampling of Scripture studies. The students could also gain practical experience in printing, carpentry, basketmaking, and farming. Comparing Ockham with other schools of its time and type, Stewart and McCann, historians of nineteenth-century English education, have noted that "it was . . . in its curriculum and appointment, far superior to the average British and National School of the period."[32] At Ockham the Crafts were able to broaden their education. In addition, William taught cabinetmaking, and Ellen needlework. In later years, when William established schools, first in Dahomey and then in Georgia, he used Ockham as his model.

The years at Ockham were, generally, happy and fruitful. The Crafts' first child, Charles Estlin Phillips, was born on October 22, 1852. But if the Crafts were happy in England, there were those in the South who still hankered after their reenslavement. In the summer of 1852, some southern visitors to London started a rumor that the Crafts longed to return to Georgia. The rumor became so widespread that Ellen was forced finally to issue a public disclaimer: "I had much rather starve in England, a free woman," she said, "than be a slave of the best man that ever breathed upon the American Continent." The incident is a clear indication of the Crafts' popularity and success, as well as the damage they inflicted on the South's already tarnished image among the British.[33]

The Crafts' development at Ockham was so impressive, they were offered the positions of superintendent and matron. They declined, however, because they intended to open a boardinghouse in London. Although a house was selected on Arundel Street in London, friends' continued opposition to the undertaking prompted the Crafts to shelve their plans. Most of their income during this period came from money William collected at antislavery meetings, his cabinetmaking, and Ellen's sewing. Later in the decade they opened a relatively successful import-export business in fancy goods in west London.[34]

William returned to the antislavery lecture circuit soon after leaving Ockham. Much of the popular antislavery agitation in this period depended on fugitives like the Crafts and Box Brown, and a handful of other black Americans, including William G. Allen, the former professor at McGrawville College in New York who was forced to flee America following the announcement of his engagement to one of his white students. Although William's lectures tended to

32. Brayley, *A Topographical History of Surrey*, I, 121–22; Stewart and McCann, *Educational Innovators*, I, 212–13.
33. *Liberator*, January 14, 1853; *Anti Slavery Advocate*, December, 1852.
34. *Liberator*, November 4, 1852, September 23, 1859; *Anti Slavery Advocate*, January, 1854.

follow the pattern established earlier with William Wells Brown, they now encompassed such topics as the role of free produce in promoting abolition. As I have shown elsewhere, the Free Produce movement had been given a new lease on life in the previous decade and had been ably promoted by Pennington and Garnet between 1849 and 1852. Whenever the opportunity presented itself, William agrued in favor of the free-produce principle. In Leeds in October, 1856, for example, he called on his audience to encourage the cultivation of cotton in British dominions as a means of undermining the South's monopoly. The theme struck a responsive chord among many concerned about British dependence on southern cotton and the consequence for Britain's textile industry of a sharp drop in cotton imports.[35]

By the end of the decade, the growing possibility of southern secession, John Brown's raid on Harpers Ferry, and the visits of Frederick Douglass, Sarah Parker Remond, William Howard Day, Samuel J. May, Robert Campbell, Theodore Bourne, and Martin R. Delany, all rekindled British interest in American slavery. In May, 1859, a handful of British abolitionists, including George Thompson and William and Ellen, met in east London to form the London Emancipation Committee (LEC) in an effort to exploit this new interest in American slavery and to silence the rising chorus of prosouthern voices among those dependent on American cotton. Both William and Ellen were members of its executive committee. The LEC, for the first time since the formation of the short-lived Anti Slavery League (1846), provided British Garrisonians a base in London. In spite of its Garrisonian inclinations, however, the LEC adopted a less strident and more conciliatory approach to other abolitionist organizations. For example, it worked relatively closely with the British and Foreign Anti Slavery Society and even endorsed the African Civilization Society, whose plans for establishing a colony of free blacks in Africa had until then been anathema to Garrisonians. The Crafts took a leading role in the LEC in the years before the outbreak of the Civil War. Their home in Hammersmith was one of the headquarters of antislavery activity in London, and visiting American abolitionists were accommodated and well entertained. William was also one of the leaders of the John Anderson Committee formed in 1861 to welcome the famed American fugitive, superintend his education, and arrange his lecture tour of Britain.[36]

35. Louis Billington, "British Humanitarians and American Cotton, 1840–1860," *Journal of American Studies*, XI (1977), 313–34; Leeds *Mercury*, October 25, 1856.
36. F. W. Chesson Diary, June 1, 1858–July 22, 1859, and July 23, 1859–April 30, 1860, in

With the revival of strong sentiments against American slavery, the Crafts decided that the time was propitious for publishing the story of their escape from slavery. The fact that no major slave narrative had been issued in Britain since the early 1850s—none had appeared since *Uncle Tom's Cabin*—further influenced their decision. *Running a Thousand Miles for Freedom* first appeared in 1860 and went through two printings in as many years. Its style shows the extent of William's literary development after only twelve years of freedom.[37] Like other narratives, *Running* explored three major themes—the struggle against overwhelming odds, oppression, and the human determination to be free. It is thus situated squarely in the tradition of popular nineteenth-century literature. Moreover, William was a living exemplar of those Victorian ideals of success through determination and self-improvement through industry and independence. Gilbert Osofsky wrote that the narrative "probably acquired some of its popularity in the 1840s and 1850s because of the excitement of these tales. The melodrama and romance of the escape—the elements Harriet Beecher Stowe skillfully weaves into *Uncle Tom's Cabin*—are less significant, however, than the evidence of the demands of courage and imagination required for the execution of a successful escape plan."[38]

Running does not give merely a description of plantation life and southern slavery; as is true of the genre, its designs are political. A major tool in the war of propaganda against southern slavery, the narrative is concerned to win adherents to the abolitionist cause. *Running* does not deviate from this tradition. The book was intended, William wrote in the introduction, not "as a full history of the life of my wife, nor of myself; but merely as an account of our escape; together with other matters which I hope may be the means of creating in some minds a deeper abhorrence of the sinful and abominable practice of enslaving and brutifying our fellow-creatures." Craft's condemnation of slavery permeates the escape story. He showed the system's persistent dehumanization

---

RED; *Liberator*, July 1, 1859; Harper Twelvetrees, *The Story of the Life of John Anderson, the Fugitive Slave* (London, 1863); A. Homer to Louis Chamerovzow, July 15, 1861, in BFASS. William was also a member of the BFASS deputation to Lord Palmerston to protest the Cuban slave trade and to persuade the government to bring pressure on Spain to close Cuban slave markets (*Anti Slavery Reporter*, July 2, August 1, 1862).

37. Although it is impossible to say, beyond all doubt, that William was the sole author of the narrative, his style, as seen in some of his later letters and reports, suggests that he possessed all the literary tools necessary to write *Running*. Chesson, who became a close associate, always referred to William as the author.

38. Gilbert Osofsky (ed.), *Puttin' on Ole Massa: The Slave Narratives of Henry Bibb, William Wells Brown, and Solomon Northrup* (New York, 1969), 24.

of the slaves, but at the same time, through a "classical" slave character like Pompey, who is aware of his oppression and conscious of an alternative way of life, he depicted the slaves' determination to free themselves by one means or another.

It is also a riveting story. Faced with "mountainous difficulties" throughout their journey from Georgia, the Crafts were in constant danger of betrayal. On the train from Macon to Savannah, Mr. Cray, a friend of Robert Collins', boarded, sat next to Ellen, and promptly tried to engage her in conversation. Feigning deafness, she managed to avoid talking to him. That was fortunate, since Cray had known her since childhood. There was another challenge on the trip from Charleston to Wilmington when a ticket salesman insisted that Ellen sign the register acknowledging that William was her slave. If she did not, they would not be able to board. But she convinced him that her heavily bandaged arm was rheumatic. And later, in Baltimore, near the end of their journey, "We felt more anxious than ever," William wrote, "because we knew not what that last dark night would bring forth. It is true we were near the goal, but our poor hearts were still as if tossed at sea; and, as there was another great and dangerous bar to pass, we were afraid our liberties would be wrecked, and, like the ill-fated Royal Charter, go down forever just off the place we longed to reach." Their fears were well founded. Minutes before the train left, an officer ordered them off—they could not continue, he said, without satisfactory proof that William was Ellen's slave. There followed a few tense and agonizing moments when all seemed to be lost. But the officer, apparently moved by Ellen's illness, finally relented and allowed them to go on to Philadelphia. This is the stuff of which great adventure novels are made. Not only do the fugitives throw off the cross of slavery, they also confront and overcome the barriers to freedom erected by the slave system and its supporters. The combination of pathos, Craft's sense of suspense and drama, and his ability to see humorous angles in the most tragic situations make this a poignant narrative indeed.

Running contains themes that appear in other slave narratives: the separation of families under slavery, licentiousness and sexual brutality of slave masters, oppression of free blacks in the South, southern Christians supporting slavery, mistrust of whites, and a sense that the fugitives are being protected and guided by a God who would ultimately lead them to freedom. Their popularity and impact were unmistakable. "This fugitive slave literature," observed the Boston *Chronotype*, reviewing Henry Bibb's narrative, "is destined to be a powerful lever. We have the most profound conviction of its potency. We see in it the easy and infallible means of abolitionizing the free States. Argument provokes argument, reason is met by sophistry. But narratives of slaves go right to the hearts of men."[39] *Running* was no exception.

As was true for many of his contemporaries, William's support of the Free Produce movement led him inevitably into the growing ranks of an alliance of abolitionists and Lancashire textile manufacturers eager to promote the cultivation of cotton by free labor in British dominions. The "cotton lobby" had its genesis in the concern among Lancashire cotton men that dependency could lead to devastating economic dislocations should their southern supplies be disrupted. That fear prompted the formation in 1857 of the Manchester Cotton Supply Association, which sought increased cotton production in India. In 1850, Thomas Clegg, a Manchester cotton manufacturer, began promoting African cotton cultivation in association with the Church Missionary Society, which had been active in West Africa. Throughout the 1850s, supplies from both these areas increased substantially but in no way affected Britain's massive consumption of southern cotton. The emergence of emigrationism among black Americans after 1855 and the growing interest in African colonization give a new fillip to the search for alternative sources. The Reverend Theodore Bourne, corresponding secretary of the African Civilization Society, went to Britain in 1859 to try to win support for his organization's plan to establish a colony of free black Americans in Abeokuta. The following year, Martin R. Delany and Robert Campbell, on their way home from Abeokuta, visited Britain—they hoped to gain financial backing for their scheme of African emigration. The result was the formation of the African Aid Society (AAS) in July, 1860. Led by prominent businessmen in London, Birmingham, Manchester, and Glasgow; colonizationists such as Dr. Thomas Hodgkin, a prominent English physician; and a number of abolitionists, the AAS wanted to encourage extensive cotton cultivation in Delany's colony. The society hoped to make the Niger the Mississippi of West Africa and, through expanded commerce and Christianity, bring "civilization" to that part of the world. Because of opposition from English missionaries in Abeokuta, and Britain's growing colonial interests in the area, the colony was never established.[40]

Here, an alliance of commercial interests and abolitionism maintained that as cotton production in West Africa expanded, Britain's dependence on southern cotton would decrease. The consequent loss of trade and profits would ultimately force the South to emancipate its slaves. This marriage of commer-

39. Boston *Chronotype*, quoted in *Anti Slavery Bugle*, November 3, 1849.
40. See Richard Blackett, "In Search of International Support for African Colonization: Martin R. Delany's Visit to England, 1860," *Canadian Journal of History*, X (1975), 307–24.

cialism and philanthropy, in many instances informed by a cultural arrogance that saw the Anglo-Saxon world, that is, Britain, as the sole bearer of civilization to the "backward and benighted" African, severely hampered the efforts of those abolitionists eager to promote the cultivation of African cotton. Many blacks were also caught on the horns of a similar dilemma. As products of their time, they too spoke of "civilizing" and "improving" Africa. And although—or, more probably, because—their plans were predicated on a broad racial affinity, they tended either to ignore or to misunderstand the relationship between British racism and British commercial interests in Africa. Craft epitomized this dilemma, and his failure to deal with it in large part accounts for his difficulties in West Africa.

The AAS sponsored a series of petitions from businessmen, particularly textile manufacturers, to the British government in 1861, asking that commissioners be sent to Abeokuta and Dahomey. In the case of Dahomey, they expressed concern about the continuing slave trade, called for the cessation of human sacrifice, and requested the establishment of "legitimate" trade. This, the AAS suggested, could be achieved through a treaty with the king of Dahomey that would provide a subsidy large enough to offset profits from the slave trade. If this failed, the society blandly recommended that Britain reoccupy the fort at Whydah and force the king to permit the entry of British commercial companies. But over the years the Dahomeans had consistently ignored or sidestepped British initiatives. Earlier efforts by British commissioners John Duncan and Frederick Forbes in 1848 had resulted in little more than a promise from the king to reconsider future participation in the slave trade. But as long as slave ships continued to break the British blockade, the king maintained, he would continue to supply the lucrative trade. He gave his assent, however, to the establishment of a few plantations outside Whydah, and many hoped these would prove ultimately the greater profitability of an economy based on free labor. But operating on the assumption that minimal concessions to British demands would forestall pressure from opponents and limit the possibility of outside attacks, the Dahomeans shrewdly manipulated British commercial interests to their advantage in wars against neighboring kingdoms.[41]

In late 1861, William decided to throw his support behind the AAS's Dahomean initiative. Craft's interest was the result of a combination of factors: his free-labor views, which converged with those of a growing sector of British ab-

41. AAS, *First Report from July 1860 to the 31st March, 1862* (London, n.d.), 26–32; *Anti Slavery Reporter*, November 1, 1862; William Johnson Argyle, *The Fon of Dahomey: A History and Ethnography of the Old Kingdom* (Oxford, 1966), 44; *African Times*, December 23, 1862.

Ellen Craft disguised for the escape from slavery
Reprinted from William Craft, *Running a Thousand Miles for Freedom*

olitionists; his work on the John Anderson Committee, which concentrated on Africa as an alternative field of labor for the fugitive; and, finally, the apparent success of Delany's and Campbell's efforts in Abeokuta. Soon after, William decided to visit Dahomey, "deeply affected," a sympathetic editor wrote, "by the recital of the atrocities perpetrated at the annual custom of the Dahomians" and impressed with "the conviction that it was his duty, as a Christian African, to undertake a Mission to the King of Dahomey." [42] One gets the distinct impression, however, that William's commendable decision was also motivated by personal considerations. Ambitious, and eager to demonstrate his skills, William found life in London confining and therefore leapt at this opportunity to leave his mark on history.

Support for William's plans came mainly from Dr. Thomas Hodgkin, of the Aborigines Protection Society, and F. W. Chesson, secretary of the London Emancipation Committee. Hodgkin, an old advocate of African redemption, was an early defender of Liberia and a supporter of the African Civilization Society and Delany's Abeokuta colony. Craft's efforts in Dahomey, Hodgkin argued, with an eye to Lancashire interests, would improve the prospects for more African cotton at a time when American supplies were becoming uncertain. Hodgkin's support of Craft's mission was premised on the belief, one he had developed in his defense of Liberia, that the commercial development of Africa would not only benefit the continent by increasing trade with Britain and America but would also give the former slave-trading countries an opportunity to atone for their past wrongs to Africa. All of this, of course, became even more urgent as American cotton shipments to Europe were threatened by the Civil War. In addition, Hodgkin said, if the mission were successful and received official endorsement from Liberia, that country's image and reputation would be enhanced. Hodgkin became William's principal advisor during the mission, even giving him information on and supplies for treating minor outbreaks of smallpox and other diseases. [43]

William toured Britain in the winter and spring of 1862, trying to raise the estimated £1,000 for his proposed one-year visit to Dahomey. He laid out his intentions to supporters at a meeting organized by Hodgkin in July. He aimed, he said, to persuade the king to give up human sacrifice, to convince him that through the adoption of "legitimate" trade, Christianity, and the cultivation of cotton, the slave trade would be eliminated, and to call on him to support the

42. *Anti Slavery Reporter*, November 1, 1862.
43. Thomas Hodgkin to President Benson, November 24, 1862, Hodgkin to Craft, October 29, 1864, both in THP.

William Craft
Reprinted from the *Harbinger*

education of his people. The introduction of agriculture and education were the foundations on which William built his plans for a change in Dahomey. The development of agriculture would make it next to impossible for the king to commandeer farmers into slave-hunting parties, and would also limit the numbers available for sacrifice. As a result, the king, motivated entirely by selfish interests, would realize that "the heads of his own people [were] too valuable to be cut off." These new circumstances would force the king to abandon "the slave trade, and the so-called 'Grand Custom.'" Like so many other advocates of the Free Produce movement and African emigration, William also believed that increased supplies of African cotton would lead ultimately to the demise of southern slavery. The plan was not simply the fantasy of an eternal optimist or misguided philanthropist. There were some signs—limited ones, to be sure— that augured well for the success of the mission. In spite of earlier intransigence, the king had signed a short-lived agreement in 1852 with Commander Forbes, leader of a British mission, to encourage the palm-oil and ground-nut trade. The precedent, William believed, justified his optimism and suggested that the king could be persuaded to recognize that "legitimate" trade was the only means of ensuring future economic security.[44]

But the mission encountered opposition from people who were convinced that this "private and unofficial essay by a person of colour, unacquainted too with the language of the Dahomians" stood little chance of succeeding. More important, Craft's intrusion into an admittedly delicate situation could, they insisted, permanently damage fledgling British commercial interests in the area. Craft and his supporters disagreed, arguing that because he was not directly connected with, though he was supported by, the British government, there was a greater chance that the king would be more amenable to his proposals. There was "something truly noble," the Aborigines Protection Society answered the cynics, "in the idea of a coloured man, himself rescued by his own exertions and those of his devoted wife from the barbarism of American slavery, so disinterestedly giving his services to the cause of degraded Africa, and even risking his own life, in the hope that by so doing he may help to prevent the shedding of innocent blood."[45]

The Foreign Office gave its blessing to the mission in November, and soon Craft set sail for Africa, brimming with optimism. But he ran into unexpected

44. *Anti Slavery Reporter*, December 1, 1862; *Aborigines Friend and Colonial Intelligencer*, January-December, 1862.

45. *African Times* December 22, 1862; Hodgkin to James Cropper, October 11, 1862, in THP; Peter Bernasko to Rev. Dear Sir, December 29, 1863, in MMS; Aborigines Protection Society, *Twenty-sixth Annual Report* (London, 1863), 12–13.

delays. Two months after leaving London, William was still sitting impatiently in Lagos, waiting for the king's return from one of his military expeditions against neighboring Abeokuta. He spent an additional three months in Why-dah, awaiting a summons from the king. When it finally came in May, William hurried off to Canna, accompanied by Peter Bernasko, Wesleyan missionary at Whydah. He received a warm welcome, and the next few days were spent in discussions and royal functions. Impressed with Craft's proposals, the king invited him to set up a merchant house in Whydah and, to show his commitment, gave William a large building in which to conduct his business. But the king's generosity proved an embarrassment when he bestowed on William five slave boys captured during a recent expedition. Unable to decline, for fear of jeopardizing the entire mission, William, the fugitive slave, had to accept the gift. Before leaving Dahomey, however, he placed the boys at Bernasko's school with the clear understanding that on his return they would be transferred to the school William planned to open.[46]

William left Dahomey in the summer of 1863, confident that he had laid the groundwork for successful efforts in the years ahead. In his report to the Dahomian Committee, formed by Hodgkin in 1861 and composed of prominent British humanitarians, he said, "The Dahomians who now make palm-oil, and grow cotton on a small scale, seem fully to appreciate my arguments, and expressed their willingness to act promptly upon my suggestions, provided I would return to Whydah and assist them in carrying it out. And as the King gave me a large place of business at Whydah and as much land and as many people as I may wish to have to teach cotton growing, I shall return there as soon as possible to assist in civilizing the people, and endeavouring, by the blessing of God, to prepare their minds for the better reception of his truth."[47] Like many of his contemporaries, notably Delany, Campbell, and Garnet, Craft saw himself and other black Americans as crucial agents in the civilizing of Africa. The scheme seemed overly ambitious, for William had no experience in cotton cultivation.

But before he returned to Dahomey in the winter of 1863, Craft was invited by the British Association for the Advancement of Science to report on his trip to Africa, and he found himself at the center of a raging controversy during the annual meeting. John Crawfund, president of the Ethnological Society, and James Hunt, president of the Anthropological Society, both read papers sup-

46. Stephen Lushington to Foreign Office, December 11, 1862, in FOD; *Anti Slavery Reporter,* January 1, 1863; *Nonconformist,* July 29, 1863.
47. *Harbinger,* November, 1863; London *Evening Star,* June 25, 1863.

porting theories that Europeans were superior and that Africans were clearly inferior. These views were not unknown to Craft; they had in fact been in incubation for some time. Ever since the appearance of Thomas Carlyle's vapid *Occasional Discourse on the Nigger Question* in 1849 and the publication of Robert Knox's research, theories of African inferiority had gained increased acceptance among a broad cross-section of the British intelligentsia. Not long after entering Ockham, William felt compelled to respond to an anonymous article in Charles Dickens' *Household Words*. Ostensibly reviewing the popular *Uncle Tom's Cabin*, the author devoted an inordinate amount of time to a refutation of what he considered the novel's "overstrained conclusions and violent extremes" and to a partial defense of American slavery, which, he maintained, had not reached the levels of barbarity associated with the Cuban system. This milder form of slavery had resulted in the natural propagation of the slave population in America, whereas the Cuban plantation had to depend almost entirely on new slave imports to replenish its labor force. However, American slavery made an uncivilized people more dependent on their owners. Uncle Tom, Aunt Chloe, and George Harris, all characters in the novel, were, therefore, exceptions, uncharacteristic of the "majority of cases . . . [who] have been depressed so far towards the state of simple beasts of burden that they have acquired the hearts and brains of horses and oxen." Living under these conditions, and denied the rights of education, "thousands of negroes [were] content to be well fed, and housed, occasionally patted on the head or played with, and when the master [found] it needful to reduce his stock, [parted] with a mere transitory brutish pang from a contented wife in Maryland, perhaps, to lie down content with a new wife in a new stall in Tennessee." With these facts in mind, the author suggested that Liberia held out the best and possibly last hope for American blacks. In an act of rediscovering the wheel, he turned to a variety of the old colonization solution long discredited by blacks and abolitionists. There were many slaveholders, he believed, who were willing to entertain the possibility of emancipation only if they were shown that blacks could be raised above their debased situation. But these slaveholders would have to educate their slaves on the plantations. Education would "make them intelligent men and women" and instill in them "the doctrines of Christianity," all necessary preconditions for becoming competent free laborers. Once the educated slaves were freed, they would continue to labor for their former masters. But this was only a temporary measure, for as the flow of immigrants from Europe increased, demand for black labor would decrease commensurately to the point where it would be confined "wholly to those districts in which the climate appears to be unsuited for field labour by white men." The surplus black population created by this displacement and "educated into love of freedom would pass over to Liberia, and form a nation on the coast of Africa, whereof America might boast for ever." These arguments, one part reworked versions of earlier schemes for Liberian colonization, and one part Gibbon Wakefield's proposal for the removal of surplus populations, were encrusted with contemporary racist ideas on black inferiority.[48]

In a masterly and surprisingly controlled response, William (possibly with the aid of John Estlin and others) dismissed these arguments as unfounded, based on ignorance of the facts, insensitive, gratuitous, and "capable of misleading and prejudicing the English mind against the coloured population of the United States." William insisted that his experience clearly showed that Stowe had not painted exaggerated pictures of Tom, Chloe, or Harris. If anything, she could be accused of understatement in her descriptions of slave masters. It was shortsighted, William argued, to attempt to depict one slave system as more humane than another, when both Cuba and America employed the same barbarous methods to maintain the system. In spite of heavy odds, and contrary to the author's belief, increasing numbers of American slaves had been escaping to Canada, being "content not to remain in slavery a moment, if they could possibly escape." Furthermore, to assume that a relatively benign system brought high rates of reproduction among slaves was to miss the lengths to which slaves went to provide for themselves independent of their masters. They supplemented their small rations, William pointed out, by "hunting in the forest at night, for racoons and oposs, and fishing by torch light, and occasionally cultivating a small portion of their masters' old exhausted land, by working at nights and on Sundays." It was strange, William concluded, that the author had chosen to palliate such a dehumanizing system of oppression and improve its image in Britain by a combination of "malignant slurs" and outright distortions.[49]

Although he had grown accustomed to such views, Craft was surprised to hear them promoted at such a prestigious gathering of scientific minds. Crawfund's paper was "The Comixture of the Races of Man as Affecting the Progress of Civilization." Superior races that had mixed with their inferiors, he argued, inevitably witnessed the decline of their civilizations. The various races were naturally quite different, with respect to mental and physical capabilities, and this led to antipathy. This law was most clearly epitomized, he said, in the

48. *Household Words*, VI (1852), 1–6.
49. London *Morning Advertiser*, October 1, 1852.

New World. In neither the Caribbean nor the United States, in places where blacks were in the majority, had the freedmen or slaves gained ascendancy over whites. In a curious twist of logic, he argued that the racist laws in the South themselves were proof of black inferiority. In fact, he concluded, the situation in the United States was caused by blacks, who were "too prone to live and labour in slavery or in special degradation, and utterly incapable of rising to an equality with the higher race among whom it has been unhappily planted." This was too reminiscent of the 1852 article in *Household Words* for Craft to keep quiet. Immediately at the conclusion of Crawfund's presentation, Craft sprang to his feet to counter the notion of natural racial antipathy. A significant number of American blacks were of mixed blood, antimiscegenation laws notwithstanding. In addition, it was social oppression, not inborn traits, that caused blacks' "special degradation." Given the opportunity, blacks consistently demonstrated their intellectual ability, and "many of them had risen to very high positions, in society." Tongue in cheek, he concluded that during his thirteen years in England he had found only one Shakespeare. The session degenerated rapidly thereafter, and the chairman ended the dispute only by declaring the meeting over.[50]

Those who attended the next session were eager for a confrontation, and their anticipation would be well rewarded. Hunt's paper was entitled "On the Physical and Mental Character of the Negro." He marshaled the arguments of experts to prove the low status of blacks. Various physical characteristics, including size of thorax and skull, demonstrated, he said, the Negro's unalterable inferiority to the European. Negroes who had become more civilized all had European blood. Only ignorance or stupidity could prompt men to oppose these scientific laws. It was Hunt's conclusion that a bright, fourteen-year-old European boy was the intellectual level beyond which no "pure Negro" ever advanced.

Craft's attack on Hunt's paper was filled with sarcastic comments. Although he was of mixed blood, he said apologetically, he was black enough to argue against Hunt. The African's thick skull was hardly proof of his smaller brain and lower intelligence, Craft said. Rather, that was God-given protection in the tropics—otherwise "their brains would probably have become very much like those of many scientific gentlemen of the present day." After reiterating many of the objections he had raised to Crawfund's paper, Craft said that the opin-

50. For the speeches of Crawfund, Craft, and Hunt, see London *Times*, August 29, 31, 1863.

ions of men like Hunt and Crawfund had little to do with "scientific fact" and were being used to justify the continued oppression of blacks.

Defending his position, Hunt stressed the importance of scientific evidence, which could hardly be refuted by what he called "poetical clap-trap, or by gratuitous and worthless assumptions." A correspondent for the Newcastle *Chronicle* observed that what was said about the Negro anatomy "was an outrage to every kindly feeling, and an insult to humanity. . . . Mr. Craft's clear, open, generous and manly countenance contrasted most successfully with that of his bitter opponents." Craft delivered his lecture on Dahomey on the last day of the conference.[51]

The dispute at the association reverberated through British intellectual and philanthropic circles for some time, adding fuel to the already acrimonious debate over race. Its significance can be gathered from the fact that Sir Richard Burton felt compelled to include a chapter entitled "The Negro's Place in Nature" in a book describing his mission to the king of Dahomey. It was Burton's way of supporting advocates of African inferiority and castigating as misguided the opinions of Craft and British abolitionists. Burton's dislike of the African is well known and requires little comment here other than that his wide travels throughout Africa lent a certain credibility to his views.[52]

The debate over "The Negro's Place in Nature" was, by 1863, rapidly assuming greater practical significance as Britain commenced a new wave of colonial expansion in Africa. No longer was the African a mere scientific curiosity. British officials sent out to Lagos and other places along the West African coast took with them their baggage of negative attitudes about African racial and cultural characteristics. On a broader international level, these views undoubtedly influenced British attitudes toward the South in the American Civil War. Crawfund, Hunt, and others of their ilk were simply providing justifications for the day when Britain might decide to recognize Southern independence. British philanthropists were acutely aware of this fact, and Craft's attack should be seen as an attempt to forestall this possibility.

With growing British interests on the west coast of Africa, the activities of the African Aid Society, and the missions of Burton, Eardley Wilmot, the French explorer Jules Gérard, and Craft, Dahomey was increasingly in the news. The country, Gérard wrote, was governed by a conniving, "cunning and cruel" king who condoned human sacrifice and exploited competing European

51. *Anthropological Review*, I (1863), 390–91; Newcastle *Chronicle*, September 19, 1863.
52. Sir Richard Burton, *A Mission to Gelele, King of Dahome* (London, 1864), Chap. XIX.

interests for his own ends. Writing under the pseudonym An African, Craft condemned Gérard for his biased reporting of events and for deliberately over-looking the fact that the "grand custom" was prompted by misguided religious belief rather than by some innate uncivilized characteristic. The problem could be solved, Craft suggested optimistically, by introducing the king and his sub-jects to Christianity. The king's hospitality, generosity, and partiality to the British offered a unique opportunity for greater missionary and commercial activity that should be seized by all those interested in the spread of Christian-ity, the destruction of the slave trade, and the expansion of "legitimate" trade. But this could never be achieved, he warned, without first eschewing racial ar-rogance. "Let us approach the abolition of human sacrifice in a temper differ-ent to that in which we have hitherto approached it. Let us undermine the faith of those of our own species who are so mentally poor; but do not let us inveigh against them as a horde of merciless, sanguinary savages."[53]

It was not long before these views came under attack. Charles Hillard, a for-mer Wesleyan missionary on the west coast of Africa, condemned what he saw as An African's willingness to condone human sacrifice. In response, Craft at-tempted to describe and explain, rather than criticize, the society, polity, cul-ture, and religious beliefs of Dahomey, and to offer some possible solutions to human sacrifice and the slave trade. All approaches to these problems, he ob-served, had to be based on peace and "averse to the homily of physical force preached every hour to the credulous folks who maintain missions to foreign parts." Difficulties were compounded because "many English gentlemen who go to Africa on affairs of Church or State do not understand the Africans, and do not care about understanding them; they set them down as idolators, or as anything else which may be loathsome and unworthy of their study." The core of any successful policy in Africa, therefore, had to be predicated on patience, concern, sympathy, and a critical understanding of the African. The "improve-ment" and "development" of Dahomey would come when the superior profits of "legitimate" trade surpassed those of the slave trade and when the spread of the gospel, through an understanding and sympathetic Christianity, eliminated the need for the superstitious custom of human sacrifice.[54]

In light of all these disputes, which had considerable effect on British per-ceptions of Africans, Craft's second visit to Dahomey was a chance to test the merits of the humanitarian-abolitionist approach to African elevation. This, of course, placed added pressure on Craft to succeed. "Urge the Africans who are

53. London *Times*, August 12, 1863.
54. *Ibid.*, September 1, 10, 16, 1863.

capable of comprehending Thee," Hodgkin implored William, "to exert themselves for the benefit and credit of their race," for only by self-improvement
could they hope to silence "Burton and the host of others [who] are doing what
they can to deprecate the African race." Sounding very much like Dickens'
Gradgrind, Hodgkin wrote Craft and insisted that facts "will best answer and
confound" opponents. There was reason to be optimistic. Before leaving in
December, 1863, Craft made arrangements with the Countess of Huntingdon's
Connexion, a small religious group with strong ties in Sierra Leone, to help
finance the establishment of his school in Whydah. The newly formed Company of African Merchants, whose secretary F. Fitzgerald had opposed Craft's
first mission, now offered him a commission as its agent in Whydah and, in a
letter to the Foreign Office, requested government support and protection for
Craft, who was to "take charge of the Company's goods and conduct their business at Whydah under arrangements which make him a participator in all the
profits to be thence derived."[55]

It is difficult to piece together exactly what William accomplished during the
three and one-half years he spent in Whydah. For most of the first three
months, he familiarized himself with local conditions and negotiated with
Dahomean authorities about establishing his school and merchant business.
Opening the school seemed to be his priority. Education, he believed, provided
the necessary foundation for the progress of all people, especially those William considered uncivilized. The educator of the backward was, in the broadest
sense of the word, a missionary to all those who had not been exposed to the
benefits of nineteenth-century education. The work of Christian missionaries
in Africa would have been greatly facilitated, he later told a meeting of the Aborigines Protection Society, if they had concentrated their initial efforts on educating native youth.[56]

But the promised support from the Countess of Huntingdon's Connexion
was slow to materialize, and, strapped for funds, William was forced to delay
the school's opening. It was, however, finally opened in mid-1864 in a building
formerly used as a slave barracoon, and by April, 1865, there were twenty students under the instruction of a trained teacher. It was an instant success. Reports from local Wesleyan missionaries constantly bemoaned the fact that
Craft's school had attracted students away from theirs. Although this competi-

---

55. Hodgkin to Craft, November 22, 1864, April 23, 1865, both in THP; Edinburgh Ladies
Emancipation Society, *Annual Report, 1864* (Edinburgh, n.d.), 2; London *Evening Star*, November
21, 1863; Company of African Merchants to Foreign Office, December 11, 1863, in FOD.
56. Aborigines Protection Society, *Thirtieth Annual Report* (London, 1867), 18.

tion did not immediately affect the school's operations, it ultimately hampered Craft's ability to raise funds in London. As money grew increasingly short, William's son Charles launched a public appeal in London in 1866 for contributions to support new students at the school. Although the school was apparently still in operation when Craft left Whydah in 1867, it seems to have survived on a minimum of resources.[57]

Craft's business activities also ran into unforeseen difficulties. His principal objective had been to prove to the king that the successful cultivation and export of cotton and other crops from Dahomey would bring greater profits than the slave trade did. Initial reports from the Company of African Merchants and the African Aid Society were full of praise for Craft's work in Whydah and for his success in winning the king's confidence. He would later report that he carried out "a large and legitimate trade" with the king and the people of Dahomey, although it is impossible to determine the precise nature of his business. On more than one occasion he sent roots to Hodgkin in England, who was responsible for running experiments to establish their medicinal and commercial value. Hodgkin was eager to join William in exploiting investment opportunities at Whydah. William also claimed that he was responsible for the "establishment" of the palm-oil trade at Whydah, a curious claim since palm oil had long been a major item in West African trade.[58]

William's successes and independence worked to his disadvantage and ultimately led to a break with the Company of African Merchants. It is clear that the company saw Craft as little more than a convenient factotum in its efforts to gain a foothold in Whydah, and had no intention of abiding by its agreement to share profits with William. As the company expanded and consolidated its commercial empire on the west coast, it came to view the contract with Craft as unnecessarily burdensome and sought an opportunity to renege on its obligations. The company got its chance in 1867. In poor health, Craft decided to return to England to recuperate. The king, however, owed the company $5,000 for goods bought on credit, and since he could not meet the debt before William's departure, the king sent him fifty slaves as payment. Unable, as a matter of principle, to accept the slaves or immediately collect the debt, William decided to set them free and "stand half the loss himself." But to Craft's

57. *African Times*, July 23, 1864; *Harbinger*, July, 1864; Rev. West to Rev. Dear Sir, May 15, 1865, in MMS.
58. *African Times*, August 28, 1864, July 22, 1865; Hodgkin to Craft, November 22, 1864, April 23, 1865, both in THP; Boston *Journal*, June 7, 1878.

utter dismay, the company rejected his decision and insisted on compensation for the full amount.[59]

Distraught, Craft abandoned any idea of ever returning to Dahomey, his plans, like those of Delany and Campbell in Abeokuta, a victim of expanding British commercial interests. He derived few rewards from his three-year association with the company. It is difficult to evaluate Craft's accomplishments in Dahomey. Although the king undoubtedly supported his efforts, it seems unlikely that he managed to bring about any significant shift in policy. In spite of the existence of a few scattered plantations near Abomey, the development of agriculture attracted little of the king's attention while Craft was in Dahomey. On the other hand, the reaction of the local Wesleyan missionary suggests that his school did achieve a measure of success.

During William's absence in Dahomey, Ellen devoted most of her energies to the education of their young family. There were now four children—Charles Estlin Phillips, named for John Estlin and Wendell Phillips; Ellen; William, Jr.; and Brougham, named after the feisty British abolitionist, Lord Brougham. Life in Hammersmith was quiet, interrupted only by visits from friends and American abolitionists touring London. In spite of the family's relatively comfortable existence and the many friends they had made since coming to England, Ellen had yearned for the day when she would be reunited with her mother. Ellen had been eleven when first separated from her mother in 1837, but they were reunited the following year when Major James Smith moved his family and slaves to Macon. The Crafts' escape in 1848 had severed all ties between mother and daughter. Following Sherman's devastating march through Georgia in 1864, Ellen and her friends the Lushingtons, teachers at Ockham, began making inquiries about her mother through Wendell Phillips and other American contacts. News soon arrived from General James Wilson, the young military commander at Macon, that Maria Smith was alive and living close to his headquarters. Ellen had money sent to Macon to cover the cost of the trip to London, and Wilson made all the necessary arrangements for Maria to join her daughter. She set sail from New York in mid-October, 1865, arriving in London three weeks later to an emotional reunion with Ellen at King's Cross train station.[60]

Although little is known about her other activities during these years, it ap-

59. *New National Era*, January 16, 1873; Chesson Diary, August 26–September 2, 1867, in RED; Boston *Journal*, June 7, 1878.
60. *Freed-Man*, December 1, 1865.

pears that Ellen continued to be involved in the abolitionist movement. She devoted a great deal of time to raising money for the work among southern freedmen, was a leading spirit in the formation of a ladies' auxiliary of the British and Foreign Freedmen's Aid Society, and worked to win support among British friends for a girls' school in Sierra Leone. Toward the end of the decade, Ellen also became involved in the fledgling Women's Suffrage Association.[61]

William's return from Dahomey coincided with a grand reunion of the international abolitionist movement in Paris. The Crafts attended the London meeting to honor Garrison and later joined their old friend on the trip to Paris. More than just a commemoration of abolitionist successes and an opportunity for old friends to get together, the conference also addressed the ticklish question of the freedmen's future and their relationship to the development of Africa. For those who had long promoted the principles of the free-labor movement and the establishment of black emigrant settlements in the tropics, the recent emancipation of American slaves and rising European interest in Africa were fortuitous, a convergence of events that should be exploited to full effect. In this context, William's account of his work in Whydah and his views on the potential of Dahomey were pertinent. The abject failure of Sir Thomas Fowell Buxton's Niger expedition to implement similar proposals twenty-five years earlier caused the advocates of African settlements little discomfort. As one optimistic French delegate told the meeting, Africa's development and advancement toward civilization necessitated the creation of settlements in the interior "where civilization shall set a good example [and] where missionaries shall preach the Holy Word." The idea won William's warm endorsement despite his problems in Whydah and the deviousness of the Company of African Merchants. At the conclusion of the conference the Crafts and Chessons toured all the major sights in Paris.[62]

The joys of the Paris visit were short-lived, however. The company was pressing for an early repayment of William's debts. His report of events in Whydah had failed to impress the company's directors. He was, they insisted, totally liable for all debts incurred. The second visit had been a financial disaster. Most of the family's limited resources had been used to finance the mission. Without the income from his import business, which he closed before going to Dahomey, the Crafts were left with no alternative but to sell the family home. It must have been a devastating blow, for the purchase of their first home symbol-

61. *Ibid.*, May 1, 1869; Chesson Diary, June 3, 1869–June 17, 1870, in RED.
62. French delegate quoted in Temperley, *British Antislavery*, 261–62; Chesson Diary, August 26–September 2, 1867, in RED.

ized, in a sense, their attainment of total freedom. With the sale of the home in late 1867, and no reliable source of income, William applied to the National Freedmen's Aid Union for a position as paid agent. But the union could not afford to employ him in that capacity.[63]

These developments undoubtedly influenced the Crafts' decision to return to America. Although it is impossible to establish precisely when they made up their minds, in 1868 they were making arrangements to leave Britain. They planned to buy a plantation in Georgia and establish a cooperative among the freedmen. As William told supporters, this would free the former slaves from the contract-labor system and help them to become independent farmers. The Crafts would secure a farm, probably on lease, buy all the needed implements, and advance money to the participants most in need, with repayment spread over a number of years. It was estimated that the project would require a capital outlay of £1,500. By December, 1868, when William began an extensive fund-raising tour of England and Scotland, the Crafts had already collected £470. Although he was unable to raise the full amount, William gained backing from many prominent British philanthropists as well as the National Freedmen's Aid Union of Great Britain and Ireland. It is interesting that the Crafts were able to raise so much money, in so short a time, on a scheme that was broached only in early 1868, less than eighteen months before their departure for America. The support his plans generated is testimony to both William's reputation among British philanthropists and his powers of persuasion. His failure in Dahomey obviously gave no one pause; in fact, it may have even enhanced interest in any scheme he proposed. He was, for many, the epitome of the bold, committed adventurer with vision. The Crafts and three of their children, Charles, Ellen, and the baby Alfred, left England for Boston in August, 1869, ending nineteen years of exile. Brougham and William, Jr., remained in England to continue their education.[64]

For seven months after their arrival in Boston, the Crafts busied themselves with preparing for their trip to Georgia and renewing old acquaintances. To many of the old abolitionist warriors, buoyed by the recent passage of the Fifteenth Amendment, the prodigals' return and their determination to labor in

63. Parish of Hammersmith, Poor Rates Book, Hammersmith Public Library, London; Craft to Committee of the National Freedmen's Aid Union, December 5, 1867, William Rowntree to Dear Friend, August 17, 1868, both in BFASS.

64. *British Friend*, December 1, 1868; Manchester *Examiner*, quoted in *Anti Slavery Standard*, May 15, 1869; Chesson Diary, June 3, 1869–June 17, 1870, in RED; Craft to Lewis Hayden, August 19, 1869, in Charles Chapman Papers, Moorland-Springarn Research Center, Howard University, Washington, D.C.; Boston *Journal*, June 10, 1878.

the state that formerly enslaved them seemed a fitting culmination of all the years of sacrifice and hardship. They were in great demand at meetings of New England philanthropists eager to expand the work among the freedmen. William spoke of their plans at assemblies organized by old friends, and to any group interested in promoting education among the freedmen in Georgia. Most of the Crafts' friends were enthusiastic. But there were a few skeptics, like Wendell Phillips, who questioned the wisdom of two of Georgia's most notorious fugitives returning to work among their former masters. Phillips thought the whole business unnecessarily risky. By the time the Crafts left Boston for Savannah in early 1870, William had managed to raise an additional $200 in gifts and secure a loan of $1,500. On the way south, they made a brief stop in Washington, where William was introduced to the secretary of the treasury by Senator Charles Sumner, and it was rumored that he would probably be appointed to an official post in Georgia.[65] Although the appointment never materialized, success in their new venture seemed reasonably assured.

The choice of Georgia was more than just sentimental, a yearning to return to their native state where some of their family still lived. It may even have been motivated, as Phillips implied, by a misplaced urge to thumb their noses at a plantocracy that had for so long denied them their liberty. Whatever the proximate reason, there is no doubt that William was moved by the same missionary zeal that took him to Dahomey. And in Georgia, too, there was work to be done, which could best be completed, William believed, by people with their experience and their intimate knowledge of the state. Similarly, he argued, the freedmen's progress in Georgia, in many respects as uncivilized as Africa, depended on an extensive education campaign that would penetrate even remote rural areas. If this was not undertaken soon, William feared, weaker people would continue to be the victims of the inevitable progress of civilization. He was a man of courage, a London editor wrote just before William left on his first mission to Dahomey, and his courage was "tempered with discretion, intelligence of a high order, and withal faith in the utility and probable success of his mission."[66] No one, not even trusted friends like Wendell Phillips, could have convinced William and Ellen that their plans were visionary.

Soon after their arrival in Georgia the Crafts went into partnership with a William Johnson, and they all moved to Hickory Hill, a plantation just across the state line in South Carolina. A crop was planted and they settled into their

---

65. *Anti Slavery Standard*, November 6, 1869; Boston *Journal*, June 14, 8, 1878; *British Friend*, April 1, 1870.
66. Aborigines Protection Society, *Thirtieth Annual Report*, 2; London *Dial*, October 18, 1862.

new life. Ellen and her daughter ran two schools at home, one for children in the day and the other for adults at night. But by the fall of 1870, all their plans lay in ruins. One night, a band of night riders set fire to the house and barn. Although the Crafts were unhurt, the entire crop was destroyed and they lost $1,000 invested in the plantation. Their experience was not unique— opponents to black advancement wreaked havoc on many farms owned or operated by blacks. In some respects, the Crafts may have been lucky to escape with their lives. By 1871, an estimated fifteen hundred to sixteen hundred murders had been committed in Georgia alone. Since emancipation, probably as many as twenty thousand blacks had been murdered throughout the South.[67]

Gathering up what little was left from the ruins of Hickory Hill, the Crafts moved to Savannah to join their son Charles, who had taken over the San Salvador House, a boardinghouse on Bay Street, facing the river. The situation was just as precarious in Savannah. Although there was little violence in the city, it appears that Charles had been deliberately deceived into believing that the boardinghouse was a viable economic proposition. Six months later, they were forced to abandon the venture after considerable losses.[68]

Even though chastened by their Hickory Hill and Savannah experiences, the Crafts remained committed to and optimistic about the prospects of farming in Georgia. There was still room for hope. The bumper cotton crop of 1870, which surpassed the best years' harvests under slavery, seemed to assure a bright economic future for Georgia. At the end of the year, the Crafts took a three-year lease, at $300 per year, on Woodville, a plantation in Ways Station, Bryan County, twenty miles from Savannah. In Bryan County, as in the other five seaboard counties, the majority of the population was black. Unlike the rest of the state, during the antebellum period these counties had large plantations where rice and Sea Island cotton were grown and where numerous slaves did the work. One quarter of all the slaveholders in the state owning more than one hundred slaves operated in these counties. The area, therefore, experienced the greatest disruption after the war as thousands of slaves left the plantations to search for a better life.[69]

Many plantations were permanently ruined. Woodville was no exception; it had been abandoned in 1864 when its owner moved to Savannah. But not all

67. Boston *Journal* June 6, 7, 1878; Dorothy Sterling, *Black Foremothers: Three Lives* (Old Westbury, N.Y., 1979), 51.
68. Mifflin W. Gibbs, *Shadow and Light: An Autobiography* (1902; rpr. New York, 1968), 13; Raddock's *Savannah, Georgia, City Directory, 1871*; Boston *Journal*, June 8, 12, 1878.
69. W. E. B. Du Bois, *Black Reconstruction in America, 1860–1880* (1935; rpr. New York, 1971), 510; Enoch Marvin Banks, *The Economics of Land Tenure in Georgia* (New York, 1905), 65–66.

slaves settled in urban areas. Some became squatters, experimenting with co-
operative farming on deserted plantations, determined to destroy the old order
and establish themselves as independent farmers. Equally determined to prevent such developments and to reassert their authority were their former masters. During Reconstruction, Charles Flynn has written, otherwise decent
people "became so outraged at 'insolent' and 'disobedient' black workers that
they struck out cruelly. Their violence reflected the sincere, elemental conviction that race defined appropriate social and economic roles." Resistance to
the legitimate demands of freedmen led to heightened agitation for land near
Savannah in 1867. Concerned about increased violence, and trying to keep the
situation under tight control, military authorities forcibly removed black squatters from land they had occupied. One Atlanta editor was so upset that he
warned of total anarchy. With typical slaveholder hyperbole, he wrote that "accounts represent the condition of things in Bryan and Camden counties as
truly alarming. The wildest days of San Domingo seem to have been re-
produced." That, of course, was utter nonsense. Although there were some up-
heavals in other seaboard counties, Bryan County remained relatively quiet
and unimportant compared to neighboring Camden and Liberty counties. According to testimony given before the congressional committee investigating
the Ku Klux Klan, Bryan County was one of the few areas in the state that
escaped Klan violence.[70]

When the Crafts arrived in early 1871, Woodville was, Ellen later recalled, "a
miserable hole, dirty and full of rats; snakes running all over the house; the
farm was overrun with weeds; and there were no fences on the place." A vast
section of the plantation was heavily wooded. In partnership with Mr. De
Lamotte, of Savannah, the Crafts set about clearing the land, planting a crop of
long-staple cotton, repairing some of the abandoned houses, and fencing about
three hundred acres, all at a cost of $400. Any hope of success, and the possi-
bility of recouping their losses at Hickory Hill and Savannah, went aglimmer-
ing when a poor harvest fetched a mere $115. At the end of the season, William
reported that the venture had lost $2,000. Disillusioned, De Lamotte withdrew
from the partnership, demanding at least partial reimbursement for his investment. These losses left the Crafts almost "totally broke." As William later

70. Manuel Gottlieb, "The Land Question in Georgia During Reconstruction," *Science and
Society*, III (1939), 372–76; Charles L. Flynn, Jr., *White Land, Black Labor: Caste and Class in Late
Nineteenth-Century Georgia* (Baton Rouge, 1983), 13; "Ku Klux Klan Report. Georgia Testimony.
Report of the Joint Select Committee of Inquiry into the Affairs of the Late Insurrection States,"
Senate Reports, 42nd Cong., 2nd Sess., Vol. II, pts. 6, 7.

admitted, his lack of any "practical experience in the cultivation of cotton or rice or in farming" accounted for the disastrous harvest. Continued failure and dwindling resources only compounded their problems. They were faced with two very difficult options. They must now either accept defeat, the predictable consequence of what Phillips insisted was a misguided and poorly conceived scheme, or give the experiment another try. Proud, determined, and, as it turned out, overly optimistic, the Crafts chose the latter. By the end of 1872, Woodville had a number of tenant farmers, the Crafts lending money and giving seeds, rations, and tools in exchange for an equal share of the crop.[71]

The new arrangement demanded an infusion of capital, and local banks and merchants were not forthcoming. Operating costs would be lowered and loans more readily secured, William decided, if they bought rather than leased Woodville. William left for New England in early 1873 and spent the entire year trying to raise $7,000, money that would be used to purchase Woodville and finance the cultivation of rice and cotton and the establishment of a school.[72] Back at Woodville, Ellen took charge of bringing a semblance of order to the shambles. Buildings were repaired and fences mended with the aid of families she had attracted as tenants to the plantation. The school that Ellen and Charles ran at home was moved to an old barn Ellen had renovated while William was in Boston. The schoolhouse doubled as a church on Sundays. Brougham, who had remained in England, arrived in December, 1873, having spent one term at Howard University, and took over the duties of running the school. Ellen could then concentrate on improving the Sabbath school. The freedmen's response to the school was more than Ellen could have anticipated. Throughout the state, blacks showed a keen interest in the establishment of schools for their children. Freedmen's Bureau officials estimated, rather conservatively, that roughly two hundred black men and women had started schools for the freedmen in at least seventy counties between 1866 and 1870. The enthusiasm for education was as infectious in the seaboard counties. Not long after Sherman entered Savannah in December, 1864, blacks opened a number of schools attended by five hundred pupils, and provided $1,000 to support teachers. Blacks in Ways Station took every advantage of the school at Woodville. By the end of 1873, there were twenty to thirty students.[73]

71. Boston *Journal*, June 12, 8, 1878.
72. Savannah *Morning News*, July 18, 1873.
73. W. E. B. Du Bois (ed.), *Economic Co-operation Among Negro Americans* (Atlanta, 1907), 77; Jacqueline Jones, *Soldiers of Light and Love: Northern Teachers and Georgia Blacks, 1865–1873* (Chapel Hill, 1980), 63; Boston *Journal*, June 12, 1878.

William returned to Georgia toward the end of 1873 with sufficient money to
buy Woodville. Although he had failed to procure the $7,000 originally esti-
mated as necessary for the purchase and successful cultivation of the plantation, William did manage to raise $2,000 from voluntary subscriptions and,
using Woodville as collateral, an additional $1,200 loaned by "other parties."
Under the agreement the loan was to be repaid in twelve installments at 10 percent interest per annum, the first payment deferred until January, 1876. But
William's stay at home was short; soon after the purchase, he was lecturing in
Boston, New York, and anywhere else people might likely contribute to their
efforts in Georgia. By the end of 1874, he had won support from a wide range
of organizations and individuals, including the Society for Propagating the
Gospel, which contributed to the church, and Harper & Brothers in New York,
which donated books for the school.[74]

Ellen was responsible for running the plantation during William's long absences. Further improvements to the one-and-a-half-story frame schoolhouse
in the spring of 1874 allowed an increase in the number of students. They
ranged in age from seven to twenty, and some came from as far away as five
miles. The school's curriculum offered reading, writing, spelling, geography,
and arithmetic; history was added in 1875. Although the Crafts patterned the
Woodville Co-operative Farm School on Ockham, they never quite managed to
duplicate Ockham's successes. Not only were there continuous financial problems, but the Crafts ran into stiff opposition from whites in the area who saw
the school as a threat to the ultimate control and discipline of black labor. The
place for blacks was in the field not the schoolhouse. Nevertheless, by 1875, the
school was the finest for whites or blacks in the entire county.[75]

Seventy-five acres of rice, cotton, and peas were under cultivation in 1874,
and additional repairs were made to fences. In an attempt to streamline operations and increase cultivation, the Crafts instituted a number of changes at
Woodville. Land was distributed to tenants and each family was expected to
manage its own crop. The Crafts continued to provide tools and rations, and
the rents received went to maintain the plantation and the school. They also
undercut neighboring planters by reducing the rent from one-third to one-
fourth of the crop and the number of days' labor given from two to one. At the
start of the 1874 planting season, there were twelve tenant families at Wood-

74. Bryan County, Deed and Record Books G and J, County Court House, Pembroke, Ga.;
Boston *Journal,* June 8, 12, 1878; New York *Times,* December 8, 1874.
75. Boston *Daily Advertiser,* July 30, 1875; Boston *Journal,* June 8, 12, 1878.

ville; four more were added the following year. Ten new buildings were constructed and all the old ones repaired by the beginning of 1876. There were
four or five oxen, used by tenants to till the soil, several yearlings, cows, and a
horse. Some tenants prospered: Joe Mallard, who was penniless when he arrived at Woodville, had by 1876 acquired two mules and twenty hogs and had
paid off his debts—all within two years. Everything seemed to be going well in
early 1876.[76]

In addition, however, there were some disquieting signs that caused the
Crafts concern. Woodville was a plantation in name only. The crops, which
were never large, were insufficient to meet the needs of the tenants, who were
compelled to spend almost one-third of their time working at nearby plantations, on unfavorable terms, to make ends meet. All the money William raised
and most of the family's savings had gone into stocking and improving Woodville, with only marginal returns. In fact, by the middle of 1875 the family was
already $1,500 in debt. Moreover, relations with neighboring white plantation
owners deteriorated alarmingly after 1874, when a number of tenants left to
take advantage of the more lenient terms at Woodville. The school only made
matters worse. But even more alarming was the Crafts' independence; many
considered them a symbol of black potential. Ellen traveled around the area in
her buggy, administering to the medical needs of the people, prodding them to
send their children to school, and teaching the women sewing and other "domestic arts." Angry neighbors viewed the experiment at Woodville as nothing
more than an attempt to subvert traditional relationships between white land-
owners and black labor.[77]

William's participation in Radical Republican politics also contributed to the
family's problems with white neighbors. When William, Jr., returned from England in 1873, he too joined the party and in 1876 was elected the first district's
alternate delegate to the national Republican convention. William was named
chairman of the Republican congressional convention for the first district,
which met in Savannah in 1874, and was later nominated for the state senate.
But he was unsuccessful, largely because Democrats who controlled the Georgia
House gerrymandered southeastern constituencies so as to destroy black Republican power. One of their actions, for example, abolished all precincts in
Chatham County in 1873, making the Savannah courthouse the sole voting
place for the entire county. This meant that some of the 6,565 eligible black

76. Boston *Journal,* June 8, 12, 1878.
77. Boston *Daily Advertiser,* July 30, 1875.

voters (over one-half of the county's total voting population) had to travel up to twenty-five miles to cast their ballots. It also meant that those who were bold enough to come to the courthouse could be more easily intimidated.[78]

The early 1870s were particularly inauspicious for the kind of experiment the Crafts undertook at Woodville. The panic of 1873 resulted in a sharp drop in both cotton prices and land values, and just when a recovery seemed imminent, a cotton crop failure, drought, and floods throughout the state extended the depression. Political troubles in the late 1860s and early 1870s and the rise of the KKK further arrested economic growth. When the Freedmen's Bank failed in 1874, many southern blacks gave up hope of ever achieving economic, social, and political equality in the South. Far more serious, a group of missionaries working in Georgia reported in 1875, was "the loss of hope, of the stimulus to save, and the driving of the Negro back to the old reckless 'hand to mouth' mode of life."[79]

In spite of these difficulties, William and Ellen viewed the future optimistically. Although the Freedmen's Bank had failed, and blacks continued to be persecuted, William wrote his supporters in 1875 of "a better feeling now in the South between the white and black people than at any time since the war." Should conditions continue to improve, he concluded, "both races will advance much more rapidly in the immediate future than in the past." That was wishful thinking—all the while, the family's enemies were planning to destroy the Woodville experiment. William left Woodville in June, 1876, to attend the national Republican convention in Cincinnati and to consult with friends and acquaintances in Boston, hopeful that continued improvements at Woodville, especially the school, would attract increased aid from traditional supporters. But the Crafts' opponents were at work, chief among them the firm of Naylor and Company. In September they circulated a letter in Boston, which was reprinted in six of the city's newspapers, accusing the Crafts of "sailing under false colors." The letter, written by Barthold Schlesinger, German consul in Boston and a successful businessman who had connections with Naylor, charged that the Crafts took money collected for the development of Woodville and put it to their personal use. William promptly rejected the accusations as nothing more than "false and malicious" rumors. But his response did little to quiet suspicions, and many who had previously supported Woodville now re-

78. Savannah *Morning News*, August 21, October 6, 1874; Olive Hall Shadgett, *The Republican Party in Georgia from Reconstruction Through 1900* (Athens, Ga., 1964), 167.
79. W. E. B. Du Bois. *The Negro Landholder of Georgia* (Washington, D.C., 1901), 666–67.

fused to contribute. William had no other alternative but to sue Schlesinger for libel.[80]

Proving libel is never easy, and the Crafts had to face a whole array of additional difficulties. Because of his diplomatic status, Schlesinger could not be tried by a jury; the case had to be adjudicated by a panel of referees. For some inexplicable reason—possibly the delaying tactics of Schlesinger and his attorneys—the case was not heard until June, 1878. In the intervening eighteen months, Schlesinger and his supporters successfully scoured the area around Woodville and in Savannah for witnesses willing to testify against the Crafts. By the time the case came to trial, they had dredged up many affidavits, including one from the sheriff of Bryan County. The Crafts did not fare so well. Whenever Ellen took witnesses to Savannah to testify, under oath, that the accusations were false, the commissioner demanded a fee of $150 each before he would take their depositions. There seemed little hope that the Crafts would be awarded the $10,000 claimed in damages.[81]

The source of the accusation turned out to be George L. Appleton, a neighbor of the Crafts. It was Appleton who first leveled charges against them during a visit to Boston in 1876. He was also responsible for finding twenty-one witnesses who signed sworn statements against the Crafts in Georgia, and he brought to the trial three witnesses, two of whom were black.[82] The Crafts, with little on which to base their case, and confronted by hostile referees, confined their testimony to the history and growth of Woodville. All was going well, Ellen testified, until the latter part of 1876 when things got "pretty warm" around the plantation. The publication of the letter was the first salvo in a carefully coordinated attack on the Crafts' work.

They had every reason to believe that neighboring planters, including Appleton, were jealous and angered by the successful experiment at Woodville, especially those who had lost tenants to the Crafts and those who opposed the education of blacks. There is no doubt that the move against the Crafts was well organized. How else could one explain the wide dissemination of Schlesinger's letter, which was also reprinted in a number of New York and Savannah newspapers; why Appleton took the trouble to procure twenty-one depositions in Georgia; or why the authorities in Savannah frustrated Ellen's efforts by insisting on the exorbitant fee of $150 for each deposition?

80. Boston *Daily Advertiser*, July 30, 1875; Boston *Journal*, June 8, 1878; Sterling, *Black Foremothers*, 56.

81. Boston *Journal*, June 7, 1878; Sterling, *Black Foremothers*, 57.

82. Savannah *Morning News*, May 28, 1878.

The referees peremptorily dismissed all attempts to show that the attack was premeditated and deliberate. They refused to entertain the prosecution's argument that the extensive reprinting of Schlesinger's letter was a carefully coordinated effort and more than just an attempt by an individual worried that the Crafts were deceiving the public. Schlesinger's letter was very specific: it accused the Crafts of being impostors, of knowingly misleading the public about what was being done at Woodville, and of diverting money collected for the plantation to their personal use. Some of the evidence presented by the defendant bordered on the fantastic. There were those who said that they had never heard of a school at Woodville; others claimed that they had but knew that it was in poor condition and attended by only a handful of pupils. Such contradictory statements had little effect on the referees. But in many respects the Crafts did not do much to help their case. William, pleading he had misplaced his account book, was unable to show how they had spent almost $7,000 collected between 1873 and 1876. More damaging was their failure to inform contributors that the original plan to establish an agricultural cooperative had been scrapped in favor of a less ambitious effort.[83]

As if this were not enough, the Crafts had also lost the support of some of their staunchest friends long before the publication of Schlesinger's letter. Begging had never been popular among abolitionists. Since moving to Woodville, William had spent considerable time away from home on fund-raising trips while Ellen supervised work on the plantation. Wendell Phillips was one of those who found William's actions unacceptable. Not only were the Crafts attempting to beard the lion in his den, a risky business at best, but William's frequent absences, Phillips insisted, jeopardized the experiment and kept him separated unnecessarily from his family. There were some who even questioned William's commitment to Woodville because he had allowed his name to be included in a list of possible nominees for the post of minister to Liberia in late 1872. Even before the appearance of Schlesinger's letter, Phillips had refused to continue supporting the Crafts. It appears from Phillips' testimony at the trial that he also wondered about the strength of William's commitment to his family. He had allowed a son, possibly Brougham, to live off friends in Washington. Phillips thought that the Crafts, in their eagerness to accomplish their goals at Woodville, had ignored the needs of their children. Schlesinger also testified that Phillips informed him in 1877 that "he did not believe a man who professed to keep a school in the South for the negro should be North all

83. Boston *Journal*, June 7, 1878.

the time begging." William Still had expressed similar views. He reported to his brother, in 1873, that two of the Crafts' sons (possibly William, Jr., and Brougham) had turned up at his house, penniless. They had been boarding in Washington and were traveling to Boston to meet their father. Still asked his brother to make some discreet inquiries about William, that "mysterious man" who left his sons with little support and his wife alone in Georgia while he spent most of his time in Boston.[84] William never tried to calm his friends' concerns; to him, the cause took precedence over family responsibilities. He seems to have had few qualms about leaving the family in London for three and one-half years while he was in Dahomey.

Not unexpectedly, the referees ruled in favor of Schlesinger. The effect was devastating: not only did the Crafts have to pay their own court costs, but support for Woodville dried up overnight. Garrison's claim that the case was "unfortunate" was at best an understatement. There was nothing left for the Crafts to do but return to Woodville. Soon after, lack of funds forced them to close the school, and their children began drifting away from Woodville in search of jobs. Charles and Brougham were later employed at the United States Postal Service; William, Jr., returned to England in 1881 and he spent the rest of his life X there; and Ellen married Dr. William Crum of Charleston.[85]

All of their parents' efforts were now directed to the cultivation of the plantation. But money was always in short supply. Like most planters, the Crafts were at the mercy of local merchants, the only ones willing to extend credit for cultivation. Banks were reluctant because planters' only collateral often was their land. Moreover, the lines of credit to cover expenses of planting crops were too small to interest banks. In this situation small-town merchants, backed by county banks that supplied the money and by a series of lien laws passed between 1866 and 1875, rushed in to fill the breach. In the spring the farmers would arrange for credit with merchants and execute a crop lien, "sometimes with the additional security of a real estate or chattel mortgage." Because the size of a crop could not be guaranteed in advance, merchants invariably insisted on that "additional security." Although in the short run this system provided sorely needed capital to struggling farmers, in the long run it left them exposed to the vicissitudes of an unpredictable crop. The result was bankruptcy for

84. Sterling, *Black Foremothers*, 53; *New National Era*, January 16, 1873; William Still to James Still, October 31, 1873, in Still Letterbook, LGC.

85. Massachusetts Supreme Judicial Court, Suffolk County Referees' Award, April Term, 1878, case no. 1752; William Lloyd Garrison to H. F. Villard, May 24, June 14, 1878, both in ASP; Sterling, *Black Foremothers*, 59; see series of letters from William, Jr., and Ellen to F. W. Chesson and Elizabeth Nichols, 1881–82, in BFASS.

many planters and small farmers. One bad harvest meant farmers would be unable to meet the exorbitant credit charges. These were then carried over, with interest, to the following year. The inevitable consequence was the wholesale execution of mortgages and the acquisition of estates by merchants. Market tensions created by this system also kept land prices well below expected levels. These conditions were further exacerbated by cotton prices, which remained unnaturally low throughout the 1880s and the first half of the 1890s. As a result, there were few prosperous farmers during this period. Most of them, Banks observed, "did not make any entrepreneur's profits; and many of them not only failed to make normal returns to labor and capital, but even sank in the business much of the capital with which they began the period."[86]

We have no way of knowing exactly what the Crafts did in the years after 1878, as there are few records extant. It is reasonable to assume that no additional acres were cultivated beyond the 75 recorded in 1880, and that the Crafts continued to grow cotton and rice. Although slightly above the average acreage cultivated by black farmers, this fits into the pattern of black landholdings in the six coastal counties up to the turn of the century. By 1903 the average size of farms in the area varied from 13 to 53 acres for blacks and from 50 to 365 acres for whites.[87] In November, 1879, the Crafts were able to repay $1,200 loaned by Boston supporters in 1873, only by borrowing an additional $2,000 at 7 percent interest from the same source eight months earlier. Eager to help the Crafts' reduced effort, their friends deferred repayment of the first installment of the new loan until February, 1884. It appears that the second loan allowed the Crafts to function relatively unencumbered until 1887, when still depressed commodity prices forced them to mortgage 500 acres on a loan of $123 from J. G. Moore, a local merchant. At about the same time, the Crafts, apparently attempting to take advantage of continuing low land prices, purchased an additional 125 acres from Alfred Clark, a neighboring landowner. This acquisition, however, did not insulate them against financial pressure brought on by low prices for the produce grown at Woodville. As a result, in May, 1888, they had to mortgage 100 acres for $450 credit from Decker and Fawcett, merchants in Savannah.[88]

Just when things seemed likely to improve—cotton prices increased slightly at the end of the decade—disaster struck. Ellen died in 1891, and William lost

---

86. Robert Preston Brooks, *Georgia Studies: Selected Writings* (Athens, Ga., 1952), 69–72; Banks, *Economics of Land Tenure*, 49–52 (quotation, 52).
87. Census of 1880: Agriculture, Bryan County; Brooks, *Georgia Studies*, 121–22.
88. Bryan County, Deed and Record Book P, County Court House, Pembroke, Ga.

the one person whose strength and determination had sustained their efforts at Woodville through the most trying times. As she had requested, she was buried near her favorite oak tree on the plantation. Ellen's death also coincided with a return to the economic, social, and political uncertainties of the years imme- diately after the end of Reconstruction. The panic of 1893 caused cotton prices to fall once again. In October, 1891, Georgia passed its first Jim Crow law, which required railroads to provide separate accommodation. The legislature also revived the dreaded whipping post for convict labor and went so far as to make it illegal to chain white and black prisoners together in chain gangs. Lynch mobs cut a devastating swath across the state, and by 1903, Georgia, with 241 lynchings, was second only to Mississippi in its barbarism. One result was a marked drop in the value of land owned by blacks—between 1893 and 1895, for example, the value fell from $15 million to $13 million.[89]

As things grew worse, many southern blacks turned increasingly to African colonization as an alternative to the lynch mobs, Jim Crow laws, and the eco- nomic pillory of low cotton prices and being dispossessed of their small farms. One Georgian captured the mood of despair when he wrote that "we have little or no voice here and our wages are so small we scarcely have enough means to subsist upon. Taxation is so pending [heavy] that we cannot hold any real estate worth mentioning." It is no surprise that 200 blacks from Waco, Texas, heeding the call of the United States and Congo National Emigration Company, sold all their belongings and camped out at a railroad station to await the arrival of a train to the coast, where they were to board a boat for Africa. Although the trip never materialized, they were joined in Atlanta by 2,500 disappointed blacks who were eager to make a new start in Africa. Interest in emigration had grown to such a pitch that southern blacks fell easy prey to ruthless speculators and impostors. For instance, in 1894 one of these impostors managed to collect one dollar each from 3,000 impoverished black farmers in Hancock County, Georgia, who were interested in African emigration. The International Migra- tion Society claimed a membership of "many thousands" as interest in emigra- tion showed a dramatic increase in the winter of 1894–95. Two ships actually left Savannah in 1895 and 1896, carrying more than 500 emigrants to Liberia.[90]

It was in this atmosphere of growing uncertainty that William chose to go

89. Du Bois, *Negro Landholder*, 669; Clarence A. Bacote, "Negro Proscriptions, Protest and Proposed Solutions in Georgia, 1880–1908," *Journal of Southern History*, XXV (1959), 476–78; Clarence Albert Bacote, "The Negro in Georgia Politics, 1880–1908" (Ph.D. dissertation, Uni- versity of Chicago, 1955), 160–61.

90. Edwin S. Redkey, *Black Exodus: Black Nationalist and Back-to-Africa Movements, 1890–1910* (New Haven, 1969), 8, 156, 208–209.

on with the experiment at Woodville. Existing conditions would have caused braver and younger men to pause and question the wisdom of continuing. It is likely that William, seventy years old, had simply decided to live out the rest of his life at Woodville. The pattern of borrowing money from Decker and Fawcett continued with predictable frequency and results throughout the decade. By February, 1896, his creditors, recognizing a good thing when they saw it, demanded a mortgage on almost the entire estate for a loan of $1,000. Two months later, apparently trying to keep some of the land in the family, William deeded the remaining 125 acres, plus all of the animals and implements in his possession, to his sons Charles, Brougham, and Alfred for a combined loan of $500. But William's debts continued to mount as Woodville's losses annually increased. He was forced to borrow an additional $536 from the Southern Bank of Georgia in November, 1897, using Woodville, already mortgaged to Fawcett Brothers, now the Southern Fertilizer Company, as collateral.[91]

Despite a partial economic recovery in America after 1895, William could do little to extricate himself from debt. In November, 1899, Southern Fertilizer sued him for recovery of the balance on the 1896 loan and won a lien on Woodville. But the lien did not guarantee repayment of the debt. So the company contrived to have the land legally returned to William. Once that occurred and William was unable to meet his debt payments, the company then moved to have the plantation sold at public auction. Under state law, because the company possessed the senior lien, proceeds from the auction first had to cover all debts owed the company; only then could the Southern Bank reclaim monies owed it. Not surprisingly, Southern Fertilizer made the highest bid at the auction and acquired Woodville for a paltry $600, which was just sufficient to cover William's outstanding debts. This dispossession signaled the end of a determined effort to make a success of Woodville. A few days before the plantation finally passed into the hands of the Southern Fertilizer Company, William died at his daughter's home in Charleston, South Carolina.[92]

It was a frustrating end to an active and productive life. Through their daring escape from Macon and their activities in Boston and then in England, the Crafts contributed immeasurably to Anglo-American abolitionism. Their escape dramatized the moral turpitude of American slavery, and their attempted recapture heightened sectional conflict in the years before the Civil War. With

91. Bryan County, Deed and Record Book U, County Court House, Pembroke, Ga.
92. Bryan County, Deed and Record Books V and W, County Court House, Pembroke, Ga.; Minutes of the Superior Court, Savannah, Georgia Department of Archives and History; Charleston *Enquirer*, quoted in Savannah *Tribune*, February 17, 1900.

Douglass, the Remonds, Garnet, Pennington, Brown, Ward, and others, the Crafts played their part in influencing British opinion against American slavery, and William's work in Dahomey may well have contributed to the final extinction of the slave trade in that kingdom. The Crafts displayed an indomitable spirit, always willing to take risks in order to achieve their objectives. The decision to return to Georgia involved considerable (some said unnecessary) risks and demonstrated their commitment to employ their knowledge and skills for the elevation of the freedman. Their friend Thomas Hodgkin, writing to an associate prior to William's departure for Dahomey, best captured the depth of commitment and determination that characterized their lives. William, he wrote, "was not to be turned aside by the many representations of the dangers which would await him. . . . His manners and address are good and pleasing and whilst making himself a pattern of independence to his class there is nothing either cringing or assuming about him."[93] The same was true of Ellen.

93. Hodgkin to William Coppinger, November 28, 1862, in THP.

Robert Campbell
Reprinted from Robert Campbell, *A Pilgrimage to My Motherland*

Chapter III

Robert Campbell and the Triangle
of the Black Experience

Heightened interest in the history of the black experience in America has always brought in its wake an examination of transatlantic contacts. The studies of the Pan-African movement and its leading lights, Henry Sylvester Williams, W. E. B. Du Bois, and George Padmore, and biographies of Marcus Garvey and Edward Wilmot Blyden testify to the need to fill the lacunae in the historiography of the connections between Africa, black America, and the Caribbean. But more than just compensation for previous exclusion is contemplated and achieved by our examining the "triangle of the black experience." Such studies also tell us something about the extent of these contacts, the reasons for their persistence, and the men and women who attempted to forge transatlantic links. What is particularly fascinating is the fact that a significant number of the pioneers in this movement were West Indians, many of whom, like their black American counterparts, returned to Africa in the nineteenth century, some as missionaries, some to seek their fortunes in the "motherland," and still others to escape the ravages of New World racism. But few of these—and Blyden is a notable exception—were able to claim the experience of having lived and labored at the three points of the triangle. The Reverend Henry Highland Garnet did work for a number of years as a missionary in Jamaica, but he died soon after his arrival in Africa. There is, however, another contemporary of Blyden's, the Jamaican Robert Campbell, whose life in Kingston and in New York, Philadelphia, and Lagos has escaped the attention of historians.

Campbell was born in Kingston on May 7, 1829. Little is known of his parents or family. His mother was a mulatto and his father a Scotsman. Campbell reports that his maternal grandmother was of pure African blood, both her parents being African born. His maternal grandfather was an Englishman, Stephen Wood, who was deputy marshal of Kingston, Port Royal, and Saint Andrew.[1] Young Campbell grew up in an exciting and volatile period of Jamaican history, one that witnessed the abolition of slavery (1833), the passage of the Enfranchisement Law (1834), which extended voting rights to a larger number of colored men and established them as a potent political and economic force on the island, and the early demise of the Apprenticeship Scheme (1838). Spurred on by these victories, the coloreds quickened the pace of protest against all remaining social and political restrictions. The plantocracy reacted predictably to these attacks on their class interests, warning of the imminent collapse of the Jamaican economy and the destruction of social and political order. The fact that the colored class showed little concern for the freedmen did not matter to the Jamaican plantocracy. The significance of the convergence of these events in the 1830s lay precisely in their challenge to white planter hegemony.

Although the coloreds as a class continued to experience discrimination after 1834, the excesses were partially cushioned by the nature of British colonialism in Jamaica. By the first census of 1844, there were 293,128 blacks, 68,529 coloreds, and 15,776 whites. Here, as indeed throughout the Caribbean, the absence of a large resident planter class obliged the numerically small white population to concede some privileges to the coloreds as an insurance against a potentially rebellious black population. Restrictions on coloreds, though nagging, therefore, could never be total. Within this admittedly limited space, coloreds were able to cut an important niche for themselves in Jamaica's economic, social, and political life. Many were porters, servants, boatmen, and sailors, but there were some small shopkeepers, lawyers, and editors as well. In fact, a noteworthy percentage of trade between America and Jamaica was controlled by colored merchants. This they parlayed into significant political power by periodically forming interest groups that were generally short-lived, and by often threatening to forge an alliance with blacks. Jamaica, they insisted, was their country: "This is our native country," William Griffiths, a colored member of the militia, said. "We have no where to go: and consider it a hardship to

1. Robert Campbell to Lord Brougham, June 25, 1861, in Brougham Papers, The Library, University College, London; information on Stephen Wood provided by the archivist at the Institute of Jamaica, Kingston.

be superseded by foreigners who have been in the country for 10 or 12 months and who brought nothing with them."[2]

The coloreds also benefited from the increase in educational opportunities following emancipation. Traditionally, what little education black Jamaicans received had been under the auspices of churches eager to promote "moral and religious education." The former slaves, many now argued, had to be prepared for freedom if they were to play a productive role in the Jamaican economy. To proprietors, however, that preparation meant "industrial education," which had as its objective the teaching of skills necessary to maintain a viable plantation economy. Whatever its objectives, Jamaican education in the 1830s was in a sorry state. The Reverend Stewart Renshaw, a visiting American missionary, writing of the shortcomings of the educational system, observed that "a few, a very few are fit for subordinate clerkships: others can read and write and possess an indefinite admiration of education . . . but the great multitude are unfit for any occupation involving the practical application of the branches they profess to have studied." Gisela Eisner has estimated that in 1833, Jamaican schools were providing education for only about one in every fifteen children in the age group five to fifteen years. By 1836, even with the rapid rise in the number of schools, brought about in part by the Imperial Educational Grant and by the continuing work of missionaries, only one in five was receiving some form of education. More schools also required a larger number of teachers. In 1836, there were only 381 teachers on the island, many of then untrained. Despite the opening of Lady Mico's Charity School for teachers in 1836 and the Baptists' Calabar College in 1843, the demand for trained teachers could not be met. The situation worsened with the withdrawal of the Imperial Grant in 1846. In an attempt to fill the void, the Jamaican Assembly established the Board of Education in 1845, but in typical fashion failed to vote sufficient funds to make it effective. Soon after its formation, the board initiated plans for a normal school specifically to train teachers for industrial schools. The plan envisaged a joint venture with the Mico School, but when this failed to materialize, the board decided to establish its own school. The Normal School was finally opened in Spanish Town in August, 1847, but, because of the shortage of funds, only six students were enrolled; two more were added in October.[3]

2. Mavis Campbell, *The Dynamics of Change in a Slave Society: A Sociopolitical History of the Free Coloreds of Jamaica 1800–1865* (New York, 1976), 49; Gad J. Heuman, *Between Black and White: Race, Politics, and the Free Coloreds in Jamaica, 1792–1865* (Westport, Conn., 1981), 72.
3. Renshaw quoted in Carl Campbell, "Development of Vocational Training in Jamaica: First

Young Campbell took advantage of these new opportunities. Following the tradition of many youngsters of his class, he became a printer's apprentice around 1840. After five years he took a job at a local printing shop, but soon decided to enter the new Normal School, where he spent two years. There are no extant records of the school's curriculum, but we do know that the board's plans to teach agriculture as a science were never implemented because a competent instructor could not be found. On leaving the school, Campbell took a job as a parish schoolmaster in Kingston. When his alma mater closed in 1852, due to lack of funds, it was reported that only twenty-three students had enrolled, sixteen of whom graduated. Campbell was one of the school's eleven graduates who went into teaching.[4]

Brighter educational opportunities, however, could not mask growing problems in other areas. By the time of Campbell's graduation, the Jamaican economy was poised on the brink of total collapse, faced as it was with lower sugar prices, removal of preferential prices for West Indian sugar on the British market, and a dramatic decrease in the island's sugar production. In this situation Campbell and his new wife, whom he married soon after graduation, found the small teacher's salary inadequate. Douglass Hall estimates that in 1847 a teacher's salary was £70 per year while a master tradesman stood to make £150.[5] More important, Jamaica's flagging economy and the high level of unemployment meant that Campbell, even with his printer's skills, could not find another job to supplement his income.

As if this were not enough, living in Kingston was nothing short of dangerous. The British abolitionists John Candler and George Alexander, reporting on their visit to the West Indies, wrote that "had we been disposed to judge of Jamaica, as a whole, by the appearance of its two principal towns, we would have formed, at once, a most unfavourable opinion of its condition. The city of Kingston with 40,000 inhabitants, bears evident marks of decay; and large portions of it, which, a few years since, were destroyed by fire remain desolate, without signs of restoration." In 1850 the country was hit by a series of devastating epidemics. The first cholera epidemic killed thirty thousand people, roughly 8 percent of the population, between October, 1850, and early 1852. Before the country had time to recover, a smallpox epidemic took more lives.

Steps," *Caribbean Quarterly*, XI (1965), 17; Gisela Eisner, *Jamaica 1830–1930: A Study in Economic Growth* (Manchester, 1961), 326–30.

4. Campbell, "Development of Vocational Training," 26–29; Campbell to Brougham, June 25, 1861, in Brougham Papers.

5. Douglass Hall, *Free Jamaica 1838–1865: An Economic History* (New Haven, 1959), 218, 228.

The death rate was so high in Kingston during the cholera epidemic that, as one historian has written, "fresh graves had to be reopened. . . . In other cases people were left dying unattended and several days elapsed before the dead were buried." One contemporary estimated that five thousand died in Kingston alone before the end of 1850.[6]

It is no wonder that Campbell decided to emigrate sometime toward the end of 1851. Although he later attributed his decision to his inadequate teacher's salary and the lack of opportunities, to remain in Jamaica would have been to tempt fate. He and his family left for Central America in early 1852. Why he chose Nicaragua and then Panama is unknown, but he might have been influenced by the fact that since 1830 a number of Jamaicans had gone to the area, especially Costa Rica, as mercenaries to fight in the civil wars that plagued those countries for almost twenty years. Indeed, Jamaican emigration to Central America increased dramatically—an estimated three thousand were working on the construction of the Panama railway in 1854. But there were few opportunities for the ambitious Campbell, who was eager to establish himself in a secure position. Not only were civil wars endemic, but American filibusters attacked periodically, bombarding and generally terrorizing the coastal towns. Not surprisingly, Campbell found "neither of these places . . . suitable as a place of abode, the society at the time consisting generally of a debased class of adventurers from almost all parts of the world, but principally from the United States."[7]

One year after his arrival in Central America, Campbell was on the move again, this time to New York. But his hopes of success were quickly dashed—no one would employ him because he was black. This was indeed a new and very traumatic experience for Campbell. A colored Jamaican—with all that his color implied in his native land—was dramatically transformed, as it were, from a brown man, who "when he had his hat on few people would know whether he was black or not," to a black person. America, it appeared, neither knew nor chose to cater to the subtleties of Jamaican race and class distinctions. The experience had a salutary effect on Campbell; it was indeed a racial baptism of fire for the young Jamaican. Finally, after Campbell spent considerable time looking for work, John A. Grey, an Englishman and an associate of Lewis Tap-

6. *Anti Slavery Reporter*, April 1, January 1, 1851; Eisner, *Jamaica*, 338; M. Campbell, *The Dynamics of Change*, 266–67.
7. Leslie B. Rout, Jr., *The African Experience in Spanish America: 1502 to the Present Day* (Cambridge, England, 1976), 268; Hall, *Free Jamaica*, 221; Campbell to Brougham, June 25, 1861, in Brougham Papers.

pan's, employed Campbell in his small printing shop in Brooklyn.[8] Campbell worked with Grey for almost two years, all the while looking around for a better position. This came in 1855 when the Institute for Colored Youth (ICY) in Philadelphia advertised for a principal, Charles Reason having recently retired.

The ICY was established in the mid-1830s with a bequest of $10,000 from Richard Humphreys, a former West Indian slaveholder. According to Humphreys' will, the money was to be used for instructing the "descendants of the African race in school learning, in the various branches of the mechanic arts and trades and in agriculture, in order to prepare, fit, and qualify them to act as teachers." The institute was plagued by financial problems during its early existence. Not until October, 1840, was the first "Farm School" opened, attended by five boys from the Shelter for Colored Orphans in Philadelphia. Not only was money to run the school in short supply, but the students continually rebelled against the "stringent rules and regulations" that governed their daily lives. Property was burned and some students ran away. As a consequence, the school was closed in September, 1843, and not opened again until March, 1845. Surprisingly, the managers decided to stiffen the rules, demanding that students follow a rigorous 5:00 A.M. to 9:00 P.M. schedule. The outcome was predictable: students again rebelled, forcing the closure of the school in April, 1846.[9]

The Board of Managers did not meet again until 1848, when it was decided to apprentice students to local black mechanics. The mechanics would accept apprentices at $50 each only if the board arranged for the students to receive literary training in the evenings. Once the terms of the agreement had been settled, the mechanics formed their own board and hired a teacher in October, 1849. Within one month of opening, thirty pupils were enrolled, the number climbing to forty-three by the end of the 1850 school term. Prodded by the mechanics, the Quaker supervisors agreed to the establishment of a day school, which was opened in 1852 with Charles Reason as principal and Grace A. Mapps as head of the female department.[10]

The agreement between the Quaker managers and the black mechanics demonstrated black Philadelphians' determination to provide their children

8. *Anti Slavery Reporter*, July 1, 1859; Campbell to Brougham, June 25, 1861, in Brougham Papers; Wilson's *Business Directory of New York City, 1852–3*.

9. *Cheyney Training School for Teachers* (Cheyney, Pa., 1914–15), 5; Linda Marie Perkins, "Quaker Beneficence and Black Control: The Institute for Colored Youth 1852–1903," in Vincent P. Franklin and James D. Anderson (eds.), *New Perspectives on Black Educational History* (Boston, 1978), 20–21; Milton M. James, "The Institute for Colored Youth," *Negro History Bulletin*, XXI (1958), 83–84.

10. Perkins, "Quaker Beneficence," in Franklin and Anderson (eds.), *New Perspectives*, 20–21.

with an adequate education in the face of widespread discrimination. The importance of education to the black community had prompted earlier attempts to start independent black schools. Throughout the nineteenth century, organizations and individuals in the black community sponsored a number of schools for black children. In 1822 the objectives outlined by the Pennsylvania Augustine Society for the Education of People of Colour reflected this spirit of commitment. "It is our unquestionable duty," the society stated in part, "which we owe to ourselves, to our posterity, and our God, who has endowed us with intellectual powers, to use the best energies of our minds and our hearts in devising and adapting the most effectual means to procure for our children a more extensive and useful education than we heretofore had the power to effect."[11] Although most of these efforts were short-lived, they did establish a tradition of black community involvement in education on which the ICY could build.

Soon after his arrival at the school, Reason introduced mathematics, book-keeping, elocution, and natural philosophy, among other subjects, to develop a sound academic curriculum. A library was opened and a lecture series on scientific subjects instituted, both free to the black community. The board also agreed to a suggestion from Sarah Douglass to merge her school for girls with the ICY. This was effected in May, 1853, and Douglass' school became the Preparatory Department of the institute. By the time Reason resigned in late 1855, the institute's future seemed assured. There were fifty-five pupils enrolled in the high school, and fifteen girls in Douglass' department. Admission standards were raised in an attempt to attract more skilled and capable students. "Although not high in the elementary branches of a plain English education," the board reported, the new standards "proved to be beyond the reaches of the great number, and required more diligence and application than they had been accustomed to use in the schools they had attended." Over the next five years, the period during which Campbell was associated with the ICY, course offerings and the number of pupils increased dramatically, and students' skills improved markedly. This growth continued, and by the end of the 1880s, almost three-quarters of the teachers in black schools in Philadelphia and Camden, New Jersey, were graduates of the institute.[12]

In the fall of 1855 the board received a number of applications in response to

11. Vincent P. Franklin, *The Education of Black Philadelphia: The Social and Educational History of a Minority Community, 1900–1950* (Philadelphia, 1979), 31.

12. Perkins, "Quaker Beneficence," in Franklin and Anderson (eds.), *New Perspectives*, 22; ICY, Annual Report, 1855, in American Philosophical Society Library, Philadelphia; C. F. H. Conyers, "A History of the Cheyney State Teachers College, 1837–1951" (Ed.D. dissertation, New York University, 1960), 112, 181.

its advertisement for a new principal and decided to employ two teachers to replace Reason. Campbell was one; the other was Ebenezer Bassett, a graduate of the Connecticut State Normal School and a former student at Yale College. Bassett was appointed principal at $600 per year, and Campbell, who was responsible for teaching natural sciences, geography, elementary algebra, and Latin, was named assistant principal at $400. Campbell's salary was raised to $600 in September, 1857. The double appointment meant that the institute could diversify and improve its curriculum. By 1856, trigonometry and higher algebra were added. During the following academic year, the high school was reorganized into introductory, junior, and senior years. In the first year geography, history, elements of natural science, and the three Rs were taught; English grammar, elementary algebra, history, bookkeeping, and elements of anatomy and physiology in the junior; and geometry, trigonometry, elements of natural philosophy, chemistry, anatomy, physiology, Latin, and mental philosophy in the senior. At the end of 1857 the board announced proudly that the institute was attracting attention and visitors from many parts of the country. "It is doubtful," the board reported, "whether the pupils of any school in the city of similar grade could have acquitted themselves more credibly." In the same year, William H. Johnson of Lancaster, Pennsylvania, a teacher with many years' experience, confirmed the board's enthusiasm and confidence after he visited briefly during the school's annual examination.[13]

Throughout his tenure, Campbell also taught evening classes. These were lecture series open to the public. The first series, consisting of twelve lectures on electricity, astronomy, and anatomy, among other topics, were all "illustrated by interesting experiments" and ran from February to April, 1856. Surprisingly, the series attracted few students, but both Campbell and the board anticipated better attendance at subsequent lectures. The second series of seventeen lectures ran from late 1856 to February, 1857. Enrollment for the early lectures seemed to confirm their optimism, but attendance fell off rapidly toward the end. A number of "leading men among the colored people" met and prepared notices promoting the classes. Although these notices were read from the pulpits of Philadelphia's black churches and had the support of the community's leading lights, attendance showed little improvement. Nonetheless, the board and its black supporters, convinced that these lectures should form an integral part of the education offered the black community, persisted in their

13. ICY, Board of Managers, Minute Book, 1855–1866, and Annual Report, 1857, both in American Philosophical Society Library; William H. Johnson, "Institute for Colored Youth, Philadelphia," *Pennsylvania School Journal*, June, 1857, p. 387.

efforts, and Campbell was commissioned to give a third series of seventeen lectures. Attendance showed only marginal improvement. In later years the series was discontinued, and prominent black Americans, like Frederick Douglass and William Wells Brown, were invited to lecture.[14]

Campbell's training at the Jamaican Normal School could not possibly have prepared him to teach such diverse subjects. Aware of his limits and driven at times by an almost frenetic desire for self-improvement, Campbell sought every opportunity to improve his skills and expand his knowledge. It was this drive that prompted him to enroll in a series of scientific lectures organized by the Franklin Institute of Philadelphia. Unfortunately for Campbell, his color got in the way of his efforts. When in November, 1856, he applied to the Franklin Institute's agent for a ticket to attend the lectures, he was informed that he would not need one until the end of the introductory week. It was obvious that the agent was stalling, in the hope that Campbell would withdraw then. But he badly underestimated Campbell's determination. Campbell's reapplication forced the agent to admit that the institute prohibited black attendance. Unable to accept that proscription quietly, Campbell wrote the managers of the institute, demanding to know if they endorsed their agent's position. Trying to skirt the issue, the managers offered Campbell a free ticket, on the grounds that he was a teacher at an incorporated institution. Confronted by Campbell's persistence and wary of setting an embarrassing precedent of selling a ticket to a black person, the managers took refuge in a patently spurious act of generosity. But Campbell would have none of it. He refused the offer, for it violated all the principles he held most dear. "Were they in the habit of presenting complementary tickets to teachers," he wrote his confidant Alfred Cope, a member of the board of ICY, "I would accept it. They are not and I shall be no exception." If the managers "deem it wrong for respectable men of different complexions to partake of knowledge in common, then let them as scientific men, let them as the assumed instructors of the public, fearlessly proclaim it. I could then pity the distortion of their judgement, but would respect their honesty. On the other hand, if they do not, why cater to the weakness and prejudice of the vulgar—why on any pretense evade a direct issue in this matter?"[15]

The offer of a free ticket was as much as the managers of the Franklin Institute were willing to concede to Campbell. His hope that scientific men would

14. ICY, Annual Report, 1856, 1857.
15. Robert Campbell to Managers, Franklin Institute, November 12, 1856, Campbell to Alfred Cope, November 17, 1856, both in Richard Humphreys Foundation, Friends Historical Library, Swarthmore College, Swarthmore, Pa.

not pander to "vulgar" discrimination was mere wishful thinking. Philadelphia's scientific and literary men had contributed their fair share to theories of black inferiority, a fact reinforced in 1858 by their response to the Banneker Literary Institute. Founded by blacks in 1853, the institute worked for the "mental improvement of its members by means of lectures, debates, etc. and the diffusion of useful knowledge among all who came within the pale of its influence." Its president, George Thomas Burrell, was librarian at the ICY, and its secretary, Jacob C. White, a colleague of Campbell's. It was White who nominated Campbell and Bassett for membership in the institute in May, 1856. Campbell played an active role in the society, sitting on a number of committees, collecting books for its library, and organizing public debates and lectures. He himself gave three lectures, "Chemistry of the Atmosphere," "Matter," and "Chemical Affinity."[16]

In April, 1858, the institute applied to join other literary societies as a member of the Literary Congress, due to meet in May. In response the congress appointed a committee of three, which attended events organized by the institute and unanimously reported in favor of including the institute as a full-fledged member. Ignoring the recommendation, the Literary Congress arbitrarily rejected the institute's application. Embarrassed, supporters suggested that the institute reapply, but they declined, insisting that "it would be a compromise of dignity to make an application after having been refused. It is a fact too evident to be gainsayed [sic] that the only objection that can be urged is founded in prejudice against color."[17]

Both incidents were symptomatic of the depth and strength of racism in the city. In fact, Philadelphia, beyond the ICY's walls, offered few sanctuaries from any kind of discrimination, vulgar or otherwise. Between 1829 and 1850, there were six major race riots in the city—many blacks were killed and beaten, and churches, schools, and homes were burned. There was also widespread segregation in churches, schools, and public transportation. It was in large measure to counteract the effects of racism that black Philadelphians created their own institutions and were so determined to make a success of the ICY.[18]

Campbell must have been well aware of the extent of American racism even in 1856 when he applied to the Franklin Institute, particularly in light of his

16. Banneker Literary Institute, Roll Book, 1854–1856, and Minutes, 1855–1859, both in LGC.
17. Banneker Literary Institute, Minutes, 1855–1859.
18. Theodore Hershberg, "Free Blacks in Antebellum Philadelphia: A Study of Ex-Slaves, Freeborn, and Socioeconomic Decline," *Journal of Social History*, V (1971–72), 183–209.

experiences in New York. This is not to suggest that that recognition would have persuaded Campbell not to apply for a ticket to the institute's lectures. On the contrary, the history of the black experience in America has clearly demonstrated that racism's defenses have only been breached by the persistent refusal of the oppressed to accept theories of their inferiority. But Campbell's lament may have hidden other motives. Responding to his letter to Cope, the Board of Managers of the ICY went to great lengths to cushion the blow of the rejection. In December, 1856, they purchased for Campbell a ticket to attend a series of lectures in the Department of Mines, Arts and Manufactures at the University of Pennsylvania. Campbell's attendance broke the color bar and, in so doing, might have represented a significant development in the fight against segregation in Philadelphia, but it had little immediate effect on the university's overall policy on the admission of blacks. W. E. B. Du Bois reported as late as 1896 that "within the memory of living men the University of Pennsylvania not only refused to admit Negroes as students, but even as listeners in the lecture halls." The board hailed Campbell's admission and the inclusion of his name in the university's printed catalog of students. "This respectful recognition," they reported, "is more deserving of notice, as an Institution in this city, one founded with benevolent intent for the encouragement of the Mechanic Arts refused on account of his color to sell him a ticket to their lectures."[19]

In spite of his successes at and contributions to the ICY, Campbell was clearly frustrated by these rather heavy-handed racial restrictions. It is, therefore, no surprise that when the opportunity presented itself, he chose to resign his position. He was invited by Martin R. Delany, in 1858, to become a member of the Niger Valley Exploring Party, which planned to inspect the area around Abeokuta, Nigeria, as the possible site for a settlement of free black Americans. Delany had already written Robert Douglass, the artist, and Dr. James H. Wilson, both of Philadelphia, inviting them to join the party. Douglass accepted, but Wilson declined and suggested Campbell as a replacement. Campbell promptly accepted and resigned from the ICY in November, 1858. The institute lost an able and well-respected teacher. Praising Campbell, the board worte that "he was a useful and energetic teacher, and with his mind fully devoted to his work would no doubt have continued a valuable aid to us." Fanny Jackson-Coppin, who would later become principal of the ICY, echoed these views. Campbell, she observed, "had the gift of imparting, and while at the

19. W. E. B. Du Bois, *The Philadelphia Negro* (1896; rpr. New York, 1967), 88; ICY, Annual Report, 1857.

Institute for Colored Youth endeared himself to its scholars by reason of that and many other worthy attributes." In December the students organized a farewell meeting in his honor, and to express their appreciation for his work, they presented him with a gold watch and chain and a copy of *Cosmos: Sketch of a Physical Description of the Universe*, the five-volume work by Alexander von Humboldt.[20]

It is difficult to determine exactly what prompted Campbell to give up a relatively secure position at the ICY for the uncertainties of Delany's effort, which was under attack from major black figures. American racism was clearly a contributing factor. On the national scene, the 1850s saw the political power of the South increase as northern politicians yielded to southern demands in a series of new laws: the Fugitive Slave Law (1850), the Kansas-Nebraska Act (1854), and the infamous Dred Scott decision (1857), in which the Supreme Court ruled that blacks as noncitizens had no rights that whites were bound to respect. Locally, his experiences with the Franklin Institute and the Literary Congress' refusal to admit the Banneker Literary Institute also convinced Campbell that there was little future for him in the United States. Most black Americans would have stayed to confront these growing restrictions, but Campbell, a West Indian, who had already shown his willingness to emigrate in search of a "better life," was not constrained by the same imperatives.

Campbell's decision was also influenced by the growing emigrationist movement among black Americans, the beginning of which coincided with his arrival in New York in 1853. In the following year, Delany convened his first emigrationist convention in Cleveland. Although this and subsequent meetings concentrated almost entirely on Haiti, Central America, and California as possible sites for the proposed colony, Delany's interest had, by 1857–1858, shifted to Africa. And in 1858, another emigrationist society—the African Civilization Society (AFCS)—was formed by the Reverend Henry Highland Garnet, and it was potential competition for Delany's Exploring Party. Proponents of emigrationism argued that a colony of black Americans would provide a homeland for those fleeing American racism and, through the production of cotton and other tropical staples, would compete with the South for world markets. Employing the economic propositions of the Free Produce movement, they hypothesized that free workers' cultivating cotton would be cheaper than slave

20. Martin R. Delany, "Report of the Niger Valley Exploring Party," in Howard H. Bell (ed.), *Search for a Place: Black Separatism and Africa, 1860* (Ann Arbor, 1971), 37–38; Fanny Jackson-Coppin, *Reminiscences of School Life, and Hints on Teaching* (Philadelphia, 1913), 156; ICY, Annual Report, 1859; Philadelphia *Public Ledger*, December 25, 1858.

labor. This competitive edge in the international market would ultimately undermine the profitability of southern cotton and force slaveholders to emancipate their slaves. The success of the colony would also create a "reflex reaction" among those who opted to stay in the United States, by enhancing their pride in black achievement and encouraging them to continue opposing slavery and race prejudice.[21]

Informing this "black nationality" was an evangelical strain, which, in language similar to that of contemporary European missionaries and humanitarians, saw black Americans as the bearers of "civilization" and Christianity to the "benighted" natives. Writing to English backers of the AFCS in 1859, Garnet articulated the missionary dimension of emigrationism. "We feel it our duty," he informed them, "as well as a privilege, to give the Gospel and Christian Civilization to our Fatherland. . . . With the blessing of God we hope to secure, as the results of our efforts, the triumph of the Gospel in Africa, and the consequent overthrow of idolatry and superstition; the destruction of the African Slave-Trade and Slavery; the diffusion of Christian principles of religion, law and order, in Central Africa; and the elevation of the race elsewhere." Campbell subscribed to the general tenets of the movement. The enterprise, he informed potential British supporters in 1859, "is of importance in the Evangelization and Civilization of Africa, and in affording an asylum in which the oppressed descendants of that country may find the means of developing their mental and moral faculties unimpeded by unjust restrictions, and is regarded of still greater importance in facilitating the production of those staples, particularly Cotton, which now are supplied to the world chiefly by Slave Labour."[22]

Throughout 1858 and 1859, Delany's movement was rent by internal dissent and bitter opposition from prominent black leaders, among them, Frederick Douglass. Delany's choosing Africa as the site of his colony elicited strong negative responses from those in the organization who, like the Reverend Theodore Holly, advocated a Haitian settlement. The third National Emigration Convention, which met in Chatham, Canada, in August, 1858, further undermined Delany's authority and leadership. Although the convention's report approved limited emigration of skilled black Americans to any country conducive to their betterment, it was couched in language uncharacteristically

21. See Richard Blackett, "Martin R. Delany and Robert Campbell: Black Americans in Search of an African Colony," *JNH*, LXII (1977), 1–25.
22. AFCS Circular, n.d., Campbell's Circular, May 13, 1859, both in BFASS.

conciliatory to other emigrationist sentiments, which had been castigated at previous meetings. The convention's aim, the report stated, was to bring all emigrationist views together in one national organization, without giving preference to any particular location. More surprising, the convention failed to endorse openly any form of emigration. All that it would do, the report stated, was "to hold its organization in readiness to put to use any openings which might be especially desired."[23]

How, then, was Delany to finance his trip without the official endorsement of the organization he had almost single-handedly created? In order to lend some legitimacy to his scheme, he attempted to form a new group, one with definite emigrationist leanings. This would, it was hoped, help generate the necessary funds. Delany turned to the Shadd family and a few other supporters in Chatham. Together they formed the African Civilization Society of Canada, which should not be confused with Garnet's society, and which disappeared almost as soon as it was established.[24] Confronted by growing black opposition, the virtual destruction of his emigrationist society, and a severe shortage of funds for his Exploring Party, Delany left for New York in November, 1858, hoping to attract support.

As was to be expected, these problems only bred skepticism and exacerbated existing internal divisions. By the time Delany went to New York, the Exploring Party had been reduced to three. Two of the original five members, Robert Douglass and Dr. Amos Aray, had withdrawn, leaving Delany, Campbell, and James W. Purnell. Campbell further increased Delany's difficulties by challenging his leadership of the party, or so Delany thought. Later he would accuse Campbell of openly consorting with the AFCS and accepting support from Philadelphia whites who advocated the total expatriation of free blacks to Africa in defiance of the strongest opposition from black Americans. There may have been some truth to the accusation, but the challenge appeared more an inadvertent consequence of Campbell's insensitivity to black Americans' passionate aversion to colonization than a carefully conceived ploy to wrest control from Delany. More to the point, Campbell might have been the unwitting tool of those Philadelphia colonizationists and supporters of the AFCS who were anxious to consolidate their position as leading proponents of black colonization in Africa. He might also have been influenced by conservative members of

23. Chatham *Tri Weekly Planet*, August 26, 1858; Delany, "Report of the Niger Valley Exploring Party," 39–40.
24. Abraham W. Shadd Ledger, November 23, 1858, in North Buxton Museum, North Buxton, Ontario.

the Board of Managers of the ICY, some of whom supported the AFCS and the American Colonization Society.

One of the leading advocates of both societies in Philadelphia was Benjamin Coates. Coates would later claim that "expediency," and an attempt to avoid the odium which blacks had for the ACS and its supporters, prompted him to suggest the formation of the AFCS. Confiding in the Reverend Alexander Crummell, he wrote of his longing for the day when "Dahomey and Ashanti as well as a larger part of the Egba and Yoruba countries—with the adjacent Kingdoms, will be Civilized and Christian States—forming part of the Greater Republic of Liberia." In fact, the emigrationist movement was given a decided boost by the publication in 1858 of Coates's pamphlet on the cotton cultivation in Africa. In it he argued that inasmuch as the profit motive created and sustained slavery, the development of an alternative, cheaper source of free-grown cotton in Africa would ultimately lead to the demise of southern slavery. This effort, he suggested, should be led and controlled by enterprising black men emigrating to Africa in small numbers over a period of years. The danger to Delany's efforts lay precisely in the fact that here was a supporter of the Colonization Society, which all blacks condemned as a proslavery organization, advocating a position in no way distinguishable from that of the Exploring Party. The presidency of Garnet notwithstanding, opponents of emigrationism were quick to expose the apparent ruse. George T. Downing called the AFCS "Mr. Benjamin Coates'" and an offshoot of the Colonization Society, both of which aimed to rid the country of the free black population. The association with Coates and other Philadelphians only increased Delany's problems and heightened his suspicions about Campbell's motives.[25]

Delany became suspicious when Campbell publicly announced, in October, 1858, that he had severed all relations with the Exploring Party. He wrote Frederick Douglass, of all people, stating that his name was being used by Delany without his sanction and "contrary to my expressed injunction." Although he supported the idea of exploring the Niger, he made it clear that he disapproved of Delany's operations. The plan was, he said, premature and

25. Benjamin Coates to Alexander Crummell, April 14, 1862, in Benjamin Coates Correspondence, Historical Society of Pennsylvania, Philadelphia; Benjamin Coates, *Suggestions on the Importance of the Cultivation of Cotton in Africa in Reference to the Abolition of Slavery in the United States Through the Organization of the African Civilization Society* (Philadelphia, 1848), 9; many black Americans agreed with Frederick Douglass when he said that Coates was the "real, but not ostensible head" of the AFCS (*Douglass Monthly*, February, 1859); Downing quoted in *Douglass Monthly*, January, 1859.

might not attract adequate financial support. It is likely that Campbell viewed the restrictions imposed by the Chatham meeting as effectively destroying the Exploring Party's chances of success. But Campbell's actions must have been influenced by other factors, which he chose not to reveal. Delany understandably regarded Campbell as a tool of his opponents. He disclosed that soon after the formation of the party was made public, a number of white Philadelphians set about undermining his position, by convincing Campbell that "we were *not ready* for any such *important* undertaking." In addition, they offered a "dissertation on the *disqualification* of the Chief of the Party, mentally and physically, *external* appearances and all." This line of argument, Delany pointed out, was so effective that many potential black supporters abandoned the cause.[26]

Whatever the validity of Delany's interpretation of events, Campbell's letter cast serious doubt on his credibility and his commitment. Delany's riposte was politically astute, raising as it did the issue of devious white influence, at a time when blacks were generally committed to independent action. More important, it provided a credible account of the reasons why the party failed to attract significant black support and why Delany was not responsible for that failure. Finally, condemning Campbell's apparent betrayal, Delany exploited American fears of outside interference in domestic affairs. Campbell, he asserted, had allowed himself to become the cat's-paw of the mission's opponents because, as a West Indian, he "did not understand those *white Americans*, and formed his opinion of *American* blacks and their capacity to 'lead' from the estimate they set upon them." As we shall see, there was some truth to Delany's broad assertions, yet it is impossible to determine whether the differences between the two men were a function simply of Campbell's West Indian background or of their competing for leadership of the Exploring Party. It is true that Campbell was not so committed as Delany to a policy of independence from white philanthropy. There is no evidence that Campbell was even remotely influenced by the first emigration convention's declaration that it was time for blacks to "make an issue, create an event, and establish a position" for themselves.[27] Nevertheless, Delany's account does appear to be an attempt to discredit black opposition, which developed independently of anything whites had to say about the

26. *Frederick Douglass Paper*, October 29, 1858, quoted in Floyd J. Miller, *The Search for a Black Nationality: Black Colonization and Emigration, 1787–1863* (Urbana, 1975), 193; Delany, "Report of the Niger Valley Exploring Party," 44.

27. Delany, "Report of the Niger Valley Exploring Party," 45, 29; Martin R. Delany, "The Political Destiny of the Colored Race," in Sterling Stuckey (ed.), *The Ideological Origins of Black Nationalism* (Boston, 1972), 205.

movement, by associating it with the deviousness of their attitudes to black organizations over which they had no control.

In addition, even Delany's supporters must have questioned his selection of Campbell, a person with no previous involvement in the movement. Delany was possibly acting in desperation to save the party. Not only had the Chatham convention destroyed his initial goals, but those to whom he first turned as potential members of the mission either declined or insisted on support for themselves and family, a demand Delany could not meet. Campbell, he explained, was accepted solely on the recommendation of Robert Douglass and James Wilson—a rather unusual way of selecting the members of such an important mission. Some even suggested that the choice of Campbell was a transparent attempt by Delany to wield absolute control over the party. If this was the case, then he badly miscalculated.

Campbell viewed restrictions imposed on the party by the Chatham convention, continuing opposition to emigrationism among the black leadership, and the formation of the AFCS as effectively destroying what little chance Delany had of successfully implementing his plans. Not only did he accept funds from whites, but by the end of the year the AFCS was receiving considerably more support from whites and blacks in Philadelphia and New York than was Delany. Campbell joined forces with the Reverend Theodore Bourne, corresponding secretary of the AFCS, in an attempt to co-opt Delany's expedition. In December, Campbell and his Philadelphia supporters, acting without Delany's approval, issued a circular that called for support of the mission. They observed that "the object of the expedition is to seek out, for a colony, a location possessing the advantages of a healthy climate, productive soil, and facilities for trade, and in which the natives are amicably disposed towards strangers, and inclined to appreciate the advantages of contact with civilization and Christianity." Those were exactly Delany's intentions before the Chatham meeting limited his objectives. Four vice-presidents of the AFCS were among those who signed the circular; another was Alfred Cope, a member of the ICY Board of Managers and a confidant of Campbell's. Others who signed were also supporters of the Pennsylvania State Colonization Society. The society subsequently agreed to contribute sixty dollars to Campbell's trip to Africa, with the clear understanding that he visit Liberia.[28]

28. Miller, *The Search for a Black Nationality*, 195; *North American and United States Gazette*, February 3, 1858; AFCS Circular, n.d., in BFASS; Pennsylvania State Colonization Society, Minute Book, Lincoln University, Oxford, Pa.

Campbell's actions not only threatened to usurp Delany's authority as leader of the expedition but also made it difficult to tell which society was responsible for the mission. This problem continued to haunt Delany until his successes in Britain in 1860 gave him sufficient leverage to assert his authority over African emigration. Campbell and the AFCS were responsible for fostering the confusion over leadership of the movement. While in Africa he corresponded regularly with members of the society, reporting on the mission. In fact, he wrote Benjamin Coates about the "Treaty" signed with the local chiefs, and it was generally believed by supporters and opponents in America and Britain that the agreement had been made with the AFCS. At a public meeting of the AFCS in March, 1860, Garnet continued the deception, announcing that he had recently received word from "our commissioners" on their progress in Africa. Garnet might have been trying to silence continuing black opposition to the mission with accounts of its success. But by the end of the year, Delany's successes in Britain, and his rise to undisputed leadership of the movement, forced the AFCS to abandon its claims. By January, 1861, Garnet would write in reply to James McCune Smith's criticism of the movement that Campbell and Delany "are not now, and probably never will be commissioners of the African Civilization Society." Campbell also publicly denied any connection with the AFCS, claiming that it was his policy to write to all other societies and individuals who had assisted him. His actions, he was at pains to point out, in no way recognized their authority over the mission.[29]

Although it should be added that Delany subsequently joined forces with the AFCS, Campbell was apparently being less than honest and might have been merely trimming his sails to adapt to the reality of Delany's triumphs. Campbell's actions seem to have been motivated more by expediency than principle, which understandably galled Delany. Acting in violation of all that Delany stood for, he and James Purnell had taken written recommendations by Coates and others to ACS headquarters, in February, 1859, in an attempt to win some financial backing for the expedition. Although the visit to Washington was unrewarding, the action provided further grist for the anti-emigrationist mill, which, given the circumstances, was something Delany could ill afford. Following his failure to win support from the ACS, Campbell left for England in April, 1859, without informing Delany. He carried letters of recommendation from Coates and others to Gerald Ralston, Liberian minister in London,

29. William Coppinger to Rev. Gurley, March 10, 1860, in ACS; *Weekly Anglo-African*, March 17, 1860, February 9, January 19, 1861.

and Dr. Thomas Hodgkin, a staunch supporter of the Colonization Society in Britain. This was more than Delany could stand. Such "mischievous interference," Delany warned, was the work of "enemies of our race."[30]

Campbell also took with him letters of recommendation to Thomas Clegg, the Manchester cotton manufacturer who had long been involved in promoting cotton production in Africa. Clegg was aware of the history of black American efforts to establish a colony in Africa. Delany and two blacks from Wisconsin, Jonathan J. Myers and Ambrose Dudley, members of the "Mercantile Line of the Free Colored People of North America," an ephemeral organization with an unknown history, had written Clegg in 1858, asking about the most suitable place in Africa for a colony. Clegg helped Campbell issue his May circular that called on British philanthropists to support the expedition. In addition, Gerald Ralston introduced Campbell to Henry Christy, a prominent industrialist and philanthropist, and to Edmund Ashworth, a Bolton cotton manufacturer and later president of the Manchester Cotton Supply Association. Christy also made it possible for Campbell to consult maps of West Africa at the Royal Geographical Society.[31]

While in Britain, Campbell held a series of meetings with the British and Foreign Anti Slavery Society and the Church Missionary Society. The CMS was vital to the expedition's plans, as the society had long been involved in missionary work in Yorubaland and, along with Thomas Clegg, had promoted cotton cultivation there. The Reverend Henry Venn, secretary of the CMS, however, declined to support the Exploring Party's scheme, claiming that the movement was in disarray and that Campbell had broken with his friends in America. More to the point, Venn observed that Theodore Bourne, who was acting as agent of the AFCS in England, could not adequately explain the relationship between Campbell and the society, except to say that "if Mr. Campbell succeeded in establishing friendly relations with the chiefs and obtained territory the Society would be able to avail themselves of his position." Venn called the entire effort "visionary" and was generally opposed to the settlement of large numbers of black Americans in the area.[32] The disorganization of the movement in America, for which Campbell was partly responsible, was

30. For a fuller discussion of these events, see Blackett, "Martin R. Delany and Robert Campbell," 1–25; Delany, "Report of the Niger Valley Exploring Party," 44.
31. Joseph Hobbins to Secretary, June 7, 1858, Jonathan Myers, Ambrose Dudley, and Martin R. Delany to Hobbins, May 31, 1858, Henry Christy to Secretary, May 19, 1859, all in RGS; Manchester *Weekly Advertiser*, July 17, 1858; *Anti Slavery Reporter*, June 1, 1859.
32. Henry Venn to Henry Townsend, October 23, 1859, in CMS.

undermining his efforts to gain support from a wide spectrum of British philanthropists.

But where Campbell failed to win the backing of Venn and the CMS, abolitionists and cotton manufacturers were quick to endorse the movement. Ashworth applied to the Foreign Office for free passage for Campbell aboard one of the government-subsidized packets running between Liverpool and Lagos. He was effusive in his praise of the party's proposal, erroneously pointing out that the expedition was self-financed and independent of any other emigration society. More important, Ashworth argued that a successful colony would lead to an increase in "commercial intercourse with the natives and settlers advantageous to all parties." Like Christy, he saw black American settlers as the "skilled cultivators" necessary for the development and successful production of cotton and other crops. Ashworth recommended that the Foreign Office give the proposed colony its official seal of protection. As a result of Ashworth's and Christy's intercession, Campbell was given free passage to Lagos and a letter of introduction from the foreign secretary, Lord Malmesbury, to the acting consul in Lagos, Lieutenant Lodder. Lodder was instructed to give Campbell and his companions the same assistance and protection he would any foreign citizen, but he was warned that her majesty's government could not "undertake to guarantee the safety of the proposed settlement in Africa." In view of black Americans' opposition and the past difficulties in securing funds, Malmesbury's assurances must have raised Campbell's spirits. But all was not well, for in Malmesbury's copy of his reply to Ashworth, the word *colony* was scratched out and replaced by the word *settlement*. British interests in the area, as we shall see, would not tolerate the existence of an independent colony.[33]

The brief trip to England was financially rewarding. By the time Campbell sailed for Africa on June 24, he had collected more than £200, the expedition's major financing. Delany arrived in Lagos with a mere $23.[34] But Campbell's visit had another and more important effect; he won the backing of British cotton interests eager for alternative sources of supply to offset their almost total dependence on southern cotton. By 1859, British mills were consuming five-sevenths of American cotton production. Textile exports were valued at one-half of total exports, and the wages of 1.5 million operatives amounted to almost £25 million. It was estimated that £150 million were invested in mills

33. Edmund Ashworth to Foreign Office, May 30, 1859, Christy to Foreign Office, July 29, 1859, Foreign Office to Ashworth, London, June 11, 1859, all in FOD.
34. Christy to Lord Russell, July 29, 1859, in FOD; New York *Tribune*, February 10, 1860.

and machinery; the total tonnage of ships in trade was roughly two million tons; and some ten thousand seamen were employed.[35]

These circumstances led to the creation of the Manchester Cotton Supply Association in 1857. Although the association did not involve itself directly in the cultivation of cotton, it aimed "to obtain as full and reliable information as possible respecting the extent and capabilities of cotton cultivation in every country where it could be grown." Prime Minister Palmerston supported the association's efforts and instructed British representatives to inform the association about the cotton-growing potential of the countries to which they were accredited. In an attempt to implement this policy, Benjamin Campbell, consul at Lagos, visited Manchester in September, 1858, to speak to the association on the prospects of cotton growing in West Africa. So it is not surprising that Robert Campbell's proposals elicited considerable interest and backing from Lancashire cotton men. Campbell would later claim that it was precisely this potential source of support that prompted him to visit Britain on his way to Africa. "I was . . . determined," he wrote Lord John Russell, "that I should visit England to secure the cooperation particularly of those who desire the development of the cotton trade in Africa."[36]

On arrival in Lagos in July, Campbell visited Lodder and made contact with the Crowther family, who informed him that the Alake of Abeokuta would welcome the emigration of black Americans especially if they settled near the Ogun River between Lagos and Abeokuta.[37] The Crowthers were influential people. Samuel, Sr., the leading native missionary of the CMS, would later become the first bishop of that region. He had accompanied the ill-fated Niger River expedition sent out under the auspices of the British government in the early 1840s. Samuel, Jr., had studied medicine at London University, and Josiah had been trained at Thomas Clegg's Manchester factory. The Crowthers were the commissioners' main contact with the chiefs of Abeokuta. Campbell spent six weeks in Lagos, impatiently awaiting Delany's arrival from Liberia, before he went to Abeokuta to lay the groundwork for meetings with local authorities. Campbell's accounts of his weeks in Lagos suggest that he had come

35. *Anti Slavery Reporter*, April 2, 1860; Frank Lawrence Owsley, *King Cotton Diplomacy: Foreign Relations of the Confederate States of America* (Chicago, 1969), 3.

36. Isaac Watts, *The Cotton Supply Association: Its Origin and Progress* (Manchester, 1861), 10, 98; W. O. Anderson, "The Cotton Supply Association 1857–1872," *Empire Cotton Growing Review*, IX (1932), 133; Cotton Supply Association, *First Annual Report* (Manchester, 1858), 8–9; Campbell to Lord Russell, July 25, 1861, in FOD.

37. New York *Tribune*, October 14, 1860.

to accept Delany's leadership of the mission. It is impossible to determine the exact point at which this occurred, but Campbell's flexibility (or, more likely, expediency) in the matter might explain his waiting for Delany.

In Abeokuta, Campbell joined forces with the two younger Crowthers to form the Abeokuta Road Improvement Society, which proposed to build a road connecting Abeokuta, Aro, and Agbamaya to facilitate cotton transport between the interior and Lagos. Samuel, Jr., had helped build cart roads in the area, and the new society planned to expand the region's rudimentary road system. The Executive Committee consisted of Campbell and C. B. Macaulay and J. G. Hughes, native catechists of the CMS. In addition, the society elected a number of English missionaries as honorary members. Campbell also assisted the Reverend Henry Townsend, head of the CMS mission in Abeokuta, in improving his printing press used to publish the *Iwe Irohin*. Campbell (and Delany after his arrival) advised Samuel, Jr., on the reorganization of the Abeokuta Lyceum, and Campbell gave the first lecture on "the Dignity of Labour" at its reopening in January, 1860. Samuel, Jr., reported that over one hundred people attended Campbell's lecture that night, forty of whom were women, an occurrence he described as a hopeful sign for the area's development.[38]

In spite of these successes, there were some disturbing signs that did not augur well for the mission. Soon after his arrival in Abeokuta, Campbell found himself at loggerheads with Townsend, who was the Alake's confidant and who was unalterably opposed to the establishment of the colony at Abeokuta. Campbell, realizing that he had to move fast, met privately with Townsend. He explained the mission's objectives and its support among leading British abolitionists. Stretching the truth a little, he suggested that the Reverend Henry Venn had intended to give him a letter of introduction to Townsend. Townsend seemed temporarily mollified by these arguments (or he may have been simply biding his time), for he accompanied Campbell to a meeting with the Alake at which the purposes of the mission were outlined. Campbell also laid the groundwork for negotiations between Delany and the "principal chiefs." All that was left for Delany to do after his arrival on November 5 was to finalize the details of the agreement. Campbell, writing the next day to friends in America, reported that "our work is really finished, except that we must make a treaty with the authorities."[39]

38. *Cotton Supply Reporter*, August, 1860; Edward Bickersteth to the General Secretary, January 4, 1860, in MMS; J. F. A. Ajayi, *Christian Missions in Nigeria 1851–1891: The Making of a New Elite* (London, 1965), 12; S. Crowther, Jr., to Venn, October 10, 1859, February 5, 1860, both in CMS.
39. Robert Campbell, "A Pilgrimage to My Motherland: An Account of a Journey Among the

The "treaty" with the Alake was finally signed on December 27 and ratified by local chiefs the following day. The choice of the word *treaty* would return to haunt Delany and Campbell, for some feared that the proposed colony would ultimately displace missionary activity. Opposition to the treaty was initiated and led by Townsend. He had already written Venn about his serious reservations concerning these "American projects," settlements of "civilized heathenism," he called them, which would increase tensions in the region. The colony stood for all the things Townsend disliked most. It would be run and controlled by blacks, who had demonstrated that they could work and plan effectively only with the supervision of white men. More important, the colony had the support of the Crowthers, whom Townsend detested with a passion. The conflict first surfaced in 1841 when Sir Thomas Fowell Buxton chose Samuel, Sr., rather than Townsend, as missionary for the Niger River expedition. When it later appeared that Samuel, Sr., would become the first bishop of the west coast, Townsend was beside himself, convinced that no black man possessed the necessary qualities of leadership. He once wrote, "There is a view that we must not lose sight of viz., that as the negro feels a great respect for a white man that God gives a great talent to the white man in trust to be used for the negro's good." That trust could not be abrogated without violating the precepts of Christ's teaching.[40]

The dispute over the "treaty" began soon after Delany and Campbell left Lagos in early 1860 and continued well into 1861. In the version published by Delany and Campbell, the colony was to consist of skilled agriculturalists who would share their expertise with the local population. In return, they were permitted to settle on Egba land not otherwise occupied, and they had legal jurisdiction over matters directly affecting the settlement. They pledged, however, to respect Egba laws and to refer disputes to a commission that would have an equal number of Americans and Abeokutans and that was empowered to impose a solution.[41]

Opposition to the treaty was orchestrated by H. G. Foote, British consul at Lagos, who informed the Foreign Office in early 1861 that the Alake and the chiefs had declared the treaty "a downright fabrication." They had merely granted Delany's and Campbell's request to establish farms among the Egba.

Egbas and Yorubas of Central Africa in 1859–60," in Bell (ed.), *Search for a Place*, 170–71; *Colonization Herald*, February, 1860; New York *Colonization Journal*, January, 1860.
40. Townsend to Venn, September 6, 1859, February 7, 1860, February 8, 1861, all in CMS.
41. Delany, "Report of the Niger Valley Exploring Party," 77–78; Campbell, "A Pilgrimage to My Motherland," 248–50.

Foote included as supporting evidence a pledge signed by nine witnesses to the agreement who stated that no treaty was made or leave given to form a colony "without the walls of Abeokuta." The Alake could not, as the treaty implied, "alienate a foot of ground" without the consent of the Council of Elders, and Foote suggested that was never given. The treaty, therefore, was nothing but "so much waste paper." Foote's interpretation was shaped by his views of British colonial interests. Britain had only recently occupied Lagos and declared that the interior was its sphere of interest. In light of this fact, Foote proudly informed his superiors at the Foreign Office, "the Alake will not accept the person of any white man who does not come to him recommended by the English consul, the Church or Wesleyan Missionaries." A colony of black Americans, who would be independent of these sanctions, posed a direct threat to British interests. Not surprisingly, Campbell's interpretation of what transpired at the signing of the agreement differed substantially. "The treaty we concluded with the authorities of the place," he wrote, "was signed by only seven chiefs, the king's signature not included. To them we were sent especially by the King, an act which seemed to indicate, either that they alone were of sufficient consequence to take part in such a matter, or that they, by common consent were deemed the representatives of the rest." The Alake, Campbell pointed out, was acting not as an executive but as chairman of "all important councils."[42]

Less pro-Egba than Foote, acting British consul McCosky shared Delany's and Campbell's view of the agreement. McCosky undertook an extensive inquiry and concluded that the Alake had in fact signed the document in the presence of the elders and that the chiefs later appended their names. Subsequent denials by the authorities were the result of political machinations, and jealous individuals even suggested that "the immigrants would erect Forts and opportunity offered they would drive the natives from the country and take possession of the soil." McCosky left no doubt that the source of the opposition was Townsend, who used the pages of his paper to attack the proposed settlement. The Alake, Townsend wrote, was totally ignorant of any treaty. More significantly, even if a treaty had been agreed to, neither Delany nor Campbell could guarantee that only skilled and educated blacks would come to the colony. But Townsend's real interests lay elsewhere. Assurances had to be given to those who had labored for the civilization and Christianization of the area, he insisted, that their efforts would not be destroyed by the newcomers, who "with certain notions of freedom, republicanism, and contempt for their uncivilized

42. H. G. Foote to Foreign Office, March 4, April 6, 1861, both in FOD; Campbell, "A Pilgrimage to My Motherland," 173–74, 179–80.

fellowmen" would seriously undermine the missionaries' work. Characteristically, Townsend rose to his own defense. "There are white men still in Abeokuta," he wrote, "who were the pioneers of this great work and through the Mercy of God still have to watch over the work that they were providentially called upon to commence."[43] This was heady stuff indeed—but it had little to do with the nature of the treaty.

Support for Delany and Campbell came mainly from the Crowthers, influenced, no doubt, by their running feud with Townsend. Samuel, Jr., wrote the Exploring Party's backers in London that the agreement was legitimate and had been signed by the king in the presence of the elders and the chiefs' representatives. The only point of dispute, and one that both Campbell and Delany glossed over, was Article I, which the Alake insisted should be interpreted as affording the immigrants "the right and privilege of farming in common with the Egba people and of building their houses and residing in the town of Abeokuta and intermingling with the population." Samuel's father subsequently confirmed that Delany and Campbell accepted that interpretation. Accordingly, he reported, "a plan was given to Mr. Campbell in Abeokuta by Chief Antambala and a place was given to Dr. Delany at Lagos by King Dosumu." Samuel, Sr., saw this as a demonstration of the party's willingness "to disperse among the large population in different towns." Both Crowthers believed that Townsend's distortions were motivated more by fear of losing his position in Abeokuta than by a genuine desire to ensure the spread of "civilization." Of the nine people who signed the letter to the Foreign Office in support of Townsend's views, one was a teacher under Townsend, another was his interpreter, and six were Sierra Leone immigrants who, Samuel, Jr., suggested, were beholden to Townsend.[44]

It is difficult to piece together exactly what transpired at the signing of the treaty. In the view of some, like Sir Richard Burton, Delany and Campbell misunderstood Egba land laws and customs. Their writings suggest, however, that they were conversant with the nuances of these laws. "Landed tenure in Africa," Delany wrote, "is free, the occupant selecting as much as he can cultivate, holding it so long as he uses it, but cannot convey it to another." Campbell agreed, though he too may have overstated the case. "The tenure of property," he observed, "is as it is among civilized people, except as to land which is

43. McCosky to Foreign Office, June 5, 1861 (in which copies of the *Iwe Irohin* are enclosed), in FOD.

44. Three letters from S. Crowther, Jr., to African Aid Society, enclosed in AAS to Foreign Office, April 22, 1861, in FOD; S. Crowther, Sr., to Venn, April 4, 6, 1861, both in CMS.

deemed common property; every individual enjoys the right of taking unoc-
cupied land, as much as he can use, whenever and wherever he pleases. It is
deemed his property as long as he keeps it in use, after that, it is again common
property." Both Delany and Campbell were also sensitive to Egba political interests. They welcomed "civilized people among them as settlers," Campbell
pointed out, but the Egba were opposed to "independent colonies, the establishment of which among them . . . would be highly inexpedient."[45]

But these views, expressed after their return to America and after Townsend's opposition was made public, might have been their way of salvaging what
they could of the treaty. Even the Crowthers' interpretation suggested that the
colony's independence was questionable, a fact that must have caused the party
some concern. Delany and Campbell knew that a colony, as they consistently
called the proposed settlement, presupposed the possession of land, recognition of the niceties of Egba land law notwithstanding. The creation of an
"African nationality," Delany wrote, depended on three "elementary principles"—territory, population and a "great staple production."[46] Their initial
version of Article I enhanced the prospects of achieving these ends; the other
did not.

Opposition to Articles II and IV seems to have been more clear-cut. Article
II guaranteed the settlers total freedom to investigate and adjudicate disputes
among themselves; Article IV, though recognizing Egba law, nonetheless gave
them unusual powers in issues where "both parties were concerned." Then,
"an equal number of commissioners mutually agreed upon" were empowered to
resolve the problem. This would have meant a large measure of independence,
a situation that did not square with the Crowthers' interpretation of the Alake's
intention. Campbell saw the articles as giving the colony "the privilege of self
government,—a municipal government—only in matters affecting the colony."
But he had no doubt that in time the colony would "assume all the functions of
a national government, for the people are fast progressing in civilization, and
the existing laws which from their nature apply only to heathens would be
found inadequate for them." Ultimately, the rulers and their people would
be influenced by the settlers to adopt more "civilized" standards of government. Until then, the immigrants "must ever remember that the existing rulers
must be respected, for they only were the *bona fide* rulers of the place. The ef-

45. Delany, "Report of the Niger Valley Exploring Party," 117; Robert Campbell, *A Few Facts
Relating to Lagos, Abeokuta, and Other Sections of Central Africa* (Philadelphia, 1860), 6, 10.
46. Delany, "Report of the Niger Valley Exploring Party," 112.

fort should be to lift them up to the proper standard and not to supersede or crush them."[47]

Whether arising from expediency or simple confusion, these views likely increased skepticism among the Egba about the intent of the colony's leaders, and confirmed Townsend's worst fears. Campbell was no emigrationist in the mold of Delany, Crummell, or Garnet, but he did subscribe to some elements of their brand of Manifest Destiny. Most emigrationists believed that blacks from the New World, the most "civilized" of Africa's descendants, were ordained to lead the continent's redemption. The proposed colony was the harbinger of African advancement and civilization. The process had already begun. The industrious and enterprising Sierra Leoneans, Campbell wrote, had brought to Abeokuta and Lagos "a knowledge of some of the useful arts" and had doubtless been "the means of inaugurating a mighty work, which, now that it has accomplished its utmost, must be continued in a higher form by the more civilized of the same race, who for a thousand reasons, are best adapted to its successful prosecution."[48] It is no wonder Campbell was so convinced that Africans would ultimately realize that the colony's laws were precisely those that ensured the successful spread of Christianity and the establishment of "civilized" government.

But expediency also played a part in Campbell's views of the agreement. The Egba, he reiterated in the summer of 1861, were enthusiastic about black Americans coming to live among them, "expecting, in return, nothing more than that we should bring with us and diffuse among them education and a knowledge of the useful arts of life." This simplistic interpretation may have been Campbell's answer to Townsend's objections about the lack of guarantees. In fact, Campbell became increasingly defensive about the entire treaty. It was agreed to, he observed, "in order that we should be able to show to the friends and patrons of our movement, as well as our people in America some tangible evidence of the results of our labours in Africa. We drew up a document, perhaps rather inappropriately called a treaty, which received the full concurrence of every native authority of any note in Abeokuta. So far as they themselves were concerned, however, this was quite unnecessary, as without such a formality we could have gone to the country and enjoyed the same privileges in common with other immigrants."[49] Following the most circuitous route, Camp-

47. Campbell, *A Few Facts*, 12.
48. Campbell, "A Pilgrimage to My Motherland," 201.
49. Campbell to Lord Russell, July 25, 1861, in FOD.

bell, if not Delany, finally arrived at an interpretation similar to the Crowthers' and only slightly at variance with Townsend's.

This kind of temporizing not only allowed Townsend to mask his true intentions with apparently legitimate grounds for disagreement but also provided others with sufficient ammunition to attack the whole scheme. One of these was Sir Richard Burton, a major opponent of all philanthropic schemes for African advancement. Interestingly enough, his concern was with Campbell, not Delany, possibly because Campbell had the effrontery to publish a travelogue of his visit to West Africa, encroaching on what Burton considered his domain. How could Campbell, Burton asked, entitle his "little volume," which he wrote "or caused to be written," a visit to the lands of his forefathers when his forefathers were more English than African? This "cullured pussun," a representative of the "needy and greedy coloured fugitives from the western world," had displayed in his "brochure," Burton gratuitously commented, monumental ignorance and deviousness. Similarly, British philanthropists, burdened with misplaced benevolence, had only confused the issue further. Replacing American with African cotton was, for the time being, totally impractical, and any scheme that ignored this fact was the work of either devious minds or charlatans.[50]

Whatever the merits of the contending views, the situation was so confused that there seemed little hope that the agreement would be implemented. In addition, British interests after the occupation of Lagos, and London's desire to keep things quiet in the interior, could not accommodate an independent black colony in Abeokuta. Finally in summer, 1861, the Foreign Office declared it "unwise to attempt to procure for the American emigrants territorial rights or privileges which might hereafter lead to disputes and rouse the Chiefs and People of Abeokuta." London had grounds for concern, for six months later the Abeokutans, in a show of defiance encouraged, the Foreign Office believed, by Townsend and other missionaries, refused to admit the British vice-consul.[51]

Delany and Campbell had left Lagos for England to try to garner further support from British abolitionists and cotton men. They received a warm welcome in May, 1860. Campbell had paved the way during his previous visit, and the Reverend Theodore Bourne, agent of the African Civilization Society, had been actively promoting the Yoruba scheme since August, 1858. Campbell's

---

50. Sir Richard Burton, *Abeokuta and the Cameroons Mountains* (2 vols.; London, 1863), I, 56–57, 95, 269.

51. Foreign Office to AAS, July 22, 1861, Thomas Taylor to Foreign Office, February 24, 1862, both in FOD.

earlier visit and Bourne's activities led many to assume erroneously that the mission was sponsored by the AFCS. Bourne consistently informed his audiences, as he did at Bolton in September, 1859, that the society's agents on the west coast of Africa were "pioneering the way for those who were to follow." Even before the Exploring Party's arrival, Bourne had informed AFCS headquarters that plans were being developed for a large joint-stock company to assist in implementing the society's scheme. He issued a circular in April, 1860, calling for the formation of a British society, with branches throughout the United Kingdom, to help the society "to carry out the objects of promoting the Christian Civilization of Africa." The circular was authorized by a committee that would later form the nucleus of the African Aid Society.[52]

But Delany, still smarting from the difficulties he encountered in America, quickly seized the initiative. Exploiting his successes in Africa and the interest that generated in Britain, he eclipsed all competitors and reasserted his preeminence in African emigration. Two days after their arrival in London, Delany and Campbell attended a meeting, organized by Bourne, at Thomas Hodgkin's home. Aware that the British were generally partial to black Americans advocating and promoting their own causes, Delany moved to assert his leadership of the movement in Britain. By June, Bourne was rather unceremoniously shunted aside as Delany took full command. Although he continued to work for the cause, "the presence of the travellers," Hodgkin lamented, proved to be more an encumbrance than a boon. Bourne's commitment and dedication were unquestionable, but supporters were courting Delany solely because of his color, and such flattery, Hodgkin warned Garnet, might ultimately discredit the entire movement for African redemption.[53]

Hodgkin's fears were unfounded; though Bourne's position was indeed undermined, Delany proved a rousing success and, in so doing, enhanced the cause of African emigration. Stimulated by Delany's visit, Bourne's original committee met in July and formed the African Aid Society. The AAS was created, Delany insisted, primarily to aid "the *voluntary* emigration of colored people from America in general, and our movement as originated by colored people in particular." Its immediate objective, Delany consistently reiterated, was to forge an alliance of British capital, African labor, and black American

52. Bolton *Chronicle*, October 1, 1859; New York *Colonization Journal*, May, 1860; *Anti Slavery Reporter*, April 2, June 1, 1860.
53. Thomas Hodgkin to William Coppinger, June 30, 1860, Hodgkin to Henry Highland Garnet, August 29, 1860, both in THP; for a fuller discussion, see Richard Blackett, "In Search of International Support for African Colonization: Martin R. Delany's Visit to England, 1860," *Canadian Journal of History*, X (1975), 307–24.

expertise on which the colony's success depended. Agreements were signed with a number of commercial firms in Glasgow "for an immediate, active and practical prosecution of our enterprise." The AAS created a special fund to finance Delany's tour of Britain, offset debts incurred in Africa, and defray the cost of return tickets to America. By the end of the year, the "Campbell and Delany Fund" had expended £167.[54]

Campbell played a relatively small role during the visit to Britain, never once challenging Delany's leadership. Although he participated in the meetings that led to the formation of the AAS, his contributions were usually limited to seconding resolutions and giving descriptions of their trip to Africa. When they were invited to the Royal Geographical Society, for example, it was Delany who gave the address on behalf of the party. Experiences in Africa had likely taught Campbell to respect Delany's ability. Events in Britain, especially Bourne's removal as the principal proponent of emigration, could not have failed to impress Campbell that Delany was the undisputed leader there. Sometime in the autumn of 1860, Campbell went back to America to promote the cause until Delany's return in January, 1861.

Any hopes of support among black Americans were dashed soon afterward. While Delany and Campbell were in Africa supporters and opponents of the AFCS had carried on a running battle, which on many occasions threatened to degenerate into a free-for-all. Their return helped to stoke the fires. James McCune Smith, one of the society's leading opponents, accused them of condoning African slavery by signing an agreement that implicitly recognized the legitimacy of all Egba institutions. Campbell rose to the defense of the party's actions. Agreements of this sort, whether with the Alake or any other government, could not be construed as recognition or acceptance of existing oppression, Campbell argued. Given that law apart from equity was cant, Campbell insisted he would respect the domestic institutions in Abeokuta "no more than James McCune Smith would respect the Fugitive Slave bill by voting under the Constitution of the United States, by virtue of which that God-defying measure is sustained."[55] But the issue had become so heated that Campbell's reasoned arguments swayed few. To make matters worse, what little support there was for the colony vanished following the firing on Fort Sumter. War between the states now seemed unavoidable, and blacks, convinced that its conclusion

54. African Aid Society, *First Report from July 1860 to the 31st March, 1862* (London, n.d.), 2–3; Delany, "Report of the Niger Valley Exploring Party," 124–25, 142; G. R. Haywood to Louis Chamerovzow, August 2, 1860, in BFASS.
55. *Weekly Anglo-African*, January 5, 19, February 9, 1861.

would see the emancipation of the slaves and a lessening of racial discrimination, turned their attention inward.

Despite all these problems, Campbell remained doggedly optimistic that the party's successes would soon spark renewed interest in African emigration among black Americans. Bedecked in African robes, he lectured in churches and halls to sympathetic audiences on the merits of the agreement, the support it had won in Britain, and the role black Americans could play in achieving its goals. He was even invited to speak to the American Geographical and Statistical Society about his experiences in Africa. Wherever Campbell spoke, his theme was the same. Africa, he told an audience at Garnet's church in New York, afforded blacks the greatest opportunity for advancement. One has no way of determining the reaction to Campbell's call to emigrate, but his commitment to the cause was unequivocal. In Africa, he said, he could "do better than here, so far as making money is concerned. He could do better than in the West Indies where he was born—than in Central America which he had tried."[56]

Campbell continued to support the scheme throughout the winter of 1861. Although major black figures remained in opposition, there were still a few signs of hope. He and Delany did everything they could to whip up support for the colony. Campbell even published an abbreviated account of his trip as an aid to his lectures. Obviously aimed at informing prospective emigrants, the pamphlet described Africa's climate and fertile soil, the availability of land, the good government that welcomed skilled foreigners, the cost of transportation, and the promise of a measure of protection from the British government. Their lecture tours of the North and Canada proved, however, to be miserable failures. Delany's plans for going back to Africa in the spring with a small number of black families from Canada, the nucleus of the settlement, failed to attract sufficient financial backing. Even the AAS's efforts in Britain were disappointing. In April, Delany wrote Lord Russell, rather plaintively, requesting support to return in June. He was unceremoniously spurned, and the whole mission was doomed.[57]

Campbell's pamphlet was extracted from his much longer work published simultaneously in London and Philadelphia. Following the pattern established by most descriptions of travels in Africa, Campbell's book was part travelogue, heavily laced with anthropological observations, and part handbook for those considering emigration. Since Delany as leader of the mission gave an official

56. *Ibid.*, December 15, 1860; Brooklyn *Daily Eagle*, November 20, 1860.
57. Delany to Lord Russell, April 2, 1861, Russell to Delany, April 23, 1861, both in FOD.

report of the journey, Campbell was free to write a lively account spiced with humorous anecdotes. He also devoted considerable space to sustained refutations of contemporary views of African inferiority and laziness, racist views found in many British works on Africa. There was, he insisted, no foundation for those assertions; in fact, it would be difficult to find "a more industrious people on the face of the earth." This was precisely the kind of statement that irked Sir Richard Burton and prompted him to spend so much time on Campbell's views. He directed the full weight of his acerbic wit and prose against Campbell and those who insisted that blacks were the equal of white men. Making allowances for what he considered typical American overstatement, Burton challenged Campbell to find one white man in Abeokuta who would endorse his position. Any "English navvy, fed on beef and beer . . . would certainly knock up a dozen Egbas," Burton boldly asserted. The problem was not African idleness, but the "malarious fever-stricken, enervating, effeminizing" climate of West Africa, which shortened the workday and the worker's life.[58] Campbell disagreed; the Egba, he maintained, displayed all the elements necessary for their own progress. All that was needed was the guidance of understanding hearts and sympathetic minds.

Campbell never wavered in his commitment to return to Africa, all the criticism of the treaty from British missionaries and the opposition of leading black Americans notwithstanding. Although Delany seemed determined to emigrate to Africa as late as August, 1862, by the end of the year, Lincoln's promised Emancipation Proclamation and increased recruitment of blacks in Union forces promised a brighter future for black Americans. Not surprisingly, Delany abandoned his scheme for active involvement in the Union's cause. For Campbell, the West Indian, there was no comparable yearning or commitment. Even before the signing of the treaty, he had expressed his determination to return to Africa. "My home," he wrote supporters in America, "shall be Africa, though I be the only person from America; and I am satisfied that any man knowing the circumstances, who is not a fool, and is solicitous for his own welfare, having too a heart to labor for the good of his race, would come to the same conclusion."[59]

When in August, 1861, it appeared certain that they would fail to enroll sufficient support for the colony, Campbell left America with his wife and four children. He spent the next five months in England, preparing for the return to

58. Campbell, "A Pilgrimage to My Motherland," 184; Burton, *Abeokuta* I, 101–102.
59. *Douglass Monthly*, August, 1862; *Colonization Herald*, February, 1860.

Abeokuta. The plan, he informed a London audience, was to "take in some land, get labourers to plant cotton, and purchase all the cotton from the natives that his means would allow and ship it to this country." In order to accomplish this, Campbell shipped £250 worth of cotton machinery to Africa in October. The following month he participated in a meeting that Dr. Hodgkin arranged. They established the "Native African Association and Their Friends" to promote "African improvement by the energy and co-operation of men of African race."[60] Although Hodgkin and others aided Campbell during his stay in London, the association was nothing more than a paper organization. Campbell and his family finally sailed for Lagos in February, 1862, with financial support from the AAS.

Campbell had to abandon his plans for returning to Abeokuta because of continuing wars in the interior and the rather delicate state of British-Egba relations brought about by the Abeokutans' refusal to accept Thomas Taylor, the British vice-consul. Campbell decided to go to Lagos, which in those days was no paradise. The sandy soil was infertile and sanitation poor or nonexistent, circumstances that influenced the lives of every inhabitant of the town. But Lagos was a natural outlet for the rich hinterlands and potentially the most important entrepôt on the west coast of Africa. The unfortunate Taylor, who was so unceremoniously refused admission to Abeokuta, reported to the Foreign Office that Lagos "our recently-acquired possession is already a prosperous, and likely to become an important colony. It has, with some impediments many of the requisites that are necessary to make it so. It is the natural sea-port, or outlet, to some of the most fertile districts in Africa—districts, too, inhabited by the most industrious and enterprising tribes in the whole country." That potential drew both Europeans and black emigrants, most from Sierra Leone, Cuba, and Brazil, who were willing to chance the frequent bouts of cholera, smallpox, and malaria, as well as the fires that devastated large portions of the town, in the knowledge that money was to be made. One suspects that Campbell's earlier experiences in Kingston prepared him psychologically for the rigors of life in Lagos. Commerce, or, more correctly, trading, was the economic lifeblood of the town; agriculture was only important as a stimulus. Out of a population of roughly 36,000 in 1868, there were 165 people in agriculture, 63 in manufacturing, and 2,871 in commerce.[61]

60. London *Morning Star and Dial*, October 17, 1861; Hodgkin to [?], n.d., in THP.
61. *Anti Slavery Reporter*, November 1, 1864; J. A. O. Payne, *Payne's Lagos and Western African Almanack and Diary for 1868* (London, 1869).

Unable to put his cotton gin to use, Campbell wrote friends in America and Britain that he planned to start a newspaper. The first number of the *Anglo-African* appeared on June 6, 1863. The choice of title is indicative of Campbell's views on the prerequisites for African progress, which were the spread of British "civilization" and the self-improvement of the race. The title also reflected his association with a New York newspaper and magazine of the same name, for which he had written a couple of articles on Jamaican emancipation. The idea that a people's progress toward civilization depended on advancement coupled with moral uplift pervaded social thinking in the nineteenth century, and Campbell marshaled his many editorial skills in order to attain these objectives. The newspaper's success was attributable to Campbell's talent as an editor and to the service it provided the small but expanding literate public, especially among Sierra Leonean emigrants. Published weekly, it sold for threepence. Usually four pages long, the paper contained a section where novels were serialized and where local literary efforts and advertisements appeared. Its news coverage kept readers informed of developments in Europe, America, and the Caribbean, as well as in Lagos. The paper's small staff consisted of local lads, some trained by Campbell, others by Townsend. Campbell must have paid a fair wage, for Townsend later lamented that one of the young men trained at his Industrial Institute, and a former employee, had left to join Campbell at wages "beyond what my head schoolmaster gets."[62]

Even before the first number appeared, however, Governor Stanhope Freeman was strongly opposed—he viewed all newspapers, including the *Iwe Irohin*, as troublemakers. The governor wrote the Colonial Office, proposing "a tax upon Newspapers published in the colony as would preclude the possibility of their succeeding as monetary speculation." Local newspapers would only fan the animosities between groups in Lagos, he warned, pointing to Sierra Leone. There, newspapers exacerbated existing sectional differences, forcing the colonial authorities to impose a "trifling check on the liberty of the press." These "worse than worthless periodicals," he told his superiors, were the major engineers of "unfortunate disputes and ill feeling" in Britain's west coast colonies. Alternatively, he urged that the government permit the publication of only one newspaper, as in Gibraltar, which would be exempted from taxes, but which would be controlled by the authorities. But the colonial secretary was aware of the controversy surrounding attempts to silence the *New Era*, published in Sierra Leone by a West Indian, William Drape. The secretary wrote Freeman,

62. *African Repository*, December, 1862; *Anti Slavery Reporter*, January 1, 1863; *Anglo-African Magazine*, I (1859), 90–92, 151–53; Townsend to Venn, June, 30, 1863, in CMS.

suggesting a more cautious approach and refusing "to sanction such a pro-
hibitory measure."[63]

In spite of the duke of Newcastle's opposition to restrictions on the *Anglo-
African*, Freeman did attempt to wield control through extensive advertising.
There were those, like the Reverend A. A. Harrison, a CMS missionary, who
suggested that the governor had paid Campbell a "considerable sum" for these
advertisements, with the result that the paper was effectively "under the influence of the Government."[64] There may have been some truth to Harrison's
claim, but throughout the life of the paper, Campbell's independence consistently galled successive governors. Campbell had few alternatives in a town
where business houses were a rare sight. Local advertisements, on which commercial newspapers have traditionally depended for the major portion of their
revenue, were few and far between. Some issues contained a handful of government advertisements, and others had no advertisements from any source. Although the front page of the first issue was almost entirely taken up by government advertisements, this was not a regular occurrence. Campbell, therefore,
could not afford the luxury of rejecting government money when commercial
advertisers were virtually nonexistent. But no governor succeeded in buying
Campbell's allegiance, by either purchasing or withholding advertisements.

If it was Freeman's intention to control the views expressed in the *Anglo-
African*, Campbell had other ideas. He declared his independence in the first
issue: "To those who have any matter to communicate of interest or importance
to the public," he announced, "we shall at all times gladly devote a portion of
our space and feel obliged for their communication. But, once and for all, we
announce emphatically, that we shall take no notice of personal disputes, or
differences among individuals, except those differences involve questions of
importance to the public, and then we can only regard them from an abstract
point of view, and if possible, without reference to individuals." When he was
later accused of editorial bias and high-handedness, Campbell reiterated his
position. "*The Anglo-African* was established," he told his readers, "to promote
the interest and welfare of Lagos and its people, and not to serve those of any
party, but in all questions to advocate the side of right—right, not in the estimation of this man or that, but in the estimation of the editor; and hence we
shall never consult any one as to what we shall say or what we shall forebear to

63. Stanhope Freeman to Colonial Office, December 6, 1862, duke of Newcastle to Freeman,
January 1, 1863, both in COD; Christopher Fyfe, *A History of Sierra Leone* (London, 1962),
280–81.
64. Harrison to Venn, September 1, 1863, in CMS.

say."[65] Although the arrogant tenor of these comments disturbed some of his readers, the statements were more a reflection of Campbell's determination to maintain his independence, and what he considered best for the development of Lagos, than a general expression of opposition to the government or antipathy toward any particular group.

Unrestricted commercial expansion, Campbell consistently argued, held out the greatest promise for Lagos' development as a major trading center. During his first visit, Campbell had been impressed by the area's expanding trade, especially at Ijaye, by the number of craftsmen, and by the cottage cotton industry at Ilorin and other towns, which, he lamented, was being threatened by an influx of cheaper and better-made fabrics from Britain. These observations suggest two important implications. First, Campbell clearly recognized that Africans had already laid the foundation and possessed some of the skills necessary for future growth. Black American settlers in the proposed colony would further refine those skills. And second, Campbell assumed that the displacement of traditional African economies by viable local commercial enterprises was a logical evolution dictated by the laws of economic growth and transformation. Yet Campbell seems to have deliberately avoided substantive contacts with any of the British commercial houses trading in the region, even the West African Company (successor to the Company of African Merchants), the brainchild of Thomas Clegg, one of Campbell's major British supporters. Clegg worked closely with the Crowthers, the two sons moving to Lokoja as agents of the company, and, as we have seen, William Craft was appointed the company's agent at Whydah in 1863 while on a voluntary mission to the king of Dahomey.[66] In spite of his friendship with Clegg and the Crowthers, Campbell's views of economic growth and African self-improvement precluded significant involvement with the quasi-monopolistic commercial houses. This, however, is not to suggest that Campbell openly opposed their activities in Lagos, for that would have been futile, but only that he thought the future of the colony lay in a proliferation of viable local enterprises aided by external businesses.

Given its position, Lagos was dependent on open trade routes to the interior. But wars in the hinterlands lasted almost continuously during Campbell's years in Lagos, impeding the town's commercial development. Commenting on the way in which the Ijayi war (1860–1865) and the constant threats of Dahomean

65. *Anglo-African*, June 6, September 9, 1863.
66. Campbell, "A Pilgrimage to My Motherland," 223–28; Hodgkin to Craft, n.d., in THP; Ajayi, *Christian Missions*, 212.

attacks on Abeokuta affected the commercial prosperity of Lagos, one contemporary observed that "trade here is in a very bad state, and we shall all be ruined if things are allowed to go on as they have been latterly. The blockage of the river Ogun, and stopping everything going up to Abeokuta when the people there were expecting an attack from Dahomey has had a very bad effect." Since trade with the interior was crucial to Lagos' economy, the government had a duty, the town's commercial elite stated, to maintain and protect trade routes by any means at its disposal. A number of British and foreign merchants in Lagos, including Campbell, petitioned the Colonial Office in September, 1863, claiming that the frequent interruption of trade had "given rise to complications with surrounding tribes on which friendly disposition towards the Government and inhabitants we rely for the successful prosecution of our trade." The petitioners called on the Colonial Office to elect a strong governor who could safeguard their interests. Captain John J. Glover, they suggested, would be just such a man.[67]

By mid-1864, however, confidence in Glover's abilities to handle the situation had almost totally evaporated. More than any of his predecessors, Glover was quick to resort to gunboat diplomacy in relations with the people of the interior. In August, 1864, at the height of the Ijayi war, he withdrew British protection from Ikorodu, giving the Egba a free hand to take that town, mainly because Ikorodu would not resume its alliance with Ijebu-Ode. Glover assumed that a tilt toward the Egba would persuade them to reopen the Ogun River to trade with Lagos. But when it became apparent that the Egba would not budge, because they doubted Glover's sincerity, he ordered them to lift the siege of Ikorodu. When the Egba refused, Glover sent in soldiers and police. The governor's objectives were obvious. He deliberately maneuvered the Egba into a position, according to Saburi O. Biobaku, "where he could take the step of armed intervention which he had premeditated as the best means of ending the interior war."[68]

This subterfuge flew in the face of all that Campbell considered honorable. Although he acknowledged that the British withdrawal from Ikorodu could be perceived as an attempted compromise with the Egba, he was at a loss to understand the reasons for allowing the Egba attack on the town. If the Ikorodians, he argued, had instigated the conflict, then they should have been brought into line by the colony, but they had not started the war. Moreover, he

---

67. *African Times*, June 23, 1863; petition enclosed in John J. Glover to Colonial Office, September 10, 1863, in COD.
68. Saburi O. Biobaku, *The Egba and Their Neighbours* (London, 1957), 75.

found it ironic that Lagos had entered into an alliance with the Egba "who had insulted our people, despoiled us of our property, and heaped every indignity they could devise upon our heads . . . while the Ikorodians who were our friends and chief customers . . . who when our supply of corn, yams and other produce of daily consumption with us, were cut off by Abeokuta, supplied us with these things and saved us from the evils of famine, should be considered the foe."[69]

Although the Egba were driven from Ikorodu, suffering heavy losses, they refused to bow to Glover's high-handed policies. Motivated more by vindictiveness than sound policy, Glover then attempted to collect compensation for the loss of British goods in Egba territory. He imposed a 2.5 percent duty on all exports from Lagos to Abeokuta and ordered European merchants and native traders resident in Lagos not to export goods to Abeokuta. Campbell immediately attacked these policies as potentially ruinous to all merchants. He could not fathom the purpose of restrictions that curtailed the activities of British subjects, who were "entitled to British protection," while permitting the Egba to operate "without hindrance." As Campbell predicted, Glover's ban forced many commercial firms to close. Campbell estimated that the number dropped by almost two-thirds in thirty months. If, he reasoned, the object of participating in the wars was to facilitate trade, then customhouses, entry permits, duties, detentions, searches, and other restrictions were unnecessary. In attempting to exact full tribute from the Egba, Glover was retarding progress and civilization in West Africa. He predicted a gloomy future for the colony if these policies went unchecked. "Everything is dark and dismal but this one fact, that the present measures of the Lagos Government if allowed their full effect must result in retrogradation—that our civilization must be arrested and the labours alike of philanthropy, Christianity and commerce, all tending to the great end of civilization, must stand still."[70]

If civilization was to be attained through unfettered commercial growth and the spread of Christianity, its survival, Campbell maintained, could only be assured by the introduction of a sound education policy. Missionaries had taken the lead in organizing schools where the rudiments of an English education could be obtained. And the "elite" of Lagos (as they chose to call themselves) founded debating, scientific, and mutual improvement societies, Masonic lodges, and gymnastic clubs. As we have seen, Campbell had helped reorganize

69. *Anglo-African*, November 11, 1864.
70. *Ibid.*, September 23, 30, 1865.

the Abeokuta Lyceum in 1860. Since he was a former schoolteacher, his views on education carried considerable weight in the colony. Campbell used his paper to promote an education system that offered more than reading, writing, and arithmetic and that deemphasized religious instruction, though he insisted that moral training was an essential ingredient of schooling. The best school system was one that attempted to develop the "moral, intellectual and physical" faculties of its students. Teaching only the three Rs was grossly inadequate and outdated. Having mastered the rudiments made students no more educated than "the possession of an ample stock of tools renders its possessor a mechanic." Students must be trained to think, to apply acquired skills, and they must be able to develop these through further study and practice. More important, education had to be made available to all, and not just the rich: "In order that civilization should extend, and that men should be lifted out of their degradation, they must be educated." Thus, "the diffusion of learning—the cultivation of the habit of correct thinking—the discipline of the mind which is the consequence of study, particularly mathematics and a few other subjects which people often think a waste of time to acquire are together with religious truths" the surest means of ensuring the development of a "respectable community."[71] Throughout his years in Lagos, Campbell showed a keen interest in the development of education, attending the annual examinations of missionary schools and periodically making recommendations for changes in their curricula.

Campbell was also active in the fledgling literary and scientific life of Lagos. In October, 1866, he was one of the founders, along with a number of prominent Sierra Leone emigrants, of the short-lived Lagos Academy, which aimed to promote literature, arts, and science. The tradition of public debate fostered by the academy and other organizations led to the formation of the Lagos Mutual Improvement Society in 1879, which attempted to stimulate interest in science and the arts. The society's debates and discussions ranged over a variety of topics, including the study of local languages, Edward Wilmot Blyden's "Mohammedanism and the Negro Race," tribal loyalties, and polygamy. Campbell was elected the society's first president, and as he had done during the lecture series at the Institute for Colored Youth, he demonstrated many of the latest scientific discoveries. But Campbell was more than just a theoretician; he conducted extensive experiments in an effort to improve many of Lagos' products. For example, in the late 1860s he developed an improved form

71. *Ibid.*, July 18, September 9, 1863, December 16, 1865. Campbell organized a series of four public lectures, in late 1863, on human physiology and other topics; admission cost two shillings.

of colza oil, which was widely used in lamps, introduced a steam mill for making salt, and manufactured soap from local materials. Not surprisingly, when the Lagos Scientific Society was formed in the late 1870s under the patronage of the colonial administrator, Campbell was elected its president. Through his participation in these societies, he helped establish a tradition of intellectual investigation in these early years of the British colony. Campbell was recognized as one of Lagos' leading minds.[72]

Once the *Anglo-African* ceased publication in December, 1865, probably because of insufficient subscriptions and advertisements, Campbell turned to a series of commercial undertakings. As he had told a Brooklyn audience in 1861, there was money to be made in Lagos and he was determined to get his share. In 1863, Campbell began supplementing his income from the paper by selling merchandise from the office of the *Anglo-African*. Toward the end of the year he apparently financed the efforts of the Reverend J. M. Harden, a black American from the Southern Baptist Missionary Society, who had established a brickmaking factory at Ebute Metta on the mainland opposite Lagos. They formed a partnership, and, when the missionary died in mid-1864, Campbell took over the factory and continued the business until 1878. Brickmaking was important in this period as Lagos residents built more brick houses in an effort to reduce the occurrence of fires. By late 1866, Campbell was also involved in the Lagos Steam Sawing and Ginning Company. Its principal shareholders and directors were some of the most prominent members of Lagos' elite. The company had at its disposal a ten-horsepower engine and a circular saw bench and was making plans for constructing buildings for cotton cleaning. Like so many other ventures, however, the company soon dissolved. One historian of early colonial Lagos wrote that "the Lagos Steam Sawing and Ginning Company Limited, established in late 1866 had a short and rather typical career, for one of the characteristic patterns in the Lagos business world, (indeed in Lagos society in general), was much fanfare at the outset of an enterprise with illness and death often following rapidly from mal-practice and non-support."[73]

With the subsequent development and expansion of the marina facing the lagoon, Campbell moved his merchandise business to this more exclusive trading area. He continued his many experiments to improve locally produced soap and to develop a more commercially useful oil. In Apapa soon after its annexa-

---

72. S. Brown, "A History of the People of Lagos, 1852–1866" (Ph.D. dissertation, Northwestern University, 1964), 257–58, 157; J. A. O. Payne, *Payne's Lagos and West African Almanack and Diary for 1882* (London, 1883); *Eagle and Lagos Critic*, January 26, 1884; Lagos *Observer*, January 1, 1884, July 6, 20, 1882.

73. Brown, "A History of the People of Lagos," 143.

tion to Lagos in the early 1880s, he established a distillery to produce what he advertised as "Africana Canna or Pure Cane Juice Spirits." In a rather unusual testimonial, the colonial surgeon called it "a more wholesome stimulant than much of the imported liquors sold in Lagos." All the local newspapers added their praise for the new product but could not guarantee its success, and the Canna soon disappeared.[74]

It is difficult to assess Campbell's many commercial undertakings, especially in a volatile period during which businesses in Lagos rose and disappeared so rapidly. One local editor attributed most of these failures to Campbell's impatience. Chiding Campbell, he asked, "Are you forgetful of such a thing as a determination of purpose? Is your life so well insured as to admit to further experimentalizing? For your own sake I deprecate the versatility of your intellect. I deny your arguments that former experiments did not pay you because I am convinced that you have relinquished many of them on the threshold of success."[75] Success in early colonial Lagos demanded patience, which Campbell seemed to lack. The ease with which he moved from one country and job to another suggests a spirit driven by an almost frenetic desire to establish a reputation and find financial security. His commercial ventures were not all absolute failures, but neither were they instant successes, and that is exactly what Campbell seemed to hanker after. He stopped publishing his newspaper, for example, just when it appeared to have gained a reputation as one of the leading papers on the west coast, with agents in Sierra Leone, Gabon, Abeokuta, and London.

Campbell saw himself as the quintessential renaissance man, ordained by history to help lead Africa to its place among the comity of "civilized" nations. But his mercurial character could not accommodate the rather mundane, patient work required to translate experiments into commercial successes. There is no doubt that Campbell's was a fertile, inquisitive, and precise mind. Many of his acquaintances in America, Britain, and Lagos would have agreed with Gerald Ralston's view that he was "a most clever and industrious man."[76] But Campbell was impatient. He had come to Africa, he once said, not to roll barrels in competition with the ordinary folk of Lagos, but to utilize his skills for the improvement of life in the colony. As soon as experiments failed to show the expected results, he abandoned them.

Campbell's frustration was increased by repeated failures to derive any eco-

74. Lagos *Times*, November 9, 1881.
75. Lagos *Observer*, July 10, 1882.
76. Gerard Ralston to R. R. Gurley, July 24, 1859, in ACS.

nomic security from his experiments. In spite of its importance as a major sea-port on the west coast, Lagos was subject to the vicissitudes of wars in the interior. The population and the volume of trade grew only gradually during Campbell's years there. Many attempts were made to rationalize its administration, each new move apparently compounding the problem it sought to rectify. For example, in 1866 the town became part of a federated "West African Settlement" under a governor-in-chief who lived in Sierra Leone. Eight years later it was placed under the governor of the Gold Coast. Two years after Campbell's death it was again reorganized and made a separate colony.[77]

But if Campbell was relatively unsuccessful as a businessman, his contributions as editor, educator, "scientist," and man of learning could not be overlooked by the colonial administration. He became the factotum of local government, holding at different times the posts of government auctioneer, stipendary magistrate, acting colonial surveyor, and acting chief clerk and warehouse keeper, and he served on the Commercial Court of Tribunal. It was, however, as acting colonial surveyor that he made his greatest contribution to the government of Lagos. He held this position four times between 1866 and 1878. In 1866 he was appointed by Glover to survey Ebute Metta and lay out plots for purchase by Lagos residents. Seven years later he reported to the Colonial Office on the occupation of land at Ebute Metta and Apapa, recommending the continued settlement of the former as vitally important to the commercial prosperity of Lagos. It is likely that Campbell's brickmaking factory at Ebute Metta influenced his recommendations.

But Campbell was never named to a permanent post in the colonial administration. Although his training as an engineer was admittedly limited to the brief series of lectures he attended at the University of Pennsylvania in 1856, and knowledge acquired through independent study, racism rather than his lack of qualifications appears to have influenced the Colonial Office's decision. His experience was not unique; in almost every British colony, there were comparable instances in which competent colonials were permitted to fill acting posts but rarely permanent positions. Twice Campbell applied unsuccessfully to become assistant colonial surveyor. In correspondence between Lagos and London, a lack of qualifications was cited as the ostensible reason for denying his application. The real reason lay elsewhere. One local official suggested appointing a European at a salary twice as high as Campbell's and supplemented by a house and horse allowance. These liberal terms, he argued, would attract

77. Sir Alan Burns, *History of Nigeria* (1929; rpr. London, 1969), 138–39.

highly qualified Europeans to the colony. When no European could be found, a Sierra Leonean was named to the post with a salary and allowance identical to Campbell's.[78] It is clear that the administration had placed a ceiling on the salaries for blacks. Such examples of blatant racism could only have heightened Campbell's frustration.

Campbell was no radical or nationalist, nor was he an ardent emigrationist. Unlike Crummell and Garnet, he showed little interest in the missionary dimension of emigrationism, although he did subscribe to the notion that New World blacks had a special role to play in the elevation of Africa. New technical skills, practical education, and "legitimate" commerce would help move Africa from its semicivilized state, one in which men neither fully Christian nor totally heathen acquired "all the vices of the white man, but know little and practice less of his virtues." At no time did he endorse the shibboleth "Africa for the African" as Delany had. But Campbell did agree with Delany's view that to succeed as a state or a nation, blacks "must become self-reliant" and, in so doing, create their "own ways and means; and a trade created *in* Africa by civilized Africans, would be a national rock of 'everlasting ages.'"[79]

This is precisely what Campbell tried to achieve in Lagos. For more than twenty years he fought for improvements in the town's economic, educational, social, and general living conditions. On January 9, 1884, ten days before his death, Campbell attended a large meeting of merchants, traders, and other leading citizens of Lagos. They emphasized the need for better education, police protection, sanitation, customs, and public works, and they indicated that Lagos should be reestablished as a self-governing colony. Campbell called specifically for improvements in sanitary conditions, something he had promoted consistently since his arrival in 1862. Through his leadership in the Lagos Academy, the Scientific Society, the Mutual Improvement Society, and the Gymnastic Club, all of which he was instrumental in founding, Campbell influenced the literary, scientific, and sporting life of Lagos. He was, according to the Lagos *Observer*, one of the town's leading citizens. "Now is the mighty fallen," its editor wrote, "and the weapons of literature (we may well nigh say)

78. For an extensive discussion of one example, see Bridget Brereton, *Race Relations in Colonial Trinidad 1870–1900* (Cambridge, England, 1979); see Henry Fowler to Pope-Hennessey, August 18, 1872, Colonial Office to Keates, March 1, 1873, Berkeley to Pope-Hennessey, April 10, 1873, Campbell to Fowler, September 18, 1872, Berkeley to Administrator-in-Chief, April 23, 1873, Campbell to Acting Colonial Secretary, September 18, 1876, Lees to Freeling, August 26, 1877, all in COD.

79. Campbell, "A Pilgrimage to My Motherland," 238; Delany, "Report of the Niger Valley Exploring Party," 120.

perish! Twelve days ago the Colony learnt with profound sorrow, the loss it has sustained in the death of one of its representative brains: this indeed being the phrase that adequately describes a man of rare intellect, and versatility of learning."[80]

If Campbell was an Anglophile, he hoped and believed that English civilization, which he considered the most technologically sophisticated culture of the nineteenth century, could help Africa develop into well-ordered, economically viable, and highly skilled societies. To this end he worked, and whenever colonial administration policies threatened the attainment of these objectives, Campbell vigorously protested. Unlike other immigrants from Sierra Leone, Brazil, and Cuba, Campbell had no cultural or historical affinity with the peoples of Lagos and the interior, a fact which makes comparative assessments of their opinions and actions difficult. He neither rejected Western culture as alien nor considered assimilation into indigenous cultures practical. Aspects of Western culture that were useful, for example, commerce, education, scientific investigation, and Christianity, had to be harnessed for the benefit of Africa. From the moment in 1858 when he accepted Delany's invitation to join the Exploring Party until his death in 1884, Campbell displayed an unfailing commitment to the "advancement" of Africa.

80. Lagos *Observer*, January 31, November 27, 1884.

John Sella Martin
Courtesy of Moorland-Spingarn Research Center, Howard University, Washington, D.C.

Chapter IV

John Sella Martin

The Lion from the West

Writing in 1859, a correspondent from Lawrence, Massachusetts, observed that John Sella Martin was "one of those self-made men, who, by the inherent force of native ability and strength of character, have risen above their surroundings, and will make a broad and noble mark upon the record of the future, as one of the brightest intellects, and whose success is only equalled by his merit and genius."[1] It was a perspicacious assessment and one that Martin would live to fulfill. Although contemporaries generally agreed with these views, history has thrown a blanket of silence over one of nineteenth-century America's most commanding orators, an indefatigable worker for freedom and equality who won considerable international fame for his work for the Union's cause during the Civil War and for black improvement during Reconstruction. And all this occurred in the relatively brief period between his escape from slavery in 1856 and his untimely death twenty years later.

Martin was born a slave in Charlotte, North Carolina, in September, 1832. His mother, Winnifred, a mulatto, was owned by a Mrs. Henderson, whose nephew, a Mr. Martin, was to marry an heiress when she came of age. Until then, Mrs. Henderson reasoned, young Martin needed sufficient distractions to keep him away from other less wealthy white women who might jeopardize her plans. So she forced Winnifred into a relationship with Martin. But he showed absolutely no interest in his betrothed. In retaliation Martin was sent

1. *Weekly Anglo-African*, October 22, 1859.

off to Virginia to manage one of his aunt's estates, and Winnifred and her two children, John Sella and Caroline, were sold to a slave trader. It was to be the first in a series of sales; but at least for the moment, Winnifred was thankful that her family was still together. The three slaves joined a coffle heading for Columbus, Georgia, where they were bought by a Dr. Chipley. Life with the Chipleys was relatively uneventful until bankruptcy forced Chipley to sell his slaves three years later. Winnifred was sold to a Reverend Terry from Troop County, Alabama, Caroline to a Mr. Young from Mobile, and Sella to Edward Powers of Columbus. The separation, Martin later recalled, was his first realization of the full meaning of slavery, of being a slave, "a slave for life—a slave without a mother or a friend who could help me."[2]

Sella learned of free blacks from the gamblers who frequented the hotel where Powers lived. Their writing also piqued his curiosity, and the young slave set about learning to read and write. He approached the white boys with whom he played marbles, but they refused to help, fearful of breaking the law. But they did play a spelling game to test one another's proficiency. By paying careful attention, Stella learned to "spell by sound" before he could read. Soon he hit upon the idea of using his skills as a marble player to achieve his ends. He entered into partnership with a white boy, less adept than he, who agreed to teach Stella to read in exchange for a regular supply of marbles. Word spread among the small slave population, and Sella became the unofficial reader for his elders. These activities complicated his master's life. Powers, a northern usurer, had lived in the South for some time, and he feared that customers might use Sella's violating the law to stop paying their debts or even run him out of town. His ban on Stella proved totally ineffective. The little money Sella received from his reading had given him a measure of independence. Moreover, he had recently heard of his mother's whereabouts and was determined to go visit her.

It took almost a year before Sella could put his plan into operation. Equipped with a pass he had written, Sella slipped out of Columbus to visit his mother sixty miles away. It was a joyful reunion. But Sella stayed too long, pleading with his mother to escape. Knowing of Terry's brutality and fearing possible recapture, Winnifred refused to accompany her son. Discovered in his mother's cabin, Sella was put in irons and shipped off to Columbus, where he remained in jail for seven months. While in prison he met a Mr. Green, who took a liking

2. On Martin's life before his escape, see *Good Words*, May 1, June 1, 1867; Baptist W. Noel, *Freedom and Slavery in the United States of America* (London, 1863), 156–64.

to him, taught him grammar, history, and arithmetic, and, more important, told him about the North and Canada. Sella was finally released when his master developed an eye problem and needed the services of his slave. As Powers' eyesight deteriorated Sella became indispensable and frequently was asked by his master to read from newspapers and books. His faithfulness was rewarded in 1850, when he was freed under the terms of his master's will. Sella's elation was short-lived, however, for members of Powers' family successfully contested the will. The young slave was bought by a black man, who subsequently sold him to a black trader with whom Sella worked for five months on the Alabama River between Montgomery and Mobile.

Sella went through a succession of masters in the next few years, working as a barber's mate, as general help in a store, as a captain's messenger on a boat that plied the Tombigbee River between Columbus and Mobile, and as a steward on a Lake Pontchartrain boat. Sella encountered predictable problems when local authorities discovered he could read, or when his masters feared he might use contacts with northerners traveling the rivers and escape. Frustrated by such uncertainties, Sella began making plans for his escape sometime in 1855. The precipitating event was a quarrel with white employees who had grown jealous of his relatively high position as steward. Never one to conceal his anger or hold his tongue, Sella thought it best to leave the boat following a heated dispute with the barkeeper. Anxious to safeguard his investment, Sella's master, John Cody of New Orleans, began searching for someone to buy his intractable slave. But instead of finding a purchaser as Cody had instructed, Sella decided to escape.

Some months before, Sella had met a black sailor from Kentucky, and this acquaintance gave him the means to effect his plan. Under Louisiana law, black sailors had to provide written evidence from whites attesting to their freedom. Unable to read and worried about his papers, the Kentuckian had requested that Sella check their validity. Here was the chance Sella had been waiting for. Knowing that it was relatively easy to replace these papers, if adequate proof could be given that they were lost, Sella concealed them and persuaded his friend to apply for a new set. Armed with free papers and permission from Cody to work on boats between New Orleans and Vicksburg, Sella secured a job on a boat on the New Orleans–Saint Louis run. But his efforts seemed to be stymied just when success appeared imminent. Not to be fooled, the boat's clerk questioned the authenticity of the papers and refused to employ Sella without further verification. After all, the papers did describe the bearer as thirty-two years old, and Sella looked at least ten years younger. Fortunately the boat's pantryman, a free black who knew Sella in New Orleans but never knew him to be a slave, agreed to testify on his behalf.

But then Sella was struck by what he called a "painful uncertainty," knowing that the pantryman would be jailed when the escape was discovered. Sella suspended his immediate plans and deliberately started a quarrel with the steward, hoping to be thrown off the boat when it docked at Vicksburg. This would allay any suspicions and make it easier for him to join the crew of another boat going upriver. But he was thwarted by a law that required white men to post a massive bond for slaves working on the Saint Louis run beyond Vicksburg. Sella had no alternative but to return to New Orleans and find a new owner who would permit him to "run higher up the Mississippi." While in New Orleans an old friend, a free black, suggested that Sella take his place on a boat traveling to Saint Louis. Aware that his friend would also have to guarantee that he was free, Sella feigned illness and declined the offer. His friend could not be suspected of collusion. Half an hour before sailing, Sella applied to the captain. Desperate to fill the position, and with little time to check his papers, the captain agreed to employ him.

The chance to escape could not have come at a worse time—the river above Cairo was usually frozen in December. It took eight days to get to Cairo, where, as he had anticipated, the boat had to stop temporarily. Seizing the opportunity, Stella informed the captain that he had to complete some business in Chicago and promised to be back before the boat resumed its journey. If getting to Cairo had been relatively simple, passing through it proved more difficult. The agent at the train station refused to sell Sella a ticket without verification from a white person that he was free. After some delay, when all appeared lost, a Californian, a passenger on the boat for whom Sella had done a favor, agreed to purchase his ticket, but only after scrutinizing his free papers, overlooking or ignoring the discrepancies that had alerted the clerk earlier. Sella arrived in Chicago a free man on January 6, 1856, twenty-four hours after boarding the train in Cairo.

Little is known of Martin's life in Chicago. Less than one month after his escape, Mary Ann Shadd, editor of the *Provincial Freeman*, wrote her brother from Chicago that she was on her way to Waukegan with Martin, who was "making an impression on the Western people, by his surprising eloquence and earnest appeals for the liberation of the slave." Martin, Shadd reported, was to help her at meetings and to act as one of the newspaper's two agents in Chicago. The other was H. Ford Douglas, a fugitive slave from Virginia, who had already made a name for himself as an outstanding orator. They met during Douglas' tour of Chicago and were instantly drawn to each other. Douglas introduced Martin to abolitionist circles and meetings throughout Illinois, where he delivered his first public lectures.[3]

Soon afterward, he moved to Detroit, where he spent nine months studying for the ministry under a local Baptist minister. Once he had completed his course of study, Martin undertook a lecture tour of Michigan in the spring of 1857. He had been working diligently to perfect his lectures and improve his delivery. Throwing caution to the wind and giving vent to hyperbole, one editor called Martin a "prodigy," a "natural orator," and "one of the most interesting and forcible speakers of his age."[4] The success of his Michigan tour brought Martin to the attention of a wider circle of blacks and abolitionists. Always tastefully dressed, even if somewhat deshabille, about medium height, "not what would be termed handsome," as his contemporary William Wells Brown wrote, "eyes clear and bright; forehead well developed; gentlemanly in his deportment," Martin rapidly became a popular feature at public meetings.[5]

Some time after this tour, Martin was ordained and called to the pulpit of the Michigan Street Baptist Church in Buffalo, New York. His first job as a free man, though exciting, posed few challenges. Like other communities in the North, Buffalo had lost many of its black inhabitants following passage of the Fugitive Slave Law in 1850, and had not yet recovered when Martin arrived in 1857. Blacks were but 1 percent of the city's population, owned just two churches, and sent their children to a single segregated public school. During his brief stay in Buffalo, Martin was active in the community and frequently participated in meetings organized by blacks in upstate New York. In September, 1858, he endorsed plans for a convention of western New York blacks that was to address the issue of voting rights and discuss the feasibility of black emigration from America. Martin also canvassed the area for Gerrit Smith, the Liberty party candidate, during the elections of 1858. Fully aware that Smith had little chance of winning, Martin was convinced that committed men had to demonstrate consistency by voting for the candidate who pledged to work for freedom and temperance. Toward the end of the year, Martin married Sarah. Nothing is known of Sarah, except that her father was a farmer of some means.

---

3. William Wells Brown, *The Black Man: His Antecedents, His Genius, and His Achievements* (1865; rpr. Miami, 1969), 243; *Provincial Freeman*, February 9, January 26, February 2, 1856; Robert L. Harris, "H. Ford Douglas: Afro-American Antislavery Emigrationist," *JNH*, LXII (1977), 217.
4. Brown, *The Black Man*, 244; Detroit *Advertiser*, quoted in *Anti Slavery Standard*, April 18, 1857.
5. *Provincial Freeman*, February 2, 1856; Brown, *The Black Man*, 245.

But Buffalo was too small and too remote for someone like Martin, anxious to be at the hub of activity.[6]

The Martins moved to Boston in the spring of 1859. By summer, Martin was well on the way to making a name for himself. While its pastor was on vacation, the congregation of the largest white Baptist church in Lawrence, Massachusetts, invited Martin to fill its pulpit. Later, when the pastor unexpectedly resigned to take up a new position in New York, Martin was engaged as "permanent supply." He also filled in at Boston's famous Tremont Temple while the pastor was away. Martin made regular appearances on the New England lecture circuit. He toured Massachusetts, Connecticut, and New York during October and November, 1859, lecturing on Nat Turner and the destiny of the Negro race in America, and reading a number of his poems, one of which, "The Mason and the Man," took almost forty minutes to deliver.[7]

Born on the day Turner was hanged, Martin saw himself as a providential replacement of the great slave martyr, destined to continue his work by different means in slightly different spheres. His birth on that fateful day, Martin later wrote, was ample vindication of Pythagoras' theory that whenever someone died, another was born in whom "the spirit of the departed found a new abode." John Brown's recent raid on Harpers Ferry was another manifestation of the antislavery instrument used by Turner. Although avowedly a man of peace, convinced that the sword should only be unsheathed as a last resort against a totally corrupt system, Martin insisted that the sword, once drawn, should not be replaced until the job was completed. Brown, he told a massive meeting at Tremont Temple, was the instrument sent to eliminate the canker of slavery. His defeat was only a temporary setback; others would follow until slavery was finally destroyed.[8]

Martin's first literary productions came on the heels of his growing popularity as an orator. Early letters to the press were so ponderous that invariably his views were lost in complex imagery. He had more success, however, with his poetry. Martin's first published poem, "The Sentinel of Freedom," was clearly influenced by Milton's *Paradise Lost*. Martin has the Flood ushering in the Sec-

6. Brown, *The Black Man*, 244; Monroe Fordham, "A Profile of the Colored Population of Buffalo, New York, in 1850" (Unpublished paper); *Frederick Douglass Paper*, September 17, 24, 1858, February 18, 1859; *Commercial Advertiser Directory of the City of Buffalo*, 1858.

7. Brown, *The Black Man*, 245; Noel, *Freedom and Slavery*, 164; *Liberator*, March 16, 1860; *Weekly Anglo-African*, October 22, 1859, November 24, 1860.

8. *Good Words*, May 1, 1867; *Liberator*, December 9, 1859; *Weekly Anglo-African*, December 17, October 29, November 5, 19, December 3, 31, 1859, January 7, 1860.

ond Coming—the waters sweep the land clean, destroying slavery and establishing equality.

> In spite of numerous warnings, of ample evidence
> The storm has begun, the thunders are pealing,
> The lightnings of truth, like the stern flashing eye
> Of Justice, that sleeps not, of vengeance unfeeling
> Are bursting from clouds in their conflict on high.

Americans, controlled by the advocates of slavery, ignore these portents and

> . . . in wild desperation,
> Are cutting their flesh as the all potent charm,
> And pouring their blood as the needed libation
> This wrath to appease, and their terrors to calm.

But this self-immolation is to no avail. Hiding behind the notion of preserving
the Union cannot forestall the inevitable; oppression and deception will be vanquished by the "deep tones" of progress' "red revolution." Only by this cleans-
ing and redemption through "fire and flood" "Shall man in his majesty stand
undegraded,/The Lord of creation, the image of God." It was a rather pre-
scient statement of the catastrophe about to befall the country.[9]

His predictions of a "red revolution" on the way to partial fulfillment in
1862, Martin turned to the question Whither America? His second published
poem, "Hero and the Slave," a lyrical ballad, is set against the uncertainty during the early months of the Civil War. The leading citizens of the Bay State
have gathered in Boston to pay their respects to the dead and praise those who
survived the Baltimore mob on April 19, 1861. The Hero, a survivor of the
attack on the 6th Massachusetts that left four dead, is receiving the plaudits of
the crowd when a fugitive slave abruptly enters. It was this Slave who had
braved musket shots and stones to rescue the injured Hero. Having nursed the
Hero back to health, the Slave left before anyone knew his identity. The Hero
is understandably elated when he hears the Slave's account of his rescue. But
Boston, engrossed in its praise of the Hero, recoils from the fugitive. White
America persists in its discriminatory tradition, viewing the white soldier as a
Hero while dismissing the black as a mere Slave. Herein lies both the moral
and the warning of the poem. Let America pause, Martin warns,

> . . . in haste of boasting
> Until justice gives us breath,

9. *Anglo-African Magazine*, I (1859), 361–62.

> Lest while building tombs of prophets
> We a prophet put to death.

It is the plea of an anguished man, a cri de coeur, for America to break with its discriminatory past

> And ascend the nation's Tabor,
> To remain transfigured there,
> With the white man and the negro,
> Standing one on either side.[10]

Here was America's greatest opportunity to live up to the principle of equal justice on which the nation was founded, but the country chose to ignore Martin and his contemporaries.

Toward the end of November, 1859, Martin accepted a call from the black Joy Street Baptist Church and began an association that lasted only three years but would provide him an important base from which to struggle against slavery and discrimination. Joy Street (formerly Belknap Street), where the church stood, was the boundary between black and white Beacon Hill. Boston's black community, 1.3 percent of the city's population in 1860, had a long and distinguished history. Although Boston was one of the most segregated northern cities in 1860, blacks had organized their own schools, temperance and abolitionist societies, churches, and self-help projects. Joy Street or the African Baptist Church was Boston's first black church. Centered around a small group who worshiped separately at Faneuil Hall after 1789, the African Baptist Church was finally established in 1805 by Thomas Paul, a recently ordained Baptist minister. In spite of a checkered history and one major split in 1840, the church continued to grow slowly and membership stood at 151 in 1859. By comparison, the Twelfth Baptist Church, formed after the split, had 263 members, its success due in large measure to the dynamism of its minister Leonard Grimes. But Joy Street prospered under Martin's leadership. By the time of his departure in 1862, there were 205 communicants. Of the two churches, Twelfth Street was considered the more liberal, action-oriented congregation; Joy Street the more "conservative." Yet Joy Street gained the sobriquet the Colored People's Faneuil Hall, for there "much of the history of black Bostonians in the middle years was planned and plotted, debated and discussed." Throughout his years in Boston, Martin built on this tradition, organizing fre-

10. J. Sella Martin, *Hero and the Slave. Founded on Fact* (Boston, 1862).

quent lectures at which he and other prominent blacks spoke on the pressing issues of the day.[11]

Martin's involvement in the community put him in the thick of the national debate raging in 1859–60 over the merits of black emigration and especially of the African Civilization Society. He was present at a convention of New England blacks on August 1, 1859, which abandoned its original call and launched an attack on the AFCS. Like many of his contemporaries, Martin took sides in this dispute, rising to the defense of the society and displaying, as one correspondent noted, "consummate argumentative power and force of reasoning." His partiality for the cause came as a direct result of his association with proponents of emigrationism such as Mary Ann Shadd and H. Ford Douglas. Douglas emerged as a leading figure in the movement at the Emigration Convention in Cleveland in 1854, arguing that a "Colored Nationality" on the American continent would demonstrate to the world that blacks were "fully capable of all the attainments that belong to civilized men." Shadd had been promoting Canadian emigration for some time, convinced that the slave power had gained the upper hand in America and was still unchecked.[12]

William Wells Brown set the tone of the 1859 meeting during his opening address. The American Colonization Society, he warned, had been given a new lease on life with the emergence of the AFCS. George Downing, president of the convention, agreed; the future of blacks lay in America, not a foreign country. Black Americans, he insisted "have not yet developed the necessary character to go among a people, to christianize, civilize, and teach them the science of government. Nor is the fault entirely ours. We have our men, but not a single representative man to spare. The debased, the indifferent, should not be shipped off to Africa. Africa is crying out already, 'Send us no more of such.'" Despite this sustained attack, not one of the AFCS's supporters came to its defense until forced to by Downing, who insisted on making the society the central point of debate. In fact, when Martin spoke during the second session, he never once mentioned the AFCS. Martin would later argue that he attempted to forestall discussion of the society's proposals, not because he

11. Weekly *Anglo-African*, December 24, 1859; James Oliver Horton and Lois E. Horton, *Black Bostonians: Family Life and Community Struggle in the Antebellum North* (New York, 1979), 2–6, 33–34, 40–43; George A. Lavesque, "Inherent Reformers—Inherited Orthodoxy: Black Baptists in Boston, 1800–1873," *JNH*, LX (1975), 513, 522–23.

12. *Frederick Douglass Paper*, September 17, 1858; H. Ford Douglas, *Speech of H. Ford Douglas in Reply to Mr. J. M. Langston Before the Emigration Convention at Cleveland, Ohio* (Chicago, 1854), 7; Mary Ann Shadd, *A Plea for Emigration; or Notes on Canada West, in its Moral, Social and Political Aspects . . .* (Detroit, 1852), 44.

thought them unimportant, but solely because he believed that the convention had not allocated sufficient time for airing the issues.[13]

Reporting on the second day, the Business Committee submitted a series of resolutions, two of which approved the necessity of increasing commercial and missionary contacts with Africa, but warned against those who, through their actions, created the false impression among whites that blacks had given up on America and were turning to Africa. Under pressure from Downing, the committee included as part of its report several resolutions passed by a meeting of blacks in Newport, Rhode Island, condemning the AFCS. That opened the floodgates. The regular business of the convention was suspended as delegates turned their attention to a discussion of the society. Brown was first into the fray. The AFCS, he argued, was not based on any coherent plan. Though not opposed to the civilization of Africa, he remained suspicious of the society if only because "it tended to the expatriation of colored people from the United States." Martin rose to the defense of the society's objectives, arguing that emigration to Africa provided the means for breaking the shackles of slavery. The successful cultivation of cotton in Africa, he insisted, would destroy the South's monopoly in the British market and so undermine the basis of slavery. Neither group offered anything new to the debate and, one suspects, almost as a direct consequence, chose instead to level charges of duplicity against each other. Martin found himself in the thick of battle, and just when it appeared that the meeting would lapse into chaos, a compromise resolution halted further discussion.[14]

In an effort to counter the opposition, Martin organized a meeting at Joy Street at which Garnet was to be the main speaker. Earlier attempts to hold the meeting had been stymied by William C. Nell and Leonard Grimes. It was Grimes, Martin said, who had refused to rent his church and who actively pressured others to reject applications from the AFCS to use their halls. Martin accused Grimes of rank hypocrisy and of deserting Garnet, his old friend. "Had I a dog," Martin overreacted, "who should treat another dog in this manner, I don't know but what I should swap him for a snake, and then kill the snake." Garnet helped matters little by charging the organizers of the convention with calling the meeting under false pretenses. The dispute produced a flurry of letters to the *Weekly Anglo-African*, which further deepened the existing bitterness.[15]

13. *Weekly Anglo-African*, September 10, 1859.
14. *Liberator*, August 26, 1859.
15. *Weekly Anglo-African*, September 17, 10, 1859; *Liberator*, September 2, 1859.

The contretemps in Boston was only the preliminary skirmish in a wider controversy that developed in New York the following spring and involved many of the same personalities. The successes of Delany and Campbell in Africa and Bourne in Britain, plus the announcement by Garnet at an earlier meeting that the AFCS was finalizing plans to send out a select group of black Americans to Africa, caused the opposition to renew its efforts. Martin hurried from Boston to participate in the New York meeting called by Pennington, Downing, and other opponents of the society. The session ended in chaos, despite Martin's feeble attempts to ensure an orderly and balanced debate. A rank novice in the art of black political infighting, Martin had believed that differences would be freely and openly discussed in an atmosphere of mutual respect. He was in for a major surprise—Boston paled by comparison to the vitriol of the New York gathering. Anti-emigrationists packed the hall in an effort to steamroll the opposition. But Garnet was up to the task. A master of manipulating meetings, Garnet disrupted the proceedings by speaking out of turn, asking impossible questions, and refusing to yield the floor. When the meeting finally ended in total disarray, Garnet had successfully prevented his opponents from passing resolutions uniformly opposed to the society. Four days later, Garnet called a pro-AFCS meeting, filled the hall with his supporters, and won an overwhelming endorsement of his position.[16]

It is doubtful that Martin remained in New York for the pro-AFCS meeting. On April 17 he dispatched a curious letter from Boston to the editors of the *Weekly Anglo-African*, announcing a break with the society. He had originally supported the AFCS, he wrote, believing erroneously that it would win the "earnest co-operation of every colored man in America." In addition, Lancashire cotton men were independently promoting African cotton cultivation, and an English company had only recently offered $10,000 to attract black cotton cultivators to Africa. Martin saw no reason for the society to continue to exist. Moreover, the AFCS seemed to have failed in its attempts to convince white America that blacks were still vigorously opposed to colonization. Although he refused to impugn Garnet's integrity, Martin concluded that the society's penury militated against the achievement of its objectives. When the society seemed likely to benefit blacks he supported it; now that he was sure it could not, Martin publicly severed all ties.[17]

This is indeed a peculiar effort, which shows that Martin could dissemble

16. *Liberator*, April 27, 5, 1860; *Weekly Anglo-African*, April 21, 28, 1860; Howard H. Bell, *A Survey of the Negro Convention Movement, 1830–1861* (New York, 1969), 232–34.
17. *Weekly Anglo-African*, May 5, 1860.

when the situation warranted it. Given the tenor of the August convention in Boston, there was no reason to suspect that the New York meeting would be dominated by cool heads and dispassionate discourse. Martin was invited solely because pro-emigrationists believed that Garnet could find no better support in his efforts to hold the line against Downing and others. It is possible that Martin was angered by Garnet's actions and concluded that continuing the dispute would only weaken the position of blacks at a time when they were under sustained attack. But this is so much at odds with his character that one suspects Martin's motives. His was an indomitable, sometimes obstinate spirit, reluctant to retreat from a position, even for the general good. Pennington saw through this speciousness and demanded that Martin "mend his pen, and tell the New York public plainly who are to blame for the turn that meeting took and which he regrets." But Martin declined, maintaining a studied silence on the society's actions.[18]

One year later he inconspicuously slipped back into the emigrationist fold, this time in support of the Haitian movement. Could it be that he was convinced that the majority of blacks supported emigration, that it was well financed, and that it in no way gave whites the false impression that blacks were anxious to flee America? At no time in Martin's brief association with the Haitian movement did he raise these apparently important issues, nor did he ever hint of plans to accept President Fabre Geffrard's offer to settle in Haiti. But one does get the distinct impression that support for the movement was based entirely on the belief that blacks should keep all options open, that they should go where it seemed most likely they could succeed.

In the months before the firing on Fort Sumter, the future looked distinctly bleak for black Americans. There were rumors of compromises and peace conventions aimed at placating the South, and in Massachusetts, pleas for reforms in state laws barring blacks from the militia fell on deaf ears. Given the situation, Martin questioned the logic of those like Downing who, in attacking Haitian emigration, called on blacks to remain and build America. Such a position seemed preposterous. How could anyone, Martin asked, love a country that has "gathered all the prejudices and proscriptions of society, all the wicked logic and devilish ingenuity of law, all the selfishness and cowardice of commerce, and the immoral expediency and inhuman corruptions of politics, and all the cant and hyprocrisy of religion, and in the fierceness of its hatred to the colored man throws them in the bomb of its cruel purposes from the mortar of

18. *Ibid.*, May 12, 1860.

its power, upon him and his race, already down-trodden and peeled." It was surely better, Martin concluded, to live in a land free from such oppression. In spite of his efforts, anti-emigrationist forces carried Boston. At a meeting in his church in May, resolutions were adopted that uncompromisingly opposed emigration and denounced the movement as "unfair and unjust, as unwise and as unchristian."[19]

But Boston blacks were beset by problems for which emigrationism seemed to offer few solutions. Throughout the antebellum period they and their white supporters had kept constant pressure on the state legislature, demanding the revocation of statutes that discriminated against blacks. With war imminent, those who wanted to preserve "Union at any cost" anxiously sought additional concessions to mollify the South. The two contending forces squared off against each other in 1859. In keeping with its having repealed laws banning interracial marriages and prohibiting segregated schools, the state legislature adopted a bill in 1859 that permitted blacks to serve in the state militia. Governor Nathaniel P. Banks vetoed the bill, however, hoping to pacify those who viewed it as evidence of a further drift toward irreconcilable sectional conflict. A meeting of blacks at Bethel Church roundly condemned Banks and appointed William Wells Brown, William C. Nell, Dr. J. S. Rock, Robert Morris, and Martin to a committee to petition the legislature in favor of a new bill. At the end of February, Morris, Martin, Rock, and Nell testified before the Committee on Federal Relations. Banks, however, was equally determined to resist these new efforts and promptly vetoed a second bill in late April. Dismayed but determined to continue the fight, Martin held a meeting at his church on April 30, and it was decided to shelve the issue temporarily and concentrate on defeating Banks in the next election. Although the issue remained unresolved, the election of John A. Andrew, a pro-abolitionist, as governor, and the outbreak of war the following year, gave blacks new hope that the pressures of war and military necessity would soon force the state to amend its exclusionary law. Almost two years elapsed before Massachusetts raised its first black regiment.[20]

Failure to win Banks's support for the amendment and growing sectional strife in 1860 must have convinced even the most die-hard believer in "Union at any cost" that the gods were indeed making America mad before destroying the country. Events in December, 1860, confirmed their worst fears. When black and white supporters of John Brown met at Tremont Temple to remember the

19. *Ibid.*, March 9, 23, 1861; *Liberator*, May 17, 1861.
20. *Liberator*, June 15, March 23, 2, January 20, 1860; Horton and Horton, *Black Bostonians*, 125–27.

martyr of Harpers Ferry, a prosouthern group rallied to stifle this deliberate act of provocation. Before Martin, the chairman, could move that the gathering be officially organized, a large group of anti-abolitionists started a general commotion in an effort to gain control of the meeting. They succeeded in electing their slate of officers headed by Richard Fry, a broker and former candidate for Congress. The well-planned coup was led by supporters of the Bell-Everett ticket, a local splinter group of the Democratic party, who advocated extensive concessions to keep the South in the Union. These were clearly "gentlemen of property and standing," lackeys, one observer called them, "of Cotton and State Street Mammon-worshippers," supported by the "pitiable tools of the Slave power; armed and equipped with poor rum and North Street bullyism." Fry came prepared with a string of resolutions, one of which condemned Brown as a madman, and one that praised Virginia for its restraint in dealing with the dangerous situation. Whenever any of the original organizers attempted to speak they were threatened with violence. Douglass did get the floor but could not be heard above the constant din kept up by Fry's supporters. A number of small skirmishes broke out in the hall, and there were shouts that some men were armed. A group of fifty policemen could not, or would not, quell the disturbance. Unwilling to concede defeat, Martin, Douglass, and others tried unsuccessfully to regain control of the meeting. When a fight involving Douglass broke out on the stage, the police moved in under orders from the mayor, closing the hall and threatening to read the riot act.

Not to be outdone, Martin announced that a meeting would be held at Joy Street that night. Soon afterwards, posters appeared on the streets, calling on the people of Boston to silence the gathering. The mayor, fearing a possible riot, called out the militia and placed the police on full alert. Worried about the church's security, the trustees considered closing its doors, but were persuaded not to when Martin said he would resign. That evening thousands milled around outside the church, protesting the meeting and threatening those entering and leaving. Inside, the organizers had taken all possible precautions against a repetition of the morning's disturbances. The meeting was addressed by John Brown, Jr., who warned that he had come prepared to meet any violence, and called on blacks to arm themselves. Speeches were also made by Martin's old friend H. Ford Douglas, who was on a lecture tour of New England, Douglass, Parker Pillsbury, and Wendell Phillips. A number of resolutions were passed, condemning the earlier disruption and accusing the mayor of duplicity and dereliction of duty. Although the presence of the militia and the police prevented attacks on the church, they could not provide protection for those leaving the meeting. A number of blacks were assaulted, and property owned by blacks on Cambridge Street was damaged.[21]

The response to the Tremont Temple meeting was symptomatic of a widening conflict between abolitionists and those who viewed them as being primarily responsible for the irreversible drift toward war. Massachusetts, commercially linked to the South, was suffering economically from the growing rift: "There is universal alarm," one observer wrote, "general financial pressure, great commercial embarrassment. The course of trade between the North and the South is interrupted, many manufacturing establishments are closed or working on short time, and there are many failures; and many workmen thrown out of employment." When Lynn, Haverhill, and Marblehead shoemakers went on strike in February, 1860, many blamed the abolitionists, arguing that the South was boycotting Massachusetts shoes in retaliation for increased antislavery agitation. Like the *Courier*, watchdog of Boston's commercial interests, many thought that there were times in a people's history when a "little deviation from the ordinary rules of demeanor are called for by circumstances," and these were particularly trying times. The city had long suffered under "the infliction of seditious meetings, addressed by a set of incendiaries who spared nothing and nobody—who have gone on actually cursing the Constitution which protects them, and gathering audiences pretending to represent the sentiments of the community." Such firebrands had been ignored for far too long, and now, reinforced by a large number of blacks and foreign agitators, they were winning more and more votes for abolitionists like Lincoln. The "quiet yet effective" manner in which the Tremont Temple meeting was disrupted pleased the *Courier*'s editors and demonstrated that Boston was slowly returning to sanity.[22]

Although other editors were more temperate, criticizing both the abolitionists for their poor timing and those who disrupted the meeting, it was clear from the tone of the editorials that the newspapermen held little hope of reconciliation. White abolitionists had no intention of desisting; neither did blacks. On January 16, Wendell Phillips lectured to a packed audience on mob law and education. When others, fearing a repeat of events at Tremont Temple, canceled an anniversary meeting on December 17 to pay homage to the three

21. Boston *Herald*, December 3, 4, 1860; Boston *Daily Atlas and Bee*, December 4, 1860; *Douglass Monthly*, January, 1861; Edith Ellen Ware, *Political Opinion in Massachusetts During Civil War and Reconstruction* (New York, 1916), 85–88; James M. McPherson, *Struggle for Equality: Abolitionists and the Negro in the Civil War and Reconstruction* (Princeton, 1964), 41–44; *Liberator*, December 14, 7, 1860.

22. Ware, *Political Opinion*, 47; Boston *Courier*, December 4, 1860.

blacks executed with John Brown, Martin used the sanctuary of his church to launch a blistering attack on slavery and its supporters. On New Year's Day, 1861, a small group of blacks gathered at the Twelfth Baptist Church to meet and commend Osborn P. Anderson for his participation in the raid. Martin praised Anderson and suggested raising a subscription for his immediate needs. He collected almost $100 that evening. Three weeks later when the Massachusetts Anti Slavery Society met, the presence of a few policemen failed to prevent attacks by a mob. Fearing further trouble, the new mayor reneged on an earlier promise to provide adequate protection, and closed the hall at which the evening session was to be held.[23]

These mob attacks were just one feature of the North's policy of appeasement. In Washington, Senator John Crittenden of Kentucky introduced a compromise plan consisting of a series of constitutional amendments that would protect slavery in the states and the District of Columbia, prohibit future interference with the interstate slave trade, and guarantee slavery south of 36°30'. Included later were the disfranchisement and colonization of free blacks. In Massachusetts the "Union savers," or conciliators, rallied in support of the Crittenden Compromise, demanding, in addition, repeal of the Personal Liberty Law, which had been adopted in 1855 as a way of undermining the Fugitive Slave Law. They met at Faneuil Hall on February 5, passed resolutions in favor of the compromise, and appointed a committee to take their resolutions to Washington. Petitions were immediately circulated throughout the state. One week later, Crittenden presented to the Senate a petition containing 23,313 signatures from Massachusetts.[24]

Blacks marshaled all available resources to counter this new assault on their limited rights. On February 6, Mr. Branning of Lee presented to the Massachusetts legislature a petition from Martin and 125 other black Bostonians that condemned these new plans and called on lawmakers to instruct their commissioners at the Virginia Peace Conference to oppose the compromise. The memorial was immediately referred to the Committee on Federal Relations. Unable to arrive at an agreement favorable to the petitioners, the committee reported out a series of resolutions against the compromise. Southern property, the committee believed, was adequately protected by existing clauses in

23. Thomas Wentworth Higginson, *Cheerful Yesterdays* (Boston, 1898), 242–45; Ware, *Political Opinion*, 88–89; *Liberator*, January 11, 1861; *Weekly Anglo-African*, December 29, 1860, January 12, 1861.
24. Ware, *Political Opinion*, 51–52; James M. McPherson, *The Negro's Civil War: How American Negroes Felt and Acted During the War for the Union* (New York, 1965), 13.

the Constitution, and the legislature, under pressure from Governor Andrew, told its commissioners not to accept the compromise.[25]

In an effort to generate additional support, Massachusetts blacks called an emergency convention at Joy Street and agreed to issue an appeal to the white citizens of the state. William Wells Brown argued that the compromise stood no chance in Congress, but Martin and others felt that the appeal would help explain the true intent of the compromise. "There never was a darker hour for the colored people of this country," Martin said. "We appeal to you to stand by us, and see that we are not unjustly treated."[26]

The firing on Fort Sumter in April temporarily lessened some of the acrimony among blacks who were debating strategies for the elimination of slavery and discrimination. President Lincoln's call to arms, and the general if somewhat frenetic expressions of patriotism which followed, understandably raised the hopes of many that the time had come for them to play a significant role in the final resolution of the conflict over slavery. On April 23, Martin chaired a meeting of Boston blacks at Grimes's church. Resolutions were submitted for Massachusetts blacks "to defend the flag of the common country against the common foe," for the legislature to remove the word *white* from the state's constitution and militia laws, for an army of fifty thousand blacks, and for the formation of armed drill companies. Repeating an earlier warning, Brown urged that the meeting temper its enthusiasm until such time as the Federal government openly stated that the abolition of slavery was one of its war aims. Martin, with the support of Downing and others, countered. Immediate and unequivocal support for the North at a time when it was militarily unprepared would give blacks "a claim upon the gratitude of the whites" at the final settlement. It was an opportunity that blacks could not miss, especially since, as Martin predicted, the initial advantages were with the South.[27]

Six days after the meeting a black drill company was formed, and in subsequent weeks the legislature received three petitions for the repeal of discriminatory militia laws. On May 15, Simeon P. Adams of Boston presented the petition signed by Martin and twenty-five others. They wanted the word *white* removed from the militia laws, because the distinction was foreign to the spirit of other Massachusetts laws, and its existence denied blacks the opportunity to participate in the defense of "the government that protects" their homes. The

25. Ware, *Political Opinion*, 53; *Liberator*, February 22, 1861.
26. *Liberator*, February 22, 1861; *Weekly Anglo-African*, March 2, 1861.
27. *Weekly Anglo-African*, May 4, 1861; *Liberator*, April 26, 1861.

second petition was for the commonwealth to amend its laws banning blacks from forming military companies; the third called on the state to ignore federal laws barring blacks from serving in state militias. In an effort to avoid open debate on the petitions, the Joint Special Committee on the Governor's Address, to which they were referred, recommended deferral to the next session of the General Court. Repeated efforts to reopen discussion on these petitions were futile. Blacks had suffered yet another defeat in their fight to amend the state's militia laws, and like their counterparts in other cities, they would have to wait until developments in the war dictated a change in federal and state policies.[28]

The failure shattered Martin's confidence in Northern resolve and raised serious doubts in his mind about its desire to face the Southern challenge. The refusal to accept blacks into the military, continual denials that slavery was central to the war, the return of fugitive slaves to their masters by some Federal officers, and the defeat of the suffrage issue in New York by a massive 2-to-1 margin, all symbolized Northern cowardice. The North refused to let "white men sell the Southerners food," he wrote Douglass, "and yet they return slaves to work on the plantations to raise all the food that the Southerners want. They arrest traitors, and yet make enemies of the colored people, North and South." Whatever the motives behind this patently absurd policy, Martin was still inclined toward the optimistic conclusion that some good would come to blacks from the conflict. What bothered him, however, was white America's refusal to concede that slavery and discrimination were directly responsible for the war. Only by recognizing this fact, Martin believed, could America work positively for the elevation of blacks to the position of full-fledged citizens. Otherwise, the country was doomed to historical hypocrisy, and blacks would find themselves again riveted at the bottom of the social ladder. "The war seems to promise something to us," he lamented, "but in the name of manhood, must our hopes depend forever upon the negative influences of Providence? Must we forever gain whatever good we have from the white man's bad?" To compound the problem, many blacks, oscillating "between the two points of social and political paralysis—from the apathy of indifference, to the apathy of despair," seemed ignorant of the war's influence on their future.[29]

This sense of deep despair was reinforced by Martin's personal difficulties. He had never been robust, and he suffered from a periodic and painful urinary infection. In the early months of 1861 while he struggled to persuade Massa-

28. *Liberator*, May 24, 1861; McPherson, *The Negro's Civil War*, 20–21.
29. *Douglass Monthly*, June, 1861.

chusetts legislators to amend the militia laws, and was actively involved in the Haitian emigration debate, his first child succumbed to an unidentified illness. In early summer, Martin decided to visit France for medical treatment, and friends suggested an antislavery tour of Britain as well. In July he wrote Gerrit Smith, soliciting financial help for his travels, and he asked Governor Andrew for a letter of introduction to Charles Francis Adams, the American minister in London. Martin probably met Andrew in mid-July to discuss the nature of his visit and the best means of winning British support for the Union's cause. In view of his earlier skepticism about America's intentions, the decision to undertake such a mission seems surprising. Andrew undoubtedly had some influence. He had been pressuring local abolitionists for months to send a mission to Britain to counter Southern influence and reduce British skepticism about Union intentions.[30]

Martin sailed for London in early August after canceling plans to visit Paris for medical attention. Why he did this is unclear, for throughout his stay in Britain, Martin suffered repeated attacks of his illness. In fact, one meeting in November had to be ended abruptly when he became ill.[31] The times were not particularly auspicious for a mission aimed at winning support for the Northern cause. Relations between Britain and America were far from harmonious in the period after May, 1861, when Britain declared its neutrality in the war. To many in the North, the declaration was tantamount to recognition of the South. Mail from America brought invectives against the British government's duplicity. In turn, such vitriol convinced many Englishmen that the North was eager to embroil Britain in the bloody dispute. Southern victories on the battlefield in 1861 only reinforced British suspicions of Union intentions and lent further support to the policy of neutrality.

To compound Martin's difficulties, British abolitionists seemed equally confounded by developments in America. Like many of their transatlantic counterparts, they looked on in disbelief as Lincoln refused to concede slavery's centrality to the war. If it were not, then on what grounds should British abolitionists, many of them peace advocates and opponents of war, justify support for the Northern cause? As far as they were concerned, there was no inconsistency in opposing slavery in the South and refusing to endorse the stated war aims of the North.

30. Martin to Gerrit Smith, July 2, 1861, in GSC; Martin to Governor Andrew, July 3, 10, 1861, Anna Loring to Mrs. Andrew, July 14, 1861, all in John Andrew Papers, Massachusetts Historical Society, Boston.
31. London *Morning Advertiser*, November 15, 1861; *Anti Slavery Standard*, December 7, 1861.

Because of nagging illness, Martin was forced to postpone the start of his lecture tour until September. Since his arrival he had devoted the greater part of his time to contacting London Garrisonians, particularly George Thompson and his son-in-law F. W. Chesson, leaders of the London Emancipation Society. It was no easy task convincing British abolitionists of Northern intentions. In early October, Thompson, never one to spend too much time on diplomatic niceties, clashed openly with Martin. As Chesson recorded in his diary, Martin had little evidence to support his contention that emancipation would result from the war and that Lincoln did intend to raise the issue sooner or later. Nothing seemed further from the truth, Chesson observed, particularly in light of Lincoln's recent modification of General Frémont's declaration freeing slaves in Missouri.[32]

Martin, however, had to persevere in trying to win over the LES. The only other abolitionist society in London, the British and Foreign Anti Slavery Society, had as a matter of policy remained silent on developments in America. Martin's overtures to BFASS leaders elicited no response. Later he would wistfully describe the society as an "antiquated affair, the members of which met but once a year for the purpose of instituting deputations, that did nothing but sprinkle rose water on the feet of a few conservative lords."[33] Martin had no alternative, therefore, but to work with those who, despite many reservations, never once slackened their attacks on Southern slavery.

Following a couple of independently organized lectures in London, Martin joined Thompson and others on a lecture tour of the Home Counties. Martin hammered away at one theme in his effort to win support for the North: for forty years, America, ignoring all warnings from concerned men, had been moving inexorably toward the present conflagration. For instance, when his friend Arthur Kinnard, M.P., expressed some dismay with Lincoln's policies, Martin rose to the defense of the Federal government. There was, he said, a deep-seated ignorance in Britain about Northern intentions, which had the unfortunate effect of increasing suspicion between the two governments. Present developments had to be viewed in the context of their historical antecedents. Salient features of that history were the slow but nonetheless perceptible growth of antislavery sentiment in the North, and the equally important increase in the level of resistance to Southern demands. Obvious examples were the North's reception of fugitive slaves and the passage of personal liberty laws.

32. F. W. Chesson Diary, September 22, 1861–December 31, 1862, in RED.
33. Howard Temperley, *British Antislavery, 1833–1870* (Columbia, S.C., 1972), 256; *Liberator*, February 28, 1862.

The outbreak of hostilities should be seen, therefore, as a different manifestation of a long-standing struggle. This dispute was brought to a head when the South illegally withdrew from the Union solely to maintain slavery. In order to survive, it would soon have to reopen the slave trade and expand its hegemony into the Caribbean. For these reasons, he concluded, the conflict was an anti-slavery war. When some of his audience questioned these conclusions, Martin responded that what really mattered was the fact that the North was at war with slaveholders and, therefore, should be supported by all those who considered themselves abolitionists.[34]

Although Martin undoubtedly won some converts to his position, it is impossible to determine how many were actually swayed by his rather tortuous reasoning. In mid-December he wrote Governor Andrew, reporting on his activities and his plans to tell Bostonians of his disappointment "with regard to my hopes of English sympathy with the North and the reason of it as well as to give many cases of mutual misunderstanding." Martin's was a thankless task, given the atmosphere of mutual distrust between the countries and Lincoln's determined resistance to making slavery a casus belli.[35] But the trip did produce some lasting personal benefits for Martin. Like many other black Americans who visited Britain, he was floored by his reception and the hospitality he received from the "best" of British society. Lords, ladies, businessmen, M.P.s, and some of the most prominent Nonconformist ministers entertained him and attended his lectures. It was they who arranged the soirée at Kinnard's in November. One of the group, Harper Twelvetrees, a prominent industrialist with dye and chemical factories in London's East End, and supporter of abolitionist causes, took Martin under his wing.

Sometime toward the end of November, Martin decided that his hectoring British abolitionists was having little effect. As a result, his lectures underwent a subtle change. Whereas in the past he had concentrated almost exclusively on the war and the need to support the North, now he seemed more concerned to attack the problem indirectly, speaking on the nature of American slavery and his personal experiences as a slave. There were more rewards and instant gratification in this approach, as Martin well knew; it was also less controversial. Following one of his lectures at Plaistow, London, in October, the Reverend John Curwen, a local Congregationalist minister, persuaded Martin to tell his

34. London *Record*, November 25, 1861; London *Morning Star*, November 27, September 19, October 14, 1861; *Douglass Monthly*, February, 1862; High Wycombe *Free Press*, October 11, 18, 1861; *Liberator*, November 29, 1861.

35. Martin to J. A. Andrew, December 13, 1861, Executive Letters, Vol. CLXXV, Box 42, in Massachusetts State Archives, Boston.

life story. Discovering that Martin's sister and her two children were still in slavery, Curwen suggested that funds be raised to purchase their freedom. A committee was established with Kinnard as treasurer, and contacts were made with their master, who agreed to their sale for £400. A number of public meetings were held at which Martin told the story of his life in slavery and his eventual escape. The congregation at Surrey Chapel raised £85 after he spoke. At a second meeting at Plaistow, where Martin had previously preached to a "congregation of navvies," the "poor of the neighborhood" thronged Curwen's church, contributing their mite to the fund. Rich and poor sent money, Curwen enthusiastically reported, and one woman said, "I have saved a penny for the collection; and every one of my family has done without something this week in order to add to it." Martin would long remember such enthusiastic support.[36]

Martin returned to America in mid-February, 1862, with approximately $2,500 for the purchase of his sister Caroline and her children, Ada and Charles. Negotiations between Martin and Caroline's master, John Dorson of Columbus, Georgia, dragged on into the summer. In April, Martin wrote Dorson, suggesting the sale be finalized immediately, and that Caroline, Ada, and Charles be sent to Boston. Dorson would have none of it. Caroline, he replied, was a Christian, a "faithful servant" and should not be exposed to Boston, that "den of social monsters and abolition infidels" where "madmen and creators of sedition as you and Wendell Phillips" live. Dorson subsequently agreed to sell the three to slave traders on their way to Kentucky, with the understanding that Martin would be given the opportunity to buy his family. In August, Martin left for Cincinnati, and the exchange was made in Kentucky between the slave traders and some friends of Martin's. There was an emotional reunion on the other side of the river between the brother and sister separated for more than twenty years. Rather than take them back to Boston, where he could not afford to support them on his meager salary, Martin settled Caroline and the children with friends in Dowagiac, Michigan, where Caroline was given a job. Before the war was over, they moved permanently to Jamaica.[37]

The ease with which the money was collected and Martin's change in the purpose of his mission raised some eyebrows in London. Some of his friends in

36. *Nonconformist*, November 27, 1861; London *Morning Star*, December 25, 1861; London *Record*, November 27, 1861; Martin to George Ruffin, October 15, 1861, in Ruffin Family Papers, Moorland-Spingarn Research Center, Howard University, Washington, D.C.

37. *Liberator*, September 5, October 24, 1862; *Nonconformist*, October 1, 1862; *Good Words*, June 1, 1867; Noel, *Freedom and Slavery*, 165–67. Martin may have left them at the Chain Lake Settlement, a colony of blacks established in 1838 in Cass County, Michigan. See James D. Corrothers, *In Spite of the Handicap. An Autobiography* (1872; rpr. Westport, Conn., 1970).

America were also bothered by Martin's actions. "We had been informed," the editors of the *Weekly Anglo-African* wrote, "that he had gone there at the urgent request of Governor Andrew of Massachusetts, to speak against the recognition of the Cotton Confederacy. It may be, however, that Mr. Martin purposes giving his attention to both matters, looking after only one at a time, giving the most important one precedence."[38] That was a dose of his own medicine. Although the reason for the shift remains a mystery, once the funds were collected, Martin reverted to his original plan of action.

The recent arrival of the Confederate commissioners James Mason and John Slidell gave Martin's agency a new fillip and provided the opportunity he needed to badger British abolitionists to sustained action against the South. The seizure of the commissioners from the British mail steamer *Trent* by Captain Charles Wilkes of the United States Navy in November threatened to bring Britain and America to blows. Many in Britain saw it as yet another example of American arrogance, an act likely to provoke conflict. Although there were heated exchanges in the weeks after the incident, tempers cooled by the end of the year, and the chances of British intervention, if ever seriously contemplated by the government, receded. But Martin was not to know that. If William Yancey, the retiring Confederate representative in London, could write his superiors as late as January 27, 1862, that he expected armed intervention by France and Britain, it is no wonder that many abolitionists continued to fear the prospect. Martin called on his audience at a farewell meeting in Plaistow on January 30 to be vigilant and consistent in their opposition to Mason and Slidell. "Their great bribe," he warned, "was free trade, and . . . though the English people would see through the fallacy of the thing, some legislators might be disposed to fall in with the notion that by recognizing the Confederacy they would promote free trade."[39]

Despite his reception in England, Martin was glad to be returning home. As he wrote his friend George Lewis Ruffin from London, although "you are the equal of white people here you feel quite alone in your equality since all are strangers." There were those who questioned his actions in England, but others were convinced, as was the Boston *Traveller*, that Martin's short stay abroad had contributed immeasurably to the Union's cause. Martin was equally sanguine, and after his return he wrote Lincoln, offering his services "to work or preach or fight to put down this rebellion." But little had changed in Martin's

38. *Weekly Anglo-African*, January 25, 1862.
39. Frank Lawrence Owsley, *King Cotton Diplomacy: Foreign Relations of the Confederate States of America* (Chicago, 1969), 83; London *Evening Star*, January 31, 1862; *Liberator*, February 28, 1862.

absence. Washington continued to ignore such offers, insisting that the war was not a struggle against slavery.[40]

Back in Boston, Martin busied himself with his ministerial duties in an effort to revitalize Joy Street, which had apparently lost some of its vibrance during his absence. That, and his attempts to purchase Caroline and her children took up most of his time during the first two months. Washington's adamant refusal to accept the help proffered by Northern blacks dampened the enthusiasm of many and shattered the hopes of others. One can only marvel at the insensitivity of those who, in this situation, called for the colonization of blacks. The Federal government's plans were reinforced by the Liberian legislature, which passed an act authorizing the appointment of commissioners to tour America to promote colonization. The legislature also earmarked a large tract of land for the new immigrants, and the American Colonization Society promised support for travel and settlement. The proposed visit of Edward Wilmot Blyden that summer, coming just after the plans were submitted to Congress, caused considerable consternation among blacks. At the end of April, Boston blacks met at the Southac Street Church to condemn the new developments. In resolutions submitted by Robert Morris and Martin, the meeting excoriated the proposals as violations of republican principles. What kind of country, they asked rhetorically, would effect plans for the compulsory expatriation of loyal citizens in the midst of a war? Such measures had no "other ground of justification than prejudice against color." The future of both North and South could only be assured, they concluded, through open competition for jobs in a rapidly expanding industrialized economy, "each making the other more faithful to the employers and more useful to themselves."[41]

There were few signs that America had ever seriously contemplated full black participation in a growing economy. Such optimism about unfettered competition was grounded more in faith than reality. Martin clearly subscribed to this article of faith. The Civil War, the crucible of fire, was the purifying agent that would cause America to fulfill its promise. This country, he told an Abington, Massachusetts, meeting held to celebrate West Indian emancipation, had sacrificed its principles in a mad scramble to attract new states into the Union. "Promise the nation that it should have a new star to dot its flag," he thundered, "and it would drag that flag through the mire of oppression and

40. Martin to Ruffin, October 15, 1861, in Ruffin Family Papers; Boston *Traveller*, quoted in *Weekly Anglo-African*, March 1, 1862; Martin to President Lincoln, July 14, 1862, in Abraham Lincoln Papers, Library of Congress.
41. *Liberator*, May 2, 1862.

injustice to secure the additional star." Now by stealth and deception, some of these states had gone to war, demanding separation. But the war involved issues larger than the mere preservation of the Union. Although the president was immobilized by an obsession with maintaining the Union at all costs, Frémont, David Hunter, and others were freeing the slaves, thus slowly but inexorably leading the "nation into the land of liberty." Even Lincoln had been forced to emancipate slaves in the District of Columbia. It mattered little to Martin that Lincoln's actions were dictated purely by political expediency. What was important was that these decisions were the first signs of recognition that the struggle was "an antislavery war."[42]

Martin was not alone in his views. The optimism about the war's outcome was shared by many of his contemporaries. Although the government's refusal to admit that slavery was the underlying cause of the war continued to rankle blacks and abolitionists, there were signs, as Martin argued, that Washington was reluctantly coming around. Black opposition to Lincoln's plan of compensated emancipation and colonization remained constant, yet there was a clear recognition that both aspects of the plan marked an effective departure from established government policies. First, it implicitly acknowledged the need to free the slaves. Once the gates were cracked, blacks argued, the rush toward total emancipation would be impossible to stop. Second, it at least conceded that expatriation had to be voluntary. Martin and others believed, correctly, that under the circumstances the vast majority of blacks would choose to stay in America. In March, 1862, Lincoln called on the border states to adopt a policy of compensated emancipation, and in April, Congress passed the District of Columbia Emancipation Act. Although there was some concern that Lincoln might veto the bill, he did not, which seemed to confirm the optimists' predictions. Lincoln's preliminary proclamation in September buoyed their spirits.

Frederick Douglass was right—the September proclamation "changed everything." No longer could the government sidestep the centrality of slavery in the conflict. But the president was a cautious man, and many were understandably apprehensive about his willingness to enforce the deadlines given the South. As in other parts of the North, a large crowd gathered at Tremont Temple to celebrate the January proclamation. Those who anxiously awaited word by telegram from Washington could not have missed the irony of the occasion. Just two years earlier, a mob had silenced their meeting; now their position had been vindicated. Speeches were made by Grimes, Martin, Anna

42. *Ibid.*, August 15, 1862.

Dickerson, Douglass, William Wells Brown, and others in an effort to relieve the tension. Jubilation followed the announcement that the president had issued the proclamation, and celebrations continued well into the night. The fact that the proclamation did not call for immediate unconditional emancipation mattered little for the moment. The die was now cast, and though blacks and abolitionists recognized the need for vigilance against any possible reversals, many were convinced that final emancipation was inevitable.[43]

Martin's optimism was dampened by recurrent illnesses that severely curtailed his activities. His inability to control these attacks was partly responsible for his decision to leave Boston for a healthier climate. But why any man suffering from pleurisy would choose London is a mystery. Dickens' London, with its "melancholy streets" cloaked "in a penitential garb of soot," seemed particularly unsuitable for someone subject to lung and other ailments. But the city appealed to Martin for reasons that far outweighed its possible deleterious effects on his health. America was unwilling to grant blacks their rights, but England, particularly the working class in London's East End, had welcomed him with open arms during his previous visit. A significant portion of the money to purchase Martin's sister and her two children had come from the men and women of the area, many of them employees of Harper Twelvetrees. A firm believer in the "elevation" of the working class, Twelvetrees organized temperance and choral societies, literary and mechanics institutes, and held frequent lectures and concerts in the hall he built next to his factory in 1861. He envisaged the hall as a church for Sunday services. Given his past contacts and popularity, Martin seemed the obvious choice to fill the pulpit. In early January, 1863, he said a sad farewell to Joy Street and left to assume his new duties in London.[44]

Martin arrived in Britain at a most auspicious time. Attitudes toward the Union had undergone significant changes following Lincoln's Emancipation Proclamation. Some derided it as nothing more than a cynical political ploy; others saw it as a definitive step in the direction of final emancipation. Gone were the concerns that the *Trent* affair or similar events would push the two countries into war. It appeared to most that the British government had finally rejected intervention in the conflict. Although many potential supporters still

43. Frederick Douglass, *Life and Times of Frederick Douglass* (1892; rpr. New York, 1962), 352–54.
44. London *Eastern Times*, January 31, 1863; W. Noble Twelvetrees to the Librarian, January 16, 1932, in Notes Re. Bromley (Typescript file, Bromley Public Library, London); Alfred Rosling Bennett, *London and Londoners in the 1850's and 1860's* (London, 1924), 99–100.

chafed at the Union's imposition and maintenance of tariffs, only a few diehards continued to insist that the right to independence was the cause of the war. Things would worsen later as the shortage of cotton devastated the lives of Lancashire operatives, but for the moment it seemed obvious to the informed that secession was, as abolitionists had insisted all along, a device to maintain slavery.

Meetings held in early 1863, even in cities like Liverpool, "a hotbed of Southern sympathy," reflected these changes. Just before Martin's arrival, a meeting organized by Liverpool pro-Unionists called for support of both emancipation and the North. It provided one of those rare occasions when the platform was shared by proponents of both sides in the war. Rising to the defense of the South, James Spence, long the South's principal advocate in Britain, and the author of the influential *The American Union*, warned against adopting the resolutions. He insisted that Lincoln's proclamation was not only unconstitutional, it was an insidious political device to encourage slave rebellion. Responsibility for the resulting carnage, Spence added, would be placed squarely on the president. Spence's histrionics had the desired effect. The prospect of even more bloodshed deterred some from endorsing Lincoln's proclamation. For others, the bloody images of the rebellion in India and the "native" revolts in South Africa and New Zealand still swirling in their minds, the fear that the proclamation would encourage slaves to turn on their masters was genuine indeed. It was a politically shrewd move by Spence. It proved next to impossible, in the midst of a war, to disprove a claim of possible insurrection by the enslaved. Only the passage of time could do that.[45] Months would pass before the fear was finally dispelled. In the meantime, Spence and other Southern supporters used the effect created to good advantage while Martin and pro-Union forces labored to counter their claims.

In spite of these hindrances, the proclamation did give new heart to British abolitionists and a fillip to pro-Northern sentiment. To date, Washington's policies had given them little to cheer about. When Martin left Britain at the end of his first visit, the situation was grim. Behind the public pronouncements of optimism lay a quixotic sense of futility. Although Martin never questioned the view that slavery was the root cause of the war, the least informed of his audiences had ample evidence from the American government to refute such claims. By early 1863, however, public opinion had definitely swung in favor of

45. London *Morning Star*, January 19, 1863; Donaldson Jordon and Edwin J. Pratt, *Europe and the American Civil War* (Boston, 1931), 115.

the North. British abolitionist societies worked feverishly to capitalize on this shift. One historian has estimated that in February alone, over forty public meetings were organized by pro-Union groups in England and Scotland, and that scores of pamphlets were published in an effort to bolster the Northern cause. Even the BFASS, for which Martin expressed so much disdain during his earlier visit, had shelved both its antiwar principles and ambivalence toward the North, and returned to active abolitionist agitation. Martin missed by two days the huge meeting organized by the LES at Exeter Hall at which ten thousand people endorsed a series of pro-Union resolutions.[46]

Allowing little time to settle into his new home and duties as minister, Martin quickly entered the fray. A few days after his arrival he joined a delegation of seventy members and supporters of the BFASS in an "interview" with Charles Francis Adams. Expressing reservations about Lincoln's contention that the proclamation was prompted by military expediency, and his exemption of those Southern states not in rebellion, the delegation nevertheless praised the president for his bold action. Adams responded that the Union aimed to "uproot Slavery as its only safeguard against all future attacks upon the principles of freedom." In a brief speech, Martin expressed his joy—and, given past experiences, his relief—that the proclamation was so warmly received in Britain.[47]

Despite his continuing poor health, Martin's spirits were buoyed by the popular support for the North, and he missed few opportunities to capitalize on it. He was the center of attraction at a large meeting organized by friends at Plaistow on February 11. Curwen had done the legwork to ensure its success, going from door to door distributing five thousand copies of two BFASS tracts on the war and handbills announcing the meeting. Although the local gentry were conspicuous, it was the "hard-handed working men from the great railway works at Stratford, the ship-building yards at Blackwall, the labourers from the docks, and the navvies from the outfall sewer works" who packed the church to applaud Martin's blistering attack on the Confederacy and its British supporters. The *Times*'s high-handed dismissal of Northern sympathizers as a "set of nobodies" did not trouble Martin. "It was a compliment to the working classes of England," he told a meeting at Woolwich some weeks later, "that they could see to the heart of the struggle, when the aristocracy no longer sympathized with humanity and suffering." Meetings like these were instrumental in en-

46. Jordon and Pratt, *Europe and the American Civil War*, 151–53.
47. *Anti Slavery Reporter*, February 5, 1862.

hancing British working-class support for the Union in the early months of 1863.[48]

There was, however, a resilient opposition led by a small camarilla of powerful Britons partial to the South. Although this group made little headway in winning new adherents to the South, Martin and his British backers were well aware of the danger of resting on their oars. In the following months, Martin joined forces with the LES, lecturing extensively in London and the Home Counties. In spite of a few catcalls from some audiences, Martin was generally well received. In each lecture he countered the arguments employed by pro-Southern advocates, expressing an almost unqualified optimism that the North would be victorious. Like many of his contemporaries, Martin perceived clear changes for the better in the North, which was no longer totally encumbered by laws and customs that excluded blacks from the exercise of their rights. Those who continued to preach the denial of black rights in the North, he told a Woolwich audience, were mere "fossils of the past—men who, like the Bourbons, never got a new idea, and never forgot an old one." The trend toward removing segregationist laws had left them in the past. To argue, as some did, that the North and the South were equally insensitive to the rights of blacks was to ignore reality. Englishmen, he warned, were being seduced into supporting the South by arguments based on blatant distortions of the facts. Responding to those like Spence who raised the bogey of slave insurrections following Lincoln's proclamation, Martin turned the issue on its head. Even if there were a rebellion, he asked rhetorically, who would say it was wrong? "Slavery was at all times a chronic state of insurrection against right—against religion, and against mankind. . . . Slavery was an institution of violence, and if the slaves did rise up against their oppressors they had a perfect right to do so, for every man had a right to be free."[49]

Martin insisted that some Southern sympathizers were influenced by erroneous newspaper reports of events in America. Others were motivated by pure self-interest, concerned that defeat for the South would jeopardize their commercial and financial investments. And there were those who simply opposed

48. London *Morning Star*, February 14, 1863; *Anti Slavery Reporter*, March 5, 1863; *Kentish Independent*, March 28, 1863. Later, efforts would be made to convince British workers that support for the freedmen would redound to their economic benefit. Thriving black workers in the South, many insisted, would increase demand for British goods and in so doing improve the lot of workers. Christine Bolt, *The Anti-Slavery Movement and Reconstruction: A Study of Anglo-American Co-operation 1833–1877* (London, 1969), 66–68.

49. *Kentish Independent*, March 28, 1863; London *Morning Star*, March 26, 1863; *Anti Slavery Reporter*, April 1, 1863.

the democratic experiment in America with its popular suffrage, freedom of religion, and voluntary national defense. For these reasons, Martin told a soirée at the Whittington Club in honor of George Thompson, many in Britain still clung to the false view that the South had gone to war to protest Northern political and economic domination. Nothing was further from the truth, he insisted. The South had seceded in a vain attempt to ensure the survival of slavery. Given this fact, and despite Lincoln's protest to the contrary, the war had evolved into a dispute over the future of slavery in America. Although many in the Federal government were slow to come to this realization, and may only have adopted an antislavery posture as a result of the war, Martin maintained that the abolitionists, in their long, persistent, and indefatigable labors, had kept the spirit of the Founding Fathers alive in the face of brutal opposition. To them was due all credit for the present wave of genuine antislavery views in the North. In light of these facts, Martin saw no reason why a country like Britain, where he had "found equality before the law," where no wicked prejudice denied him the "enjoyment of the obligations and privileges of a man," should do anything other than support the cause of abolitionism.[50]

The spring and summer of 1863 brought a rising tide of public agitation by pro-Confederate forces in Britain. Led by Spence and financed by merchants who had reaped substantial profits from the Southern trade, they intended to rouse public opinion to the point where the government would be forced to recognize the South. The devastation of the cotton famine provided them a golden opportunity, which they hastend to exploit. Southern clubs were organized by Spence in every major town in Lancashire and in most of the towns in Derbyshire, Cheshire, and Yorkshire during 1863. He extended his agitation to northern England, paying unemployed workers to pack meetings to ensure the adoption of pro-Southern resolutions and to prevent disruptions by pro-Northern supporters. The intrinsic value of popular support in the battle for the hearts and minds of the British aside, Spence's efforts should also be seen as part of a larger strategy that led to John Roebuck's motion in Parliament in July when he called for recognition of the South.[51]

Faced with this well-organized and adequately financed operation, pro-Northern supporters were forced to move quickly to cushion its effects. But principled opposition to slavery, though vital, was not enough in the battle for public opinion. Too many questions about the North's intent remained un-

50. London *Morning Star*, February 26, 1863; Chesson Diary, 1863, in RED; *Liberator*, March 20, 1863.
51. Owsley, *King Cotton Diplomacy*, 176–77.

answered; and the lingering fear that Lincoln's proclamation would result in bloodshed continued to influence many of the undecided. Even among the ranks of the truly committed, there was considerable indecision, and even some disagreement, about the best course to follow. The formation of the Freed-Man's Aid Society in April, 1863, bore all the signs of compromise among Northern backers. Curwen, the author Thomas Hughes, Martin, and Chesson were among the principal movers in founding the society. Rather than tackle Spence head on, the society chose to concentrate on raising money to aid the many destitute slaves who were fleeing Southern plantations in droves. The approach was not without merit, for the society could avoid becoming mired in the debate over recognition—it could leave that to others—and by eschewing participation in heated political discussions, it could appeal directly to all sectors of the public. This was precisely the position taken by Sir Thomas Fowell Buxton in his opening remarks at the society's inaugural meeting on April 24. Although Hughes demurred if only slightly, expressing fear that Parliament had not rejected possible recognition, Martin as a member of the Executive Committee seemed content to toe the line.[52]

The business of countering Southern support was left to abolitionist societies. In early May a LES meeting at Finsbury Chapel attracted a crowd in excess of two thousand people. Resolutions supported the Federal government, praised Lincoln for his bold initiatives, and called on the British government to ensure that no vessels of war for the Confederacy were being built or equipped in England. As he had done so often in the past, Martin delivered a scathing attack on the South, in what Chesson described as a "brillant speech." There was, he warned, a very real danger that should the South succeed, it would then build a slave empire in Central America with the aid of Spain, which would draw Britain inevitably into a war to protect its colonial possessions.[53]

As abolitionists and Confederate supporters anxiously awaited the submission of Roebuck's motion to Parliament, Martin and M. D. Conway, a former slaveholder who was now an abolitionist, joined forces in a series of lectures in London. Martin's speech at a meeting organized by the LES at Cross Street Chapel, Islington, in early May, contained most of the arguments he employed against the South. He spoke of his own experience in slavery and of abolitionist efforts to destroy "a hellish institution and a curse to the continent of Amer-

52. London *Morning Star*, April 27, 1863; Chesson Diary, 1863, in RED; "Freed-Man's Aid Society" (Broadside, in BFASS); Bolt, *The Anti-Slavery Movement*, 59.
53. London *Morning Star*, May 7, June 2, 1863; *Liberator*, May 29, 1863; *Anti Slavery Standard*, June 6, 1863; Chesson Diary, 1863, in RED.

ica." Those few in Britain who supported the Confederacy, he added derisively, were nothing more than sycophants aping the views of their "pet aris-
tocrats." They possessed not one original thought on the issues involved in the
war—because "the aristocracy had taken a pinch of snuff, those parties to be
fashionable began to sneeze." When combined with moving accounts of his life
in slavery, such caustic wit had the desired effect of winning support for the
North from most of Martin's audiences. At the end of these meetings, petitions
were signed, calling on the House of Commons to support the government in
its bid to enforce provisions of the Foreign Enlistment Act that prohibited the
recruitment of Britons to fight in foreign wars.[54]

As the date for Roebuck's motion drew nearer, both sides stepped up their
efforts to win public support. Toward the end of May, Roebuck addressed a
massive meeting of eight thousand at Sheffield and urged recognition of Southern independence. All was not clear sailing, and Roebuck had to contend with
numerous disruptions by Northern supporters in the audience. In spite of
efforts to amend resolutions, in the end Roebuck carried the day. His speech
contained nothing new; he accused the North of trying to establish an empire,
of hating blacks as much as it hated slavery, and the South was portrayed as
bravely trying to secure its independence. Slavery, Roebuck asserted, was a
necessary evil, or, more correctly, a system that protected the slave from unnecessary hardships. "Time, patience, and the education of the black man, all
must go hand in hand, and it will be the result of time, of education, of patience
which will drag them out of the condition in which they now are."[55]

As it was with so many Southern backers, Roebuck spent considerable time
exposing the contradictions in Northern opposition to slavery. How, they
asked, could one be against slavery and at the same time hate blacks? Ignoring
their own demands for consistency, pro-Southerners insisted that slavery was a
form of stewardship, preparing blacks for full citizenship; they did not even
suggest how slaves who were denied an education could ever reach the levels of
free men who had gone to school. It was this contradiction that Martin and
others attempted to exploit in letters to the press and in meetings, in the weeks
before Roebuck submitted his motion. For every town carried by Roebuck,
there were countless meetings that urged the government to maintain its neutrality. In a letter to the London *Morning Star*, Martin took Roebuck to task for
his distorted reasoning. Accepting that blacks were still denied political rights
in the North, Martin insisted that this was "against the spirit of Northern law

54. North London *News*, May 9, 1863; *Anti Slavery Reporter*, June 1, 1863.
55. Sheffield and Rotherham *Independent*, May 27, 1863.

and the protest of a large part of the Northern people." In the South, however, "[blacks'] social, political, and even religious rights are trampled under foot . . . according to law, and with the unanimous consent of its inhabitants." There were, moreover, irrefutable signs that blacks were being slowly accorded the rights of citizens in the North. They were commissioned as surgeons in the army, "a coloured ambassador has been received in Washington, coloured soldiers are received on an equality with white soldiers, and there is at this moment presiding over one of the wealthiest presbyteries of the city of Brooklyn, New York, a coloured man who is not yet forty years of age." There were no comparable developments in the South, which continued to enforce the subjugation of its black population. Britain, Martin concluded, had to make a historic choice: either support those struggling for their freedom or cast their lot with oppression.[56]

The ignominious defeat of Roebuck's motion in the House of Commons in July gave Martin and others only a brief respite in the struggle against Confederate supporters. But there was news of dramatic successes for Northern forces at Vicksburg and Gettysburg. It was obvious even to the most stouthearted defenders of the South that the North could not now be defeated. The best they could possibly hope for was that stalemate on the field of battle would increase pressure on Britain to intervene as mediator. Despite these shifts in Northern fortunes, the devastation of the cotton famine in Britain and the activities of Southern clubs in the Midlands demanded continued vigilance on the part of abolitionists. In early September, Martin took the fight to the enemy, delivering two lectures in Preston, long a stronghold of Southern support. As in the past, these lectures covered familiar ground. Like Satan, Jefferson Davis had gone to war "to gratify the aspiration of his inordinate ambition, that he might keep for ever those that believed in his sway behind his triumphal car of sin and death." To support the South was to join the legions of the wicked who were bent on snuffing out the lamp of liberty.[57]

But even as Northern supporters continued to record victories over their opponents, there still remained a nagging worry that the tide could turn at any moment. This jumpiness is reflected in the speed with which Martin responded to a rumor in August that Jefferson Davis had proposed to enlist 500,000 black troops in the Confederate army, promising fifty acres of land at war's end for each of those who joined. This was pure fabrication. If anyone in the Confederacy contemplated such a move in 1863, wisdom dictated that it be

56. London *Morning Star*, June 4, 27, 1863; *Anti Slavery Reporter*, July 1, 1863.
57. Preston *Guardian*, September 5, August 29, 1863.

kept a secret. As late as January, 1864, Davis felt compelled to silence similar proposals from a handful of generals as "injudicious to the public service." The idea was later revived in the closing years of the war as the South scrambled to find sufficient manpower to fill the ranks of its depleted armed forces. But Martin was not to know that Davis would reject such a plan as anathema to Southern interests. That the delicate balance of British public opinion might tip in favor of the South haunted Martin. All things considered, his fears were not unfounded. He was genuinely worried that adopting such a proposal would seriously weaken Northern support in Britain. It was to be expected, he wrote the London *Morning Star*, that Davis' declaration might initially prompt a number of slaves to join the Confederacy, but the first encounters would bring home to them the contradiction of fighting for the continuation of their enslavement. But Martin salvaged some good out of what he considered a rather bizarre turn of events. The South, he argued, could ill afford to put in gray the very men who produced the food that kept their armies in the field. More important, the new policy undermined the very basis on which the Confederacy argued for its independent existence. What need, he concluded, was there for a separate government if slavery was to be abolished?[58]

The departure of Mason in September convinced many that the South was finally on the retreat. But abolitionists were taking no chances; now in flight the enemy had to be pursued and destroyed. The work in London and vicinity was led by the LES, and its attack centered on the ships being built for the South at the Laird shipyards. Martin teamed up with William Craft, who had recently returned from Dahomey, at one of the society's meetings in London. Resolutions were passed that condemned slavery as a violation of Christian precepts and called on the British government to frustrate attempts "to equip vessels of war" for the Confederacy. The identical themes were repeated at subsequent gatherings in early October. These efforts were further reinforced by Henry Ward Beecher's successful whirlwind tour of Britain in the summer and autumn. The decision by the British government in October to seize the Laird vessels before they left port was yet another vindication of the Northern cause and the methods employed by their British supporters to influence public opinion.[59]

Each victory brought increased activity among British abolitionists. With

58. London *Morning Star*, September 9, 1863; Clement Eaton, *Jefferson Davis* (New York, 1977), 258.
59. London *Morning Star*, September 22, October 2, 24, 1863; London *Patriot*, September 24, 1863; *Anti Slavery Reporter*, October 1, November 2, 1863.

Mason in Paris, the burden of promoting the Confederacy was now solely Spence's. Apparently undaunted by news of Southern defeats on the battlefield, the British government's seizing the Laird ships, and the undeniable growth of British popular support for the North, Spence shifted his emphasis in November to the formation of influential pro-Confederate societies, which, like the Manchester Southern Independence Association, aimed to whip up backing for the South. In December, Spence reactivated the otiose Southern clubs in many northern towns and apparently recorded some successes. Neither side pulled many punches. Meetings of opponents were frequently disrupted and sympathizers were attacked and beaten. Abolitionists rose to the challenge, organizing frequent lectures at which Martin played an active role. Washington Wilkes lectured twice in Bedfordshire in late October; Captain T. Morris Chester, a black from Harrisburg, Pennsylvania, lectured in London; William Craft in Dulwich; George Thompson in Islington and Ryde in early November; and Martin, Frederick Tomkins, and Thompson in London in mid-November. Other lectures were organized by the LES and the Manchester Union and Emancipation Society at Brighton, Greenwich, Exeter, and Pendleton. When a pro-Southern meeting was called in Leicester on December 2, members of the local emancipation society packed the hall, elected their own chairman, and made life difficult for the speaker.[60]

But Spence persisted in his activities. Late in November he held a successful meeting in Glasgow in spite of opponents' disruptive efforts. It was clearly Spence's way of reactivating public sentiment in one last desperate attempt to pressure Parliament into recognizing the South. His speech contained nothing startlingly new. He appealed to his audience's sense of racial affinity. The South, traditionally loyal and peaceful, was overwhelmingly of British descent, but the North, always "turbulent, arrogant, and seditious," was inhabited by a large number of foreigners. He concluded that America comprised two distinct peoples, one characterized by "bluster, speeches, dispatches, the things called sermons from the men called ministers of religion," the other displaying "calm, silent resolution." Those, therefore, who argued that secession was an attempt to divide the nation were simply ignoring reality. The war, he stated, had nothing to do with slavery. That was a political device designed by Northern advocates to deceive international opinion. It was a war pursued in part for greed and in part for empire. It was incumbent on Britain, having introduced

60. Owsley, *King Cotton Diplomacy*, 176–78; *Anti Slavery Reporter*, January 1, 1864; London *Morning Star*, November 12, 25, 1863.

slavery in America, to interpose itself more forcefully to bring about a cessation of hostilities. With an obvious eye on previous failures, Spence seemed to be shifting his emphasis. No longer was he insisting on recognition of the South by Britain, but instead urged the government to "enter into relations with the other Powers of Western Europe, . . . to influence a restoration of the blessings of peace."[61]

The following day Martin rushed off a letter to the London *Morning Star*, questioning Spence's contentions and denouncing his request for a change in British policy. He dismissed as utter nonsense Spence's claim that slavery would be abolished once the South was independent. Secretary of State Judah Benjamin had expressly stated in a series of dispatches to his European emissaries that slavery was to be excluded from all diplomatic discussions. The Confederacy's constitution recognized and protected the right of individual states to maintain slavery. No nation serious about its independence, Martin concluded, could abolish its pivotal institution. To do so would lead to economic ruin. To suggest, as Spence had done, that Northern arrogance had pushed the two sections toward separation was clearly not borne out by the facts. It was the Southerners who held sway in national politics until 1860. They controlled the administration and "guided the politics and shaped the fashion of dress; they have made the laws, appointed its officers, and established the rules of etiquette; they have . . . bound merchants with their patronage, and let loose slave-traders upon the seas; in short, they have done all the evil which has been done to the American character—from the stultification of great men like Webster, till they become moral pigmies, to the transforming of little men, like Buchanan, into giants of evil." Having sown the wind, the South was now reaping the whirlwind. "Governing their plantations by the revolver and the poor whites by the bowie-knife, what is more natural than that the Southerners should melt the private revolver into the cannon of the public battlefield, and beat their bowie-knifes into swords of rebellion." The South, Martin observed, was not "the first national dog that in snatching at the reflection of the bone in the water lost the one in its mouth."[62]

It was a devastating attack on Spence and his shrinking group of supporters. Efforts to revitalize Southern clubs in December never got off the ground, largely because of the activities of Martin, Wilkes, Thompson, Conway, and

61. James Spence, *Southern Independence: An Address Delivered at a Public Meeting in the City Hall, Glasgow . . . 26th November, 1863* (Glasgow, 1863), 7–8, 15–17, 23, 24; *North British Daily Mail*, November 27, 1863; London *Morning Star*, November 27, 1863.
62. London *Morning Star*, December 1, 1863.

others. The more Spence retreated in the face of superior odds, the more frequently he asserted that Southern independence would lead to emancipation. Ironically the reiteration of that "promise" cost Spence his position as Confederate financial agent. His opponents, keeping up the pressure, gave no quarter. Martin traveled to Glasgow in early December for a public meeting organized by Scottish abolitionists with the express purpose of silencing whatever little support Spence may have garnered two weeks earlier. Determined to give pro-Unionists a taste of their own medicine, Southern supporters turned out in force. Despite the chairman's pleas, speakers were greeted with hisses and constantly interrupted from the hall. Martin added little to the points expressed in his recent letter to the London *Morning Star*. But his unmeasured attack on Spence for continuing to serve the South when he had been relieved of his official duties elicited catcalls from Spence's supporters in the audience. The situation threatened to degenerate into a free-for-all when someone attempted to introduce a motion accepted at the Spence meeting. Although the motion was defeated, Spence must have chuckled up his sleeve at his opponents' discomfort.[63]

Two weeks later, Martin was on the move again, this time to Hull, where he delivered two lectures under the auspices of the Union and Emancipation Society. The content of these speeches established a clear pattern that Martin would follow for the rest of his stay in Britain. To some extent it reflected a feeling among Northern supporters that the kind of lecture needed to counter Spence and his ilk was no longer necessary now that they had been effectively defeated. The discussions of the issues involved in the war were now broadened to include the narrative of his life and an extensive peroration on the nature of equality among the races. The recent dispute between William Craft and the leaders of the Ethnological and Anthropological societies at the British Association for the Advancement of Science had raised some concern that racial prejudice, long thought to be an American sickness, was now raising its ugly head in Britain. Those who argued that slavery had been the crucible in which the uncivilized African was introduced to the moral influences of Christianity were, Martin argued, deliberately falsifying history. "Southern Christianity" had been more damaging than useful to the slave's development. It had deliberately kept the slave subservient only to argue that he was inferior. If, he observed, "the proudest and most learned of the men of the polished nations had

63. *North British Daily Mail*, December 12, 15, 1863; London *Morning Star*, December 17, 1863; *Anti Slavery Reporter*, January 1, 1864; *Anti Slavery Standard*, January 9, 1864.

been brought up in the condition of the slave they would have been equally as ignorant." All blacks needed was freedom from oppression, both slavery and discrimination, and an opportunity to cultivate their intellectual faculties. His experience, like those of Douglass, Pennington, Craft, Brown, and others, was ample testimony to the soundness of this argument.[64]

Martin started making plans for his return to America in early 1864. George Thompson's departure for America on January 23 might have been the stimulus. As early as September, 1863, Martin had told a Preston audience of his ·anxiety to return home to publicize the extent of British support for the Union. Now that the opposition was vanquished, there was no reason to extend his stay. His year in Britain had been an eventful one; it was clearly the pivotal year in the competition for British support. British abolitionists had buried their differences over the policies of the Federal government following Lincoln's proclamation, and rallied to the challenge thrown down by Southern emissaries. Their success in winning significant public support, the government's neutrality and its seizure of the Laird ships in October, Mason's ignominious departure from England, and Spence's failure to create viable pro-Southern organizations, all spelled doom for Confederate interests in Britain. Efforts in 1864 were simply mopping-up operations.

Martin's stay in England had been most rewarding. By all accounts his fledgling church in Bromley had flourished, and he was liked and respected by his working-class congregation. His experience with the church created an abiding respect for the working class. He also became acquainted with some of Britain's leading men—John Stuart Mill, Goldwin Smith, John E. Cairnes, F. W. Newman, John Bright, and Richard Cobden, to mention only a few. His talents flourished in such illustrious company, and at no time, except for the rare occasion when Southern supporters poured out their venom on him, did anyone question his competence. But all Martin's successes did little to compensate for continuing poor health. The pressures of a hectic lecture schedule, which involved considerable travel, and ministering to the needs of his congregation proved too much. His doctors, therefore, suggested he return to America. On April 4 the LES held a soirée to bid Martin farewell. Most of his friends were there, and those who could not be present sent letters praising his work. Many people were well aware that Martin had been the vital cog in the effort to influence British opinion in favor of the North. John Bright summed it up best: "By his numerous and able letters to the newspapers, and his many eloquent

64. Hull and Lincolnshire *Times*, December 26, 1863; Northampton *Mercury*, January 23, 1864.

speeches at large meetings in London and elsewhere, he has had a great influence upon public opinion here."[65]

When Martin sailed a few days later, his destination was New York, not Boston. Successes in Britain seemed to demand a larger, more influential field. The pulpit at Shiloh Presbyterian Church had only recently become vacant. It was the largest black Presbyterian church in the country and in the past had had such prominent ministers as Pennington and Garnet. Although ordained a Baptist, Martin had been associated with a Congregationalist chapel in London, and this could have facilitated the transition from one denomination to the other. But there were some problems. The Shiloh congregation seemed to exist in a state of perpetual excitement, and had forced the resignations of both Pennington and Garnet. Although Martin accepted a call from the church one month after his return from England, his testimonies were not presented until February, 1865. For whatever reasons, there were some who opposed his appointment. Soon after submission of his testimonies, a special committee was established to investigate "charges derogatory to his moral character." Although he was cleared of any wrongdoing, it seemed a particularly inauspicious way to begin a new ministry.[66]

Martin's association with Shiloh was short-lived, interrupted by frequent extended trips to other cities and another visit to England. Given the delay in presenting his testimonies to the church, it is reasonable to assume that Martin had to find alternative means of supporting his family. He might have acted as stated supply for the church until he was installed in March. But this would have been insufficient to meet his daily needs. Like so many contemporaries, Martin had to supplement his meager income with fees from lectures. His success in Britain and his popularity as a speaker made the lecture circuit far more lucrative than the pulpit. As the war moved into its final phases many were eager to hear about British responses to the struggle. Martin had more invitations than he could reasonably handle. A few days after his return to America, a committee of prominent New Yorkers, including William Cullen Bryant, Theodore Tilton, Sydney Howard Gay, Henry Ward Beecher, and James McCune Smith, invited Martin to deliver a lecture on his work in Britain. In spite of postponements due to errors in scheduling, two thousand people attended the

65. London *Evening Star*, April 7, 1864; *Anti Slavery Reporter*, May 2, 1864; *Liberator*, April 8, 1864; *Anti Slavery Standard*, May 21, 1864; Sarah Agnes Wallace and Frances Elma Gillespie (eds.), *The Journal of Benjamin Moran, 1857–1865* (2 vols.; Chicago, 1948), II, 1267; New York *Evening Post*, May 31, 1864.

66. Records of the Third Presbytery of New York, in PHS; New York *Evening Post*, June 14, 1864.

meeting at Cooper's Institute in mid-June at which Martin expanded on a theme employed frequently in his British lectures, and one he would return to periodically during a later tour, namely, that loyalties in the war were determined largely by class considerations. A portion of the upper class, he argued, did not want victory for either side, hopeful that the war would destroy an important competitor. Another section of this class stood firmly behind the South, opposed as they were to American democracy and fearful that it would ultimately affect political developments in Britain. "They feared for the commercial and naval supremacy of England," he told a New Bedford audience later. "There is nothing they fear so much as a revolution, and in no country would a revolution be so terrible as in England, owing to the brutal character of the people." Similarly, the position taken by the upper middle class was due solely to extensive commercial contacts with the South. Members of the lower middle class, mainly its Dissenting ministers and its professionals, were by "nature and by grace," however, Northern supporters. The lower class, almost without exception, Martin boldly asserted, were friends of the Union, some on abolitionist grounds, others for "political and philanthropic reasons combined." All in all, he concluded, the majority were Union supporters.[67]

On unflagging working-class endorsement of the North, Martin consistently reiterated, hinged British popular support for the Union. The "energetic movements of the nameless masses," he asserted, controlled the actions of the ruling classes. In an anonymous letter to the New York *Evening Post*, he wrote: "The poor sufferers of Lancashire could never be cajoled or influenced with a false-hearted sympathy with a people seeking to be received into the community of Christian nations, avowedly with slavery as the 'corner stone' of their edifice; their simple, common-sense judgment conducted them to a true appreciation of the great principle involved in this desolating war, and their faith in the constancy and courage of the northern people leading them to the final triumph of truth, justice and liberty." Despite the evidence of Spence's success, the limited opposition Martin encountered during his visits to Glasgow and Preston, and the fact that some Lancashire towns ravaged by the cotton famine openly supported the South, Martin did not modify his convictions. He knew from experience in the East End of London and other cities that the "nobodies," as the *Times* derisively dismissed them, were at the center of popular support for the Union. They also knew that defeat for the North could affect

67. New York *Daily Tribune*, June 1, 2, 1864; New York *Evening Post*, June 14, 1864; *Anti Slavery Standard*, June 18, 1864; *Liberator*, June 3, 1864; *National Principia*, June 16, 1864; New Bedford *Evening Standard*, January 1, 1865.

class conflicts in Britain. "The upper class in England," he told a Philadelphia meeting, "are doing all in their power to make the lower class feel their dependence on the aristocracy, and they look forward to the time when the aristocracy will be able to crush the lower classes. The feeling of lower classes in England towards the aristocracy is most bitter, and once despair once settles down on them it will be the precursor of the enactment of a bloody scene." Northern victory, Martin believed, would redound to the benefit of the British working class.[68]

International support for the Northern cause, the cause of right against evil, mattered little, Martin insisted, if blacks failed to take the lead in the rehabilitation of America. Although Providence had provided the means through which black equality could be achieved, the work of "actual elevation" had to be initiated and carried out by blacks. The South must be defeated, for the future of black Americans was "wrapped up in this contest with probabilities more terrible or glorious, as the issue shall turn out, than even that [the future] of the white American." Defeat would have little effect on white Americans; for blacks, however, the result would mean possible expatriation and hatred "springing from wounded national pride." The quarter of a century necessary to reconcile the South "to the flogging" it received would give black Americans a splendid opportunity to prove their worth, which would necessitate constant sacrifice and active participation in the postwar reconstruction of America. Financial contributions to aid sick and wounded soldiers were an important beginning. Martin joined Douglass, J. Mercer Langston, and others in a series of lectures in January and February to benefit the Ladies' Bazaar Association, which raised money for the soldiers.[69]

But Martin would spend the rest of the decade outside America. In April, 1865, the American Missionary Association announced that Martin had been appointed its agent in Britain and representative to the May anniversaries in London. The AMA's expenses had increased dramatically in the last year as its work expanded among Southern freedmen, and existing American contributions were not enough. Martin, who had been associated with the AMA since his return from England, was a logical choice; his popularity enhanced the association's chances of winning substantial support from British philanthropists deluged with requests for contributions from a host of competing freed-

68. New York *Evening Post*, October 22, 1864; see Mary Ellison, *Support for Secession: Lancashire and the American Civil War* (Chicago, 1972); Philadelphia *Inquirer*, January 26, 1865.
69. Philadelphia *Inquirer*, January 25, 1865; New York *Evening Post*, February 1, 8, 9, May 21, 1865; New York *Daily Tribune*, May 18, 20, 1865.

men societies. But because of an attack of influenza in April and his church's reluctance to release him, Martin did not leave until May 10.[70]

Martin missed most of the important anniversary meetings because of that delay. Since his departure from England in April, 1864, a number of prominent Americans had been collecting money for the freedmen. Levi Coffin spent twelve months in Britain raising an estimated $100,000 in "money, clothing, and other articles" for the Western Freedmen Aid Commission. He was replaced by Dr. D. A. M. Storrs of Cincinnati in May, 1865. Coffin was largely responsible for the reactivation of the defunct Freed-Man's Aid Society, of which Martin was a founding member. In an effort to improve coordination and efficiency, a number of regional and national societies banded together in May to form the National Committee of the British Freed-Men's Aid Association (BFMAA). Martin's late arrival was the least of his immediate concerns. In a situation of open competition for limited and jealously guarded resources, the AMA's lack of official contacts with British freedmen associations impeded Martin's efforts. Under these circumstances, Martin's wide circle of friends proved relatively ineffective. Those with official sanction, such as Storrs and Charles C. Leigh, agent of the National Freedmen's Relief Association of America, with whom Martin traveled from Boston, were warmly welcomed at meetings of the BFMAA; Martin was not. His problems were complicated by a debilitating attack of neuralgia soon after his arrival in London. While other agents were busy making contacts he was confined to bed.[71]

Before he had totally recovered, Martin dispatched nine letters to newspapers, hoping to win some endorsements, and arranged a number of public lectures through old friends. But he had to tread carefully; too many endorsed meetings would irk some who could either be useful allies or formidable foes. He chose to act cautiously, making appropriate deferential gestures to those who mattered. In spite of his anxiety to get started, Martin reined in his impatience and requested a private meeting with Sir Thomas Fowell Buxton, chairman of the BFMAA. Only if that failed to produce tangible results, he wrote home, would he consider acting independently. But Martin's popularity in England annoyed some competitors. In an effort to defuse a potentially explosive situation and at the same time put some controls on Martin, Frederick Tomkins of the BFMAA arranged a meeting with Martin, Storrs, and Leigh.

70. New York *Evening Post*, May 8, 1865; *American Missionary*, June, 1865; Martin to George Whipple, April 29, 1865, in AMA.
71. Martin to Dear Sir, May 26, 1865, in AMA; Levi Coffin, *Reminiscences of Levi Coffin* (1876; rpr. New York, 1968), 664, 703–704; Bolt, *The Anti-Slavery Movement*, 59.

Both Storrs and Leigh protested that they had been accused by some newspapers of begging in Britain while Martin and the AMA escaped censure. Martin responded that he had been commissioned by the AMA to "lay the facts before the People and give them an opportunity to give without asking a gift," and this he intended to do. Fearing that things were getting out of hand, Tomkins suggested that these differences would hurt the cause if they were not resolved. The only alternative was for Martin to do as Storrs and Leigh had done and place himself under the BFMAA's direction. Martin resisted, insisting that the AMA had given him no authority to accept such a proposal. Angered by Martin's response, Storrs and Leigh stormed out of the meeting. Taking full advantage of the impasse, Tomkins conceded that although Martin could conceivably be successful without the society's imprimatur, he would find things most uncomfortable if it publicly denounced him. There were some members of the society, Tomkins observed, who were openly hostile to the AMA and who would relish public expression of their animosity. Martin had to accept Tomkins' offer, but he did manage to salvage a degree of independence. He insisted on the right to inform his audiences that they could designate the AMA as the recipient of donations and that all donations were to be "equally divided between the Society—not at different times; but whenever donations were made." It was the best he could do under the circumstances. But there was a price to pay for such a peace. Martin's meetings had to have the society's seal of approval, but he was responsible for organizing and financing them.[72]

Although restricting Martin's freedom to exploit his popularity to full effect, the arrangement did have the distinct advantage of making the AMA known to the public without the open recriminations engendered by competition. There were, however, other problems. In spite of the agreement with Tomkins, there were some who openly tried to isolate Martin. Things came to a head in mid-June when Arthur Albright, secretary of the Birmingham and Midlands Freedmen's Aid Association, attempted to exclude Martin from a public meeting in Birmingham organized to welcome American agents to Britain. Albright, a man apparently driven by nervous energy, was perpetually embroiled in disputes with his co-workers. On this occasion he insisted that the AMA could not take part because it was a sectarian organization controlled by Congregationalists. When Martin dismissed his accusation as unfounded, Albright resorted to a technicality: having not been included in the initial vote of welcome, the

72. Martin to Dear Sir, June 4, 9, May 31, 1865, all in AMA; London *Daily News*, June 1, 8, 1865.

AMA's representative could not speak at the meeting. Martin at first threatened to boycott, but later changed his tactics, rallying outside pressure to have his name added to the resolution of welcome. Albright reluctantly gave in, but then attempted to limit Martin's speaking time while giving Storrs and Leigh free rein. Martin's threat to remain silent forced Albright to relent. Although he had won the day, Martin knew that Albright's opposition could ultimately stymie all his efforts. In an obvious gesture of reconciliation, he met privately with Albright following the public meeting and came away with the impression that they had parted friends.[73]

But Martin had to pay a price for this victory. Had he not accepted the society's endorsement, there was little chance that his agency would have succeeded. For a number of reasons, the society had insisted that visiting Americans receive its seal of approval before going into the field. Great mischief had been done the cause, Louis Chamerovzow, secretary of the BFASS, wrote the AMA, "by parties coming over here, for some ostensible object, loosely recommended by persons more or less known on your side, and who succeed in collecting considerable sums of money, the appropriation of which, is never accounted for, and upon the expenditure of which there is no check." But there was more to it than just this concern to avoid fraud. At its center lay a desire to wield a measure of control over American visitors. Martin was quick to recognize this fact. His situation was made even more difficult by the fact that both Leigh and Storrs had been invited to Britain with the express purpose of making contacts with certain denominations; Leigh with the Methodists, and Storrs with the Congregationalists and Baptists. As if this were not enough, there were some in the AMA who questioned the wisdom of accepting the society's endorsement. Martin found himself in an unenviable bind. But there were a few rays of hope. Dismayed by Leigh's attempts to control the funds coming out of Britain, Storrs refused to hold any further meetings with him. Martin moved to take advantage of the break by teaming up with Storrs. He also attempted to break through the confines imposed by the London society's endorsement by mailing circulars containing information on the AMA to every freedmen's aid society in Britain.[74]

By mid-July, there was still no sign that the society's endorsement had borne fruit. In fact, the society seemed to be deliberately ignoring Martin. He tried on five different occasions to meet Tomkins, who had yet to arrange a single

73. Martin to Dear Friend, n.d., in AMA; *Midlands Counties Herald*, June 15, 1865.
74. Chamerovzow to Dear Sir, July 5, 1865, Martin to Dear Sir, June 21, 30, July 4, 1865, all in AMA; Lewis Tappan to Martin, July 3, 7, 1865, both in Lewis Tappan Papers, Library of Congress.

meeting, and each time Tomkins evaded him. More disheartening was the fact that Martin's letters to local societies had elicited only three replies, all unfavorable. Faced with these apparently insurmountable obstacles to his agency, Martin decided to shift his field of operations to Scotland. Using aristocratic contacts in London, Martin obtained letters of introduction to Norman Mac-Leod, the duke of Argyll, the lord provost of Glasgow, and other prominent Scots. The field, he wrote London and New York, was fresh and could be worked under very favorable conditions. In the first flush of enthusiasm, he thought raising $100,000 well within the range of possibility. But things were not all that rosy. For example, Glasgow's extensive commercial links with the South made it particularly lukewarm toward those promoting the cause of the freedmen. But Martin did have the support of James Sinclair and other members of the Glasgow Freedmen's Aid Society, which was formed in November, 1864. Using Glasgow as his base, he planned to visit other Scottish cities, "organize societies where none exist and try and awaken an interest in those that do exist."[75]

But nagging problems militated against Martin's getting an early start. His list of endorsements was so impressive that he felt constrained to find a chairman of comparable stature for his proposed meeting, and his arrival in Glasgow coincided with the general holiday exodus of aristocratic and middle-class Scots from the cities to the countryside. In a situation bordering on the comical, Martin spent most of August wandering around Scotland looking for a chairman, returning to Glasgow "as chairmanless as when we went and a good deal more moneyless." This lack of immediate success only increased his frustration. Not only was Shiloh demanding his return, but Martin was haunted by the prospect that the AMA, not knowing the difficulties he faced, would question his commitment and diligence. Having little to show for his expenditure of over £1,000, Martin complained of oscillating between "a sense of guilty extravagance and a sense of fear in accounting" to the association. It was an understandable dilemma.[76]

While Martin searched in vain for a chairman, Tomkins was busy making plans for Storrs and Leigh to tour Scotland. This threatened to destroy an earlier agreement by which Storrs and Leigh concentrated on England, leaving Scotland to Martin. Just when it appeared that Martin's diligence would bear fruit he was informed that Storrs had already organized meetings in Edinburgh

75. Martin to Dear Sir, July 3, 12, 1865, both in BFASS; Martin to Tappan, September 28, 1865, in AMA; Glasgow *Herald*, August 3, 1865.
76. Martin to Dear Sir, August 12, 15, 1865, both in AMA.

and Dundee. Angered by this affront and the open violation of the agreement, Martin threatened to organize competing meetings. Tomkins, he argued, had not only failed to organize any meetings for him in England, but the head of a regional society had no authority to hold public meetings in other areas. The Scottish field was the sole province of Scottish friends and should not be encroached on by those who were bent on capitalizing on the work of others. Although he warned London that he had no intention of relinquishing his position, Martin left the door open for possible compromise. In an effort to break the deadlock, Sinclair suggested that Tomkins consign the planned meetings to Martin "or at least make some arrangements with him by which he will give the sanction of his Scots names . . . and his presence to the meeting, in connection with any other delegate you desire to send." Tomkins apparently demurred, for in early September, Martin left Scotland to confer with the London society. The result was a series of joint lectures in Scottish cities in subsequent weeks.[77]

Before returning to Scotland, Martin attended the quarterly meeting of the British Freed-Men's Aid Associations in Bristol. The meeting, Martin wrote home, was a "great failure." Not only was it poorly organized, but the American delegates had no opportunity to make their views known in the area. Martin had earlier expressed an interest in holding public meetings around Bristol, but none of these materialized. He did take some comfort, however, in the fact that his persistence had resulted in small but nonetheless symbolically significant remittances to New York. The agreement that contributions collected as a result of the Scottish meetings would be shared equally between the AMA and Storrs augured well for the future.[78]

In the following weeks Martin and Storrs held a series of public meetings in Glasgow, Dundee, Aberdeen, and Perth. All, with the exception of the first Glasgow meeting, were well attended, and at the conclusion of each, local committees were formed to collect funds for the freedmen. Slavery, he told a Glasgow meeting, had "struck its roots so deep in the soil" that it could not be pulled up without leaving "a great hole . . . showing where the accursed thing stood." He appealed to his audiences to lend all possible assistance to fill the holes. Britain, he argued, had long been viewed as the world's moral arbiter.

77. Martin to Tappan, September 9, 1865, Martin to Dear Sir, August 19, 15, 1865, all in AMA; Martin to Dear Sir, August 18, 1865, in BFASS.
78. Martin to Dear Sir, September 16, 1865, in AMA; Martin to Dear Sir, August 26, 1865, Martin to Aspinall Hampson, August 3, 1865, both in BFASS; Bristol *Daily Post*, September 15, 1865; *Freed-Man*, October 1, 1865.

"When the poor wounded negro race lay bruised and wounded by the wayside, and the Pharisees and Levites among the American people passed him by on the other side, the Good Samaritans of Great Britain not only cried out against the sin, but did what they could to relieve the bondmen, and at a great sacrifice, which was the best proof of their sincerity, emancipated the slaves in the West Indian Islands." Following that tradition, all humanitarians were morally obliged to help the freedmen through this difficult transition period.[79]

But matters were not that simple. Lurking behind the popular support for American emancipation, an influential group of men, like Thomas Carlyle, John Crawfund, and others, argued that blacks were simply inferior to whites and incapable of improvement. Martin and Storrs spent a considerable portion of their lectures dismissing these arguments as immaterial in the present situation. Many of the recently emancipated, Martin told a Dundee audience, had shown their determination to be productive workers. But there were many impediments in their path. Former masters, for example, had made it difficult for them to acquire suitable land, and the desolation of war had made "profitable labour" almost impossible. Under these circumstances, discussions of the "capacity of the negro" were totally irrelevant; attention should be directed instead toward providing the freedmen with the means to survive the coming winter.[80]

This approach only sidestepped the issue temporarily. As pressure from opponents mounted, Martin was forced to address the issue more extensively at the annual meeting of the National Association for the Promotion of Social Science. As William Craft had done two years earlier, Martin sought to answer the question of "negro inferiority." There was no such thing as "natural inferiority," he asserted, "except on the Darwinian theory that all races, at some period of development, are inferior." If this were true, which he seriously doubted, the argument that justified black enslavement on the grounds of "inherent" inferiority was utterly erroneous. If, following the logic of the theory, the Negro was in a transitional state from "the brute to the man, he is simply where all races have been at some point in their history; and if any other race has finally risen to superiority, so may the Negro race eventually rise." But Martin dismissed the theory as fallacious, until such time as someone "catches

79. *Perthshire Advertiser*, October 5, 1865; Aberdeen *Free Press and Buchan News*, October 3, 1865; *Peoples Journal*, September 30, 1865; *Liberator*, November 3, 1865; Glasgow *Herald*, October 4, 1865.

80. Dundee *Courier and Argus*, September 27, 1865; Glasgow *Herald*, September 23, 1865; Helen M. Finnie, "Scottish Attitudes Towards American Reconstruction, 1865–1877" (3 vols.; Ph.D. dissertation, Edinburgh University, 1975), II, 289–92.

and exhibits a specimen of speaking ourang-outangs, or of a speechless race of man, or till I am shown a gorilla with a thumb that is not as long as its fingers." The "negro's inferiority" or laziness, Martin insisted, was nothing but a red herring conjured up by the Negro's enemies to confuse the issue of American Reconstruction and to avoid tackling the central concern, namely, the total emancipation of labor in America. "If the labourer does not progress in the arts," he averred, "the employer cannot progress in the science of labour. The form of labour must therefore remain stationary, which, in our time, is the same as being retrograde in character."[81]

The tenor of the debate grew increasingly acerbic in the wake of the Morant Bay Rebellion. Word of the rising of Jamaican peasants led by Paul Bogle and its brutal suppression by Governor Edward John Eyre reached Britain in November and immediately sparked renewed interest in the debate over the "negro's position" in society. The black Jacquerie "thirsting for the blood of their social superiors," Charles MacKay, a leading Negrophobe, wrote, had thrown those humanitarians with "nigger on the brain" into consternation. It seemed obvious to MacKay that Carlyle's predictions had come to pass. Americans should take warning from these events and rein in the intemperate desires of those who were insisting on black equality. Martin's compatriot Sarah Parker Remond, who had been living in England since 1859, discerned a marked change in British attitudes toward blacks. Planter interests, she asserted, were now on the rise, and since the Civil War "Southern Confederates and their natural allies, those former West Indian planters, have united together to endeavour to neutralise the interest felt for the oppressed negroes, and to hold them up to scorn and contempt of the civilised world."[82]

With the exception of his speech at the Social Science Association meeting and some periodic comments, Martin fought shy of open confrontation with Negrophobes. That would have deflected attention away from his duties at a time when it appeared he had reconciled (or possibly papered over) differences with Tomkins. His tour of Scotland with Storrs had been a success in more than one respect. Remittances to the AMA stood at £1,500 by the end of October. But more important, a mixture of patience and determination in his dealings with the London society had won Tomkins' grudging admiration. In late Oc-

81. J. Sella Martin, *The Cotton Question: Free Versus Slave Labour* (Glasgow, [1865]), 9–13; London *Times*, October 13, 1865; *Freed-Man*, November 1, December 1, 1865.
82. *Blackwood's Edinburgh Magazine*, XCIX (1866), 581; Remond quoted in Bolt, *The Anti-Slavery Movement*, 35.

tober, Martin, Storrs, and others attended the annual meeting of the Congregational Union of England and Wales in Bristol. The union's decision to call on its member churches to make a collection for the freedmen in January, Martin wrote home gleefully, promised to raise in excess of £10,000, most of which, he predicted, would go to the AMA because of its Congregationalist affiliations.[83]

Just when things seemed to be most promising, Martin's commitments to his church forced him to return home. It was not an easy decision. He anxiously wrote the AMA in September, suggesting a replacement and requesting an extension of his leave until the new agent familiarized himself with the field. The Reverend John Holbrook of New York was sent to replace Martin in early October, and his church reluctantly agreed to an extension of six weeks. Martin sailed for America on November 11, depressed about leaving a situation he had nurtured so patiently. He had been forced to decline twenty-six invitations from churches. His friend Dr. MacLeod wondered why Martin was being recalled from such an important assignment to a pulpit that could be easily filled, and Holbrook expressed some concern that the cause would suffer without Martin's knowledge and guidance. "I must confess," Martin wrote before his departure, "that my heart is sick at the thought of depending upon a people who are not willing to make so small a sacrifice as is required here."[84]

Martin's return was the worst of all possible situations. He never quite forgave Shiloh for compelling him to return, which only heightened tensions with the congregation, and his premature departure affected the flow of funds to the AMA. "He is well and favourably known all over the Kingdom," Holbrook wrote, "he is a colored man and a freed slave and these tell wonderfully and enable him to go *any* where and everywhere and to secure a hearing and he is a very able and acceptable speaker." Holbrook's difficulties were further increased by Tomkins' continuing insistence that he place himself under the guidance of the London society. With Martin gone, Holbrook found the Scots less inclined to lend further assistance to the AMA, which meant that "the good opinions developed were allowed to die without follow up." Holbrook's solution to the problem envisaged a direct appeal to the United Presbyterian, Free, and

83. Bolt estimates that more than £3,000 went to the AMA from this source (*The Anti-Slavery Movement*, 88–89); Martin to Dear Sir, October 26, 27, 1865, both in AMA; Bristol *Daily Post*, October 27, 1865; *American Missionary*, August, 1866.
84. Martin to Dear Sir, November 1, 1865, John Holbrook to Secretary of the AMA, October 31, 1865, both in AMA; Martin to Hampson, October 12, 1865, in BFASS.

Established churches of Scotland. It was not a novel proposal, for Sinclair and Martin had toyed with the idea in the summer of 1865 before shelving it.[85]

Constrained by many of the same difficulties Martin encountered, Holbrook suggested a series of new approaches. Even before these could be reviewed, however, New York decided that Martin's absence was directly affecting Holbrook's ability to raise substantially new support. But Martin's church stood in the way of his early return to Scotland. Wishing to avoid unnecessary conflict with Shiloh, M. E. Strieby, secretary of the AMA, spoke out against a new appointment for Martin, on the grounds that his "church would make trouble, and arouse the Presbyterians against us and *prompt them to give him trouble in Scotland.*" The association's decision was complicated unexpectedly by Holbrook's sudden reevaluation of Martin's abilities. Praise was now replaced by what Holbrook considered a more balanced judgment. Although Martin's ability as a public speaker was unquestioned and his reputation in Scotland was good, "some of our best friends," Holbrook confided, "say he lacks in *business* tact and adaptation. Mr. Sinclair of Glasgow said he did not succeed in private solicitation and business management. His color and antecedents are in his favor as a public speaker, but make him timid and hesitating in private approaches."[86]

To make matters worse, serious differences developed between Martin and the AMA, which hindered chances for reappointment. A new mission meant resignation from his pastorate. Recognizing the difficulties involved, the association tried to cushion the blow by first offering to name him one of its secretaries, but later withdrew the offer, fearing that some members would oppose the appointment of a black secretary. It was more than Martin could stomach. An association that had long espoused equality was now bowing to rank prejudices. Saying he would accept nothing less than a secretaryship, and fully aware of his indispensability to the association in Britain, Martin informed Strieby that the African Civilization Society had made a bid for his services. Unfortunately for Martin, the society's offer was a two-edged sword. Although it caused the AMA some anxious moments, forcing serious reconsideration of their original proposal, it placed Martin in an unfortunate quandary. What would other blacks think of his taking an inferior position in a white organization? Being dismissed and ridiculed as a "whiteman's lichpital [*sic*]" would not be dif-

85. Holbrook to Secretary of the AMA, December 4, November 27, 1865, Martin to Secretary of the AMA, November 11, 1865, all in AMA.
86. M. E. Strieby to Whipple, January 23, 1866, Holbrook to Strieby, February 9, 1866, both in AMA.

ficult to accept, he told Strieby, but he could not lose the respect of the "colored people of New York" and continue to be useful. Many blacks would view his "position to be antagonistic to their own in refusing their offer to accept the one from the AMA," so he must be able to say "and to prove, that the whites in working for negroes will do as much for me as those from whom I turn away."[87]

One thing was certain, the AMA could not afford a long, potentially costly battle over a relatively trivial issue. Faced with a debt of over $30,000 in May, Strieby warned that the association faced imminent bankruptcy due to the expenses of expanded work among the freedmen and an unexpected drop in remittances from Britain. The AMA accepted Martin's suggested compromise, naming him a special secretary for the duration of the mission. Martin resigned his pastorate in April and sailed for London soon afterward, accompanied by Dr. William W. Patton of Chicago.[88]

If things had been difficult before, existing differences among British supporters of the freedmen threatened to restrict Martin's usefulness. The BFMAA National Committee had been torn apart in the aftermath of the Morant Bay Rebellion. There were those like Thomas Hughes and Tomkins who demanded that the committee adopt the cause of the rebels as part of its support for all former slaves while others argued that the committee should confine itself to problems in America. In the wake of the dispute, Tomkins and his supporters withdrew to form the British and Foreign Freedmen's Aid Society. The rump, under the leadership of Fowell Buxton, was revamped and renamed the National Freedmen's Aid Union of Great Britain and Ireland (NFAU).

The rebellion had a significant influence on British attitudes toward the American freedmen. Many advised Americans to tread warily in their dealings with the freedmen if they hoped to avoid such savage responses to the beneficence of former masters. From around England came word, in late 1865 and early 1866, that the times were decidedly inauspicious for holding meetings for the freedmen. The vigor with which these views were promoted finally prompted Martin to respond in September, 1866. Englishmen who for more than thirty years had lent their support to abolitionist causes were in danger, he warned, of "prostituting the well-earned influence of their nation to the support of a great wrong." Proslavery sentiment, forced to retreat in the face of Union victory in the Civil War, was again raising its sinister head behind the

87. Martin to Strieby, March 27, 20, 1866, both in AMA.
88. Strieby to Homer, William Patton, and Martin, May 21, 1866, in AMA; *American Missionary*, May, 1866; *Freedmen's Aid Reporter*, May, 1866.

smokescreen of the Jamaican rebellion. Support for President Johnson's efforts to rehabilitate the Confederate states (a policy designed to reestablish the status quo ante) could not conceal the naked racist designs of proslavery supporters in Britain. "It makes one's heart ache," Martin lamented, "to find these fallacies and inconsistent fooleries more rife in England than they are now in America: not among the common people, it is true; and yet many of these, the sycophantic followers of the great, out-Herod Herod in the meanness of their welfare and the vileness of their weapons." At this critical juncture, when America was slowly but perceptibly coming to the realization that blacks must be entrusted with full political rights, it was incumbent on Britain, Martin insisted, to reaffirm its support for the equality of all men, and arrest the growth of this racist cancer.[89]

Martin spent a few days in London, making contacts and renting a home for his family in Islington. A week later he was on his way to Scotland. Earlier in the month, Holbrook and Patton, following up on Martin's initial contacts, had addressed the General Assembly of the United Presbyterian Church and won its official support for the AMA. Subsequent collections netted £690, of which £640 was transmitted to New York. Soon after his arrival in Scotland, Martin arranged a number of public meetings and issued a series of broadsides that called on local ministers to support the cause by inviting him to preach in their churches. The visit had been planned, however, with the express purpose of attending the general assemblies of the Church of Scotland and the Free Church. Following addresses by Martin and Patton, both assemblies agreed to support the AMA's efforts, the Church of Scotland recommending collections by its churches in July and August and appointing an officer to receive and transmit these funds to New York. Little came from the appeal to the Free Church, which Martin later described as "hot in feeling, bigoted in denominational preference, narrow in doctrine and policy."[90] He left Scotland in early June for western England to fulfill a number of engagements organized by the NFAU, with whom he had agreed to cooperate. Past experiences with Tomkins suggested this was the best approach. Martin nevertheless tried to keep his options open, steering a delicate course between contending freedmen's aid groups.[91]

89. London *Daily News*, September 4, 17, 1866; Bolt, *The Anti-Slavery Movement*, 41–44; Martin to Whipple, May 19, 1866, in AMA; *Freedmen's Aid Reporter*, May, 1866.
90. Martin to Whipple, October 2, 1866, Martin to Dear Brethren, July 3, 1866, both in AMA; Finnie, "Scottish Attitudes," II, 360, 448–49, III, 29–33; *Freed-Man*, June 1, 1866.
91. Martin to Hampson, May 30, 1866, in BFASS; Martin to Strieby, June 16, 1866, in AMA.

Martin carried on where he had left off in 1865. Appeals to British humanitarians aimed to fill the void created by the ravages of the war, which destroyed
the southern economy and left thousands homeless or orphaned. Southerners
had fled in droves, he pointed out, taking with them necessary skills and capital
that had not been replaced because conditions in the area were unstable, and
the freedmen, jealously guarding their liberty, had understandably shown little
inclination to return to the land. Once the stigma associated with cotton cultivation and slavery was removed (and Martin insisted that that would soon
occur), then the former slave, now an independent laborer, would go back to
the land. In the interim, the destitute had to be fed and clothed, and the unlet-
tered educated. Although America was capable of providing for all these needs,
it was, Martin argued, still shackled by its past antipathy toward blacks. Britain,
which was responsible for the introduction of slavery in America, and which
had done so much to ensure its abolition, was now morally obliged to support
this worthy cause. This form of reparation, as Martin called it, also had a decided economic dimension, for an educated, self-reliant, and dignified labor
force would soon be producing cotton at levels demanded by British industry.
Appealing directly to the strong missionary movement in the West Country, he
suggested that support for the freedmen's education would ultimately "produce
people fitted to go into Africa and Christianize it." Blacks, he later told an Edinburgh audience, were "naturally susceptible to religious influences. They had
shown that in their patient endurance during the civil war, rather than rise
upon their oppressors with the insurrectionary knife, though they had shown
also their courage in the field when a proper opportunity was afforded them."
Martin continued to use this approach in his lectures, an approach that relied
heavily on long-held beliefs among British humanitarians. The future of blacks
in the New World, many believed, depended on their ability to function as independent and free laborers. Their education and exposure to Christianity
would, as Robert Campbell argued, make them particularly suited for spread-
ing Christianity and civilization in Africa. The likes of Carlyle and Knox might
have dismissed Martin's views as the rantings of a deranged mind, but for many
in Britain this approach held out the greatest hope for the future of blacks
everywhere.[92]

Martin's plan of action involved using London as headquarters and making
periodic forays into the provinces to address public meetings. This, he cal-

92. *Weekly Review*, July 7, 1866; Exeter and Plymouth *Gazette*, June 8, 1866; Bristol *Daily Post*,
June 7, 1866; *Freedmen's Aid Reporter*, June, 1866.

culated, would reestablish him as *primus inter pares* among American agents
in Britain, and improve the AMA's stature among British humanitarians.
Nothing else could have persuaded him to cede temporarily the Scottish field
to Patton and Holbrook, for he had always considered Scotland his domain.
This method of operation was also prompted by the urgent need to counter
opponents in the NFAU, and Tomkins' renewed efforts to win Martin's allegiance to the British and Foreign Freedmen's Aid Society. Although Martin
remained neutral in disputes between the union and the society, an indiscretion
by Patton provided Tomkins with enough ammunition to discredit the mission.
Ignoring Martin's advice, Patton had evidently shown Tomkins AMA correspondence about its poor financial situation, information that Tomkins used to
chastise the association in the pages of the *Freed-Man*. Unaware of past differences, Patton made matters worse by declining the proffered endorsements of
the NFAU. Opponents took full advantage of the opportunity, refusing the
association a percentage of collections made in Britain, voting instead to send
all monies, in one instance, to the Western Freedmen Aid Commission in Cincinnati, even though Martin had been the main speaker at many of their public
meetings. As a result, Martin wasted considerable time and energy during the
summer, writing letters to friends and newspaper editors and attending the
meetings of both societies, "drawing teeth," as he put it, where necessary and
rebuilding old bridges where prudent. He also busied himself with efforts to
persuade prestigious Congregational churches around London to make donations that would be used to build schools in the South, holding out the promise
that these schools would be named for the congregations. Unfortunately his
plan fell victim to the famine in India and a cholera epidemic in England.
Under these circumstances, the needs of the freedmen seemed less desperate.
With little to do, Martin spent part of August trying to collect money already
raised by United Presbyterian churches. The trip was worth the inconvenience,
for he was able to send £350 to New York in mid-August.[93]

The departure of most of the American agents in September opened up new
possibilities for Martin. While preparing the ground for his work in Scotland
later in the year, Martin was approached by the NFAU with a plan for joining
forces in a series of public meetings. His neutrality was now paying dividends.
Yet he demurred, insisting that the union first grant the AMA equal status with
the Cincinnati commission, which up to that point had been receiving the bulk
of its contributions. Until a decision was made, Martin demanded that his ex-

93. Martin to Whipple, August 18, 1866, Martin to Dear Brethren, August 4, 1866, Martin to
Strieby, July 14, October 6, 1866, all in AMA.

penses be met by the union. This was clearly unprecedented, for customarily the NFAU expected visiting agents to cover their own expenses. But Martin would not budge; he saw no reason why money raised through his efforts as the AMA's agent should go to any other group. Moreover, he wrote Aspinall Hampson, the AMA was the only permanent society in America with a long, honored history of work among blacks. Although a considerable portion of contributions sent from Britain to the commission had been utilized to meet operating expenses, the association, because of its efficient organization, was able to earmark most of its money for work among the freedmen. In spite of these arguments, the union refused to accede to Martin's demands. Instead they voted to send contributions to the AMA through the commission, at the same time making it abundantly clear that insisting on total equality would work to Martin's disadvantage during the remainder of his agency. Given the influence of the union, Martin had to conclude that periodic contributions from this quarter were preferable to a battle over equal recognition for the association.[94]

But Martin suffered another debilitating attack of ague and "catarrhal fever" in October, which forced postponement of gatherings scheduled for Reading, Pecham, Luton, Leeds, Huddersfield, and Bradford until after the middle of November. As he had done in the past, Martin used these public meetings as forums from which to launch a series of blistering attacks on the purveyors of racist views in Britain, and to increase interest in the cause of the freedmen. He was convinced that there existed a direct link between slavery and civil war in America and the growth of racist sentiment in Britain. All the concerns expressed about the effects of immediate emancipation, the reluctance of blacks to work, their lack of intelligence, and theories about their proximity to the ape in the "Chain of Being" were attempts to rehabilitate former slaveholders and return the freedmen to the ranks of the servile. In order to reverse this trend, concerned men and women must redouble their efforts in behalf of the freedmen. Large crowds and contributions boosted Martin's hopes. Following the Huddersfield gathering, he wrote optimistically that popular reaction to the Jamaican rebellion and responses to his public meetings showed a definite swing in favor of the freedmen.[95]

Despite NFAU pleadings, Martin cut short the tour and headed for Scotland

94. Martin to Whipple, October 2, 1866, Martin to Strieby, October 6, 1866, Martin to Whipple and Strieby, October 20, 1866, all in AMA.
95. Reading *Mercury*, November 17, 1866; Leeds *Mercury*, November 23, 1866; Huddersfield *Examiner*, November 24, 1866; Bradford *Observer*, November 29, December 6, 1866; Martin to Strieby, November 24, 1866, in AMA.

in early December, partly to continue promoting the cause there, but also to try the hydropathic method as a possible cure for his ailments. If the situation seemed bleak in Scotland at the end of 1866, an editorial in the prestigious *Scotsman*, attacking the local ladies' freedmen aid society, seemed to put paid to any hope of increasing support in Edinburgh. Although not avowedly anti-AMA, the editorial nonetheless chastised an "imperfect" American Congress for passing what it considered illegal constitutional amendments. Those in Britain who favored Radical Reconstruction policies, the editors argued, were involving themselves directly in the internal affairs of America. Refusing to accept any replies to its editorial, the newspaper, by associating Scottish aid for the freedmen with foreign interference in American politics, dealt a serious blow to Martin's chances in Edinburgh. When he left Scotland, he was convinced that the editorial had affected contributions, even from those who supported the cause. Furthermore, appeals to church general assemblies had brought only marginal returns. Contributions from Scotland would only increase, Martin wrote, if the AMA sent an agent to work directly with churches. Busy in the temporarily more productive English field, and evidently basking in his acceptance by the union, Martin saw no reason to waste his time in Scotland.[96]

Not only had Scotland proved a disappointment, but Martin was now solely responsible for all of Europe and Britain. It was obviously too much for any one person, and especially for someone whose health was uncertain. Before returning to the lecture circuit in England, Martin decided in late December to pay a quick call on supporters in Paris and Geneva. He returned saddened by the lack of support in Paris, but buoyed by the prospects in Geneva, which, he wrote headquarters rather ambitiously, could act as a stepping-stone for subsequent visits to Russia. His rosy view of potential support on the Continent is reflected in the fact that soon after his return to London he began studying French with a private tutor.[97]

But the lessons had to be fitted into breaks between lectures organized by the NFAU. The major portion of this new tour took place in Yorkshire, covering most of the cities and towns omitted from the previous visit. The sizable turnout in Malton was a welcome relief after the disappointingly small crowd at an earlier meeting in Croydon. At the conclusion of the lecture in Malton, it was decided to form a local auxiliary of the union and Martin was invited to return

96. Martin to Strieby, December 15, 1866, Martin to Whipple and Strieby, December 29, 1866, both in AMA.
97. Martin to Whipple and Strieby, December 29, 1866, January 7, 1867, both in AMA.

as soon as his schedule permitted. At Scarborough the deputation held one public meeting, visited Sunday schools, held a special meeting for children, and Martin preached at two chapels. Three meetings at York netted only £200, and Martin hoped that £100 would be sent to the AMA. These returns discouraged him. In nine months he had managed to raise only £1,000 for the association, much less than he had collected during his last visit. Martin wondered whether his agency had exhausted its usefulness. "I am willing to continue as you may determine," he wrote home in late January, "but having had such sanguine expectations in regard to receipts from this country blasted and having worked night and day to recover my spirits by finding new fields and [?] new agencies and being convinced that large returns from here may not be looked for I am anxious to be relieved of the burden of responsibility which tells greatly on my health and spirits." The request to return was repeated frequently during the remaining eighteen months of his mission, each time eliciting pleas that he continue and praise for his work. Given the AMA's reliance on support from Britain, it could afford to do little else.[98]

It appears certain that Martin had now had his fill of the agency. Although he continued a hectic schedule of nightly lectures in January and February, collections and subscriptions were disappointingly low. Anxious to report some successes, Martin temporarily shifted his focus of activities to Geneva, where, after a second visit in January, his contact Pasteur Philippe reported optimistically on potential support from the city. Martin returned to London, determined to take up the challenge. The successful exploitation of this new area, he wrote, required a full-time agent on the spot. With his French studies almost completed, and the British field continuing to produce only paltry returns, Martin intended to abandon Britain for the Continent. But New York was less enthusiastic and refused to endorse his plan until another agent arrived. In the midst of this gloom, Martin found one small ray of hope. In early 1867, Lord Stanley, the British foreign minister, agreed to receive a deputation from the NFAU to discuss the possible disposition of a £60,000 surplus from the Lancashire Relief Fund. The union had every reason to hope that the government would allow the release of the money for work among the freedmen. Martin's spirits were lifted temporarily by this new development and in February he returned to the lecture circuit.[99]

98. Martin to Dear Brethren, January 26, 1867, in AMA; Croydon *Chronicle*, January 20, 1867; Malton *Gazette*, January 26, 1867; Scarborough *Mercury*, February 2, 1867; *Freedmen's Aid Reporter*, February, 1867; Thomas Phillips to Hampson, January 21, 1867, in BFASS.
99. Martin to Dear Brethren, January 26, 1867, Martin to Whipple, February 4, 1867, both in AMA.

Following another attack of fever, which forced cancelation of a return engagement in Malton, he lectured in Leicester, Hull, and Newcastle in late February and early March. Responses to these meetings only depressed Martin. Audiences in small towns like Malton were sizable and enthusiastic, but contributions rarely exceeded £15. Attendance in the larger towns like Leicester, where they had hoped for more substantial contributions, was however, unexpectedly slight. People on whom abolitionists and supporters of the freedmen had long depended for a significant portion of their backing were now engrossed in the national debate over reform, and they seemed to have little time for causes thousands of miles away. Yet, one local editor insisted, there was "an undercurrent of sympathy at work in this country in behalf of the Freedmen in America." He was convinced that under less trying circumstances, a speech of such "fact, philosophy, and good feeling" as the one delivered by Martin would have enlisted the "attention of a much larger audience." For someone already depressed by his inability to attract more contributors, this was cold comfort.[100]

The arrival in March of the Reverend J. A. Thome of Cleveland, the new agent he had been impatiently awaiting, jolted Martin out of his depression. But earlier experiences with Patton had made Martin wary of agents with whom he had had no previous contacts. Thome, however, proved to be the perfect foil for Martin. He was considerate and deferential to a fault. Martin, Thome wrote, "is one of the noblest men I know; he is very able, as a speaker, as a dealer with men personally, as a manager of affairs, as a counsellor. His judgement is quite reliable, his insight into men is quick and clear, his temper is good, usually I guess, and his spirit is I think Christian." What a far cry from Holbrook's assessment of Martin's abilities! The feeling was mutual. Martin found Thome to be prudent and modest. "His gentlemanly deportment, and Christian considerations," Martin observed, "have completely won me and as I learn all others who have made his acquaintance here."[101]

Martin returned from a visit to Paris to be on hand when Thome arrived and to introduce him to important people in the movement. They planned to use the weeks before the May anniversary meetings to lay the groundwork for a rejuvenated agency. Several meetings were organized for London and the Home Counties in late March as a means of introducing Thome to the public. Under

100. *Midlands Free Press*, February 16, 23, 1867; Leicester *Chronicle and Leicestershire Mercury*, February 16, 1867; Hull *News*, March 2, 1867; Newcastle *Chronicle*, March 12, 1867; Malton *Gazette*, March 16, 1867; Phillips to Dear Friend, February 22, 26, 1867, both in BFASS; Martin to Strieby and Whipple, March 9, 1867, in AMA.

101. J. A. Thome to Strieby, April 3, 1867, Martin to Whipple and Strieby, April 13, 1867, Martin to Whipple, August 18, 1866, all in AMA.

this new plan, Martin was to concentrate on the Continent while Thome worked Britain, both periodically coming together at important public meetings in Britain. Martin also put out tentative feelers in Russia through Ira Aldridge, the black American Shakespearean actor, and suggested that Cassius M. Clay, the American minister at Saint Petersburg, might be willing to introduce him to potential supporters there. Martin left for Brussels in early April, hoping to influence some of his contacts to establish a committee similar to the one recently formed in Paris. They hoped to raise 250,000 francs in France, but achieving that goal remained problematic because of the threat of war between France and Prussia.[102]

The period of waiting before the anniversary meetings and the threat of war on the Continent dampened any optimism Thome's arrival might have generated, and again Martin asked to be relieved of his duties. The illness of his four-year-old daughter and his increasing alienation from the NFAU leadership only exacerbated the situation. By April, union meetings had become inconsequential as public interest turned to the more pressing issue of the proposed reform bill in Parliament. Martin was convinced that the union was foundering. Its efforts were now concentrated on procuring the Lancashire Relief Fund's surplus and on organizing a massive public meeting at the London Tavern, a last-ditch attempt to win new support for the cause. Although optimistic about the former, Martin was less sanguine about the latter, even though he was convinced that the AMA would be the largest recipient of any funds collected. His gloomy prognosis might also have been the result of differences over his role in the anniversary meetings abolitionists planned for Paris in July. Although he was invited to participate, the union insisted that he attend as part of its delegation rather than as a representative of the AMA. This he flatly rejected. Martin's problems also affected Thome's work. Just one week after his laudatory letter, Thome reported that Martin had not been "very communicative to me, nor very helpful," nor had he responded to Thome's "proposals for joint action." Indeed, Thome concluded forlornly, Martin seemed "to have given over this field as quite hopeless. Yet . . . he is quite encouraged by the interview I had with him on Saturday last." Martin even refused to attend the anniversary meetings. His disappointment and frustration were clearly responsible for these wild fluctuations in mood.[103]

102. Martin to Dear Brethren, May 3, 1867, Martin to Whipple and Strieby, April 13, 1867, Thome to Strieby, April 3, 1867, all in AMA; John Hodgkin to Esteemed Friend, March 27, 1867, in BFASS; *East Sussex News*, April 5, 1867; *Freedmen's Aid Reporter*, April, 1867.
103. Thome to Strieby, May 10, 1867, Martin to Dear Brethren, May 3, 1867, both in AMA.

Settlement of the dispute between France and Prussia improved Martin's chances for success on the Continent only marginally. But this was offset by word from Clay that there was little to be gained from a visit to Russia. Martin sat idly in London for three weeks, waiting for the planned meeting with Lord Derby about the Relief Fund's surplus. What worried him even more was the fact that he had no definite engagements for the next three months. Such idleness, at the very moment when the association was in dire need of support, rankled. But the officers in New York continued to discourage his return to America, where Martin thought he could do the most good, and tried to impress on him the importance of his mission even in trying circumstances.[104]

If Martin or anyone else had hoped for a speedy disposition of the Relief Fund's surplus, they were to be sadly disappointed. Initially, the NFAU suggested to Lord Derby, who, incidentally, was also chairman of the Lancashire Cotton Famine Fund Committee, that a Chancery Court dispensation could free the surplus for use in areas other than the one it was intended to cover. This approach proved much too difficult. The deputation, of which Martin was a member, suggested using a short act of Parliament to accomplish its objectives. Always the consummate politician, and fully aware of the many suggestions for the surplus' use, Derby refused to commit himself. Others, he pointed out, wanted to put the money toward building a hospital in Manchester; some said it should be returned to the donors. The decision, he concluded, would have to be taken by the Lancashire committee. Acquisition of the surplus proved elusive, not only because of competition from other worthy causes, but also because of internal wrangling in the NFAU over this and many other issues.[105]

These disputes and the failure of the deputation contributed to Martin's growing alienation from the union. Armed with weighty letters of recommendation from the duke of Argyll and others, Martin left for the Continent in mid-June, hoping to win financial support from prominent Frenchmen and Germans. The visits to Berlin and Paris were not successes. Although he did manage to elicit a few small contributions, no one was willing to involve himself in the work of organized committees. When the rump of an old committee, organized by Leigh, refused to transfer the few florins in its coffers to the AMA because the money had been raised initially for the Cincinnati commission,

104. Strieby to Martin, May 17, 1867, Cassius Clay to Strieby, May 13, 1867, Martin to Dear Brethren, May 18, 25, 1867, all in AMA.
105. Bolt, *The Anti-Slavery Movement*, 110–11; London *Daily News*, May 25, 1867; London *Morning Star*, May 25, 1867.

Martin threw up his hands in despair and returned to London. As had occurred in the past, failure prompted him to ask again to be released. Although he had not abandoned all hope of French support, he had serious doubts about his abilities and usefulness. Funds were so short that his wife took in lodgers, and he deferred paying doctors and clothiers, using what little money he did have to continue his activities in cities like Amsterdam. Frankly, he wrote home, his was not a temperament that could "long submit to constant failure, especially when the money flies as it does here." [106]

In addition, Martin had virtually severed all contacts with the NFAU. Things came to a head in the weeks leading up to the Paris conference. Just as disputes in Britain during the antebellum period were rooted in conflicts among American abolitionists, these differences were also the result of events in America. The formation of the American Freedmen's Union Commission (AFUC) in May, 1866, ushered in a new period of divisiveness among those evangelicals associated with the AMA and those, like Garrison, who advocated a secular approach to work among the freedmen. Almost as soon as it was formed, the AFUC began to disintegrate. The Cincinnati branch defected to the AMA, and the Chicago and Cleveland branches soon followed. The issue was further complicated by the fact that the Freedmen's Bureau, and particularly its head, General O. O. Howard, openly endorsed the work of the association. [107]

These conflicts had a direct impact on Martin's relationship with the union and exaggerated his sense of frustration at its failure to organize effective lecture tours. Repeated visits to small towns like Malton produced but few more contributions. Never in the habit of hiding his feelings, Martin protested these engagements by simply staying away. This did not endear him to the leaders of the NFAU, and although they continued to work together, the relationship turned increasingly sour. The union's suggestion that he attend the Paris meeting as one of its delegates only made the situation worse. The fate of the deputation to Lord Derby and the continuing personal feuds in the union reinforced Martin's conviction that the NFAU had become moribund. The union's support for the AFUC in the dispute with the AMA, and its decision to invite William Foster Mitchell, a Nantucket Quaker, to visit Britain as its agent, proved to be the last straw.

The union once again tried to silence Martin, this time by granting him only

106. Martin to Dear Brethren, August 2, 13, July 12, 1867, all in AMA.
107. Richard Bryant Drake, "The American Missionary Association and the Southern Negro, 1861–1888" (Ph.D. dissertation, Emory University, 1957), 15–23.

ten minutes at the last session of the Paris conference. By comparison, Garrison, an AFUC delegate, was given thirty minutes. Martin seriously considered boycotting the meeting but was persuaded by Thome and Coffin "to fire off his gun." Ignoring the imposed limitation, Martin spoke for twenty-five minutes. Angered by such blatant attempts to keep him quiet, Martin delivered one of his finer speeches, one that Thome, obviously partial, thought was as effective as Garrison's. Although the speech contained little that was new, Martin made sure that the association was competently defended against Garrison's charges of sectarianism. "Mr. Garrison says his Society is the largest non-ecclesiastical Freedmen's Aid Society in America. The term ecclesiastical we do not accept," Martin responded, "because we are supported by, and employ in, our work members of every evangelical sect. But the term 'religious but non-sectarian' we can and do accept." Martin's quarrel was not with Garrison, for he had an abiding respect for the early abolitionists. Although there were periods when the intransigence of some Garrisonians drove Martin to distraction, he never missed an opportunity to praise Garrison. Martin's speech was both a defense of the association and a message to the union that he was determined not to quit the field.[108]

But the field continued to be frustratingly unproductive. Coffin's presence raised his hopes that old contacts in Switzerland and Germany could be used to better effect. But a cholera epidemic in September quickly destroyed that possibility. Anxious to avoid open disputes with Mitchell, whom he considered grasping and overly ambitious, Coffin decided to forgo public appearances while in Britain, and he concentrated instead on visiting old friends. But this did little to relieve Martin's frustration and sense of defeat brought on by almost total inactivity. He and Thome decided to mark time, hoping that the situation would improve after the Congregational Union meeting in October.

One gets the distinct impression that Martin's failures also began to affect his perception of reality. With little money coming in from other sources, he turned almost in desperation to the Lancashire Relief Fund. The union's inability to effect a quick dispensation of the surplus, however, seemed to spur him on to new activity in late September. Martin believed he could influence an early decision in favor of the freedmen. He told New York that some members of the Derby government who, he insisted, had to remain anonymous were

108. Thome to Strieby, September 9, 1867, in AMA; *Special Report of the Anti-Slavery Conference, Held in Paris . . . on the Twenty-sixth and Twenty-seventh August, 1867* (London, 1867), 51–52; Drake, "The American Missionary Association," 24.

convinced that his speech at the May meeting with the prime minister would be crucial. Armed with this information, Martin planned to meet William E. Foster, M.P. for Bradford, "to instill into him my own hopes about the fund." Foster, he hoped, would then put him in touch with the undersecretary for foreign affairs. Nothing came of this scheme, and, driven to reality by the need to increase remittances to New York, Martin was forced to seek assistance from more traditional sources.[109]

Just when things seemed to be at their worst, an event occurred that threatened to end Martin's relationship with the AMA. Someone, whose name the association refused to disclose, had evidently accused Martin of living in luxury and traveling first class. Although the charge irked Martin, the fact that the association relayed it anonymously and demanded an explanation was an outrage. He threatened to resign immediately if his name was not cleared. He reminded headquarters that he had ignored life-threatening illnesses, which were so serious that insurance companies would not sell him a policy, in laboring for the association. Traveling first class protected him from inclement weather, which could bring on attacks of the fever. Martin's anger and disappointment were understandable.[110]

Thome found the AMA's actions unconscionable, but, try as he might, he initially failed to persuade Martin to await a response to his letter before severing relations with the association. Martin, he wrote, was "worthy of trust" and had to be trusted if he were to be retained in the service of the association. Thome seemed on the point of despair. "I think he is hopelessly estranged," he wrote New York somberly. "The responsibility of cutting off the help in which I have trusted for the winter's work, and of diminishing the proceeds, must rest where it belongs." But Thome persisted in his efforts to mollify Martin, and by the end of the month, he anxiously reported that his colleague had "regained his equanimity" following a letter of reconciliation from Strieby.[111]

The break with the union, and the adoption of Mitchell as its principal lecturer, left Martin with no other option but to retreat to Scotland, the area where he had recorded his greatest successes. Since his arrival Thome had continued with limited success to exploit the field. The return to Scotland was

109. Martin to Dear Brethren, October 4, 1867, Thome to Strieby, September 9, 1867, both in AMA.
110. Martin to Dear Brethren, November 10, 1867, in AMA.
111. Thome to Strieby, December 14, November 25, 8, 1867, Martin to Dear Brethren, December 20, 1867, all in AMA.

logical, given the unfavorable situation in England. But the move was made all
the more urgent by AMA policies. Supported by matching subventions from
the Freedmen's Bureau, and anxious not to lose promising school properties
in the South, the association had incurred considerable debts in its effort to
expand educational facilities for the freedmen. Almost $50,000 of the associa-
tion's total debt of $87,726 in 1868 had been spent for that purpose. Thome
and Martin began this new phase of the campaign in Paisley in mid-October,
conducting services at Free, United Presbyterian, and Baptist churches. They
held an organizational meeting in Glasgow in early November to explain the
association's needs. Hindered by constitutional restrictions that limited federal
government intervention in this sphere and by southern insolvency, philanthropic organizations, Martin insisted, had to take the lead in educating the
freedmen. Although northern whites were the logical and immediate choice as
teachers in the South, Martin argued that in the long run, blacks, who were
acclimated to southern conditions, would ensure the success of the work. Recognizing this fact, the AMA had decided to establish normal schools for blacks
in the South. At Martin's and Thome's suggestion, it was decided to hold a
large public meeting in early 1868 with the duke of Argyll as chairman.[112]

In the intervening weeks Thome and Martin held a series of meetings in
Edinburgh, Dundee, Perth, Blairgowrie, Paisley, Greenock, Montrose, and
Port Glasgow, following which local committees were established to collect
funds. The poor state of the economy, however, kept contributions to a minimum. After the Edinburgh meeting, Martin reported that "the people who
gave £100 two years ago gave only £25 yesterday. And the majority who gave
£25 before declined to give anything at all this time." Although Thome expected £200 from Dundee, he saw these gatherings as preparing the ground
for increased contributions following the Free Church Assembly in May. The
Glasgow meeting, attended by four thousand, was a rousing success. Even the
duke of Argyll, traditionally a lukewarm supporter of total black enfranchisement, enthusiastically endorsed the principle of black equality. Martin and
Thome were understandably pleased. The Glasgow committee formed to solicit contributions for the association subsequently raised £851. People in other
cities seemed similarly inspired. Edinburgh, for instance, contributed £600
while elsewhere lesser amounts were raised. Things were looking up in early

112. Drake, "The American Missionary Association," 100, 279; Finnie, "Scottish Attitudes,"
II, 468–70; Glasgow *Herald*, November 8, 6, 1867; Paisley and Renfrewshire *Gazette*, October 26,
1867; Thome to Strieby, October 14, 1867, in AMA.

1868, so much so that Thome felt confident he could return home without seriously affecting the flow of contributions from Scotland.[113]

Thome's proposed departure rekindled Martin's desire to leave Britain. He had been in the field nearly three years, and despite his initial optimism and hard work, he had failed to realize the amount of contributions anticipated. Periodic illnesses only increased his despondency. Martin's long absence also meant that he had lost contact with day-to-day events in America. It was clear from his speeches that he had begun to repeat himself. They lost some of the sting characteristic of earlier deliveries, and as a substitute for substance, he found it necessary to rely increasingly on humor. Thome was quick to realize this. Martin, he observed, had in "some respect the advantage over any man. His disadvantage as compared with myself, is that he has been too long here, away from the field of which he speaks." Thome suggested that Martin return home temporarily so as to reacquaint himself with developments and gain new ammunition for the work in Scotland. Martin's anxiety to leave led him to interpret an obscure reference in one of Strieby's letters as permission to go. Anticipating confirmation from New York, he hurried off to London to prepare his family for departing with Thome in late February.[114]

Whatever the AMA's feelings about Martin's repeated requests, it could not afford to have its most important agent leave Great Britain. Thome's departure depressed Martin. In spite of increased contributions from Scotland, he painted a gloomy picture of diminishing returns and rising expenses. Unlike Thome, he was not convinced that the Free Church Assembly would recommit itself to the association and name a date when a collection would be made. Martin persevered, however, and in the weeks before the General Assembly, he held periodic meetings with church leaders in an effort to win their support for simultaneous collections. The situation was further complicated by deep-seated disputes within the church over a proposed merger with the United Presbyterian Church. Martin's most delicate task, he informed the AMA, was to convince those who were in favor of a collection that their support would not be exploited by opponents. Although the assembly declined to name a spe-

113. Thome to Strieby, December 30, 1867, January 14, 7, February 1, 1868, Martin to Dear Brethren, December 20, 1867, all in AMA; Dundee *Courier*, January 7, 1868; Montrose, Arbroath, and Brechin *Review*, January 10, 1868; Blairgowrie *Advertiser*, January 11, 1868; *Perthshire Advertiser*, January 16, 1868; Glasgow *Herald*, January 28, 1868; *Freed-Man*, February 1, 1868; Finnie, "Scottish Attitudes," II, 65–70, III, 79.
114. Thome to Strieby, January 7, 1868, Martin to Dear Brethren, December 20, 1867, January 17, 1868, all in AMA.

cific date, it did vote for a future collection for the association. It is not clear
when, or even if, the collection was ever made, but the vote did raise Martin's
spirits temporarily. The labor of the past three months had not been totally
unproductive.[115]

The vote of the Free Church freed Martin from what had become a most
trying agency. There was no longer any reason to stay in Britain. Strieby's repeated pleas that he remain were unavailing. The field, he pointed out, was now
exhausted. The £400 remitted in April was really the most that could be expected from Britain now or in the immediate future. More than anything else,
however, he worried about his wife's serious illness, which demanded that she
be moved to a warmer climate. "I am willing myself to stay and do whatever
work I can find to do notwithstanding the irksomeness of partial failure," he
wrote, "but my wife's health is anything but reassuring and my own is nothing
like as good as it was. Besides a chronic trouble I feel more and more exhaus-
tion from long Railway journies and greater susceptibility to cold after heated
meetings and perspirative efforts."[116]

Martin sailed for America in early August after a trying but relatively successful agency of three years. He was pivotal to the association's international
efforts to win support for its work among the freedmen. He had his greatest
success in Scotland, where he labored mightily to gain the backing of churchmen, philanthropists, and the public. He was clearly aided by Scottish suspicions of any attempt by London to dictate policy. The reaction to Tomkins'
trying to enter the Scottish field without the endorsement of leading Scots tes-
tifies to this strong sense of independence from metropolitan control. When it
mattered, as it did in the Tomkins affair, Martin could rally his Scottish friends
in order to reassert his primacy in that field. And when things seemed gloom-
iest in England, he was guaranteed a haven in Scotland. Martin never developed a similar rapport with his English co-workers. His refusal to accept un-
critically the leadership of men like Tomkins and Albright, and his insistence
that the AMA be recognized as an equal partner, militated against more harmonious relations. None of these problems existed in Scotland. There, he was
his own boss. His success in Scotland is even more significant, given old abolitionist antagonisms. The Glasgow Freedmen's Aid Society, whose leaders had
long been stalwart Garrisonians, was in its endorsement of the AMA breaking
with tradition and supporting an association with which Lewis Tappan, an old

115. Martin to Dear Brethren, May 28, April 14, March 1, February 19, 1868, all in AMA;
Finnie, "Scottish Attitudes," III, 24–26.
116. Martin to Dear Brethren, April 4, June 26, 1868, both in AMA.

arch-enemy, was strongly identified. Not even Garrison's visit in 1867 was able to shake the firm commitment of Scots Garrisonians to Martin and the AMA.

Martin left Britain with a heavy heart; the country that had welcomed him with open arms in 1861 had turned decidedly racist by 1868. At no time during his most recent visit did he feel constrained to write home, as other blacks had done in the past, about his reception by the British. In fact, he informed a Leicester audience that when he "returned to America he would have to say that the name of England was anti-slavery, but that rich, cultivated, aristocratic, fashionable England was pro-slavery." Even some supporters of the freedmen found it necessary to distance themselves from notions of black equality. E. S. Beesley, a noted defender of working-class interests, for instance, publicly declared himself no "negro-worshipper. I don't consider a black man a beautiful object," he wrote, "and I daresay he sings psalms more than is good for him. Some negroes may be men of ability and elevated character, but there can be no doubt that they belong to a lower type of the human race than we do, and I should not really like to live in a country where they form a considerable part of the population." Following the massive freedmen's aid meeting in Glasgow in January, the Glasgow *Herald* addressed the thorny issue of black freedom and equality in one of its editorials. Rejecting arguments justifying black slavery, the editors nonetheless castigated the duke of Argyll for taking too sanguine a view of the "negro's capabilities." Argyll's praise of Martin as a fine specimen of "negro intellect" was totally misplaced, for "the reverend gentleman has more of white than negro blood in his veins, and consequently is more closely allied to the higher than the inferior race." Martin's reply fell on deaf ears. Pride in his black ancestry meant nothing to ethnologists of this school; what mattered most was the apparently irrefutable fact that Martin owed his intelligence, "eloquence . . . pathos and humour" to his "white blood."[117]

All of this seemed inconsequential when compared to the effects of the agency on Martin's health. The attacks of neuralgia, ague, liver disorder, and "catarrhal fever," which periodically immobilized him, recurred with increasing frequency in this period, so much so that Sarah wrote the AMA that her husband would not survive if he did not reduce his work load. "Night traveling which I have been compelled to do, has kept in constant germination the seeds of an old disease, ague and liver complaint," Martin informed Whipple and

117. Beesley quoted in Douglas A. Lorimer, *Colour, Class and the Victorians* (Leicester, 1978), 191; Leicester *Chronicle and Leicestershire Mercury*, February 16, 1867; Glasgow *Herald*, February 1, January 30, 1868.

Strieby, and these illnesses were complicated by exposure to inclement weather. Ague fits, which he had shaken off easily in the past, were so persistent that they weakened him to the point where only "quinine and such remedies" brought any relief. All the evidence suggests that opium or, more likely, laudanum was prescribed for his ailments. The frequency of use and the dosage are unknown, but by late 1867, Martin was apparently addicted. In many instances, work was only possible after "a dearly bought release from personal pain and by opiates."[118]

By midcentury, opium and laudanum had become the most regularly prescribed treatment for a whole range of painful illnesses, including consumption, coughs and colds, pelvic troubles for women, cancer, rheumatism, and neuralgia, and was even found in soothing syrups for babies. One contemporary British medical text recommended the use of opium "to mitigate pain, to allay spasm, to promote sleep, to relieve nervous restlessness, to produce perspiration and to check profuse mucous discharges from the bronchial tubes and gastro-intestinal canal." Martin found himself under this "yoke of mysery," as De Quincey called it, as he struggled to relieve severe pain. But Martin never lost his sense of humor. When doctors recommended that he cut his hair close after a particularly painful attack of "catarrhal fever," he wrote that though it did help, some people mistook him for a Chinaman.[119]

These illnesses and the effects of laudanum probably accounted for the fluctuations in mood so evident in the closing months of his agency. But there was also concern for Sarah's frail health. Prior to leaving London, Martin wrote the AMA, suggesting an appointment in the South. But when the association offered Plymouth Church in Georgia, he declined, insisting that experience had taught that trouble invariably followed whenever ministers were not directly selected by the congregations they were to serve. His experiences at Shiloh had left some bitter memories. "I should never go to a church again that I did not deliberately choose," he told the association. Martin returned to New York without any immediate prospects for employment. He spent a considerable portion of the weeks of inactivity following his return in Saratoga, New York, recovering from a severe attack of lung congestion and taking the waters.[120]

118. Martin to Dear Brethren, November 10, 1867, Martin to Whipple and Strieby, October 20, 1866, Sarah Martin to Whipple and Strieby, October 27, 1866, all in AMA.
119. David F. Musto, *The American Disease: Origins of Narcotic Control* (New Haven, 1973), 70; Thomas De Quincey, *Confessions of an English Opium-Eater* (London, 1886), 1–3; Martin to Whipple, November 17, 1867, in AMA.
120. Martin to Whipple, October 30, 1868, Martin to Dear Brethren, June 26, 1868, both in AMA.

Without pulpit or agency, Martin had little else to do. It appears that he began negotiating with the Fifteenth Street Presbyterian Church in Washington, D.C., during the fall and was called to the pulpit later that year. The move to Washington put him at the hub of political activity in Reconstruction America. The election of Ulysses Grant as president and the imminent departure of Johnson promised a speedier growth in black political rights. Black Washingtonians, their stature and numbers enhanced by the residence of men such as J. Mercer Langston, George B. Vashon, Downing, Martin, and later Douglass, now assumed the mantle of black leadership. It was a logical evolution, as black Americans were directly affected by policies emanating from the White House and Congress. Living in Washington also provided Martin with an opportunity to dabble in behind-the-scenes political dealings. He obviously relished lobbying in the halls of Congress. When it came time to name the new American minister to Haiti, he busied himself in private meetings with Senators Charles Sumner and Henry Wilson in an effort to have Douglass nominated. Although he failed, it was clear that Martin took these activities seriously and that he intended to continue to walk the corridors of Congress, promoting the interests of black Americans. Unfortunately, recurrent illness curtailed his active participation in some of the major events in this period. Although he attended the National Colored Convention at Union League Hall in mid-January, he was not an active participant. In recognition of his commitment to the cause, the convention nonetheless elected him a member of its Executive Board.[121]

The convention was the immediate precursor of the first Colored National Labor Convention, which met in Washington in December, 1869. Martin's long association with and promotion of workers' interests in both Boston and London drew him naturally toward others with similar concerns. Throughout his most recent tour of Britain, he had taken every opportunity to explain the needs of black southern workers to his audiences. Those, like Carlyle and MacKay, who argued that the freedmen were lazy and did not want to work, Martin averred, were ignorant of the fact that whenever reasonable wages were available, blacks had willingly gone to work. In many instances, former slaveholders had combined openly with racist organizations, like the Ku Klux Klan, to force the freedmen to work in situations from which they had only recently been emancipated. This, and not an aversion to honest labor, was responsible, Martin insisted, for the freedmen's understandable reluctance to return to the

121. Martin to Whipple, December 23, 1868, in AMA; *Anti Slavery Standard*, January 30, 1869; *New Era*, February 10, March 17, 24, 1870; Martin to Frederick Douglass, April 24, 1869, in FDP.

plantation. Now that freedom had been attained on the battlefield, the path toward "civilization" for the freedmen lay through honest, dignified labor. Given their skills and the needs of national and international industries, success would be assured if the freedmen continued to cultivate cotton. "But only wait till our frolic is over," he said in 1866, "and we ourselves will see that the staple which enslaved us is yet to elevate us. We stood in nakedness two hundred and fifty years to produce it for others to be clothed withal; but hereafter out of its mystic web we shall weave the garments of self-respect, the turban of our manhood and the banner of our progress and equality." The South had the land and the capital; the freedmen, the labor. All that was needed was for the former slaveholders to disabuse themselves of "the bugbear" that the freedmen were hankering after "their daughters and sisters for wives," and an alliance of labor, capital, and land could be effected that would make the South "the mistress of the world's manufacturing industry."[122]

Martin viewed the attainment of these objectives with particular urgency, for he was convinced that black Americans had just twenty-five years after the defeat of the South to show their mettle before a national backlash set in. This is why the growth of racism in Britain caused him such anguish. Conclusions about black inferiority were being drawn without first permitting the freedmen an opportunity to redeem themselves. "Our demand for fair treatment is made," he wrote the Glasgow *Herald*, "in the interest of civilization; for it is admitted on all hands that the negro has some very good natural qualities, and that his worst traits are those of falsehood and dishonesty which we have every right to father upon slavery, and that they are no lovers of bloodshed, tyranny, or needless revolution." Martin called for a suspension of judgment on the "negro's place among races till education shall have done for him what it has for other educated peoples viz. tested their qualities and fixed their place."[123]

Open resistance by southern interests and their northern supporters to the freedmen's demands for land, education, and civil and political rights prejudged, in Martin's view, the outcome of this new experiment. The plight of black workers in the late 1860s was cause for deep alarm. Opportunities for fair employment were limited, and organized labor had openly rejected black participation in unions. The recently formed National Labor Union (NLU) ignored the pleas of leaders such as William Sylvis and A. C. Cameron, and bowed to pressure from constituent unions that practiced racial exclusion. The

122. *Freed-Man*, March 1, 1866.
123. Glasgow *Herald*, February 1, 1868.

Typographical Union of Washington, for instance, refused membership to
Lewis Douglass, Frederick Douglass' son, solely on the grounds of race. The
persistence of Sylvis, Cameron, and others, however, seemed to have paid off
when the 1869 annual meeting of the NLU admitted nine black delegates.
They were urged to form local organizations and elect representatives to subsequent congresses. One resolution captured the essence, or, more correctly,
the hoped-for effect, of this new direction. The NLU, it stated, knew "no
north, south, east, west, neither color nor sex, on the question of the rights of
labor." Isaac Myers, a Baltimore caulker, and one of the black delegates, spoke
for other black laborers when he said that "the white laboring men of the country have nothing to fear from the colored laboring man. We desire to see labor
elevated and made respectable; we desire to have the highest rate of wages that
our labor is worth; we desire to have the hours of labor regulated as well as to
the interest of the laborer as to the capitalist. Mr. President, American citizenship for the black man is a complete failure if he is proscribed from the
workshops of the country."[124]

Myers was the principal mover in the formation of the Colored National
Labor Union (CNLU). When black workers gathered in Baltimore in July to
elect delegates to the NLU congress, Myers and others issued a call for a meeting of blacks in Washington. In the months leading up to the December conference, local meetings were held in many black communities to select representatives. The convention, attended by over two hundred delegates from some
twenty-two states, reflected the sense of urgency with which many blacks
viewed the plight of black workers. The convention also attracted a number of
white labor leaders, many of whom addressed its sessions. The meeting's links
with the Negro Convention movement were indisputable—it too spoke of the
need for temperance, education, industry, and economy among blacks. But unlike its predecessors, this convention also aimed specifically to counter white
trade-union exclusion, to organize black workers in the South, to promote ways
of achieving better wages, to form cooperatives and land and building associations among black workers, and to stop the importation of Chinese laborers.
"Coolie" labor, a form of disguised slavery, threatened to cheapen the value of
labor and undermine the chances for black workers to achieve their goals. "Our
motto," the convention declared, "are liberty and labor, enfranchisement and

124. Sumner Eliot Matison, "The Labor Movement and the Negro During Reconstruction,"
JNH, XXXIII (1948), 433–38; Myers quoted in Charles V. Wesley, *Negro Labor in the United States,
1850–1925* (New York, 1927), 162–63.

education! The spelling-book and the hoe, the hammer and the vote, the opportunity to work and to rise, a place on which to stand, and to be and to do, we
ask for ourselves and children as the means in the use of which, under God, we
are to compass these achievements which furnish the measure, the test, and
justification of our claim to impartial treatment and fair dealing." Its demands
included fair employment practices, open apprenticeships, fair wages, and the
division of public lands for homesteading. The adoption of these policies,
the convention argued, would lead ultimately to a "superstructure capacious
enough to accommodate on the altar of common interest" all workers—Irish,
black, German; the "poor white" in the South and the white mechanic in the
North; even the Chinese laborer now being exploited on southern plantations.[125]

Martin played an active role in the convention and was elected to the Executive Board of the Labor Bureau, which was formed to provide continuity between annual meetings. He was largely responsible for preventing the exclusion
of some whites who were opposed by Langston on the grounds that they supported the Democratic party. Blacks, Martin insisted, could not afford the luxury of rejecting white friends solely on the basis of their political affiliations.
He also argued for women's total participation in the meeting. But the optimism with which the delegates returned home was short-lived. Efforts to establish local black unions were only marginally successful. In an attempt to
achieve one of its goals, a large CNLU meeting in February, 1870, elected
Myers its agent to tour the South. Myers held two organizational sessions in
Norfolk and Richmond in April, but there is no evidence that others were held,
or even what success followed from Myers' efforts. By the union's second annual meeting in January, 1871, its objectives clearly had not been fulfilled. Organizational drives were held, the CNLU recording state assembly meetings in
Tennessee, Texas, Alabama, Missouri, Georgia, and North Carolina. But no
permanent organizations emerged from these state gatherings, and the CNLU
was defunct by 1872, a victim of the NLU's inability to enforce its interracial
policy.[126]

As efforts were being made to improve the condition of black workers, and

125. Colored National Labor Convention, *Proceedings of the Colored National Labor Convention
Held in Washington, D.C., on December 6th, 7th, 8th, 9th and 10th, 1869* (Washington, D.C., 1870), 20,
18, 11, 31; Wesley, *Negro Labor*, 173; Matison, "The Labor Movement," 456; Joseph E. Taylor,
"The Colored National Labor Union, Its Birth and Demise, 1869–1872" (M.A. thesis, Howard
University, 1959), 10–13; *New Era*, January 13, February 17, 1870; *Anti Slavery Standard*, December 18, 1870.
126. Wesley, *Negro Labor*, 181; Matison, "The Labor Movement," 464–67; Taylor, "The Colored National Labor Union," 67–68; *New Era*, April 21, 1870.

ensure political rights, black leaders in Washington and other cities sought ac-tively to protect civil rights gained in 1866. Whenever the law was broken, as in the case of segregated transportation, blacks organized to bring pressure on the authorities for the removal of these insidious legacies of antebellum discrimi-nation. Martin and his family found themselves at the center of such a battle. In late November, 1869, Martin enrolled his nine-year-old daughter in the white Franklin School. The principal, unaware of the child's racial background, gladly accepted her. When it became known that young Martin was black, she was sent home immediately. Martin's insistence that his daughter attend that school, and no other, opened a can of worms. Washington had shown little inclination to provide adequate primary education for its children, white or black. At the end of the 1860s, the public schools were unable to accommodate more than 25 percent of all children in the city. A law passed in 1862 required Washington, Georgetown, and the county to establish public primary schools for blacks. The shortcomings of these schools were patently obvious by the end of the decade; the black schools could accommodate only 33 percent of the school population between the ages of six and eighteen.[127]

In an apparent attempt to solve some of these problems, Congress proposed merging the black and white school boards in early 1869. Some blacks, Martin among them, pressured President Johnson to veto the bill, arguing that black students would suffer from the merger. In the early fall, however, a number of black and white residents of the city's fourth ward petitioned for a mixed school in their neighborhood. City officials seemed partial to the request, but before they could act, the dispute over Martin's daughter's admission to the Franklin School broke. Expelling her was clearly illegal. Martin had followed the neces-sary procedures and had obtained permission for his daughter to attend the school from George B. Vashon, one of the black trustees. Soon after her expul-sion, Martin returned her to the school, but she was again sent home until the corporation's attorney could rule on the legality of her admission. But Martin would brook no delay. Anxious to avoid "white flight" and stymied by Martin's intransigence, the school authorities allowed the young girl to attend the Franklin School as a visitor. When Martin protested this move, the trustees suggested what must stand as one of the most bizarre devices employed to avoid integration: young Martin could be admitted as a white student. But Martin would have none of it. Unable to break the impasse, both sides looked to the

127. Lilian G. Dabney, *The History of Schools for Negroes in the District of Columbia, 1807–1947* (Washington, D.C., 1949), 117, 107, 111, 67.

school board's attorney for resolution. Refusing to pull either party's chestnuts out of the fire, the attorney avoided the issue by insisting that he would wait until the entire school board solicited his views.[128]

It is not clear if the situation was ever resolved in Martin's favor, but the dispute effectively postponed the issue of integrated education in the city for decades. Martin's insistence, some would have called it intransigence, did nothing for his popularity in some quarters of black Washington. A public meeting of the Board of Trustees of Colored Schools adroitly avoided making a statement. Black and white speakers seemed concerned to downplay the dispute and ended the meeting without discussing the issue. A correspondent for the Philadelphia *Press* may have been speaking for many when he wrote that though not illegal, it was "impolitic for a colored parent to insist upon sending his child where her presence would prove disturbing. Such conduct serves only to postpone a solution which will come about by gradations, but which will, nevertheless, surely come." Integrated education would have to wait on developments in the twentieth century. Charles Sumner did attempt to resolve the dispute by introducing a bill in early January that called for school desegregation. Although the city council did request that Congress act on the bill, national developments and congressional plans to reorganize city government effectively killed any chance that it would be passed. As a result, black children continued to attend segregated schools.[129]

Although personally devastating, such disappointments must have been partially offset for Martin by the successful formation of the CNLU. The conference endorsed the *New Era*, of which Martin was editor, as its official organ. Plans for a new paper had been under consideration by a small group of black Washingtonians since early 1869. Under the original plan developed in March, Douglass was to occupy the editor's chair and Martin would be the associate editor. But when Douglass showed little enthusiasm for moving to Washington, Martin was named resident editor and editor-in-chief, and Douglass' son Lewis, chief compositor and manager of the printing office. Operating expenses for six months were estimated at $5,000; by March, $2,500 had been raised. Part of Douglass' hesitation was due to the inability of the small group of black Washingtonians to guarantee adequate capitalization. His reservations

128. Washington *Daily Morning Chronicle*, December 1, November 26, 27, 30, 1869; *Anti Slavery Standard*, December 4, 1869, January 8, 1870; Constance McLaughlin Green, *The Secret City: A History of Race Relations in the Nation's Capital* (Princeton, 1967), 100–101.
129. Green, *The Secret City*, 101; *National Republican*, January 11, 8, 1870; Washington *Daily Morning Chronicle*, November 29, 1869; *New Era*, May 5, 1870.

dampened the group's enthusiasm and forced a temporary suspension of plans. Negotiations with Douglass continued through the summer, however, and in August, Martin suggested a compromise that answered Douglass' reluctance to assume the editorship but made no mention of his concerns about the paper's finances. Martin agreed to take the job as editor only if Douglass would be the corresponding editor. In addition, Martin insisted on a number of guarantees, the most important being that editorial policies were to be solely his responsibility. Nor was he to be involved in the financial management of the paper unless directly asked by the business manager.[130]

Martin's demands must have been accepted, and Douglass' concerns partly allayed, for the first issue of the paper appeared in January, 1870, with Martin as editor and Douglass as corresponding editor. The paper's future seemed promising: located in Washington, and the official organ of the CNLU, the *New Era* seemed destined to fill the void left by the *Weekly Anglo-African*. Martin's editorial philosophy, though distinctly partisan, was nevertheless nonsectarian. "We as a Northern people," he wrote Douglass, "should use the advantages that belong to our position in free Society to lay bare mere party machinations and so draw out the best intelligence of those of whom we speak while at the same time we should fearlessly express the peculiar grievances of those who might become victims of even the radicals. I insist in short upon our organ being the *Radical* of the radicals." The first issue was a bit more specific. The paper, Martin told his readers, would support a homestead act as one means of improving life in rural America and curtailing the power of land speculators; promote black labor organizations; oppose "coolie" immigration; give its hearty support to the Republican party as the party of the people; and support all efforts to eliminate proscriptive schools.[131]

The goddess of liberty on its masthead, the *New Era* resembled many of its contemporaries in style and layout. Its four pages were devoted to a mixture of news and literature. For example, the inaugural issue carried the first installment of an original story by Frank J. Webb, the novelist. The paper would become an important publisher of black literary expressions. It also included frequent articles by Martin R. Delany, George B. Vashon, William James, and other notable figures. Two articles appeared under Sarah Martin's byline. The first, "Cotton," was a verbatim reproduction of a portion of Martin's speech to

130. Martin to Douglass, August 24, March 29, April 24, 1869, Douglass to Martin, April 5, 1869, all in FDP; Douglass, *Life and Times*, 399.
131. Martin to Douglass, August 24, 1869, in FDP; *New Era*, January 13, February 3, 1870.

the British National Association for the Promotion of Social Science in October, 1865, which raises some doubt about the originality of Sarah's second
article. That sort of deception is difficult to understand, as Martin did not
complain about a shortage of suitable material. Letters covering a wide range
of topics were published frequently. Breaking an age-old tradition, Martin
rarely published any of his own speeches, and on the few occasions when he
did, they appeared in précis. In spite of its high standards, the paper was, as
Douglass had feared, never quite able to meet its operating expenses. It carried
few advertisements, and its yearly subscription rate of $2.50 was insufficient
to cover costs. Periodic pleas did produce some new subscriptions, but not
enough. Its difficulties were compounded by the fact that few blacks seemed
willing to act as agents, and it appears that at least in the first month of its existence, a significant number of subscribers were white.

Working at the editor's desk was a full-time, consuming job. Soon after the
appearance of the first number, Martin announced his retirement from the
ministry and the pulpit of the Fifteenth Street Presbyterian Church after just
one year as its minister. It was to be his last ministerial appointment. He had
apparently taken the position as a last resort, when nothing else materialized
following his return from London. Martin's years away from the pulpit while in
Britain had to some extent distanced him from the church, and his rejection of
the AMA's offer of the Plymouth Church suggests that he was really seeking a
position outside the church. The memory of disputes with the congregation at
Shiloh did not help matters. He had always been critical of the church's conservatism. Forever shackled by "pecuniary interests," ministers spent too much
time and energy, he said, raising money for their own support and the building
of churches. As a consequence, they were obliged to pander to the wealthy,
whose influence invariably forced most to accede to the wishes of the "powers
that be. So that though the church is an ark containing at least pairs of all truths
worthy to be preserved, yet the doors are sealed so tightly to keep out the flood
in iniquity, that the ministers can no more get out than those called sinners can
get in."[132] The result was increased proscription. He had left the Baptists for
the congregationalism of the Presbyterians. Now it appeared that even the relative freedom of the Presbyterian church could not satisfy his need to be rid of
ministerial restrictions.

132. London Emancipation Society, *The Martyrdom of John Brown. The Proceedings of a Public
Meeting Held in London on the 2nd December, 1863, to Commemorate the Fourth Anniversary of John
Brown's Death* (London, 1864), 19.

But other forces were at work here. Although ecclesiastical rules could be easily circumvented, Martin could find no simple answers to his nagging, persistent questions concerning the relationship between the church and the oppressed. He had grown tired of titles, he told his congregation, for they were serious impediments to the task at hand. They were "sometimes the watchword of superstition among followers, and often a sign of mere egotism in the wearer." When Bishop Daniel A. Payne of the AME church wrote him enthusiastically in 1868, announcing dramatic increases in the size of congregations since emancipation, he was unmoved. He dismissed that change, attributing it to "the love of animal excitement among all ignorant people, and their regard for high-sounding titles, as well as the seductiveness of social class meetings, where they enjoyed at once the pleasure of boasting about their spiritual strength and enjoyments and gratified the gregariousness of their natural disposition." Such views were in part a reflection of contemporary notions about the "hereditary fetichism" of backward peoples, as well as a realization of the wide gap that had developed between the minister, partial to rather abstruse intellectual sermons, and his congregation, whose members were still moved by the robust fire-and-brimstone sermons. Martin had clearly lost touch with his communicants. He had also come to question the need for separate black congregations, an attitude that could only have angered many in his church. Convinced that blacks were now on the verge of attaining political equality, with the passage of the Fifteenth Amendment, he insisted that every opportunity should be taken to push for social equality. That was only attainable through direct challenges to all forms of social proscription wherever they existed. It was for this reason that he enrolled his daughter in a white school. Under these circumstances, the maintenance of racially exclusive institutions, like the church, severely hampered the drive for total equality.[133]

Burning his bridges to the church was a dangerous gamble. His claim that an editor needed the "freedom of secularity" to be most effective, though true, did not pay the bills. If this rather optimistic view had indeed influenced his decision, Martin must have felt vindicated when it was announced in April that subscriptions to the paper had topped seven thousand, and that the decision had been taken to incorporate "The New Era Printing and Publishing Company," capitalized at $15,000.[134] His stock and popularity rose with the success of the paper, and Martin found himself at the center of activity in early 1870.

133. *New Era*, January 20, 1870; Martin to Dear Brethren, July 10, 1868, in AMA.
134. *New Era*, April 14, 1870.

He was principal speaker at celebrations commemorating the passage of the Fifteenth Amendment in both Washington and Richmond. For those who had struggled long and hard for the rights of black Americans, the passage of the amendment was a justified culmination of a worthy cause, and ample grounds for hope. One editorial in the *New Era* announced, rather prematurely, the disappearance of the Negro as America had known him and the arrival of a citizen of equal rank. There is no place, Martin told the Washington celebrants, "except perhaps in a heathen land, where the personal and political rights of the negro are not duly respected." But one local editor's reaction to his Richmond speech brought Martin up short. The amendment, this editor insisted, was a "monstrous Federal cancer, sending its roots deep into the States." And if Martin was sanguine about imminent racial equality and contacts, then the editor sought to disabuse him of such misplaced notions. Martin, he wrote, "cannot bear the idea of having to go to churches and theatres where there are none but negroes; whereas a white man always wants to attend such places in company with whites only. The negroes can never be respected until they respect themselves. They have the same rights as whites to build churches, hotels and theatres. Let them do so, and let them exclude the whites. That's the way to get even with us." For the time being, Martin chose to ignore these stormy petrels, placing his hopes instead on a nation that had gone through the trials of civil war and, in the wake of destruction, had initiated bold policies for political and social reconstruction.[135]

With the summer came increasing signs that all was not well in Martin's family. How he must have questioned the wisdom of severing ties with the church. He had left Buffalo in 1859, frustrated by the constant struggle to make ends meet. The situation at Joy Street in Boston was marginally better. With a congregation of 205 in 1862, Joy Street was relatively comfortable. It was able to raise sufficient funds to install a new organ in 1860 and periodically supplemented Martin's salary from the proceeds of concerts. But it was never enough.[136] Even at Shiloh, reputedly the best-paying black pulpit in the country, life was unpredictable. The Fifteenth Street Church offered few improvements, but it did provide a salary that, if Martin had maintained his position,

---

135. *New Era*, February 10, April 7, 14, 28, 1870; Peter Rachleff, "Black, White and Grey: Working Class Activism in Richmond, Virginia, 1865–1890" (Ph.D. dissertation, University of Pittsburgh, 1981), 304–307; Richmond *Daily Dispatch*, April 23, 20, 21, 1870.

136. *Weekly Anglo-African*, December 15, 1860, January 5, 1861; *Frederick Douglass Paper*, March 1, 1859.

would have meant the difference between indebtedness and solvency. That he chose not to stay set the stage for his subsequent troubles. His optimism about the *New Era* was never fully realized. Subscriptions continued to lag behind expected levels, and the joint-stock company never materialized. As a result, Martin found himself deep in debt.

In May he wrote the AMA about Sarah's illness and his doctor's advice that he move the family south. Martin chose Mobile and requested an appointment as a missionary at an annual salary of $1,000. The projected move appeared designed more to meet his pressing financial needs than to help Sarah recover. In fact, she remained in Washington after his departure for Mobile. Martin left Washington in July, owing Douglass over $100, a debt Douglass only recovered when his son Charles took possession of some furniture that Sarah still had. Martin's plan to retain his job at the *New Era*, making periodic trips to Washington from Mobile, was totally impractical, given the paper's straitened circumstances and his fragile health. Douglass was already having second thoughts about his involvement as the paper's debts increased. All his earlier fears had been realized. But Douglass was a proud man; rather than stand aside and see the paper collapse, he chose to take control. His decision guaranteed the immediate survival of the paper but only at the prohibitive cost of $10,000.[137]

Leaving Washington was just the first in a series of moves, desperate attempts by Martin to cut a niche for himself in reconstructed America. But beneath it all, there was also a yearning to return to the South. He had contemplated that many times before and had written in his narrative, published in Scotland in June, 1867, "to go back to that soil, to stand there as a man, and work on an equality with other people, to labour for the elevation of my race, to preach the everlasting gospel of Jesus Christ, is to me a prospect indescribable in pleasure, and will be in its realization one of the greatest blessings that God can give me." Some things had changed since then, but his desire to go back to the South was undiminished by time. Even while nursing the *New Era* through its infancy Martin applied for the post of special agent in the Treasury Department. It was not his first and would not be his last attempt to procure a government appointment. Although the Treasury Department rejected his application, he was named a Post Office Department "special agent" stationed at Mobile. It is possible that he had already received this appointment when he

137. Charles Douglass to Dear Father, July 14, August 9, 1870, both in FDP; Martin to Dear Brethren, May 18, 1870, in AMA; Douglass, *Life and Times*, 399–400.

applied to the AMA. Why, then, did he not mention it in his letter to the association, and why emphasize Sarah's illness as the major cause for the move to Mobile?[138]

What at first glance looks like deception should be seen in the context of Martin's burning desire to achieve the distinction, and the financial security that went with it, to which he felt entitled. After all, America was his home, and, as he had said so many times before, the country owed the former slave reparations, a measure of compensation for past exploitation. All Britain had received him with open arms, he had even been invited to meet Queen Victoria at Balmoral Castle, yet America seemed determined to deny him an opportunity to achieve personal security and distinction. Impatient to succeed and unwilling to persevere unnecessarily, Martin was incensed and frustrated by these denials.

Unfortunately, Martin's job with the Post Office lasted only a few months. Later that year he moved his family to New Orleans and spent most of his time lecturing and moving in local black Republican circles. His series of lectures at Straight University, founded in 1869 by the AMA, won him considerable praise but little money. Sarah was active in local charities, and in March, 1871, she was elected secretary of the "Hathaway Home for the Poor and Friendless," which provided accommodation and medicine for the indigent aged and trained the young in "industrial pursuits." When Horace Greeley visited the city in late May, Martin, along with P. B. S. Pinchback, A. E. Barber, C. C. Antoine, F. C. Antoine, and William G. Brown, all prominent Louisiana blacks, met with the famous New York editor to discuss the future of the freedmen. Although the meeting produced nothing of substance, it did identify Martin with some of the leading black figures in Louisiana Republican politics. His agreement to write frequent articles for the *Louisianan* also provided him with a useful outlet for any political aspirations he might have harbored.[139]

Involvement in Louisiana politics was the last thing any sane outsider should have contemplated. That Martin chose to, and entered the fray with customary abandon, is not surprising. By the time of his arrival, Louisiana politics had already degenerated into a series of bizarre, bitter squabbles between Governor Henry Clay Warmoth and contending factions led by Lieutenant Governor Oscar J. Dunn. Opposition to Warmoth coalesced following his veto of the so-

138. *Good Words*, June 1, 1867; *New Era*, September 1, 1870; Harris, Abbot *et al.* to George Boutwell, February 28, 1870, in Treasury Department Records, National Archives.
139. *Louisianan*, March 16, 1871, December 22, 25, 29, 1870, January 12, February 19, May 21, 28, June 1, 1871.

cial equality bill in 1868 and his refusal to endorse the public education law and to sign the civil rights bill passed in 1870. Although he vetoed these bills, considered by many blacks and white Radicals to be the only guarantees of black social equality, Warmoth engineered passage of a series of bills that radically increased his powers. Perhaps the most emotionally charged was a law enabling Warmoth to succeed himself in office, something his opponents saw as yet another attempt by the governor to dictate the political future of the state. The governor's appointment of a number of Democrats, former Confederates such as General James Longstreet, to prominent positions only added insult to injury. Dunn and others moved quickly to isolate Warmoth from the party at the Republican convention in August, 1870. Sensing that his opponents would have difficulty maintaining their ranks, Warmoth ignored the convention's decisions and actively canvassed the state for the party in the November elections. A Republican victory could not disguise the deep rifts within the party, which continued to widen in early 1871 over the naming of a U.S. senator from Louisiana, as well as Warmoth's veto of a number of bills considered important by a group of powerful legislators.[140]

This was the situation when Martin arrived in New Orleans. It was complicated further by disputes between leading black political figures. Old alliances and friendships were strained to the breaking point as Dunn, Pinchback, C. C. Antoine, and others jockeyed for position. Martin's association with Pinchback, which served as a useful introduction to New Orleans society and politics, carried with it some unnecessarily burdensome obligations. When friendship between Pinchback and Antoine turned to animosity in 1871, Martin could not avoid taking sides. He also found Antoine's whispered accusations about Pinchback's financial dealings particularly repulsive. And Pinchback, after all, was second only to Dunn in the state's black political hierarchy, a fact that could not have escaped Martin's attention. Furthermore, Warmoth was the governor and, as such, the dominant force in the party. Martin had long held the view, one he promoted sedulously in his *New Era* editorials, that the Republican party was the party of black people and, therefore, had to be supported and protected from those who sought to destroy its work for the freedmen.

These factors might help explain why Martin joined the political fray in August, 1871. While Warmoth was away in Mississippi convalescing after a riding accident, his opponents, sensing an opportunity to turn the party against him,

140. Althea D. Pitre, "The Collapse of the Warmoth Regime, 1870–72," *Louisiana History*, VI (1965), 162–65; Henry Clay Warmoth, *War, Politics and Reconstruction: Stormy Days in Louisiana* (New York, 1930), 89–93, 164.

called a state convention at the Mechanics' Institute, site of the state legislature. But the move failed when Warmoth got wind of the meeting and hurried
back to New Orleans. Aware of the governor's return, the opposition led by
Dunn and local customs officials went to the Custom House, which they controlled, and appointed marshals to keep Warmoth and his supporters out. Warmoth countered by inviting his supporters to withdraw and join him for another
meeting at Turners' Hall. He succeeded in attracting 95 of the 118 delegates to
the Mechanics' Institute convention, one of whom was Pinchback; C. C. Antoine, Dunn, and others declined the offer. Martin addressed the Turners' Hall
meeting, pledging black cooperation, Warmoth later recounted, and denouncing the Custom House clique. One local reporter, absolutely beside himself
with joy at Republican discomfort, wrote that Martin "gave the Custom House
clique a few straight from the shoulder, which blows brought down the house."[141]

Such support in the midst of opposition from some of the state's leading
black politicians could not go unrewarded. In less than one month, Martin was
nominated by Warmoth to fill the position of division superintendent of public
education for the fourth division, recently vacated by General J. McCleary. In
his haste to show his approval of Martin's unsolicited and unexpected backing,
Warmoth ignored the law that nominations had to come from the superintendent of education. Superintendent Thomas Conway, in New York on business,
could do nothing but express mild surprise at the speed of the appointment
while pledging support for it. As was to be expected, the *Louisianan* fully approved. Martin's association with education reformers and commitment to "the
elevation of his race by education," an editorial observed, would benefit the
fourth division. Not only was Martin "able and worthy," another paper wrote,
but the nomination confirmed Warmoth's sincerity and acknowledged the
"claims of the colored man to an equal participation in the positions of honor
and trust."[142]

Given the political climate, Martin's nomination seemed doomed from the
start. Warmoth's success at outmaneuvering his opponents only heightened
their determination to remove him from office. There were calls for his impeachment in early fall, and C. C. Antoine and others were unlikely to forget
Martin's attack in August. Their chance for revenge came quickly; the fourth

141. Warmoth, *War, Politics and Reconstruction*, 186; Pitre, "The Collapse of the Warmoth Regime," 167–69; Ella Lonn, *Reconstruction in Louisiana After 1868* (1918; rpr. Gloucester, Mass.,
1967), 96–103; *Louisianan*, August 13, 1871; New Orleans *Daily Picayune*, August 12, 10, 1871.

142. Thomas Conway to Warmoth, September 2, 1871, No. 752, in Henry Clay Warmoth Papers, Southern Historical Collection, Library of the University of North Carolina at Chapel Hill;
Attakapas *Register*, quoted in *Louisianan*, August 27, 17, 1871.

division included Caddo Parish and its principal city, Shreveport, Antoine's political home base. When Martin visited Shreveport in late September and was invited to lecture at a local church, Antoine and his supporters disrupted the meeting. There are conflicting reports of what took place. Antoine accused Martin of conducting religious exercises in the church when he was no longer a minister, and of being drunk and playing cards in New Orleans. As a result, some of the congregation refused to listen to Martin and left. Next day, Antoine reported, Martin got into a shoving match with William Harper, an associate of Antoine's, who disarmed him when Martin attempted to draw a pistol. However, this account is so at variance with another report, and what we know of Martin, that one has to question its veracity. Although it was Antoine's local opponents, with their own ax to grind, who first brought the incident to light, the speed with which he moved to exploit the situation suggests ulterior political motives. Although Martin might have appeared drunk at times from the constant use of laudanum, a mixture of 45 percent alcohol and 55 percent opium, he had never tried to pass himself off as a minister after severing ties with the church. In addition, accusations that Harper threatened to "take the top of his [Martin's] head off" with his pistol ring true, for Harper, a self-educated former slave and future state senator, had a reputation as a fighter of no mean order. On one occasion when the Klan threatened him, Harper armed himself and dared them to carry out their threat.[143]

For Antoine and others, Martin was a symbol of Warmoth's power and intransigence, and so was ripe for attack. But before that materialized, Martin went to work as division superintendent. It was an unenviable task. For many minor politicians, the education act of 1870, which established the office of division superintendent, provided an unexpected opportunity to line their pockets. Thousands of dollars were fleeced from the state to pay the salaries and expenses of school administrators, many of whom were illiterate. In addition, conditions in the division were appalling. There were no high schools; primary schools could accommodate only a trifling percentage of the student population; teachers' salaries were particularly low; schools were open an average of three months during the year, and when they were, the teacher-student ratio was 1 to 46. Martin's duties as division superintendent included organizing and conducting conferences, encouraging and assisting teachers' associations, and reporting the number of teachers in schools. In spite of the many shortcomings, such as employers' holding too tenaciously to the past and

143. New Orleans *Republican*, October 6, 1871; *Louisianan*, October 19, 1871; Charles Vincent, *Black Legislators in Louisiana During Reconstruction* (Baton Rouge, 1976), 117.

the employed being "too presumptuous as to the future," Martin wrote optimistically in his annual report that the log schoolhouse and the academy "are
issuing lights which will correct the two-fold confusion and cause the owners of
the soil to see that they are not independent of the tillers, and aid the tillers in
understanding that they can not be independent of the owners."[144]

Within days of submitting his report, Martin left for Boston, where he spent
a few months. While there, he received word that the state senate had voted
against his nomination as division superintendent. Antoine and some Warmoth
opponents had had their say on this score. There were other developments as
well. Dunn's death in November was followed by a temporary respite in the political jockeying, and Warmoth had an opportunity to name a more amenable
successor. As the movement for his impeachment gained momentum, Warmoth
recalled the senate in December to vote on Dunn's successor, convinced that his
candidate, Pinchback, would carry the day. True to tradition, the senate and
Warmoth were quickly at one another's throats, and when Pinchback emerged
as the victor by a single vote, there were cries of fraud. Many thought Warmoth's recall of the senate illegal, and in a direct assault on his authority a
group of fifteen senators, Antoine among them, agreed to vote as a bloc on "different reform measures," including amendments to registration, election, and
constabulary laws, general appropriation bills, revenue and license bills, and
confirmation of nominations. When Martin's nomination was taken up on February 20 the bloc held firm, accounting for almost two-thirds of the negative
votes.[145]

While in Boston, Martin attended the city convention called to elect delegates to the Negro convention meeting planned for New Orleans in May. In his
address, Martin roundly condemned the choice of New Orleans. Although the
brief report of his speech offered no explanations, the recent rejection surely
accounted for Martin's views. Martin was chosen an alternate, but officially participated in the convention when a delegate was forced to withdraw. The meeting's location and composition to a large extent determined the issues discussed. Louisiana political disputes hung like a pall over the proceedings, and a
great deal of statesmanship was necessary to keep the convention from degen-
erating into a local fight. But national disputes also intruded and threatened on
numerous occasions to disrupt the deliberations. The major contention cen-

144. Lonn, *Reconstruction*, 80–81; Vincent, *Black Legislators*, 90; State Superintendent of Public
Education, *Annual Report, 1872* (New Orleans, 1873), 233, 227–28.
145. Pitre, "The Collapse of the Warmoth Regime," 170–73; James Haskins, *Pinckney Ben-
ton Stewart Pinchback* (New York, 1973), 101; *Louisiana Senate Journal*, Extra Session, 1871,
pp. 234, 28.

tered on splits in the Republican party. Many suspected that Charles Sumner, who had long guarded the interests of blacks, might accept the nomination of the Liberal Republicans and oppose Grant in the November elections. The failure of Grant's administration to enforce civil rights laws, and Sumner's popularity, prompted many blacks to question their unbending allegiance to the Republican party. Fearful that some would bolt the party, motions were submitted reiterating support for Grant. As president, Douglass tried to ensure continuing loyalty. "As far as the colored people are concerned there are but two parties in this country," Douglass told the meeting at its closing session, "the Democratic and Republican parties. Men may change as they please, and factions split off in one direction and the other, wearing different and specious names, but one is always the party of progress and the other the party of reaction. For colored men the Republican party is the deck, all outside is the sea."[146]

For Martin, however, things were not all that straightforward; his experiences in Louisiana and the party's failure to enforce the law had set him adrift. He was not yet quite willing to abandon the Republican ship, aware that the majority of blacks supported Grant and the party unquestioningly. Nor was he partial, as he said some months before, to "bolting in our party." When the resolution of unconditional support for Grant and condemnation of the bolters was submitted to the convention, however, Martin wondered why Republicans, as the majority party in both houses of Congress, had so singularly failed to ensure the civil rights of blacks. Although opposed to the Liberal Republican convention as the "opening wedge to divide the Republican party," and doubtful that Sumner would join their ranks, Martin concluded that if blacks were not given their civil rights he would abandon the party. When Henri Burch facetiously inquired where he would go and who would accompany him, Martin responded angrily that he would act independently and try to persuade others to join him. But Martin fought shy of announcing a break with the party, and Douglass expressed some relief at the decision. "There was one man in the convention who surprised us by the calm and gentlemanly manner with which he handled every question upon which he ventured to speak, and that was John Sella Martin. For his ability and eloquence we were quite prepared. We had witnessed both in Boston and elsewhere but from some cause we had feared that his political life at the South had injured and soured him. . . . Few men in the South have it in their power to be more useful than John Sella Martin."[147]

146. Boston *Daily Globe*, March 29, 1872; *New National Era*, May 2, 1872.
147. *Louisianan*, July 20, 1871, March 28, April 11, 14, 18, 1872; *New National Era*, May 9, 2, 1872.

The length of the commentary suggests that all was not well, and that Douglass realized Martin had been soured by his experiences. The Republican party's failure to halt increasing violations of black rights only compounded Martin's dismay. Soon after the convention, he left for Shreveport, where he remained until the end of the year. It may well have been an act of bravado, a determination to beard the lion in its den. Louisiana politics was continuing along the destructive course charted in 1868, and now there was a split in Republican ranks. The Liberal Republican convention in Cincinnati, in May, nominated Greeley and B. Gratz Brown to oppose Grant and Wilson in November. In Louisiana, Warmoth's differences with Grant and the local Custom House clique led him into the Greeley camp. During the spring and summer, the various groups held separate conventions to nominate candidates for the elections. The Grant faction met in April; the Pinchback supporters in May; and the Liberal Republicans in August. At the August convention a special committee was named to approach the Democrats, the Reform Republicans (a splinter Democratic group), and the Pinchback faction on the possibility of a fusion ticket. When that initiative collapsed, Pinchback returned to the fold, throwing his support to Grant. The remaining contenders then met and agreed to a fusion ticket with a Democratic candidate for governor and with members of other groups for lesser offices.[148]

Martin's official break with the party came in late June following its convention in Baton Rouge. Hopes for reconciliation between the contending factions were dashed when the Custom House group carried the day and refused to entertain any ideas of compromise. It was more than Martin could stand. "The Packard corruption, conspiracy and tyranny," he wrote Pinchback, "has triumphed over the will of the colored people. By keeping Republicans divided they have driven thousands from the ranks and organized a defeat. The only hope of the negro in this State rests in the Liberal-Republican Party. Henceforth I am one of them." It was one thing to castigate Packard, Antoine, and others—Martin had constantly done that in the past—but quite another to make the giant leap to the Liberal Republicans, especially since its nomination of Greeley, an "erratic, unpredictable and irresponsible" person whose abolitionist credentials were questionable. The party, an odd assortment of high- and low-tarriff men, civil service reformers, disgruntled Republicans, reform Democrats, and many who simply wished to see Grant out of the White House, left a great deal to be desired. Although its platform insisted on acceptance of

148. Pitre, "The Collapse of the Warmoth Regime," 174–75; Warmoth, *War, Politics and Reconstruction*, 161, 197–98.

the Thirteenth, Fourteenth, and Fifteenth Amendments, its call for anmesty for southern rebels and its appeal to "white supremacist Southerns" stirred the ire of many old abolitionists. Faced with this situation, many adopted Douglass' aphorism—the Republicans were the deck and all else the sea.[149]

Although understandably incensed by the political machinations at Baton Rouge, Martin decided to change parties because of sheer frustration and his personal assessment of the political alignments in the state. Martin had never taken too kindly to determined opposition, and the ease with which he took offense and gave full vent to his acerbic tongue often drove him to intemperate public denunciations of his opponents. For the time being, however, he chose to control his vitriol, convinced that the Liberals stood a real chance of winning the elections. Warmoth had cast his lot with Greeley, and for all intents and purposes, Pinchback seemed disposed to the Liberals in June. Pinchback shrewdly kept his own counsel, but Martin, piqued by the results of the Baton Rouge meeting, publicly announced that he backed the Greeley ticket. He wrote Greeley in mid-July of his decision. Eager to trumpet his support among the "intelligent" portion of black America, Greeley promptly published the letter in which Martin expressed anger at Republicans who took the black vote for granted and who, in Louisiana, devised a battery of fraudulent schemes to ensure continuing support. These men, mainly federal officeholders, "have more time and facilities for reaching our race than any other class, and they use their opportunities, first of all, to discredit the loyalty of all colored men who are independent of them, and next, to put the most ignorant colored men from the country on Parish Committees, headed by white carpet-baggers, and into Conventions dominated by the Custom-house at New Orleans." The Liberals now offered an alternative, Martin observed, and with the possible support of Pinchback, Greeley could receive thirty thousand black votes in the state.[150]

Even if all this were true, Martin still had to explain why he had bolted the party of black Americans, a practice he never condoned. Abandoning his customary blunt, straightforward approach to problems, Martin employed the most tortuous reasoning in a desperate attempt to portray Greeley as an abolitionist and the "journalistic founder of the Republican party." Lauding Greeley's constant support for black rights, Martin excoriated Grant's blundering, ineffective leadership of the country. If any word could be used to charac-

149. *Louisianan,* June 22, 25, 1872; James M. McPherson, "Grant or Greeley? The Abolitionist Dilemma in the Election of 1872," *American Historical Review,* LXXI (1965), 44; William Harlan Hale, *Horace Greeley, Voice of the People* (New York, 1961), 259; Glyndon C. Van Deusen, *Horace Greeley: Nineteenth Century Crusader* (Philadelphia, 1953), 404.
150. New York *Daily Tribune,* July 15, 1872.

terize Greeley, it was surely not *consistent*, and Martin must have known of the mercurial editor's reputation for flitting from one cause to the other. What the New York *Tribune* chose to view as a "process of ratiocination which all logicians will commend," the *New National Era* dismissed as rank political opportunism by Martin. "So far from being the apostle of the Abolitionist press," Douglass wrote, "it is notorious that he [Greeley] merely followed in the wake of the persecuted Garrison, Gerrit Smith, Wendell Phillips, and other eminent Abolitionist leaders, who are now wisely favoring the re-election of Grant. We do not remember that Horace Greeley ever opened his lips in an Abolitionist meeting in his life, and it is all nonsense for Mr. Martin to serve a purpose to exalt Greeley to the dignity of an Abolitionist apostle, for he never was and is not anything of the kind."[151]

Pinchback's decision to return to the Republican fold may have caused Martin some concern, but it did not deter him from actively entering the election campaign. In late August, Martin delivered a series of speeches to local Greeley clubs, which mushroomed in the weeks after Greeley's nomination. In his first address to the Shreveport Greeley Club, he called on blacks to accept the "proffered hand of the white man," whom he now believed to be sincere, and insisted that incompetent blacks be removed from the party's ticket and replaced with representative black men or "good white men." One local editor could not resist the temptation to compare the dignified Martin with the black rowdies and blackguards, "the most ignorant and credulous class," who attended Grant meetings. Anxious to capitalize on Martin's support, some liberals suggested his nomination for superintendent of public education, but the party's convention in September chose instead to name him one of its candidates for the Louisiana House. Douglass' fears and Antoine's suspicions that Martin harbored political ambitions seem to be borne out by these developments. Martin would have pleaded innocence, however; duty dictated that he enter the political arena as a foil for dishonest carpetbaggers, scalawags, and their black henchmen, most of whom he saw as incompetent. The nomination of those blacks for political office, Martin maintained, not only ensured continued white political dominance but also gave comfort to racists who believed that blacks were inferior and, therefore, should not be afforded equal rights.[152]

The Shreveport *Times* set the tone for the elections following the selection of the local Liberal slate. In an editorial to the "Colored People," it insisted

151. *Ibid.*; *Louisianan,* July 20, 1872; *New National Era,* July 18, 1872.
152. Shreveport *Times,* August 24, 25, 28, 29, September 1, 5, 8, 18, 24, 26, 1872.

unblushingly that, unlike Grant, Greeley had won the backing of lifelong abolitionists. Grant, on the other hand, "had been all his life a negro hater" and was being supported in the state by those who were opposed to the present order in the South and who yearned for a return to the old ways. William Kellogg, the Republican candidate for governor, was no different; he in fact was the head of a conspiracy, which, the editors announced, had only just come to light, to oust Antoine if he were elected and replace him with a white person. The plot was hatched by Republicans "because their object is to keep the negro down, and build up in Louisiana, as everywhere else, a bondholding, landgrabbing, railroad aristocracy." The tenor of the campaign rarely rose above the level set by the editors of the *Times*.[153]

Even before the votes could be counted, the *Times* raised the specter of fraud as the "dusky cohorts" tramped to the polls to cast their ballots. The early returns from Caddo Parish, over 70 percent of its population black, gave the Liberals a comfortable edge. It was later announced that the Liberals had carried the parish. The Grant party had been "flaxed," the *Times* chortled, in spite of Republican ward bosses' attempts to control the black vote. Before the Liberals could savor their victory, however, claims of voter intimidation and fraud were made throughout the state. At one polling station in Morningside, a town in Caddo Parish, a hawk-eyed Republican registrar was refused entry, but through the window he could see three hundred ballots cast for the party and he heard many Liberal supporters openly admit that they were trounced. Yet when the ballots were counted, the Republican tally had dwindled to just seventeen votes.[154]

The final outcome of the elections was kept in doubt as Warmoth and his opponents jockeyed for supremacy. Almost as soon as voting stations closed, contenders were arguing over the composition of the returning board, which, under Louisiana law, was authorized to count returns and declare the winners. As if to confirm recent history, the situation was complicated by board members being removed either because they were candidates for statewide office or because they were accused of malfeasance. As the contending groups knew, a board under Warmoth's control would declare for the Liberals; one under Kellogg, for the Republicans. It was no surprise that two returning boards emerged—the one beholden to Grant Republicans announced the election of

153. *Ibid.*, September 26, 1872.
154. *Louisianan*, November 16, 5, 6, 1872; New Orleans *Daily Picayune*, November 12, 16, December 5, 1872; New Orleans *Republican*, November 14, 1872.

Republicans; the other, Liberals. Both factions moved to take control. Armed with a court order, Warmoth's opponents took possession of the legislative chambers in the Mechanics' Institute, installed a Republican government, adopted a motion calling for Warmoth's impeachment, and named Pinchback acting governor. Not to be outflanked, Warmoth acquired a court order declaring Pinchback's election illegal, a ruling Pinchback chose to ignore. While both groups continued to shadowbox, Martin and his Liberal colleagues languished in a limbo between state power and total obscurity. On December 10 the Warmoth faction held a massive public meeting in New Orleans at which a committee of one hundred was chosen to petition Grant and visit Washington to confer with Congress. The next day Warmoth declared the Mechanics' Institute government illegal and organized an alternative government at City Hall. On December 12, Grant recognized the Pinchback government, and the following day, in an effort to drive home his decision, he informed the committee that its visit to Washington would serve little purpose.[155]

But the Liberals and their "government" at City Hall under John McEnery had no alternative but to send the committee to Washington; persuading Congress of the election's illegality was their only hope of ousting Kellogg. Although Martin was not one of those originally selected, he later joined a smaller committee that left for Washington on December 15. Why he persisted in this charade is a mystery. His late addition to the "sorehead committee," as the New Orleans *Republican* dismissed it, allowed opponents to charge that he was the token black included at the last moment to soften the stigma of racism long associated with all of its other members. This most "unscrupulous of negro carpet-bag adventurers," this "miserable subterfuge of a colored man," had allowed himself to become the cat's-paw of southern racists.[156]

Initially Martin ignored these rebukes and actively participated in the work of the committee, which met on December 19 with the president and the Supreme Court justices in an attempt to persuade them to examine the legality of certain rulings made since the elections. But the Court demurred. The following day the committee issued a public statement outlining the law and the facts of the case and petitioned Congress for relief. Three days later, forty-four members signed a lengthy document that explained recent events in Louisiana. The installation of the Kellogg government, they declared, was a usurpation of

155. Pitre, "The Collapse of the Warmoth Regime," 179–85; New Orleans *Daily Picayune*, December 10, 1872.
156. New Orleans *Daily Picayune*, December 14, 15, 16, 1872; New Orleans *Republican*, December 31, 18, 1872.

all legal authority, a coup d'état that threatened the legal fabric of American society. Nothing came of the appeal as Congress dispersed for Christmas and a number of the committee's members returned home. A smaller committee of ten remained in Washington to prepare for another appeal at the start of the new session. These Louisiana businessmen with extensive links to northern commercial houses were well suited to exploit all possible avenues to bring pressure on Congress to investigate. When they met in January the congressional committees heard accounts of electoral fraud, intimidation of black voters, judicial deception, and questionable actions by Warmoth. Caddo was at the top of the list of those parishes where blacks were intimidated. Testimony from an array of witnesses did little to enlighten the committees, however. The result, of course, was utter confusion. Reports issued by the committees denounced the actions of most of those involved in the dispute, yet the election results were allowed to stand, despite the committees' agreeing with claims that there were many questionable judicial decisions. True to form, nothing was resolved, and two separate governments continued to function in Louisiana, one under Kellogg, the other under McEnery.[157]

Those with a fine sense of the theatrical marveled at developments in New Orleans and in Congress, and Martin, recognizing the futility of it all, chose to abandon ship and remain in Washington. In fact, he never took his seat in the McEnery legislature. Given his betrayal of the "party of black America," it took extreme bravery or exceeding recklessness to return to Washington as a member of the Liberal committee. Some castigated him for joining the "sorehead committee," but Douglass and a number of other black Washingtonians, aware of Martin's experiences in Louisiana, and a bit more forgiving, held out a hand of reconciliation. They met with Martin soon after he arrived in the city in an effort to persuade him to abandon his position. "While we do not agree with Mr. Martin in this matter," Douglass wrote diplomatically, "we do not fail to recognize his ability as a worker in the cause of human rights and the services he has rendered." The gentle approach worked; within a month, Martin had publicly disassociated himself from the Liberals and apologized for his "political aberration." The Liberals' "uniform courtesy and flattering consideration" throughout their association, Martin explained, compared favorably with the "personal ill-treatment" of those he once considered his political allies in

157. See *Senate Reports*, 42nd Cong., 3rd Sess., No. 457; *House Executive Documents*, 42nd Cong., 3rd Sess., No. 91; New Orleans *Republican*, December 22, 1872; New Orleans *Daily Picayune*, December 22, 27, 1872; New York *Daily Tribune*, December 20, 24, 25, 30, 1872.

the Republican party. The Liberals' promises and the acceptance by prominent southerners of the Thirteenth, Fourteenth, and Fifteenth Amendments raised his expectations for an "end to every form of Ku-Kluxism" and for the enfranchisement of blacks. This was the bait that led him into the snare of the Liberals. That "hour's mistake," he admitted, had done considerable damage to the "credit of 20 years' devotion" to his race and had weakened his standing in the party he had done so much to build. "I am not willing to block up the pathway of my future usefulness," he concluded, "by adding to my mistake" when in the estimation of friends "my position places me in antagonism to my race, while my heart is as warm and true toward it as ever."[158]

It was a humble and a bold move by Martin, and such humility ensured a relatively easy return to the fold of his former political associates. Within two weeks he was again in demand at public meetings in Washington. Black Washington's elite also forgave his lapses and welcomed him back to their salons. When the *New National Era* was reorganized in early February, Martin and Lewis Douglass were the co-editors. It is impossible to determine how many of the editorials were Martin's. The association was short-lived, however. When financial difficulties forced the *Era* to merge with the *New Citizen*, a competitor, Martin decided to quit. Although he appears to have opposed the merger, his decision was based on continuing financial problems and the need for a stable job. There were even rumors that he was seriously reconsidering returning to the pulpit.[159]

There is no evidence that Martin ever became a minister again, and there are few clues as to what he did after leaving the *Era*. He did remain in Washington, where he participated on the fringes of local politics. It was announced in October that Senator S. B. Conover of Florida had invited Martin to accompany him on a trip to Florida, where Martin was to give a series of lectures. There is no way of knowing if Martin did, but in late 1873 he joined the lecture circuit in an effort to provide for his family.[160] There were few signs of improvement in the months ahead, although national black political activities at the end of the year temporarily took Martin's mind off his woeful financial situation. America seemed to be growing increasingly tired of the issue of black rights. In southern states the amnesty act of 1872 paved the way for the return to power of old Democrats and new conservatives, and from the Supreme Court came un-

158. New Orleans *Republican*, January 10, 1873; *Louisianan*, January 25, 1873; *New National Era*, January 16, 1873, December 27, 1872.
159. *New National Era*, April 24, February 6, 13, 20, March 13, 1873.
160. *New National Era and Citizen*, October 23, November 20, 1873.

mistakable warnings that the protection afforded blacks by recent constitutional amendments was subject to interpretations upholding the power of state legislators to abridge the rights of citizens.

In the wake of these developments, 309 black delegates, representing twenty-seven states, gathered in Washington in December to devise a strategy for pressuring Congress to pass a more stringent civil rights act to protect, as one resolution expressed it, "all classes of citizens in the enjoyment of their civil and public rights without distinction as to race or color." Peter H. Clark of Ohio, who, like Martin, had temporarily abandoned the Republicans in the last election, best expressed the concerns and hopes of the Civil Rights Convention. He insisted on the total integration of schools and the removal of all forms of segregation. "I do demand social equality," he thundered, "I demand the right to qualify myself for first-class manhood in the same institutions and under the same circumstances as the white man practices, and when I have that leave it to ourselves whether we will mingle together or not." Following an audience with President Grant, convention delegates petitioned Congress for the passage of a civil rights bill "protecting citizens from denial and proscription in enjoying common carriers and hotels, public places of convenience and refreshment, amusement, and the like." Black citizens, they argued, should not be compelled to attend segregated schools or be denied the constitutional right to trial by a jury of their peers.[161]

But the convention and its appeal to Congress were not sufficient to raise Martin's spirits. The jockeying for prominence, which so characterized many black national conventions, beset the Washington meeting. One group coalesced around George Downing, who was named interim president of the National Council, and another around Frederick Douglass, Jr., and Martin. Prior to the formal elections for the National Council in mid-January, Downing and thirty-nine others, a handful of them members of the council, issued a public appeal to both houses of Congress for a civil rights act that guaranteed integrated education and impartial juries. There was nothing in the appeal that violated the convention's position or, for that matter, any stand taken by Martin on the issues. But Downing had stolen a march on Martin. Signed by forty black Washingtonians, the appeal enhanced Downing's stature and gave the false impression that he was acting in his capacity as council president. What galled Martin most was the fact that many believed the letter to be a true re-

161. Herbert Aptheker (ed.), *A Documentary History of the Negro in the United States* (2 vols.; Secaucus, N.J., 1951), II, 640–41; *New National Era and Citizen*, December 11, 18, 1873.

flection of black views. Although its objectives were generally accepted, Martin roundly condemned its barbed threats, and stated his conviction that Congress, left to its business, would grant blacks full civil rights. Downing's letter did contain a veiled threat, but no more than any other letter of its time would have expressed: "We want our rights and no more than our rights. Nothing short of them will satisfy us. If driven to the wall it must be by those who having the strength, may, if they will, secure them." Such bullying, Martin responded, was preposterous and typical of Downing, who was "always doing something to endanger the cause of equal school rights." Martin gave vent to his frustrations in invective. He saw no reason why the race should have to suffer "from an article in which the grammar is bad, the sense is confused, the style is coarse, and the tone is fit only for an egotist who occasionally assumes the airs of a braggart."[162]

Aware that he had the upper hand, Downing studiously ignored Martin and instead worked behind the scenes to isolate him. When the National Council was named a week later, Martin's name was absent. Refusing to recognize the legality of the votes for the council, Martin withdrew from the Civil Rights Convention altogether. But Downing's was a pyrrhic victory. It would have been much easier to control Martin from within the convention; on the outside he could take potshots, unencumbered by any organizational responsibility. As it turned out, Charles Sumner's death gave Martin a forum for an attack on Downing. He was named "orator of the evening" at a public meeting in late February to honor the memory of one of black America's most ardent supporters. Downing was conspicuously absent and missed what must rank as one of the finest speeches of the age. Long famous for his oratorical skills, Martin surpassed himself that evening.[163]

His being chosen principal speaker squared the series between himself and Downing, but it also increased the vitriol to a level reminiscent of 1859–60, when disputes over the African Civilization Society almost brought them to blows. In succeeding weeks, pro- and anti-Downing forces argued over the proposed Sumner monument. Competing meetings were held in early February to make arrangements for a statue. Exploiting his organizational base to full advantage, Downing called for the formation of a national Sumner monument association at a private meeting of his supporters. Two weeks later, Martin publicly castigated Downing's Star Chamber association. Black America, he ar-

162. *New National Era and Citizen*, December 18, 1873, January 1, 1874; Washington *Daily Morning Chronicle*, January 10, 9, 1874.
163. *New National Era and Citizen*, February 26, 12, 1874; *Louisianan*, April 4, 1874; Washington *Daily Morning Chronicle*, January 16, 1874.

gued, had outgrown its small coterie of leaders who, ignoring the wishes of the ordinary man, insisted on acting as their spokesman. It was time that "the people" be given an opportunity to speak for themselves. Martin urged them to form local Sumner associations that would solicit and deposit in banks money raised in their respective areas. This would also safeguard against the failure and fraud that occurred when a similar attempt was made to build a Lincoln monument. When sufficient funds were collected, delegates from local associations could meet to form a truly national society. "If you get together here a lot of clerks and caterers, employees of Government, and the Board of Public Works, and try to make them dictators of the donations of the sovereign people, you will have made a mistake as to the fitness of the times and as to the feelings of people."[164]

That was a low blow aimed at Downing, a caterer in Congress. The meeting quickly degenerated, dividing almost evenly on the question. Attempts by cooler heads failed to effect reconciliation, and for the next three months both sides fired broadsides at each other from the safety of their own trenches. Martin was accused of all manner of sins. G. Snowden, a Downing man, charged that he had pocketed most of the money raised for the Lincoln monument, and Martin threatened to sue. Unaware of his addiction to laudanum, some again accused him of drunkenness. Having contained himself for far too long, Downing now gave full vent to his rage. Comparing himself to Martin, he wrote that "I have no imputation upon me either in this District, in Mississippi, in Louisiana, in Virginia, New York, in Massachusetts, in England or anywhere else of being an inebriate, a debauchee, a collector of funds under false pretenses, a purloiner of other persons' property, a defrauder of creditors. I have never seen the need of changing my name." That was enough for Martin; he abandoned the field to Downing, leaving friends to defend his good name. Such drivel, Martin would write later, could only have come from a man "going crazy." As in the conflict over the African Civilization Society, Martin chose to retreat in the face of superior acerbity.[165]

Pleas for reconciliation fell on deaf ears, and Martin, stung by the bitterness he had done so much to initiate and sustain, started his perennial search for a new field and a job that paid a regular salary. Again he turned to the government and, with the aid of such prominent senators as John Sherman, Hannibal

164. *New National Era*, April 2, 1874; Washington *Daily Morning Chronicle*, March 12, 13, 27, 1874.
165. *New National Era*, April 9, May 23, June 4, 1874; Washington *Daily Morning Chronicle*, April 3, 4, 9, 11, 16, 1874.

Hamlin, and Frederick Frelinghuysen, applied to the Treasury Department for a position as a special agent. Within a month of his application, he was appointed an agent at Shieldsboro, Mississippi, a small port on St. Louis Bay, a relatively short distance from New Orleans. Martin's duties involved the prevention of smuggling and the collection of proper customs revenues. It was not the most stimulating job, but it provided a guaranteed income and put Martin within striking distance of New Orleans. There seemed to be some compelling force drawing him toward the city where he had spent so many years as a slave. It is even possible that Martin had come to realize that those incessant attacks of pleurisy and other ailments, and his dependence on laudanum, had marked him for an early grave. The bitterness of the contretemps with Downing did not help matters.[166]

Martin's stay in Shieldsboro was brief. By early fall, he was back in New Orleans and in the thick of local politics again. Given other alternatives, few would have chosen to return to Louisiana at this time. The state had not recovered from the disputed elections of 1872. White conservatives, determined to destroy the Kellogg administration and win power in November, organized the White League in March, 1874. The league terrorized the state in the months before the elections. A pitched battle was fought in the streets of New Orleans between the White League and the police in September. When the police were forced to retreat, leaving forty-four dead, Kellogg and other state officials took refuge in the Custom House. Within four days, federal forces had restored order. Republicans nevertheless continued to bicker, and the convention at Baton Rouge was held together not by party loyalty but by recognition of the threat from Democrats and the league. Blacks, like Lieutenant Governor Antoine, insisting on greater black representation in the party, were forced to settle for less. In a public address issued in late September, the Kellogg administration was accused of ignoring black aspirations and of refusing to consult black elected officials. "Neither the influence nor the opportunity has been permitted to us to shape or control any policy," averred the Republicans led by Antoine. "We have retrograded rather than advanced under the administration; and had it not been for some of the inflexible white Republicans, we would long since have been where political hope is a stranger, and republican justice could

166. Martin to Secretary of the Treasury, June 9, 1874, George B. Vashon to B. H. Bristow, August 4, 1874, Charles Hays to Bristow, July 8, 1874, J. A. J. Creswell to James Marshall, July 17, 1874, Lawrence Minor to Bristow, July 27, 1874, all in Treasury Department Records; *New National Era*, July 30, 1874; *Louisianan*, August 15, 1874.

not have reached us." It was time, they argued, for the governor to acknowledge by his actions the fact that blacks were largely responsible for his election.[167]

Martin would have nothing to do with the address. His experience with the Liberals' and Democrats' total control and the subversion of the Cincinnati platform in 1872 had taught him a lesson: Republican administrations had to be supported by blacks if they ever hoped to achieve full equality. Republicans of Louisiana, he told a Sixth Ward Club meeting, "must vote down the disunion slaveocrats spirit until the last man who remembers he was a master shall have passed from the face of the earth!" But what angered Martin most was the cringing, supplicating tone of the address. In this he was correct. After castigating Kellogg for his policies, and insisting on recognition of black contributions to the party's success, the address ended on a surprisingly quiescent note: "We have been wronged, outraged and massacred by the whites, without cause or provocation, until the air is heavy with our sighs, and the waters of Louisiana are reddened with our blood; as citizens, we cannot retaliate, and as christians we bear our afflictions as becomes our faith." Such "talk about the vassalage of the black man," Martin told a meeting of New Orleans Republicans, was sheer humbug. Martin tried unsuccessfully to alter the tone of the address; he was also concerned that such statements underestimated, if they did not completely overlook, the ineluctable laws of progress. In this sense, he was much more sanguine about the future than were Pinchback and others. It was in the interest of northern capital and political power that the Union be forever united and free. Blacks, free and spending millions of dollars, were much more attractive to American capital than if they were enslaved. For these reasons alone, the North would never countenance the return to slavery. It was, therefore, for blacks working through the Republican party to ensure that there was no retreat from gains already made. That demanded bold initiatives by blacks, not supplication. When Democrats and White Leaguers temporarily occupied and organized the legislature following the disputed elections in November, 1874, and only gave way in the face of superior forces deployed by General Philip Sheridan, Martin found all the evidence he ever needed to support his contention: the future was in a strong, determined Republican party enforcing the law and controlling reactionary forces.[168]

Reality, however, quickly defied such optimism. Clinging tenaciously to the party was more a reflection of Martin's determination not to repeat the mis-

167. Vincent, *Black Legislators*, 183–85; *Louisianan*, October 3, 1874.
168. *Louisianan*, January 16, 1875, October 10, 3, 1874; Vincent, *Black Legislators*, 187.

takes of 1872 than it was a recognition of political facts. The passage of the
Civil Rights Act in 1875 would have lent additional color to his roseate view of
the future, but common sense should have told him that the South was well on
the way to recapturing its old dominance and reversing earlier gains. The evidence was everywhere. White New Orleanians were implacably opposed to
equal treatment for blacks, and although the war and Reconstruction had
wrought important changes, blacks were still discriminated against in jobs, on
public transport, in the opera house, and in theaters, and in many instances
white merchants just simply refused to serve them. A string of lawsuits after
1869 attests to black New Orleanians' refusal to accept such treatment quietly.
But they were sailing into the wind, and the going was exceedingly slow. A mass
meeting of whites in September, 1875, declared that "the compulsory admix-
ture of children of all races, color and condition in the schools, in the same
room and on the same benches, is opposed to the principles of humanity, re-
pugnant to the instincts of other races, and is not required by any provision of
the laws or constitution of this State."[169]

In spite of such resistance to the attainment of equal rights, blacks in the
Crescent City refused to cower. Upper-class blacks organized a number of self-
help associations, literary societies, and clubs. Martin was instrumental in the
formation of the New Orleans Atheneum Club in early 1875, serving as president until its reorganization in June. At meetings, members and guests presented original essays, which were discussed, and sometimes they listened to or
sang songs. Martin was also a member of the Louisiana Progressive Club,
which was founded in 1874. Among its thirty-six members were influential
black politicians, such as Antoine, Pinchback, and William G. Brown, wealthy
black Creoles, and a few white politicians. In spite of past differences, Martin
was at home in the company of "cultured" men like Antoine, Pinchback, James
H. Ingraham, and Brown.[170] No longer constrained by what he considered the
relatively sterile intellectual environment of the church and largely free from
the hostilities that seemed to follow wherever he lived, Martin was on the
threshold of a new phase of his life.

He joined Pinchback, Brown, and Burch as Louisiana delegates to the Convention of Colored Newspaper Men in Cincinnati in August. The idea for such
a convention had been under discussion for almost a year, its objective being to
explore ways of making black papers self-sustaining. Fourteen newspapers were

169. John Blassingame, *Black New Orleans 1860–1880* (Chicago, 1973), 113, 185–96.
170. *Ibid.*, 147–48; *Louisianan*, January 30, February 27, April 3, June 5, 1875.

represented at the meeting. Concerned that the meeting would be poorly attended if limited solely to editors, the organizers broadened its concerns and invited clergymen and others "interested in the intellectual development of the colored race" to participate. Under this broad rubric, the Cincinnati convention was a direct descendant of earlier national convention meetings; like its predecessors, it was not without its share of disputes. There were those who were unaware that the meeting's objectives had been expanded and expressed dismay at the presence of so many who were not editors. And from Washington came a query from the National Council (formed by the Civil Rights Convention) concerning the authority to call a national convention of any kind without first gaining its approval. But there were some important achievements. The convention agreed to the formation of the Centennial Committee, which was to select a number of editors responsible for producing histories of the black experience in America. Eighteen categories were suggested, including "Origin of the Negro," "The Ancient Glory, or the Foot-prints of the Negro in All Ages," and "One Hundred Years with the Negroes' Muse." It was a revolutionary idea, and one that would have made the jobs of later historians much simpler if it had ever produced results. The convention also agreed to establish the Press Association, and issued a call for a national convention in Nashville in April, 1876. Martin actively participated in the convention, chairing the Committee on the Press Association. He was also the keynote speaker at a public meeting. Entitled "Friends of the Union," Martin's speech was a brief history of British support of the war and Northern determination to maintain the Union. Its Southern friends were those who supported the Republican party and the cause of black equality. Governor Kellogg, he reiterated, had been a good governor for all Louisianians. "He has protected their person as far as possible, fostered their interest, recognized their ability, and, what is as good as all this, he had brought about a better feeling between the races than exists anywhere in the South."[171]

Folks in New Orleans cringed. In reporting his speech, the *Louisianan* italicized his praise of Kellogg in utter disbelief, but held its fire, refusing any editorial comment. If no one else was, Martin at least remained convinced that opposition to Kellogg was grist for the mill of the White Leaguers. He insisted to the end that the future of blacks was tied inextricably to the Republican party, whatever the nature of the administration.

The year between the Cincinnati convention and Martin's death in August,

171. *Louisianan*, August 14, 1875; *Convention of Colored Newspaper Men, Cincinnati, August 4th, 1875* (N.p., n.d.), 4–6; Cincinnati *Daily Gazette*, August 5, 1875.

1876, is an absolute mystery. The evidence suggests that he went to Massachusetts, where his wife and daughter lived after the convention. Sometime later
he drifted back to New Orleans. It appears that he also lost his job with the
Treasury Department during this period. The fact that there is no mention of
him in local newspapers suggests that he possibly fell from favor with the city's
black political leaders after his Cincinnati speech. On August 11, 1876, a servant found him in bed "breathing irregularly," a half empty vial of laudanum
next to his bed. He died soon after, despite attempts by doctors to save his life.
The autopsy report sheds little light on the actual cause of death. From the
scanty evidence available, indications are that he committed suicide. The drug-
gist who sold him half an ounce of laudanum the day before his death testified
that the amount taken was insufficient to kill Martin, and suggested that he may
have taken "another poison." Others who knew him well spoke of increasing
despondency brought on by continuous illness and failure to find a job.[172]

Black America had lost one of its finest workers at the relatively young age
of forty-four. In the space of just twenty years, from his escape to Chicago
until his death in New Orleans, Martin had done enough to leave his mark on
nineteenth-century Afro-American history. Other men took twice as long to
accomplish half as much. His work in Britain after the war sustained the AMA
at its moment of greatest need, and in spite of many obstacles, his indomitable
spirit kept alive British support for the Union during the conflict. Few of his
contemporaries challenged Douglass' view that Martin was one of the era's
finest orators. Garnet, his colleague in the African Civilization Society, wrote
in praise of the lion who roared from the West. He wielded the pen with as
much facility. Frequent letters to the press as well as editorials in the *New Era*
showed his command of the written word. He was charming, yet formal, quick
to befriend others, yet never thought twice of denouncing them publicly when
he thought them wrong. But above all else, Martin was driven by an obsession
to achieve. He could never quite fathom why hard work had resulted in such
few rewards. One suspects that his impatience was fueled by the knowledge
that his illnesses might one day prove fatal and so cut him off short of his goals.
His friend and mentor Douglass was aware of this and, try as he might, could
not get Martin to persevere, to see a project through to the end. When Douglass heard that Martin had accepted a position at the *Louisianan* in 1871, he
wrote pleadingly, almost desperately, imploring him to pull "steadily in his

172. New Orleans *Republican*, August 12, 16, 1876; Death Certificate, New Orleans Health Department; New York *Daily Tribune*, August 15, 1876.

present harness." That was too tall an order. Pulling hard demanded patience, a virtue Martin never cultivated. And back of all this weakness and its attendant failures hung the addiction to laudanum, the result of a desperate battle to relieve incessant pain. Like the daughter of Hawthorne's Rappaccinni, Martin found himself equally at risk from the medicine as from the disease.

William Howard Day when young
Reprinted from B. F. Wheeler, *Cullings From Zion's Poets*

Chapter V

Marching On

The Life of William Howard Day

On the eve of William Howard Day's retirement from the Harrisburg, Pennsylvania, School Board, after twenty years of service, a black newspaper boldly asserted that "whoever has read the doings of the race at the north the past quarter of a century has seen Prof. William Howard Day's name among the worthies and always in a conspicuous place."[1] In the eighty years since that was written, Day, like so many of his contemporaries who devoted their lives to uplifting the race, has virtually disappeared from the pages of American history. Rediscovered temporarily in the 1950s, at which time his grave in Harrisburg's Lincoln Cemetery was rededicated by W. E. B. Du Bois, Day has again slipped into relative obscurity. Day would not have anticipated such oblivion. He knew well that America and its debilitating racism always contrived to underestimate the contributions of blacks to its history. But he firmly believed that that was an aberration, the product of greed and ignorance, which could be tempered if not destroyed by determined political agitation and education. His life was dedicated to righting the wrongs besetting American society, and no wrong, he insisted, was greater than the oppression of black Americans.

Day was born in New York City on October 16, 1825, the youngest of John and Eliza Day's four children. John Day, a sailmaker, had a long and distinguished career in the American navy. He was a veteran of the War of 1812, and

1. Cleveland *Gazette*, March 19, 1898.

the wars against the Barbary pirates in the Mediterranean. He saw service in the bloody naval engagements on Lake Champlain in the row galley *Viper*, under Commodore Thomas Macdonough. Years later his proud son recalled that he fought "on the deck of the row-galley, until all his fellows fell beside him, until his blood and theirs rose up to his ankles, literally washed the deck, and dyed the waters around them. The marks of that battle he carried to his grave." Less than one year after the cessation of hostilities, John Day was drafted into the naval expedition under Commodore William Bainbridge sent to the Mediterranean to protect American commercial interests against continuous attacks from the Barbary states. Relations among the United States, Algiers, Tripoli, and Tunis had been strained since the outbreak of the American Revolution. American ships were frequently impounded and their crews pressed into slavery. Diplomatic efforts to stop these actions met with little success. Frustrated by these failures and anxious to display the country's naval might, Congress declared war on Algiers in February, 1815, and dispatched two squadrons to the area, one under Bainbridge, the other under Commodore Stephen Decatur. While Decatur harassed Algerian shipping, finally forcing the dey into a treaty, Bainbridge took his fleet directly to Carthagena, Spain, and from there to Tunis and Tripoli. This show of force had the desired effect. The fleet was on its way home by October, 1816, and America had established its right to trade in the area free from attacks. Five months after he returned to the United States, John Day was honorably discharged.[2]

Not long after his return to America, John married Eliza Dixon. Little is known about Day's mother. In a period when women were expected to limit their vision to the hearth, Eliza was an active participant in the community. She was a member of the John Street Methodist Church, "the mother church of Methodism in this country," and a founding member of the first African Methodist Episcopal Zion church. She was the spiritual leader of the family, and the Days' home soon became the major center of AME Zion activity in New York. All of the church's early leaders were guests at the Days' home, and William was baptized by James Varrick, the denomination's first bishop. Eliza was also active in the fledgling abolitionist movement and frequently attended its public meetings. She had to flee for her life from a mob that attacked an abolitionist meeting at Chatham Street Chapel in 1833. It was a foretaste of things to come. For

---

2. Wilmington *Daily Commercial*, April 20, 1870; William C. Nell, *The Colored Patriots of the American Revolution* (1855; rpr. New York, 1968), 282–83; Ray W. Irwin, *The Diplomatic Relations of the United States with the Barbary Powers, 1776–1816* (Chapel Hill, 1931), 176–82; B. F. Wheeler, *Cullings From Zion's Poets* (Mobile, 1907), 117.

three days in July, 1834, the city was held to ransom by anti-abolitionist mobs that destroyed black homes and churches. Even after the mobs were dispersed, the Days kept their home barricaded. Neighbors rallied to protect themselves and their property. At night, Day later recalled, "we barricaded our windows . . . we watched on our arms, . . . our neighbors heated water to give the mob a warm reception . . . and we had a man walking up and down with a sword on his side, to give the alarm when the mob came."[3] That they survived relatively unscathed was due more to their own vigilance than the ability of authorities to maintain order.

Eliza Day must have felt particularly vulnerable during those attacks as she attempted to protect her four young children. John had died tragically sometime in 1829, when he fell from a ship and drowned. Eliza's young family had to depend totally on her limited resources, supplemented by support from her elder son, who found a job on board one of the ships plying the coastal trade routes.[4] But Eliza was determined to provide her youngest child with the best possible education. At the age of four, William was sent to a private school on White Street run by a Mr. Levi Folsom and his family. William was a bright, diligent student, and in two years he was reading passages from the Bible. Following the transfer of the New York Manumission Society's school to the Public School Society in 1834, William enrolled at Public School No. 2 on Laurens Street, headed by Ransom F. Wake. It was here that William had his first taste of black organization and protest. In March, 1834, over 150 students of the city's black grammar schools, led by Henry Highland Garnet, William, and others, formed the Garrison Literary Society, named in honor of the Boston abolitionist. Members ranged in age from five to fourteen, and meetings were held every Saturday afternoon, at which original compositions were read and discussed. Black improvement would gain momentum, the preamble to its constitution read, if "youth of color distinguish themselves by their good conduct and intellectual attainments." But leaders of the Public School Society, many of them members of the local auxiliary of the Colonization Society, bristled at the name adopted by the young men. In a rather heavy-handed attempt to force the students to drop the name, the society banned their using school property for meetings. But the black students persisted, and in a show of defiance, they re-

3. Wilmington *Daily Commercial*, April 20, 1870; Harrisburg *Telegraph*, September 6, 1897; Armagh *Guardian*, October 14, 1859; Leonard L. Richards, *"Gentlemen of Property and Standing": Anti-Abolition Mobs in Jacksonian America* (New York, 1970), 28–29, 113–14; *Star of Zion*, March 10, August 18, 1898.
4. *Star of Zion*, April 28, 1898; Harrisburg *Telegraph*, September 12, 1872.

fused to bow to the pressure. The board of the Philomethan Society, a local black organization, came to the rescue and granted the students permission to use their rooms.[5]

Although the Garrison Literary Society was short-lived, the fact that it had named William, just nine years old, its assistant librarian must have boosted his confidence. Because there were no public high schools for blacks in the city, William's mother had to reach deep into her meager resources in an effort to continue her son's education. She enrolled him in a private school on West Broadway run by the Reverend Frederick Jones of Northampton, Massachusetts. It is not known how long William attended this school. But during one of its public examinations, a visitor, J. P. Williston of Northampton, was so impressed with William's performance that he presented him with a special prize. Williston, an ink manufacturer, was a prominent figure in temperance and abolitionist circles in Hampshire County. Two weeks later, Williston was back in New York, determined to persuade Eliza Day to allow him to adopt William. After some soul searching, she consented, fully aware that this was the only way to guarantee William's education.[6]

The move to Northampton was a dramatic turning point in young William's life. The five years spent there provided him with most of the tools needed to survive and prosper in nineteenth-century America. The Willistons were a warm family. One son later remembered the "fine little fellow" being treated with equal respect and afforded all the privileges of the white family. William was enrolled at the common school taught by the Reverend Rudolphus B. Hubbard and he was an instant success. In spite of his warmth and affection, Williston was a hard taskmaster, a firm believer in the doctrine of hard work, thrift, self-respect, self-control, and self-abnegation. He required that the children earn what money they spent on their "own pleasure or gave to a worthy object." Although William was in school, he was also expected to acquire a trade. Williston placed him in the print shop of the *Hampshire Herald*, a newspaper he had established some years before. By the time William left North-

5. *Emancipator*, April 1, 15, May 27, 1834; Herbert Aptheker (ed.), *A Documentary History of the Negro in the United States* (2 vols.; Secaucus, N.J., 1951), I, 151–52; Daniel Perlman, "Organizations of the Free Negro in New York City, 1800–1860," *JNH*, LVI (1971), 195; Bishop J. W. Hood, *One Hundred Years of the African Methodist Episcopal Zion Church* (New York, 1895), 321; Carlton Mabee, *Black Education in New York State from Colonial to Modern Times* (Syracuse, 1979), 21–23.

6. Hood, *One Hundred Years*, 321–23; *Star of Zion*, December 3, 1891; Martin L. Williston, "Reminiscences From the Life and Character of Deacon John P. Williston" (Typescript, in Forbes Library, Northampton); *Hampshire Gazette*, January 11, 1901.

ampton in 1843, he was a skilled printer. Williston, recognizing his adopted son's intellectual skills, also gave him a room in his factory where William taught a class of black men, mainly fugitive slaves temporarily settled in the area.[7]

Northampton allowed William time and space to develop, free from the pervasive racism of a big city like New York. Although he would never forget the riots of 1834 and the continuous threats of violence from angry white mobs, Northampton did offer a needed respite, and demonstrated to the young man that there were some whites who still clung to the vaunted principles of freedom, equality, and brotherhood. He attended school and openly competed with white children, regularly sat by the side of his foster-father in the choir of the local church, worked with white apprentices and master printers at the *Hampshire Herald*, and no one expressed shock or protested his presence. It was an experience he would carry with him for the rest of his life. He later became a passionate defender of interracial political agitation. Day saw himself as the perfect example (a symbol) of black potential freed from the shackles of American racism. Afforded similar opportunities, others could achieve as much as he had.

His training and experiences at Northampton promised a bright future for William. He was well educated and seemed destined to follow in the footsteps of many of his classmates who had enrolled in prestigious New England colleges. He had set his sights on attending Williams College in Massachusetts. But if life in Northampton had sheltered him temporarily from the daily pressures of American racism, his wish to attend Williams and the angry protests it generated from southern students jolted William back to reality. His white classmates could attend the college of their choice, but William would have to find a school whose leadership had not succumbed to racist pressures. Oberlin was the only college that had adopted a policy of open enrollment. Williston was also one of its earliest supporters. It was, therefore, the logical choice for William, especially as he could earn his keep either in its print shop or, during the long winter-vacation months, in schools where students taught blacks in the North and Canada.

In June, 1843, William wrote R. E. Gillett about a vacancy in the print shop at Oberlin and gave details of his qualifications for attending the college. He had successfully completed examinations in Latin and Greek conducted by Beriah Green, principal of Oneida Institute, New York, as well as courses in

7. *Star of Zion*, April 28, 1898, December 3, 1891; Williston, "Reminiscences."

English, chemistry, botany, and algebra. After further language examinations by John Morgan and James Fairchild of Oberlin, William joined the 1843 freshman class of over fifty students, the only black in the group and only the third black to enter its collegiate course.[8] William left Northampton with mixed feelings. Williston had done all within his power to provide for his adopted son. But he was an unrelenting taskmaster and disciplinarian who insisted on keeping a close watch over William. Williston's son remembers his father as being so inflexible that "obedience became a fixt habit, and the very thought of insubordination or trespass was practically absent from the mind of the child." Now eighteen and free from the daily supervision of his foster-father, William bristled at Williston's incessant meddling and the constant stream of letters to Oberlin officials to warn them of William's weaknesses. He was particularly worried about William's "habit of procrastination," his aversion to manual labor, and his susceptibility to flattery. Two years after William entered Oberlin, Williston still found it necessary to write, warning that his ward "ought to be guarded against personal vanity and a love of dress. So fond was he of adjusting his dress that he wore the paint off the floor in the place where he stood before the looking glass in his chamber."[9] William's growing sense of independence, reinforced by constant praise from his peers, made such hectoring even more galling.

Williston's concerns were not totally unfounded. Tall, good-looking, and always dapperly dressed, William quickly became a favorite particularly with the ladies. He was also well aware of his intellectual abilities and oratorical skills, which won him a great deal of praise. But his academic and social successes imposed additional burdens on the young man. As a black college student, in a society that accepted as faith black intellectual inferiority, William found himself under constant scrutiny. Blacks saw him as a symbol of rights and hopes denied; whites, as an exception to the rule of black inferiority. Although the latter could in many circumstances be ignored, one had to live up to the expectations of the former. If for no other reason, then, William approached his vacation teaching duties with added determination. Like other Oberlin students, he had to go in search of a school. During his years as an undergraduate, he taught school in Buffalo and among fugitive slaves in Ontario. The difficulties

8. Day to R. E. Gillett, June 29, 1843, in File 7/1/5, OCA; William J. Simmons, *Men of Mark: Eminent, Progressive and Rising* (1887; rpr. New York, 1968), 978; *Star of Zion*, December 3, 1891.
9. Williston, "Reminiscences"; Williston to Rev. A. Mahan, July 17, 1845, Williston to H. Hill, February 14, 1845, both in File 7/1/5, OCA.

these small schools faced, and the pride they took in their successes, were William's first major exposure to black self-help organizations. Day would dedicate the rest of his life to the spread and improvement of education for blacks.[10]

During the school year, William divided his time between studies and work among the small black community in the college town. He became a leading figure in the community, a popular speaker at most of its public meetings. When the Reverend Charles Turner Torrey died in a Maryland prison, William drew up a series of resolutions condemning the abolitionist's imprisonment and the governor's refusal to release him. He also teamed up with Sabran Cox and visited nearby towns, lecturing and singing antislavery songs. Cox, born a slave in Virginia, had settled in Oberlin in 1839 and attended public school and the college's preparatory department. These activities won William considerable praise in the black community and drew the expected fire from Williston, who was convinced that such recognition bred immodesty. His doubts were partially confirmed when word arrived that William was in debt. That, Williston insisted, was the inevitable consequence of William's susceptibility to flattery.[11]

If Williston was right, and the evidence suggests that he had some grounds for concern, then William had not conformed totally to the college's traditions. Oberlin students were expected to live a spartan existence. Its program envisaged the "training of a band of self-denying, hardy intelligent efficient laborers, of both sexes, for the world's enlightenment and regeneration." William clearly was not one of those "threadbare and emaciated students" who met in classrooms of "dilapidated buildings to hear ragged professors sound the clarion call for world reform." Having experienced some hardship and the relative comforts of life at the Willistons', William had no intention of voluntarily adopting a spartan way of life to conform to Oberlin traditions. His tailored clothes set him apart from his fellow students. It was one way of asserting his individuality. The Reverend Charles G. Finney's assertion that "glee, fun, hilarious mirth, games, charades, and pleasure seeking grieve the Holy Spirit, destroy [the] heart, darken [the] mind . . . and break up . . . fellowship with the Father, and His Son Jesus Christ" meant little to William. He simply did not

10. *Star of Zion,* April 28, 1898; *Pennsylvania School Journal,* March, 1899, J. Mercer Langston, *From the Virginia Plantation to the National Capitol* (1894; rpr. New York, 1969), 87; Robert Samuel Fletcher, *A History of Oberlin College from Its Foundation Through the Civil War* (2 vols.; Oberlin, 1943), I, 424, 245–49.
11. William F. Bigglestone, *They Stopped in Oberlin: Black Residents and Visitors of the Nineteenth Century* (Scottsdale, Ariz., 1981), 59–60; Oberlin *Evangelist,* June 10, 1846, March 17, 1847; Fletcher, *History of Oberlin,* I, 251; Williston to Hill, December 17, 1846, in File 7/1/5, OCA.

accept the notion that such self-denial was a necessary precondition of Christian existence. This rejection may explain why William declined to enter the ministry after graduation.[12]

William was chosen one of eleven speakers at commencement exercises, a fitting tribute to his leadership as an undergraduate. Since his arrival at Oberlin he had been a regular and popular speaker at various meetings. His address, "The Millennium of Liberty," was his first published statement on the nature of oppression and the prospects for liberty in the United States. America, he argued, had turned its back on liberty and was using its unlimited power to prop up despotism, so much so that its supporters had come to accept such actions as a natural duty of government. As a result, the country was in danger of establishing a civilization based on and sustained by despotism, and civilizations founded on despotism rather than the "rights of humanity," he warned, were doomed to failure. But there was still time to retreat from the brink of disaster. After all, America had been founded as an outpost of liberty against European despotism, a land of hope for humanity, where civil and religious liberty could flourish. America needed to reaffirm its original principles. But even if it did not, William remained optimistic that liberty and the forces for good would be victorious. "You may bury the seeds of Liberty in a coffin of adamant beneath the tread of many generations," he asserted, "you may heap upon it an iron soil; but it shall burst its cerements, and with an omnipotent power shall upturn the kingdoms built upon its graves."[13]

The conviction that the principles of liberty embodied in the Declaration of Independence and the Constitution would ultimately rise above present efforts by proslavery advocates to distort their intent placed Day ideologically in the Liberty party camp. Not that he ever openly castigated those who accepted the Garrisonian interpretation of the Constitution, but Day was much more hopeful about the future of blacks in American society. It could not have been otherwise. His life to that point spoke eloquently in favor of good men performing good deeds on behalf of the oppressed. The Willistons had treated him as an equal, and so had his contemporaries at college. Oberlin and the surrounding community were an oasis in a wilderness of oppression. Another black student, J. Mercer Langston, remembered that on Sundays "colored persons could be seen seated in conspicuous places in the only church in town, worshipping after the manner of those in whose midst they lived, and no one molested or

12. Fletcher, *History of Oberlin*, II, 809, I, 489–93; Hood, *One Hundred Years*, 324.
13. Oberlin *Evangelist*, October 13, September 1, 1847.

disturbed them." Blacks, he concluded, were welcomed as equals "in the best families." It is no wonder that soon after graduation, Day became an active proponent of the Liberty party and its successor, the Free-Soil party. He was named an Ohio delegate to the national convention that met in Buffalo in October, 1847.[14]

It is not clear what Day did after graduation. Like so many of his contemporaries, he seems to have divided his time between the lecture circuit, where he was in constant demand, and work in the Negro Convention movement, neither of which guaranteed a regular income. But whatever he did, Day's actions were motivated by a commitment to promote the interests of blacks. He was named secretary of the national Negro convention in Cleveland in September, 1848. The formation of the Free-Soil party and the platform adopted at Buffalo were the focuses of dispute at the meeting. Many, like Samuel Ringgold Ward, viewed the new party and its tempered platform as a betrayal of abolitionist principles. Others called for endorsement of the new party, arguing that it was the only option available to blacks following the demise of the Liberty party. The convention toyed with the idea of open endorsement but in the end decided to remain neutral.[15]

This was not an inauspicious beginning for the young graduate. Although Martin Delany had cause to question portions of his report, it was generally accepted that he had performed admirably. He also joined Frederick Douglass, Henry Bibb, and others on the committee that prepared the "Address to the Colored People of America."[16] But though the national meeting dealt almost entirely with general concerns, blacks in Ohio were organizing for a concerted drive to eliminate legalized discrimination in the state. These activities would consume Day's energies for the next seven years. In early December, an Oberlin meeting named him chairman of a committee to prepare an address to blacks in the county and the state. The meeting pledged to vote only for those who supported equal rights, wondered about paying taxes when blacks were generally disfranchised, and called on friends of the fugitive to redouble their efforts.

Ohio's black code was considered to be among the most restrictive of any northern state. Although the constitution of 1802 permitted blacks to reside in

14. Langston, *From the Virginia Plantation*, 102; *Emancipator*, November 10, 1847.
15. "Report of the Proceedings of the Colored National Convention, Held at Cleveland, Ohio, on Wednesday, September 6, 1848," in Howard H. Bell (ed.), *Minutes of the Proceedings of the National Negro Conventions, 1830–1864* (New York, 1969), 8–15; Jane H. Pease and William H. Pease, *They Who Would Be Free: Blacks' Search for Freedom, 1830–1861* (New York, 1974), 195–99; *Signal of Liberty*, April 13, 1848, in Reel 5, BAP.
16. *North Star*, November 17, 1848.

the state, it denied them the vote. Legislation in subsequent years severely cir-
cumscribed the rights of blacks to settle, gain an education, testify in court
cases involving whites, and serve in the state militia. These proscriptions had
come under increasing attacks from blacks and abolitionists since 1830. In state
conventions that met regularly for the next eight years, blacks in Ohio attempted through public appeal and the ballot to bring about reform. The recent election of a number of Free-Soilers to a legislature almost equally divided
between Democrats and Whigs increased expectations of positive change.
Throughout the 1849–50 session, the Free-Soilers used their balance of power
to stymie proslavery Democrats and win repeal of laws prohibiting black testimony and requiring blacks to post bond when reentering the state. The legislature also placed on the statute books a law that obligated townships to allocate
a prorated share of school funds for black education. It was a stunning if limited
success and an augury, many blacks hoped, of more sweeping reforms.[17]

These expectations were not met; the successes of 1849–50 would never be
duplicated. But blacks were not to know that. The state convention that met in
Columbus in January, 1849, concentrated almost all its energies on the elimination of the "black laws." Day was one of seven delegates from Lorain County.
The convention named a committee to petition the legislature for the removal
of the black laws. It also endorsed the creation of two funds, one to employ a
black lecturer to canvass the state in favor of repealing the laws, and the other to
hire a lawyer to test the legality of discriminatory school laws. In its "Address to
the Citizens of Ohio," the committee headed by Day called for the removal of
"negro pews" in churches, for school privileges in common with others, for the
admission of blacks who were insane to state asylums, for the right to testify in
cases involving whites, and finally for the removal of the word *white* from the
state constitution. "We ask," the address concluded, "that we may be one people,
bound together by one common tie and sheltered by the same impartial law."[18]

Although a state agent was never officially hired, Day seems to have filled the
breach temporarily as agent of the Colored American League of Oberlin, collecting money for the campaign.[19] A state league was officially organized, with

17. David A. Gerber, *Black Ohio and the Color Line, 1860–1915* (Urbana, 1976), 3–5; Leonard
Erickson, "Politics and Repeal of Ohio's Black Laws, 1837–1849," *Ohio History*, LXXXII (1973),
171–73; *North Star*, January 12, 1849; Oberlin *Evangelist*, February 28, 1849.

18. "Minutes and Address of the State Convention of the Colored Citizens of Ohio, Convened
at Columbus, January 10th, 11th, 12th and 13th, 1849," in Phillip S. Foner and George E. Walker
(eds.), *Proceedings of the Black State Conventions, 1840–1865* (2 vols.; Philadelphia, 1979), I, 226–34;
Anti Slavery Bugle, January 26, 1849; *North Star*, January 26, 1849; Columbus *State Journal*, quoted
in *Anti Slavery Standard*, January 25, 1849.

19. Cleveland *True Democrat*, December 24, 1849.

J. L. Watson of Cuyahoga County as president and Day as corresponding secretary, at the state convention in Columbus in January, 1850. The league aimed to create local auxiliaries and employ a number of lecturers to influence the upcoming constitutional convention to remove voting restrictions on blacks. There were grounds for optimism. Not only had the legislature already lifted some proscriptions on blacks, but in areas such as Lorain County and other parts of the Western Reserve, blacks had voted, some in contravention of state law, others through exploiting loopholes in the law. Day was without doubt the dominant figure at the Columbus meeting, insisting that it concentrate on the issue of voting rights. He was elected to address the constitutional convention on behalf of black Ohioans, and was named one of the lecturers to canvass the state. In addition, the meeting agreed to petition the legislature to appoint a superintendent of black schools and recommended Day for the post.[20]

Day saw these new legislative enactments as a sign that Ohio, if not America, was moving slowly but ineluctably toward a time when all restrictions on blacks would be lifted. He reiterated his optimism in a poem read at an August 1 celebration in Cleveland:

> The onward rushing tide of time
> Advancing to its goal,
> The bark of man upon its breast,
> Rearing after the soul,
>
> All told of man's high destiny;
> And made the Saxon feel
> That for him it was best to be
> Defender of his weal.

All of this was reinforced by the election of Dr. Norton Strange Townshend as Oberlin representative to the constitutional convention. Townshend, considered by many the father of agricultural education in America, was a trustee of Oberlin College and one of the principal proponents of equal rights for blacks in the state legislature. As delegates to the convention gathered in Columbus, Day wrote William H. Seward of New York, asking his views on the "benefit to the colored man in the States where he has been permitted to vote." A positive reply from Seward, he observed, would be useful in the struggle for voting rights. Supporters and opponents of equal suffrage for blacks swamped the convention with petitions. Some opponents argued for the removal of blacks

20. "Minutes of the State Convention of the Colored Citizens of Ohio, Convened at Columbus, January 9th, 10th, 11th and 12th, 1850," in Foner and Walker (eds.), *Proceedings*, I, 243–53; Cleveland *True Democrat*, January 21, 22, 26, 30, February 2, 14, 1850.

from the state, others for increased restrictions on their rights, and still others
for the maintenance of the status quo. Supporters simply called for the excision
of all invidious racial distinctions so as to make the suffrage laws conform to
the spirit of equality that informed the national and state constitutions.[21]

The black state convention that met in Columbus in January, 1851, devoted
almost all its energies to devising ways to influence the constitutional convention. H. Ford Douglas of Cleveland, among others, rejected such efforts as
futile. The "Constitution of the United States," he argued, "is pro-slavery,
considered so by those who framed it, and construed to that end ever since its
adoption." It was, therefore, patently contradictory for any black man to vote
"under the United States Constitution." Day led the opposition to this interpretation. Douglas' error, he insisted, was not separating the Constitution itself
from the "construction" of the Constitution employed by those who wished to
see blacks oppressed. If, he argued, it was framed to establish justice, then by
the same token it must be opposed to injustice: "If it says plainly no person shall
be deprived of life, *liberty*, or property, without due process of law, I suppose it
means it." Blacks had to use all available means in their fight to attain equality
before the law. Day came down squarely on the side of the anti-Garrisonians in
his interpretation of the intent of the Constitution. "I consider the Constitution the foundation of American liberties," he asserted, "and wrapping myself
in the flag of the nation, I would plant myself upon that Constitution, and using
the weapons they have given me, I would appeal to the American people for the
rights thus guaranteed."[22]

Day's arguments carried the day, and the convention named him to a committee of seven to visit Governor Reuben Wood. The meeting with Wood was
fruitless—he simply refused to intervene in support of an equal franchise law.
Undaunted, the convention named Day chairman of a committee of three to
prepare an address to the constitutional convention. Blacks, the address stated,
were citizens of the United States by virtue of the fact that they were born in
this country, had fought and died for it, and had been regular taxpayers. But the
convention ignored such arguments and accepted the recommendations of its
Committee on the Elective Franchise to deny blacks the right to vote. James
Loudon, representative from Brown County, best expressed the view of those

21. Fletcher, *History of Oberlin*, I, 356, 388; Cleveland *True Democrat*, August 10, 1850; Ohio,
*Report of the Debates and Proceedings of the Convention for the Revision of the Constitution of the State of
Ohio, 1850–1851* (2 vols.; Columbus, 1851), I, 56–75; Day to William H. Seward, May 6, 1850,
Seward to Day, May 16, 1850, both in William H. Seward Papers, Reel 6, BAP.
22. "Minutes of the State Convention of the Colored Citizens of Ohio, Convened at Colum-
bus, January 15th, 16th, 17th, and 18th, 1851," in Foner and Walker (eds.), *Proceedings*, I, 261–63.

opposed to an extension of the franchise: "A majority of the people I represent, without regard, I may say, to whether they are of the Democratic party or the Whig party, believe with the fathers of this State that this should be a State for the white man only."[23]

Even before the constitutional convention concluded its business, Day had decided to move to Cleveland. Larger than Oberlin, it held out greater prospects for someone anxious to establish himself in a recognized profession. He had been reporting from the black community for the Cleveland *True Democrat* since 1850, and after moving to Cleveland, he became a compositor and local editor of the paper. Day had also announced the date of his marriage to Lucy Stanton of Cleveland, whom he had met at Oberlin, where she was the first black woman to complete the collegiate course of study. Lucy was born in Cleveland in 1831, the only child of Samuel and Margaret Stanton. Samuel died before she was two, and Margaret married John Brown, a free black from Virginia, who had been Samuel's partner and who was a prominent figure in the city. Lucy grew up in a predominantly white neighborhood and attended a white school until a local minister protested her presence. In response, John Brown built a school for black children at his own expense. Lucy probably attended this school before enrolling at Oberlin. Little is known of her years at college, except that she was elected president of the Oberlin Ladies Literary Society in her senior year. She was also selected to give one of the orations at the commencement exercises in 1850. Following graduation, she taught at a black school in Columbus until her marriage to William in 1852.[24]

Physically and psychologically, the move was a minor one. Although blacks were a meager 1.3 percent of the city's population in 1850, their numbers were on the increase. But more important, Cleveland, like Oberlin, had a good record of race relations. Segregation in public accommodations was rare, and when it did occur, it was usually short-lived. Most theaters and other public facilities did not segregate their black patrons. This is not to suggest that there was no discrimination in Cleveland. Both William and Lucy, for instance, were

23. Ohio, *Report of the Debates and Proceedings*, II, 550–54; "Minutes of the State Convention, 1851," in Foner and Walker (eds.), *Proceedings*, I, 269–72; Cleveland *True Democrat*, February 5, 1851; *Anti Slavery Bugle*, February 22, 1851; Loudon quoted in Frank Quillin, *The Color Line in Ohio: A History of Race Prejudice in a Typical Northern State* (1913; rpr. New York, 1969), 64.

24. Russell H. Davis, *Black Americans in Cleveland* (Washington, D.C., 1972), 49, 59–60; Ellen N. Lawson, "Lucy Stanton: Life on the Cutting Edge," *Western Reserve Magazine*, X (1983), 9–10; Ellen N. Lawson and Marlene Merrill, "The Antebellum 'Talented Thousandth': Black College Students at Oberlin Before the Civil War," *Journal of Negro Education*, LII (1983), 146; Fletcher, *History of Oberlin*, II, 524, 534; Oberlin *Evangelist*, September 11, December 17, 1850; *Frederick Douglass Paper*, May 13, 1852.

refused membership in the Cuyahoga Temperance Society. After some protest it was agreed to admit only William, but a small group later withdrew to form the Freedom Temperance Lodge, which admitted both.[25] Acceptance by many whites in Cleveland partially protected Day against the more blatant and pervasive forms of racism that his contemporaries in other cities experienced. Where others came to view America's professions of liberty and equality with growing skepticism because of their experiences with racism, Day continued to hold out hope for imminent change.

The two positions clashed at the January, 1852, black state convention in Cincinnati. American refusal to grant blacks full equality, J. Mercer Langston, C. H. Langston, H. Ford Douglas, and Peter H. Clark argued, left blacks no alternative but to explore the possibilities of voluntary emigration. Although they declared the policies of the American Colonization Society anathema to blacks, they endorsed emigration as "the only relief from the oppressions of the American people" and argued that its success would "react favorably upon the institution of slavery." Day and others, like John I. Gaines of Cincinnati, roundly condemned pro-emigrationists for deflecting black interest away from the struggle against slavery and racial discrimination, and for abrogating their responsibilities as black leaders to fight for the rights of full citizenship. The debate was not new. Three years earlier, J. Mercer Langston had raised the issue at a similar meeting. There, too, the dispute resulted in the adoption of a minority report opposing emigration. This meeting was no different; but this time the majority voted against any form of emigration.[26]

The meeting also reiterated its desire to publish a newspaper that could represent the views of blacks in the state. A fund of $1,000 would be raised through the formation of a joint-stock company, and agents to sell the stock would be selected. The paper would be published by a committee of three chosen by the stockholders. The 1850 state convention had also attempted to publish the "Voice of the Oppressed," a newspaper edited by Day and C. H. Langston. Day worked for almost a year but failed to get the project off the ground. He reported his failure to the 1851 meeting and suggested it elect a replacement. The Committee on the Press reported in favor of a renewed

25. Cleveland *True Democrat*, July 22, 1850, February 25, 1851; Lawson, "Lucy Stanton," 11; Kenneth L. Kusmer, *A Ghetto Takes Shape: Black Cleveland, 1870–1915* (Urbana, 1976), 10–15.

26. "Proceedings of the Convention of the Colored Freemen of Ohio, Held in Cincinnati, January 14, 15, 16, 17, and 19, 1852," and "Minutes and Address of the State Convention, 1849," both in Foner and Walker (eds.), *Proceedings*, I, 223, 276, 279; *Frederick Douglass Paper*, February 5, 1852.

effort and suggested retaining Day and Langston as editors.[27] But as had been the case at previous meetings, nothing came of the decision taken at Cincinnati. When a convention of blacks met in Cleveland in September and declined to act, Day decided to go it alone. His plan was to publish a pilot issue, await the response, and then decide on its future. The first issue of the *Aliened American* appeared in April, 1853, and was generally well received, although some, like the New York *Daily Tribune*, questioned the wisdom of publishing another black weekly. Day, the editor of the *Tribune* warned, was fishing "with a naked hook—or rather with the frying pan—and so is quite unlikely to catch any but the slowest chubs." Although well-intentioned, the warning was unnecessary, for Day had already announced that the paper would not appear regularly if the first issue failed to generate a substantial number of subscriptions. For the next few months, he toured the Northeast, meeting leading black figures, in an effort to attract further financial backing. Day must have felt confident of continuing support, for he issued the second number in August.[28]

Unfortunately our knowledge of the paper is limited to one extant copy. Its motto declared that it would promote education as a vehicle for the development of blacks and "defend the rights of humanity." The content reflected these objectives. The first of its four pages contained poems and an original story by Lucy S. Day. There were also book reviews and a typical smattering of news clipped from exchanges. Day assembled a prominent editorial staff. Both Samuel Ringgold Ward and J. W. C. Pennington agreed to be corresponding editors, and Dr. S. C. Murray, Amos Beman, and Martin R. Delany were to act as regular correspondents. It was an auspicious beginning, but the support of well-known individuals could not guarantee its success. Although Day had purchased a press and so could produce each issue at minimal cost, no paper could survive solely on the subscriptions it garnered. Although the annual subscription rate of $1.50 was well within the reach of many blacks, it never generated sufficient funds to meet normal operating expenses. Moreover, the liberal *True Democrat* and its successor, the *Leader*, which gave extensive coverage to events in the black community, militated against the need for a newspaper aimed exclusively at blacks. As a result, the paper ceased publication sometime in 1854,

27. "Minutes of the State Convention, 1851," "Minutes of the State Convention, 1850," and "Proceedings of the Convention, 1852," all in Foner and Walker (eds.), *Proceedings*, I, 227, 264–66, 253–54, 280; Cleveland *True Democrat*, February 9, 11, 1852; Harrisburg *Telegraph*, July 3, 1886.

28. New York *Daily Tribune*, quoted in *Frederick Douglass Paper*, May 13, January 7, September 2, July 22, 1853; Cleveland *True Democrat*, April 12, August 24, 1853; *Anti Slavery Standard*, September 17, 1853.

and Day's attempt to revive it as a monthly failed soon after the publication of the first number.[29]

These failures did not diminish Day's optimistic view of the future of American society, and the role blacks had to play in its development. Those whites who continued to discriminate against blacks, who insisted that blacks were inferior, and those blacks who had grown impatient with America, promoting instead voluntary emigration, Day maintained, were violating, on one hand, the precepts of Christianity and the tenets of the Constitution and, on the other, were abrogating their responsibility to stay and fight for their rights. America would always fall short of its objectives, he insisted, as long as it failed to develop all of its potential, and that included its black citizens. A country or government, he wrote, "is strong not as it progresses in territory, but as that country develops its own resources, as it advances in education, in general intelligence, and in a strict sense of justice." Black leaders and their white supporters, therefore, had to take two approaches to education: first, they must prepare blacks to assume the responsibilities of untrammeled citizenship; second, they must disabuse whites of erroneous notions of superiority based on racism. The achievement of these goals, of course, assumed that blacks would stay in America. Equally, Day accepted as immutable the principle that the Constitution recognized the equality of man. Like Lysander Spooner, he maintained that blacks were born "under the United States Constitution, and entitled by it, to all the rights and immunities of other citizens." These rights had been subverted by those who used the power vested in state and national governments to disfranchise and ostracize blacks through law, public opinion, and community regulations, all in deliberate distortion of the spirit and the intent of the Constitution. Blacks, he argued, had to take the leading role in the struggle to eliminate these denials of constitutional rights.[30]

One of these distortions was the insistence that blacks were not citizens of the United States. Day confronted this position on two fronts. First, he demanded to be shown clauses in the Constitution that specifically excluded free blacks from all rights and immunities of citizenship. Exclusion was the work of later generations who were largely responsible for ignoring blacks' contributions to the defense and development of America. Day was particularly proud

29. *Aliened American*, April 9, 1853; Davis, *Black Americans in Cleveland*, 49; Kusmer, *A Ghetto Takes Shape*, 29; *Frederick Douglass Paper*, May 19, 1854.
30. *Aliened American*, April 9, 1853.

of his father's role in the battles on Lake Champlain and in the Mediterranean. America, he asserted, should never be allowed to forget what John Day and others had done. In the wake of the Fugitive Slave Law, and the state constitutional convention's refusal to accord blacks their rights, Day decided to organize a celebration in memory of those who had fought and died for America since the War of Independence. The veterans who could be identified and who were strong enough to make the journey were invited to Cleveland. The date was chosen to coincide with the anniversary of the battle of Lake Champlain. Seven or eight veterans of the War of 1812 were present, including John Julius and John B. Vashon of Pittsburgh. The services of these men, Day told the audience, had not been recorded. It was time that sensible men pay homage to those who had defended their country. "We hold it up, that men who have denied its truths may observe, that the ignorant may be enlightened, and that white Americans may be divested of excuse for basing their exclusive liberty upon the deeds of their fathers. We, today, advance with them to the same impartial tribunal, and demand, that if the reason be good in the one case, it be made to apply in the other." Turning to whites in the audience, Day warned that continued denial of full equality in the face of such evidence could have serious political and social consequences. Blacks had always been "faithful subjects" and powerful allies, but "an enemy, in your midst, we would be more powerful still." Given this history, he saw no reason why blacks should be denied those rights guaranteed white Americans: "We ask for liberty; liberty here—liberty on the Chalmette Plains—liberty wherever floats the American flag. We demand for the sons of the men who fought for you, equal privileges."[31]

Day did all he could to exploit the momentum created by the meeting, but with little success. The country adamantly refused to recognize the validity of such arguments and continued to deny blacks their constitutional rights. In Ohio, there was irrefutable proof, in the wake of the recent constitutional convention, that blacks had little chance of achieving equal rights. To make matters worse, there were some in state government willing to reverse the limited gains made in 1849–50. A bill before the legislature proposed, among other things, to ban the settlement of blacks and mulattoes from other states, and to register all black and mulatto children born after January, 1854. It was patently absurd, yet it attracted considerable support. Although it was finally shelved, the major-

31. Cleveland *True Democrat*, September 9, 1852; *Frederick Douglass Paper*, October 1, 1852; *The Loyalty and Devotion of the Colored Americans in the Revolution and War of 1812* (Boston, 1861), 3–4; Nell, *The Colored Patriots*, 277–84.

ity of blacks took its very submission as another sign of Ohio's racist intransigence. Yet there were those who took comfort from its defeat—Ohio, they believed, was moving, albeit slowly, in the right direction. But Day considered the victory pyrrhic and insisted that more had to be done by Free-Soilers to rid the state of the last vestiges of discrimination. His attempts to persuade local Free-Soilers to adopt a resolution denouncing continued discrimination and expressing the party's commitment to work for its elimination failed to elicit any response. "Oppression," he was forced to conclude, "almost always overleaps itself, by forcing to its aid, some whose interest may demand disobedience to its behest."[32]

As the situation grew increasingly ominous, blacks met in state convention at Columbus in January, 1853, to map out strategies to deal with the problems. Recognizing the relationship between slavery and discrimination, the convention agreed to form the Ohio State Anti Slavery Society. The new organization was at best ephemeral. Day and others believed that the difficulties besetting blacks in Ohio had to be addressed on a national level, and since 1851 they had been pressing for a national convention. That year the state meeting named Day, J. McCarter Simpson, and C. H. Langston to a committee to correspond with other blacks on the desirability of holding such a meeting. The committee's initial suggestion for a gathering in September, 1851, in Buffalo generated little response. The following summer, Day wrote Douglass that black leaders in New York, Pennsylvania, Connecticut, and other states were now prepared to attend a meeting, and recommended that Douglass, in his capacity as president of the last national meeting, issue a call for a convention to meet in Pittsburgh in September. Nothing came of these efforts until July, 1853, when blacks met in national convention in Rochester.[33]

A meeting of Cleveland blacks named Day, Justin Holland, and Galen Malvin its delegates to the national convention. The success and unanimity of that meeting led those who had participated in its sessions to hope for concerted action. For the first time in almost twenty years, most of the major national black figures had gathered together in a convention. Day took understandable pride in the fact that he was partly responsible for the meeting. He was elected

32. *Frederick Douglass Paper*, December 24, October 15, 1852; *Anti Slavery Bugle*, December 25, 1852; Cleveland *True Democrat*, September 13, 1852.
33. "Minutes of the State Convention, 1851," in Foner and Walker (eds.), *Proceedings*, I, 266; *Official Proceedings of the Ohio State Convention of Colored Freemen Held in Columbus, January 19th–21st, 1853* (Cleveland, 1853), 4; *North Star*, April 3, 1851; *Frederick Douglass Paper*, August 6, 1852.

one of its vice-presidents and a committee of one to report on the condition of blacks in agriculture. By far the most significant achievement of the convention was its decision to form the National Council of Colored People, a black "shadow cabinet" to promote and protect black interests. Day and John I. Gaines were named Ohio's representatives on the National Council. The convention also agreed to explore the possibility of establishing a manual-labor college for blacks.[34]

Day's involvement in the convention enhanced his image and brought him national prominence. One reporter thought him equal to Douglass in ability, with a voice that "mingled persuasion with authority." Another correspondent went even further. Day, he wrote, "is a young man, even yet beardless, though good looking, with much more mental force, seemingly, than physical—looks as though he consumes midnight oil when soft, sweet repose should cradle him—looks, emphatically, a hard student." This "exquisitely fine appearing gentleman" seemed destined, the reporter thought, for great things. Before returning to Cleveland, Day visited New York to see his mother, who was now remarried, to meet prospective supporters of his newspaper, and to lecture. Both he and his paper were praised as worthy examples of black enterprise. Day spoke in turn to the importance of sustaining the convention and working for the successful implementation of its decisions.[35]

But deep fissures soon appeared in the façade of unanimity and optimism presented by the Rochester convention, and Day seems to have been largely responsible. It is difficult to fathom the exact causes of these differences, but it is likely that Day and other Ohioans had grown increasingly suspicious of eastern dominance of the convention movement. All their earlier efforts to convene a national meeting had been turned aside by Douglass, whose interests were then centered on third-party politics. It was not until early 1853 that Douglass finally attended to the pleas of Day and others, prompted in part by the emergence of an emigrationist movement among blacks. To make matters worse, the councils created by the convention were dominated by easterners. Matters came to a head at the first meeting of the National Council held in New York in November. Although it lacked a quorum, the president James McCune Smith decided to continue, as some delegates had traveled long distances. Day did not

34. "Proceedings of the Colored National Convention, Held in Rochester, July 6th, 7th, and 8th, 1853," in Bell (ed.), *Minutes*, 6, 18–19, 29–33, 45–46; Cleveland *True Democrat*, June 15, 1853.
35. *Frederick Douglass Paper*, August 5, July 22, 1853; New York *Daily Tribune*, July 15, 1853.

arrive until after most of the major decisions had been made. The council had
voted, for example, to establish committees on business relations (with headquarters in Philadelphia), on protective unions (based in New York), and
on publications (centered in Boston). Officers of the council had also been
elected, Day being named corresponding secretary. And they had ratified an
earlier decision to locate the proposed manual-labor college within one hundred miles of Erie, Pennsylvania. With the exception of the college's location,
the meeting firmly established eastern ascendancy on the council. These decisions galled Day, who immediately called for a suspension of the proceedings,
citing the lack of a quorum. Smith refused and the gathering degenerated into
a squabble between Day and William C. Nell on one side and those who supported Smith on the other. Rather than resolve differences privately, Smith
ridiculed Day's concerns publicly. The "Buckeye boy, or as they now call him
the 'little Protestant,'" Smith wrote Douglass, not only had failed to inform the
council of his possible late arrival, but seemed bent on derailing all of their
decisions. According to Smith, Day also demanded another council meeting
specifically to amend the constitution, and when the motion failed for lack of a
seconder, he warned that Ohio would be compelled to reexamine its commitments to the council.[36]

Having been publicly derided by Smith, the proud Day would brook no attempts at reconciliation. He was now set against the council and, in the next
few months, did everything within his power to destroy it. The fact that he controlled the *Aliened American* only increased the degree of bitterness. Deter-
minedly opposed to the council, Day was not above using some questionable
methods when excoriating his opponents. For example, ever since Delany's call
for an emigration convention in August, 1853, Day, an arch-anti-emigrationist,
had given the movement what Delany called "oblique support." Day could not
be considered partial to emigrationism. When the issue was first broached by
J. Mercer Langston in 1849, Day was against it, and when the 1852 state convention in Cincinnati considered a resolution for a national emigrationist
meeting, Day led the opposition. His recognition of Delany's efforts, whether
oblique or open, was Day's way of undermining the council and its eastern
leaders, who, to a man, were anti-emigrationists. The publicity given the emigrationist movement in the *Aliened American* drove Douglass and the other
council supporters to distraction. Prior to Day's decision to publicize the move-

36. Howard H. Bell, *A Survey of the Negro Convention Movement, 1830–1861* (New York, 1969),
169–70; *Frederick Douglass Paper*, December 2, 1853.

ment, Delany had bitterly resented being ignored by Douglass, who had printed everything he could lay his hands on that castigated emigrationists. By the end of the year, however, Douglass was complaining, rather sheepishly, that Day was filling his paper with pro-emigrationist statements and articles and deliberately ignoring rejoinders from their opponents.[37]

Day took his criticism of the council's plans even further, denigrating efforts to establish the manual-labor school. There were schools, like the New York Mechanics' Institute, that openly enrolled blacks, he pointed out. Given this fact, Day saw no reason why blacks should expend limited resources on establishing a school the success of which could not be guaranteed. Those who were in favor of the manual-labor school angrily dismissed Day's claims. The Rhode Island State Council, for example, argued that the New York school emphasized the theoretical rather than the practical side of manual-labor education. Day's opposition, they insisted, was based on the fallacious argument that "the money it will cost can be put to a more advantageous use without giving us the benefit of knowing what that more advantageous use is." Although "worthy of the light proceeding from an Ohio Day," his explanation obviously did not satisfy his critics. Peter H. Clark and others thought the school would be too expensive, but Day was motivated in large part by his desire to increase western leverage in a movement dominated traditionally by easterners. He was, after all, almost simultaneously involved with the Albany Manual Labor University in Athens County, Ohio, a school modeled on Oberlin College and with aims very similar to those of the proposed manual-labor college.[38]

As the date for the Emigration Convention drew nearer, the tempo of the dispute between supporters and opponents quickened. The situation was exacerbated by differences between Day and Douglass and his associate editor, William Watkins. A group of blacks in Columbus pledged to "uproot the design of the coming convention in Cleveland," convinced that the majority of blacks were opposed to its objectives. In an effort to defuse the situation, Douglass wrote that union, cooperation, and devotion to a common cause were what the times demanded, not public denunciations. Douglass withdrew from the dis-

37. "Minutes and Address of the State Convention, 1849," and "Proceedings of the Convention, 1852," both in Foner and Walker (eds.), *Proceedings*, I, 223–25, 279; *Frederick Douglass Paper*, November 25, October 28, 1853, January 13, 1854; Floyd J. Miller, *The Search for a Black Nationality: Black Colonization and Emigration, 1787–1863* (Urbana, 1975), 141–44.

38. See *Annual Catalogue of the Officers and Students of the Albany Manual Labor University, at Albany, Athens County, Ohio, 1857–8 and 1858–9* (Athens, 1859), for a good example of the school's work; Athens *Messenger and Hocking Valley Gazette*, September 22, 1854; *Frederick Douglass Paper*, April 29, 1853, April 28, May 26, 1854; Bell, *A Survey*, 172–74.

pute with Day, using the traditional ploy of promising to say no more on the subject while restating the accusation, pleading innocently that no offense was meant. This also left room for Watkins to continue the debate with Day.[39]

The National Council's future seemed to be in doubt long before its annual meeting in Cleveland in July. Day was determined to have his way; either the council concede that its decisions in New York were unconstitutional, or he would disrupt the proceedings. His plans were aided considerably by the absence of five members who would likely have endorsed the actions of the New York meeting. The entire Ohio delegation plus Nell lined up behind Day. Whenever crucial decisions came to a vote, they left—the meeting then lacked a quorum. Try as he might, Douglass could not forge a compromise to save the council. His suggestion that the delegates vote to ratify, seriatim, decisions made at New York was dismissed by Day, who recognized that endorsing any one decision would in effect legitimize them all. The alternative, Day insisted, was a complete overhaul of the council to include a significant number of Ohioans. Unable to accept such demands, the meeting voted to adjourn. But adjournment did not increase the chances of survival. In fact, recriminations grew increasingly acerbic in the following months as Ohio withdrew from council business. No prominent Ohioan attended the 1855 national convention in Philadelphia, and the last council meeting in May, 1855, was a decidedly New York affair.[40]

Rather than leave the council, Day had chosen to stay simply to prevent its functioning. The demise of the council benefited no one and could only have increased Day's frustration and his isolation from other black leaders. Part of the problem may have been a direct result of his sense of his own importance— after all, ever since his graduation he had heard only praise for his abilities from other blacks, and such heightened expectations had to be fulfilled. In this he was not alone; other blacks with comparable educational attainments labored under similar pressures. Men such as James McCune Smith, William G. Allen, Alexander Crummell, George B. Vashon, Henry Highland Garnet, J. Mercer Langston, and Charles Reason, all college or university graduates, were part of this black "intellectual elite." Many considered them pivotal individuals in the struggle for black equality. Therefore, when the disputes in the council set Day apart and excluded him from what he considered his rightful position among black leaders, he defied his opponents to function without him.

39. *Frederick Douglass Paper*, March 10, February 17, 1854, October 28, 1953.
40. *Ibid.*, July 28, September 1, 8, 1854; Bell, *A Survey*, 176–78.

He saw himself as the Young Turk, the western rebel, capable of forcing the old eastern leadership to admit him into the inner sanctum as an equal. And when this failed, Day began to act less like the astute politician he considered himself and more like a bull in a china shop. The alternative, of course, was to embrace Delany's emigrationist designs, but Day's well-known opposition militated against such a shift. His "oblique support" for Delany continued after the convention, largely because he wished to remain a thorn in the council's side. His boycott of the next council meeting widened divisions among black leaders and effectively killed any chances for a revival of national convention meetings. The Philadelphia meeting in 1855 was a rather tame affair, the last of its kind before the Civil War. Just when the tide seemed to be running against black interests, with the passage of the Fugitive Slave Law and the Kansas-Nebraska Act, black leaders found it increasingly difficult to forge a united front.

One wonders why Day's recent experiences in Ohio had not tempered his opposition to the council. In early January, 1854, he was admitted to the senate press gallery following a motion by his friend Norton Townshend. When opponents realized what had occurred, they hurriedly submitted a counterproposal to have Day expelled. One senator explained that he wanted to discourage "amalgamation of principle, amalgamation of politics, as well as amalgamation of races, believing all fusions of politics and persons degrade the original purity of both." The motion won the support of the majority of senators, many of whom had originally voted to admit Day. That created a furor. Townshend and others denounced the vote, and protest meetings organized by blacks called for a reversal of the decision.[41] The expulsion could not have come as any great surprise to Day and it forced him to question his rather rosy picture of American society. While in New York for the council meeting in November, he and his wife had ridden unmolested on the Sixth Avenue Railroad, which had a long history of refusing to carry black passengers except in segregated cars. Day was obviously elated. The "people are gaining," he exulted. "Time was when these things could not be. We went as gentlemen and ladies. We were treated as such. No white person in the car seemed to be at all astonished, and of course *we* were not. We found that a white lady in the car could politely ask a favor of us, as of any other gentleman, and we tried as politely to gratify her as if she had been colored." He was clutching at straws, an abolitionist editor observed, in

41. *Anti Slavery Standard*, February 11, 25, 1854; *Forest City Democrat*, January 23, 24, February 17, 1854; New York *Times*, January 20, 1854; Athens *Messenger and Hocking Valley Gazette*, September 28, 1854; Davis, *Black Americans in Cleveland*, 52.

hopes that though the city was still afflicted "with the malady of colourphobia," it was by such liberal action showing signs of convalescing.[42] Nothing was further from the truth. Within two years, in fact, Pennington was forced to take the company to court when one of its conductors ejected him from a white-only car.

In spite of his prominence and popularity in Cleveland, life was becoming increasingly burdensome for Day and his young wife. Their first two children had died in infancy, and Day's health had suffered from all the pressures of running a newspaper single-handedly. More important, the paper, despite pledges of support, was a drain on the family's limited resources, even though Lucy's stepfather, a man of considerable means, had likely subsidized it. By the middle of 1854, Day was making plans to transfer the paper to a committee of black investors, leaving him free to concentrate on editorial responsibilities. When the plan fell through, the paper folded. Day now turned to his liberal friends in the city for a job. Sometime before the end of 1854 he was named librarian of the Cleveland Library Association, a forerunner of the city's present library. But some had grave misgivings about naming a black person to such an important and visible position. The association, one local editor lamented, had decided "to throw itself into the arms of the Abolitionists."[43]

Day's tenure could not have lasted more than nine months, for sometime in the fall of 1855 he began to plan for a move to Canada. Poor health, the failure of his second newspaper venture, continued discrimination, and America's dogged resistance to the pleas of blacks for their rights, all contributed to his decision to seek his fortune elsewhere. In September he and Lucy purchased a forty-acre farm from a Reverend Clark in Dresden, Ontario. The *Provincial Freeman*, published by blacks in Chatham, commented on the move and announced that Day had agreed to act as its corresponding editor.[44]

Whatever the reasons for going to Canada, becoming a farmer seemed completely out of character. Even if he was simply practicing what he had preached to blacks for many years, living on a farm was never a serious part of Day's plans for his future. Day, the sophisticated, urbane gentleman, stimulated by life in the city, could not have taken to life in the country. His expectations and plans

42. *Anti Slavery Standard*, December 31, 1853.
43. Lawson, "Lucy Stanton," 11; Davis, *Black Americans in Cleveland*, 59–60; Cleveland *Leader*, January 1, 10, 1855; *Anti Slavery Standard*, January 13, 1855; Cleveland *Plain Dealer*, December 28, 1854.
44. Cleveland *Leader*, June 5, 1855; *Anti Slavery Standard*, February 2, 1856; *Provincial Freeman*, January 19, 5, 1856, September 29, June 9, 1855.

would never be realized there. For the moment, he planned to establish a lumbering business with George De Baptiste, of Detroit, but the partnership never materialized. By May, 1857, Day was living in London, a year later in St. Catherine's, Ontario, and by the end of 1858 in Chatham. He seems to have spent most of his time on the lecture circuit, addressing the problem of continued segregation in Canadian schools. Although the rights of blacks to an education were codified by the Common School Act of 1850, those whites who opposed attending school with blacks could, according to the law, petition for separate schools. Even where separate schools did not exist, as in Chatham, black students were forced into segregated buildings. Although there were limited signs of improvement in the late 1850s, the pleas of Day and others went largely unheeded.[45]

As his reputation grew in the province Day became one of the more popular figures on the lecture circuit. He was in constant demand. In comparing Day to the eloquent British abolitionist George Thompson, one paper wrote: "We have heard many pulpit and platform orators in our day, but we have heard few whose performances were marked with greater solidity of substance, or felicity of style." Day, the editor concluded, "takes his audience by surprise, captivating by 'thoughts that breathe, and sorrows that burn.'" He lectured on a wide range of topics, including "the humanizing tendency of the principles of mutual dependence" and "The Proscribed Races of France and Spain." This popularity, however, masked Day's growing isolation from black leaders in America and, to a lesser extent, in Canada. The battles in the National Council five years earlier still rankled. This seems to be the only logical reason for his consistent refusal to join the editorial staff of the *Provincial Freeman*. Even his old friend H. Ford Douglas felt compelled to comment publicly that Day had not "put himself in a proper position to give the colored people the benefit of his classical education and fine literary attainments."[46]

Day did not, however, totally ignore developments in America, especially when the issue was continued discrimination against blacks. But even here his actions were prompted by personal experiences. He had committed himself,

45. Day to Gerrit Smith, March 27, 1856, in GSC; *Provincial Freeman*, January 9, 1856, May 16, 1857, March 29, 1856; Hildreth Houston Spencer, "To Nestle in the Mane of the British Lion: A History of Canadian Black Education, 1820 to 1870" (Ph.D. dissertation, Northwestern University, 1970), 95–123.
46. St. Catherine's *Journal*, October 29, November 12, 19, December 24, 1857, January 7, 1858; Chatham *Tri-Weekly Planet*, March 4, 1858, August 6, 1857; *Provincial Freeman*, May 16, 30, 1857.

after his expulsion from the Ohio Senate gallery, to resist vigorously such ignominy. In September, 1855, he and Lucy were denied cabin passage on the
steamer *Arrow* running between Detroit and Toledo. They refused to accept
alternative accommodations and instead decided to sue John Owen, owner of
the steamer. But that demanded money, and although blacks in Detroit were
willing to support the suit, Day still had to ask old friends for additional assistance. In March, 1856, he wrote Gerrit Smith for a loan of $300 or $400 to
help defray the cost of the trial. Whether Smith sent the money is unclear. It
seems more likely that Day used Lucy's house in Cleveland as collateral for a
loan. The case, which took two years to get to the Michigan Supreme Court,
was a further drain on their already depleted resources. Refusal to accommodate the Days, their lawyer argued, violated all state laws governing carriers. In
response, the defendant insisted that carrying a black person in a cabin violated
customs of navigation on Lake Erie, as no carrier permitted blacks to use cab-
ins. A violation of this custom would contravene the regular course of business
and inconvenience the majority of passengers. Writing the decision for the
court, Judge Manning separated rights from regulations. In the first instance,
everyone has a right to be carried, and the Days were not denied that right.
They were, however, refused a cabin on the reasonable assumption that allowing blacks to travel that way would have violated custom and impaired business.
Day's was just one of a number of suits by which blacks periodically but generally unsuccessfully tested the legal barriers of racial exclusion in public
transportation.[47]

Even before the case got to the Michigan Supreme Court, Day was deeply
involved in a clandestine plot that would rock the nation. In April, 1858, John
Brown targeted Day as one of his possible supporters among blacks in Canada.
They had met years before at Oberlin, where Brown's father was a trustee.
Brown delivered his "skeleton pamphlet," their code name for his "Constitution," to Day two months after its completion. When Brown returned to
Chatham, he wrote Day to ask him to attend the meeting on May 8 at which the
constitution was to be ratified, but Day declined, claiming he was busy with
"the mechanical part of the pamphlet" and lamenting the slow pace of the
work. Day, however, promised to have a draft of the constitution ready in time
for the convention, which attracted forty-six delegates. Brown won easy ratification of his constitution and three days later dispatched his lieutenant John Henry

47. *William Howard Day* v. *John Owen*, in *Michigan Supreme Court Reports* (1858), V, 520; Day to
Gerrit Smith, March 27, 1856, in GSC; *Anti-Slavery Standard*, October 30, 1858.

Kagi to St. Catherine's to help Day print the final version. Day later recalled that they worked with a small handpress, in "a little eight by ten shanty across the Canadian line."[48] Brown had to postpone the attack on Harpers Ferry when Colonel Hugh Forbes, a British soldier of fortune whom he had employed to train his troops, disclosed the plans to Senators Wilson and Sumner of Massachusetts. Although the senators had supported Brown's efforts, they refused to condone the attack. When the raid finally occurred in October, 1859, Day was in England on a fund-raising trip.

Acquiring the handpress rekindled Day's interest in publishing a new black weekly. He had deliberately avoided extensive cooperation with the *Provincial Freeman* since his arrival in Canada, but now that the paper was defunct, he was anxious to fill the void. Raising the $900 needed to start a paper was more difficult than Day had anticipated. None of his old benefactors were willing to invest in another risky venture. Day's uncertain finances led him to move his family to Chatham in the summer of 1858. He had to find a job that guaranteed a regular income in order to support Lucy and his daughter, Florence Nightingale, born some months earlier. Day began teaching at the fugitive slave settlement in Buxton run by the Reverend William King.[49]

The move to Chatham also put Day in touch with his old friend Martin R. Delany, who had moved there from Pittsburgh in 1856. In the period since the first Emigration Convention in 1854, Delany had been working to implement his plans for a colony of free blacks. The initially proposed site in Central America was shelved, and Delany turned his attention to Africa, particularly the Niger Valley. The lack of adequate financial support and opposition from major black figures, however, were serious impediments. In addition, divisions within the movement centered around Theodore Holly, the leading advocate of Haitian emigration. Holly had visited Haiti in July, 1855, with the endorsement of the National Board of Commissioners, the organization Delany created to oversee emigrationist activities between conventions. He won support for his proposed settlement from Haitian authorities, although the financially straitened Episcopalian church refused to back his plans for a missionary station. In spite of these setbacks, Holly's proposal remained a viable alternative to

48. John Brown to Day, April 16, 1858, Stanley Smith Papers, Day to Brown, April 17, 1858, Villard Papers, Day to Brown, May 3, 1858, Harriet Tubman Papers, all in Reel 11, BAP; Boyd B. Stutler, "John Brown's Constitution," *Lincoln Herald*, L-LI (1948–49), 20–24; Fred Landon, "Canadian Negroes and the John Brown Raid," *JNH*, VI (1921), 181; Harrisburg *Telegraph*, October 12, 1887.
49. Day to Smith, June 21, 1858, in GSC; Lawson, "Lucy Stanton," 11.

Delany's scheme. While Day was busy organizing John Brown's convention in
April, 1858, Delany was trying to raise money for his expedition to Africa.[50]

In view of Day's staunch opposition to emigration, it is surprising that he
participated in the third emigrationist convention, which met in Chatham in
August, 1858, and even more surprising that Delany allowed him to be elected
president. Left with nothing but a rump organization since the departure of
H. Ford Douglas and William Monroe and the death of James Whitfield, Delany
was obviously desperate to present a united front to his critics. Of the leaders at
the first convention in Cleveland, only Holly was in attendance. Day, too, may
have been anxious to return to the ranks of black leaders, even if it meant being
president of an organization that had outlasted its usefulness. Although Delany's
leadership of the movement was not openly challenged at the convention, it is
clear that his ability to effect policy was now in some doubt. Although the convention's address supported limited emigration to any country where blacks
could exist unfettered, it was uncharacteristically conciliatory in tone. In fact,
emigration was not even positively asserted. The most the convention would do
was prepare itself "to put to use any openings which might be especially desired." The constitution was also amended to accommodate "all colored people
interested, and all who really sympathized" with the organization, and to change
its name to reflect a new, catholic approach that took "cognizance of all matters
properly concerning the colored people."[51] That surely was not what Delany
intended by an emigrationist organization.

This change in the group's *raison d'être* was engineered by Day and reflected
the strong anti-emigrationist feelings of many blacks in Chatham. Although he
favored Haiti, Day told the meeting, he nonetheless felt "equally bound in
Canada to use every effort to unite the colored people's interest in that of our
British brothers here, to know no separate interest; and in the United States to
use all honorable means to hasten the day of enfranchisement and freedom."
Those were not the words of an emigrationist anxious to see the establishment
of a colony or a settlement outside North America for blacks to live free from
slavery and racism. Only Holly seemed to recognize, or was willing to denounce, this new direction. He would brook no conciliation and withdrew from
the organization rather than consent to the destruction of its objectives. Later,
following Delany's return from Africa, Holly spoke again of these changes,
which were effected when "the platform which discountenanced emigration to

50. Miller, *The Search for a Black Nationality*, 162–64.
51. *Ibid.*, 179–81; Martin R. Delany, "Report of the Niger Valley Exploring Party," in Howard
H. Bell (ed.), *Search for a Place: Black Separatism and Africa, 1860* (Ann Arbor, 1971), 37–40.

the Eastern world" was overthrown and "a quiet conservatism inaugurated under the presidency of Professor William Howard Day." Holly could do nothing to stem the tide or stop Day. Months later, Day took his opposition to emigrationism to the Ohio State Negro Convention; at the meeting years before, he had led the charge against suggestions that blacks leave the country. Even though he was an emigrant, he was still opposed to emigrationism, he said. Labor and self-sacrifice were necessary "to make a home in a foreign land." Most blacks, he felt, had not arrived at that point in their development where they were willing to make such sacrifices. Once they did, there would be no need to move to another country, as these were the same attributes needed for achieving their rights at home. From this rather tortuous reasoning, Day concluded that there were no circumstances under which blacks should leave America. At no time did he think it necessary to explain why he had emigrated. Of course he would never concede that he lacked the ability to fight for his rights in America. It was this sort of reasoning that baffled and angered Holly. Delany's commission from the National Board to visit the Niger expressed Day's unequivocal opposition to emigration. The expedition, it stated, was being undertaken for "the purpose of science and for general information; and without any reference to, and with the Board being entirely opposed to any Emigration there as such."[52]

Day may have grown to understand the palpable contradictions of his antiemigrationist position, for soon he was to leave Canada for a four-year exile in Britain. When he returned in 1863 it would be to New York, not Chatham. The suggestion for the visit to Britain came from the Reverend William King, the founder of the Buxton Settlement. Ever since he had moved his handful of freed slaves to the farmland just outside Chatham, King had insisted on maintaining an extensive educational system. He was a firm believer in the intellectual capabilities of blacks, and the settlement school should prepare students for the standard classical education, as well as provide them with particular skills. The first school was started in April, 1850. One year later, there were more whites at Buxton than in the district school, which was soon forced to close its doors as more of its students transferred to the settlement's school. A second school was built in 1856 to accommodate the growth in the student population. Two years later a third was built, with a total enrollment of 250. Day taught at one of these schools and was an elder in the local Presbyterian church.

52. Chatham *Tri-Weekly Planet*, August 26, 1858, February 21, 1861; "Proceedings of a Convention of the Colored Men of Ohio, Held in the City of Cincinnati, on the 23rd, 24th, 25th and 26th Days of November, 1858," in Foner and Walker (ed.), *Proceedings*, I, 333, 335; *Anti Slavery Bugle*, December 4, 1858.

Lucy was a Sabbath school teacher and conducted two "singing schools" with a Mrs. Johnson.[53]

Despite its successes, the settlement faced constant shortages. An economic recession in the late 1850s exacerbated the settlement's problems and forced King to develop plans to diversify the community's economy. Neither Canada nor America had the capital or the inclination to invest in his new scheme to rescue the settlement. It was for these reasons that he planned to visit Britain in the summer of 1859. The trip, King believed, would also provide him with an opportunity to raise money among philanthropists for his schools. Aware of British partiality to black American advocates of their causes, King invited Day to join him. The two arrived in Dublin in July. By the end of August they had raised over $1,000. The visit finally netted well over $6,000. Soon after their arrival they attended and addressed the Irish Presbyterian General Assembly. Like all of his black compatriots, Day expressed his happiness at being on free soil where slavery could not exist, and condemned proslavery churches and their ministers. In many respects, it was a traditional antislavery speech and followed the pattern established by black American visitors to Britain in the 1830s. Day appealed to his listeners' known opposition to slavery, called on them to raise their collective voice against it, and recommended possible projects that warranted their support. Day deviated little from this technique through- out the tour.[54]

At the close of the assembly, King's friends organized a massive public meet- ing chaired by the lord mayor of Dublin. King spoke of his firsthand knowledge of slavery in Louisiana, its internal slave trade, the cruelty of the system, both physical and moral, and the barriers erected to prevent emancipation. He then described Buxton, noting its achievements and the work of its colonists. The object of the visit, he informed his audience, "was to get funds to erect schools and endow them, to erect places of worship, and to have academies where young men could be educated so that they could enter college." Some of these, King believed, could be the means of developing Africa. Then Day spoke, giv- ing a history of slavery in the South and discrimination in the North. Slavery, he argued, had to be isolated by international public opinion and by efforts such as Buxton supported by philanthropists who were willing to invest in their belief

53. Victor Ullman, *Look to the North Star: A Life of William King* (Boston, 1969), 148–51; *Pro- vincial Freeman*, July 25, 1859; *Liberator*, December 24, 1858; Lucy S. Day to E. Strieby, May 21, 1864, in AMA.

54. William King, "Autobiography" (Typescript, in William King Papers, Chatham Public Li- brary, Chatham, Ontario); Ullman, *Look to the North Star*, 256; Miller, *The Search for a Black Nationality*, 223; Londonderry *Guardian*, July 12, 1859.

in the equality of man. The failure of such experiments would give more ammunition to those who were for the continuation of slavery. Success, on the
other hand, would "rise as a signal light, casting its brilliancy over the whole of
slave-land, and eventually would prove a blessing not only to slaves themselves
but to the whole country."[55]

After spending roughly three weeks in Dublin, where a committee was
formed to collect contributions, King and Day visited and lectured in Waterford. By early September they were in Belfast. Their first lecture was a rousing
success. King gave his account of developments at Buxton and called on the
audience to support its educational work. He was followed by Day, who delivered one of his finest speeches. Replete with weighty imagery, it was one part
sermon and one part traditional oratory. God, he warned, has the power to save
the lost Christian, a "wanderer out upon the sea of life," or to destroy those
who chose consistently to deny the hand of fellowship to others. It was the duty
of Christian men and women, concerned with the welfare of the less fortunate,
to ensure that the tentacles of American slavery did not extend to Canada. The
free states of the North had singularly failed to stop the advance of slavery's
influence, and the result was that all blacks, free and slave, were oppressed.
Slavery's toadies "like a pestilence, skip all over the land; you find them in the
Custom-houses, Post-offices—everywhere; its ministers like their prototype in
the Garden of Eden, crawl up into the sacred desk, and leave their slime all over
the Bible and its pages. The result of this union—a union of meanness—is felt
like the lice of Egypt, everywhere."[56]

King and Day generated considerable interest in Buxton wherever they went.
In a decade still very much under the sentimental influence of Stowe's *Uncle
Tom's Cabin*, the combination of the philanthropic onetime slaveholder, now
working for the elevation of his former fieldhands, and the free black who epitomized the intellectual potential of all blacks, was a guarantee of success. One
suspects that King was deliberately given the sobriquet Clayton, the benevolent
character in Stowe's novel *Dred*, to exploit this sentimentalism to full advantage.
At each lecture King spoke first, extolling Buxton and pleading for support to
continue its good work. This set the stage for Day, who placed the settlement in
the context of the struggle against American oppression. Although he had
never been a slave, he told a gathering in Armagh, he had been proscribed by

55. *Douglass Monthly*, August, 1859; *Liberator*, October 14, 1859; King, "Autobiography";
Chatham *Tri-Weekly Planet*, October 20, 1859.
56. *Liberator*, October 14, 1859; Chatham *Tri-Weekly Planet*, October 20, 1859; Waterford *Mail*,
August 11, 1859; *Banner of Ulster*, September 29, 8, 1859.

the system for twenty-five years, and when, he continued, "I went away to learn something I was followed by it pointing its long bony fingers at every corner; and even in the houses of Almighty God I found its evil influences." Day recounted some horrifying stories, which clearly moved his audiences. The attack on his mother and other abolitionists at an antislavery meeting in New York in 1833 and the white mob attack on the black community in 1834 were just two examples of the influence of slavery on free black men. How could a free society, one that prided itself on its democracy, continue to condone such actions and deny free blacks their rights? "The business of Government is to protect all men within its pale," Day insisted, "and the Government that does not protect all men is not just."[57] Many left these meetings convinced that America stood on the brink of some calamitous upheaval. Under these circumstances, it was the responsibility of Christians to hold the line against the spread of this dangerous contagion, lest it cross the Canadian border. Buxton stood as an obvious bulwark against American slavery.

The visit to Ireland was unquestionably a success, marred only by Day's not being allowed to use the assembly room in Lisburn for a public meeting. When it was suggested that he apply to the Court House for its rooms, Day refused on the grounds that it was inappropriate for the gathering. As a result, they were unable to hold a meeting in Lisburn, in spite of protests from supporters.[58] King and Day left Ireland for Scotland two weeks later on the second leg of their tour, visiting Glasgow, Dundee, and other cities. They arrived in Edinburgh in mid-November. It was a homecoming of sorts for King, who was educated in Edinburgh in the 1840s, and had left for America under a cloud of controversy during the Free Church's conflict with abolitionists, led by Frederick Douglass. Douglass and many Scots abolitionists, especially the Glasgow Emancipation Society, had insisted that the church return money it collected in the South in 1843. The money, stained with the blood of slaves, abolitionists argued, should not be accepted by British Christians, especially not by a church that had only recently severed ties with the Established Church. The leadership of the Free Church successfully resisted the pressure to return the money, and some in the church, like King, who had expressed concern about the decision, thought it best to emigrate. Interestingly enough, the surviving leaders of the church now headed the welcoming committee for King and Day in Edinburgh.[59]

57. *Banner of Ulster*, October 20, 1859; Armagh *Guardian*, October 14, 1859.
58. *Banner of Ulster*, October 18, 1859.
59. C. Duncan Rice, *The Scots Abolitionists, 1833–1861* (Baton Rouge, 1981), 142; *Anti Slavery*

King went to London in December to meet a number of British phi-lanthropists interested in the establishment of black American colonies in Af-rica. Their plan, King later recalled, "was to plant Christian Colonies in the western coast of Africa under British protection. These colonies would teach the Chiefs that it was more profitable for them to raise Cotton and sugar than to sell their slaves." Theodore Bourne's similar proposals had already won en-dorsements from George Thompson, a longtime opponent of African colo-nization; Lord Brougham, the famous British abolitionist; and Thomas Clegg, a substantial Manchester cotton manufacturer. The agreement between De-lany, Campbell, and the Alake of Abeokuta for the establishment of a colony of skilled black Americans increased the chances for successful implementation of the scheme, and King's cherished hope of using his Buxton students in the work of African redemption seemed assured of fulfillment.[60]

King returned to Canada temporarily in late December, leaving Day in Scotland. He planned to return in the spring with another partner to carry on the work. Following King's departure Day attempted to breathe new life into his efforts to raise money for a press in Canada. But other black Americans were touring Britain at the time, competing for available support. Among others, the Reverend W. Troy of Windsor, a pro-emigrationist, was pleading on behalf of fugitives, and the Reverend W. Kinnard was raising money to build schools and churches in Canada. Day's circular, "The Bible, the School, and the Press, For the Fugitive Slave," generated only marginal support. In addition, there was growing suspicion among British philanthropists that these appeals increased the risk of fraud. There were complaints that money collected for worthy causes in America was being diverted to defray agents' expenses. Greater supervision and control by abolitionist organizations were the only means of ensuring honesty. Day met a number of abolitionists in an effort to persuade them to support his plans. He attended a public meeting in Glasgow in Febru-ary, where George Thompson spoke, and he was present at the annual meeting of the Glasgow New Association for the Abolition of Slavery in April, but there is no evidence that Day won appreciable support from Scottish societies.[61]

Day moved his base of operations to London in May, and he took with him

---

Advocate, January, 1860; *Caledonian Mercury*, November 17, 29, 1859; Chatham *Tri-Weekly Planet*, December 24, 1859; King, "Autobiography"; Ullman, *Look to the North Star*, 258–59.

60. King, "Autobiography"; Bolton *Chronicle*, October 1, 1859; Manchester *Guardian*, Septem-ber 5, 21, 1859; Delany "Report of the Niger Valley Exploring Party," 77–78.

61. See King papers for title of Day's circular; Manchester *Guardian*, January 1, 1860; Glasgow *Examiner*, October 6, April 7, 1860; *Anti Slavery Advocate*, April, 1860; GES, Minute Book 4 (1845–1876), in Smeal Collection, The Mitchell Library, Glasgow.

the endorsements of many prominent Scots. His departure from Scotland coincided with the arrival of Delany and Campbell in London. But the move was
more than just a simple coincidence. Word of Delany's successes reached Britain long before he did, and in April, Bourne put in motion plans to establish a
British organization to facilitate the colonizing effort. His circular announced a
British society to promote the "Christian Civilization of Africa, by means of
Christian colored settlers from America and to instruct the native in improved
modes of art, manufactures and the cultivation of the soil." Most of its supporters became the nucleus of the African Aid Society, formed in July, 1860.
Delany worked to establish his preeminence in the movement in the weeks immediately after his arrival in London. He met little resistance even from
Bourne, who inadvertently had done so much to facilitate Delany's success in
Britain. Delany possibly drew Day into his plans, in an effort to lend legitimacy
to his leadership of the movement. After all, Day was president of the association that commissioned Delany and Campbell to visit Abeokuta. The fact that
the Chatham meeting had limited the purposes of the expedition mattered
little at this juncture. Day, having not raised as much money as he hoped,
probably leapt at the opportunity to reassert his nominal presidency of the organization. There were now obvious benefits to be derived from identification
with Delany. Blacks in Canada and America, long opposed to all forms of African colonization and emigration schemes, had to be educated, Day now asserted, "to the idea of what, as a people and as individuals, they can accomplish
in view of openings in Africa by the hand of Providence." Such education
would be greatly facilitated by establishing a "well-conducted press located in
Canada, surveying the whole field of coloured peoples' activities, and truthfully
recording results."[62]

Although Day attended the founding meetings of the African Aid Society in
July, he deliberately tried to separate his interests and Delany's. While Delany
stressed the need for British support for his proposed colony Day concentrated
on raising money for his press. For example, when Delany visited Brighton at
the end of August, he lectured on "Africa and the African race." Soon afterward, Day addressed a different audience on the problems confronting black
Americans in the United States. Even though the local press identified Day
with Delany's Canadian organization, there is no evidence that they were working together. They did, however, come together briefly toward the end of De-

62. New York *Colonization Journal*, May, 1860; *Anti Slavery Reporter*, June 1, 1860; Miller, *The
Search for a Black Nationality*, 225; *Bond of Brotherhood*, October, 1860.

lany's tour, and for the first time Day, rather surprisingly, expressed unequivocal support for the African colony. The colony, he argued, would provide black Americans and their British supporters with the means to break the southern monopoly by producing cotton of the same quality, first in Africa and later in the West Indies and other British colonies. In the colony the "bone and sinew" of Africa would be directed by black American exiles in Canada who were skilled in the cultivation of cotton. Its success would have a direct bearing on Britain, where many workingmen and manufacturers were dependent on a continuing supply of cotton from the South, a supply that could be interrupted at any moment, Day insisted, by either unfavorable weather or a slave insurrection. This was indeed a traditional emigrationist argument, but Day used it so rarely that one can only suspect him of harboring ulterior motives. His principal concern continued to be the publication of a newspaper in Canada. Even before the formation of the African Aid Society, Day had been busy throughout London trying to raise £1,000 for his press.[63]

But Day's interest in the newspaper project seemed to evaporate within the year. He may have found it increasingly difficult to attract sufficient funds, but it does appear more likely that the outbreak of the Civil War caused him to concentrate on other matters. With Delany's departure for Canada in December, 1860, Day became the only spokesman in Britain for the colony, and, interestingly enough, he chose to increase his public endorsements of the colony. But like most other things associated with Delany's scheme at the time, Day's increased fervor was ill-timed and opportunistic. What interest there was for the colony among black Americans almost disappeared after the firing on Fort Sumter. Now that war between the states had begun, many who had originally supported emigration as an alternative to living in an oppressive society saw some future in a postwar society freed from slavery. Under these altered circumstances, it was the duty of all black Americans, they argued, to stay and contribute to the defeat of the South.

Day seems to have directed most of his energies in 1861 to promoting the work of the African Aid Society. The ASS, he told a Leeds audience, aimed to use blacks in Canada as pioneers who "with the lamp of liberty and the light of God's Gospel, should go into Africa, the land of their fathers, and through the

63. Delany, "Report of the Niger Valley Exploring Party," 140–41; Brighton *Herald*, September 8, 1860; *Douglass Monthly*, February, 1861; Clerkenwell *News*, August 8, July 28, 1860; *Anti Slavery Reporter*, September 1, 1860; *Nonconformist*, August 8, 1860; Leeds *Mercury*, December 8, 1860; Halifax *Guardian*, December 22, 1860.

cotton, and palm oil, and dyewoods of that country lift up the African continent, and in a few years produce a supply of cotton to set-off against the American slave-grown cotton." He returned to this theme at a public lecture following the annual meeting of the Birmingham Ladies Negroes' Friend Society in
November. After narrating the story of Delany's successful trip to Africa, Day
pointed out that cotton cultivation there would be in Britain's interests, for the
supply would be continuous. Capital from Britain, used by skilled black Americans instructing African labor, would ensure the commercial development of
Africa. Moreover, Day concluded, if the "natives of that country are to be civilized, it must be not only by the influence of religion, but by the exertion of
those united by the ties of blood." At a meeting of the Birmingham auxiliary of
the AAS, also attended by Henry Highland Garnet, Day argued that "with the
light of God's truth in one hand, and political economy in the other," the society would elevate "their brother black men."[64]

Since Day had abandoned his plans for the newspaper, and by late 1861 it
was obvious that the proposed colony in Abeokuta would not materialize, why
did he not return to his family? Although it is impossible to determine with any
precision exactly when he made the decision, Day took the opportunity of the
visit to put distance between himself and Lucy. She had been a woman of some
means, but Day's suit against John Owen, as well as his numerous newspaper
schemes, had probably exhausted most of the family's resources. Lucy and
Florence received little money from Day during his stay in Britain. It is doubtful that he even had sufficient money to survive in England. He held a number
of temporary jobs, acting on two occasions as "stated supply" for Gerald Massey
in Hull and for Father Gavazzi in Burton-on-Trent, though he was not officially
ordained. He also taught for a short time at a school in Lincoln. Later, Louis
Chamerovzow, secretary of the British and Foreign Anti Slavery Society, informed his friends at the American Missionary Association that Day was one
of those few black Americans in Britain who had taken advantage of British
support and exploited it for their personal gain. Money raised by Day and King
was properly remitted, but what Day had managed to elicit for his proposed
paper simply went to cover his living expenses, and none of it was returned to
contributors after the scheme collapsed. Chamerovzow wrote that Day had

64. Leeds *Mercury*, December 2, June 1, 1861; *Douglass Monthly*, October, 1861; Chatham *Tri-
Weekly Planet*, February 21, 1861; *Anti Slavery Reporter*, November 2, 1861; London *Morning Star
and Dial*, December 16, 1861; *Midlands County Herald*, December 19, November 7, 1861; African
Aid Society, *The American Crisis and the Slave Trade. Report of a Public Meeting, Held in the Town Hall,
Birmingham, on Friday, December 13, 1861* (Birmingham, 1861), 7.

"obtained contributions which must in the aggregate have amounted to a considerable sum, but at length in consequence of doubts being raised as to their appropriation, he left the country." Chamerovzow intimated that Day had also borrowed money from a female artist and had never repaid it. In obvious desperation, Lucy turned to dressmaking in order to survive. She found her husband's action incomprehensible. As far as she was concerned, they had been a happily married couple in 1859. After repeated inquiries from Lucy concerning his return, Day replied that "uncongeniality of disposition" had been responsible for their estrangement and calmly suggested she get a divorce.[65]

Day left England in early December, 1863, and settled in New York. He was obviously pleased to be back in America and to renew old acquaintances, his reputation enhanced by his stay in Britain. On New Year's Day, 1864, he spoke at a large meeting celebrating the first anniversary of Lincoln's proclamation. His participation represented a return to the black leadership fold, which he had abandoned ten years before. Four days later he was the principal speaker at a meeting organized by the American Freedmen's Friend Society. Formed in October, 1863, the society, a black organization, drew most of its members from New York and Brooklyn. Its aims went beyond those of other freedmen organizations in that it sought to address the physical and educational needs of freedmen and to persuade those still enslaved to abandon their masters. Never a peace advocate, Day delivered a speech that was a call to arms, a restatement of his position that blacks traditionally had fought for their freedom. As an example he cited Cinque, one of the *Amistad* rebels, and Nat Turner, leader of the Virginia slave rebellion. Blacks were not strangers to war. The Civil War was simply the final stage of a long-standing battle between freedom and oppression, begun in 1776, a war to stop the most "deliberate murder enacted through all time, a war to reinstate those souls into the immortality which the black hand of immorality has effaced."[66]

65. Lucy S. Day to Strieby, May 21, 1864, Lucy S. Day to George Whipple, April 26, 1864, Chamerovzow to Dear Sir, July 5, 1865, all in AMA. For problems with impostors, see London *Patriot*, June 25, 1863, and *Anti Slavery Reporter*, May 2, 1864. Lucy later applied for a teaching position with the AMA in the South; she was refused, possibly because of her separation, which many at the time saw as a character deficiency. She was sent as a teacher to Georgia by the Cleveland Freedmen's Association in 1866 and later moved to Florence, Mississippi, where she taught. She finally divorced William in 1872, married Levi Sessions of Mississippi in 1878, and lived in Chattanooga, Tennessee, in the 1880s and 1890s, before moving to Los Angeles, where she died in 1910. See Lawson, "Lucy Stanton," 12; and J. A. Thome to Whipple, March 17, 1864, in AMA.

66. Amos G. Beman, "Scrapbook, II," in Amos G. Beman Papers, Collection of American Literature, Beinecke Library, Yale University, New Haven; New York *Tribune*, January 5, 1, 1864.

Day became involved in the work of the American Freedmen's Friend Society soon after he arrived in New York. In May he and the Reverend James Gloucester, president of the society, toured Missouri, Illinois, and Iowa, raising money for the society, and getting a firsthand account of the freedmen's needs. Day's association with the society and his frequent speeches to black and abolitionist meetings increased his visibility and reaffirmed his reputation as one of black America's finest orators and leading figures. In October he attended the National Convention of Colored Men in Syracuse. It was the first of its kind since 1855 when disputes, in which Day had been prominent, led to the early demise of the National Council. Day played a relatively minor role in this convention. He was nominated as one of two temporary secretaries, and was elected a member of the Permanent Organization and Publishing committees. Those who had been at Rochester in 1853 and at Cleveland the following year must have wondered if the proceedings at Syracuse were simply a reenactment of the debacle of those earlier meetings. No sooner had the convention agreed to the formation of the National Equal Rights League, to "encourage sound morality, education, temperance, frugality, industry, and promote everything that pertains to a well-ordered and dignified life," than a dispute arose regarding the site of its headquarters. When Philadelphia was suggested, representatives from Ohio substituted Cincinnati or Cleveland. After considerable discussion, the meeting voted in favor of Cleveland. When the convention reassembled for its evening session, however, a motion was made to substitute Philadelphia for Cleveland. Obviously more sensitive than previous meetings to the feelings of western blacks, the convention struck a compromise, naming J. Mercer Langston of Ohio to the presidency and locating the league's headquarters in Philadelphia.[67]

Invitations to speak at meetings kept Day busy throughout the rest of 1864 and most of 1865. The thematic thrust of his speeches could not be considered novel; they were, however, moving reaffirmations of Day's conviction that blacks had always been in the forefront of American history. Their involvement in the Civil War was only the most recent example of this fact. Yet America myopically refused to recognize these contributions and continued to deny blacks unrestricted participation in the system that they had done so much to build and secure. Blacks, he wrote William C. Nell on the eve of a meeting to

67. J. Gloucester and Day to Smith, August 19, 1864, in GSC; *Missouri Democrat*, May 28, 1864; "Proceedings of the National Convention of Colored Men, Held in the City of Syracuse, New York, October, 4, 5, 6, and 7, 1864," in Bell (ed.), *Minutes*, 3–7, 18–19, 29, 36, 39.

commemorate the death of Crispus Attucks, "must tell the truths of our people to the nation, until it shall learn to do justice." The nation had to be "shamed back to first bloodshed and first principles." Day returned to this theme frequently in subsequent months. In spite of continued oppression, blacks had not remained idle, but had done their part "towards industry, thrift, good order and an improved Social State." Driven by a desire for freedom, they had sacrificed their lives to improve America. Now they demanded to be included on an equal basis with every other American. Not that Day expected full justice immediately, not "today, nor tomorrow, but the next day, as surely as that four years of war have passed, and 200,000 black Minervas, fully armed, had sprung from the brain of the white Jupiter of this land." His motto, he told a meeting in New York, was "Ask for justice—ask respectfully—of those who have withheld it; but ask earnestly, and sleep on your arms." America was now standing at a historic crossroads, and the direction it elected to follow would, Day insisted, be determined in large measure by the vigilance of blacks and their white supporters. Should they not succeed in wresting the franchise from a reluctant nation, then all would have been in vain. But characteristically Day remained optimistic about America's future. This hope sounded a theme movingly echoed by Martin Luther King almost one hundred years later:

I see . . . the States reorganized merely sufficiently so to include every native male 21 years of age of some kind, whether he be black as night or white as the icicle that's dwindled by frost from the purest snow and hangs on Dian's temple. I see this Government made one by black and white hands, yielding up to the black man thus, effort after effort a portion of the Government control. I see the schools thrown open for the black child as for the white. I see black and white priests ministering together at the altars of religion. I see black men elected to petty and then to higher offices in the State. I see preferment open to the black man, even to the Presidential chair. I see everywhere respect for brains and worth moral and material. I see everywhere the recognition of the Norman principle, "Man is man and no man is more." I see, therefore, internal peace unbroken for ages. I see a pure government striving for the interest of the weaker members of it. I see power everywhere stooping to protect the poor. I see a nation clinging to justice, the admiration of the world. I see a civilization, not of head merely, but of heart—a civilization unlike except one which this tyrant-ridden world has ever seen— a civilization manufactured out of the world of thoughts, world sympathies, world loves.[68]

68. *Anti Slavery Standard*, August 12, 1865, December 3, 1864, April 1, June 10, 1865; *Liberator*, August 11, March 24, July 14, 1865; *Anglo-African*, August 12, 1865; New York *Evening Post*, November 29, 1864; Colored People's Educational Monument Association, *Celebration by the Colored People's Educational Monument Association in Memory of Abraham Lincoln, on the Fourth of July, 1865, in*

Such hopes for the future were shattered with the assassination of Lincoln, Johnson's policies toward the rebel states, and the refusal of northern states to enfranchise their black population. But Day's optimism was also tempered by an awareness that blacks had to struggle continuously if they were ever to achieve full equality. They had to be "a bell-rock tower, standing erect amid the stormy waters, where, during the day, the bell was rung, where during the night the fire was kindled, so that men are not saved from the wreck, but saved from being wrecked at all." In these troubled times the shoals of presidential preferences and local political inertia stood as barriers to black progress. There was also considerable work to be done among the freedmen. Day's commitment to black progress put him at the center of black activity during the next five years. He was secretary-general of the Freedman's American and British Commission, successor to the American Freedmen's Friend Society. For the most part, the commission worked with other freedmen associations, procuring clothes for the needy and recommending teachers for schools. There is no evidence that the commission ran its own schools but it did recruit teachers for schools established by other societies. Day was also a member of the Justitia League of New York City. Little is known of the league, but it apparently worked to ensure that black soldiers were given due recognition, and to amend the state constitution to give blacks the vote.[69]

Day was also a regular fixture on the lecture circuit. Invitations poured in from most of the eastern states. In November he addressed a meeting organized by blacks in Harrisburg, Pennsylvania, to honor returning soldiers. In April, 1866, he joined Garnet, General O. O. Howard, and Senators Trumbell and Wilson at an emancipation celebration in Washington, D.C. Four months later he was the main speaker at another emancipation celebration in Hartford, Connecticut.[70] Day also worked closely with the Pennsylvania State Equal Rights League, an auxiliary of the National Equal Rights League. The Pennsylvania league had plans to employ Day as its state lecturer and agent at a fee of $25 per lecture paid by local chapters. But the majority of local chapters were in

---

the Presidential Grounds, Washington, D.C. (Washington, D.C., 1865), 10–18; Day to Daniel Ullman, April 12, 1865, in Daniel Ullman Papers, Reel 15, BAP; New York *Tribune*, August 2, 1865, November 28, 29, 1864.

69. Day to J. Miller McKim, May 21, 1866, in Anti-Slavery Collection, Cornell University Library, Ithaca, N.Y.; Colored People's Educational Monument Association, *Celebration*, 18; *Anglo-African*, November 4, August 26, 1865.

70. Harrisburg *Telegraph*, November 11, 1865; L. R. Kelker, *History of Dauphin County* (3 vols.; New York, 1907), II, 548–49; *Anti Slavery Standard*, April 28, 1866; Hartford *Courant*, August 1, 2, 1866; David O. White, "Addie Brown's Hartford," *Connecticut Historical Society Bulletin*, XLI (1976), 63.

such dire financial need that the league was forced to cancel the agreement.[71]

Dependence on lecture fees as one's main source of income leads to a rather precarious existence, and Day had clearly had his fill of such a way of life. In an effort to ensure a small but regular income, he decided to become a minister. Despite his solid religious upbringing, this was a radical departure from his earlier decision not to seek his fortunes inside the church. But his association with the *Zion Standard*, organ of the African Methodist Episcopal Zion church, may have brought about a change of heart. Day became lay editor of the paper in 1866, and sometime during this period he joined Wesley Zion Church in Washington, D.C. Not long afterward, he was ordained by Bishop J. J. Clinton during the formation of the Virginia Conference.[72]

Day was actively involved in New York blacks' efforts to remove constitutional limitations on their right to vote. Prior to the state constitutional convention, blacks established several committees to gain support from local political figures. At a meeting in September, 1866, Day and other blacks called for the formation of a state central committee to represent blacks' interests and to work for the election of legislators favorable to equal suffrage. The meeting also recommended that a state convention be held in Albany in mid-October. Day was elected president of the convention, which devoted its energies to the issue of voting rights. He could not have missed the similarity to the earlier Ohio conventions, which had failed to convince white legislators that blacks had a case. Here, too, it was asserted that the "elective franchise in this republic is not a gift, but a right belonging to all native-born men." But by 1866, that sentiment must have lost some of its potency in light of white America's refusal to accept it. Yet Day and his contemporaries had few alternatives. The principle had to be reiterated until such time as America recognized its legitimacy and applied it to all citizens.

Day insisted in his presidential address that blacks adopt an independent position in an effort to influence both parties. Although this ran counter to the belief that black interests were best served by the Republican party, Day knew that the party's hold on the state was tenuous. Only a slight margin separated the two parties, which won four elections each between 1862 and 1869. At the convention and in the legislature, Republicans endorsed the principle of black suffrage, but they disagreed on the political consequences. Moreover, in prac-

71. Pennsylvania State Equal Rights League, Minutes of the Executive Board, 1864–1868, Day to William Still, February 14, 1866, both in LGC.

72. Hood, *One Hundred Years*, 324–25; *Star of Zion*, April 28, 1898.

tical terms, Republicans recognized that equal suffrage would result in an increase of less than 8,000 voters, not enough to offset possible defections to the opposition. With the issue in doubt elsewhere and Democrats committed to exploit it in forthcoming elections, state Republicans opted to soften their stand. It did them little good. In 1867 the Democrats carried the state by roughly 50,000 votes, their strongest showing in years. Although other factors contributed to the Republicans' defeat, black suffrage was undoubtedly important. When the issue of equal suffrage was finally put to the voters in 1869, removing the property qualification was defeated, 282,403 to 249,802. Like others, New York blacks would have to await passage of the Fifteenth Amendment.[73]

Even while Day worked for the elimination of voting restrictions in New York, he was actively seeking jobs in the South. He made an extensive lecture tour through Maryland and Delaware in the summer of 1867, and two months later Major General E. M. Gregory, assistant commissioner of the Freedmen's Bureau, offered Day the position of superintendent of schools for the freedmen in those states. Since its formation the bureau had been working with local black communities to promote education, supplying money and materials to build schools. In Baltimore and Wilmington, for example, blacks could call upon white supporters for assistance and guidance. The Baltimore Association for the Moral and Educational Improvement of the Colored People (1864) and the Delaware Association for the Moral Improvement and Education of the Colored People (1866) were the two major white groups in favor of black education. Similar nineteenth-century organizations also aimed to blend reading and writing with the "moral habits" of honesty, thrift, cleanliness, and punctuality in an effort to educate the "whole man." Their objective, Gregory observed, was "to rouse the colored people . . . to be prompt, active, self-sustaining, and independent in the great work of educating themselves and their children to prepare them for the important duties that should soon devolve on them, as free citizens of a free country." Blacks needed little prodding; nor, one suspects, did they give undue attention to pleas from such as Gregory. Wherever they could they held festivals to raise money to purchase lots for schools and then applied to the bureau or one of the associations for support.[74]

73. Phyllis F. Field, *The Politics of Race in New York: The Struggle for Black Suffrage in the Civil War Era* (Ithaca, 1982), 148, 169–76, 199; New York *Times,* June 6, 1866; *Anti Slavery Standard,* September 29, October 27, June 15, 1866; New York *Tribune,* October 18, 19, 1866.

74. Gregory to Day, September 14, 1867, in BRFAL; Baltimore *American,* July 4, 7, 22, 1867; *Delaware Republican,* June 27, 1867; Hood, *One Hundred Years,* 325; Wilmington *Daily Commercial,* November 15, October 5, 1867; Jacqueline J. Halstead, "The Delaware Association for the Moral

But some people in Maryland and Delaware refused to accept either the fact that the war had ended or that their former slaves should be granted the rights of citizenship. Governor Gove Saulsbury of Delaware denounced efforts to elevate blacks as "futile and subversive to the ends and aims for which American government was established, and contrary to the doctrines and teachings of the Fathers of the Republic," and some whites in small towns and villages took matters into their own hands and destroyed schools built by blacks. There were, however, a few signs of hope. In Baltimore, for instance, the city council passed an ordinance in June, 1869, that required the Board of School Commissioners to build separate schools for blacks, and those institutions would be subject to all the rules governing the white schools. By the time Day submitted his first report in January, 1868, he optimistically stated that even in localities where opposition had been great, indifference seemed to have taken its place.[75]

Although Day's headquarters were in Baltimore, he spent most of his time traveling, visiting some of the most remote areas, anywhere a community needed the bureau's assistance to build and maintain a school. His job often involved more than a superintendent's regular duties. On a number of occasions he intervened to free children who had been captured and illegally indentured. Day's arrival coincided with the bureau's attempts to coordinate all educational efforts for the freedman. By the end of 1867, most teachers from freedmen's groups and missionary societies were reporting to Day. Even the Oblate Sisters of Providence, a black Roman Catholic order that ran a girls' school and an orphanage, kept Day informed of their work. After four months Day reported, with some satisfaction, that there were 5,852 students in 120 schools taught by 150 teachers (104 blacks and 46 whites).[76]

There were, however, pockets of resistance that threatened to undermine Day's efforts. In Baltimore and Cecil County, Maryland, county commissioners and boards of education refused to accept black schools transferred to their jurisdiction. As a result, bills, including salaries, remained unpaid, and schools were kept open only because of the teachers' dedication. As one Baltimore commissioner observed, the bureau's establishing black schools was an

Improvement and Education of the Colored People: Practical Christianity," *Delaware History*, XV (1972), 20–21.

75. *Delaware House Journal*, 1869, p. 24; Baltimore *American*, June 8, 26, 1, 1867; Wilmington *Daily Commercial*, November 19, 1867; Halstead, "The Delaware Association," 22; Day to E. C. Knower, January 8, 1868, in BRFAL.

76. Day to Knower, January 8, 28, 1868, Day to Brooks, February 22, 1868, Oblate Sisters of Providence to Day, October 22, 1867, all in BRFAL; Day to George Whipple, October 17, 1867, in AMA; Baltimore *American*, October 17, 2, 1867, January 7, 1868.

"act of gratuity, and stretch of authority unwarrantable." Blacks, some of this ilk insisted, were "mere sojourners" among white Baltimoreans, and so were not entitled to state funds for education. Wiser heads ultimately prevailed, but Day and others at the bureau could only wait until the issue ran its political course.[77]

They seem to have circumvented most of the roadblocks thrown up by local white opponents. But there were some areas, particularly the southern counties of Delaware, where resistance to black education showed no signs of abating. In addition, an unusually harsh winter seriously affected school attendance. In April, Day reported rather gloomily that the highest attendance at any one school in Cecil, Caroline, and Somerset counties, Maryland, and Kent and Sussex counties, Delaware, was twenty-two. Furthermore, the Baltimore association's treasury was almost depleted. But the suggestion that black communities increase their contributions to the association's missionary fund met significant resistance. The bureau was faced with the prospect of taking over the association's schools. Day nevertheless reported optimistically on the progress of his work. The number of schools and teachers had increased, and though attendance dropped during early 1868, signs of recovery were clear by April. In May the bureau, convinced that the worst was over, allocated additional funds for the construction of schools throughout the area.[78]

Just when the situation seemed to be improving Day was relieved of his duties following a reorganization of the bureau. Under these new arrangements, officials in Washington were in charge of a streamlined operation and several offices in Maryland and Delaware were eliminated. Although Day's relationship with the bureau ended somewhat prematurely, he was proud of his accomplishments. He had on many occasions outmaneuvered the opponents of black education, reconciled differences among blacks that could have become impediments, and worked wherever he could to defuse white opposition to black education. The appointment also afforded Day a unique opportunity to implement his views on education. Although his work among fugitive slaves in Canada in the 1840s and again at Buxton in the late 1850s had been rewarding, he had never been in a position to determine educational policy. As superintendent, he could utilize all the powers of his office to encourage and, where necessary, cajole blacks to work for improved education, which he saw as imparting

77. Baltimore *American*, April 16, 18, 19, 1868, November 27, December 4, 11, 17, 1867, January 13, 1868.
78. Wilmington *Daily Commercial*, June 1, 1868; Cormer to O. O. Howard, April 10, 1868, Day to Knower, June 12, 1868, both in BRFAL.

knowledge and instilling those principles necessary for the development of cultured individuals. Day tried to persuade blacks to act in what he considered a dignified manner, for dignity was the hallmark of cultured men. Unfettered emotionalism at prayer meetings, for example, violated all that Day considered "correct in well-ordered life." Although he made some allowances for "early training, and for religious enthusiasm intensified by 'protracted effort,'" he thought the "present state of things injurious to the Colored People." Such pleas fell on deaf ears, for Day's sense of propriety seemed more appropriate to the staid proceedings at his church than to the traditions of southern black prayer meetings.[79]

Before leaving the bureau, Day attended the Border State Convention, which was held in Baltimore in August. Black Republicans wanted to organize their constituents to pressure local legislatures for equal rights, to insist on suffrage, and to appeal to whites to eliminate inequities. Blacks in Baltimore, for instance, had been fighting with the city council over the types of schools available to their children and the employment of black teachers in black schools. Schools for blacks were limited to the primary grades, and there were only white teachers in city schools. The dispute was still raging when the convention assembled. Such injustices, ample evidence of continued discrimination against blacks, provided a convenient rallying point.[80]

Although threatened with disruption, the convention completed its business without incident. Day was unquestionably a dominant force. He delivered three major speeches, reaffirming how proud he was of black participation in the country's armed forces and insisting that because of such sacrifices, those veterans and all blacks were deserving of full citizenship. As he had done so many times, Day again discussed the nature of the Constitution, the role of blacks in American history, and the importance of educating black children. Total freedom, he reiterated, could only be attained through self-sacrifice, hard work, and education. Blacks were involved "in a battle, not such as of five years ago, but of brains," and their every attempt received national scrutiny "as one looks to a waif on a stream to see which way the current was going." Blacks therefore had to do all within their limited power to educate themselves to assume their rightful position in society. The achievement of these goals, the convention agreed, necessitated united and concerted activity in favor of the Republican

79. Day to Knower, February 7, 1868, John Kimball to Day, August 14, 20, 1868, Day to Kimball, August 15, 18, 21, 1868, C. H. Howard to O. O. Howard, August 14, 15, 1868, all in BRFAL.
80. Baltimore *American*, July 25, 29, June 10, July 1, 2, 8, 1868; Wilmington *Daily Commercial*, June 10, 1868.

party. Every black voter should cast his ballot for Grant and Colfax. Anyone who did not should be "stamped a traitor to his race, an enemy to his ancestors, and a political murderer of his children's rights." Day was named chairman of the committee to write an address on behalf of the convention. He called for the adoption of an amendment guaranteeing blacks the right to vote, arguing that since amnesty was awarded "to the men who rose in arms against the Nation," the country could do no more than grant full citizenship to "its friends, who fought under the nation's flag, and helped maintain its honor."[81]

The address was issued in the weeks prior to the National Colored Convention, which met in Washington, D.C., in mid-January, and formed the basis of the convention's demand for a constitutional amendment granting the vote to blacks. Day, one of the delegates from Delaware, was named a vice-president, a member of the National Executive Committee and several other committees, and chairman of the Committee on Census. Not since the early state conventions in Ohio had Day played such a prominent role in a black meeting. The convention dealt with several pressing issues, including education, the settlement of public lands in the South, and the need to improve census enumerations of blacks. But all of these were overshadowed by the suffrage issue. Day and six others were appointed to lobby members of the Senate Judiciary Committee. Although Senator Wilson, chairman of the committee, could not guarantee passage of a constitutional amendment, the delegation left convinced that the chances for its adoption were good.[82]

Day returned to Wilmington, where he had settled after leaving the bureau. His promotion of black education and political equality in the city and state since 1867 had established him as one of the state's most influential blacks. In Wilmington, blacks faced a host of problems. The city council, for instance, had been particularly intractable in its refusal to appropriate funds for black education. In 1868 the Delaware association requested money for constructing schoolhouses for all students "without distinction of race or color." The council's appropriation of $5,000 was used to build the Howard School. When it was completed, however, and the association recommended that the school become part of the city system, opponents on the council and the board of education

81. *Anti Slavery Standard*, January 30, 1869, August 15, 1868; Baltimore *American*, August 5, 6, 1868; Wilmington *Daily Commercial*, August 5, 1868; Leroy Graham, *Baltimore: The Nineteenth Century Black Capital* (Washington, D.C., 1982), 173–76.
82. *Anti Slavery Standard*, January 23, 30, 1869; Wilmington *Daily Commercial*, January 19, 1869; Carol E. Hoffecker, "The Politics of Exclusion: Blacks in Late Nineteenth-Century Wilmington, Delaware," *Delaware History*, XVI (1974), 64.

William Howard Day
Reprinted from B. F. Wheeler, *Cullings From Zion's Poets*

raised a howl of protest, insisting that the public school system had been established expressly for whites. But faced with Reconstruction acts mandating
equal access to education, the school board agreed to a compromise. The board
would administer the association's schools, but blacks were not allowed to pay
city school taxes and so were automatically excluded from school board elections. Blacks denounced this restriction as a flagrant violation of their rights,
and at a meeting in early January, 1869, Day was named to a committee of ten
to draft a memorial to the state legislature. They called for the granting of
equal educational opportunities through equal taxation. Later that month another meeting reaffirmed that demand and circulated a petition for submission
to the state legislature. In spite of efforts by supporters, the legislature refused
to act on the petition. Delaware did not adopt a school law permitting separate
education until 1875, long after other border and southern states had done so.[83]

Despite these setbacks, this was a period of heightened expectations and
hope. Most blacks in Delaware endorsed Douglass' shibboleth: the Republican
party was the only ship, the one sanctuary, in a stormy sea. The removal of all
existing impediments to political equality, therefore, necessitated the defeat of
the Democratic party. Although Day had urged blacks to adopt an independent
line during the New York elections of 1866, he was a proponent of this approach. The Democratic party, he told the fifth annual convention of the
Pennsylvania State Equal Rights League, was vainly attempting to defy history,
to "dam up the stream of liberty which has its fountain-head in the heart of
God," by resisting the enfranchisement of blacks. Blacks, in turn, owed a "debt
of gratitude" to the Republican party for the emancipation of the slaves and the
passage of the Thirteenth, Fourteenth, and Fifteenth Amendments to the Constitution, a debt they were obliged to repay in the elections of 1870.[84]

The hopes of blacks were embodied in these legislative enactments, and the
passage of the Fifteenth Amendment was celebrated throughout the country.
The long years of struggle had been justly rewarded. In Wilmington, the "day
of jubilee" included a gun salute, the suspension of business for one day, religious services, a massive parade with participants from Delaware, Maryland,
eastern Pennsylvania, and New Jersey, and a mass meeting at which Day was the

83. Wilmington *Daily Commercial*, December 31, 1868, January 20, March 16, 17, 1869; *Delaware
Republican*, January 7, March 18, April 12, 1869; Halstead, "The Delaware Association," 37; Ronald
L. Lewis, "Reverend T. G. Steward and the Education of Blacks in Reconstruction Delaware,"
Delaware History, XIX (1981), 161; *Delaware Senate Journal*, 1869, pp. 183, 203, 237, 110, 467,
521–22.
84. *Anti Slavery Standard*, September 25, March 27, 1869; Wilmington *Daily Commercial*, April
30, 1869; *Delaware Republican*, March 4, 1869.

principal speaker. Although he said nothing new, Day's speech was a masterly oratorical performance. He again reiterated his contention that blacks were largely responsible for their own freedom. "I recognize . . . the good hand of God, I acknowledge the positive effort of the Republican party, and I admit the acts of the Democratic party as occasion for that positive act," he told his listeners, "but I recognize another influence as combining with these, and without which the work would not have been completed. That influence (and I repeat merely the facts of history) is our own. With all due respect to others, we have won the recognition which we celebrate today." It was now up to blacks to protect what they had gained after years of suffering and struggle. That, Day maintained, could be achieved only through "self-help, social and moral development, political elevation [and] full enfranchisement."[85]

But repaying the debt of gratitude to Republicans was no easy task in Delaware, where Democrats held almost hegemonic control of state and local government. Only in Wilmington were Republicans able to break that stranglehold. Ratification of the Fifteenth Amendment and the enfranchisement of 4,500 blacks raised Republicans' hopes for victory in November, and J. Sella Martin, J. Mercer Langston, and other well-known blacks were brought in to canvass the state. The Democrats countered by exploiting to full effect the one fear that haunted most southern whites: the ascendancy of former slaves. The Democrats called on whites to join the "White Man's Party," a move that put Republicans on the defensive. Republicans, one editor insisted, were not interested in introducing blacks into public schools, churches, and public office. Their only desire was to see blacks have "their own churches, their own schools, and the necessary protection to ensure them a fair chance to earn an honest livelihood." Such reasoning had little effect on those who hankered after the old order, or those who feared the rise of black political power through the Republican party. Day had a taste of things to come when he visited the village of Laurel, Sussex County, for a Fifteenth Amendment celebration. Long before the meeting convened, rumors were circulated that the speakers would be attacked and run out of town. Fortunately, the meeting was held without incident. Election day in Wilmington was another matter. A white vigilante group, the Old Church Rangers, attacked blacks in a number of districts. Acting in arrogance and ignorance, the Rangers were stunned by the determined resistance they encountered; every attack was repulsed and blacks threatened to turn the

85. Wilmington *Daily Commercial*, April 20, 16, 15, June 3, 1870; *Delaware Republican*, April 18, 14, February 24, July 11, 1870.

city into a battleground. Fearing increased disturbances, city authorities called out the troops to protect black voters, and Day pleaded with blacks to avoid confrontations with white mobs. Where the Rangers failed, Democratic tax collectors succeeded—they listed thousands of blacks as "dead" or "having left the state." When the ballots were counted, the Democrats had carried the state by over 2,000 votes.[86]

Day spent most of 1869 and 1870 away from Wilmington, lecturing in other parts of the state and attending meetings in Philadelphia and Harrisburg. He concentrated on promoting the interests of blacks in the Harrisburg-Philadelphia-Wilmington area. His previous affiliation with the Pennsylvania State Equal Rights League provided him with the necessary organizational base from which to launch this new phase of his career. The disappointment over the election results in Delaware and the violence during the Fifteenth Amendment celebrations finally forced Day to broaden his interests. Not long afterward, he joined forces with the Montana Agricultural Emigrant Aid Association, a black organization formed in Philadelphia in January, 1871, to promote black emigration to the newly created territory. The association pledged to assist the "worthy but poor and their families" who wished to move from places where "the avenues of profitable labor and trade are so generally occupied by men who already have means . . . and where their energies must remain comparatively unproductive for years to come" to a fertile area where their talents could flourish. Day was named vice-president, as was Henry Highland Garnet, and his old friend William Nesbit, the main force behind the association, was elected president. Day was also named to help O. L. C. Hughes of Harrisburg collect funds. It is not known how many emigrants the association assisted, or even how long it survived. Hughes did tour San Francisco, Salt Lake City, and Montana in the spring and then lectured throughout eastern Pennsylvania in an unsuccessful effort to promote the association's scheme. Only a handful of blacks actually settled in Montana, and it is impossible to determine how many of them went west under the auspices of the association.[87]

Prior to assuming his duties as collecting and traveling agent of the association, Hughes had to find a buyer for his newspaper, the *Progress of Liberty*, pub-

86. Harold B. Hancock, "The Status of the Negro in Delaware After the Civil War, 1865–1875," *Delaware History*, XIII (1968), 62; *New National Era*, October 6, 1870; *Delaware Republican*, November 10, October 3, April 21, May 9, 1870.

87. Harrisburg *Telegraph*, May 8, 11, April 17, 1871; *Montana: A State Guide Book Compiled and Written by Federal Writers' Project* (New York, 1939), 57–58; Clark C. Spence, *Territorial Politics and Government in Montana, 1864–89* (Urbana, 1975), 13–15; "Ho! For the West" (Broadside, in LGC); Hoffecker, "The Politics of Exclusion," 64.

lished in Harrisburg. Since his return from Britain, Day had been looking for an opportunity to launch a new paper. His work as lay editor of the *Zion Standard* had lasted only one year before he accepted the post at the Freedmen's Bureau. When Hughes offered to sell his newspaper, Day and C. M. Brown, a Harris-burg businessman and one of the association's directors, bought it and changed its name to *Our National Progress*. Business and editorial responsibilities were separated in an effort to ensure financial solvency. Brown devoted most of his time and energy to raising money through subscriptions and advertisements, leaving Day free to run the paper. The work of self-elevation, expanding educational opportunities, and harnessing the political potential of blacks, Day believed, called for the establishment of as many newspapers as blacks could afford to support. But Day was also motivated by personal considerations. The paper gave him an opportunity to return to a profession he relished and one for which he was well qualified. As he put it, "One cannot easily shake off the hopes and aspirations of earlier years—hopes born in the storm of conflict created by the enslavement of his brethren."[88]

But one could not run a newspaper for any length of time simply on well-placed hopes. As a supporter of the Republican party, the paper benefited from periodic party largesse, especially around election time, but that was no substitute for guaranteed income from advertisements and subscriptions. The initial rate of $1.50 per year was clearly insufficient to cover expenses, and Day and Brown were forced to increase the price to $2.25 by early 1874. The paper was published simultaneously every Saturday in Harrisburg, Wilmington, Philadelphia, Camden, and New York. Day and Brown saw it as the "organ of the Middle and Border States," the only "national organ" of blacks between Washington, D.C., and New York. The large number of advertisements from areas as far afield as Portland, Maine, and La Porte, Indiana, suggests that the paper achieved a wide circulation.[89]

These efforts helped to keep the paper afloat, but they could not guarantee its survival. Although in March, 1874, Day could boast with some justification that the paper had the largest circulation east of Washington, D.C., he could do nothing to forestall its demise nine months later. Attempts had been made to improve efficiency by moving all operations to Harrisburg in 1872, and Brown had widened his area of appeal for subscriptions and advertisements. Yet income continued to lag behind expenditures, further limiting the scope of the

88. *Delaware Republican*, February 23, 1871; Harrisburg *Telegraph*, August 30, July 2, 1871 (hereinafter cited as *Telegraph*); *New National Era*, March 16, 2, April 27, 1871.
89. *Our National Progress*, March 14, 1874.

paper. Problems were increased when Day accepted a clerkship in the Pennsylvania auditor-general's office in January, 1873. It is conceivable that Day could have divided his time between the new office and editor's desk without further impairing the paper's flagging fortunes. But with the appointment came the expectation that he would actively work for the party during campaigns, something that involved extensive travel around the state. In addition, the *Telegraph's* relatively impartial coverage of the black community possibly lessened the need for a black newspaper. More damaging, however, was the economic depression of 1873. By January, 1875, the paper was in serious trouble, and Day and Brown proposed to broaden their partnership into a joint-stock company capitalized by two thousand shares at $5.00 each. Meetings were held in a number of cities but failed to attract enough subscribers. As a result, the paper ceased publication soon afterward. It was to be Day's last newspaper undertaking, although he did try unsuccessfully to revive the paper as the official organ of the AME Zion church. The 1876 General Conference endorsed the proposal, named Day editor, and suggested that each minister contribute at least $4.50 per year to finance the operation. The following year the bishops angrily reported that the first issue had yet to appear and questioned Day's use of money already collected. Unable to elicit a satisfactory response from Day, the bishops suspended the agreement and immediately started making plans for a new venture.[90]

Day had moved to Harrisburg in 1872, anxious, one suspects, to put some distance between himself and the violence of Delaware politics. Although he continued to be a regular speaker at Republican meetings in Delaware, the chances of electing a Republican administration sympathetic to blacks seemed rather remote. Pennsylvania, on the other hand, with its much larger black population and stronger Republican machine, held out greater hope of success. There was optimism, for instance, that black votes could help elect a Republican administration in 1871. During the previous election the Democrats had used every possible device to whip up antiblack hysteria. To elect a Republican mayor, the Harrisburg Democratic paper warned, was to fulfill the promise of John Brown. The "pride of race" dictated that white Harrisburg residents

90. "Our National Progress" (Broadside, in LGC); *Our National Progress*, March 14, 1874 (there is only one copy extant); David Henry Bradley, Sr., *A History of the AME Zion Church* (2 vols.; Nashville, 1956, 1970), II 196–98; John Jamison Moore, *History of the AME Zion Church in America* (York, Pa., 1884), 326–33; Hood, *One Hundred Years*, 107–109; on the plight of black newspapers in the late nineteenth century, see Emma Lou Thornborough, "American Negro Newspapers, 1880–1914," *Business History Review*, XL (1966), 467–90.

vote against "the party the negroes vote for." Political equality, the editor trumpeted, was a prelude to social equality and ultimately amalgamation. But back of it all was the fear, bred of an unblushing racism, that these "new and highly perfumed African voters" held the balance of political power in the state and could help elect the majority of "Congressmen and members of the legislature." Some blacks were said to be voting Republican early and often—the claim was a transparent device to hide Democrats' pandering to racism.[91]

Democratic leaders were well aware of the potential power of the black vote in closely contested elections. Traditionally, Republican strength in the state's two major cities, Philadelphia and Pittsburgh, was offset by Democrats' ascendancy in rural areas. That balance was now endangered by the newly enfranchised black voter allied to the Republican party. In an attempt to neutralize that alliance, the Democrats employed a two-pronged attack. First, they pleaded with and encouraged blacks to vote for Democrats, arguing that Republicans were taking the black vote for granted and not providing any tangible rewards for such support. Second, they employed brazen racism, raising the specter of black political ascendancy, racial equality and amalgamation, in an effort to win white votes from Republicans. The Republicans were equally aware of the importance of the black vote and developed their own strategy to counter Democratic efforts. In every election, they waved the "bloody shirt," reminding Pennsylvanians that it was Democrats' intransigence and lack of patriotism that led to and sustained the slaveholders' rebellion. Democrats were also adamantly opposed to black political equality and had resisted it every step of the way. On the other hand, Republicans, the party of Lincoln, the Great Emancipator, had labored to ensure that equality.

Following defeat in the 1870 elections, some Democrats began to question the utility of the racist appeal and sought instead to curry favor with black voters, either by promises of minor patronage jobs or by flagrant bribery. Then the Republicans, who were unable to offer a larger number of patronage jobs for fear of alienating white supporters, chose to wave the bloody shirt more furiously and invoked more stridently the memory of Lincoln. Any black who ignored such an appeal was either a traitor to his race or an ingrate. The Republicans' tone suggests that the Democrats were already making some small inroads into the black vote. Later, as Republicans failed to fulfill promises

91. *Delaware Republican*, July 6, September 7, 1871; Wilmington *Daily Commercial*, September 4, 1871; Chambersburg *Public Opinion*, October 10, 1871; *Telegraph*, October 11, 7, 1871; Harrisburg *Patriot*, October 6, September 6, 14, 23, 1870 (hereinafter cited as *Patriot*).

of increased patronage appointments the ranks of black Democrats would grow. But for the moment the number of blacks who broke ranks remained relatively small.

The Pennsylvania State Equal Rights League had been working since 1869 to establish itself as the main political broker of black votes. In return for getting out the black vote for Republicans, the league expected its leaders to receive a suitable number of government jobs. When preferments failed to materialize, however, some in the league jumped ship. In an effort to hold the line against Democratic advances in the early 1870s, the league regularly condemned the Democrats as the party that supported slavery, excluded blacks from the workplace, deprived them of an education, and encouraged mob attacks on black communities. The black person who voted for such a party, in light of these facts, was a traitor. Day's description of a black Democrat was typical: "He was a horrible looking object, hideous to behold, a man without any brains—if any brains, no heart—if any heart, no conscience—if conscience, gum elastic, that can stretch so great as to take in anything, however rotten and corrupt."[92]

Black political clout in Harrisburg was predicated on two interrelated factors: there was an old and stable community, which was centered primarily in two wards of the city, and there was a benign segregation, which, after 1870, accepted the social, cultural, and educational separation of the races but also led to the creation of political alliances. As a result, blacks were able to utilize their population concentrations to win political office and, under certain circumstances, wrest concessions from the party machine. Although blacks lived in every ward of the city, 60 percent lived in the eighth and the sixth wards in 1870. There were three significant concentrations of blacks: the first between the capitol and the Pennsylvania Railroad lines; the second bounded by Reilly, Calder, Sixth, and Third streets; and the third in "Balm town." The majority of blacks who came to Harrisburg, many having left Virginia and Maryland, gravitated to those areas in the years after 1870. "Sibletown" became notorious—in its warren of alleys and narrow streets was some of the worst housing in the city. One local editor lamented in 1875 that there were six "dens of infamy" on just one street, all operating "without any interposition of the strong arm of the law." In spite of efforts to close them, the "houses of ill-fame" continued to tarnish the community's image. But Sibletown was not unique in this

92. *Telegraph*, October 4, 11, 10, May 31, June 23, 1871.

regard. The city's unpaved roads, open sewers, and frequent epidemics were infamous. Although attempts were made to remove some of the shanties inhabited by "a worthless class of people, colored and white, who made them the headquarters of desperate men and debased women," urban beautification was still two decades away.[93]

Residential segregation was just one manifestation of a much wider malaise that militated against social contact between the races. For example, there were separate Decoration Day celebrations to honor those who died in the Civil War. Whites marched to white cemeteries to lay wreaths on the graves of white soldiers; and blacks decorated the graves of black soldiers buried in a black cemetery in Pembroke, just outside the city limits. In spite of state laws, most black schoolchildren completed their education in all-black schools. Only the few who went on to high school were ever integrated into the larger school system. Conditions were no better in the last third of the nineteenth century. It was reported in 1884 that there were only two firms that offered blacks "anything like decent employment." Furthermore, "not a city paper, a dry goods dealer, or a shoe dealer in this city pay one dollar for employment to colored clerks or apprentices." There were restaurants that refused to serve blacks and hotels that denied them accommodation. When in 1885 a group of black and white Republicans visited a city restaurant, the proprietor refused to serve the two black members. By the end of the century, there were in effect two Harrisburgs—one was white, the other was black.[94]

Despite continued segregation and poverty, the black community remained relatively stable. For instance, 14 percent of blacks owned their own homes, and the majority lived in nuclear families. The average number of children per family was two. In fact, 81 percent of families had three or fewer children. Although 45 percent of black workers were unskilled laborers in 1880, roughly 13 percent, a comparatively large number, were tradesmen, professionals, and businessmen. Most of the city's black leaders came from the latter group.[95] Segregation allowed them to marshal the community's collective resources to improve living conditions. Blacks created a vast array of independent social, cultural, and po-

93. Michael Nestleroth, "The Black Community of Harrisburg, 1880–1910: A Study of the Black Community of a Small Northern City" (M.A. thesis, Lehigh University, n.d.), 13–14; *State Journal*, December 15, 1883; *Telegraph*, April 13, 1875, September 9, 1878, November 12, 1881, February 13, 1882.
94. *Telegraph*, July 8, 1885, November 10, 19, 1877, May 22, 1873, May 29, 31, 1872; *State Journal*, December 27, April 5, 1884.
95. Nestleroth, "The Black Community of Harrisburg," 11, 16–17.

litical institutions to address their particular needs. There were churches and social clubs, debating and literary societies, baseball and cycling teams, and a host of political organizations.

These associations were often the bases from which blacks addressed wider issues. They were willing to acquiesce to social separation in their daily lives, but they flatly refused to condone or accept policies that were contrary to their interests. Throughout the latter part of the century, for instance, they struggled to improve educational conditions for their children. They were concerned about the number and standard of black schools and about the hiring of black teachers in black and "mixed" schools. Prior to the war the education of black children in Pennsylvania had been governed by Section 24 of the 1854 school act. This required school directors in districts with twenty or more black students to establish segregated schools. Where no schools were provided, black children were to be admitted to traditionally white schools. Such segregation was based on a belief in black intellectual inferiority. When asked why blacks were not admitted to Philadelphia schools, the president of the school board replied unashamedly, "In no strictly colored school are the same requirements exacted that are called for in the other schools. Colored teachers are not asked to know as much as white teachers, colored children have easier examinations, regularity of attendance is not insisted upon, and there is great laxity of discipline."[96]

After the war, blacks throughout the state increased their protests against exclusion. At an 1870 meeting, blacks in Harrisburg expressed their determination that their children not be "kept back by an insufficient number of school houses, nor for want of graded schools, nor by the inability of any teacher therein." Two years later the Union Republican Club, a black political organization, appointed a committee to talk to the school board about improving black schools. Blacks in other parts of the state were also actively working for better education. In October, 1871, blacks in Allegheny City challenged the need for separate schools but failed to elicit a response from school directors. A few months later, blacks in Reading held a series of meetings to protest the school board's decision to deny their children admittance to white schools. The board's action was prompted by a liberal director's admitting a black student to the school closest to his home rather than the designated black school that was miles away. In reprimanding their colleague, the board ordered all teachers to

96. Edward J. Price, Jr., "School Segregation in Nineteenth-Century Pennsylvania," *Pennsylvania History*, XLIII (1976), 124; Ira V. Brown, "Pennsylvania and the Rights of the Negro, 1865–1887," *Pennsylvania History*, XXVIII (1961), 46; *Pennsylvania School Journal*, August, 1881.

ignore similar independent actions in the future. Blacks in Reading established one committee to test the legality of the board's decision in court, and another to persuade the board to rescind its decision. The board, however, stood firm, and black children continued to attend segregated schools.[97]

In late 1874, Day organized a meeting of blacks to explore ways for improving school facilities and the types of courses taught. Those in attendance appointed a committee, headed by Day, to meet with the school board and to visit, inspect, and report on the four black schools in the city. Day's petition to the board in early 1875 objected to conditions in the South Street and Calder Street schools, particularly the poor grading system, and he asked for better accommodations. The board's response is not known, but two months later the board sent to committee a resolution to purchase land in the eighth ward for building a school. In any case, the board's actions on school integration continued to be governed by the 1854 act. When black parents from the first ward petitioned the board to allow their children to attend Lochiel, the local white school, the directors insisted that the children be enrolled in the black school on Eleventh Street. The board's refusal was typical of educational policy throughout the state. Faced with comparable intransigence, blacks from around the state turned to the legislature for relief. While Congress was considering the Sumner bill, with its provision for school integration, the state legislature was debating the merits of what came to be called the "mixed school" bill. As election day approached, opponents launched a sustained attack on proponents of school integration. As a result, both bills were allowed to languish in committee. Democratic successes at the polls sealed the fate of the bills, though a lame-duck Congress did pass the Sumner bill without its school provision.[98]

These defeats undoubtedly impeded the struggle for school integration, but they in no way silenced blacks' demands for improved conditions in Harrisburg's existing black schools. By the mid-1870s they were calling for night schools to accommodate the growing number of blacks eager to continue their education. The importance of education to the black community and Day's long association with efforts to improve educational opportunities for blacks were the main reasons he decided to run for the board from the eighth ward in 1873. His defeat was a temporary setback, but five years later he became the first black

97. Price, "School Segregation," 127–29; *Telegraph*, October 5, 7, 1870, July 5, 1872; Reading *Times and Dispatch*, January 16, 24, February 20, 1872.
98. Price, "School Segregation," 130–32; Frank B. Evans, *Pennsylvania Politics, 1872–1877: A Study in Political Leadership* (Harrisburg, 1966); 125–26; *Telegraph*, December 11, 17, 1874, January 6, March 3, May 26, 1875.

elected to the board. He was a member for the rest of the century, with the exception of brief periods in the 1880s when he declined renomination.[99]

The continued struggles seem to have borne some fruit by the end of the 1870s. For the first time, three black boys were enrolled in the city high school for boys, and the following year eight black girls were attending the girls' high school. There were also reports of marked improvement in the black schools, which were "well graded" and from which transfers were made "with the same regularity and system as in the other schools." One local editor was convinced that Harrisburg's black schools were the best in the state.[100] These were the first cracks in the system of school segregation, and there was similar progress in other parts of the state. Black students, for example, were admitted in 1879 to Central High School and the Girls' Normal School in Philadelphia, and the following year Pittsburgh school directors permitted blacks to enroll in district elementary and high schools. Black leaders now sought to capitalize on these initial successes. The 1879 meeting of the Pennsylvania State Equal Rights League demanded the establishment of black schools in areas with sizable black populations as well as "colored teachers for colored schools and a share in the number of teachers where there are mixed schools." The league ultimately wanted to remove the laws that permitted separate schools. Until then, however, black children had to be educated—even if that implied an apparent endorsement of segregation. The league's 1880 meeting adopted resolutions to rescind laws allowing separate schools, and members praised colleagues in Allegheny City for getting separate schools abolished. In 1881 the league revealed plans for a stepped-up campaign against those laws, and when a bill abolishing racial distinctions in common schools won bipartisan support from legislators, it was a clear recognition of black voters' potential power in state elections. Unfortunately, the 1881 law contained no provisions for punishing offenders, and in practice it affected only those areas where the small number of black residents made maintaining separate schools prohibitively expensive.[101]

Separate schools continued to exist in Harrisburg and other parts of the state, but the issue lost some of its potency after 1881. When, for example, a General Deven offered in 1883 to build a separate school for blacks in Sibletown so as to limit contact between the races, blacks were quick to denounce segre-

99. *Telegraph*, February 4, 11, 20, 1878, September 1, 8, October 15, 16, 1873, January 5, 1876.
100. *Ibid.*, June 4, 1881, August 3, 1880, May 25, 1879; *Pennsylvania School Journal*, November, 1879, October, 1880.
101. Price, "School Segregation," 132–37; Brown, "Pennsylvania and the Rights of the Negro," 55–56; *Telegraph*, August 21, 1879; Altoona *Tribune*, August 19, 1880; *Lawrence County Guardian*, August 19, 1881.

gation. Later protests were tempered, however, by the recognition that cate-gorical opposition to separate schools effectively denied black children the op-portunity for an education and black teachers the chance for employment. There were five black teachers in the system in 1888, all in black schools. It was obvious that the board had no intention of hiring black teachers for mixed schools. Even Day's presence on the board seemed to have little effect. When the Eleventh Street School was made a mixed school, the one black teacher was released while all the white teachers were retained. White teachers also taught in black schools. The situation was patently unfair, insisted a local black editor, for it gave the white teacher three opportunities for employment in the system. Although the 1881 law allowed black children to attend any school in their dis-trict, it did not address the question of employing black teachers. The board's policy was governed by the unwritten law that no black teachers would be hired in mixed schools. Was Day a party to this understanding? He was, without doubt, largely responsible for opening up the city's high schools to black stu-dents, but why, as a member of the teachers' committee, he failed to recom-mend black teachers remains something of a mystery. If Day "deserved credit for the opening of the door of the high school to colored children," the same editor reasoned, "then he deserved censure for not protecting the interest of colored teachers located here."[102] Community concerns about black teachers in black schools to a limited degree facilitated continued segregation, but respon-sibility for the perpetuation of the system, in violation of legal restrictions, must be placed on the board and on those who believed in racial segregation.

All these efforts to win equal opportunities in education were predicated in large part on the ability of blacks to influence political developments in the city and the state. The election of sympathetic legislators and local officials in-creased black political clout and ensured favorable legislation. The elections of 1872 provided the first opportunity, since the passage of the Fifteenth Amend-ment, for blacks to flex their political muscle. Three months before the presi-dential and gubernatorial elections, they formed the Union Central Republi-can Club, an umbrella organization of affiliated ward clubs, each committed to enlist an assigned quota of members. At its first meeting the club pledged to work for the election of the entire Republican ticket. Day was a pivotal figure in the effort to rally blacks behind the Republican party. In early August he joined his old friends J. Mercer Langston, William D. Forten, and William Nesbit at a

102. *Telegraph*, June 23, 1883, October 26, 1888; *Home Journal*, August 11, June 30, 1883; *State Journal*, July 19, 1884, December 22, 1883.

massive rally of black Republicans in Carlisle at which both the Democrats and
Liberal Republicans came in for some scathing denunciations. He served with
C. M. Brown and Major John W. Simpson on the invitations committee for the
Pennsylvania State Equal Rights League's convention in Harrisburg a few days
later. A vote for the Democrats, the league argued, was a vote for a return to
slavery; support of the Liberals, an exercise in futility. Day was also a regular
on Republican platforms throughout central Pennsylvania, and he addressed
large audiences in Shippensburg, Mechanicsburg, Middletown, Reading, Altoona, and Christiana. In early September he was one of the principal speakers
at a rally organized by Harrisburg Republicans at the capitol. "The hand of
Almighty God," he said, "seems to be connected with the success of the great
Republican party, and it cannot go backward, but must go forward." No black
person, true to his race, could forsake Grant and the party now, for "not a black
man, from one end of the nation to the other, can have an honest word of complaint against General Grant." Day called for endorsing the entire ticket. A few
days before the elections he left on another campaign swing through Reading,
Altoona, and Baltimore. Throughout, his message was the same: "Give four
years more of power to the Republican party, and thereby fifty years more
of peace to the nation."[103]

Widespread black participation in the elections and the success of Republicans led one local party stalwart to announce: "The prejudice on the subject of
color and race is fast disappearing. It has no longer a lodgement in the Republican party." The election of William D. Forten as a state presidential elector
was sufficient evidence of this change of heart among Republicans. The claim,
however, was definitely premature. Blacks, for example, were still excluded
from jury duty, and the state constitution had not been officially purged of its
racial restrictiveness. In early January, 1873, blacks met at Wesley Union to
protest their exclusion from juries and to demand the removal of the word *white*
from the state constitution at the upcoming constitutional convention. But in
spite of these legacies of the past, there were a few rays of hope after the elections. Day's unceasing work for the party led the Republicans to offer him a
clerkship in the auditor-general's office. Although the position was minor, no
black could possibly decline it on the grounds that it was inadequate and undig-
nified. The appointment was more important for its symbolism than as a statement of the party's intentions. As one black editor observed, Day acted cor-

103. *Telegraph,* November 1, October 21, 5, 9, 3, September 30, 12, 10, August 31, July 29, 5, 12,
18, 1872; Baltimore *Sun,* November 2, 1872; *Louisianan,* November 30, 1872; Carlisle *Herald,* August 8, 1872.

rectly when he accepted, though if offered "as a recognition of his service to the party in the late campaign, it is somewhat slight, yet it makes an advancement, and so he is doing the cause a service in accepting." Day's appointment and Forten's election were small but significant investments in the future, and ensured, for the time being, continued support for the party from major black figures in the state.[104]

Before he went to work for the auditor-general, Day married Georgie F. Bell in Philadelphia. His bitter differences with Lucy had dragged on until she obtained a divorce in 1872. The evidence suggests that Day had severed all contacts with Lucy and Florence, and since his return from Britain in 1863 he had refused to support them. Lucy had held a number of teaching jobs among the freedmen and had been the sole provider for their child. Little is known about Georgie, except that she was from Washington, D.C., where Day met her when he joined the Wesley Zion Church in 1866. The wedding was attended by most of Philadelphia's prominent black citizens. The couple went to Harrisburg, where they were met by a welcoming committee. Black Harrisburg would not be outdone by Philadelphia. The Days were escorted to C. M. Brown's home, where they were serenaded by the Excelsior cornet band and presented with gifts. Guests had traveled many miles just to be part of black Harrisburg's premier social event of the year. Georgie, twenty-four years Day's junior, was content to live in the shadow of her husband. Unlike Lucy, who had been an active member of black organizations in Cleveland and Canada, Georgie limited her public involvement to a few church auxiliaries.[105]

Not long after his wedding, Day left on a tour of the northern and western counties. The Pennsylvania State Equal Rights League wanted to capitalize on Emancipation Day celebrations in an attempt to highlight black accomplishments and emphasize work still to be done. Blacks attending a meeting in Harrisburg stated that gains had been made, but they had to keep "knocking until the barriers of prejudice and unchristian sentiment shall be removed, and we enjoy the schools, churches, positions in commercial affairs, and all trades." This was the message Day delivered during his tour. Blacks had achieved their freedom through a trial by fire, he told a Titusville meeting; liberty had been attained through suffering, death, and the destruction of southern slavery. When the debris was finally cleared away and "the old foundations for crime

104. *Telegraph*, January 17, 13, 15, 1873, November 12, 1872; *New National Era*, February 6, 1873.

105. *Telegraph*, June 4, 6, 1873; Census of 1880: Population Schedules, Pennsylvania, Dauphin County.

removed, we shall see new light upon the habitations of cruelty; we shall see the nation's prosperity secured; we shall see a new temple rising—a Temple of Liberty—beautiful and grand, the home of freedom and free men." Not only had blacks' successes to be defended against those who yearned for the old order, but blacks and their white friends had to commit themselves to remove all vestiges (the debris) of the oppressive past so that a new, egalitarian society might arise.[106]

For Day and most of his colleagues, this new society could only be achieved through the Republican party. The election of Democrats or members of a third party would threaten recent gains and impede progress to full equality. The league's annual meeting endorsed this position, arguing that the Republican party alone was the "true exponent of the highest progressive sentiment of the day" and was capable of securing to all Americans "the complete exercise of their constitutional and natural rights." The Grant administration showed no signs of reneging on the party's commitment to a free South, and locally the party seemed to be taking positive steps to recognize the contributions of its black supporters. At the state convention, two blacks, John Conway of Philadelphia and C. M. Brown, were named to minor posts, and in Harrisburg, George Galbraith was elected secretary of the party's executive committee.[107]

For the moment, most blacks were content with these minor and often token appointments, which they saw as signs that the party's heart was in the right place. However, blacks had to become directly involved in the system by running for elective office. Day was aware of this when he ran for the school board from the eighth ward. Although he was opposed by other Republicans, Day won the primary by a rather comfortable margin. The strength of the party seemed to ensure his election. Some local Republicans were convinced that a victory on election day would finally bury a comatose Democratic party. In spite of these optimistic predictions, the Democrats refused to leave the field of battle. Again, they did all they could to portray the Republicans as the black man's party. Blacks in the eighth ward, they argued, controlled municipal nominations for alderman, school director, assessor, and constable and so gave "the white trash the candidates for city council and for judge of elections." There were even rumors that some black Republican candidates in the eighth ward had sold out to the Democrats. Although the rumors were politically motivated and meant to embarrass Day and other black candidates, there were signs that

106. *Telegraph*, July 16, August 2, 1873; Titusville *Herald*, August 2, 1873.
107. *Telegraph*, August 13, 20, 1873, January 19, 1874.

some blacks were already growing wary of the Republicans. In late September a meeting of eighth ward "unconditional Republicans" elected a committee of seven, including Day, to discuss with "doubtful Republicans" their views on the party's ticket. It is not known how or whether differences were actually resolved, but the split in the ranks was ominous. The Republicans carried the state, county, and city in the fall elections, but Day was defeated in his first bid for office.[108]

Black defection from the party in Harrisburg had its roots in local issues, but it nonetheless reflected a widening rift among Republicans, many of whom were increasingly frustrated by Senator Simon Cameron's dominance of the state party machine. Day, however, viewed the trend with alarm. On the eve of the mayoral elections he led more than six hundred Republicans in a call for a meeting of all those opposed to a third party. The focus of local opposition was David Chester, head of a third party called the Peoples' Republican party. Republicans were deeply concerned that a split black vote would result in a victory for the Democrats. Day led the charge against the Chesterites in a series of meetings just before the elections. John D. Patterson, the Republican candidate, was worried enough to break tradition and speak on his own behalf at all the meetings. The Chesterites, Day insisted, were disaffected individuals who threatened to undermine blacks' precarious position in the city. Chester and the Democrats denounced Day and Patterson as "carpet baggers," men from other cities attempting to dictate the future of Harrisburg natives. The criticism was unfortunate and unfounded, for many residents had been born outside the state. As Day put it, the accusation was ludicrous and insulting to a considerable segment of the city's population. The election results show that concerns about a Democratic victory were not that farfetched. Patterson won by a mere 133 votes, and although Chester received only 22 votes, it is likely that all the bickering did cost the party some votes.[109]

The minor split in the local ranks of black Republicans was an indication of things to come. But for the moment, the party continued to master the opposition, and black leaders felt secure enough to involve themselves in wider political issues. The Pennsylvania State Equal Rights League's annual address captured this feeling of optimism. There were no signs of discouragement, it asserted. On the contrary, blacks "have obtained jury rights and admission to the common schools in some parts of the State, [and have been] elected to

108. *Ibid.*, October 15, 16, September 8, 26, 1873; *Patriot*, September 8, 30, 1873.
109. *Telegraph*, January 26, February 6, 13, 15, 18, 1874; *Patriot*, January 28, 1874.

offices of trust, and appointments of honor and responsibility, all in answer to our united effort." For the first time, the league addressed issues other than social and political equality. Democrats were condemned for advocating free trade, a policy threatening all workingmen, especially blacks, the majority of whom were laborers. Nor could the league ignore the fact that both Sumner's bill and the mixed-school bill had run into stiff opposition. In a public appeal the league called on the president for open endorsement of Sumner's bill, for all citizens must be protected from "insult and outrage on the highways of the nation and secured in all their 'public rights.'" Continued outrages against blacks in the South further tempered the league's optimism. But blacks could see how far the country had traveled in just four years and conclude, not unreasonably, that the Republican party, with some prodding, was still committed to their advancement.[110]

But there were some in Harrisburg, like the editor of the *Telegraph*, who expressed serious doubts about the usefulness of continued appeals to Washington. Congress, he maintained, was no longer inclined to eliminate remaining inequities, and the "African race must depend more upon their individual action than upon acts of Congress to obtain what they consider their rights." That was easier said than done, especially in a period of quickening resistance to legitimate demands for full equality. Moreover, Day and others in the league knew that their influence as leaders was predicated on the general advancement of their people. Only after the elimination of all vestiges of past discrimination would the *Telegraph*'s exhortation have some merit. Not that Day belittled the significance of individual achievement. On the contrary, he firmly believed that individual advancement and recognition were symbolically important and an incentive to others. The appointing of blacks to public posts, including his own as clerk, acknowledged their ability and potential. Day was named to a board of examiners by the state superintendent of education James Wickersham. They were to report on the desirability of adding Lincoln University to the state's normal-school system. Day would have agreed with the *Telegraph* that his appointment was "an official recognition of the rights of the colored people of the State."[111]

These appointments depended on continued Republican control of the state, and all the signs pointed to a Democratic sweep of state offices in November, 1874. Day could do nothing directly about the rifts in the party brought on by

110. *Telegraph*, August 18, 22, October 20, 1874; "To His Excellency, The President of the United States" (Broadside, in LGC).
111. *Telegraph*, September 22, August 25, 1874.

the growing strength of Independents opposed to the Cameron machine. But he could work to rally the estimated fifteen thousand black voters. They might prove sufficient to carry the state for the Republicans, despite the divisions. This is why he undertook a lecture tour of the state in the weeks before the election. Wherever he went, his message was the same: this election was pivotal in blacks' struggle to attain full equality. They were "the advance guard of the party looking out . . . to see that which must come." There was enough evidence in the Republican party's record, he told a Williamsport audience, "to command the worthy respect of its lovers down to eternity. No matter if we do not receive the recognition immediately, the colored man will certainly receive his reward and has already in the glorious freedom he has received." It was the duty, therefore, of all blacks to vote the "ticket from top to bottom." If the eighth ward was typical, then blacks overwhelmingly voted for the party, but the Democrats won in a landslide. More immediately, the defeat of the auditor-general Harrison Allen meant that Day was out of a job.[112]

After the election, friends in the eighth ward tried to persuade Day to run for the school board. Flattered by the suggestion, Day declined, aware that another defeat could permanently wreck his chances of achieving elective office. He did pledge his support for the party's nominee, but in doing so, he issued a warning that must have raised eyebrows among the party faithful. He would not assist anyone, Day announced publicly, who was "too nice to vote for a colored man merely because of his color, and too much of a Christian to regard a colored citizen as anything else than a Pariah or Soodra of society." His statement could not be dismissed out of hand. Even the *Telegraph* thought the issue important enough to warrant a lengthy editorial. The author pleaded with black voters to remember that the party of Lincoln had been responsible for their advances. Prejudice still existed, he admitted, but patience was necessary, since biased attitudes could not be eliminated immediately. Continued agitation, he said, increased rather than diminished prejudice. Searching for examples of Republican recognition of blacks in the state, the *Telegraph* could do no better than dredge up the party's only election of a black to statewide office. The party in Pennsylvania had "honored herself, and vindicated the traditions of her earliest history, by electing a negro by an unprecedented majority one of her Senatorial electors in 1872, to cast the vote of this great State for the man whose life, since the war began, has been one devoted to struggle for the secu-

112. *Ibid.*, October 28, 29, November 16, 1874; Williamsport *Gazette and Bulletin*, October 31, 1874.

rity of RIGHT, and the extirpation of wrong against their race."[113] There were many who had grown weary of such platitudes and had abandoned the party, but Day was still willing to give Republicans the benefit of the doubt.

Out of a job, Day divided his time between efforts to rescue *Our National Progress* and work for the church. He was unquestionably the most prominent member of the AME Zion church in eastern Pennsylvania, if not in the entire state, the principal force behind both the growth of the church's Sabbath school program in the 1870s and the formation of the Wesley Union Christian Association, which promoted education among its members. Besides being president, he was also head of its astronomy section. There were an additional six sections, covering such subjects as biblical geography and history. The association's school complemented the work of the public schools and in some instances provided the only educational opportunities available to black children. Day's promotion of education in the church was recognized at the 1875 annual meeting of the Philadelphia and Baltimore Conference. He was named secretary of its Missionary Association and secretary and general agent of its Educational Fund Society. One year later he achieved national prominence in the church with his election as secretary-general.[114]

Work for the church in no way diminished Day's interest in politics. On the eve of the 1875 elections, he was invited by the Republican State Committee to canvass the western, central, and northern counties. All was not clear sailing. At Altoona, someone in the audience kept up a constant barrage of abuse, and the meeting almost degenerated into a free-for-all. During the parade after the meeting, people threw rocks at the band but no one was injured. But Altoona was the exception, for Day was warmly received wherever he lectured. One partisan editor in Pittsburgh reported that Day's speech was a "masterful effort," which was guaranteed to have a strong, positive effect. When the Republicans carried the elections, Harrisburg Democrats were understandably chagrined and blamed their defeat on the solid black vote. Blacks in the South were splitting their votes as interest dictated, the Harrisburg *Patriot* fumed, but those in the North continued blindly to cast their ballots for Republicans. Black votes determined the outcome of the elections in the two important swing states of Ohio and Pennsylvania. In states such as these, where the parties were evenly balanced, the black vote was an "unmixed evil," in the editor's view. "[A] mass of voters who cannot adjust themselves to the decision of political issues

113. *Telegraph*, February 1, January 30, 1875.
114. Bradley, *History of the AME Zion Church*, II, 48; *Telegraph*, May 25, 29, 1875, November 24, 27, 1874, March 21, December 27, 1876.

on their merits are not fit to take part in political contests and are quite as dangerous to the welfare of the party they assist as to that of the party they oppose." The threat was unmistakable, but until Democrats showed a willingness to accept the legitimacy of black interests, or Republicans refused to fulfill their promises, blacks had no alternative but to continue to support the party of Lincoln. The *Telegraph*, however, hailed Day's contributions to the Republican victory. "As an effective speaker Mr. Day ranks high; and his accomplishments are highly esteemed and his labors gratefully acknowledged by those who join him now exulting over our hard earned victory."[115]

Day may have expected that such praise and recognition of his contributions to the party's success would have resulted in another government job. But no offers were forthcoming from the new administration, and, disappointed by this slight, Day temporarily retreated from active participation in Republican politics. There were other ominous signs of Republican insensitivity and ingratitude. John Gaitor, the only black Republican candidate for city office, was crushed by his Democratic opponent in the February elections, which were dominated by Republicans. The *Patriot* chortled, wondering aloud about the willingness of white Republicans to vote for a black candidate; the *Telegraph* fidgeted, nervously searching for an explanation. Day's earlier concern that there were people in the party who treated blacks as pariahs was borne out by Gaitor's defeat. Yet Day was unwilling to break with the Republicans at this juncture, even though many of their policies and actions toward blacks were distasteful. The Democrats, however, were worse. As a result, Day reluctantly continued to support the Republicans. As the 1876 elections approached he did what he could to assist the party locally, but did not undertake his customary lecture tour.[116]

In mid-1877 it was rumored that Day was near death from a bout of consumption that confined him to bed for more than eight weeks. His doctors recommended a change of climate, but whether he actually left Harrisburg is not known. He had recovered sufficiently, however, to participate in election campaigns later that year. He was a member of a local committee that issued an address in September, condemning the Democratic party and rejecting suggestions that blacks join forces with the Greenbackers. But the choice of words in the resolution of support must have caused some Republicans to wince. The committee may even have meant it as a subtle warning. Given the fact, the reso-

115. Pittsburgh *Daily Commercial*, October 22, 1875; *Patriot*, November 5, 1875; *Telegraph*, November 5, October 4, 5, 21, 1875.
116. *Telegraph*, November 1, 2, January 16, February 11, 18, 1876.

lution read, that blacks traditionally supported the Republican party "because it has professed to be and in numerous instances has been our only political hope . . . in the present contest in Pennsylvania we see no reason to change our allegiance." But gentle prodding did not shake the party's conviction that it held a monopoly on the black vote. After all, blacks could never forget that the Democrats were the party of slavery and discrimination. Day did undertake a local tour for the party, but one gets the distinct impression that his heart was not in it. Whatever doubts Day harbored about the party's willingness to work for black candidates were partially allayed when he was nominated for the school board from the eighth ward and won the election by a comfortable margin. Day had, by 1878, established himself as the city's leading black citizen. That in part accounted for his success. His prominence and importance to the party also meant that no Republican could stand idly by and witness another defeat like Gaitor's.[117]

Day brought to the job considerable experience as both a teacher and an administrator, something few other board members could claim. He had also been at the center of efforts to improve educational opportunities and facilities for black children since his arrival in Harrisburg. Although most restrictions had been eliminated by law or by court injunction, there was still a great deal to be done in the city. No black students had been admitted to the city's high school, and only a few black teachers had been hired by the board. Public school education in Harrisburg in 1878 was hardly ideal. Schools were generally overcrowded, the curriculum needed overhauling, teachers were inadequately trained, and it was estimated that the board's deficit was somewhere in the region of $120,000. All these problems, a local editor observed, were directly attributable to poor management. The common-school system, he wrote, "has been made a complex machine, which is difficult for the ordinary taxpayer longer to understand, a costly feature of the Government, the revenues for whose support are exhausted in salaries at once too high and undeserving of the talent engaged, in architecture that is an abortion, in sinecures which are a disgrace, and an extravagance which now amounts to a criminal waste." In an effort to reduce the deficit, the new board slashed all teachers' salaries above $400 by 10 percent and attempted to reduce the number of teachers on its payroll by eliminating certain courses from the curriculum.[118]

117. *Ibid.*, September 26, October 20, 26, 30, November 2, July 11, 18, August 4, 1877, February 4, 11, 20, 1878.
118. *Ibid.*, June 10, 1878, December 21, 1876, February 7, March 31, August 14, 29, 1877, September 17, March 19, 1878.

During his first term on the board, Day served on the important "Finance," "Supplies," and "Teachers, Examinations and Transfers" committees. The teachers' committee, apparently the most active, was responsible for hiring and firing; salaries; and special investigations of teachers' conduct. Day was secretary of this committee for 1879–1880. A considerable amount of time was spent on the rather tedious and often bitter business of hiring and dismissing teachers. Although the superintendent's 1878 report spoke glowingly of an increase in the number of qualified teachers (graduates mainly of the girls' high school) available to the board, that did not eliminate completely the political maneuvering for appointments. In fact, the board expended considerable effort in selecting teachers and determining their salaries. In some instances, as in 1879, the whole board voted to reject suggestions for appointments made by the teachers' committee. In a clear attempt to control hiring, teachers' contracts were limited to the life of the board that hired them. As a result, teachers were hired or dismissed without notice or explanation. There were numerous instances of teachers requesting hearings to protest their arbitrary dismissal.[119]

There was fortunately more to the job than the tedium of deciding which teachers to hire and retain. Day was at the center of efforts to reduce truancy. Many of the main offenders, he informed his colleagues, had deceived their parents into believing they were attending school. His proposal, which the board adopted, ordered teachers to inform parents when children were absent, and the penalties included possible fines or suspension. Although this new approach did reduce absenteeism, truancy remained a problem for the rest of the century. The board could do little to improve conditions. A large number of working-class parents had to choose between their children's education and a job that helped the family survive. Day promoted a modest expansion in the number of schools along with a public campaign geared to impress on working-class parents the importance of education. He also supported the establishment of night schools. Recurring deficits, however, seriously curtailed many of these plans.[120]

Hidden behind these nagging problems were some successes. There was improvement in the curriculum, as well as a limited expansion in enrollment. Black students especially had broken through the barrier preventing their enrollment in the city's high schools. Less than one year after Day joined the

119. *Ibid.*, September 7, 1881, February 5, April 2, July 2, 1879, July 6, 1881; Harrisburg School District, Minute Book, 1879–1883, Board of Education, Harrisburg.
120. *Telegraph*, February 2, 1881, June 24, 1879, August 5, 1881, August 2, 1882; Harrisburg School District, Minute Book, 1879–1883.

board, four black students, one girl and three boys, passed the examination and were transferred to the high schools. All of these reforms and improvements led the editor of the *Telegraph* to reassess his evaluation of the schools just nine months after his blistering indictment. The schools had since improved their organization and were now "managed in a manner to afford the daily profit of every dollar expended. . . . Directors, superintendents and teachers are all doing their full duty conscientiously."[121]

Given these improvements, in which Day played a pivotal role, it came as something of a surprise when he announced in 1884 that he would not accept renomination for a third term. There were some, like James H. Howard, editor of the *State Journal*, who condemned Day's tepid support of demands for increases in the number of black teachers. Such criticism could have only minimally affected Day's decision. He was more concerned with the expansion and improvement of the school system than with the race of those who taught in it. Two other factors were more important, however: a serious bout of illness, which Day insisted was the only reason why he declined renomination, and his temporary break with the Republican party soon after his election to the board in 1878. There is no doubt that Day was very ill in the winter of 1883–84, but he also had grown weary of his isolation from former political allies and dreaded the prospects of possible defeat. At least Howard thought this was the proximate reason behind Day's decision. Although Day had done much "to advance the educational interest of the colored youth of this city," for which the people would always be grateful, Howard believed that Day was trying to "save himself from the humiliation of defeat." Seeing "the blood on the moon," Howard wrote rather quaintly, Day "wisely declined to stand for slaughter."[122]

Assessing his accomplishment, Day observed proudly that he had seen a "grammar school established where children of color, (for whom previously no such provision was made), could attend; the same class of children admitted to the two high schools; and two young men of the same class, graduate therefrom, and engaged today as teachers." When, he concluded, "I consider the strides which all this indicates that the Nation, the State and the city have taken, and when I see today in the law no distinction in school privileges, on account of the color of the hair, the shape of the nose or the hue of the skin, I feel that any honorable man can now guard the interest of these in common with the interest of all." It was a reasonable if personal testimonial, the

121. *Telegraph*, December 1, May 25, 1879; *Star of Zion*, March 31, 1898.
122. *State Journal*, February 9, 16, April 12, 1884.

claims of which few would deny, but Day failed to address all the reasons for his departure.[123]

Day's break with the Republicans was not sudden, although it did surprise most of those who worked with him. He had never wavered in his support for the party and had received some rewards for his services. "I am a Republican at every election from the presidential to the fence viewers," he once stated categorically, "and while the Democratic party acts as they do now, I must firmly oppose them." Had either party changed significantly in four years to warrant such a dramatic reversal? Since 1871, when Ohio Democrats adopted "new departurism," the national party had come under the control of moderates eager to devise a long-range plan for a return to power. The features of new departurism involved a simultaneous acceptance of Reconstruction, which party leaders hoped would improve their standing among northern voters, and opposition to federal enforcement of the new constitutional amendments, which they calculated would consolidate their position in the South. The new policy coincided with growing disillusionment among some black leaders with Republican reluctance to appoint blacks to office, the continued exclusion of blacks from juries, and increasing corruption and lawlessness in the South. Peter H. Clark, J. Sella Martin, and George T. Downing insisted that the party was taking blacks for granted. By 1874, Democrats were actively working to improve their image among black leaders and were undoubtedly aided by Republican indecisiveness on civil rights, corruption in the South, and the party's abysmal record on patronage. Pennsylvania, which had acquired a reputation as one of the nation's most corrupt states, one in which the Cameron machine held absolute sway and paid little attention to black political aspirations, epitomized these problems. Democrats were quick to capitalize on popular demands for reform, concentrating most of their criticism on the Republican Treasury Ring, which had hired Day in 1873. Harrison Allen was at the center of all these disputes. His refusal to open his accounts to a citizens' committee in 1873 lent credence to Democratic accusations that Republicans were illegally using state funds for private loans and speculation. Later, Allen's voluntary statement of state deposits showed that a considerable portion had gone to banks in which leading party figures had vested interests. In addition, these loans were "without collateral or interest"—at a time when the interest rate was 5 percent.[124]

123. *Telegraph*, February 6, 4, 1884; Harrisburg School District, Minute Book, 1879–1883.
124. Lawrence Grossman, *The Democratic Party and the Negro: Northern and National Politics,*

Day kept his counsel, never once publicly commenting on these developments. He continued to canvass the state for the party even after his departure from the auditor-general's office, yet he was overlooked, as were most of his black co-workers, for patronage positions. The Republicans, for example, carried the November, 1875, gubernatorial elections by a mere 12,000 votes, at a time when the black vote was estimated at 15,000. Although other factors (the school question possibly the most important) determined the final outcome, black leaders could claim, with some justification, that the black vote had provided the margin of victory. Yet no blacks were offered patronage jobs. Day's rejecting the nomination for the school board in 1875 might have been prompted by increasing disenchantment with the party's policies toward blacks. But he continued to work for the party while old friends such as William Still of Reading and Robert Purvis of Philadelphia crossed over to the Democrats.

This rift among black leaders widened perceptibly after 1875 and directly affected the operations of the Pennsylvania State Equal Rights League (ERL). Since its formation in 1864, the league had never wavered in its support for the Republican party. Now growing disillusionment with the party's treatment of blacks threatened to shatter its existence. Still and Purvis had left the fold, and now Day refused to attend its annual meetings in 1876 and 1877. The league, however, retreated behind the security of uncritical party affiliation rather than address the questions raised by the disaffected. The split provided Democrats an unexpected opportunity to make inroads into traditionally solid Republican support. For example, they sent paid organizer Thomas Younger, a black Louisianian, to work among blacks in Harrisburg. Younger had some success, and a black Democratic organization was formed in the eighth ward in early September. Younger's efforts were facilitated by Day's expulsion from the Laboring Men's Club of the Eighth Ward. Day's claim to being a "free republican" carried little weight. His former allies in the eighth ward sent an unmistakable warning to anyone thinking of following Day's lead. Rising to the challenge, Day denounced his "would-be oppressors, white and black" and pledged to continue to fight for blacks' freedom from "political bondage." Apparently trying to hold the line against Democratic incursions, the Republicans brought in James Howard, a black lecturer from Chicago, and reminded blacks of the Democrats' past by waving the bloody shirt even more frantically. Condescending editorials in the *Telegraph*, portraying blacks as passive spectators while Repub-

---

1868–1892 (Urbana, 1976), 15, 24–26, 37–38, 52–54; August Meier, "The Negro and the Democratic Party, 1875–1915," *Phylon*, XVII (1956), 173; Williamsport *Gazette and Bulletin*, October 31, 1874; Evans, *Pennsylvania Politics*, 115–16.

licans battled the forces of evil, only angered Day and convinced him of the efficacy of his actions.[125]

When Forten and others demanded a pledge of loyalty to the party as a prerequisite for membership in the ERL, Day was not the only one who decided that the time had come to leave and create a new organization. The People's League (PL) was formed in Pittsburgh in August, 1878. Its platform roundly denounced the party pledge as "unconstitutional and impolitic" and promoted the "intellectual, industrial, mechanical, and social improvement" of all blacks regardless of party affiliation. Forten and the ERL did not remain silent in the face of what they considered ingratitude and apostasy. Forten arranged a public meeting in Pittsburgh, an obvious attempt, a Democratic paper asserted, to win back the large number of blacks in the city who had severed ties with the Republicans. Forten, however, could offer only praise for the party's previous record, and yet he had to concede publicly that blacks had not been awarded a fair share of the political spoils. But as long as the party continued to support the principle of equal rights for all, he insisted, blacks should ignore "the small question of office" and work toward that end. The meeting prepared the ground for the ERL's annual gathering in Pittsburgh. In an apparent effort to defuse a potentially explosive situation, the meeting devoted most of its time to questions on which there was some consensus. Its resolutions were largely concerned with continued discrimination in education and had little to do with traditional political issues. But try as it might, the ERL could not avoid divisiveness, a situation its opponents fostered. A delegation from Pittsburgh forced the league to reject its credentials when it refused to take the oath of loyalty to the Republican party.[126]

That rejection set the stage for the PL organizational meeting a week later. Although its officers were drawn equally from the western, central, and eastern parts of the state, its leadership was dominated by two Harrisburg residents, Day and C. M. Brown. Day wrote its first major public address, which condemned the ERL for expelling those who refused to take the pledge. Even if all blacks were attached to the Republican party, the address questioned the wisdom of blindly endorsing the defections that had "been grievous to us for several years past." The PL's first convention was scheduled for Pittsburgh in October, a few weeks before the elections.[127]

125. Philadelphia *Inquirer*, August 16, 1876; Evans, *Pennsylvania Politics*, 283–84; *Telegraph*, September 4, 19, 20, 23, 25, 1878; *Patriot*, September 3, 6, 23, 1878.
126. Pittsburgh *Daily Commercial*, August 21, 22, 2, 1878; Pittsburgh *Post*, August 21, 2, 3, 1878.
127. Pittsburgh *Post*, August 30, 31, 1878.

Both organizations held a series of meetings leading up to the Pittsburgh convention, for success could seriously influence the choice blacks made in November. At Lancaster, for example, Forten denounced the PL, arguing that his organization was forced to include the pledge in its constitution only after some members had begun "to stray from the Republican household and follow false gods." The Republican party, he boldly asserted, was "the grandest and noblest political organization" the world had ever known. A few hours later, it was Day's turn to address a People's League meeting. The new league, he said, was the only means of freeing blacks from the tyranny of a handful of people in the ERL. Later, in Marietta, Day took the differences between the two organizations a stage further by publicly announcing his support for the Democrats.[128] Surely that was not the action of a "free republican." Like so many others who had broken with the Republicans, Day, especially since his recent expulsion from the Laboring Men's Club, had few alternatives but to change his party allegiance.

The ERL had no intention of allowing its opponents an untroubled convention. Many of its members attended, prepared to do battle on the slightest pretext. Day countered by attempting to limit possible conflict. A relatively peaceful gathering would enhance their image and bring them added support; a chaotic meeting would work to their disadvantage. Evidently Day did manage to extract a promise that political issues would be avoided and that issues of larger concern to blacks would be addressed. The absurdity of the compromise betrayed the PL's insecurity, and confirmed suspicions that Day was desperately trying to keep the situation under control. The agreement survived disputes over the election of a committee to issue a public address. Day moved that the committee be named by C. M. Brown, the convention's president, but opponents insisted that it be elected from the floor. As a compromise, the committee had members from both sides of the aisle. Resolutions for improving educational facilities and opportunities for black children were quickly passed without dissent. Just when it appeared that the agreement would hold, George Galbraith, Day's former co-worker, submitted a pro-Republican resolution. Galbraith's refusal to honor the compromise shattered the meeting's delicate harmony. Threats were hurled as opposing factions tried to silence one another, and Galbraith had to be rescued by friends. Although peace was restored, policemen in the hall could not guarantee personal safety. The wording of the address submitted to the convention only added fuel to the fire. Al-

128. Lancaster *New Era*, September 27, 1878; *Patriot*, October 7, 1, 1878.

though the original condemnation of the ERL was softened, the address repeated the claim that blacks were being terrorized by a cabal of black figures who demanded party fealty. More important, Galbraith's resolution provided Democratic supporters with an opportunity to submit a counterproposal favoring their party. On the second day of the convention, Younger castigated the compromise tone of the address, and he recommended an endorsement of the Democratic party. Pandemonium followed as opponents jockeyed for control of the stage. Again the police were forced to intervene but could do little to stop the free-for-all. In the mad scramble, the address disappeared, stolen, supporters of the PL insisted, by their opponents. Faced with utter turmoil and the threat of open violence, Brown adjourned the convention.[129]

Back in Harrisburg, Day unleashed a torrent of abuse against the "pimps and valets" of Republicans who secretly orchestrated the disruption of the convention. Pittsburgh, he wrote, was scraped "for filthy material to attempt the degrading, murderous work." For the first time, Republican leaders condoned the use of "bullies, state prison birds, bummers, and cut-throats" to break up a black convention. The spectacle of blacks attacking one another was reprehensible and due entirely to Galbraith's flagrant disregard of the agreement to which he had been a party. Galbraith dismissed Day's accusation as utter nonsense. He denied making any compact and ridiculed Day's assertion that the convention was nonpartisan. Day, he asserted, was using his "Three Party Act" to hide "his own duplicity and triple dealing." Stung by Galbraith's accusation, Day resorted to sarcasm. He insisted categorically that Galbraith had broken the pledge not to introduce political resolutions, and he questioned whether Galbraith was even capable of writing the response to his original letter. Day concluded that "it is rather more insolent than he usually is, and is therefore beneath any further notice." Day could haughtily withdraw from the dispute with Galbraith, but he could not ignore the fact that his plans had sadly misfired. The debacle in Pittsburgh had successfully nipped the PL in the bud.[130]

Defeated in his efforts to create an alternative organization, Day had no recourse but to throw in with the Democrats. It must have been a bitter pill to swallow—until then, Day's Republican credentials had been impeccable. Ironically, this new affiliation can only be explained in terms of Republican failures, not new and positive approaches to blacks by Democrats. Day harked back to Gaitor's defeat as symptomatic of Republican dissembling and recounted

129. Pittsburgh *Daily Commercial*, October 16, 17, 1878; Pittsburgh *Post*, October 16, 17, 18, 1878; *Telegraph*, October 17, 1878.
130. *Patriot*, October 19, 18, 1878; *Telegraph*, October 18, 1878.

Senator Don Cameron's questioning Harrison Allen about Day's appointment. In recognizing Day, Cameron supposedly argued, the party was recognizing the claims of other blacks. Most of the jobs proffered by Republicans, Day wrote, were an insult to black intelligence and an affront to their support for the party. It was time for blacks to "assert their power" by showing the Republicans how much they depended on black votes. Day's newfound popularity among Democrats must have disturbed him. Their cheers and invitations to lecture throughout central Pennsylvania were not signs of greater support for black interests. Splitting the black vote would improve the party's electoral fortunes, and having one of the state's premier black figures in their corner improved those chances immeasurably. But Day's departure failed to turn enough blacks away from the Republican party. In the end, the *Telegraph* could claim with some justification that the "colored men of the city" were deserving of "commendation for their faithful adherence to the Republican party," despite the efforts of people such as Day who had sold their souls and destroyed their reputations for a mess of Democratic pottage.[131]

Now that he had abandoned the party, Day's earlier concerns about blacks being treated like pariahs by Republicans were realized. Harrisburg was, after all, a Republican-controlled city in the 1870s, and even his position on the school board was not sufficient cushion against political isolation. His rather pompous claims that the days of the ERL were numbered and its burial imminent were totally misplaced. The league did survive after significant reforms. The same could not be said for those blacks who dared to challenge Republican hegemony in the city. But the party had to adopt a more cautious approach toward Day if only because his defection did little damage to his reputation in the black community. Rather than openly denounce him, Republicans chose to heap scorn and ridicule on his association with the Democrats. Any other policy might alienate those who would not countenance open denunciations of one of their leading citizens. "O tempora, O mores" was the way the *Telegraph* greeted Day's election as sergeant at arms at the Democratic state convention in July, 1879. When Cumberland Democrats organized a picnic and invited Day, the *Telegraph*'s reporter could not control his sense of the absurd. Here was a picnic attended by Day, a former Republican; and by William Wallace and Samival Randall, who were both competitors for the party's leadership. "William Howard O'Day," a member of the Irish-dominated Democratic party,

131. *Telegraph*, November 8, October 29, 1878; *Patriot*, October 28, November 2, 4, 1878.

wandered aimlessly "all by himself, his hands in his pockets, and nobody taking any notice of him or his swallow-tail coat. The committee thought he looked hungry and slily slipped him a dinner ticket, but the Hon. W. O'H. D. was crowded out from the first table, the unterrified not relishing the idea of sitting at meat with him, and some who were acquainted with him wanted to know 'What the divil does the dom naygur want here, onyhow?' He finally got a square meal in front of his swallow-tail, but they didn't ask him to speak, all the same."[132]

Such sarcasm had little effect on Day's reputation in the black community. He continued to be the dominant figure in all matters of interest to blacks other than political issues. In late 1879, for instance, he was named president of the Citizens Association, a black organization formed to participate in the welcoming ceremony for President Grant. Although it is true that few of those who participated in the bitter feud over the PL actually belonged to the association, most of its members were avowed Republicans. Yet they continued to work together and to provide some semblance of cohesiveness to the community in the wake of the PL debacle. As Day said on the eve of the 1880 elections, when he was actively canvassing for the Democrats, "the mass of the colored men of Harrisburg and I . . . are personal friends, for they know my devotion to their best interests. They come to me for advice; we consult together; they talk pleasantries and even politics with me, without the bitterness." It is likely that Day viewed the association as an alternative power base. But its brief history suggests that it generally followed a nonpartisan line. It organized an Emancipation Proclamation celebration in early 1880, at which Day and the Republican mayor spoke, and a Fifteenth Amendment celebration two months later. At the latter event, most of the leading participants were Republicans as well as active members of the ERL and the recently formed Union Club, a city organization of black Republicans.[133]

Divisions did exist, however, on the best means of promoting black political interests. Day worked for Democratic candidates, but most blacks continued to support the Republicans. The Union League, formed in August, 1880, was yet another attempt by black Republicans to establish a centralized city organization capable of bringing out the black vote on election day and acting as the principal spokesman for the black community. It was also closely affiliated with the ERL, which still backed the Republican party. In response to Day and

132. *Telegraph*, September 29, July 16, 21, August 20, 22, September 26, 27, 1879.
133. *Ibid.*, March 31, April 6, January 14, 3, 1880, December 5, 1879; *Patriot*, October 15, 1880.

others who condemned Republicans for ignoring blacks' contributions to the party, the ERL's annual meeting commended the party for its appointing blacks to offices in Harrisburg and Pittsburgh. The fact that these were minor offices mattered little; the party's intentions were good. However, the Union League's threat to drive Democrats into the "last ditch again and all those who sympathize with them" was nothing but blustering. As long as the Republicans refused to afford blacks a fair share of the spoils, Day could claim, as he did throughout the 1880 campaign, that such threats were disingenuous. The "republican party of ten years ago was not the republican party of today," he told a political rally in Steelton. The "negro was as good as a white man with the republicans if he behaved himself, but now he is either made a serf or a 'hewer of wood and a drawer of water.'" Blacks were simply being exploited by white Republicans for political reasons. A vote for the Democrats, he argued, would improve the bargaining strength of blacks with both parties. The election results brought Day and his Democratic allies little satisfaction, and to many the Republicans appeared invincible in Pennsylvania.[134]

These setbacks had little effect on Day's reputation in Harrisburg. Only two months after the Republican victory in the presidential elections, which Day had so actively opposed, he was renominated for the school board by Republicans in the first and second precincts and by Democrats from the first precinct of the eighth ward. Ironically, he lost the Democratic primary and won the Republican and defeated his Democratic opponent by 35 votes, a relatively comfortable margin in an election dominated by the Republican party.[135] His reelection put Day in something of a quandary. The party for which he, despite ridicule, had done so much had refused to endorse him, yet the party he had abandoned had nominated him and ensured his election. His victory in the February elections marks Day's slow return to the Republican fold. Unfortunately it coincided with the emergence of the Independent movement and increasing division within the party. Here again Day found himself swimming against a strong current of discontent among blacks. While he was contemplating a return to the party, there were those who were moving in the other direction because Republicans refused to recognize black stalwarts' contributions. Increasing black representation in party councils, the *Telegraph* editorialized, would only widen discord. All blacks could do was to follow the old course and,

134. *Telegraph*, November 3, August 4, 7, 13, July 5, 10, 26, 1880; *Patriot*, October 8, 2, 6, 1880; Altoona *Tribune*, August 9, 1880.
135. *Telegraph*, February 16, 17, January 24, 28, 31, 1881.

like the Pennsylvania State League (PSL), successor to the ERL, continue to support the party while calling for some gesture in recognition of black allegiance.[136]

These were the difficult and unfortunate circumstances under which Day returned to the Republican party and the mainstream of black political organizations in the state. In August, 1882, he was named a Harrisburg delegate to the annual convention of the PSL. But there were some who were understandably reluctant to welcome him back. Not only had he attempted to discredit the ERL and create a rival organization in 1878, but he had actively worked for the Democrats, the sworn enemy of black people. Such a person, said Johnstown delegate H. P. Derrit, should not be pardoned and allowed to participate in the league's affairs. But Day had his defenders, who argued that he was contrite, recognized past errors, and committed himself to work for the Republican party and the election of General James Beaver as governor. Day did not speak in his own defense, but later in a vote of thanks to Beaver, who addressed the meeting, he announced that he would vote for "the model citizen, the Christian gentleman, the gallant soldier, General Beaver." Although the debate over his readmittance lasted well over an hour, most delegates were willing to forgive Day's temporary digression. It was better, after all, to have a man of Day's reputation working *for* the party. A unified black leadership, moreover, guaranteed greater leverage with those who dispensed jobs and influenced the selection of delegates. In spite of Day's efforts and those of the league, Beaver and the Republicans were swamped in the gubernatorial elections. The *Telegraph*'s worst fears were realized, and Day found himself on the outside again, having backed a loser in two consecutive gubernatorial elections.[137]

Rather than shelve their demand for greater representation, blacks took the opportunity of the defeat and the Independents' continued growth to reiterate their claims for greater consideration from the party. The time seemed particularly propitious. The greater the strength of the Independents, the more likely that party regulars would have to depend on a solid black vote at elections, and there were signs in early 1883 that the situation was improving in Harrisburg. By June, there were blacks in important positions—school direc-

136. *Ibid.*, February 10, July 30, August 1, 2, 1881, June 8, 1882; *Lawrence County Gazette*, August 19, 1881.
137. *Telegraph*, November 9, 6, October 23, August 16, 15, 1882; Williamsport *Gazette and Bulletin*, August 16, 1882.

tor, councilman, constable, post office employee, sanitation policeman, school principal, and two policemen. Day was also elected chairman of the Republican county convention in June. It was the first time that a black man had been elected to such a position in the state, and the Democrats could not miss the opportunity to poke fun at Day's new renown. "There have been political conventions in this city which had some funny episodes," reported the *Patriot*, "but the republican county convention of yesterday took the cake as a travesty on the putative dignity of such bodies." The "versatile politician" from the eighth ward had beaten back a challenge from "the white trash who had caught it right and left, and a number of delegates from the county were observed to mop their eyes with their bandanas." The *Patriot* gleefully manipulated the irony of a party electing a dissident to chair its convention only a few months after he had ceased supporting the opposition. Even the city's black newspaper had to temper its joy at Day's election—the question of the party's motive was understandable. James H. Howard had been insisting for some time that blacks were entitled to have delegates representing them at Republican county and state conventions. Although conceding that Day's chairmanship was some compensation for not securing a black delegate, Howard wondered if the honor "was tendered as molasses to catch flies."[138]

Howard's fears were borne out by subsequent events. Day's election was to be the highest office attained by any black in the local party. Howard's challenge to the party to reassess its policy on electing black officers and delegates was studiously ignored. "The Republicans of Dauphin county know too well that we have never had in the way of representation what we are entitled to. They must go a step further," he warned, "so that we may be assured that there are no snakes in the grass." At a time when many blacks were becoming increasingly disillusioned with Republicans, especially in light of their inactivity following the Supreme Court's decision that denied congressional power to grant or enforce civil rights in states, Howard's plea that the party "place its arms around all of its adherents, and give equal representation and equal protection" was sound advice. Rather than address these issues, the party pleaded innocent in the matter of the Supreme Court decision and, with notable insensitivity, questioned the value of the Civil Rights Act (1866). The act, the *Telegraph* believed, had done more harm than good, had "retarded civil rights by giving the most ignorant and self-important among the colored race an excuse to thrust

138. *Telegraph*, June 26, 1882, June 27, February 21, 1883; *Patriot*, June 27, 1883; *Home Journal*, June 30, 9, 1883.

themselves into social positions from which white men under similar circumstances, would very properly be ejected."[139]

The Court's decision and Republican inaction angered many blacks; some threatened to stay away from the polls in November, others contemplated joining the Democrats, and still others, like the PSL, continued their uncritical support of the party. But there were a few, like Howard, who tried to shake the party out of its lethargy by pleading for increased black representation. For six months, as mugwump sentiment gained ascendancy in the party, Howard hammered away at the Republicans. The leadership had to assure black representation on the party's central committee, not "as members at large, but as full members, and let such men be recognized as will truly represent the colored vote and who will ask for and contend for proper representation in the State Convention." A lack of black unity and the unwillingness of many capable blacks to become embroiled in party politics only added to the problem. As a result, blacks were "deprived of the enjoyment of rights . . . justly ours." But the fact remained that Republicans adamantly refused to share political power with an important segment of the party. Some were even convinced that party leaders made a "regular practice of setting up colored men as targets, simply to fire their ballots at." At the city convention in April, the party rejected Howard's nomination of Frisby Battis as a delegate to the state convention. Battis' defeat was predictable, and Howard could only lament that though Republicans were willing "to take the votes of their colored brethren it goes against the grain to give their votes to confer an honor upon a colored man." The alternative, of course, was to shift party allegiance. For the moment, at least, Howard was not willing to take that leap, but he did warn that the party was in imminent danger of losing the black vote.[140]

Howard's frustration with Republican parsimony was symptomatic of a much broader disillusionment among blacks and heralded the growth of organized black Democratic organizations. In late April, seventy-five blacks gathered in Pittsburgh at the Inter-State Convention of Colored Men of the Northern States to discuss the future in light of the recent Supreme Court decision, continued violence in the South, and their own failure to generate greater support from the Republican party for their cause. Although the meeting openly dis-

139. *Home Journal*, June 30, 1883; *State Journal*, December 22, 1883; *Telegraph*, October 18, November 3, 1883.
140. *State Journal*, April 19, 12, 5, March 8, 1, February 2, January 12, 1884, December 15, 1883; *Telegraph*, April 7, 8, 1884, November 3, 1883.

avowed party politics, it was clear to all who attended that disenchantment with the Republicans had been a major impetus to the convention. Many were also concerned that older, recognized black leaders, those so intimately involved with the Republican party and so committed to its political survival, had deliberately attempted to silence questions about the party's policies. These Young Turks could either openly switch party allegiance and embrace the Democrats, or they could declare black neutrality. W. S. Scarborough of Wilberforce University tried to sort through the dilemma facing the meeting. "The colored people," he pleaded, "cannot afford to be rash or take hasty actions. An independence movement had been suggested as a way out of the dilemma. But what does that mean? If it means action with the Democratic party," Scarborough saw little hope of success "until after the day of judgement." If, on the other hand, it meant "thinking and acting for themselves, then it will be a step in the right direction." But, he concluded, blacks still had to marshal their energies in efforts to influence the Republican party. Frederick Douglass was even more blunt: "If it is true that we want to break away from the Republican party, let us do so. If we want to affiliate with the Democrats, let us so say. If we are to form an Independent party, let us go about it and give it to the world." Douglass and Scarborough were simply forcing the hands of those who contemplated an alternative to provide justification for such action. Blacks may review Republican faults, Douglass argued, and "paint it as black as the devil, and I will show you a party blacker still." When George Downing suggested that the convention adopt a resolution condemning both parties for ignoring blacks' interests, and postponing all endorsements until after both parties' conventions, when blacks could critically appraise their intentions, he was denounced as a Democratic wolf in Republican sheep's clothing. As the convention drew to a close, the Young Turks had clearly fallen short of their objective. No one seemed willing to chart a course through the unknowns of independent black political activity.[141]

Day kept his distance from all these developments, due partly to a long illness and also, one suspects, to his increasing disenchantment with politics. He decided not to run for a third term on the school board, and he directed his energies instead to working for the AME Zion church. He was admitted officially to the Philadelphia and Baltimore Conference at its annual meeting in April, 1884, following his suspension from the Virginia Conference. In spite of

141. Pittsburgh *Commercial Gazette*, April 30, May 1, 2, 1884; Pittsburgh *Post*, April 30, May 1, 1884; *State Journal*, March 22, April 5, 26, May 3, 1884; *Telegraph*, May 3, 1884.

earlier differences with church leaders over the publication of its newspaper, the meeting called on the General Conference to name Day editor of the *Star of Zion*. There was little chance of that happening, especially since Day supported Bishop Hillery in his dispute with Bishop Hood, the church's senior bishop. According to Hood, Hillery was accused of intemperance and making immodest advances to women congregants. Hillery was cleared by the Kentucky Conference, but under church rules the chairman of the investigating committee (Hood, in this case) had the authority to appeal the decision to the General Conference. In an apparent effort to outflank Hood, Hillery charged him with maladministration and won the support of the appeals committee, which met in Philadelphia. Day acted as Hillery's counsel in Philadelphia and, in so doing, probably alienated a number of prominent bishops. Consequently, when Hillery was removed from office by the General Conference, Day found himself on the losing side, effectively destroying any chances he might have had of being named editor of the church paper.[142]

It is impossible to determine with any accuracy what caused the dispute between Day and the board of bishops. His support for Hillery, based on their long friendship, might also have had other sources as well. Hood was critical of Day's decision to devote less time to the fledgling Virginia Conference, which needed his expertise, and more to the Philadelphia and Baltimore Conference, one of the church's stronger conferences. Day had also failed to publish the minutes of the 1876 General Conference, and he had refused to hand over the manuscript minutes when ordered to by the board of bishops. Day's subsequent opposition to the church's plans to establish the Zion Hill Collegiate Institute in Pittsburgh only exacerbated the situation. Apparently, Day persuaded the governor to veto a legislative appropriation of $5,000 for the institute, arguing that the government should not condone or actively promote the establishment of a segregated college. As a result, Day was suspended from the Virginia Conference and removed as secretary-general. These differences were later reconciled, and Day resumed the office of secretary.[143]

Day's problems with the national church seem to have had little effect on his reputation in Pennsylvania. The mere fact that the Philadelphia and Baltimore Conference recommended him for the post of editor suggests either that larger internal disputes existed in the church or, more probably, that Day's standing in

142. Hood, *One Hundred Years*, 122–25; *State Journal*, October 27, December 15, 1883, May 17, 19, 1884.
143. Bradley, *History of the AME Zion Church*, II, 99–103, 150–51.

the conference was such that he could overcome any local opposition these differences may have created. There is no doubt that Day was the dominant figure at Wesley Union in Harrisburg, or that he wielded considerable influence over the other AME Zion churches in central Pennsylvania. Ever since his arrival in Harrisburg he had involved himself in the life of many of these churches, lecturing, raising money for construction, and promoting black Sunday school education. It was not surprising that the conference chose to ignore Day's disputes with the board of bishops and ask that he tour the state on behalf of its educational efforts. Starting in September, 1884, Day visited Union, Lycoming, Columbia, and Northampton counties, lecturing, preaching, and raising money "in the interest of Christian education" in Lewisburg, Milton, Watsontown, Montandon, and Bloomsburg, among other places. He held a ten days' camp meeting at Lewisburg attended by thousands, both black and white. The success of the tour was even more remarkable, since it was undertaken at the height of an election campaign.[144]

The lecture tour was part of the conference's plan to establish a Junior Biblical Institute to train church licentiates. The idea for the institute was first proposed in 1883, and since then Day had been actively involved in raising funds for its establishment. His support and work for the institute might also explain his opposition to the Zion Hill Institute. The 1884 conference named him general representative, collecting agent, and honorary secretary of its education committee with responsibility for the collection of funds and organization of the institute. Day's initial tour in September allowed the first group of students to begin their studies in February, 1885, under his tutorship. Most of the money was used to purchase books for a library. It was the duty of the AME Zion church, he insisted, to train qualified men for the pulpit, especially since other denominations were expanding educational facilities for their ministers. Day continued his fund-raising activities in 1885, appealing mainly to white denominations in central and eastern Pennsylvania for support to educate black students at Wesley Zion Institute, the denomination's college in New Bern, North Carolina. Wesley Zion Institute grew and flourished in the last years of the nineteenth century, but there is no information on the fate of the Junior Biblical Institute, not even if its efforts were incorporated into Livingstone College, the successor to Wesley Zion Institute.[145]

144. *Telegraph*, November 28, August 5, December 9, 1884; *State Journal*, November 15, July 26, August 2, December 13, 1884.
145. AME Zion Church, Philadelphia and Baltimore Conference, *Minutes, 1885* (Carlisle, Pa., n.d.), 44–45; *Telegraph*, October 20, November 18, 21, 1885; Gettysburg *Star and Sentinel*, November 17, 1885.

Day was elected presiding elder of the conference at its annual meeting in April, 1885, a fitting recognition of his contributions to the church. He played a leading role at the meeting, serving on two committees and preaching one of the annual sermons. He was also responsible for arranging a visit by a conference delegation to the White House. Although two of the denomination's leading bishops were part of the delegation, Day was named its official spokesman. The election of a Democratic president in the very year that Day had returned to the Republican fold must have caused him some discomfiture as they sat waiting for the president. His statements to President Cleveland reflected a growing spirit of black independence from and disillusionment with Republicans, but he also unmistakably indicated that for the first time since the Civil War, blacks had to depend on a Democratic president to protect their rights. The understandable uncertainty about the future was reflected in the conference's "State of the Country" report. "We need to eschew mere partisan teaching, partisan training, partisan expectation and party necessity," Day and others wrote. "We need to trust more in God and in ourselves, and less in Party and Party expediency." Where one year earlier George Downing had failed to secure a statement of independence from the conference of blacks in Pittsburgh, the election of Cleveland succeeded. Blacks were not seekers of office, nor were they politicians, Day told the president, except as "in the judgement of the powers that be [they] may be considered a portion of the body politic." Party labels mattered little, Day observed, for Cleveland was president not of a party, but of a nation, and it was their duty to work for the time when "no man in this land shall be too poor to have rights and no man too poor to be protected in them." Cleveland was courteous but made no promises, and the delegation had to be content with the president's cordial reception and the fact that the election of a Democrat had not interfered with the traditional visit to the White House when the conference met in Washington, D.C.[146]

As presiding elder, Day supervised a district including Washington, D.C.; York, Pennsylvania; Arlington, Virginia; and Montgomery County, Rockville, and Baltimore, Maryland. Fulfilling his duties involved considerable travel which tested his frail health. One year after his appointment Day was forced to relinquish his position because of poor health. But he continued to play an active role as general missionary of the conference and as a major figure in the church's efforts to promote education.[147] Despite the pressures of church re-

146. *Star of Zion*, May 15, April 24, June 3, 1885; *Telegraph*, April 18, 1885; Philadelphia and Baltimore Conference, *Minutes, 1885*, 46.
147. *Telegraph*, April 15, May 20, 22, 24, 25, 1886.

sponsibilities and recurring bouts of illness, Day tried to keep in touch with political developments in Harrisburg. Although he never regained the stature he once held among Republicans, he remained an important figure in the party, devoting most of his time to improving black representation at Republican conventions. Attaining these positions grew in importance as black influence on the party waned. The issue of black representation, in effect, became a substitute for black failure to alter Republican attitudes and policies. This failure increased frustration and quickened the pace at which black leaders crossed over to the Democrats, and that in turn stiffened Republican resistance to black demands. By late 1885, there were a number of black political organizations with varying degrees of affiliation to the Republican party. The membership of the Old Reliable Club, for instance, differed from that of the PSL, both avowedly Republican; and there were those like Day who continued to work in the party but declined to join any black political organization. Whatever their organizational affiliation, most of the leading black figures were united in their determination to gain increased representation in the party's councils. At the city and county convention in June, 1886, Day moved to have C. W. Harley, an "unflinching gentleman in his intercourse with his fellow men and a veteran soldier," elected a delegate, arguing in vain for the recognition of black rights.[148]

Having failed to impress upon the Republicans their determination to be adequately represented, a number of blacks and a handful of white supporters turned to Day as a possible independent candidate for the state house. Flattered by the call, Day astutely mulled over the request for four months before deciding against entering the race. A successful election, he responded, needed substantial sums of money, which none of his supporters could guarantee. He had only recently cleared a debt of roughly $16,000, and he had no intention of being saddled with similar burdens. Moreover, there was little evidence to suggest that an independent candidate could win in 1886. All he could do was siphon votes from the Republicans, thus ensuring a Democratic victory. Day seemed determined to give Republicans another chance. Blacks had a right to expect recognition from a Republican administration, he insisted, "not simply as messengers and watchmen, not simply as janitors, but as qualified clerks as well." Although he disclaimed any intention of drawing a color line, Day objected "to the usual setting aside of a man simply because of his color. *Let colored men have a chance.* The 'Republican' who cannot say that is *not* a Re-

148. *Telegraph*, June 15, 14, 1886, October 14, 15, 1885; Lancaster *New Era*, October 14, 1885.

publican." Relieved, the *Telegraph* praised Day's magnanimity, but offered no hope of future recognition, and a Republican victory in November produced no appreciable change in party policy.[149]

Prior to announcing his decision not to run, Day had completed a series of articles for the *Telegraph* entitled "Uncle Sam's Color-Line." There is little original in these articles, but they do give some insight into Day's thinking in this period. What concerned him vitally was the country's resistance to the equal employment of black youth. Most of this, he wrote, was directly attributable to the racism of white workers, who pressured "Christian Republican" businessmen to dismiss those blacks they had hired. Such views on the relationship between white and black labor were overly simplistic but understandable, coming from someone who placed great store in those middle-class ideals that were the foundations of Republican economic policy. In addition to his business partnership with C. M. Brown, Day had been one of the principal investors in a self-weighing and self-registering scale developed by A. B. Hanacher in 1873. Nothing is known of the scale's fate or the profitability of Day's investment, but his economic associations with leading businessmen and manufacturers, and his long opposition to working-class political organizations, suggest that ideological blinkers had narrowed his view of what caused black exclusion in Harrisburg.[150]

Interestingly enough, Day devoted considerable space in the "Uncle Sam's Color-Line" articles to a discussion of racial discrimination and segregation among Masons. His experiences with the Cuyahoga Temperance Society in Cleveland in the early 1850s still rankled, no doubt. Such discrimination violated all the tenets of Free Masonry, Day insisted. "If it be said," he wrote, "that the Grand Lodge of Pennsylvania and most of the State authorize . . . color-distinction, then we say it not only proves the universality of this color-line, but that the Grand Lodge is wrong, is violating Masonic law, is removing the ancient land-marks, and ought not to be obeyed." Until such time as white Masons recognized this fact, blacks had no alternative but to create their own independent organizations. Day was a prominent figure in the Grand United Order of Odd Fellows and a regular participant in the activities of its eastern Pennsylvania lodges. Most organized black activities in Harrisburg were conducted under the auspices of one or other of the lodges. In fact, all the city's major black figures were Masons or Odd Fellows. Day belonged to Brotherly Lodge No. 896, by far the most influential lodge in the city. He also played a

149. *Telegraph*, October 30, September 17, 1886.
150. *Ibid.*, September 8, 1883, July 31, August 21, 28, September 4, 1886.

leading role in the order's national affairs and was frequently chosen to deliver its biannual addresses. The order provided an alternative to institutional dependence for its members, and its attractiveness, one authority has argued, stemmed from "the perceived nature and impeccability of its goals, works, reputation, secrecy, status, and social power."[151]

The lodge also provided Day with a vital organizational base from which to conduct political campaigns. He would rely on it again in early 1887 when he decided to run for the school board. His desire to return to the board may even have influenced his decision not to accept the offer to run for the house. Day was nominated by the first and second precincts of the eighth ward. His only opponent in the primary was the incumbent Young, who had replaced him at the last election, but who failed to win the endorsement of the second precinct. Without unanimous party support, Young had little chance of winning the election and withdrew from the race. Young's withdrawal guaranteed Day's victory; otherwise, the recent alliance of Democrats and the Knights of Labor could have captured the seat. Many blacks viewed that alliance as a device to defeat the Republican party and reverse the few gains they had made. Here was ample proof, Day believed, that his invective against white labor was warranted. Day won handily in an election dominated by the Democrats, who gained control of the mayor's and comptroller's offices and twelve of twenty-five seats on the school board.[152]

The return to the board seemed to give Day a new lease on life. There were some issues, like the establishment of night schools, which had yet to be resolved. Day eagerly pushed for the implementation of plans already adopted by the board, and he must have felt some satisfaction when the first two schools were opened in October. The response was unanticipated, and by February the board was considering proposals for expanding available facilities to meet the rising demand. There were, however, other projects that failed to elicit any response from the board. One week after his return, Day offered a series of resolutions aimed at protecting teachers who were forced to miss work because of illness. Under this plan teachers were to be paid their full salaries minus the amount paid substitutes. But the proposals were too innovative and were tabled after cursory consideration.[153]

151. *Ibid.*, December 7, 1872, July 15, August 3, 1881, September 3, 1884, October 16, 1882, August 28, 1886, October 26, 1888; Philadelphia *Inquirer*, October 6, 1886; Loretta J. Williams, *Black Freemasonry and Middle Class Realities* (Columbia, Mo., 1980), 4.

152. *Telegraph*, January 31, February 5, 16, 17, 1887.

153. *Ibid.*, June 11, July 13, October 26, 1887; Harrisburg School District, Minute Book, June, 1886–May, 1890.

In spite of his frail health and increased responsibilities on the board, Day maintained a heavy schedule of commitments. For instance, he accepted an invitation to deliver a series of emancipation celebration speeches in Gettysburg, Chambersburg, Williamsport, Lock Haven, Bellefonte, and Erie in October. He also continued to participate in the work of the church and was appointed general superintendent of the Sunday School Association and general missionary, intellectual instructor, and supervisor of missions of the Philadelphia and Baltimore Conference. All these activities, plus Day's leading role in promoting an educated ministry, particularly his work with the Junior Biblical Institute and his raising funds for students' scholarships, prompted church leaders, many of whom had been critical of his part in the Hillery affair, to nominate him for an honorary doctor of divinity degree from Livingstone College. Day received the degree during the General Conference at New Bern, North Carolina, in 1888. It was a fitting tribute, ample recognition of his labors for the church since 1866.[154]

On the eve of the award, a correspondent to the *Telegraph* observed that Day was "still one of the leaders of the people," someone who had not "lost any of his old-time power."[155] Although age had done little to cool the ardor of his oratory, many were more constrained in their assessment. To some, he was a disappointment because he had failed to fulfill an early promise of greatness. Day seemed to possess all the qualities for leadership—he was well educated, urbane, a gifted orator, and an indefatigable worker. He nevertheless remained on the periphery of black leadership. This could be attributable in part to his wanderlust, the ease with which he moved from one occupation to another, never staying long enough to record any major successes. To be sure, he was no different, on this score, from many of his contemporaries, equally gifted men, who also failed to establish an abiding reputation in their lifetimes. But Day's shortcomings were also the result of a conscious decision to try his hand at professions for which he considered himself eminently qualified and which white America, in its arrogance, considered beyond black capabilities. Day chose to work in Harrisburg rather than a major city, and this too must have affected his chances for achieving national stature. Yet wherever he went, he struggled in the interest of his people, never reluctant to condemn those who deliberately placed stumbling blocks in the way of progress. This is why he left the Republicans in 1878, and why even after he returned, he was never fully rehabilitated. Although he would continue to support the party's candidates

154. *Telegraph*, May 4, 5, 8, 25, April 26, 1888, October 22, 5, 26, 1887.
155. *Ibid.*, June 13, 1888.

and run for office under its banner, the fact that Republicans continued to give scant consideration to black demands militated against Day's being considered again the dominant black Republican in central Pennsylvania.

The presidential election of 1888 underscored the nature of this new relationship between Day and Pennsylvania Republicans. Gone were the days when he was commissioned to canvass the state for the party. Now he simply limited himself to periodic appearances and then only if they did not involve special arrangements. As election day approached, Republicans grew increasingly restless over Democratic advances among blacks especially in pivotal states like Pennsylvania. The Democratic State Colored League, led by William Still and his son R. G. Still, William Battis, and James H. Howard of Harrisburg, and G. G. Anderson and W. S. Brown of Allegheny City, provided an organized alternative to those who continued to insist on toeing the old line. Republicans, they argued with some success, had become the party of capital, of "combines and trusts, which rob the laborers and enable men to become millionaires in an hour, in a day." Although efforts to organize a national black Democratic association collapsed in Indianapolis in July, it was obvious to most Republicans who took time to examine the facts that the Democrats could win sufficient votes in November to tip the scales in favor of Cleveland. Some in the party tried unsuccessfully to involve Day in the elections, since they were aware that his active endorsement would offset Democratic gains. Ever since the national Republican convention, for instance, friends in western Pennsylvania had repeatedly invited him to lecture. Yet he consented only during a visit to Mount Pleasant after he attended the Allegheny Conference of the AME Zion church. He also spoke for the party when he attended the semi-annual meeting of the board of bishops in Asheville, North Carolina, in October. That was the extent of his involvement with the party.[156]

Sometime in 1888, Day decided to dedicate most of his time to the school board and the church. He was by the end of the 1880s one of the board's elder statesmen, and his honorary degree undoubtedly enhanced his stature. He delivered the keynote address at the commencement exercises of the boys' high school, in June, 1888. The occasion allowed Day to express his position on the merits of the high school (the "people's college," he called it), which belonged to the people and was established for their benefit. Its importance lay not in any claim to aristocratic distinction, but in its curriculum and the "usefulness with which it was intended to serve the whole people, high or low, rich or poor, in

156. *Ibid.*, October 9, September 17, July 16, 26, 27, August 25, 1888; *Patriot*, October 20, 6, 21, 22, 1888.

the graded and necessary preparation for an American's duties." Expanding on this theme some years later, Day maintained that in order to be most effective and have the greatest utility, high schools must open their doors to everyone without regard to social standing. "Enter these portals in the name of God and country and justice and liberty and equality," he pleaded with graduating students, "no clogs in your limbs, no fetters on your brain . . . through the mist and dark of this hour to the sun-lit plains above you." Day also worked tirelessly to improve facilities and promote literacy. He was an avid supporter of the public library system and led efforts to establish a library at Lincoln, one of the city's predominantly black grammar schools. Concerts were organized by the community, with the proceeds going toward the purchase of books for the school library.[157]

The Biblical Institute continued to operate under Day's supervision in Harrisburg, though there is no evidence that plans for a permanent establishment were ever realized. Most of those who completed the course of study did so under his guidance. His dedication to the church was unquestionable. Whenever unexpected problems arose, Day volunteered his services, temporarily filling vacancies, for example, on occasions when ministers were unable to meet their commitments. In addition to being secretary-general, he also served as secretary of the General Board of Home and Foreign Missions. But Day's relationship with colleagues was subject to periodic, angry disagreements, which appear trivial from this distance. There is little doubt that he held many of the church's leaders in contempt for what he considered unacceptable inadequacies. Never one to brook much opposition to his views, Day demonstrated an extraordinary insensitivity, responding to criticism in unjustifiably harsh tones. Such aloofness and high-handedness angered many and only increased the frequency of disputes. When the address he had written for the board of bishops to present to President Harrison was altered and published in the *Star of Zion* in 1890, Day rather haughtily announced that it was not his work and that the writer clearly suffered from "*cacoethes scribendi*, OR DIARRHEA OF WORDS," an affliction he had never contracted. Such rhetoric made few friends. Yet there were times when Day could be accommodating in the midst of heated disputes—though it was he who chose the grounds on which to be magnanimous.[158]

157. *Telegraph*, March 2, 15, December 28, 1889, June 11, 1892, June 20, 1888; Harrisburg School District, Minute Book, June, 1886–May, 1890.
158. *Telegraph*, March 29, 13, May 22, 1889, April 19, October 9, 1890; Huntingdon *Globe*, March 14, 1889; AME Zion Church, Philadelphia and Baltimore Conference, *Minutes, 1890* (N.p., n.d.), 54; *Star of Zion*, January 2, October 30, 1890.

This attitude seriously affected Day's chances of becoming a bishop. Although his name was regularly submitted to the quadrennial conferences that elected bishops, Day could never muster more than a handful of votes. It is likely that none of the bishops who dominated church conferences relished the thought of having Day as a colleague. His best chance came in 1892, during the General Conference in Pittsburgh, which one surprised local reporter described as containing all the fury and blustering of a political convention and little of the staid synodical gathering. In the final tally, Day received only 1 vote, whereas there were 129 votes for the leading candidate. His election to a third term as secretary-general, at an increased salary, must have softened the blow of being rejected.[159]

In 1891, Day was unanimously elected president of the school board to complete the unexpired term of the late George Nelson Fry. Earlier he had been named president *pro tem* for two months during the illness of the previous incumbent. Day's first major duty was to lay the cornerstone for the new high school, the building of which he had actively promoted since his election to the board. The board made some significant decisions during Day's tenure, the most important of which was to provide free textbooks to all students. This policy, supporters argued, would greatly facilitate free education and would encourage higher levels of attendance. Day was also elected president of the Dauphin County Directors' Association, a pressure group of school directors, formed in 1889. He served in this capacity until 1895 and was instrumental in the growth of the organization, which, one report observed, did so "much for the improvement of the schools and the advancement of the cause of education in the county."[160]

The success with which Day ran the board prompted W. H. Middleton to nominate him for a full term in June, 1892. Middleton praised Day as "a model presiding officer," insisting that "there was never a more able president of this Board." The unanimous election was a fitting recognition of years of service to the city and a thoroughly uncharacteristic tribute to a black man by his white colleagues. No other city would rise to comparable heights in Day's lifetime. Blacks would have to wait until the advent of the civil rights movement in the middle of the twentieth century to gain similar recognition. Day was well aware

159. Pittsburgh *Times*, May 23, 1892; Pittsburgh *Post*, May 5, 7, 10, 13, 24, 1892; *Star of Zion*, May 12, 19, 26, 1892, July 24, 31, 1885; *Telegraph*, May 18, 20, 21, 25, 1892.

160. Harrisburg School District, Minute Books, June, 1890–November, 1893, and June, 1886–May, 1890; *Telegraph*, March 8, September 2, October 4, 1890, January 1, February 13, April 30, May 6, 7, 1892, November 15, 1894; *Pennsylvania School Journal*, April, 1893.

of the significance of his election. "You emphasize most fully," he told his colleagues, "that in your opinion the accidents of birth or circumstances are matters over which a man can have no control, amounts to nothing when considering the interest of thousands of children committed to your care for tuition and training in the public schools." He took the opportunity to relate the case of a low-born clerk—an obvious personal analogy—who was versed in the classics and science and yet was rejected because of his social status. "In English his style was so superior, that he was first in his class, but because he was a clerk and because he earned his living by work, and obeyed the Divine injunction to man to toil, he could not graduate with his honors, he could never, in that condition of things, live down the fact wrought into the mental caliber of the community, that because he was not one of the favored ones, and was a clerk, he could never expect to succeed." At last the clerk had found an oasis of reason, Day implied, in a desert of prejudice. The disappointment of not going to Williams College, the riots that threatened his family, Ohio's refusal to give blacks the vote, America's persistent denial of black equality, all of these burdens of race were lifted ever so slightly by this small but significant recognition of black capabilities. The son of a black sailmaker had risen, through his own exertion, to the eminence of president of the board, exactly when America seemed determined to deny blacks all their rights by first denying their humanity. Blacks were proud of Day's accomplishments but were not lulled into believing that white America's attitudes were therefore going to change.[161]

As president, Day chaired all meetings, determined the composition of standing committees, and represented the board at public functions. His final duty as president was the dedication of the high school in June, 1893. But most of the president's work was more mundane and involved a great deal of political maneuvering. The selection of textbooks, for example, sometimes generated considerable discussion whenever special interest groups felt slighted. The adoption of Pleam's *Book of Opening Exercises* produced a storm of protest. At public meetings the book was condemned as "the thin edge of the entering wedge driven by the Roman Catholics to get the Bible out of the schools." Assurances from the board that it was meant to supplement not replace the Bible proved unacceptable. Local "patriotic orders" petitioned the board for reconsideration. A motion to reconsider failed by the narrowest of margins, and the board was forced to expend time and energy in subsequent weeks defending its

161. *Telegraph*, June 11, 7, 1, 1892; Harrisburg School District, Minute Book, June, 1890–November, 1893.

policies. Day thoroughly enjoyed his year in office and the opportunity it gave him to work with directors and presidents from other cities. Why he was not reelected remains something of a mystery; past presidents had served more than one term. It is possible that Day declined reelection, but this is speculation. According to one observer, Day presided over the board with "fairness and dignity," and his knowledge of parliamentary rules greatly facilitated its operations.[162]

Day was elected to two additional terms following the expiration of his presidency in 1893. Such was his reputation in the eighth ward that no one considered contesting the seat. He was the only candidate for the board from either party to run unopposed in 1893. Yet he continued to keep his distance from black political organizations and only involved himself periodically in local Republican politics. Neither hectoring nor beseeching produced results for blacks, who with rare exceptions found themselves excluded from party councils. Day was regularly elected an eighth-ward delegate to the party's city and county conventions, where he worked for increased black representation. He promoted George Galbraith's candidacy for county auditor in 1890, arguing unsuccessfully that "colored men have not had recognition in proportion to their fealty to the party." Two years later, Norris H. Layton of Harrisburg pleaded with the state convention to elect Day a delegate to the national convention. Thirty-five thousand black voters, Layton said, were looking to the party for some gesture of recognition. Hiding behind the niceties of parliamentary procedure, the chairman avoided the issue by ruling Layton out of order. There is no evidence that Day encouraged these efforts. He had apparently resigned himself to the inescapable fact that Pennsylvania Republicans had no intention of recognizing the contributions of black supporters.[163]

There were few alternatives available to blacks at this juncture. Not only were Republicans totally intransigent, but Democrats made no meaningful gestures in their direction. The formation of the State Colored League, the Democratic organization headed by Still and Howard, though an obvious nuisance, failed either to elicit more favorable responses from Republicans or, for that matter, frighten them into showing more flexibility. To complicate matters further, other black organizations, like the state Afro-American League, spent

162. *Telegraph*, June 11, 5, July 1, August 6, 16, September 3, 8, November 17, 1892; Harrisburg School District, Minute Book, June, 1890–November, 1893.
163. Harrisburg *Times*, quoted in *Star of Zion*, January 22, 1891; *Telegraph*, April 20, 1892, August 11, 12, 27, 1890, August 8, 1892, January 2, February 22, 1893; Harrisburg School District, Minute Book, 1893–1897.

an inordinate amount of energy on internal squabbles as individuals vied for position. The bickering was so debilitating that the Republican national office simply ignored the state league and imperiously named Alderman J. B. Raymond of Altoona to head the election campaign among blacks in 1896. The decision angered league leaders, many of whom refused to work with Raymond. But their weakness afforded few alternatives other than sitting out the election, which many were unwilling to do. Their position was made even more untenable when black regulars endorsed Raymond's election. For the first time in years, Day joined the fray, but even here he was being consistent, choosing to remain within the party rather than trying to influence it from without.[164]

Day devoted most of his last years to the church and the improvement of education as he retreated from political involvement. But his work was frequently interrupted by recurring illness, which on more than one occasion threatened his life. In August, 1895, for instance, he suffered a stroke and partial paralysis and he had to curtail his activities for almost a year. But he still attended to his duties at the board whenever he could. Two major issues faced the board in the 1890s—the implementation of compulsory-attendance laws and, less important, the need to establish an equitable system of teacher selection. Compulsory attendance, though laudable and generally supported by all members of the board, posed a serious problem in a city where schools were already overcrowded. In some primary schools, in fact, students were forced to sit on the floor. The board made every effort to ease the situation by expanding existing facilities or building new ones. Four new schools were built in 1896, including the Wickersham School in the eighth ward. Yet attendance did not markedly increase. Under the law, all children between the ages of eight and thirteen were obliged to attend school, and precinct assessors would compile a final tabulation. As it turned out, assessors were unable to provide reliable figures consistently. When the tally was accurate, though, the board had to deal with parents who refused to send their children to school. Some thought that those parents should be imprisoned, but others prevailed and the board adopted a policy that students who were consistently absent had to pass an examination before being readmitted. Although there were some successes, certain areas of the city remained largely untouched by the law. The eighth ward had one of the highest attendance figures—of 338 children, only 2 were not attending classes regularly. Clearly, Day's influence on his constituency was

164. *Telegraph*, October 26, 22, 19, 15, September 16, 1896, October 29, 13, 1894; *Patriot*, October 12, 1896, August 22, 1890; John E. Bodnar, "Peter C. Blackwell and the Negro Community of Steelton, 1880–1920," *Pennsylvania Magazine of History and Biography*, XCVII (1973), 206.

considerable. Although attendance did increase during his tenure, the problem was not resolved until well into the twentieth century.[165]

Day avoided becoming embroiled in disputes surrounding the board's policy of competitive examinations for teachers. When he was first elected in 1878, he and the board spent considerable time on selecting and dismissing teachers. Primary school teachers were usually chosen from among the best graduates of the high school and were generally sponsored by the board member from their constituency. This mutual understanding, however, did not exist when it came to dismissing a teacher or headmaster. Open competitive examinations, a policy adopted to alleviate this problem, operated adequately until some on the board moved for reversal. An indignant public condemned these new developments and called for a return to free competitive examinations. "Our public schools must be preserved from the blight of sectarian or political influence of any kind," one meeting demanded. "No secret or death-bound order, Protestant or Catholic, has the right to enter our schools and proscribe men and women of any religion, any faith, or any race or form of belief."[166]

Although Day avidly supported competitive examinations as the most efficient means of selecting teachers, he stayed clear of the controversy, choosing to devote his time to the work of the school directors' organization. Even after he relinquished the presidency of the Dauphin County Directors' Association in 1895, he remained an active member of the state organization. In early 1899 he was asked by the board and the association to address the association's annual convention on the importance of organizing school libraries. Members recalled his success in the eighth-ward schools and in raising money to purchase books for the Junior Biblical Institute and Livingstone College. The library act of 1895 stimulated community interest in establishing local public libraries, and Day seized the opportunity to exploit this enthusiasm to rally support for expanding educational opportunities. School libraries had become more than just the repositories of textbooks, he told the meeting. Many books were taken home by students and "very honestly and earnestly studied by other members of the family, sometimes the whole family associating at specified times to listen to the reading aloud by the pupil or some one else." That increased community support facilitated the work of school directors. "The more the work for the schools is sustained by the community," he concluded, "the more effective our

165. *Telegraph*, July 29, December 23, 1897, October 7, June 20, May 28, 30, January 3, 1896, September 17, August 2, 1895; *Star of Zion*, May 20, August 12, 1897; *Pennsylvania School Journal*, July, 1896; AME Zion Church, General Conference, *Minutes, 1896* (Charlotte, N.C., 1896), 36.
166. *Telegraph*, September 23, 5, August 8, 1896.

school work in discipline and other ways; and the nearer, therefore, we come together in such efforts, and make our efforts, both of the community and Directors, center upon the same work for each, the better."[167]

Sometime in 1897, friends began making preparations to celebrate Day's fiftieth anniversary in education. Even since his graduation from Oberlin he had been involved in education either as a teacher, an administrator, or a school director. No other contemporary could boast of such a record, nor had any other member of the board served as long as Day. But most important, Day's election to the presidency of the board made him the preeminent black school director in the country. He was, a contemporary observed, "one of the grandest and most refined men of this country regardless of race." Such a person deserved extraordinary commendation. The local committee arranged a gala event to commemorate the anniversary. The testimonial lasted six days, and those who attended heard papers on every aspect of Day's life and work. At the end, there was a massive reception and banquet attended by local dignitaries, leaders of the church, and members of the board. By September the testimonial committee had collected $450 from all over the country. Although another bout of illness, and the hysteria over the war in Cuba, threatened to mar the occasion, the testimonial was a rousing success and a fitting tribute to an old warrior, a man, one admirer observed, "at whose feet we would gladly bow to learn lessons of wisdom."[168]

The greatest praise and recognition came from Day's colleagues in the church, many of whom were too young to know of his earlier work in behalf of the race. Despite his frail health, Day continued to receive invitations to lecture at churches throughout the country and never once missed an annual meeting of the Philadelphia and Baltimore Conference. His work as secretary-general of the General Conference, to which he was reelected in 1896 and 1900, and as secretary of the board of bishops involved traveling to North Carolina, where most of the meetings were held. Yet he ignored the hazards to his health in order to attend to the duties of his office. Day particularly enjoyed participating in the month-long centennial celebrations of the church in New York in 1896. He was the last remaining link to the fathers of the church: he had been baptized by James Varrick, its first bishop; his mother had been one of the

167. Harrisburg School District, Minute Book, 1897–1900; *Telegraph*, November 12, 1896, November 18, 1897, January 8, 1898; *Pennsylvania School Journal*, March, 1899, March, 1897.
168. *Telegraph*, April 14, 30, 1898; "Program and Hand Book of Howard Day Testimonial, 1847–1897," Dauphin County Historical Society, Harrisburg; *Star of Zion*, February 11, 1892, January 13, 6, 27, March 3, 17, 31, April 28, October 6, 1898.

church's first members; and the Days' home had been used as a temporary meeting place in the 1820s. It was left to Day to give the opening lecture on the history of the church. Many of the major black figures of the period delivered papers—Booker T. Washington, the rising star from Tuskegee; T. Thomas Fortune, the premier black editor; and P. B. S. Pinchback, former lieutenant governor of Louisiana; and others. Day could not have missed the similarity between this occasion and the conventions in the 1850s, which brought together the talent of black America. Back then their objectives were straightforward: slavery and its handmaiden, discrimination, had to be destroyed. Although the former had been eliminated, the latter had survived and was prospering.

But there were other, more personal regrets that weighed heavily on Day. Hidden behind his status as elder statesman, a survivor of the great antebellum struggles, was the sad recognition that he no longer played a pivotal role in the problems confronting black America. The country, many believed, had moved beyond the simple dichotomies of the antebellum period and consequently required new black leaders who could provide a remedy for American racism. There were occasions when Day roundly condemned the inefficacy of these new approaches, as he did in opposing Washington's education policy. But these were rare. Day remained an optimist, a firm believer in the ineluctable progress of history. He was fond of reminding audiences that he had lived through three eras of American history—slavery, war, and freedom—a progression that even those who hankered after the past could never reverse.[169]

Although he continued to participate in church events, regularly attending meetings, and retained the positions of general missionary, intellectual instructor at the Junior Biblical Institute, and supervisor of missions for the Philadelphia and Baltimore Conference, Day's frail health forced him to curtail many of these commitments. This is why he decided not to seek reelection to the board in 1899. After eighteen years on the board, the time had come, he told his constituents, to devote some time to writing his autobiography. Since joining the board he had witnessed substantial development and progress. No schools were now closed "against any properly behaved boy or girl, and as nearly as may be every pupil stands on a level. Rights and privileges are sacredly regarded and color is no bar to a pupil in any department of educational work of the public schools in the city of Harrisburg." A resolution

169. *Telegraph*, September 6, May 21, 1897; *Star of Zion*, September 17, October 15, 29, November 5, 1896.

adopted by the board in June captured the importance of Day's contribution to education in the city. When he first joined the board, "the question of a High School was then an idea. Since your entrance into the school work in this city many, varied and important changes have taken place, the enrollment of pupils is now near 9,000, modern school buildings have been erected including the High School building, which is a credit to the city and stands as a monument for education, its facility comparing well with the foremost institution of its kind in the country. You have done your part in this important and noble work, and deserve the acknowledgement and endorsement from your compeers in the Harrisburg School Board."[170]

Day had done more than just his part in promoting education in the city; he was a dominant figure, an innovator and a thinker. Few of his colleagues would retire from the board with more recognized accomplishments. Unfortunately, Day never completed his memoirs, for he suffered another stroke soon after his resignation. The community he had served so long was stunned but was determined to show its appreciation. Even though Day was confined to bed, they met at Wesley Union in October to celebrate his birthday and later presented him with a gold medal. It was clear to all his friends that he would not survive this recent stroke. Day died on December 2, 1900, at the age of seventy-five, after a sometimes painful illness of six months. He was buried four days later in Harrisburg's black cemetery following services at the new Wesley church, another of the projects for which he had worked so hard.[171]

Harrisburg residents of both races had long considered Day the leader of his race in the city; there were many who even placed him among the city's first men. But Day was no race leader in the mold of Martin R. Delany or Henry McNeal Turner. Nor, for that matter, did he see himself as one of the new breed of leaders, those who eschewed political involvement and sought the salvation of the race in economic and social segregation. What mattered most to Day was the belief that blacks had always been in the vanguard of movements for change in America and had contributed to the country's independence and protection. That was evidence enough of the race's worth and capabilities, its right to equal status and citizenship. Although he devoted his life to the removal of economic, social, and political inequities, Day never once demanded

170. *Telegraph*, May 28, 1898, January 2, 6, 1899, May 10, 1900; *Star of Zion*, September 30, 1897, September 1, June 9, 1898; Harrisburg School District, Minute Book, 1897–1900.
171. *Telegraph*, December 3, November 26, 20, October 2, 1900, February 22, 1899; *Pennsylvania School Journal*, January, April, 1901.

special dispensations as reparations for wrongs committed against blacks. All he asked was that America stop creating racist impediments to black progress. Treated equally, blacks would progress as any other race.

Day clearly was living proof of black potential. He was, one observer wrote in 1865, "a fine specimen of what a colored man can be made by culture and education." Not all blacks would attain comparable levels, but once unfettered from slavery, they had shown remarkable progress and potential in just three decades. By the century's end, they were faced with a more menacing form of oppression, a new and more subtle impediment to progress, which necessitated, Day believed, heightened forms of resistance. That included political agitation, not the abnegation of one's constitutional right to participate in and perhaps influence the system. The fact that Day lived to see a reversal of gains made during Reconstruction and increased black exclusion did not diminish his faith in the efficacy of this principle. The race's future also necessitated the creation and survival of black institutions, the links that bound the black community. Churches, Masonic orders, and other societies were all indispensable, and Day actively promoted them. The progress of the race, he once wrote, was embodied in the success of the church, which had also "risen from the discomfort of poverty and their enforced condition; risen from the clutches of the mob which sought their harmless lives; risen from the ashes of their dwellings and the embers of their churches fired by the torch of the incendiary; risen from their Golgotha and their Calvary of suffering to respectability and recognition and power, over the law and by the law." Education, the vehicle for the creation of cultured men, would ensure and facilitate this progress. Day's record as an educator is unmatched by any of his contemporaries. The essence of his life is embodied in one of his many eulogistic poems:

> Forward
> Why not march on?—Why not reap the fields
> Of harvest from the seed now sown today,
> And reaching heaven's gate, lay down her load
> And say, "Here, Lord, the sheaves Thou gavest me."[172]

172. Colored People's Educational Monument Association, *Celebration*, 10; Hood, *One Hundred Years*, x–xi; Wheeler, *Cullings From Zion's Poets*, 126.

Conclusion

Assessing the condition of black America in 1854, Martin R. Delany observed that despite pleading, cajoling, badgering, and reasoning, America had adamantly refused to acknowledge that blacks were either citizens or freemen. The twin pillars of American oppression, slavery and discrimination, each operating relatively independently and sustaining its own institutions, had been built to deny blacks the rights and privileges granted whites. These institutions were so ingrained in the economic, social, political, and intellectual fabric of American society that blacks had little chance of effecting immediate fundamental changes, without first denying their own history and racial identity. In the spirit of 1848 and the struggle of European peoples to overthrow monarchical despotism, Delany offered a solution that entailed the systematic emigration of selected black Americans to areas where they could become part of a colored majority, areas free from the canker of slavery and racism that had destroyed the spirit of 1776. Power and freedom, he argued, only come to those who are "an essential part of the *ruling element* of the country in which they live." Blacks, he concluded, had grown tired of living on mere sufferance and were determined to forge a new and radical alternative.[1]

Although based on sophisticated reasoning, Delany's suggested solution was nothing new. Emigration had always been a clear and reasonable alternative to

1. Martin R. Delany, "The Political Destiny of the Colored Race," in Sterling Stuckey (ed.), *The Ideological Origins of Black Nationalism* (Boston, 1972), 195–97.

staying in America. The appeal of his proposals had more to do with conditions in the 1850s and the fact that he envisaged the voluntary emigration of certain skilled black Americans. America seemed poised on the brink of disaster, driven, many believed, by forces beyond its control. How else could one explain the insanity of the Fugitive Slave Law or even the Kansas-Nebraska Act, northern concessions to southern slavery? In every dispute between the "great political parties," Augustus Washington, the Hartford daguerreotypist, wrote in 1851, blacks had been sacrificed. The time had come for blacks to mark out an independent course and become architects of their own fortunes, for "neither Colonizationists or Abolitionists have the power or the will to admit us to any honorable or profitable means of subsistence in this country." Unless blacks could force emancipation and "then the perfect social and political equality of the races, human nature, human pride and passions, would not allow the Americans to acknowledge the equality and inalienable rights of those who had been their slaves." Unlike Delany, Washington saw the independent course of action as eschewing the formation of specific organizations and promoting in-dividual initiative.[2]

Delany and Washington represented two wings of the same expatriation movement. The "Children of Sisyphus," in Orlando Patterson's phrase, had toiled for far too long in a system that simply refused to recognize their talents or grant them their rights. Those who thought otherwise were deceiving the people, Washington believed, by "clinging to long cherished prejudices, and fostering hopes that can never be realized." But emigration had vast implica-tions for the future of black Americans, opponents insisted. It assumed that blacks had no future in America, the country of their birth, one they had done so much to cultivate and defend. In so doing, advocates of expatriation unwit-tingly gave ammunition to those racists who believed that America was a coun-try created by whites for whites. Ever since the emergence of organized protest against the American Colonization Society, blacks had insisted that America was their country: "Here we were born—here bred—here are our earliest and most pleasant associations—here is all that binds man to earth, and makes life valuable. And we consider every colored man who allows himself to be colo-nized in Africa, or elsewhere, a traitor to our cause."[3] Others were less strident, but such views were a fair representation of black sentiment in the antebellum period.

2. Washington quoted in *African Repository*, September, 1851.
3. *Ibid.*; William Lloyd Garrison, *Thoughts on African Colonization* (1831; rpr. New York, 1969), Pt. II, p. 35.

The country's intransigence in the face of indisputable historical evidence could not mask blacks' significant role in America's defense and development, and if for no other reason, they were therefore entitled to all the privileges of full citizenship. Such intransigence had to be openly challenged and the country shamed back to first principles, to "first bloodshed," in Day's words. The contributions of such martyrs and veterans of America's wars as Crispus Attucks, John Day, John B. Vashon, and the host of blacks who defended New Orleans against British attack could never be denied or allowed to go unheralded. Thus Day organized the Cleveland celebrations in their honor and William C. Nell produced a history of that involvement. Blacks, Day told the Border State Convention in 1868, were "enrolled, enlisted and marched in solid column in the wars of the Revolution and helped equally with the white man to redeem this country and make it the 'land of the free and the home of the brave.' So in the war of 1812 and 1815. It was no new born zeal that led the colored men down into the breach in the last war. It was their interest in the interest of the Government. Braver men never went to battle, and at Fort Wagner they threw their bodies against the flagstaff to keep the stars and stripes from falling."[4]

This sense of responsibility and loyalty never muted black condemnation of American oppression and in fact imposed a certain duty to lead the assault against the bastions of slavery and discrimination. This is why Pennington insisted on taking the lead, why he demanded a return to the Negro Convention meetings in the early 1840s, why he created the Union Missionary Society, and why at the outbreak of the Civil War he, Day, and Martin maintained that blacks had to participate in the destruction of the "peculiar institution." Lincoln might temporize, but blacks were convinced beyond all doubt that it was a war of attrition against a system that was the foundation of American oppression. Black resistance had exposed the system's weaknesses, heightening the many contradictions between the principles of freedom that motivated the Founding Fathers and the compromises that recognized and permitted the continuation of slavery. The revolt of Cinque and others aboard the *Amistad*, Nat Turner's Insurrection, and the rising tide of fugitive slaves were ample evidence of black initiative and resistance. These men, Day told an Emancipation Jubilee in New York, had all "the same inspiration of liberty as Kosciusko and Washington. Nat Turner was beheaded and quartered, but the spirit of liberty in him could not be reached. It did not rest in that mangled carcass. Chains

4. Baltimore *American*, August 5, 1868.

could not bind it, for it was immaterial. Every drop of Turner's blood had since risen up instinct with life and demanded repentance and retribution."[5]

They saw no immediate discrepancy in fighting for the preservation of America while at the same time attacking its shortcomings. "Heaven forbid that we, Colored Americans, should indignantly lay a finger upon the chord of harmony of this Union," Pennington observed in 1839. "But while we love our country, and love her prosperity, we dare not love her sins and abuses."[6] Here was the subtle difference between Pennington and other anti-emigrationists and Delany. To them, slavery and discrimination generally operated in different spheres, but the latter fed upon the former. Without slavery, racial discrimination—its Jim Crow laws and traditions—would be more vulnerable. The history of the black experience in the antebellum North gave some credibility to this interpretation, for while there were lingering restrictions, there were also discernible improvements. Hence Pennington's rather roseate view of black progress at the 1843 World Anti Slavery Convention. There was indisputable evidence, he maintained, that blacks had progressed, as had American society since the mid eighteenth century. His life history was evidence enough of both black potential and progress.

Here was the law of progress at work. With Saint-Simon, Fourier, Comte, and others, Pennington insisted that man was basically good and, once freed from unnecessary restrictions, would turn away from oppression and hate. None of the people discussed in these essays would have questioned the merits of Comte's observation: "To me it appears that amelioration is as unquestionable as the development from which it proceeds. . . . Taking the human race as a whole, and not any one people, it appears that human development brings after it, first in the radical condition of man, which no one disputes; and next, in his corresponding faculties, which is a view much less attended to." There might be temporary deviations, but the progress toward perfection was ineluctable, occurring incrementally over time, by what Day called "installment[s] of Good." Thus, when blacks gathered in Boston in 1861 to protest Massachusetts' participation in the peace convention and its possible support of the Crittenden Compromise, William Wells Brown counseled them to sit still, for "the law of progress shall give the black man his freedom." Such a sanguine view of the future was totally out of character. Brown and most of his contemporaries believed with Albert Brisbane, the American Fourierist, that Nature,

5. New York *Tribune,* January 5, 1864.
6. J. W. C. Pennington, *An Address Delivered at Newark, New Jersey at the First Anniversary of West Indian Emancipation, August 1, 1839* (Newark, 1839), 12.

having implanted in man an instinct for social progress that would ultimately lead to the "attainment of his Destiny," also reserved for "his intelligence the noble prerogative of hastening this progress, and of anticipating results, which, if left to the gradual movement of society would require centuries to effect."[7]

Although some progress had been made, there was still a great deal to be done. Black and white abolitionists' attacks had resulted in many cracks in the edifice of oppression. Still slavery survived and expanded. Hastening progress would require continuous assault on slavery as the foundation of the hierarchy of American oppression. Slavery, Pennington told a Leeds meeting, was "a great tree, having four enormous roots, and those roots piercing down through all its politics; another through its religion; another through all its education; and another through all its social education; and the tree spread out its branches and bore ten thousand kinds of bitter, nauseous and accursed fruit." The need to defend slavery against assaults from fugitives, abolitionists, and free blacks led to the creation of discriminatory laws and customs. This effort to ensure slavery's perpetuation depended on denying the existence of a class that was both black and free. Hence the host of such laws in the North. Yet blacks had progressed, demonstrating what Pennington called the "law of self-preservation" and, in so doing, had become the "dread of their oppressor." Blacks, Martin informed British critics of the Union, had shown unquestionable signs of progress and were, by 1863, to be found in many branches of American life from which they had been previously excluded.[8]

The discrimination against blacks in the North, Martin insisted, contravened "the spirit of Northern law and the protest of a large part of the Northern people; but [their] social, political and even religious rights are trampled underfoot in the South according to law, and with the unanimous consent of its inhabitants." Others failed to discern such niceties, however. H. Ford Douglas, like other blacks who subscribed to the Garrisonian view of the Constitution, argued that it was undeniably proslavery. Article I, Section 2, gave the South disproportionate strength in the House of Representatives through the three-fifths formula; Article I, Section 8, gave Congress power to suppress insurrections; Article I, Section 9, postponed a ban on the slave trade for

7. Comte quoted in Robert Nisbet, *History of the Idea of Progress* (New York, 1980), 255–56; Day to Salmon P. Chase, March 30, 1862, in William H. Seward Papers, Reel 11, BAP; *Liberator*, February 22, 1861; Brisbane quoted in Merle Curti, *The Growth of American Thought* (New York, 1951), 371.

8. Pennington quoted in Leeds *Mercury*, August 5, 1843; J. W. C. Pennington, *A Lecture Delivered Before the Glasgow Young Men's Christian Association and Also Before the St. George's Biblical, Literary and Scientific Institute, London* (Edinburgh, n.d.), 20; Martin quoted in Preston *Guardian*, September 5, 1863; Sheffield and Rotherham *Independent*, May 27, 1863.

twenty years; and Article IV, Section 2, provided for the return of fugitives from labor. Although the words *slaves* and *slavery* were not expressly mentioned in the Constitution, it was generally understood by James Madison and other Founding Fathers that southern interests were to be protected. Given these facts, emigrationists saw no reason to prolong their stay in America.[9]

What, then, prompted Martin and others to turn to the Constitution as the document of last resort in their effort to win freedom? Day, for instance, was convinced that H. Ford Douglas had erred in confusing construction with the Constitution itself. Although he conceded that the government and the Supreme Court were proslavery, he considered the Constitution the "foundation of American liberties." It had been drawn up to protect all men regardless of their station; justice denied one was justice denied all. As far as Pennington was concerned, the debate was largely moot, for neither the Constitution nor the Declaration of Independence created any new rights; they only reaffirmed man's natural rights. The Declaration simply recited certain truths concerning the universal rights of mankind that are "as old as creation, and consequently do not depend upon this, or any other declaration, pro or con, for their existence." Man, after all, was endowed by his Creator with certain inalienable rights, which no government had the power to limit or deny.[10]

Here was a reiteration of the theory of natural law in which the individual, not the state, is the "only ultimate reality," whose right to life, liberty, property, and the pursuit of happiness could not be alienated by the state. It was also on the whole a broad reaffirmation of Paineite republicanism. Although neither Day nor Pennington subscribed to Lysander Spooner's vision of anarchism, it is clear that they agreed with a large portion of his analysis. Laws not based on the universally recognized rights of man were arbitrary and a mere reflection of those in power. More important, Spooner argued, nothing in the Articles of Confederation or state constitutions raised slavery above "a mere abuse sustained by the common consent of the strongest party, in defiance of the avowed constitutional principles of their government." Such laws, Day argued, clearly did violence to the "innate energy" that motivated the Founding Fathers.[11]

9. London *Morning Star*, June 4, 1863; "Minutes of the State Convention of the Colored Citizens of Ohio, Convened at Columbus, January 15th, 16th, 17th, and 18th, 1851," in Philip S. Foner and George E. Walker (eds.,), *Proceedings of the Black State Conventions, 1840–1865* (2 vols., Philadelphia, 1979), I, 261; Staughton Lynd, *Class Conflict, Slavery and the United States Constitution* (Indianapolis, 1967), 159, 153–54.

10. "Minutes of the State Convention, 1851," in Foner and Walker (eds.), *Proceedings*, I, 262, 270–71; Pennington, *An Address*, 10.

11. Curti, *The Growth of American Thought*, 103–104; Eric Foner, *Politics and Ideology in the Age of the Civil War* (New York, 1980), 21; Spooner quoted in Lewis Perry, *Radical Abolitionism, Anarchy*

Pennington took the argument one step further, rejecting the notion that a benevolent God, in his infinite wisdom, could have created a world of such depravity. Did a wise Providence "who is the author both of the world and of his own word, and who beholdeth the end from the beginning, foreseeing all that should take place in the world, make a world in which evil should take place to which the word he has given has no practical application?" God could not have committeed such a serious blunder in the organization of his "moral government." The question, then, is not whether the Bible condemns slavery "without any regard to circumstance," but whether slavery is consistent with the spirit of the gospel. Those who searched the Bible for evidence of slavery were deliberately distorting the issue so as to force comparison between one form of slavery and another, between the tyranny of one slaveholder and the apparent benevolence of another, to lead to the conclusion that one form or individual was preferable. By this means, they were able to justify the institution's existence. But the fact that the Bible records the existence of slavery in antiquity is not the issue, only "what it reveals as consistent or inconsistent with the moral nature of God, what is obedient or rebellious before his throne." This universalism insisted that God is infinitely good and so could only have decreed that *all* men were to be saved. It assumed, Merle Curti has argued in another context, "the Fatherhood of God, the Brotherhood of Man and the possibility of universal salvation by character." [12]

None of these views could countenance the prospect of voluntary or compulsory emigration, for such a policy rejected the primacy of natural law, the dictates of the Bible, and the law of progress, all of which seemed to require that blacks stay at home. The emigrationist response that a successful settlement would have a positive "reflex reaction" on all who chose to stay in America seemed farfetched to Day and Pennington. Day's "oblique support" of Delany's Emigration Convention in 1854 was a convenient device employed to challenge Frederick Douglass and other members of the eastern establishment. His move to Canada in the mid-1850s can be considered a temporary retreat from the fray in Ohio, for throughout his stay he continued to oppose all forms of emigration. Pennington, in the midst of recovering from his problems with alcoholism, expressed support for Garnet's African Civilization Society, par-

and the Government of God in Antislavery Thought (Ithaca, 1973), 195–96; *Aliened American*, April 9, 1853.

12. J. W. C. Pennington, *A Two Years' Absence, or a Farewell Sermon, Preached in the First Congregational Church by J. W. C. Pennington, November 2nd, 1845* (Hartford, 1845), 22–23; Curti, *The Growth of American Thought*, 161.

ticularly its missionary objectives, something Pennington had favored since the formation of the Union Missionary Society (1841). Martin, on the other hand, was a defender of both African and Haitian emigration in the late 1850s, largely on account of the influence of Mary Ann Shadd and H. Ford Douglas, two emigrationists who had helped him in his first months of freedom. The belief of George Downing and others that conditions would improve if blacks abandoned the busy, congested city, where competition for limited resources exacerbated tensions, for the calm of rural America seemed to Martin devoid of historical justification.[13] Yet two years later he was on a mission to Britain, arguing that the Union held out the best hope for both the slave and the free black.

Permanent removal from America appealed to few. For every Augustus Washington, there were scores who saw no alternative to staying at home and battling the system. Many found it necessary to escape temporarily from the oppressive atmosphere of northern discrimination to the freedom of Britain or one of its colonies in the Caribbean. Although this exile afforded them an opportunity to reevaluate their lives and at the same time marshal international opposition to American oppression, they invariably returned home as soon as circumstances permitted. Of all the leading antebellum black figures who went abroad, only Samuel Ringgold Ward and Sarah Parker Remond did not return. For Campbell, the Jamaican, however, America held no attraction. Long before Delany turned his attention to war-torn America, as his plans for a colony in Abeokuta fell victim to British imperial designs, Campbell was on his way to Lagos.

Delany's and Garnet's failure to establish a colony in Africa, and the early demise of Redpath's and Holly's Haitian scheme, temporarily eliminated one serious alternative in the future of black Americans. The "optimism" of those who advocated staying at home seems to have been borne out by developments in the months following the firing on Fort Sumter. The law of progress was apparently at work, pushing the country toward the final extirpation of an institution that had been the bane of every black American. If it was beyond the ken of most whites, blacks knew in 1861 that a war between the states was a war over slavery. Should the Union succeed, and few blacks doubted that it would, then slavery would be destroyed. Victory would give blacks the necessary breathing space—Martin rather somberly predicted twenty-five years—to develop and demonstrate their talents. Increased educational opportunities, the

13. *Weekly Anglo-African*, February 23, March 9, 1861.

right to vote, the elimination of petty discriminatory laws, all pointed to a bright future. The fact that the country took six years to adopt three constitutional amendments guaranteeing these rights was ominous but predictable, given the bitterness engendered by the war.

No one underestimated the work to be done in the years following the surrender. With the exception of Campbell, a special case, they all worked for varying lengths of time among the freedmen. The Crafts boldly (some friends said recklessly) returned to Georgia, where they had been slaves; Martin to New Orleans, where he had been enslaved; Pennington to Mississippi and Florida; and Day to Delaware and Maryland. All approached the task from the same perspective: Freedom could be defended only if the freedmen established an independent economic existence, were exposed to the civilizing effects of education, and were guaranteed the right to vote. The future would be assured, Martin observed in 1866, when the issue of "whether humanity can flourish under a black skin . . . is settled." The hands that recently fought to free the country from slavery were now ready to rebuild the South. Once the euphoria of freedom had worn off, he predicted, the freedmen would return to the plantations if fair wages could be guaranteed. If the former master would rid himself of his prejudice and unite his capital and land with the labor of the skilled freedman, they could make the South "in many important respects the mistress of the world's manufacturing industry." Although the vast majority of freedmen generally envisaged a different future, one built around the ownership of land, this solution, formulated at the height of uncertainty in 1866, held out the greatest chance for success. Four years later, Martin and other black leaders, taking their cue from the freedmen, would demand some form of land redistribution. For the moment, however, the "Triple Alliance," as Delany called it, seemed a reasonable alternative to the chaos besetting the South.

But Martin also insisted that it was necessary for blacks to develop "habits of self reliance and feelings of self respect," which would come with their involvement in trade and commerce. "We know the value of our blood," he boldly asserted, "let us begin to learn the value of gold." Not that he underestimated the resilience of prejudice. In comparing the British and the American, he once observed that the former used a person's culture to determine his worth while the latter was willing to trample "his own education under foot in the mire of a senseless prejudice, from fear to do what all other gentlemen of the world feel disgraced in not doing—of recognizing the equality of a gentleman." While such prejudice continued to exist blacks had to depend upon one another. "Turn to your own people with trust and confidence, and don't ask the white people to trust you until you set the example of trusting your own colour," Martin advised the people.[14]

No one assumed that these objectives were easily obtainable or, for that matter, that America was willing to divest itself of its attitudes and policies toward its black citizens. At least for Day, overcoming such difficulties was the measure of true greatness, and blacks had long demonstrated their willingness and ability to resist American oppression. He constantly alluded to American racism's many impediments to black progress, and black challenges to the system were symbolized by the ship caught in dangerous waters, battling adverse currents and storms. These were not a people who would willingly submit, and the ingenuity displayed in resisting American oppression, Day insisted, would see the freedman through the uncertainties of Reconstruction. Even in the 1890s, when it was clear that America had reneged on promises of equality for its black citizens, Day's belief never faltered. Those like Booker T. Washington who advocated a form of appeasement were denying that history of resistance. At a meeting in 1897 commemorating the discovery of the unmarked graves of two fugitive slaves who had killed themselves rather than be returned to slavery, Day chose to reiterate his position. The history of black progress, he argued, is to be found in the story of little men combatting oppression and so forcing the country to address existing inequities. "It is not that they were rich or honored in life," he said of the two fugitives, "it is not that they accomplished great achievements, but poor and unqualified as they were, they knew how to be free and live and die in the enjoyment of liberty after they had attained it." The new gravestones he called "Memorial tablets" to that tradition.[15] Here was the conviction that struggle ensured progress, but accommodation guaranteed stagnation and ultimately regression.

But the battle against oppression in America, they all insisted, depended on the moral and material support of all liberty-loving people. Despotism, which "respects not the limits consecrated to Jehovah," Day told his graduating class, affects everyone by denying the individual's birthright. Humanity is a unit with common interests, and the denial of the rights of anyone threatens the interests of all. "Homo sum; nil humanum alienum puto," was how Pennington, following Terence, put it: I am a man; I regard as foreign to me nothing related to the family of man. Nations or groups within nations might advance, he ar-

14. *Freed-Man*, March 1, 1866; *Special Report of the Anti-Slavery Conference, Held in Paris . . . on the Twenty-sixth and Twenty-seventh August, 1867* (London, 1867), 50; *New Era*, September 1, 1870.
15. Chatham *Tri-Weekly Planet*, September 12, 1858; Harrisburg *Telegraph*, September 6, May 21, 1897.

gued, but neither could attain their full potential until all constituent parts of humanity, all races, all nations, were free from oppression and had every opportunity to progress toward happiness. These were the foundations on which the movement for equality in America was built. The elimination of oppression in one area, West Indian emancipation being a case in point, redounded to the benefit of all oppressed peoples. They took seriously the reciprocity and solidarity inherent in internationalism. Tyrants throughout the world, declared the Ohio State Convention of 1852, were "united against the oppressed, and therefore the Russian Serf, the Hungarian Peasant, the American Slave and all oppressed people, should unite against tyrants and despotism." In a gesture of solidarity with the "glorious struggle" of German and Hungarian nationalists, the meeting agreed to support the efforts of Gottfried Kinkel and Lajos Kossuth. Day spearheaded the drive in Cleveland. Later he recalled that black support was prompted by a recognition that liberty and oppression were one the "world over, and that the oppressed must succeed in securing rights and privileges only by combining together." When the issue of American assistance in the Irish struggle came up in 1886, Day declared that there had never been a movement to assist oppressed nationalities which had not been supported by "the sympathy and mites of the colored citizens."[16]

Black Americans' success in Britain in the antebellum period and the sympathy and support they generated for the cause of freedom in America were ample testimony to the efficacy of internationalism. They continued this work during and after the Civil War—Day, for example, on a limited basis in the early 1860s. Although William Craft spent a large portion of the period in Dahomey, he kept in touch with developments and promoted the cause whenever he could. Ellen was an active participant in women's auxiliaries of freedmen societies. Pennington did visit Britain in 1861, determined to exploit his earlier success in behalf of the Union, but troubles in Liverpool shattered his plans. No other American, black or white, did more for the Union or the freedmen than Martin did. He logged thousands of miles and delivered scores of lectures throughout England and Scotland during the war, and on his final mission to Britain, which lasted more than three years, he raised thousands of dollars for the American Missionary Association. Their efforts over forty years resulted in contacts with a broad cross-section of the British public, from the aristoc-

16. Oberlin *Evangelist*, October 13, 1847; Leeds *Mercury*, August 5, 1843; *Anti Slavery Reporter*, June 28, August 9, 1843; "Proceedings of the Convention of the Colored Freemen of Ohio, Held in Cincinnati, January 14, 15, 16, 17, and 19, 1852," in Foner and Walker (eds.), *Proceedings*, I, 277; Harrisburg *Telegraph*, July 3, 1886.

racy of Stafford House to the "hard-handed working men of the great railway works at Stratford."[17]

Yet all these activities and their abiding optimism in the future of America could not ensure a measure of personal satisfaction and accomplishment. Not that any of them would have acted differently, had they been given another opportunity, for circumstances imposed a duty to work for the improvement of their fellow men which none could deny. From the ranks of the oppressed, they successfully exploited the limited opportunities provided by the system. They were the ones who stood to benefit most from the system they were attacking, yet they chose to work for the general good. But America's resistance to pleas for reform, its refusal to exorcise the demon of discrimination, first broke the will and later the spirit of many of its critics. William Craft went to his daughter's home in Charleston to die, his property at Ways Station having passed into the hands of creditors, his experiment in black farming in Georgia a shambles. Martin, always in frail health, but driven to distraction by the system, succumbed to an overdose of laudanum. Pennington, the doctor of divinity, fell prey to the bottle and died in obscurity. Day may have avoided a similar fate by simply narrowing his sights and withdrawing to the provincialism of Harrisburg. The frequency with which they moved suggests that these were driven people unable to find a niche for themselves in a thriving society. America rewarded whites of lesser talent but refused to afford blacks the full range of opportunities. Having experienced slavery and hardship, and having by their own initiative and dogged determination acquired an education and all the trappings of civilized men, they refused to remain "hewers of wood and drawers of water." This accounts for both their wanderlust and their impatience. Having come that far, they saw no reason why America could not afford them an equal opportunity to achieve a relatively comfortable existence.

But even more frustrating was the intellectual isolation racism engendered. Not one white Hartford minister was inclined to exchange pulpits with Pennington prior to his successful trip to Britain in 1843 and his warm reception by some of Britain's leading divines. After his return, a few rather sheepishly invited him to address their congregations. Such an intellectually gifted man as Pennington, who had taught himself Greek and Latin, was frustrated by this isolation. He was able to forgive the limits imposed on him at Yale as a young man, but he yearned for the stimulation of his intellectual peers. A lack of intellectual contacts denied the attainment of self-culture, man's destiny, which

17. London *Morning Star*, February 14, 1863.

came about only through intercourse with superior minds through "books and lectures, the curbing of animal spirits, participation in the political duties of a free republic" as the Transcendentalist William Ellery Channing argued. Many, like Pennington and Martin, complained bitterly of the black church's inability to provide them with needed intellectual stimulation. Martin finally left the pulpit, frustrated by its conservatism; Day avoided involvement until 1866, and when he did join, he spent an inordinate amount of time fulminating against what he considered the intellectual backwardness of its leadership. Try as he might, Pennington could not bring himself to leave. After all, in spite of its shortcomings, the church was the one major institution controlled by blacks. Augustus Washington may have summed up the dilemma best when he wrote: "Strange as it may appear, whatever may be the colored man's natural capacity and literary attainments, I believe that, as soon as he leaves the academic halls to mingle in the only society he can find in the United States, unless he be a minister or lecturer, he must and will retrograde. And for the same reason, just as in proportion as he increases in knowledge, will he become the more miserable."[18]

These people nevertheless articulated black hopes and aspirations. Unlike their successors who emerged in the period after Reconstruction, these "representative colored men" would never have contemplated advising their "followers" to eschew political agitation. Those who exhorted blacks to postpone political involvement and concentrate on acquiring a limited education and money would have met with universal condemnation. No one who came of age in the 1830s would have suggested such a dichotomous approach. They viewed education as a necessary precondition for all development, an important agent in the establishment of moral government. There may have been some differences of opinion on the exact method of educating blacks, but each one labored untiringly to promote education among his people. In spite of his many personal problems and his frequent moves, Pennington always found time to run a school. In 1845 he requested a leave of absence from his church so he could pursue a classical education. Blacks, he told his congregation, were yet to be "moulded," and he predicted that "*the last half of the present century will be our great moral battle cry*," which would require an educated leadership.[19] When he retired from the Harrisburg School Board in 1899, Day had been involved in education for more than fifty years, as teacher of fugitive slaves in Ontario and

18. Channing quoted in Curti, *The Growth of American Thought*, 356; *African Repository*, September, 1851.
19. Pennington, *Two Years' Absence*, 6.

in Lincoln, England, as superintendent of schools for freedmen in Maryland and Delaware, and, for almost thirty years, as a school director in Harrisburg. The Crafts ran what was clearly the finest school in Bryan County until local opponents contrived to discredit their work. Campbell taught school in three countries, and Martin briefly acted as superintendent of the fourth division in Louisiana.

But education was only one feature in the struggle for equality. The right to vote and work free from discriminatory limitations was equally important. Day fought long and unsuccessfully to eliminate restrictions on blacks in Ohio, as did Pennington in Connecticut. Such restrictions as existed in most northern states, they argued, were in direct contravention of constitutional guarantees. But American racism proved much too resilient, and the two-party system limited the range of options available to blacks, once Republicans reneged on the promises of Reconstruction. Martin captured their dilemma in one of his editorials: Remember, he wrote, that "one cannot fight a whole party, unless he has honesty enough to go over to the ranks of the enemy. The Republican party, for instance, is the only party which has ever done you any good, and were it the very devil bringing you a boon, you have a right to believe the Lord sent it."[20] Yet two years later he had joined forces with the Liberal Republicans, and Day would later join the Democrats. Although both subsequently returned to the fold, there was no alternative for the victims of oppression. Some joined the Democrats and many flirted with the idea of developing a third party, but none of these options offered much hope at a time when both parties appealed to the racist instincts of the country. But whatever the impediments to equal participation, they had worked too hard for far too long to ever contemplate voluntary withdrawal from active political involvement.

These people were among the standard-bearers for black America, extolling its strengths and virtues; its emissaries to the outside world; its exhorters, pleading with blacks to work for their own improvement. Employing what James McGregor Burns calls a "structure of action," they nudged blacks from all walks of life—"among the interstices of society"—to work for their own elevation. Here were symbols of black potential, America's finest examples of Horatio Alger accomplishments, defying the restraints of slavery and discrimination. What heights of success they, and by extension, other blacks could have attained in the absence of such impediments. Here was the quintessential transforming moral leadership—"affiliative leadership," Allison Davis calls

20. *New Era*, April 14, 1870.

it—at its best, one that does not aim to master and exploit people to satisfy its own irrational drives, but sets out to help them "identify and use their own abilities more fully in the service of themselves and society." It was a leadership of change, not fundamental radical reorganization, but reformation, advocating the fulfillment of America's revolutionary republican principles.[21] Their efforts were assaults on the barriers to man's potential imposed by an oppressive society, as well as beacons guiding succeeding generations.

21. James McGregor Burns, *Leadership* (New York, 1978), 3–5; Allison Davis, *Leadership, Love and Aggression. As the Twig Is Bent: The Psychological Factors in the Making of Four Black Leaders* (New York, 1983), 9.

Selected Bibliography

Contemporary Materials

Manuscripts

American Anti Slavery Society Papers. Boston Public Library.
American Colonization Society Papers. Manuscript Division, Library of Congress.
American Missionary Association Papers. Amistad Research Center, New Orleans.
John Andrew Papers. Massachusetts Historical Society, Boston.
Anti-Slavery Collection. Department of Rare Books, Cornell University Library, Ithaca, N.Y.
Amos G. Beman Papers. Collection of American Literature, The Beinecke Rare Book and Manuscript Library, Yale University, New Haven.
Black Abolitionist Papers. Microfilm.
British and Foreign Anti Slavery Society Papers. Rhodes House Library, Oxford University, Oxford.
British Colonial Office Documents. Public Record Office, London.
British Foreign Office Documents. Public Record Office, London.
Brougham Papers. The Library, University College, London.
Bureau of Refugees, Freedmen and Abandoned Lands. Record Group 105. National Archives.
Thomas Clarkson Papers. The Huntington Library, San Marino, Calif.
Church Missionary Society Papers. Church Missionary Society Archives, London.
Frederick Douglass Papers. Microfilm. Library of Congress.
Raymond English Deposit. The John Rylands University Library of Manchester, Manchester.
Estlin Papers. Dr. Williams's Library, London.
Leon Gardiner Collection. The Historical Society of Pennsylvania, Philadelphia.

Sydney Howard Gay Papers. Rare Book and Manuscript Library, Columbia University, New York.

Glasgow Emancipation Society Papers. Smeal Collection, The Mitchell Library, Glasgow.

Harrisburg School District Papers. Board of Education, Harrisburg, Pa.

Thomas Hodgkin Papers. In possession of Hodgkin family, Warwickshire.

Richard Humphrey Foundation. Friends Historical Library, Swarthmore College, Swarthmore, Pa.

Institute for Colored Youth Papers. American Philosophical Society Library, Philadelphia.

Jay Family Papers, etc. Rare Book and Manuscript Library, Columbia University, New York.

William King Papers. Microfilm. Chatham Public Library, Chatham, Ontario.

Harriet Martineau Papers. Cumbria Record Office, Kendal, England.

Methodist Missionary Society Papers. The Methodist Church Overseas Division (Methodist Missionary Society), London.

Oberlin College Archives. Oberlin College, Oberlin, Ohio.

Royal Geographical Society Papers. Royal Geographical Society, London.

Ruffin Family Papers. Moorland-Spingarn Research Center, Howard University, Washington, D.C.

Gerrit Smith Collection. George Arents Research Library, Syracuse University, Syracuse, N.Y.

Lewis Tappan Papers. Microfilm. Library of Congress.

Records of the Third Presbytery of New York. Presbyterian Historical Society, Philadelphia.

United States Treasury Department Records. National Archives.

Henry Clay Warmoth Papers. Southern Historical Collection, Library of the University of North Carolina at Chapel Hill.

Books, Pamphlets, and Articles

Aborigines Protection Society. *Twenty-sixth Annual Report*. London, 1863.
———. *Thirtieth Annual Report*. London, 1867.

African Aid Society. *The American Crisis and the Slave Trade. Report of a Public Meeting, Held in the Town Hall, Birmingham, on Friday, December 13, 1861*. Birmingham, 1861.
———. *First Report from July 1860 to the 31st March, 1862*. London, n.d.

African Methodist Episcopal Zion Church, General Conference. *Proceedings, 1884*. New York, n.d.
———. *Proceedings, 1888*. Wilmington, N.C., 1888.
———. *Minutes, 1896*. Charlotte, N.C., 1896.

African Methodist Episcopal Zion Church, Philadelphia and Baltimore Conference. *Minutes, 1885*. Carlisle, Pa., n.d.
———. *Minutes, 1887*. Carlisle, Pa., 1887.
———. *Minutes, 1889*. N.p., n.d.
———. *Minutes, 1890*. N.p., n.d.

———. *Minutes, 1891.* N.p., n.d.

American and Foreign Anti Slavery Society. *Annual Report, 1848.* New York, 1848.

———. *Annual Report, 1849.* New York, 1849.

———. *Annual Report, 1850.* New York, 1850.

———. *Annual Report, 1851.* New York, 1851.

———. *Annual Report, 1852.* New York, 1852.

Armistead, Wilson. *A Tribute to the Negro Being a Vindication of the Intellectual and Religious Capabilities of the Colored Portion of Mankind.* Manchester, 1848.

Bearse, Austin. *Reminiscences of Fugitive-Slave Law Days in Boston.* 1880; rpr. New York, 1969.

Bell, Howard H., ed. *Minutes of the Proceedings of the National Negro Conventions, 1830–1864.* New York, 1969.

Blassingame, John, ed., *Slave Testimony: Two Centuries of Letters, Speeches, Interviews and Autobiographies.* Baton Rouge, 1977.

Bowditch, Vincent Y. *Life and Correspondence of Henry Ingersoll Bowditch.* 3 vols. Boston, 1902.

Bristol and Clifton Ladies Anti Slavery Society. *Special Report of the Bristol and Clifton Ladies Anti Slavery Society; During Eighteen Months, from January 1851 to June 1852; With a Statement of the Reasons of its Separation from the British and Foreign Anti Slavery Society.* London, 1852.

British Association for the Advancement of Science. *Report of the Thirty-third Meeting of the British Association for the Advancement of Science Held at Newcastle-upon-Tyne in August and September 1863.* London, 1864.

Brown, William Wells. *The Black Man: His Antecedents, His Genius, and His Achievements.* 1865; rpr. Miami, 1969.

Burton, Sir Richard. *Abeokuta and the Cameroons Mountains.* 2 vols. London, 1863.

———. *A Mission to Gelele, King of Dahome.* 2 vols. London, 1864.

Butler, J. C. *Historical Record of Macon and Central Georgia.* Macon, 1879.

Campbell, Robert. "Effects of Emancipation in Jamaica." *Anglo-African Magazine,* I (1859), 151–53.

———. *A Few Facts Relating to Lagos, Abeokuta, and Other Sections of Central Africa.* Philadelphia, 1860.

———. "A Pilgrimage to My Motherland: An Account of a Journey Among the Egbas and Yorubas of Central Africa in 1859–60." In *Search for a Place: Black Separatism and Africa, 1860,* edited by Howard H. Bell. Ann Arbor, 1971.

———. "Struggle for Freedom in Jamaica." *Anglo-African Magazine,* I (1859), 90–92.

Coffin, Levi. *Reminiscences of Levi Coffin.* 1876; rpr. New York, 1968.

Colored National Labor Convention. *Proceedings of the Colored National Labor Convention Held in Washington, D.C., on December 6th, 7th, 8th, 9th and 10th, 1869.* Washington, D.C., 1870.

Colored People's Educational Monument Association. *Celebration by the Colored People's Educational Monument Association in Memory of Abraham Lincoln, on the Fourth of July, 1865, in the Presidential Grounds, Washington, D.C.* Washington, D.C., 1865.

Congregational General Association of Connecticut. *Minutes.* Hartford, 1840.

————. *Minutes*. Hartford, 1841.

————. *Minutes*. Hartford, 1842.

————. *Minutes*. Hartford, 1843.

————. *Minutes*. New Haven, 1844.

————. *Minutes*. New Haven, 1845.

————. *Minutes*. New Haven, 1846.

————. *Minutes*. New Haven, 1847.

————. *Minutes*. New Haven, 1848.

————. *Minutes*. New Haven, 1856.

Congregational General Association of New York. *Minutes*. Whitesboro, N.Y., 1839.

————. *Minutes*. Hamilton, N.Y., 1840.

Craft, William. *Running a Thousand Miles for Freedom*. 1860; rpr. New York, 1969.

Delany, Martin R. "Report of the Niger Valley Exploring Party." In *Search for a Place: Black Separatism and Africa, 1860*, edited by Howard H. Bell. Ann Arbor, 1971.

De Quincey, Thomas. *Confessions of an English Opium-Eater*. London, 1886.

Douglass, Frederick. *Life and Times of Frederick Douglass*. 1892; rpr. New York, 1962.

Edinburgh Ladies Emancipation Society. *Annual Report, 1864*. Edinburgh, n.d.

————. *Report of the Proceedings at a Public Meeting of the Edinburgh Ladies Emancipation Society Held at Queen's Street Hall, Friday the 28th December, 1849*. Edinburgh, n.d.

Foner, Philip S., and George Walker, eds. *Proceedings of the Black State Conventions, 1840–1865*. 2 vols. Philadelphia, 1979.

Garrison, William Lloyd. *Thoughts on African Colonization*. 1832; rpr. New York, 1969.

Higginson, Thomas Wentworth. *Cheerful Yesterdays*. Boston, 1898.

Hood, Bishop J. W. *One Hundred Years of the African Methodist Episcopal Zion Church*. New York, 1895.

Hooker, John. *Some Reminiscences of a Long Life*. Hartford, 1899.

Jackson-Coppin, Fanny. *Reminiscences of School Life, and Hints on Teaching*. Philadelphia, 1913.

Johnson, J. F. *Proceedings of the General Anti Slavery Convention Called by the Committee of the British and Foreign Anti Slavery Society and Held in London from Tuesday, June 13th to Tuesday, June 20th, 1843*. London, 1844.

Langston, J. Mercer. *From the Virginia Plantation to the National Capitol*. 1894; rpr. New York, 1969.

London Emancipation Society. *The Martyrdom of John Brown. The Proceedings of a Public Meeting Held in London on the 2nd December, 1863, to Commemorate the Fourth Anniversary of John Brown's Death*. London, 1864.

Martin, J. Sella. *The Cotton Question: Free Versus Slave Labour*. Glasgow, [1865].

————. *Hero and the Slave. Founded on Fact*. Boston, 1862.

————. "The Sentinel of Freedom." *Anglo-African Magazine*, I (1859), 361–62.

May, Samuel. *The Fugitive Slave Law and its Victims*. 1861; rpr. Freeport, N.Y., 1970.

Moore, John Jamison. *History of the AME Zion Church in America*. York, Pa., 1884.

Nell, William C. *The Colored Patriots of the American Revolution*. 1855; rpr. New York, 1968.

Noel, Baptist W. *Freedom and Slavery in the United States of America*. London, 1863.

Peace Congress. *Report of the Proceedings of the First General Peace Convention Held in London, June 22nd, 1843, and the Two Following Days.* London, 1843.

———. *Report of the Proceedings of the Second General Peace Congress Held in Paris on the 22nd, 23rd and 24th of August, 1849.* London, 1850.

———. *Report of the Proceedings of the Third Peace Congress, Held in Frankfort, on the 22nd, 23rd, and 24th August, 1850.* London, 1851.

Pennington, J. W. C. *An Address Delivered at Newark, New Jersey at the First Anniversary of West Indian Emancipation, August 1, 1839.* Newark, 1839.

———. *Christian Zeal. A Sermon Preached Before the Third Presbytery of New York, in Thirteenth Street Presbyterian Church, July 3, 1853.* New York, 1854.

———. *Covenants Involving Moral Wrong Are Not Obligatory Upon Men: A Sermon Delivered in the 5th Congregational Church, Hartford on November 17, 1842.* Hartford, 1842.

———. *The Fugitive Blacksmith; or Events in the History of J. W. C. Pennington Pastor of a Presbyterian Church, New York, Formerly a Slave in the State of Maryland, United States.* In *Great Slave Narratives,* edited by Arna Bontemps. Boston, 1969.

———. "The Great Conflict Requires Great Faith." *Anglo-African Magazine,* I (1859), 343–45.

———. *A Lecture Delivered Before the Glasgow Young Men's Christian Association; and Also Before the St. George's Biblical, Literary and Scientific Institute, London.* Edinburgh, n.d.

———. *The Reasonableness of the Abolition of Slavery at the South. A Legitimate Inference from the Success of British Emancipation, an Address, Delivered at Hartford, Conn. on the First of August, 1856.* Hartford, 1856.

———. "A Review of Slavery and the Slave Trade." *Anglo-African Magazine,* I (1859), 93–96, 123–26, 155–59.

———. "The Self-Redeeming Power of the Colored Races of the World." *Anglo-African Magazine,* I (1859), 314–20.

———. *A Text Book of the Origin and History of the Colored People.* Hartford, 1841.

———. *A Two Years' Absence, or a Farewell Sermon, Preached in the First Congregational Church by J. W. C. Pennington, November 2nd, 1845.* Hartford, 1845.

———, ed. *A Narrative of Events in the Life of J. H. Banks, an Escaped Slave, From the Cotton State, Alabama, in America.* Liverpool, 1861.

Plato, Ann. *Essays; Including Biographies and Miscellaneous Pieces in Prose and Poetry.* Hartford, 1841.

Simmons, William J. *Men of Mark: Eminent, Progressive and Rising.* 1887; rpr. New York, 1968.

Spence, James. *Southern Independence: An Address Delivered at a Public Meeting in the City Hall, Glasgow . . . 26th November, 1863.* Glasgow, 1863.

Still, William. *The Underground Rail Road.* Philadelphia, 1872.

Tiffany, Nina Moore. "Stories of the Fugitive Slaves, I: The Escape of William and Ellen Craft." *New England Magazine,* I (1890), 524–30.

Warmoth, Henry Clay. *War, Politics and Reconstruction: Stormy Days in Louisiana.* New York, 1930.

Weiss, John, ed. *Life and Correspondence of Theodore Parker.* 2 vols. London, 1863.

Wheeler, B. F. *Cullings From Zion's Poets.* Mobile, 1907.

Newspapers and Periodicals

African Repository, 1851–52.
African Times, 1862–65.
American Freedman, 1866–68.
American Missionary, 1860–69.
Anglo-African (Lagos), 1863–65.
Anti Slavery Advocate, 1852–62.
Anti Slavery Bugle, 1847–58.
Anti Slavery Reporter, 1843–67.
Anti Slavery Standard, 1840–70.
Baltimore *American*, 1867–68.
Charter Oak, 1838–48.
Chatham *Tri Weekly Planet*, 1857–60.
Christian Freeman, 1843–45.
Cleveland *True Democrat*, 1849–53.
Colored American, 1837–41.
Delaware Republican, 1867–71.
Douglass Monthly, 1859–63.
Freed-Man, 1865–68.
Freedmen's Aid Reporter, 1866–67.
Harrisburg *Patriot*, 1870–1900.
Harrisburg *Telegraph*, 1870–1900.
Home Journal/State Journal, 1883–84.
Lagos *Observer*, 1882–84.
Liberator, 1831–65.
London *Daily News*, 1865–67.
London *Evening Star*, 1862–64.
London *Morning Star*, 1861–67.
Louisianan, 1870–75.
New National Era, 1870–74.
New Orleans *Daily Picayune*, 1871–72.
New Orleans *Republican*, 1871–76.
New York *Evening Post*, 1864–65.
New York *Daily Tribune*, 1864–65, 1872–76.
Nonslaveholder, 1850.
North Star/Frederick Douglass Paper, 1848–60.
Oberlin *Evangelist*, 1844–50.
Pennsylvania Freeman, 1850–55.
Provincial Freeman, 1854–59.
Shreveport *Times*, 1872–73.
Slave, 1851–52.
Star of Zion, 1885–1900.
Washington *Daily Morning Chronicle*, 1869–74.

Weekly Anglo-African, 1859–65.
Wilmington *Daily Commercial*, 1867–71.

Secondary Materials

Books

Ajayi, J. F. A. *Christian Missions in Nigeria 1851–1891: The Making of a New Elite.* London, 1965.

Argyle, William Johnson. *The Fon of Dahomey: A History and Ethnography of the Old Kingdom.* Oxford, 1966.

Banks, Enoch Marvin. *The Economics of Land Tenure in Georgia.* New York, 1905.

Biobaku, Saburi O. *The Egba and Their Neighbours.* London, 1957.

Blassingame, John. *Black New Orleans 1860–1880.* Chicago, 1973.

Bolt, Christine. *The Anti-Slavery Movement and Reconstruction: A Study of Anglo-American Co-operation 1833–1877.* London, 1969.

Bradley, David Henry, Sr. *A History of the AME Zion Church.* 2 vols. Nashville, 1956, 1970.

Campbell, Mavis. *The Dynamics of Change in a Slave Society: A Sociopolitical History of the Free Coloreds of Jamaica 1800–1865.* New York, 1976.

Dabney, Lilian G. *The History of Schools for Negroes in the District of Columbia, 1807–1947.* Washington, D.C., 1949.

Davis, Russell H. *Black Americans in Cleveland.* Washington, D.C., 1972.

———. *Memorable Negroes in Cleveland's Past.* Cleveland, 1969.

Du Bois, W. E. B. *The Negro Landholder of Georgia.* Washington, D.C., 1901.

———, ed. *Economic Co-Operation Among Negro Americans.* Atlanta, 1907.

Eisner, Gisela. *Jamaica 1830–1930: A Study in Economic Growth.* Manchester, 1961.

Evans, Frank B. *Pennsylvania Politics, 1872–1877: A Study in Political Leadership.* Harrisburg, 1966.

Field, Phyllis F. *The Politics of Race in New York: The Struggle for Black Suffrage in the Civil War Era.* Ithaca, 1982.

Fletcher, Robert Samuel. *A History of Oberlin College from Its Foundation Through the Civil War.* 2 vols. Oberlin, 1943.

Franklin, Vincent P., and James D. Anderson, eds. *New Perspectives on Black Educational History.* Boston, 1978.

Green, Constance McLaughlin. *The Secret City: A History of Race Relations in the Nation's Capital.* Princeton, 1967.

Grossman, Lawrence. *The Democratic Party and the Negro: Northern and National Politics, 1868–1892.* Urbana, 1976.

Hall, Douglass. *Free Jamaica 1838–1865: An Economic History.* New Haven, 1959.

Heuman, Gad J. *Between Black and White: Race, Politics, and the Free Coloreds in Jamaica, 1792–1865.* Westport, Conn., 1981.

Horton, James Oliver, and Lois E. Horton. *Black Bostonians: Family Life and Community Struggle in the Antebellum North.* New York, 1979.

Jordon, Donaldson, and Edwin J. Pratt. *Europe and the American Civil War.* Boston, 1931.

Kusmer, Kenneth L. *A Ghetto Takes Shape: Black Cleveland, 1870–1915.* Urbana, 1976.

Lonn, Ella. *Reconstruction in Louisiana After 1868.* 1918; rpr. Gloucester, Mass., 1967.

Mabee, Carlton. *Black Education in New York State from Colonial to Modern Times.* Syracuse, 1979.

McPherson, James M. *The Negro's Civil War: How American Negroes Felt and Acted During the War for the Union.* New York, 1965.

Miller, Floyd J. *The Search for a Black Nationality: Black Colonization and Emigration, 1787–1863.* Urbana, 1975.

Murray, Andrew E. *Presbyterians and the Negro: A History.* Philadelphia, 1966.

Nisbet, Robert. *History of the Idea of Progress.* New York, 1980.

Owsley, Frank Lawrence. *King Cotton Diplomacy: Foreign Relations of the Confederate States of America.* Chicago, 1969.

Richards, Leonard L. *"Gentlemen of Property and Standing": Anti-Abolition Mobs in Jacksonian America.* New York, 1970.

Sebba, Gregor, ed. *Georgia Studies: Selected Writings of Robert Preston Brooks.* Athens, Ga., 1952.

Siebert, Wilbur H. *The Underground Railroad in Massachusetts.* Worcester, Mass., 1936.

Sterling, Dorothy. *Black Foremothers: Three Lives.* Old Westbury, N.Y., 1979.

Strother, Horatio T. *The Underground Railroad in Connecticut.* Middletown, Conn., 1962.

Temperley, Howard. *British Antislavery, 1833–1870.* Columbia, S.C., 1972.

Ullman, Victor. *Look to the North Star: A Life of William King.* Boston, 1969.

Vincent, Charles. *Black Legislators in Louisiana During Reconstruction.* Baton Rouge, 1976.

Ware, Edith Ellen. *Political Opinion in Massachusetts During Civil War and Reconstruction.* New York, 1916.

Warner, Robert A. *New Haven Negroes: A Social History.* New Haven, 1940.

Wesley, Charles V. *Negro Labor in the United States, 1850–1925.* New York, 1927.

Wyatt-Brown, Bertram. *Lewis Tappan and the Evangelical War Against Slavery.* Cleveland, 1969.

Articles

Bacote, Clarence A. "Negro Proscriptions, Protest and Proposed Solutions in Georgia, 1880–1908." *Journal of Southern History*, XXV (1959), 471–98.

———. "Some Aspects of Negro Life in Georgia 1880–1908." *Journal of Negro History*, XLIII (1958), 186–213.

Bell, Howard H. "The Negro Emigration Movement 1849–1854." *Phylon*, XX (1959), 132–42.

Billington, Louis. "British Humanitarians and American Cotton, 1840–1860." *Journal of American Studies*, XI (1977), 313–34.

Brown, Ira V. "Pennsylvania and the Rights of the Negro, 1865–1887." *Pennsylvania History*, XXVIII (1961), 45–57.

Campbell, Carl. "Development of Vocational Training in Jamaica: First Steps." *Caribbean Quarterly*, XI (1965), 13–34.

Du Bois, W. E. B. "Georgia Negroes and Their Fifty Millions of Savings." *World's Work*, XVIII (1909), 11550–54.

Erickson, Leonard. "Politics and Repeal of Ohio's Black Laws, 1837–1849." *Ohio History*, LXXXII (1973), 154–75.

Gottlieb, Manuel. "The Land Question in Georgia During Reconstruction." *Science and Society*, III (1939), 356–88.

Halstead, Jacqueline J. "The Delaware Association for the Moral Improvement and Education of the Colored People: Practical Christianity." *Delaware History*, XV (1972), 19–40.

Hancock, Harold B. "The Status of the Negro in Delaware After the Civil War, 1865–1875." *Delaware History*, XIII (1968), 57–66.

Harlan, Louis R. "Desegregation in New Orleans Public Schools During Reconstruction." *American Historical Review*, LXVII (1962), 663–75.

Hoffecker, Carol E. "The Politics of Exclusion: Blacks in Late Nineteenth-Century Wilmington, Delaware." *Delaware History*, XVI (1974), 60–72.

Landon, Fred. "Canadian Negroes and the John Brown Raid." *Journal of Negro History*, VI (1921), 174–82.

Lavesque, George A. "Inherent Reformers—Inherited Orthodoxy: Black Baptists in Boston, 1800–1873." *Journal of Negro History*, LX (1975), 491–525.

Lawson, Ellen N. "Lucy Stanton: Life on the Cutting Edge." *Western Reserve Magazine*, X (1983), 9–12.

Lawson, Ellen N., and Marlene Merrill. "The Antebellum 'Talented Thousandth': Black College Students at Oberlin Before the Civil War." *Journal of Negro Education*, LII (1983), 142–55.

Matison, Sumner Eliot. "The Labor Movement and the Negro During Reconstruction." *Journal of Negro History*, XXXIII (1948), 426–68.

McPherson, James M. "Grant or Greeley? The Abolitionist Dilemma in the Election of 1872." *American Historical Review*, LXXI (1965), 43–61.

Meier, August. "The Negro and the Democratic Party, 1875–1915." *Phylon*, XVII (1956), 173–91.

Pitre, Althea D. "The Collapse of the Warmoth Regime, 1870–72." *Louisiana History*, VI (1965), 161–83.

Price, Edward J., Jr. "School Segregation in Nineteenth-Century Pennsylvania." *Pennsylvania History*, XLIII (1976), 121–37.

Schwartz, Harold. "Fugitive Slave Days in Boston." *New England Quarterly*, XXVII (1954), 191–212.

Stutler, Boyd B. "John Brown's Constitution." *Lincoln Herald*, L–LI (1948–49), 17–25.

Warner, Robert A. "Amos G. Beman, 1812–1874: A Memoir of a Forgotten Leader." *Journal of Negro History*, XXII (1937), 200–21.

White, David O. "Augustus Washington: Black Daguerreotypist of Hartford." *Connecticut Historical Society Bulletin*, XXXIX (1974), 14–19.

———. "Hartford's African Schools, 1830–1868." *Connecticut Historical Society Bulletin*, XXXIX (1974), 47–53.

Theses and Dissertations

Bacote, Clarence Albert. "The Negro in Georgia Politics, 1880–1908." Ph.D. dissertation, University of Chicago, 1955.

Brown, S. "A History of the People of Lagos, 1852–1866." Ph.D. dissertation, Northwestern University, 1964.

Bruser, Lawrence. "Political Antislavery in Connecticut, 1844–1858." Ph.D. dissertation, Columbia University, 1974.

Conyers, C. F. H. "A History of the Cheyney State Teachers College, 1837–1951." Ed.D. dissertation, New York University, 1960.

Drake, Richard Bryant. "The American Missionary Association and the Southern Negro, 1861–1888." Ph.D. dissertation, Emory University, 1957.

Finnie, Helen M. "Scottish Attitudes Towards American Reconstruction, 1865–1877." 3 vols. Ph.D. dissertation, Edinburgh University, 1975.

Howard, Victor. "The Anti Slavery Movement in the Presbyterian Church, 1835–1861." Ph.D. dissertation, Ohio State University, 1961.

Johnson, Clifton. "The American Missionary Association, 1846–1861: A Study of Christian Abolitionism." Ph.D. dissertation, University of North Carolina, 1958.

Nestleroth, Michael. "The Black Community of Harrisburg, 1880–1910: A Study of the Black Community of a Small Northern City." M.A. thesis, Lehigh University, n.d.

Spencer, Hildreth Houston. "To Nestle in the Mane of the British Lion: A History of Canadian Black Education, 1820 to 1870." Ph.D. dissertation, Northwestern University, 1970.

Taylor, Joseph E. "The Colored National Labor Union, Its Birth and Demise, 1869–1872." M.A. thesis, Howard University, 1959.

Thomas, Edward H. "An Analysis of the Life and Work of James W. C. Pennington, a Black Churchman and Abolitionist." Ph.D. dissertation, Hartford Theological Seminary Foundation, 1978.

Index

with Downing, 277–79; mentioned, 335, 389, 391, 394–97
Martineau, Harriet, 102
Mason, James, 207, 218–19, 222
Miller, John, 41–42
Mitchell, William Foster, 245–47
Montana Agricultural Emigrant Aid Association, 336
Morris, Robert, 197, 208
Myers, Isaac, 255–56

National Freedmen's Aid Union of Great Britain and Ireland, 235–36, 238, 240–41, 243
National Labor Union, 254–56
National Negro Convention: in 1831–1833, pp. 7–9; in 1848, p. 295; in 1853, pp. 56–57, 304–305; in 1855, pp. 308–309; in 1864, p. 324; in 1869, p. 332
Nell, William C., 194, 197, 306, 308, 324, 389
Nesbit, William, 336, 345
New York Vigilance Committee, 28, 49, 52, 57–59
Niger Valley Exploring Party, 74, 149, 151–52, 182

Oberlin College, 291–94, 297, 299, 307, 312

Parker, Theodore, 92, 94
Paton, Andrew, 51–52
Patton, William W., 235–36, 238, 242
Paul, Nathaniel, 12–13, 27, 41, 97
Payne, Daniel, 23, 261
Pembroke, Stephen, 57–59
Pennington, J. W. C.: in slavery, 2–3, 43; escape, 3–5, 43–44; family of, 1–3, 16, 32, 36, 43, 58–59; education of, 9; on education, 16–19, 82–83; teacher, 10, 15–16, 73, 80–83; ministry of, 11, 15, 38, 73, 80–84, 223; works with national Negro conventions, 7–9, 12–15, 56–57, 389; visits to Britain, 28–30, 35, 42–53; 79–80; at World Anti Slavery Convention, 19–20, 27–29, 390; attends peace congresses, 28–29, 45, 47–48; supports missionary work, 22–27, 33, 35, 55, 389; elected moderator, Hartford Central Association of Congregational Ministers, 31; editor, 31; freedom purchased, 32, 51–53; visits Jamaica, 33–34; on emigration, 33–36, 48, 74–77, 195–96, 393–94; and anti-colonization, 6–8, 27, 41–42, 53–56; supports free-produce movement, 35, 46–48, 104; marriages of, 16, 36, 39–40; and rela-

tions with Garrisonians, 48–53, 63–70, 100; receives honorary degree, 48; works for Underground Railroad, 57–59; fights segregated transportation, 59–62, 310; elected moderator, Third Presbytery of New York, 63; and problems with alcohol, 70–73; imprisoned in Liverpool, 79–80; works with freedmen, 80–82; mentioned, 96–97, 137, 222, 301, 389–93, 395–99
Pennsylvania State Equal Rights League: rift in, 358–61; mentioned, 326–27, 334, 336, 340, 344, 346–50, 362, 365
Pennsylvania State League, 365, 367, 372
People's League, 359–61, 363
Phillips, Wendell, 90, 121, 124, 127, 132, 198–99, 206, 272
Pillsbury, Parker, 68, 198
Pinchback, P. B. S., 264–66, 268, 270–71, 274, 281–82, 384
Purnell, James W., 152, 156
Purvis, Robert, 14, 358
Putnam, Lewis, 54

Ralston, Gerald, 156–57, 179
Reason, Charles, 144, 308
Redpath, James, 76–77, 394
Remond, Charles Lenox, 27, 41, 97
Remond, Sarah Parker, 104, 232, 394
Remsen, Peter, 10
Richardson, Anna, 46–47
Rock, J. S., 197
Roebuck, John, 214–17
Ruggles, David, 14, 60

Schlesinger, Barthold, 130–33
Shadd, Mary Anne, 188, 193, 394
Sherman, James, 28, 31
Sinclair, James, 229–30, 234
Slidell, John, 207
Smeal, William, 50
Smith, Gerrit, 73, 189, 203, 272, 312
Smith, James, 88, 121
Smith, James McCune, 14, 27, 74, 156, 168, 223, 305–306, 308
Spence, James, 211, 213–15, 219–22, 224
State Colored League (Penn.), 376, 380
Still, William: works with Underground Railroad, 58–59; joins Democrats, 358, 376; mentioned, 133
Storrs, D. A. M., 226–33
Strieby, M. E., 234–35, 249–50, 252
Sturge, Joseph, 32, 46
Sumner, Charles, 253, 258, 269, 278, 313

BLACK HERITAGE